Still Sick 3

［スティルシック］

BLADE COMICS pixiv

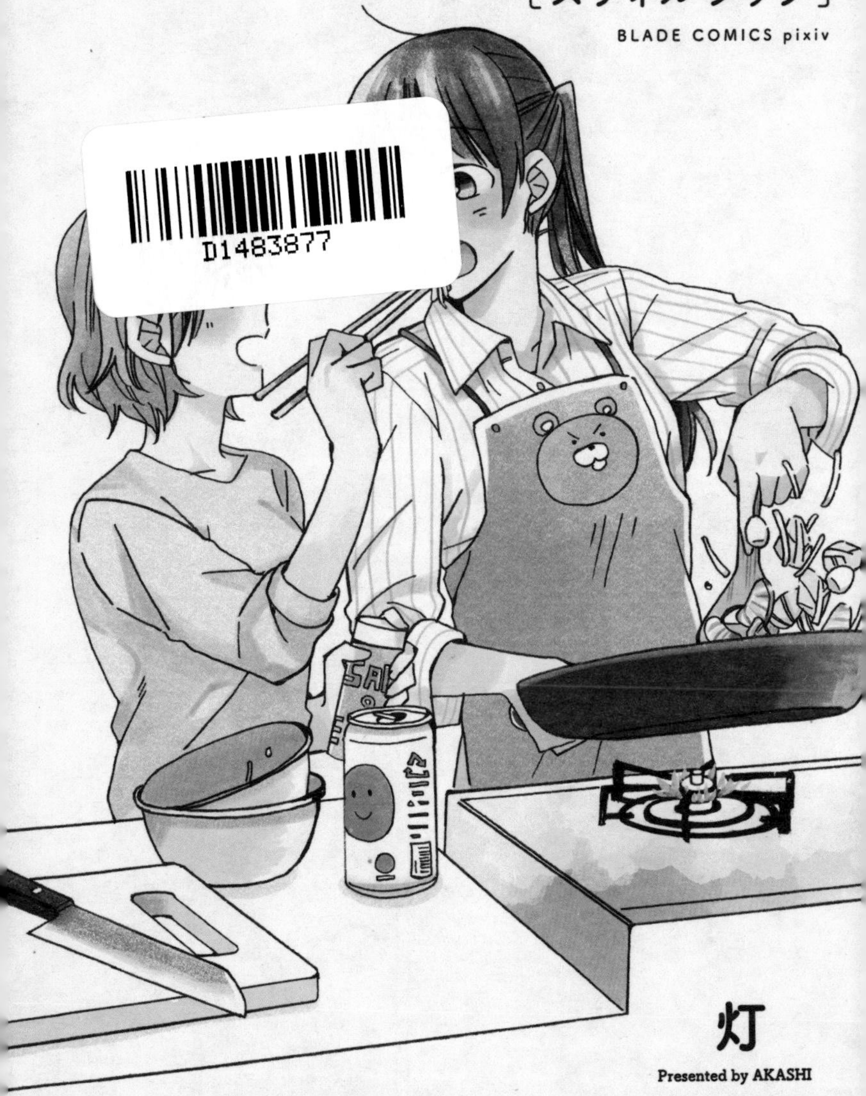

灯

Presented by AKASHI

[CONTENTS]

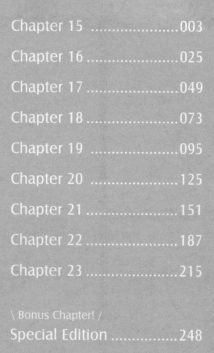

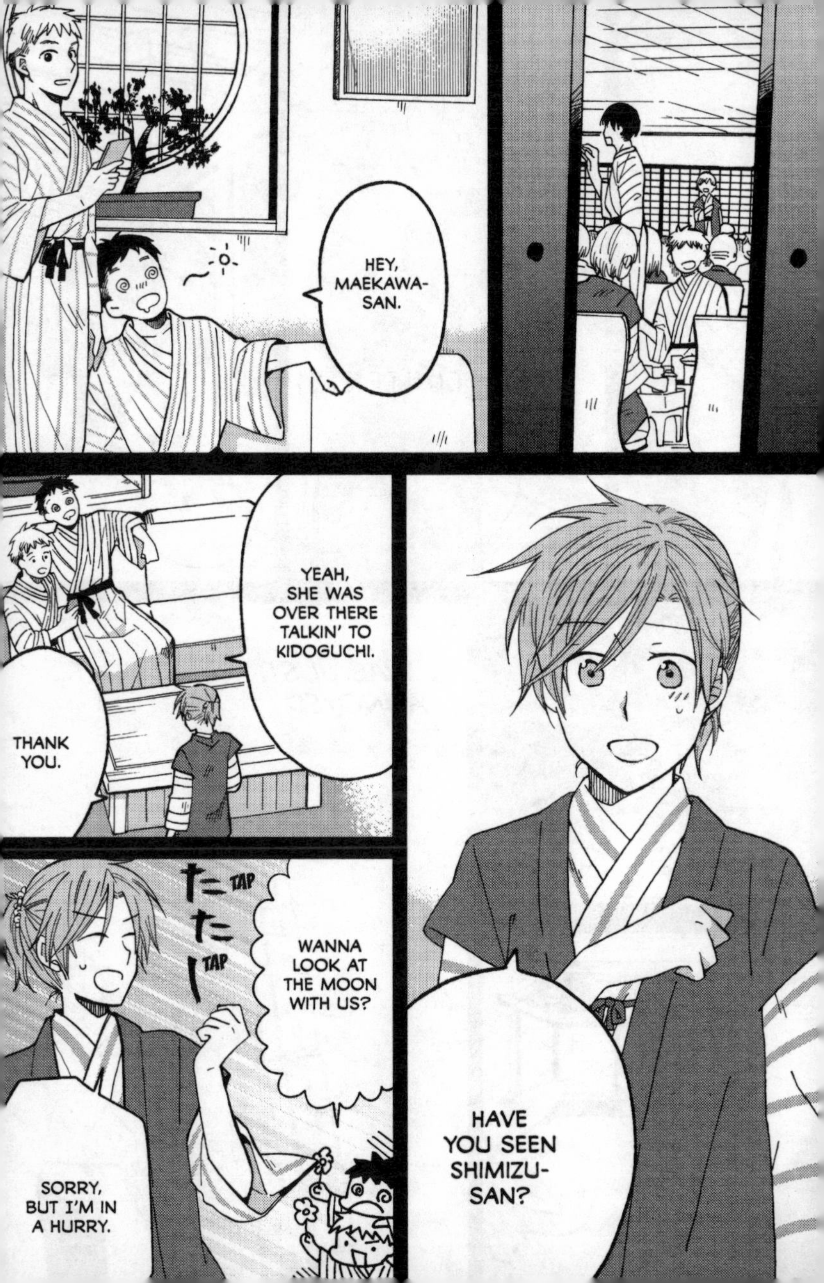
HEY, MAEKAWA-SAN.
HAVE YOU SEEN SHIMIZU-SAN?
YEAH, SHE WAS OVER THERE TALKIN' TO KIDOGUCHI.
THANK YOU.
TAP
TAP
WANNA LOOK AT THE MOON WITH US?
SORRY, BUT I'M IN A HURRY.

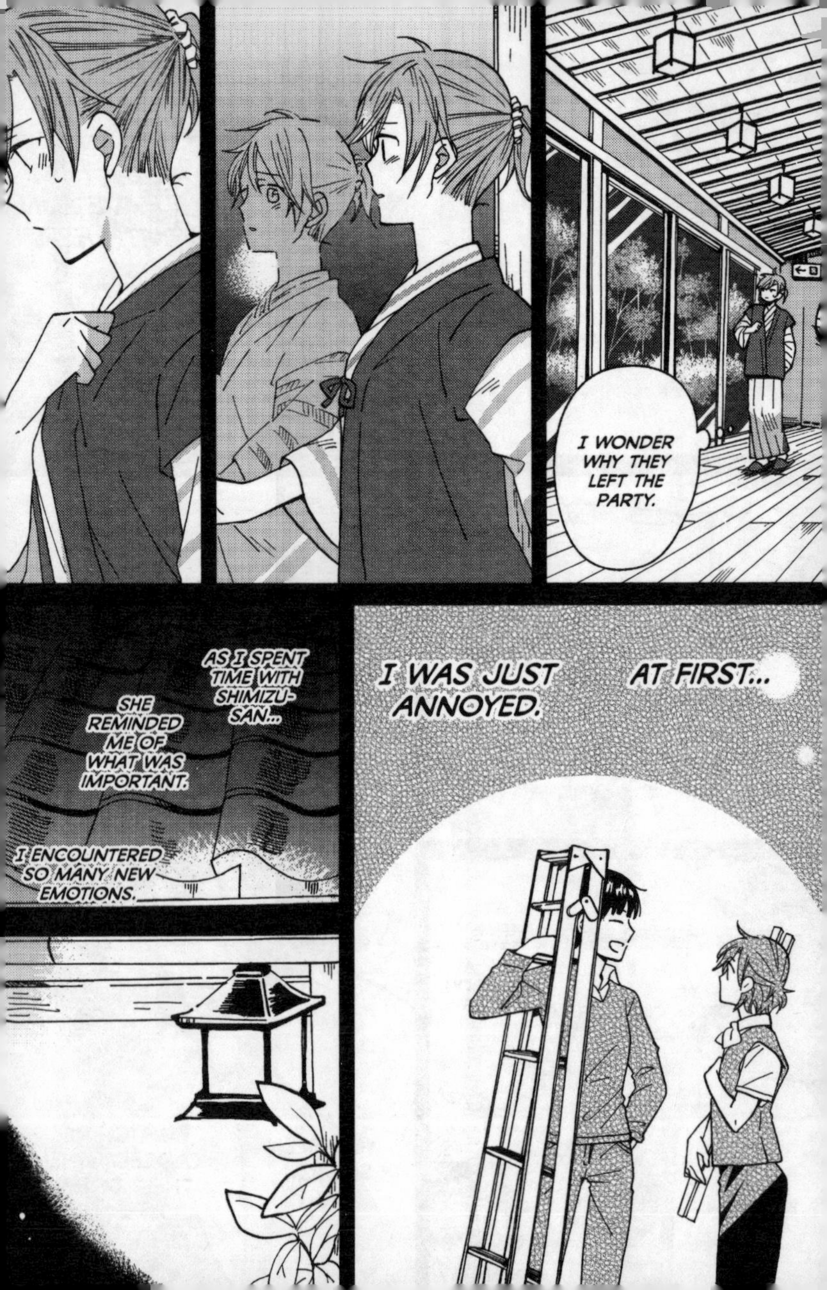
I WONDER WHY THEY LEFT THE PARTY.
AT FIRST...
I WAS JUST ANNOYED.
AS I SPENT TIME WITH SHIMIZU-SAN...
SHE REMINDED ME OF WHAT WAS IMPORTANT.
I ENCOUNTERED SO MANY NEW EMOTIONS.

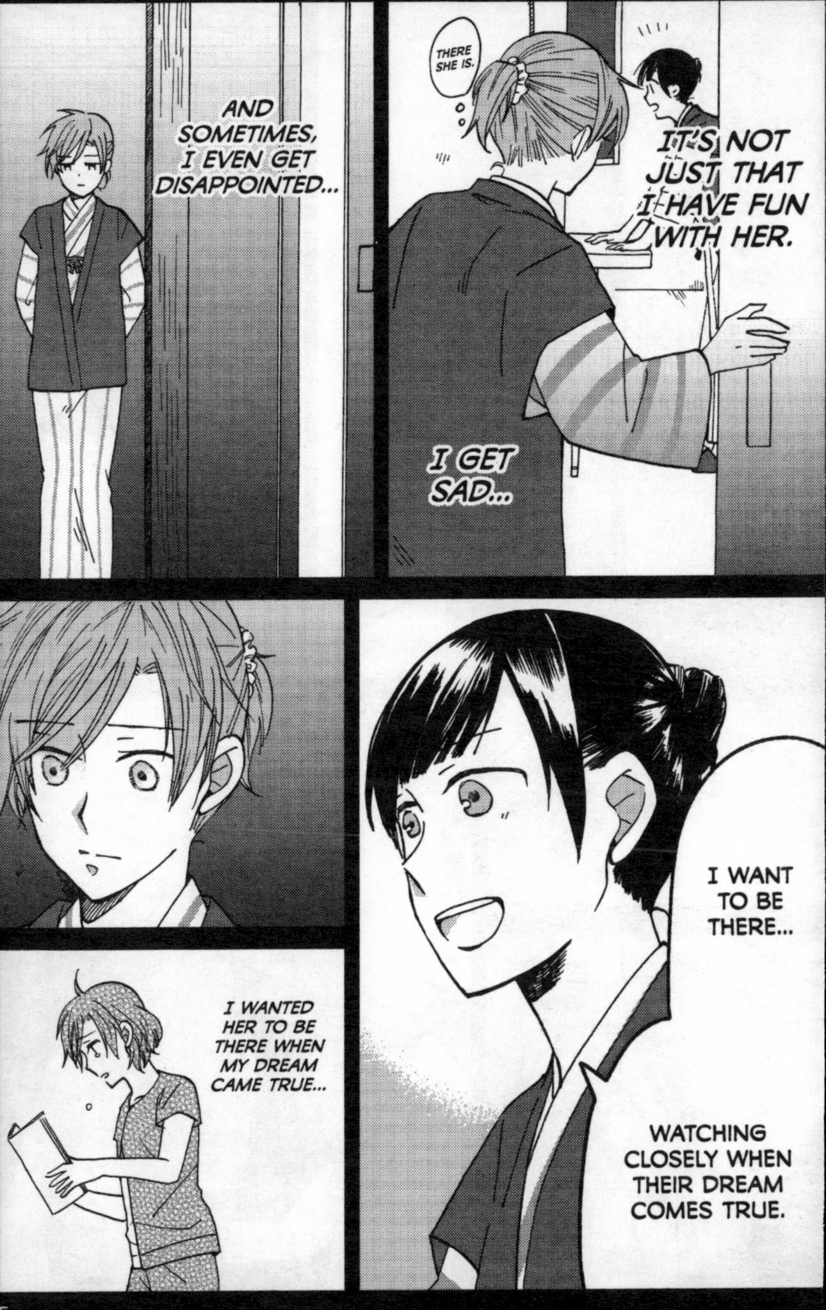
THERE SHE IS.
IT'S NOT JUST THAT I HAVE FUN WITH HER.
I GET SAD...
AND SOMETIMES, I EVEN GET DISAPPOINTED...
I WANT TO BE THERE...
WATCHING CLOSELY WHEN THEIR DREAM COMES TRUE.
I WANTED HER TO BE THERE WHEN MY DREAM CAME TRUE...

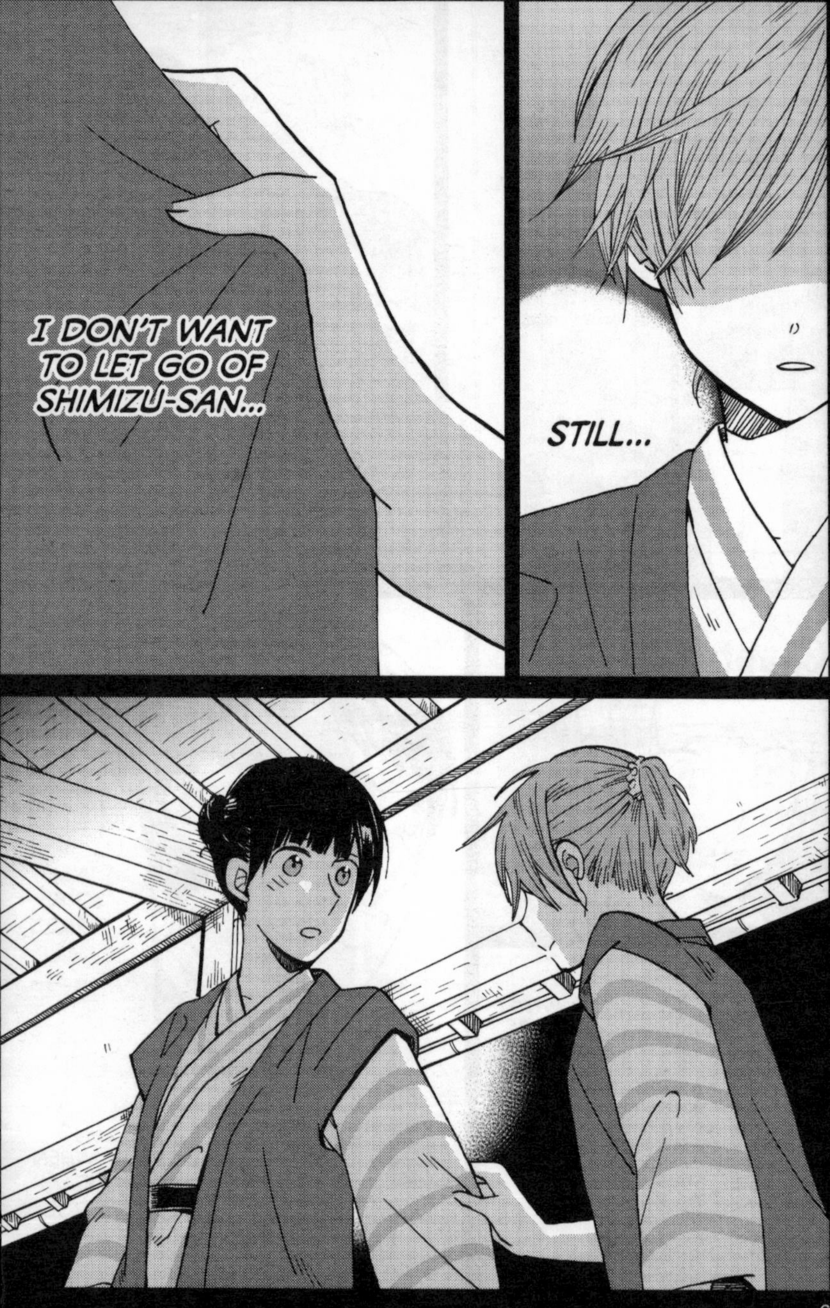
STILL...
I DON'T WANT TO LET GO OF SHIMIZU-SAN...

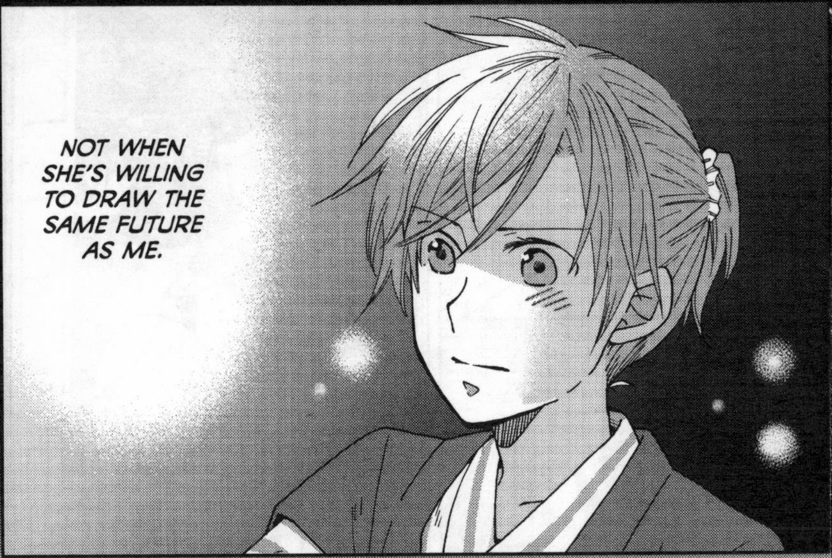
NOT WHEN SHE'S WILLING TO DRAW THE SAME FUTURE AS ME.

Chapter 15

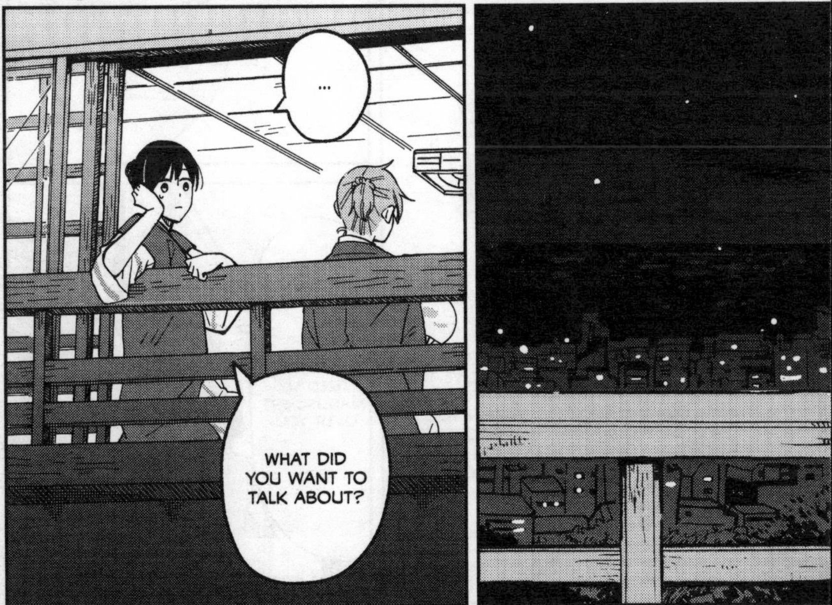
...
WHAT DID YOU WANT TO TALK ABOUT?

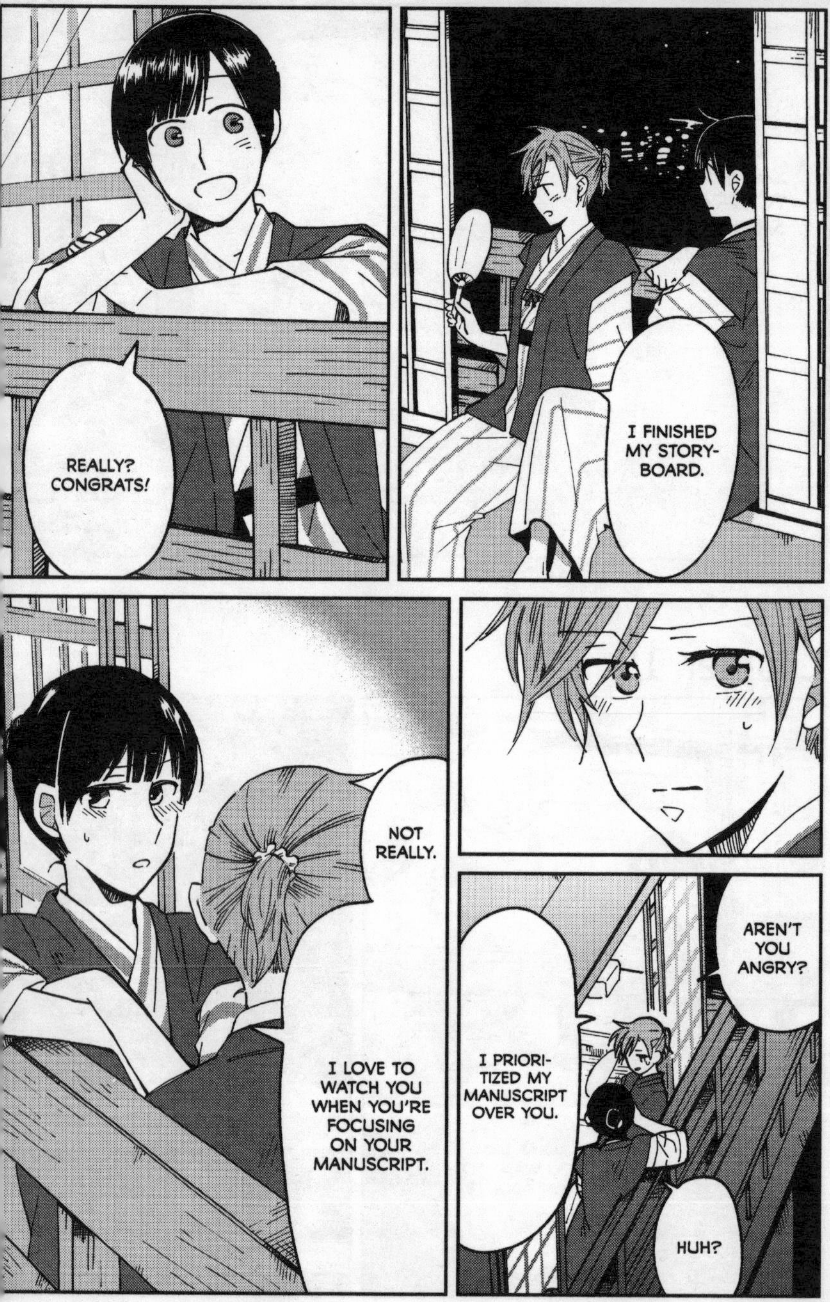
I FINISHED MY STORY-BOARD.
REALLY? CONGRATS!
AREN'T YOU ANGRY?
I PRIORI-TIZED MY MANUSCRIPT OVER YOU.
HUH?
NOT REALLY.
I LOVE TO WATCH YOU WHEN YOU'RE FOCUSING ON YOUR MANUSCRIPT.

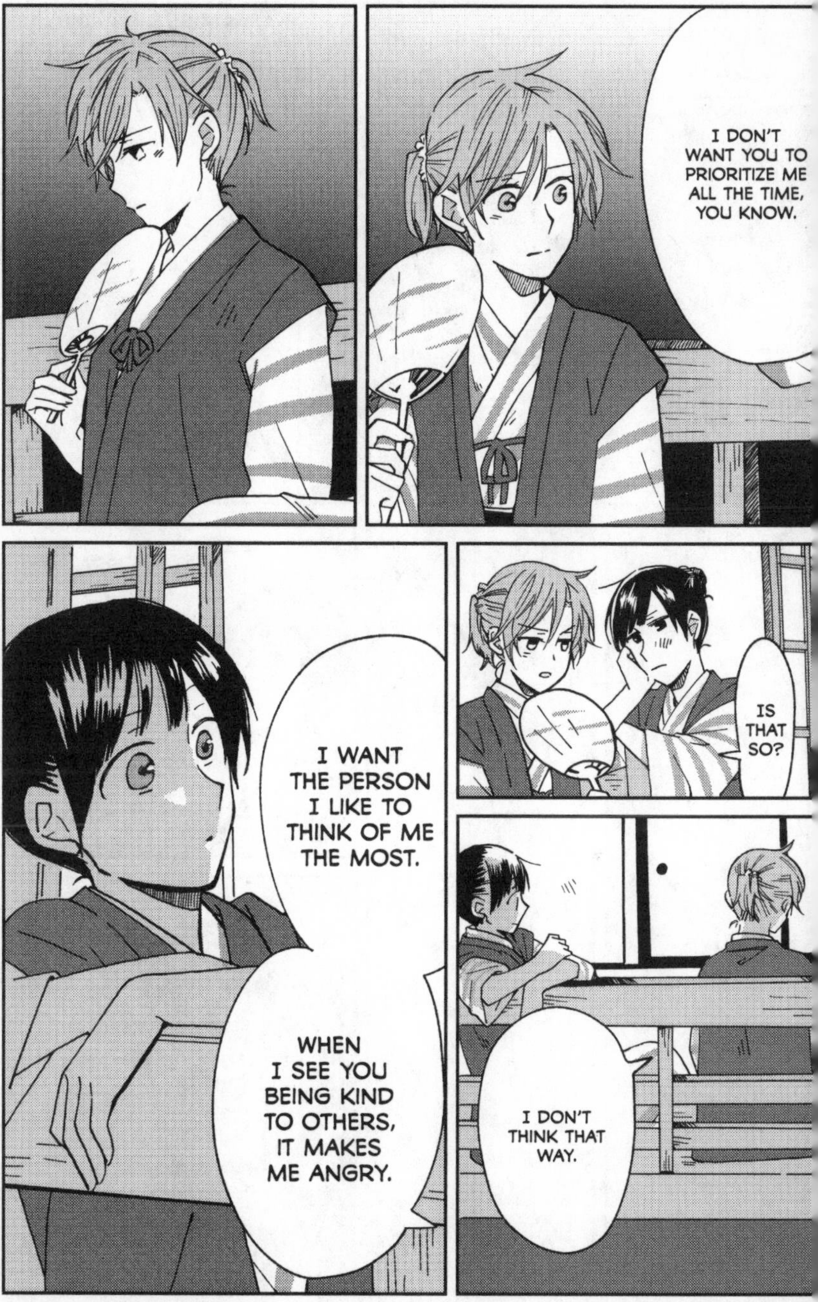
I DON'T WANT YOU TO PRIORITIZE ME ALL THE TIME, YOU KNOW.
IS THAT SO?
I DON'T THINK THAT WAY.
I WANT THE PERSON I LIKE TO THINK OF ME THE MOST.
WHEN I SEE YOU BEING KIND TO OTHERS, IT MAKES ME ANGRY.

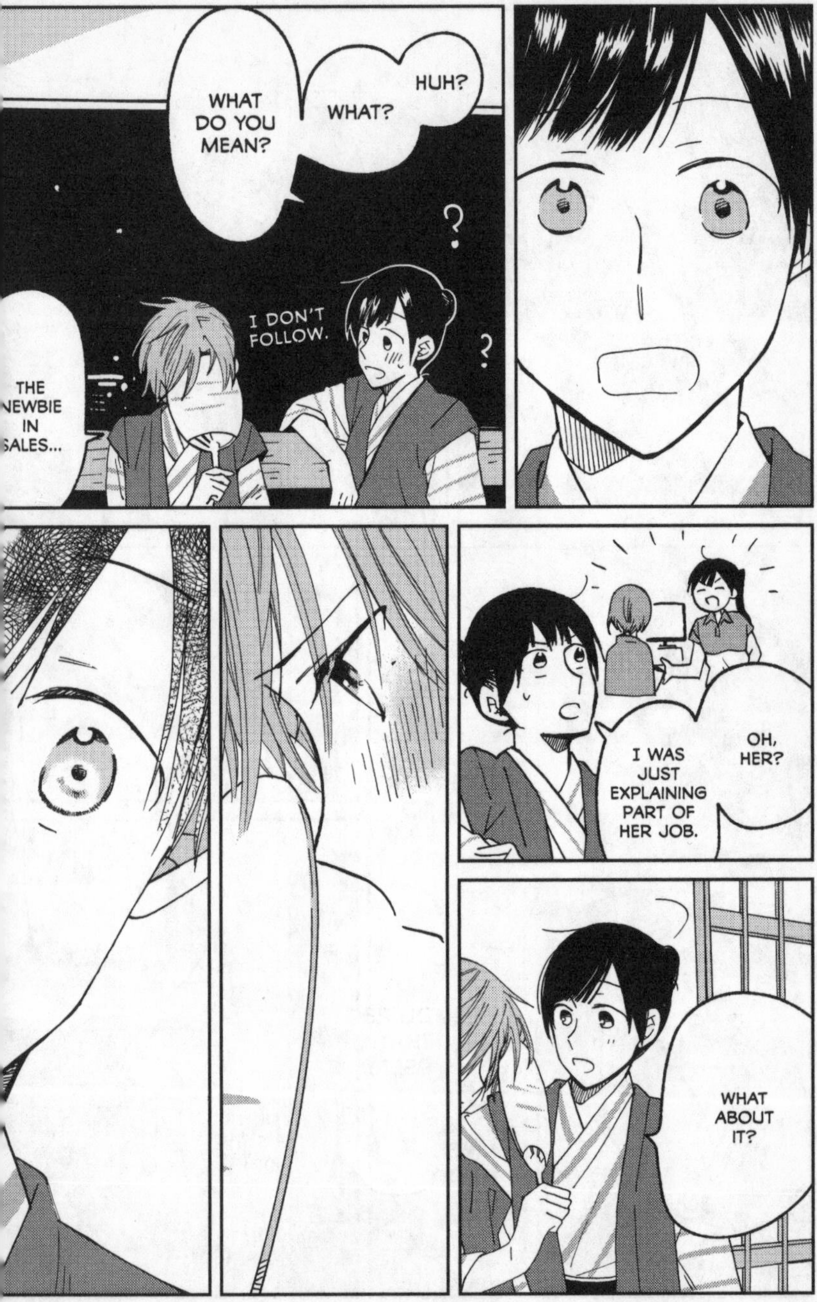
HUH?
WHAT?
WHAT DO YOU MEAN?
I DON'T FOLLOW.
THE NEWBIE IN SALES...
OH, HER?
I WAS JUST EXPLAINING PART OF HER JOB.
WHAT ABOUT IT?

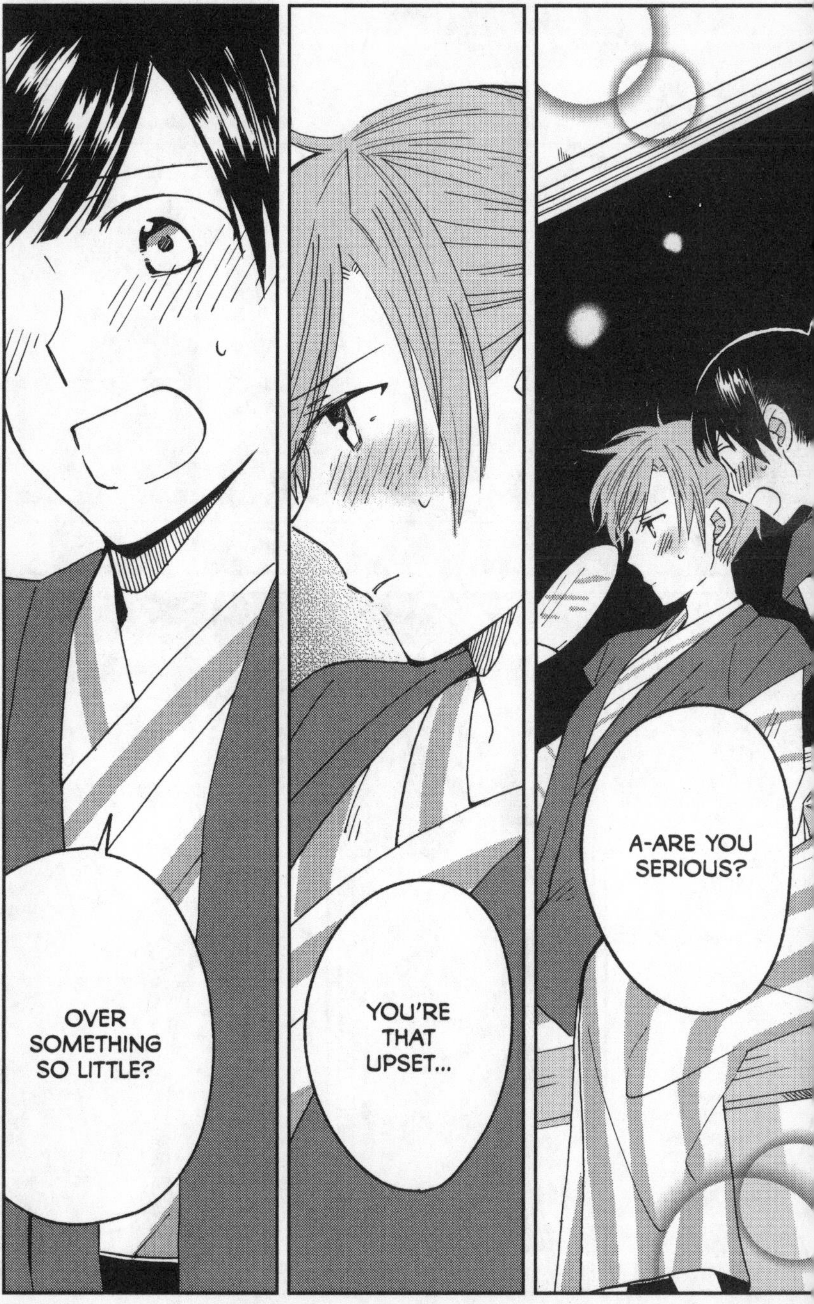
A-ARE YOU SERIOUS?
YOU'RE THAT UPSET...
OVER SOMETHING SO LITTLE?

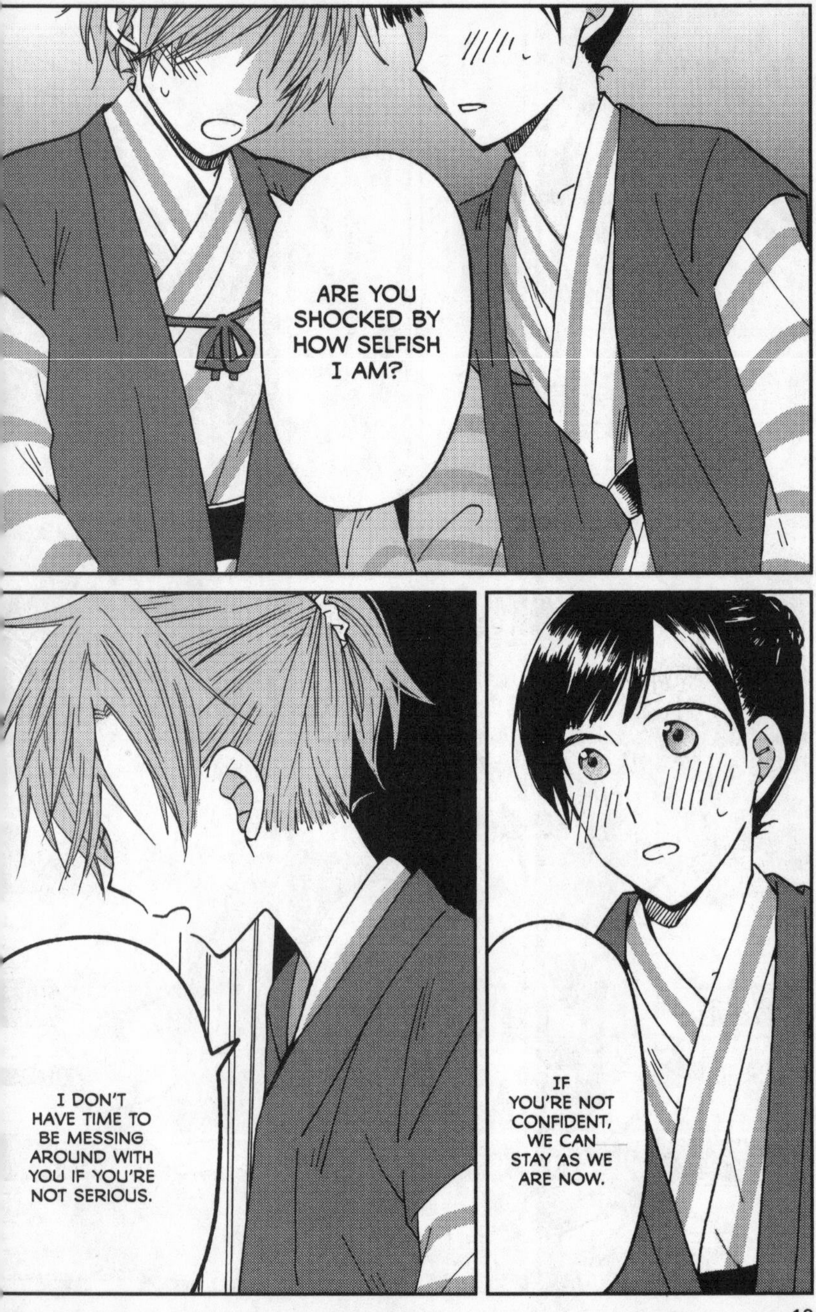
ARE YOU SHOCKED BY HOW SELFISH I AM?
IF YOU'RE NOT CONFIDENT, WE CAN STAY AS WE ARE NOW.
I DON'T HAVE TIME TO BE MESSING AROUND WITH YOU IF YOU'RE NOT SERIOUS.

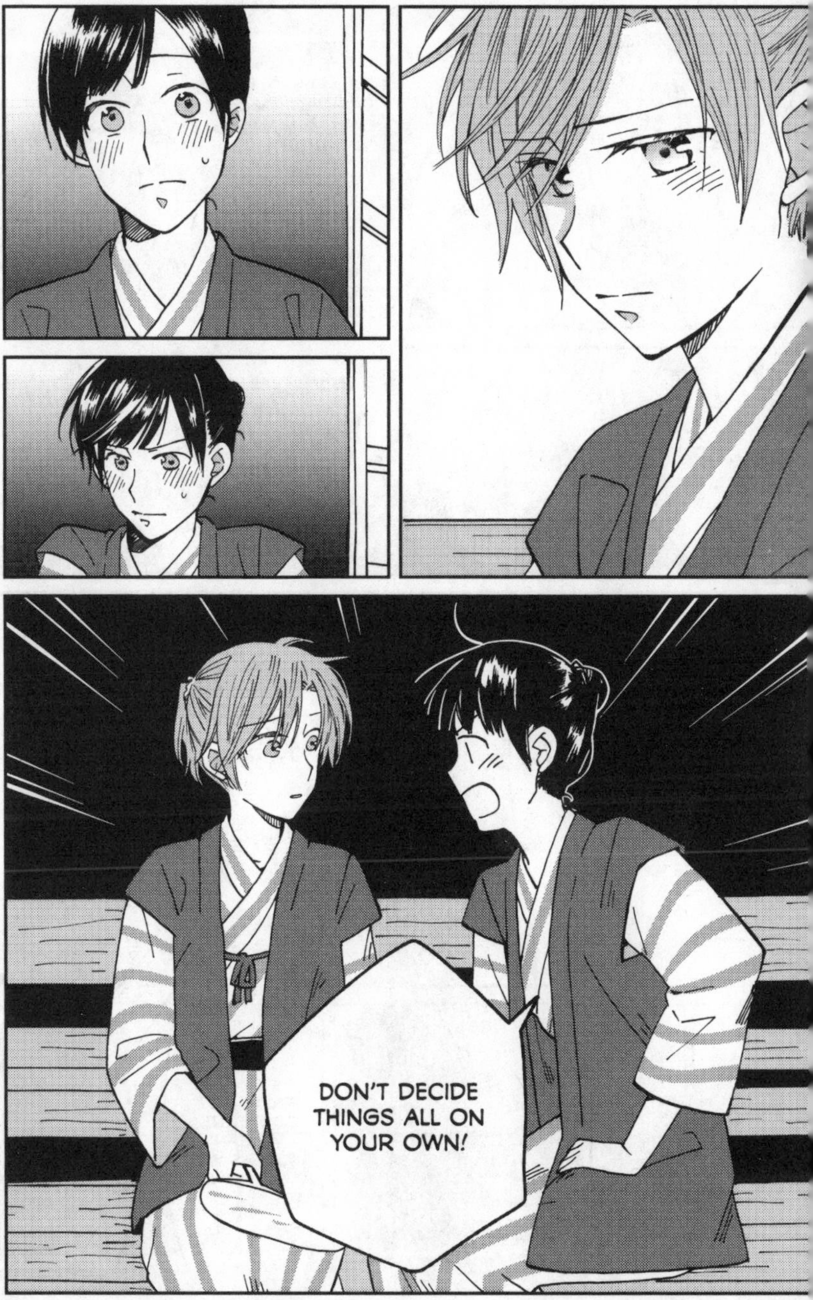
DON'T DECIDE THINGS ALL ON YOUR OWN!

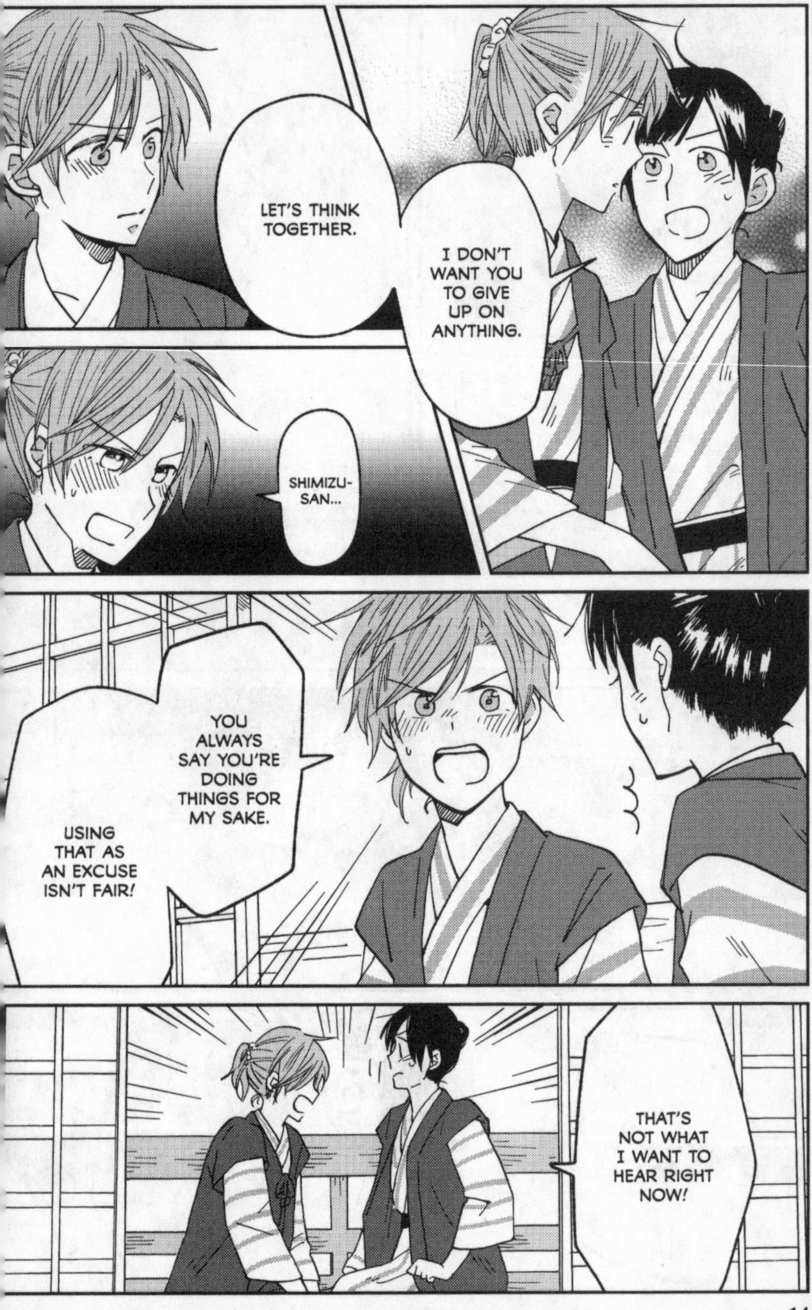
I DON'T WANT YOU TO GIVE UP ON ANYTHING.
LET'S THINK TOGETHER.
SHIMIZU-SAN...
YOU ALWAYS SAY YOU'RE DOING THINGS FOR MY SAKE.
USING THAT AS AN EXCUSE ISN'T FAIR!
THAT'S NOT WHAT I WANT TO HEAR RIGHT NOW!

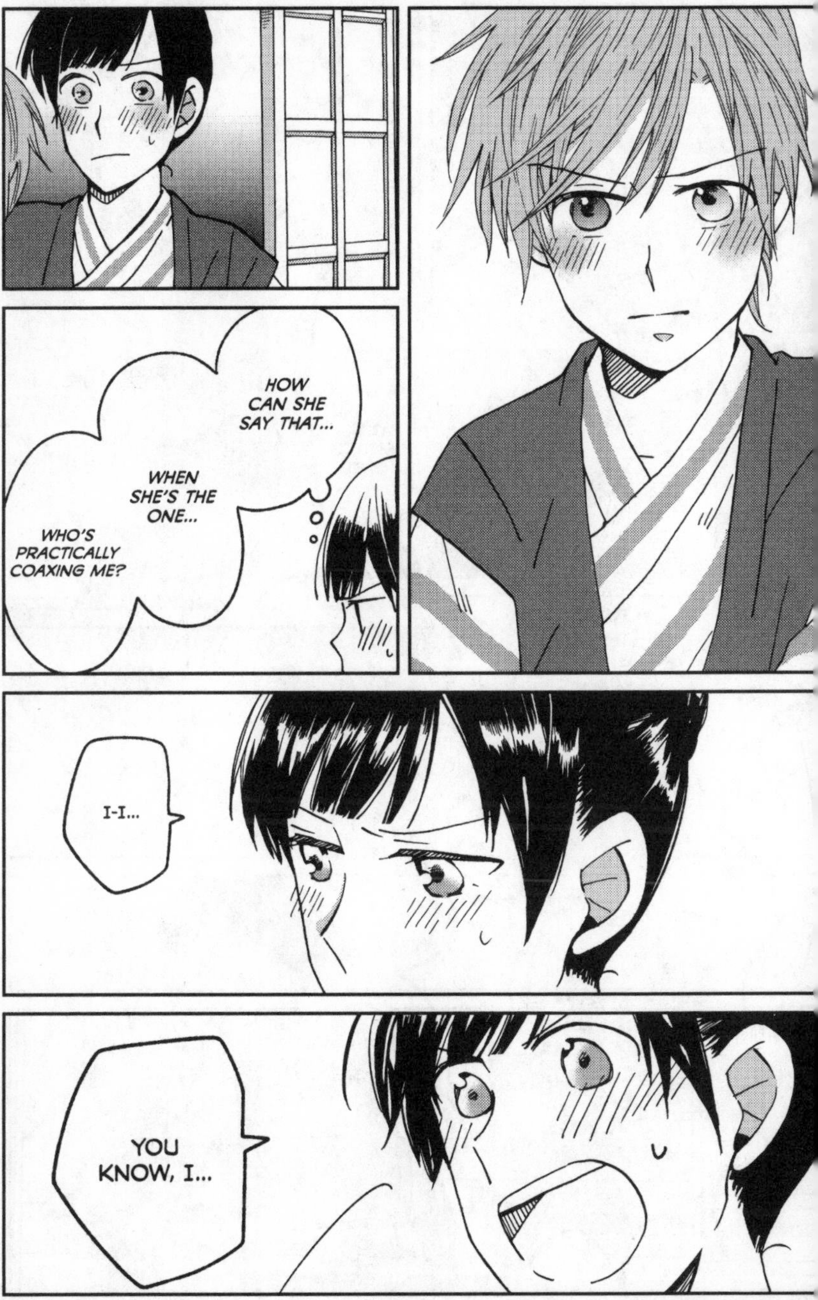
HOW CAN SHE SAY THAT...
WHEN SHE'S THE ONE...
WHO'S PRACTICALLY COAXING ME?
I-I...
YOU KNOW, I...

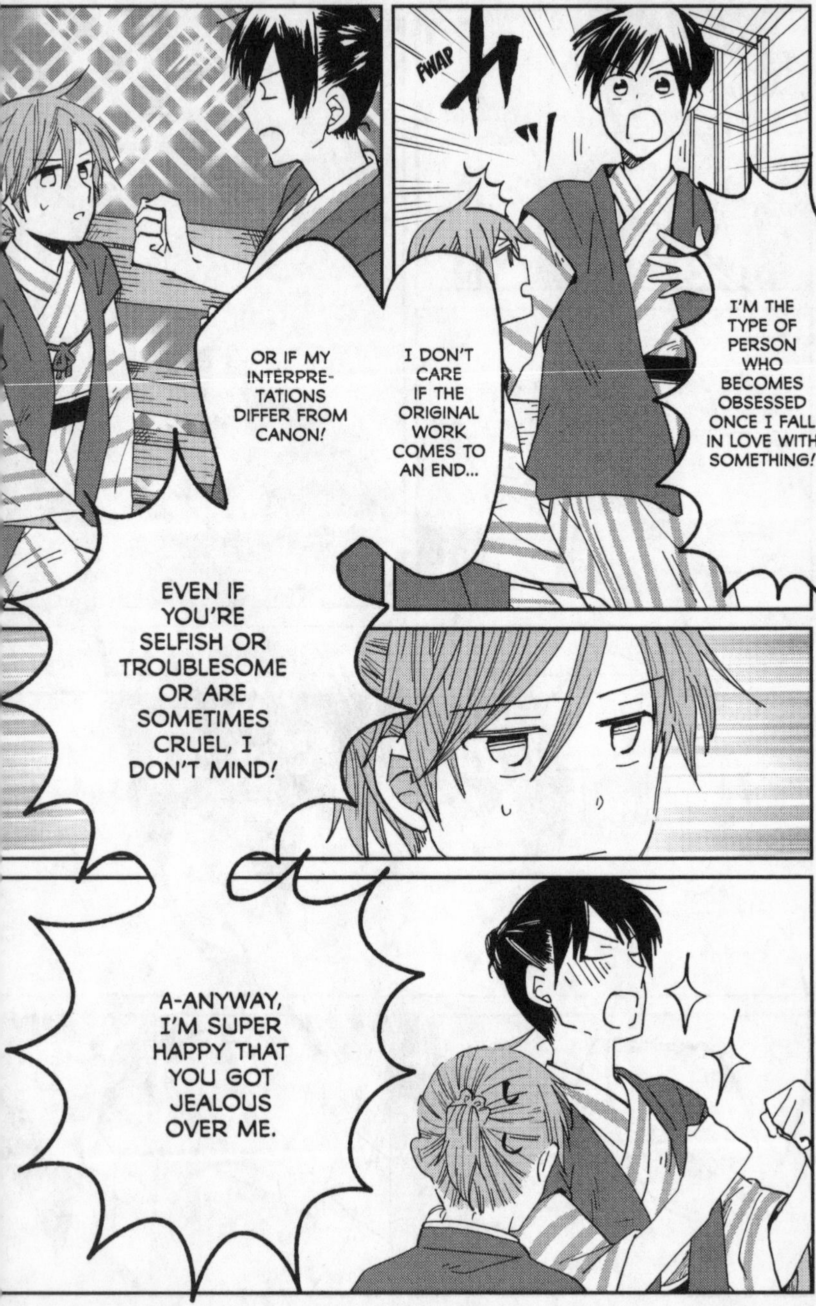
FWAP
I'M THE TYPE OF PERSON WHO BECOMES OBSESSED ONCE I FALL IN LOVE WITH SOMETHING!
I DON'T CARE IF THE ORIGINAL WORK COMES TO AN END...
OR IF MY INTERPRETATIONS DIFFER FROM CANON!
EVEN IF YOU'RE SELFISH OR TROUBLESOME OR ARE SOMETIMES CRUEL, I DON'T MIND!
A-ANYWAY, I'M SUPER HAPPY THAT YOU GOT JEALOUS OVER ME.

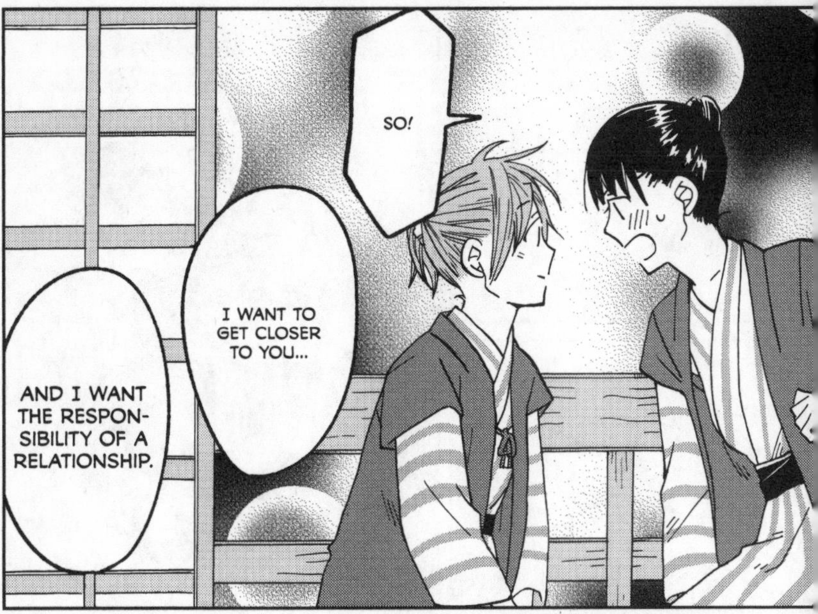
SO!
I WANT TO GET CLOSER TO YOU...
AND I WANT THE RESPON-SIBILITY OF A RELATIONSHIP.

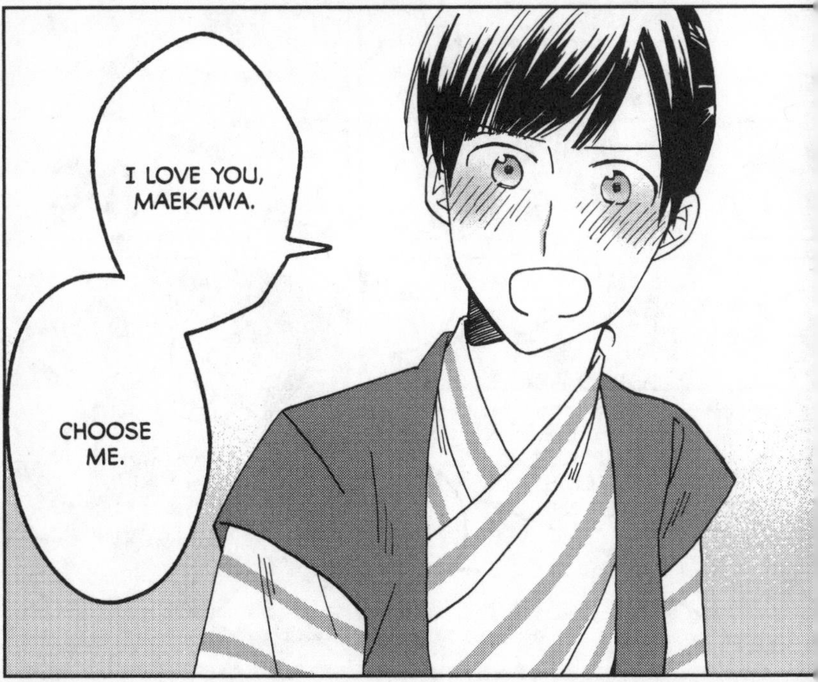
I LOVE YOU, MAEKAWA.
CHOOSE ME.

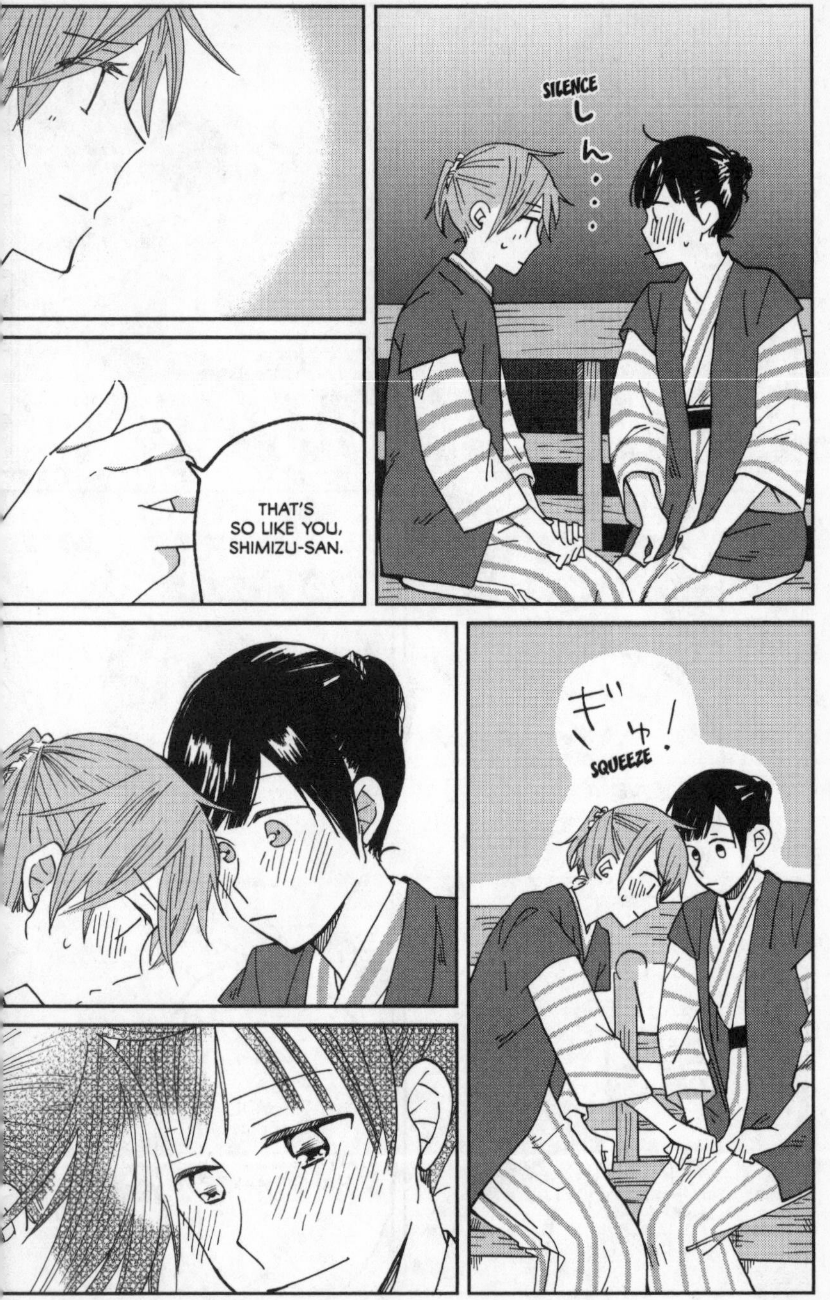
SILENCE
しん・・・
THAT'S SO LIKE YOU, SHIMIZU-SAN.
ぎゅ!
SQUEEZE

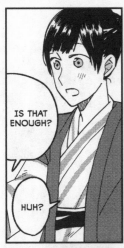

Y-YEAH!
SHAKE ぶん SHAKE ぶん
I'M GLAD YOU AGREE.
IS THAT ENOUGH?
HUH?
ARE YOU SATISFIED WITH JUST A HANDSHAKE?

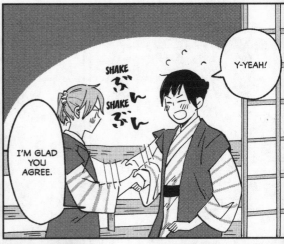

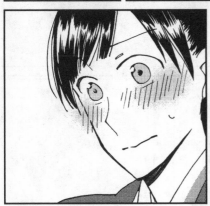

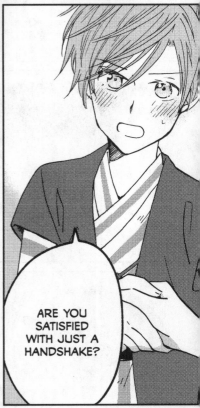

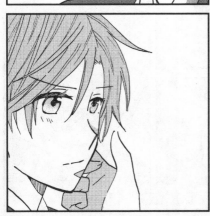

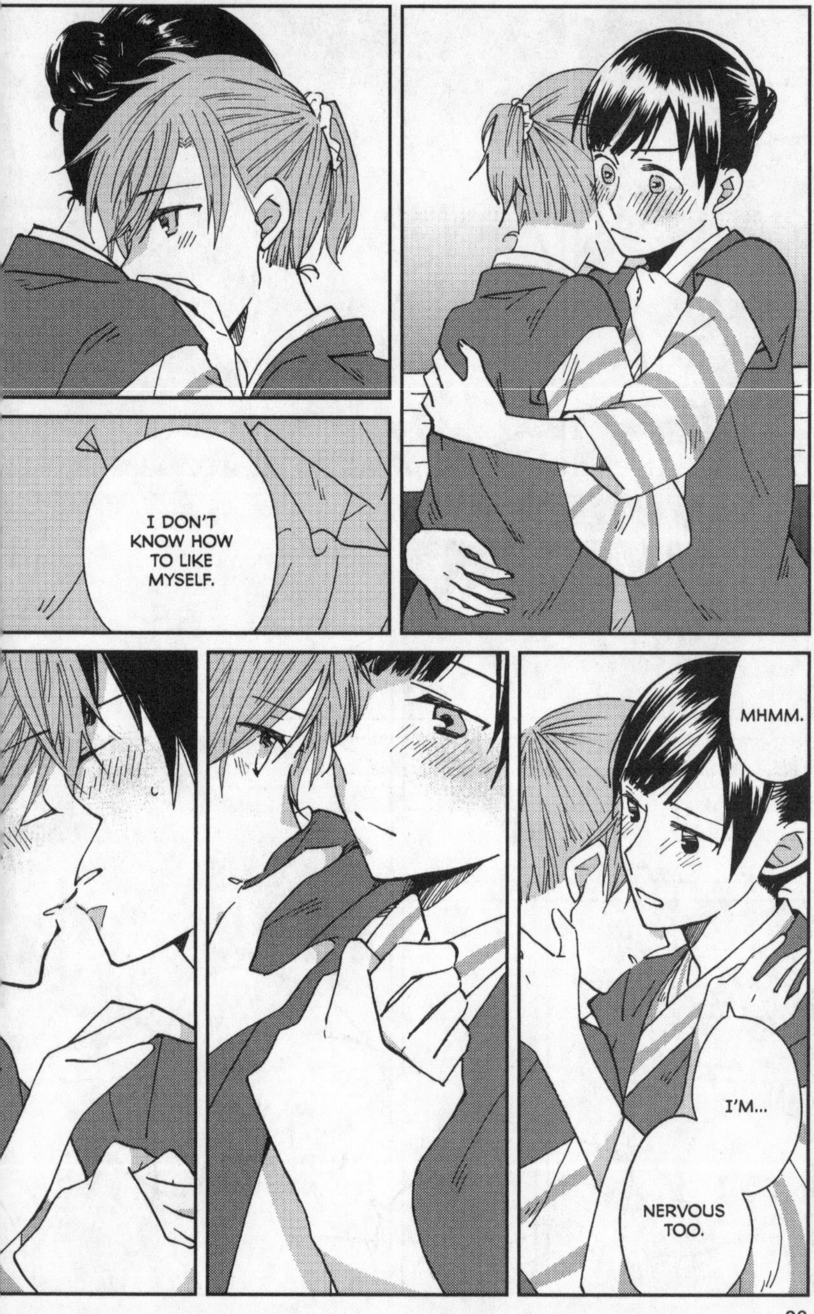
I DON'T KNOW HOW TO LIKE MYSELF.
MHMM.
I'M...
NERVOUS TOO.

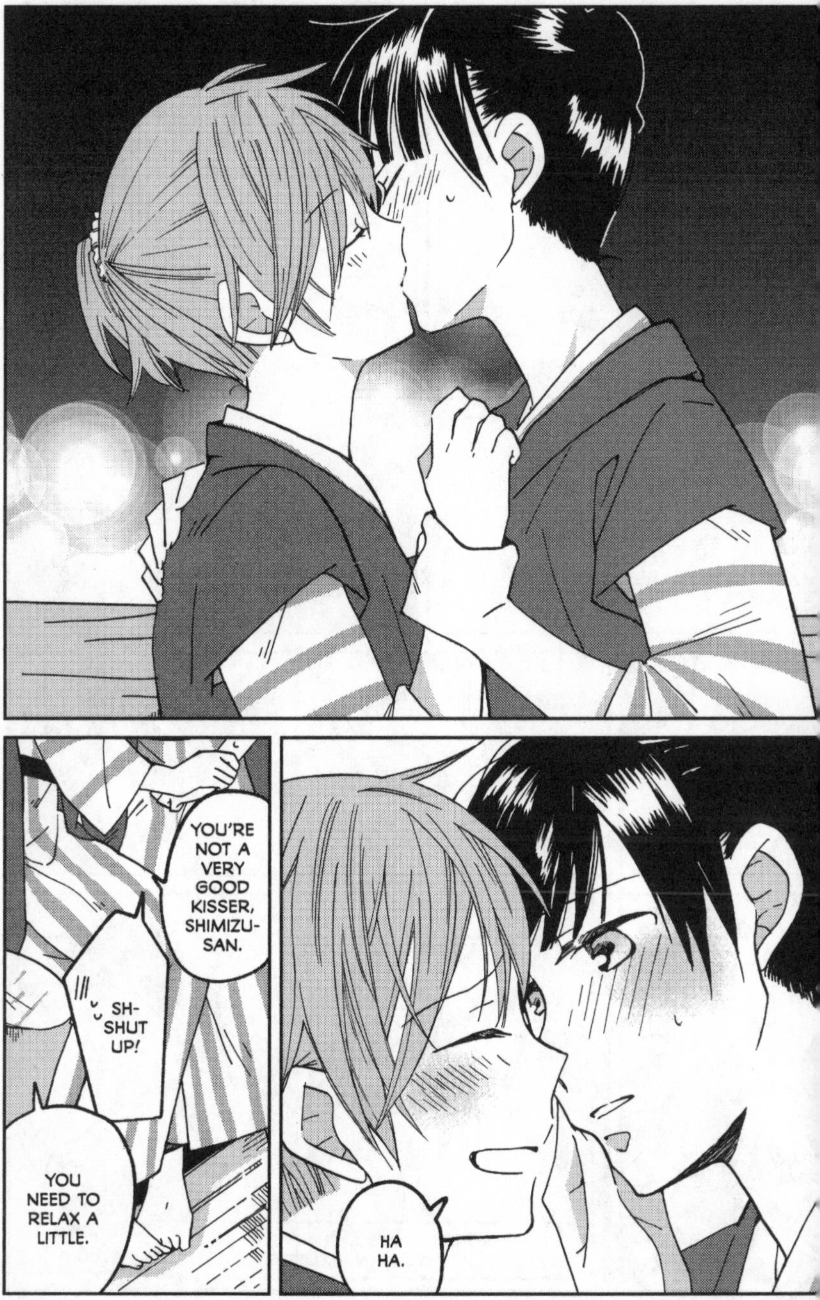
HA HA.
YOU'RE NOT A VERY GOOD KISSER, SHIMIZU-SAN.
SH-SHUT UP!
YOU NEED TO RELAX A LITTLE.

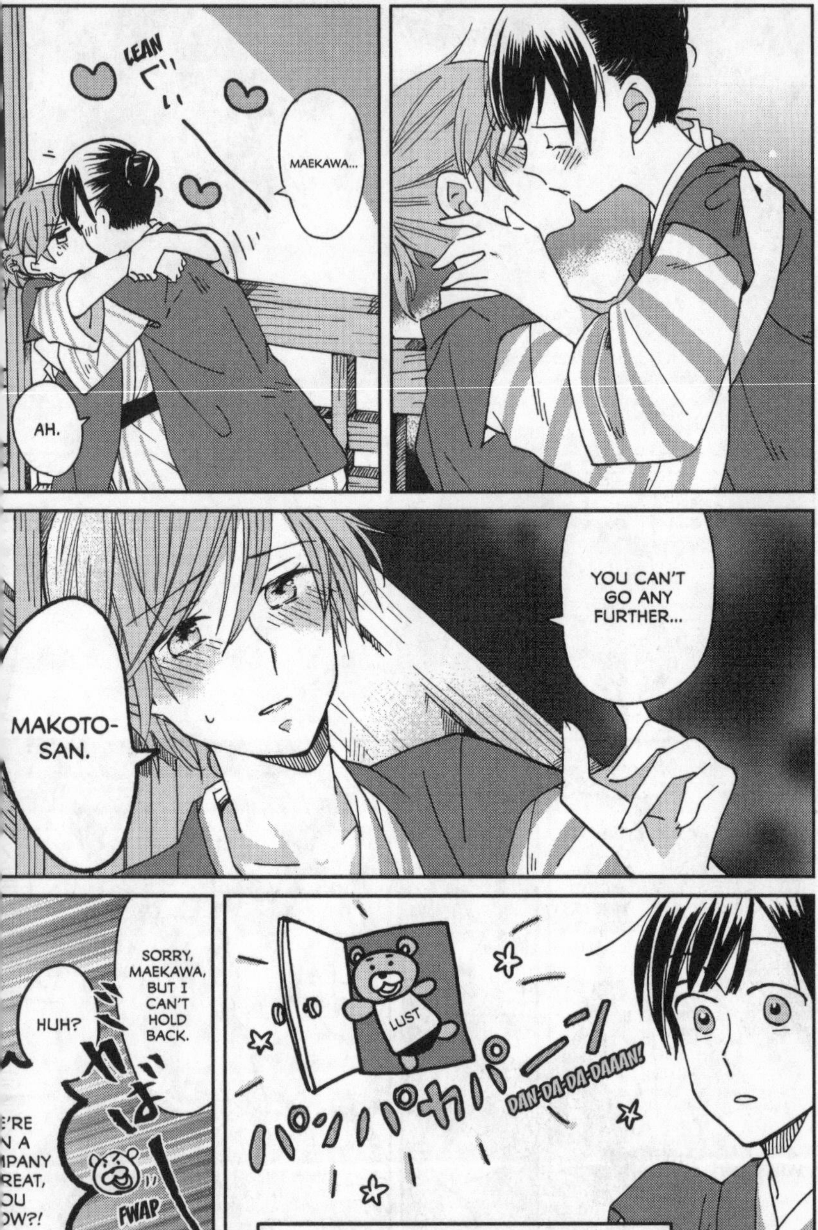
MAEKAWA...
LEAN
AH.
YOU CAN'T GO ANY FURTHER...
MAKOTO-SAN.
LUST
DAN-DA-DA-DAAAN!
SHIMIZU-SAN'S CARNAL DESIRES HAVE BEEN RELEASED!
SORRY, MAEKAWA, BUT I CAN'T HOLD BACK.
HUH?
FWAP
E'RE N A MPANY REAT, OU OW?!

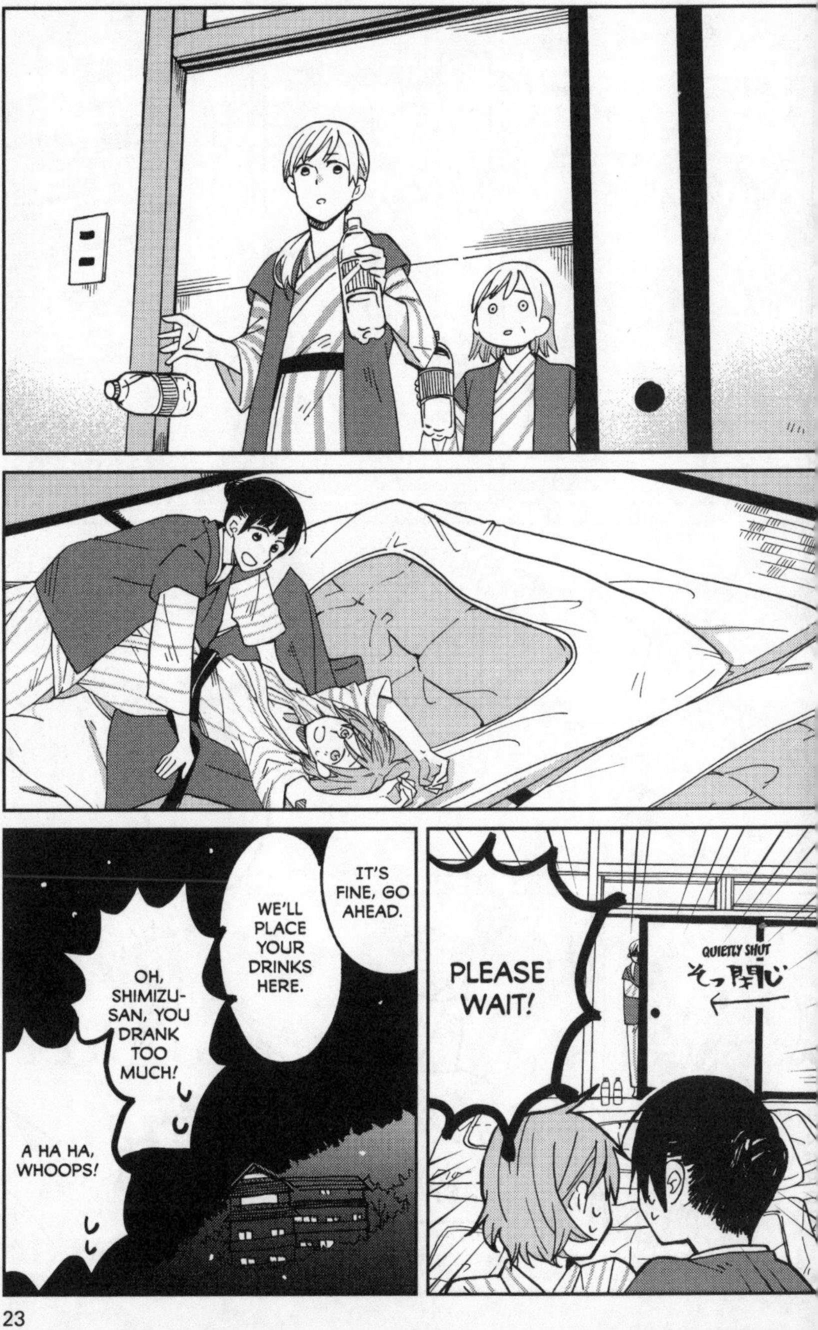
PLEASE WAIT!
QUIETLY SHUT
そっ閉じ
IT'S FINE, GO AHEAD.
WE'LL PLACE YOUR DRINKS HERE.
OH, SHIMIZU-SAN, YOU DRANK TOO MUCH!
A HA HA, WHOOPS!

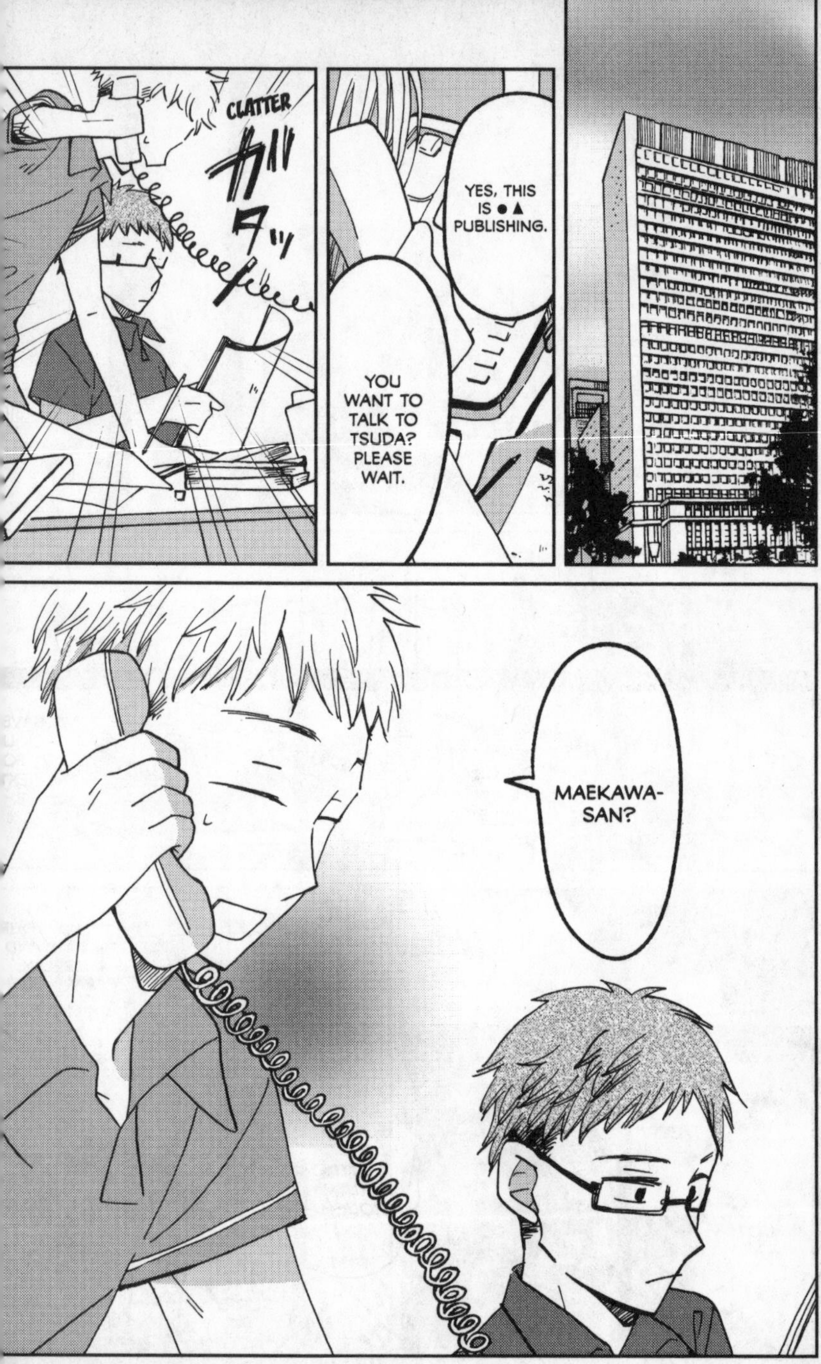
YES, THIS IS ●▲ PUBLISHING.
YOU WANT TO TALK TO TSUDA? PLEASE WAIT.
CLATTER
ガタッ
MAEKAWA-SAN?

Chapter 16

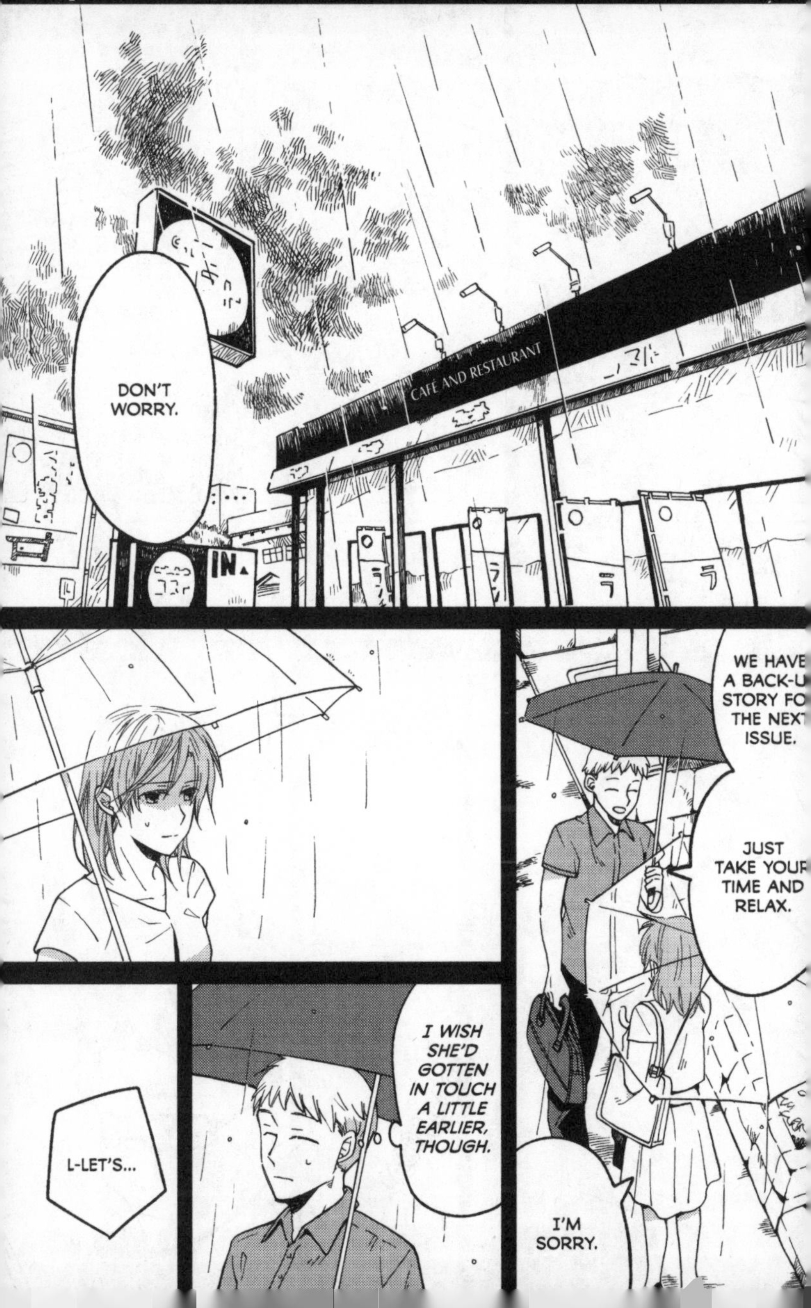
DON'T WORRY.
CAFÉ AND RESTAURANT
IN
WE HAVE A BACK-U STORY FO THE NEXT ISSUE.
JUST TAKE YOUR TIME AND RELAX.
I'M SORRY.
I WISH SHE'D GOTTEN IN TOUCH A LITTLE EARLIER, THOUGH.
L-LET'S...

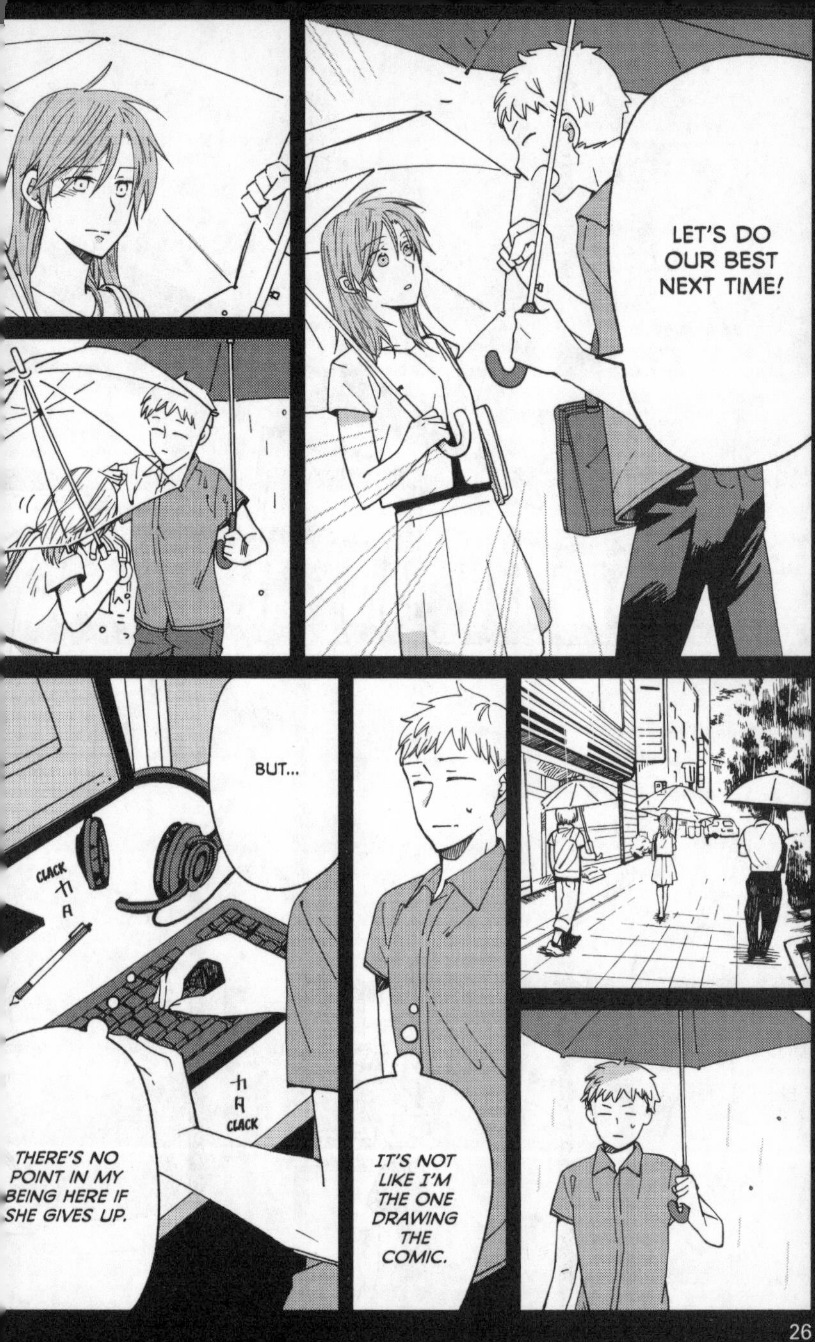
LET'S DO OUR BEST NEXT TIME!
IT'S NOT LIKE I'M THE ONE DRAWING THE COMIC.
BUT...
CLACK
CLACK
THERE'S NO POINT IN MY BEING HERE IF SHE GIVES UP.

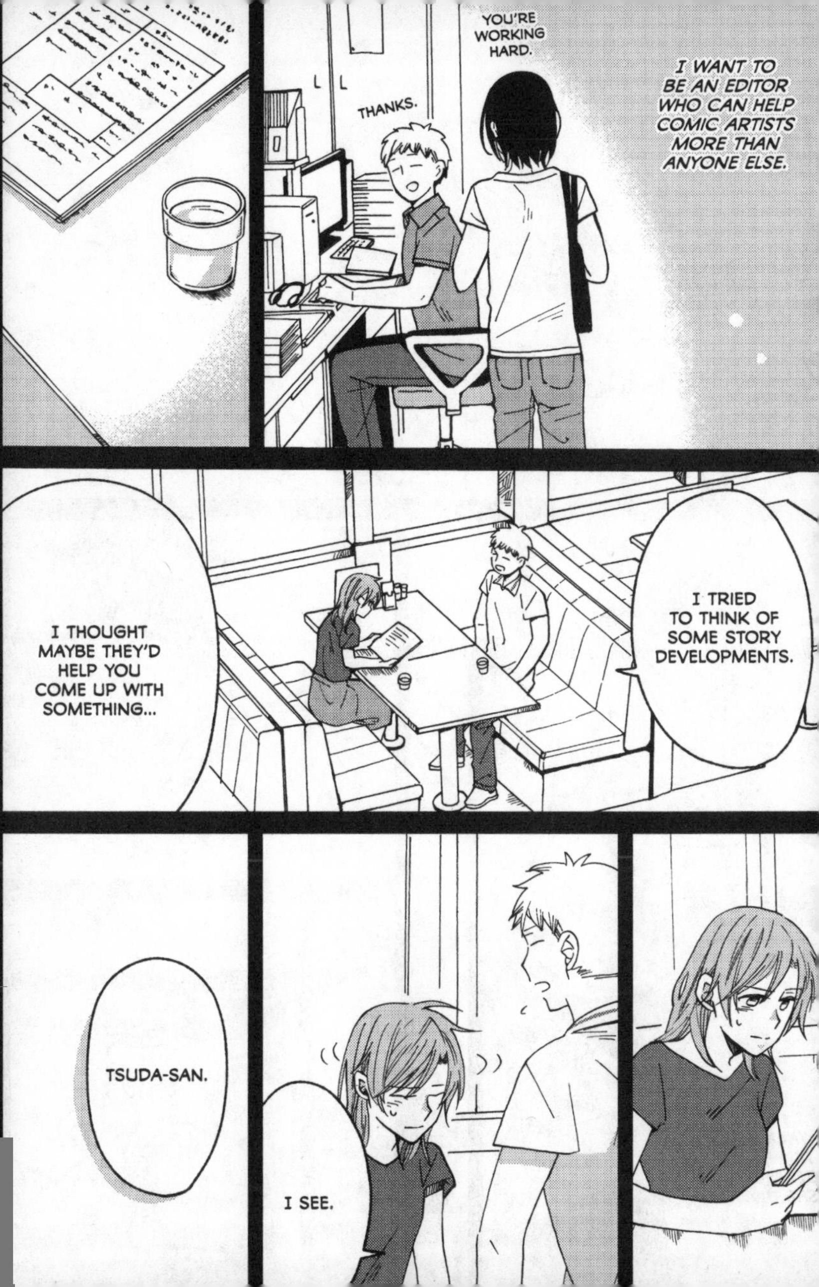
I WANT TO BE AN EDITOR WHO CAN HELP COMIC ARTISTS MORE THAN ANYONE ELSE.
YOU'RE WORKING HARD.
THANKS.
I TRIED TO THINK OF SOME STORY DEVELOPMENTS.
I THOUGHT MAYBE THEY'D HELP YOU COME UP WITH SOMETHING...
I SEE.
TSUDA-SAN.

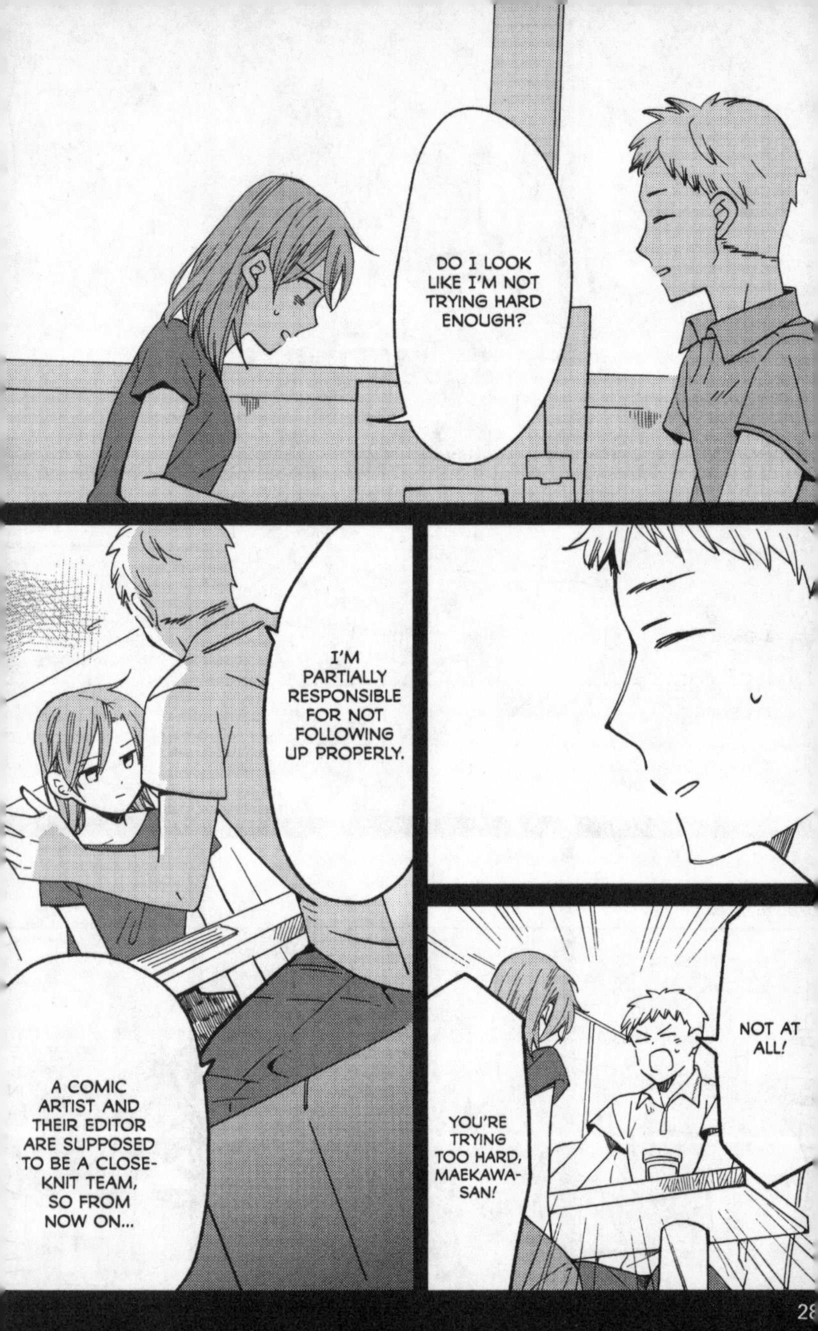
DO I LOOK LIKE I'M NOT TRYING HARD ENOUGH?
NOT AT ALL!
YOU'RE TRYING TOO HARD, MAEKAWA-SAN!
I'M PARTIALLY RESPONSIBLE FOR NOT FOLLOWING UP PROPERLY.
A COMIC ARTIST AND THEIR EDITOR ARE SUPPOSED TO BE A CLOSE-KNIT TEAM, SO FROM NOW ON...

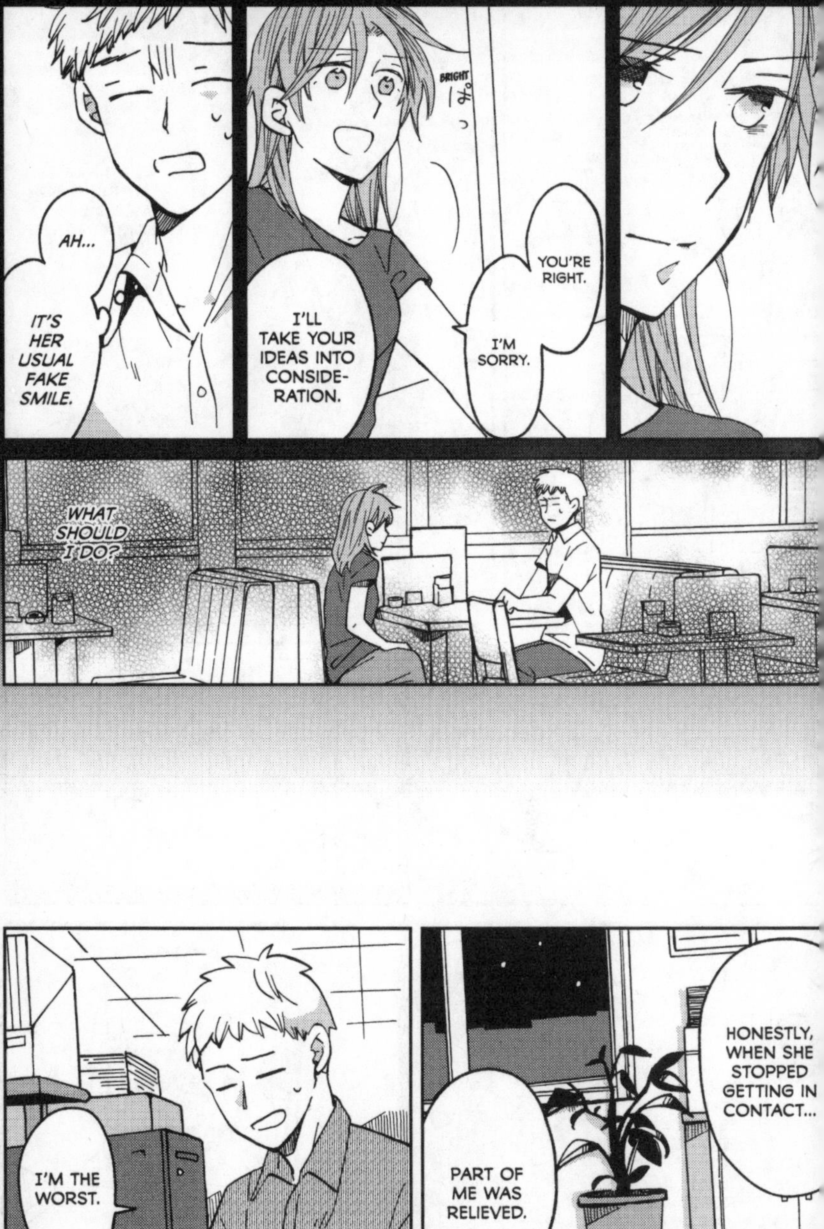
BRIGHT
ぱっ
YOU'RE RIGHT.
I'M SORRY.
I'LL TAKE YOUR IDEAS INTO CONSIDE-RATION.
AH...
IT'S HER USUAL FAKE SMILE.
WHAT SHOULD I DO?
HONESTLY, WHEN SHE STOPPED GETTING IN CONTACT...
PART OF ME WAS RELIEVED.
I'M THE WORST.

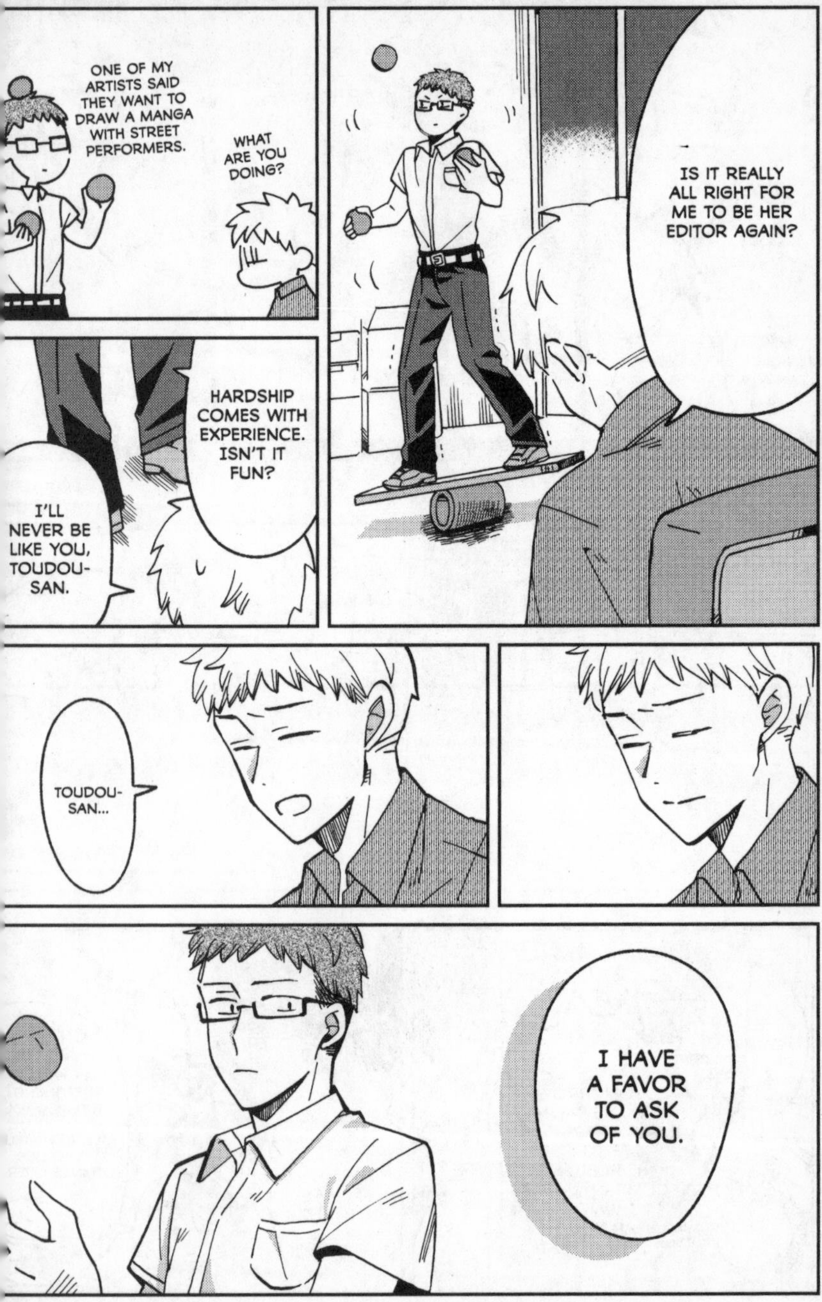
IS IT REALLY ALL RIGHT FOR ME TO BE HER EDITOR AGAIN?
WHAT ARE YOU DOING?
ONE OF MY ARTISTS SAID THEY WANT TO DRAW A MANGA WITH STREET PERFORMERS.
HARDSHIP COMES WITH EXPERIENCE. ISN'T IT FUN?
I'LL NEVER BE LIKE YOU, TOUDOU-SAN.
TOUDOU-SAN...
I HAVE A FAVOR TO ASK OF YOU.

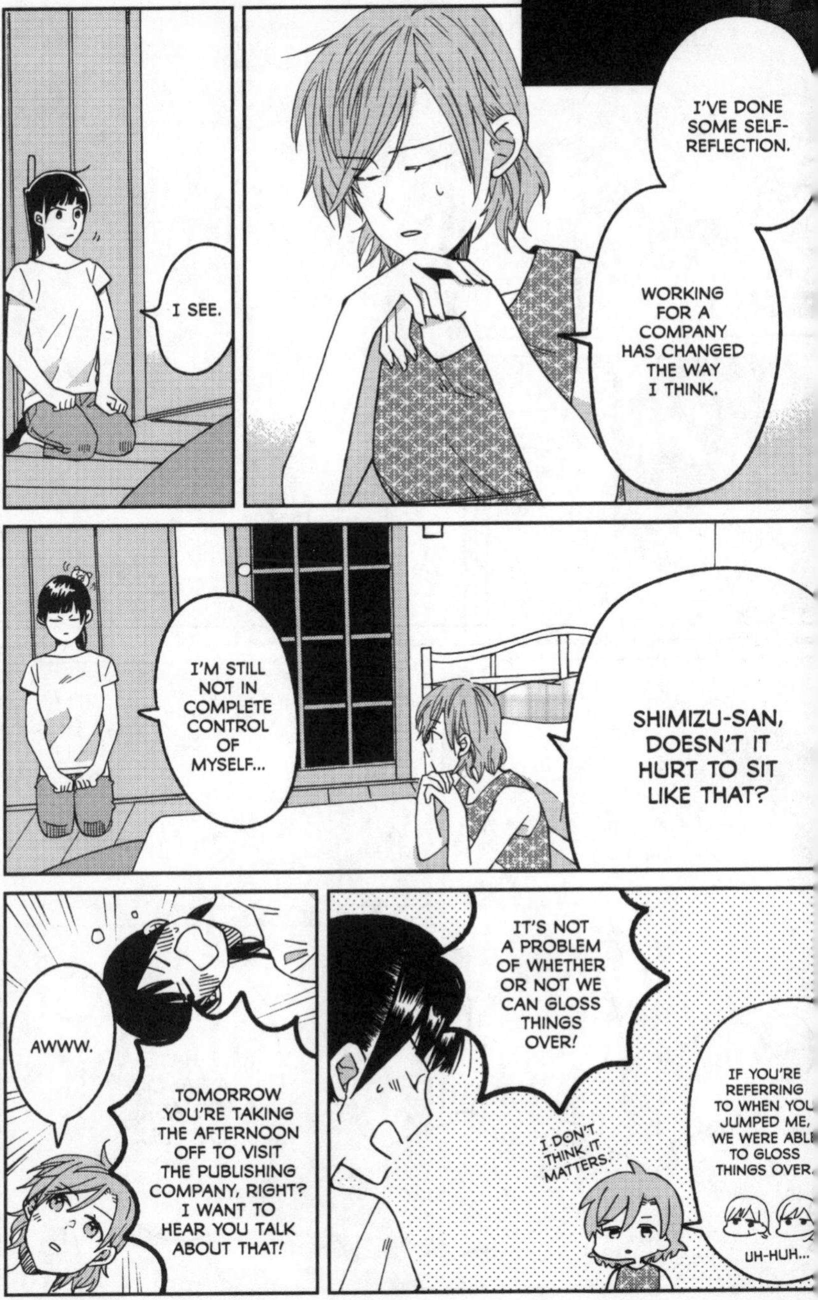
I'VE DONE SOME SELF-REFLECTION.
WORKING FOR A COMPANY HAS CHANGED THE WAY I THINK.
I SEE.
SHIMIZU-SAN, DOESN'T IT HURT TO SIT LIKE THAT?
I'M STILL NOT IN COMPLETE CONTROL OF MYSELF...
IF YOU'RE REFERRING TO WHEN YOU JUMPED ME, WE WERE ABL TO GLOSS THINGS OVER.
UH-HUH...
IT'S NOT A PROBLEM OF WHETHER OR NOT WE CAN GLOSS THINGS OVER!
I DON'T THINK IT MATTERS.
AWWW.
TOMORROW YOU'RE TAKING THE AFTERNOON OFF TO VISIT THE PUBLISHING COMPANY, RIGHT? I WANT TO HEAR YOU TALK ABOUT THAT!

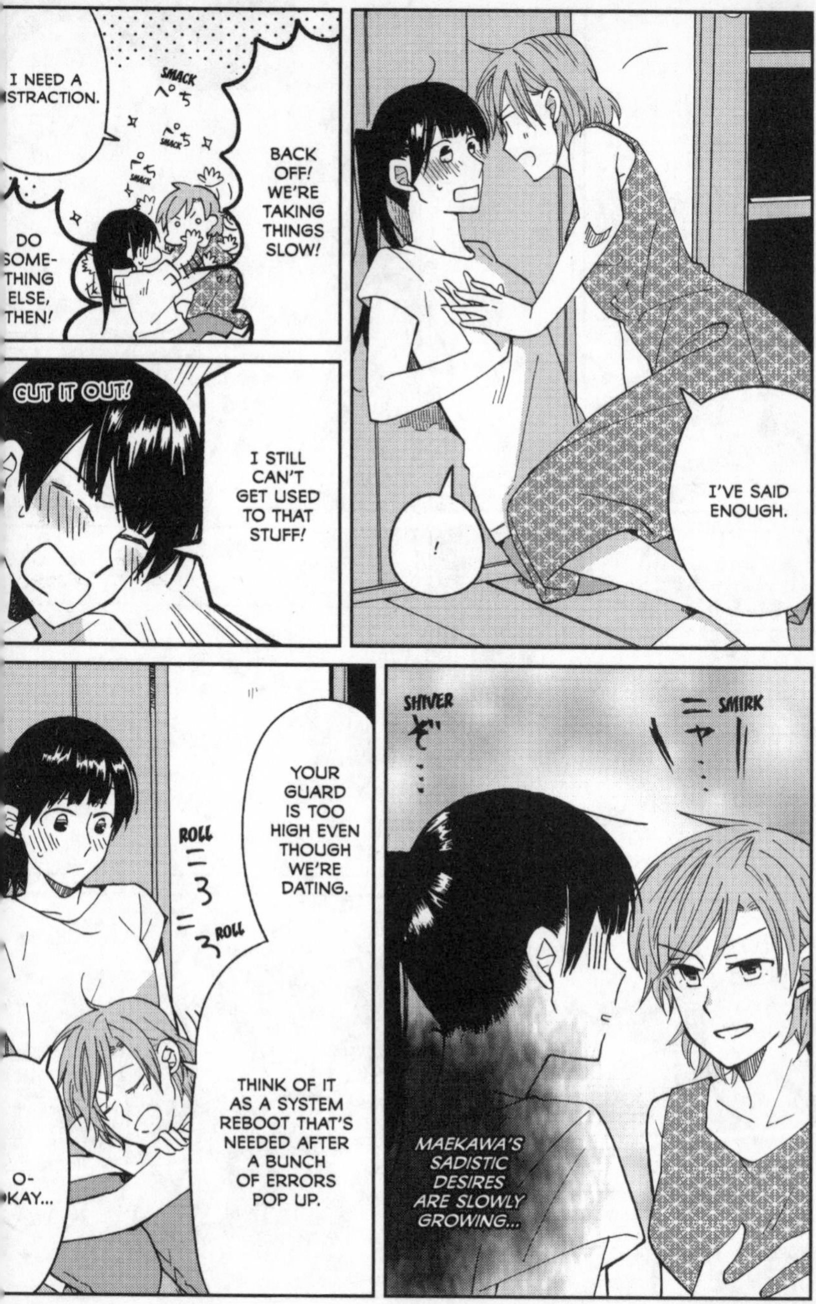
I NEED A
ISTRACTION.
SMACK
SMACK
SMACK
DO SOME-
THING
ELSE,
THEN!
BACK OFF! WE'RE TAKING THINGS SLOW!
CUT IT OUT!
I STILL CAN'T GET USED TO THAT STUFF!
!
I'VE SAID ENOUGH.
YOUR GUARD IS TOO HIGH EVEN THOUGH WE'RE DATING.
ROLL
ROLL
THINK OF IT AS A SYSTEM REBOOT THAT'S NEEDED AFTER A BUNCH OF ERRORS POP UP.
O-
KAY...
SHIVER
SMIRK
MAEKAWA'S SADISTIC DESIRES ARE SLOWLY GROWING...

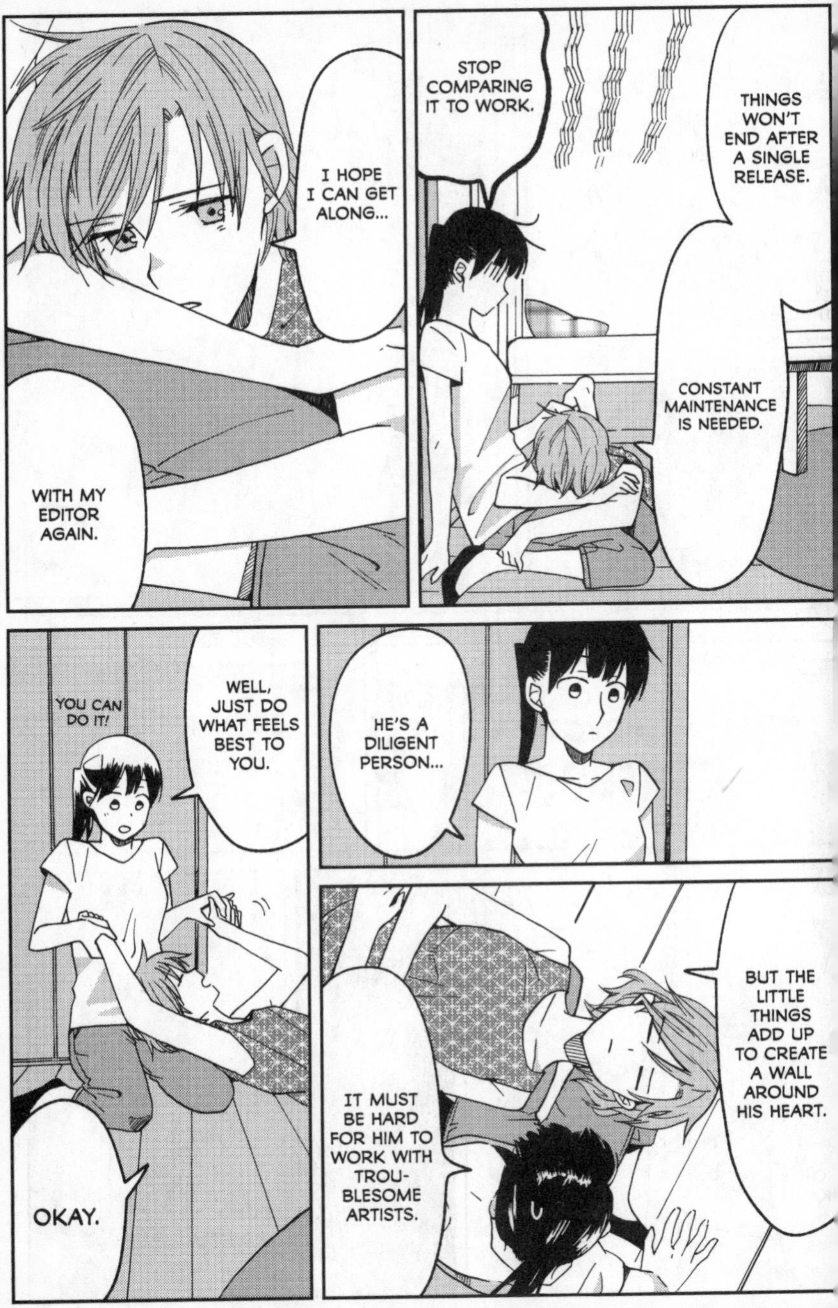
THINGS WON'T END AFTER A SINGLE RELEASE.
CONSTANT MAINTENANCE IS NEEDED.
STOP COMPARING IT TO WORK.
I HOPE I CAN GET ALONG...
WITH MY EDITOR AGAIN.
HE'S A DILIGENT PERSON...
BUT THE LITTLE THINGS ADD UP TO CREATE A WALL AROUND HIS HEART.
IT MUST BE HARD FOR HIM TO WORK WITH TROU-BLESOME ARTISTS.
WELL, JUST DO WHAT FEELS BEST TO YOU.
YOU CAN DO IT!
OKAY.

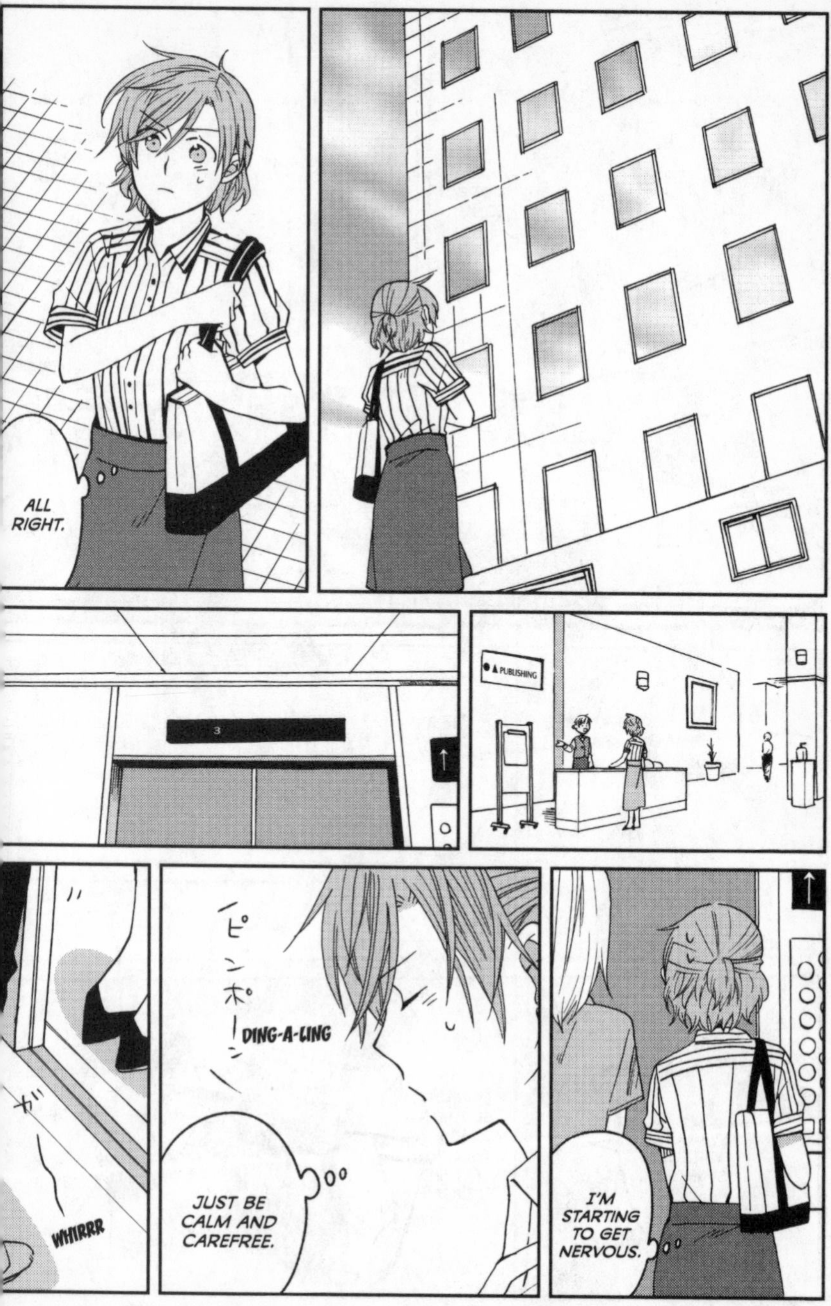
ALL RIGHT.
● ▲ PUBLISHING
3
I'M STARTING TO GET NERVOUS.
ピンポーン
DING-A-LING
JUST BE CALM AND CAREFREE.
WHIRRR

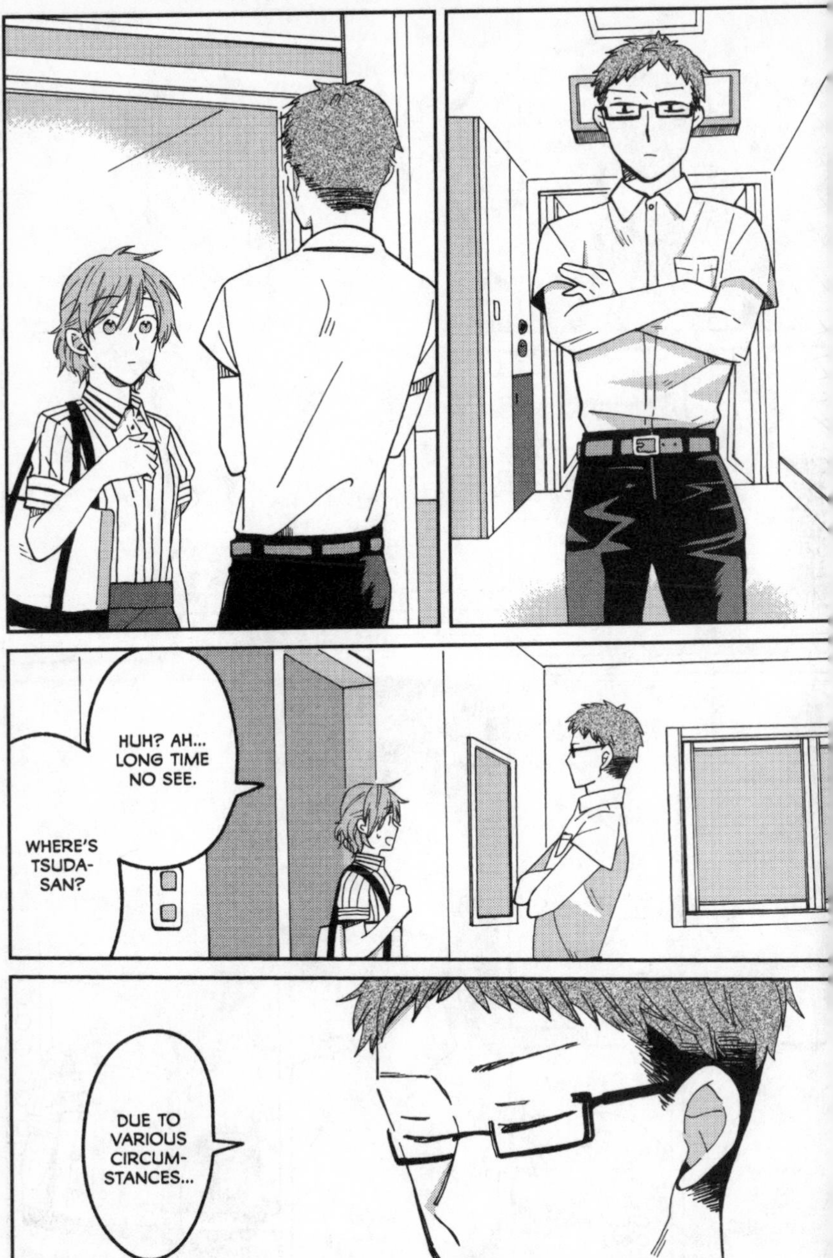
HUH? AH... LONG TIME NO SEE.
WHERE'S TSUDA-SAN?
DUE TO VARIOUS CIRCUM-STANCES...

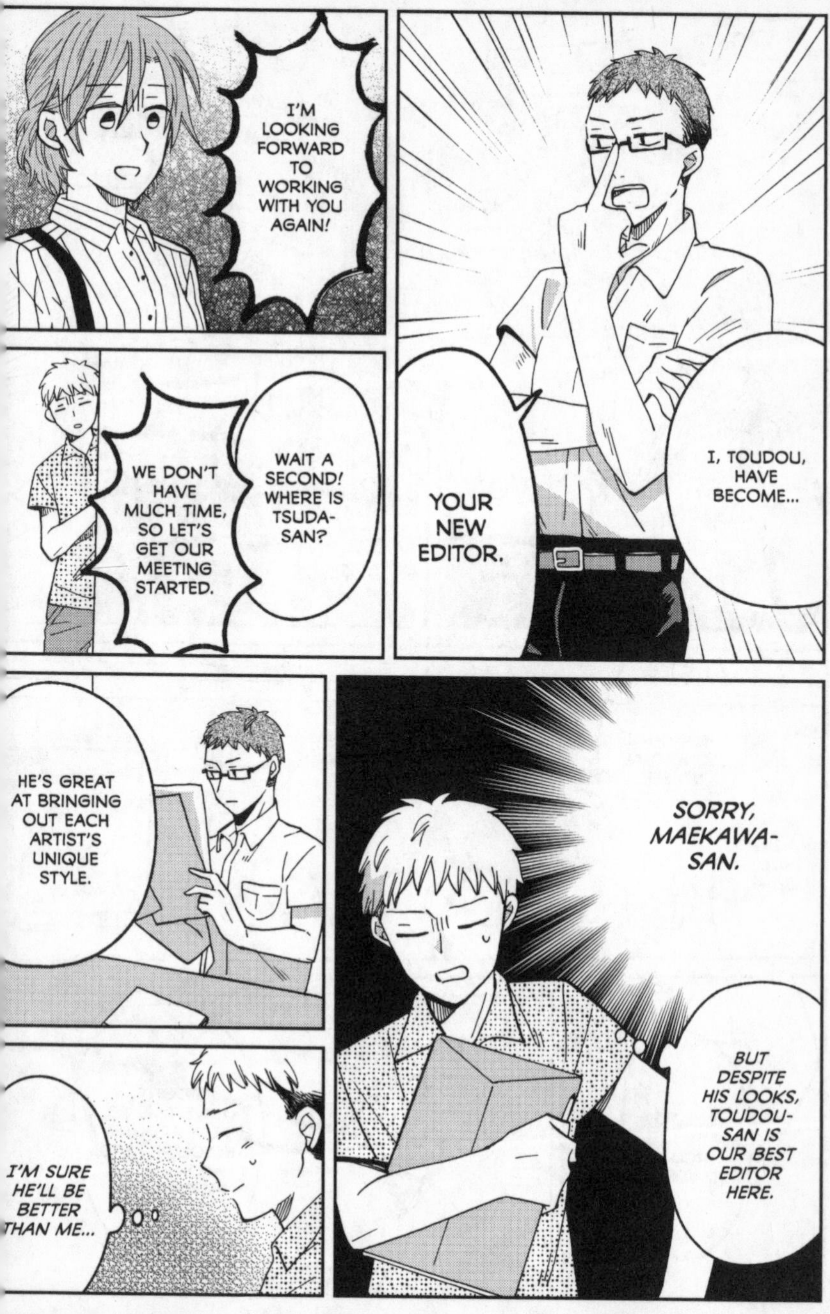
I, TOUDOU, HAVE BECOME...
YOUR NEW EDITOR.
I'M LOOKING FORWARD TO WORKING WITH YOU AGAIN!
WAIT A SECOND! WHERE IS TSUDA-SAN?
WE DON'T HAVE MUCH TIME, SO LET'S GET OUR MEETING STARTED.
SORRY, MAEKAWA-SAN.
BUT DESPITE HIS LOOKS, TOUDOU-SAN IS OUR BEST EDITOR HERE.
HE'S GREAT AT BRINGING OUT EACH ARTIST'S UNIQUE STYLE.
I'M SURE HE'LL BE BETTER THAN ME...

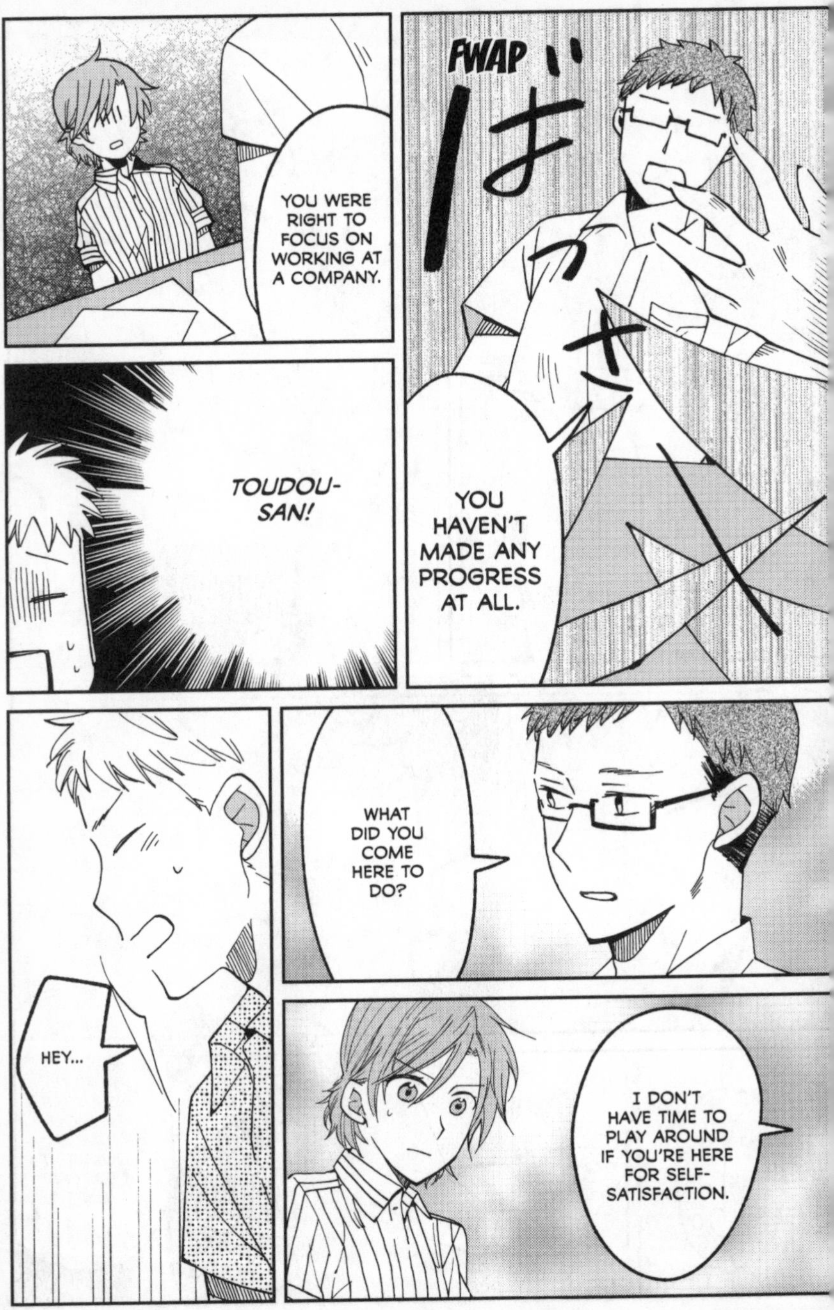
FWAP
YOU HAVEN'T MADE ANY PROGRESS AT ALL.
YOU WERE RIGHT TO FOCUS ON WORKING AT A COMPANY.
TOUDOU-SAN!
WHAT DID YOU COME HERE TO DO?
I DON'T HAVE TIME TO PLAY AROUND IF YOU'RE HERE FOR SELF-SATISFACTION.
HEY...

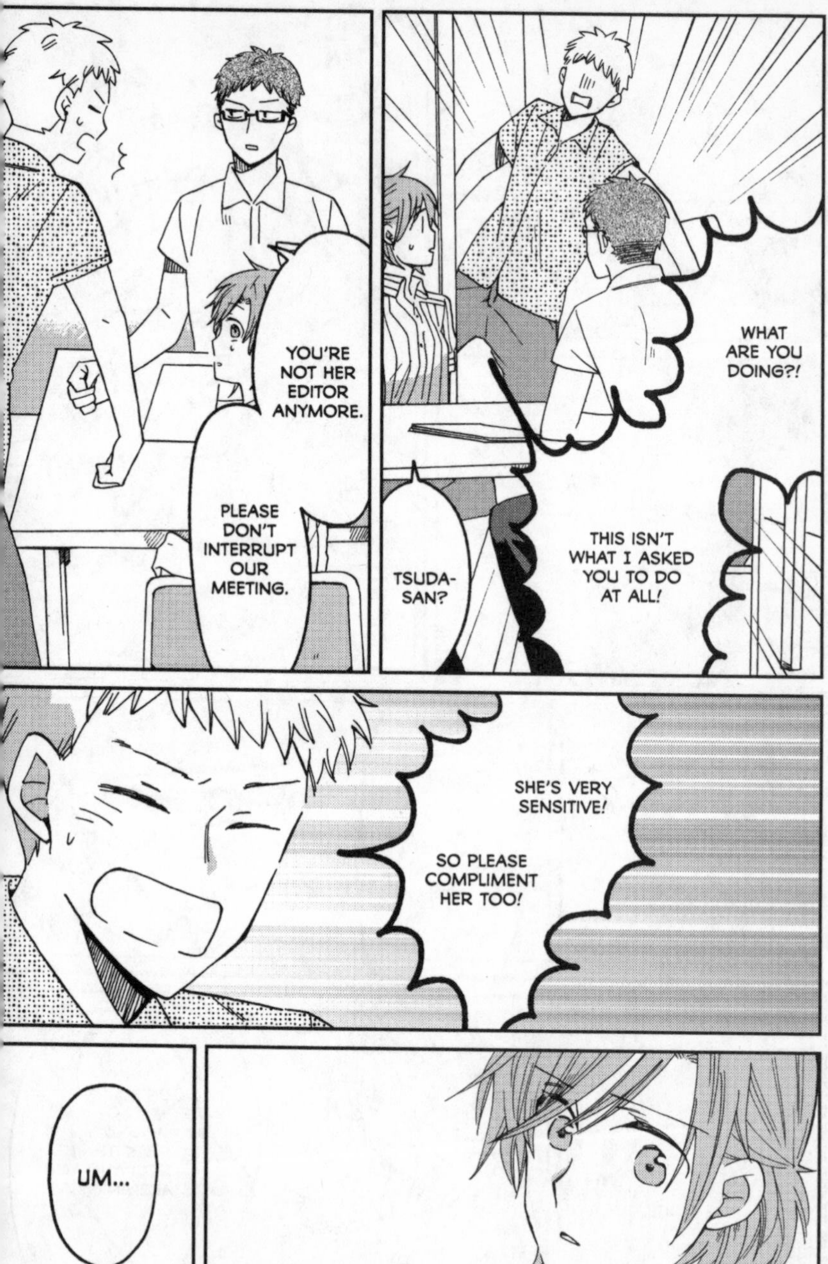
WHAT ARE YOU DOING?!
THIS ISN'T WHAT I ASKED YOU TO DO AT ALL!
TSUDA-SAN?
YOU'RE NOT HER EDITOR ANYMORE.
PLEASE DON'T INTERRUPT OUR MEETING.
SHE'S VERY SENSITIVE!
SO PLEASE COMPLIMENT HER TOO!
UM...

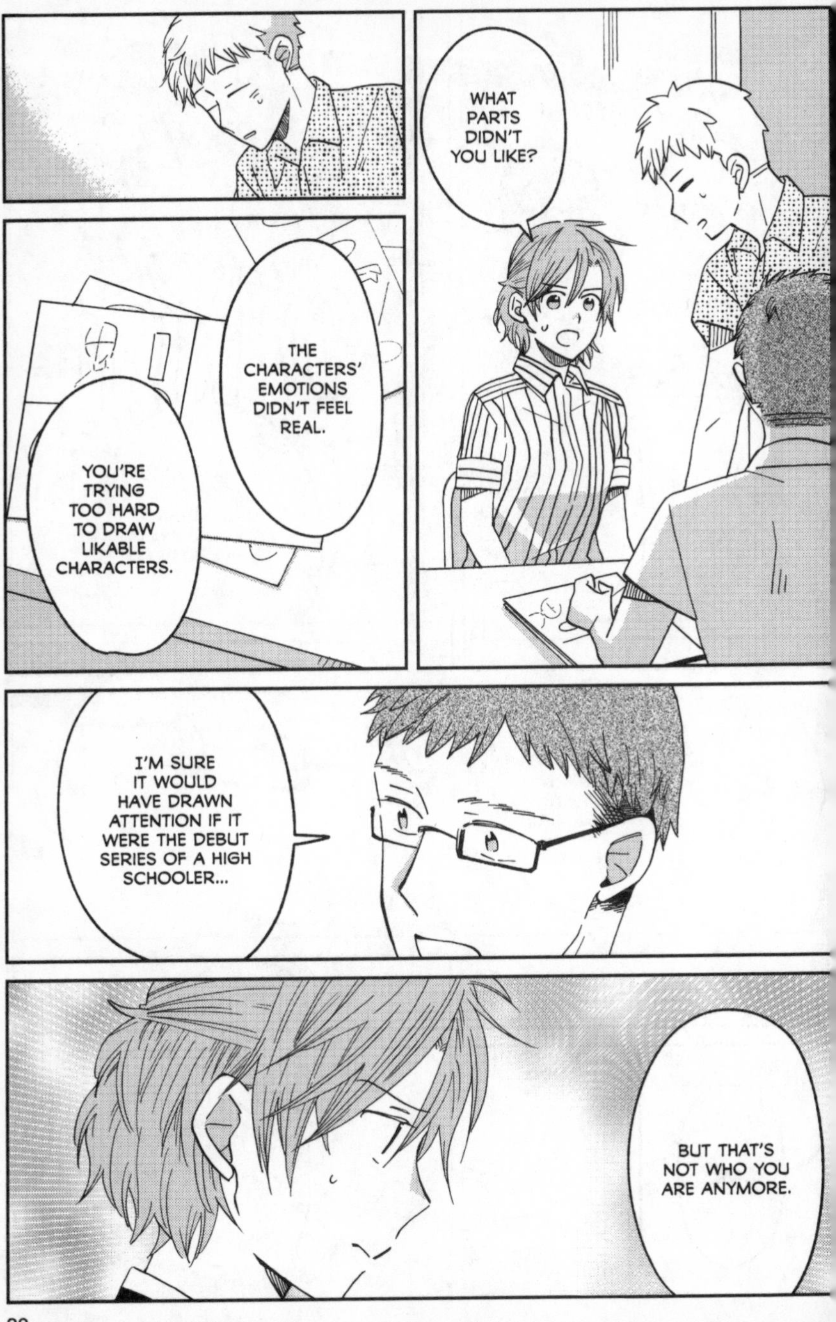
WHAT PARTS DIDN'T YOU LIKE?
THE CHARACTERS' EMOTIONS DIDN'T FEEL REAL.
YOU'RE TRYING TOO HARD TO DRAW LIKABLE CHARACTERS.
I'M SURE IT WOULD HAVE DRAWN ATTENTION IF IT WERE THE DEBUT SERIES OF A HIGH SCHOOLER...
BUT THAT'S NOT WHO YOU ARE ANYMORE.

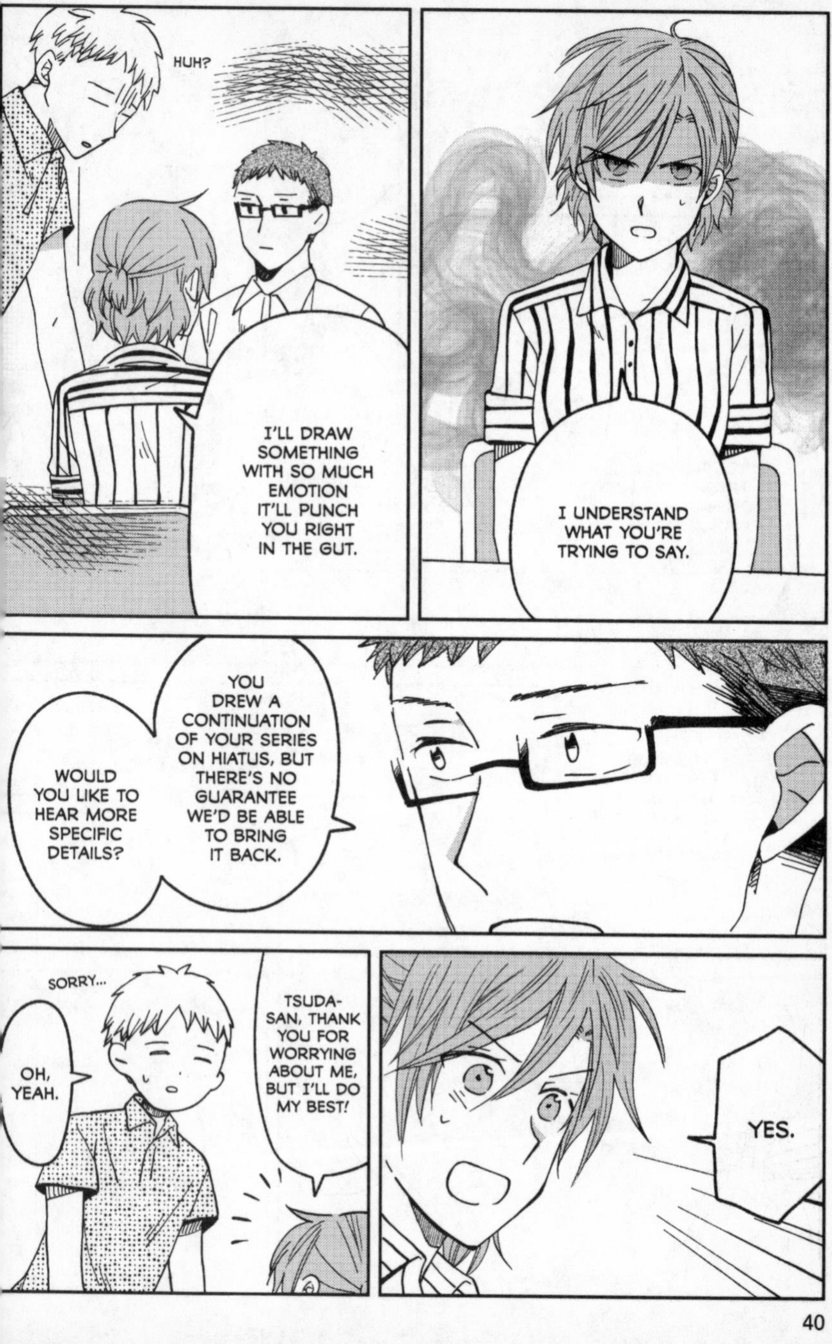
I UNDERSTAND WHAT YOU'RE TRYING TO SAY.
I'LL DRAW SOMETHING WITH SO MUCH EMOTION IT'LL PUNCH YOU RIGHT IN THE GUT.
HUH?
YOU DREW A CONTINUATION OF YOUR SERIES ON HIATUS, BUT THERE'S NO GUARANTEE WE'D BE ABLE TO BRING IT BACK.
WOULD YOU LIKE TO HEAR MORE SPECIFIC DETAILS?
YES.
TSUDA-SAN, THANK YOU FOR WORRYING ABOUT ME, BUT I'LL DO MY BEST!
OH, YEAH.
SORRY...

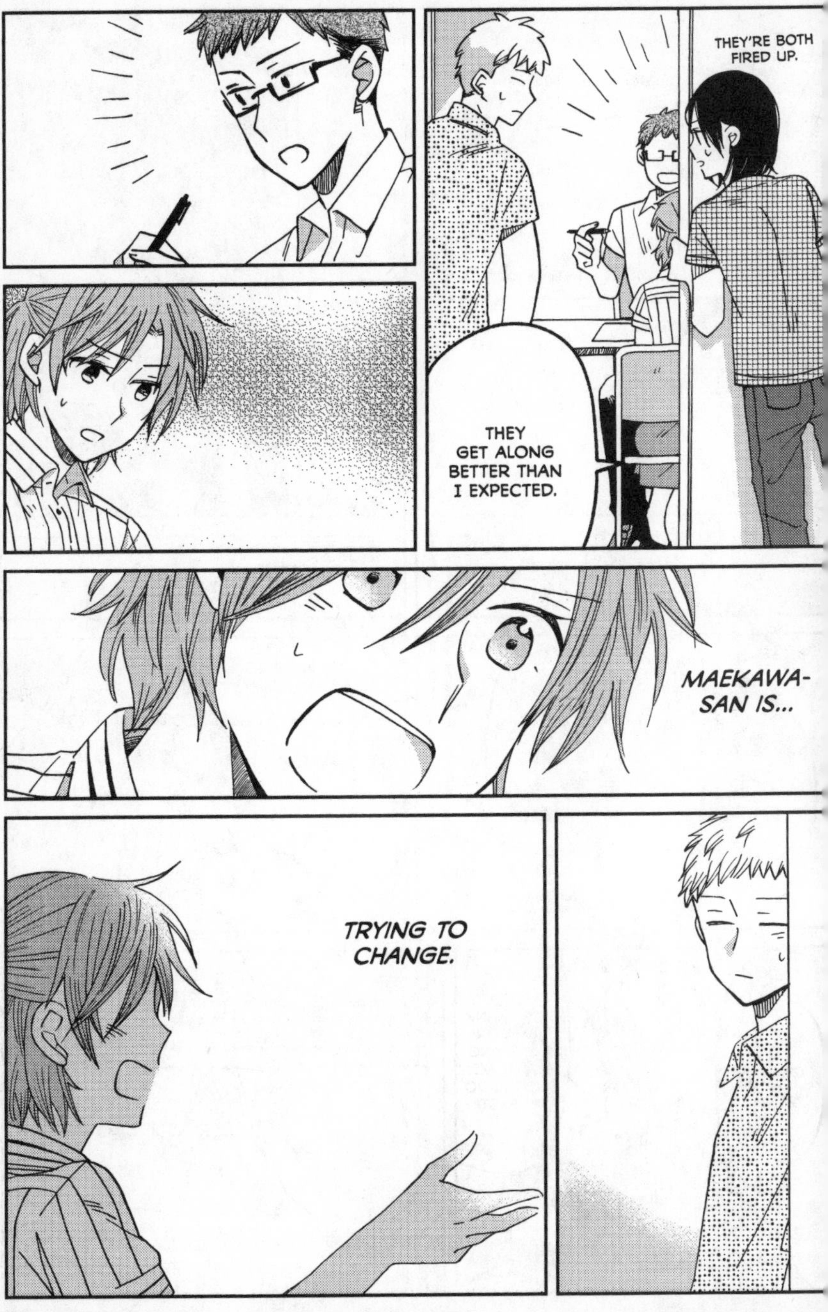
THEY'RE BOTH FIRED UP.
THEY GET ALONG BETTER THAN I EXPECTED.
MAEKAWA-SAN IS...
TRYING TO CHANGE.

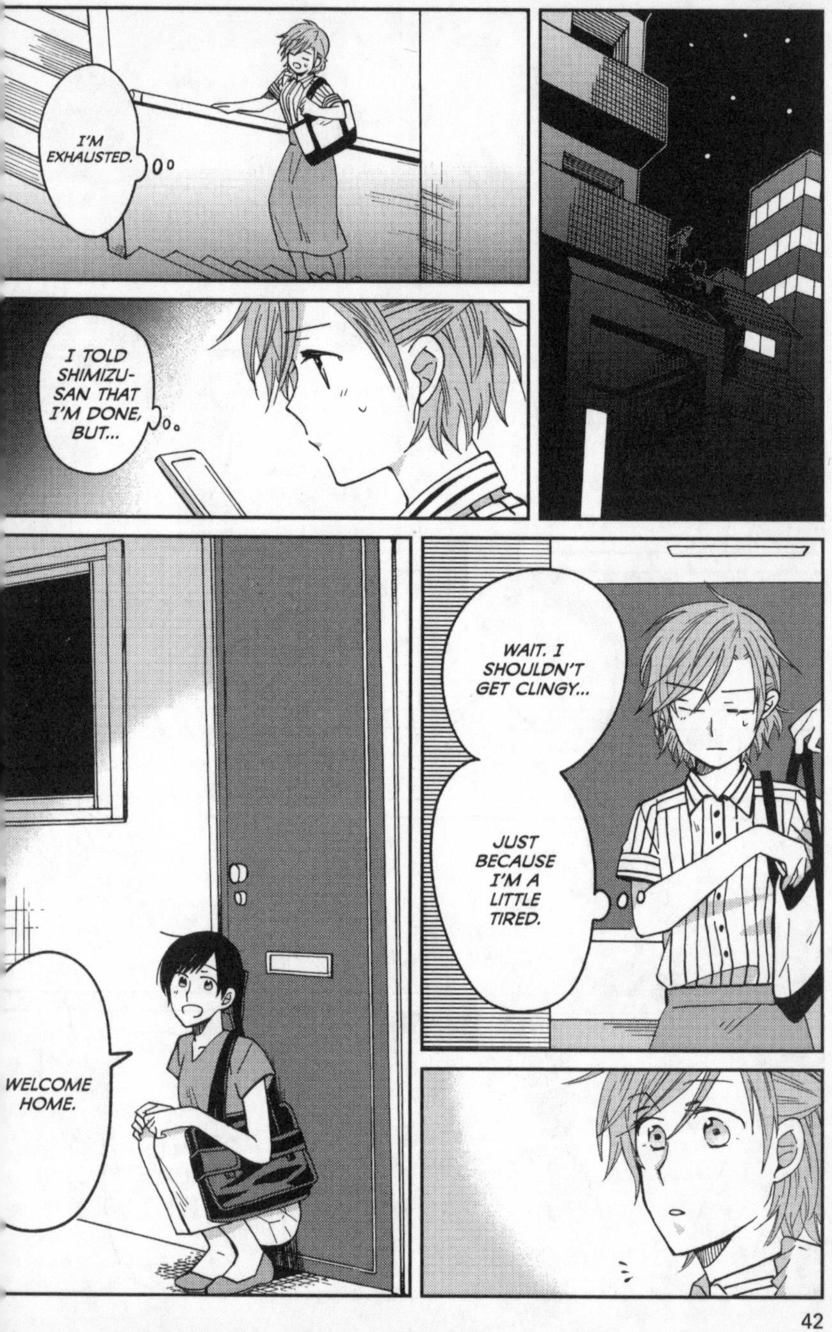
I'M EXHAUSTED.
I TOLD SHIMIZU-SAN THAT I'M DONE, BUT...
WAIT. I SHOULDN'T GET CLINGY...
JUST BECAUSE I'M A LITTLE TIRED.
WELCOME HOME.

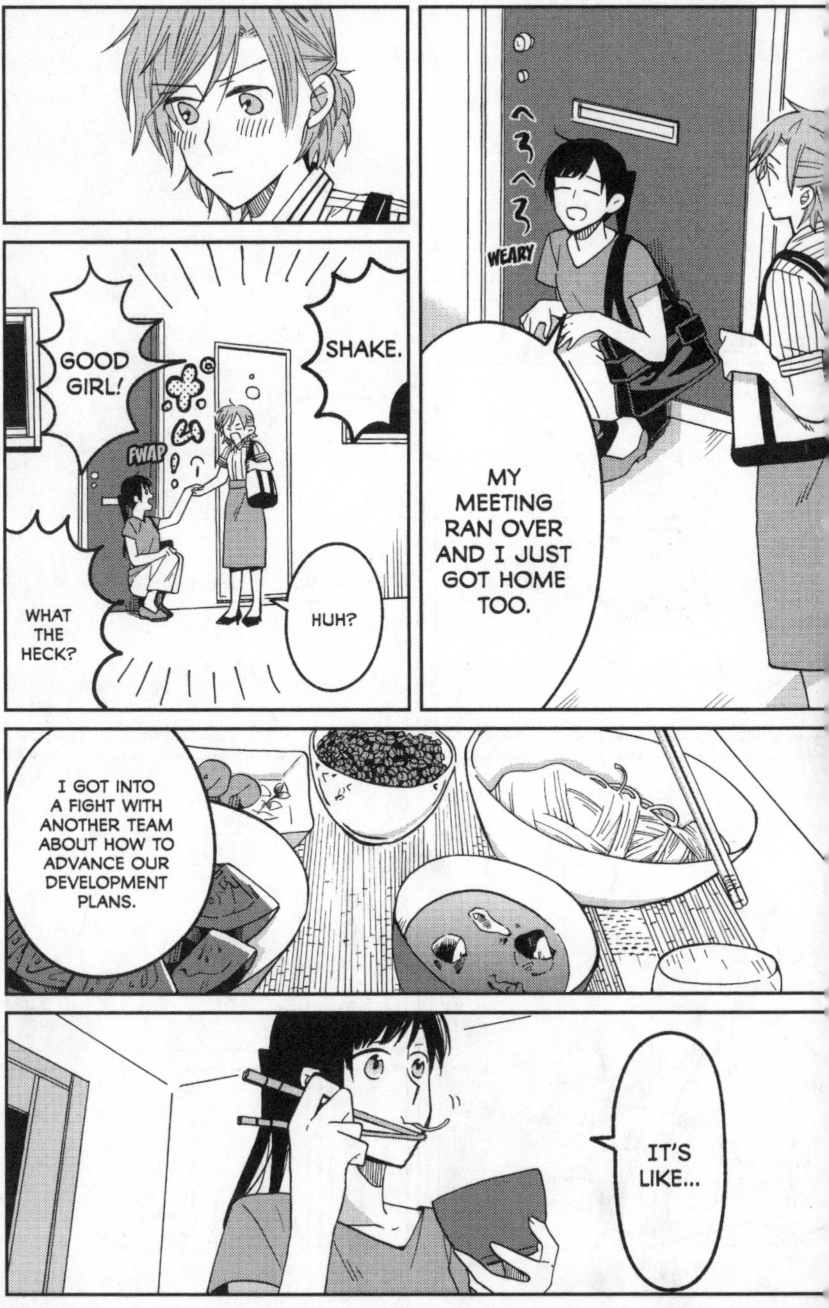
へろへろ
WEARY
MY MEETING RAN OVER AND I JUST GOT HOME TOO.
SHAKE.
GOOD GIRL!
FWAP
HUH?
WHAT THE HECK?
I GOT INTO A FIGHT WITH ANOTHER TEAM ABOUT HOW TO ADVANCE OUR DEVELOPMENT PLANS.
IT'S LIKE...

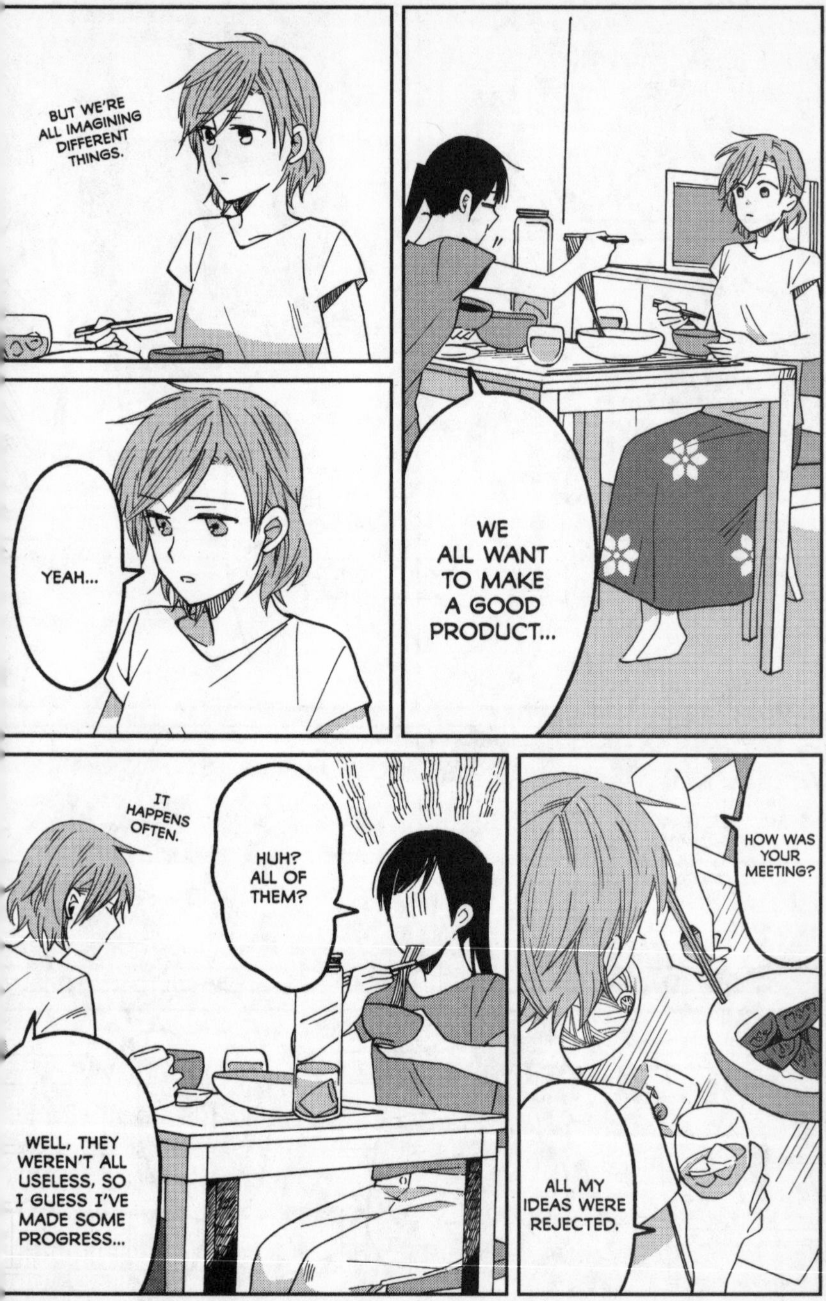
WE ALL WANT TO MAKE A GOOD PRODUCT...
BUT WE'RE ALL IMAGINING DIFFERENT THINGS.
YEAH...
HOW WAS YOUR MEETING?
ALL MY IDEAS WERE REJECTED.
HUH? ALL OF THEM?
IT HAPPENS OFTEN.
WELL, THEY WEREN'T ALL USELESS, SO I GUESS I'VE MADE SOME PROGRESS...

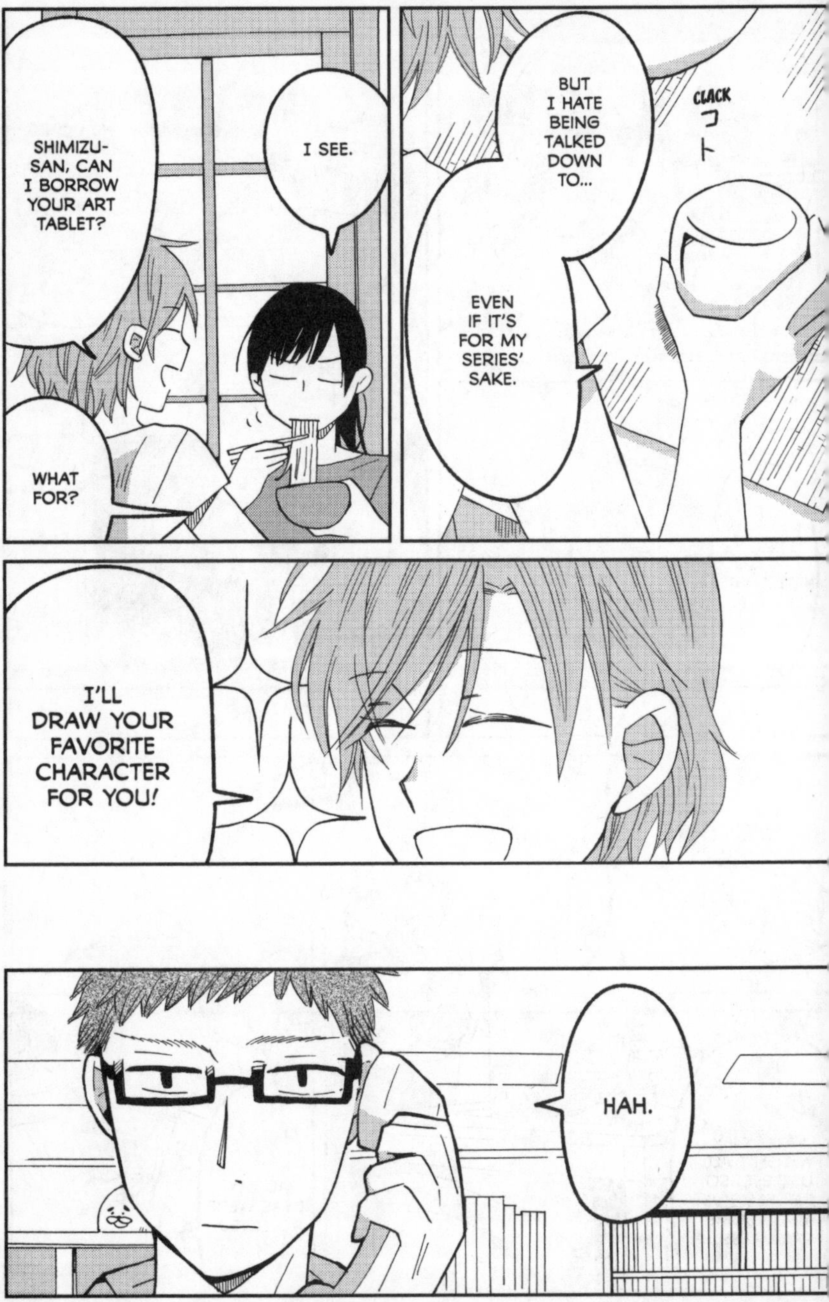
BUT I HATE BEING TALKED DOWN TO...
EVEN IF IT'S FOR MY SERIES' SAKE.
CLACK
コト
I SEE.
SHIMIZU-SAN, CAN I BORROW YOUR ART TABLET?
WHAT FOR?
I'LL DRAW YOUR FAVORITE CHARACTER FOR YOU!
HAH.

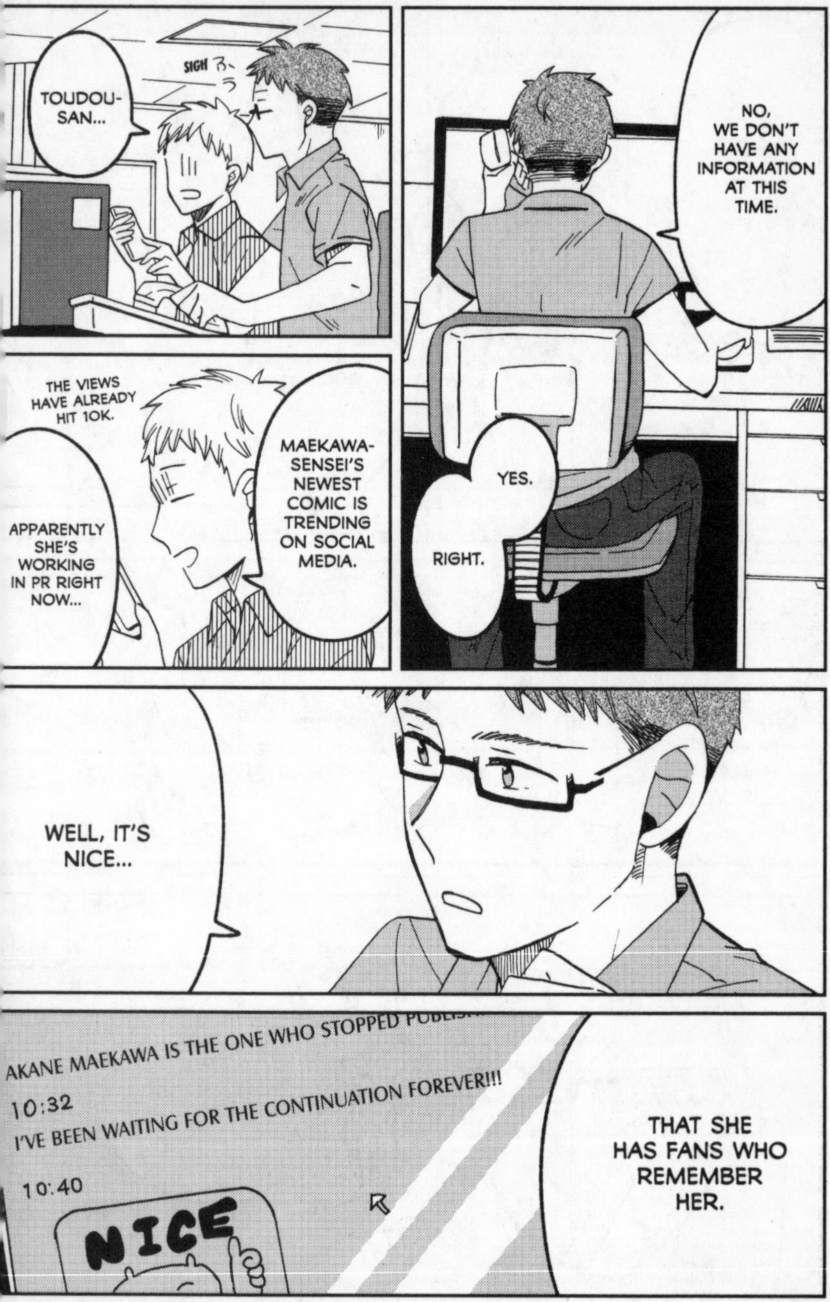
NO, WE DON'T HAVE ANY INFORMATION AT THIS TIME.
YES.
RIGHT.
SIGH
TOUDOU-SAN...
MAEKAWA-SENSEI'S NEWEST COMIC IS TRENDING ON SOCIAL MEDIA.
THE VIEWS HAVE ALREADY HIT 10K.
APPARENTLY SHE'S WORKING IN PR RIGHT NOW...
WELL, IT'S NICE...
THAT SHE HAS FANS WHO REMEMBER HER.
AKANE MAEKAWA IS THE ONE WHO STOPPED
10:32
I'VE BEEN WAITING FOR THE CONTINUATION FOREVER!!!
10:40
NICE

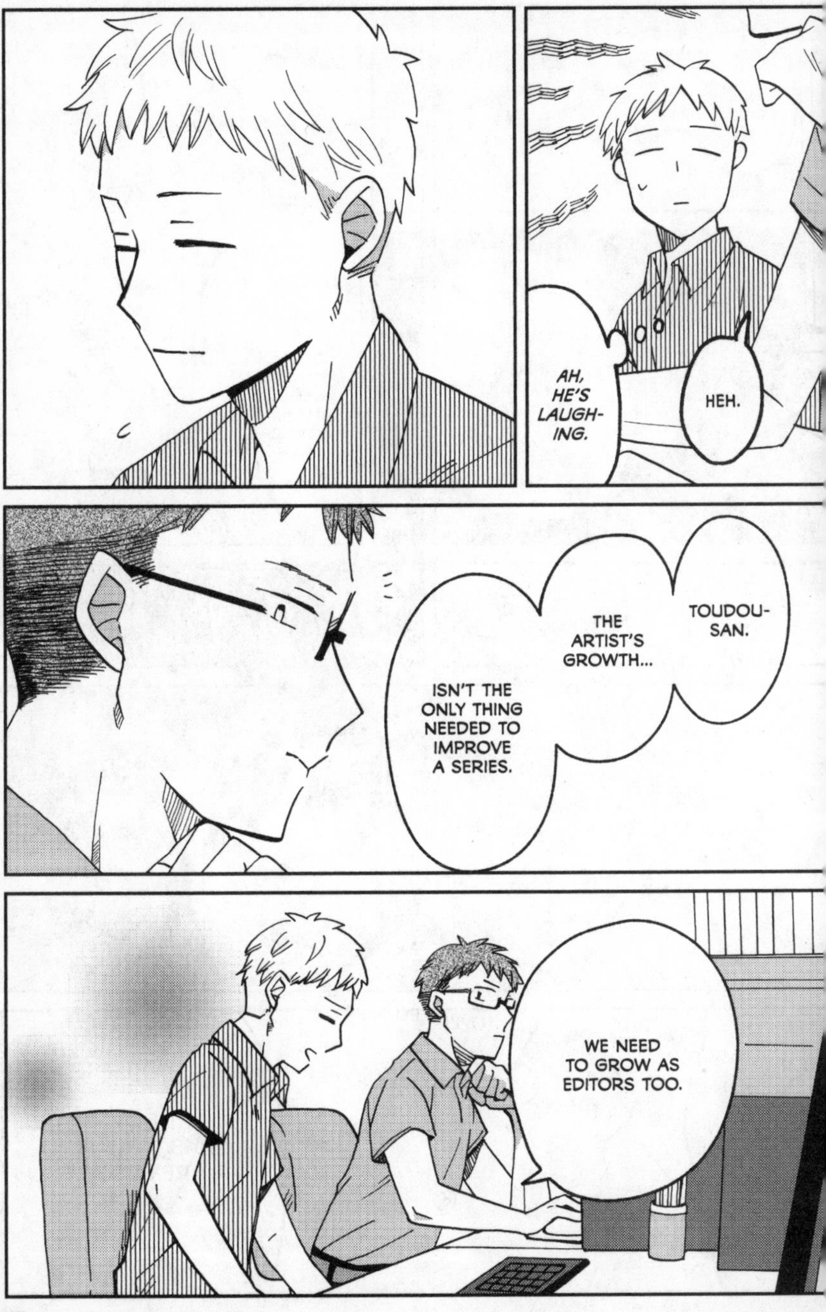
HEH.
AH, HE'S LAUGHING.
TOUDOU-SAN.
THE ARTIST'S GROWTH...
ISN'T THE ONLY THING NEEDED TO IMPROVE A SERIES.
WE NEED TO GROW AS EDITORS TOO.

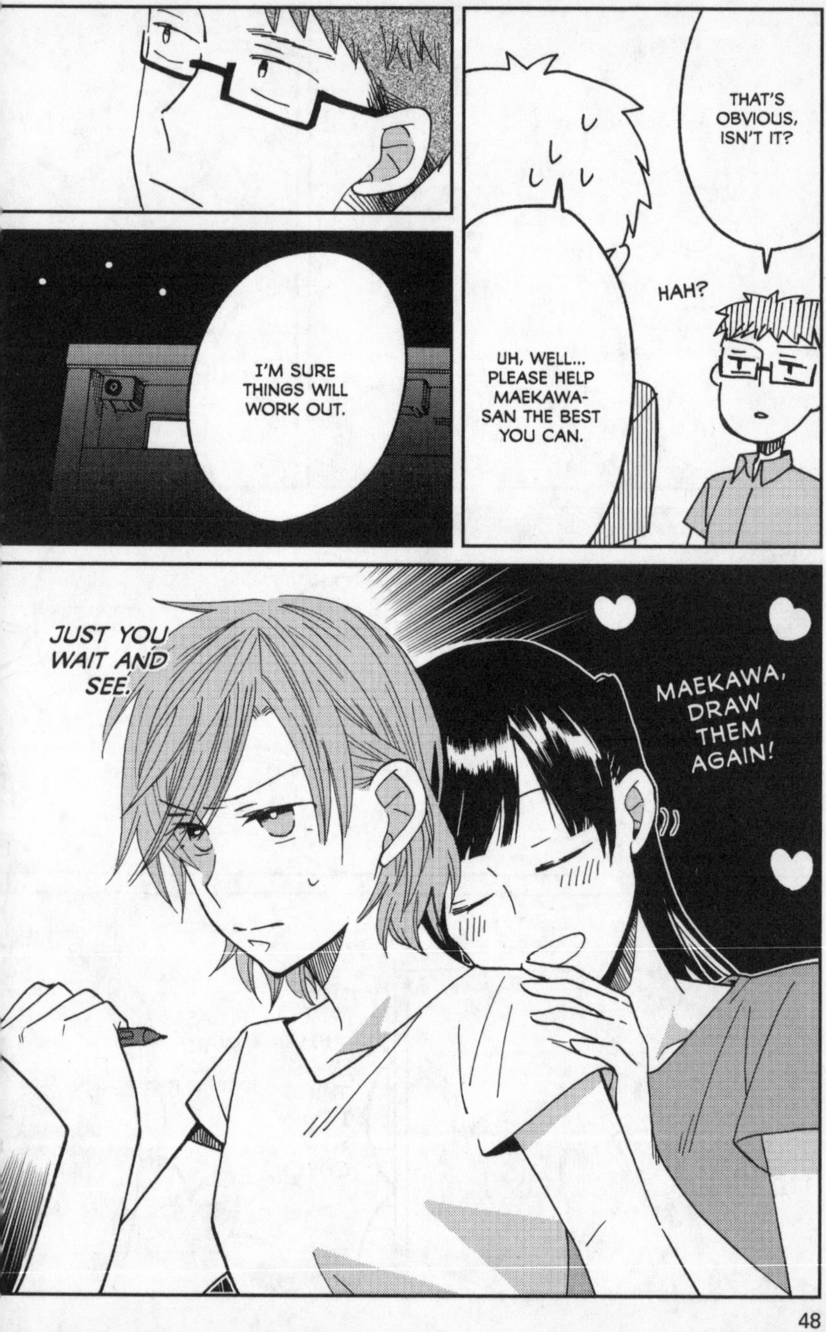
THAT'S OBVIOUS, ISN'T IT?
HAH?
UH, WELL... PLEASE HELP MAEKAWA-SAN THE BEST YOU CAN.
I'M SURE THINGS WILL WORK OUT.
MAEKAWA, DRAW THEM AGAIN!
JUST YOU WAIT AND SEE.

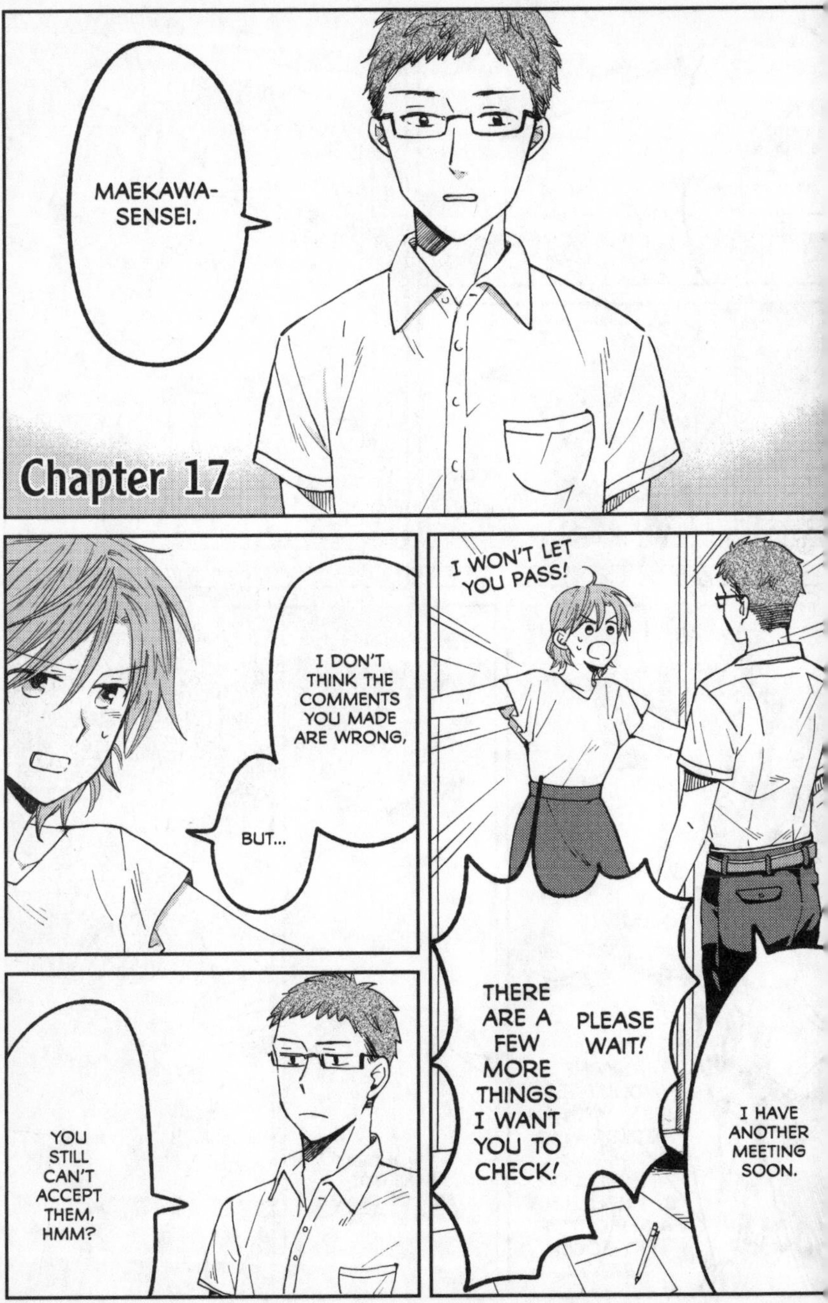
Chapter 17
MAEKAWA-SENSEI.
I WON'T LET YOU PASS!
PLEASE WAIT! THERE ARE A FEW MORE THINGS I WANT YOU TO CHECK!
I HAVE ANOTHER MEETING SOON.
I DON'T THINK THE COMMENTS YOU MADE ARE WRONG, BUT...
YOU STILL CAN'T ACCEPT THEM, HMM?

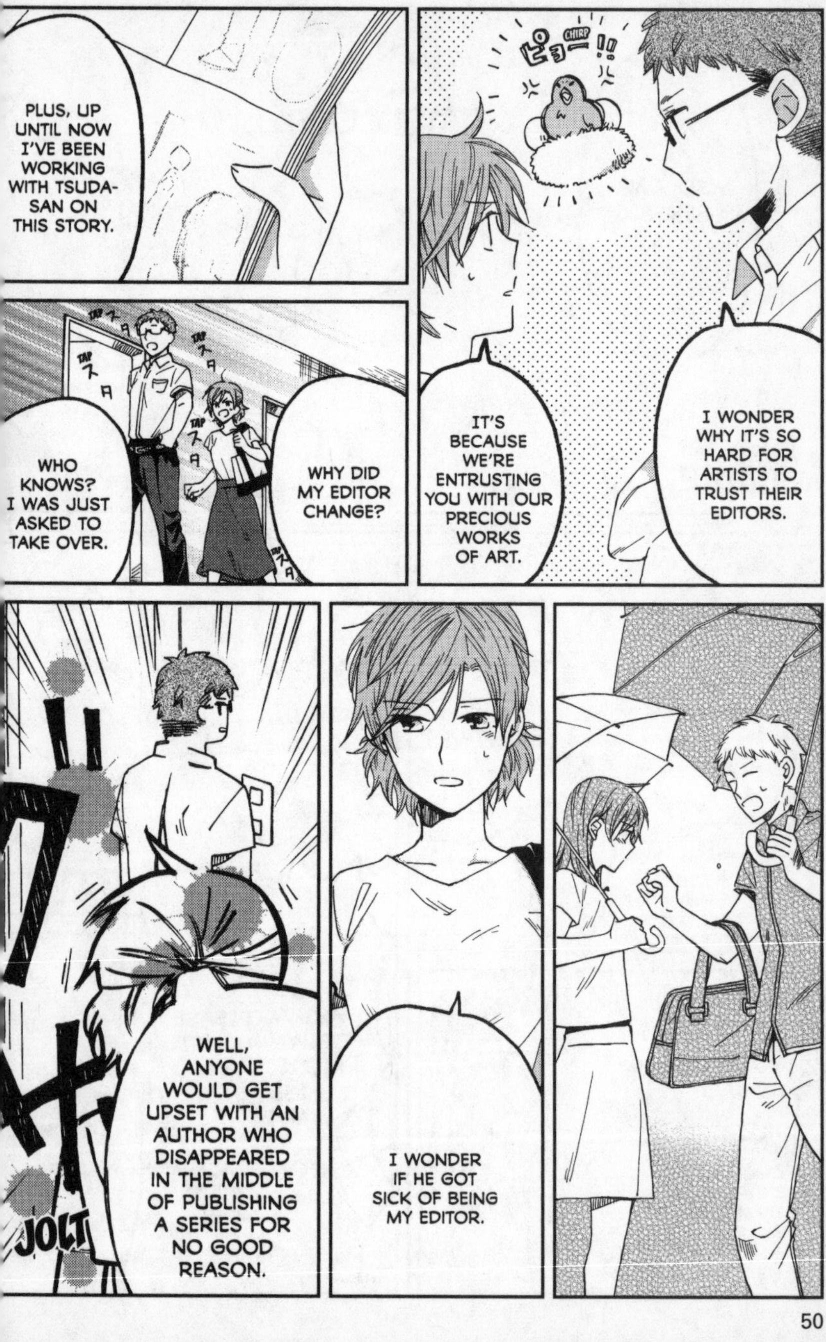
ピョー!!
CHIRP
I WONDER WHY IT'S SO HARD FOR ARTISTS TO TRUST THEIR EDITORS.
IT'S BECAUSE WE'RE ENTRUSTING YOU WITH OUR PRECIOUS WORKS OF ART.
PLUS, UP UNTIL NOW I'VE BEEN WORKING WITH TSUDA-SAN ON THIS STORY.
TAP
TAP
TAP
TAP
TAP
WHY DID MY EDITOR CHANGE?
WHO KNOWS? I WAS JUST ASKED TO TAKE OVER.
I WONDER IF HE GOT SICK OF BEING MY EDITOR.
WELL, ANYONE WOULD GET UPSET WITH AN AUTHOR WHO DISAPPEARED IN THE MIDDLE OF PUBLISHING A SERIES FOR NO GOOD REASON.
JOLT

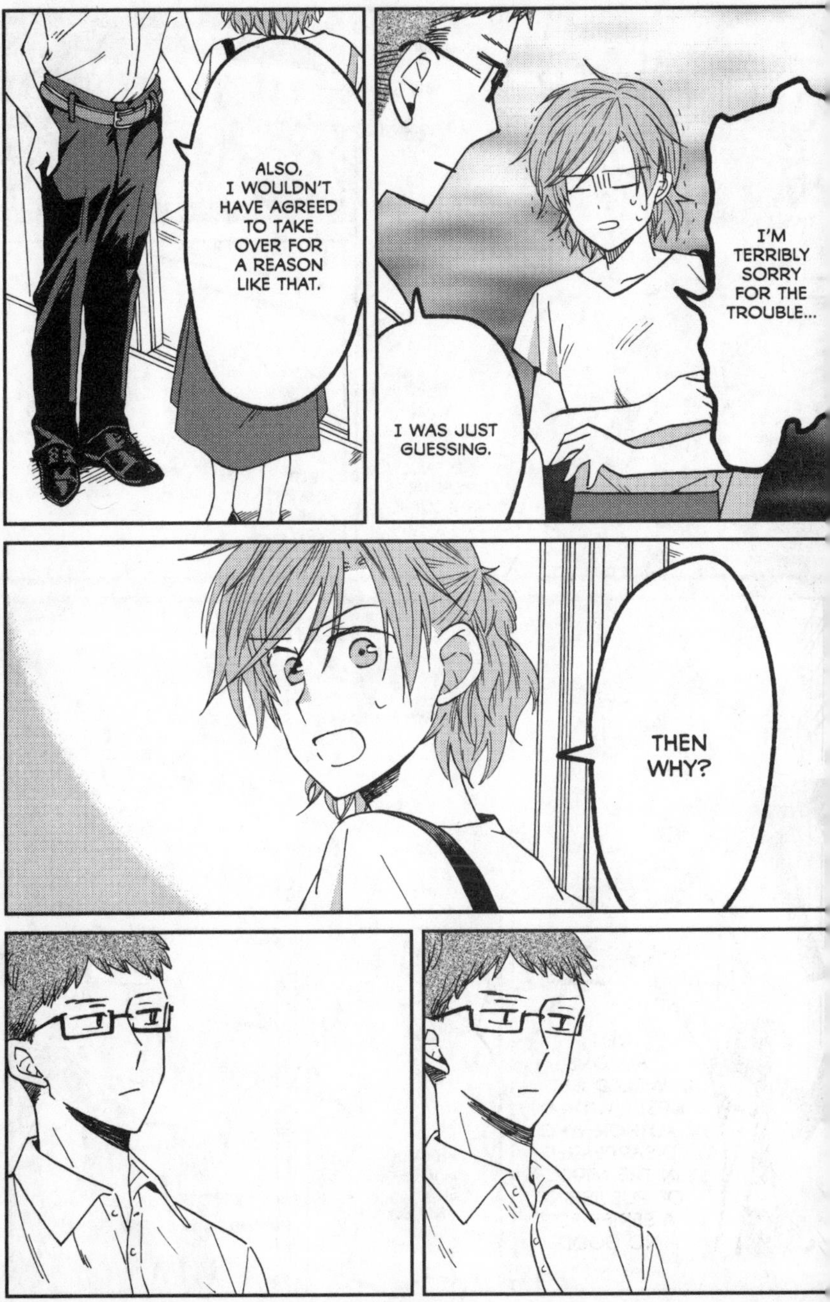
I'M TERRIBLY SORRY FOR THE TROUBLE...
I WAS JUST GUESSING.
ALSO, I WOULDN'T HAVE AGREED TO TAKE OVER FOR A REASON LIKE THAT.
THEN WHY?

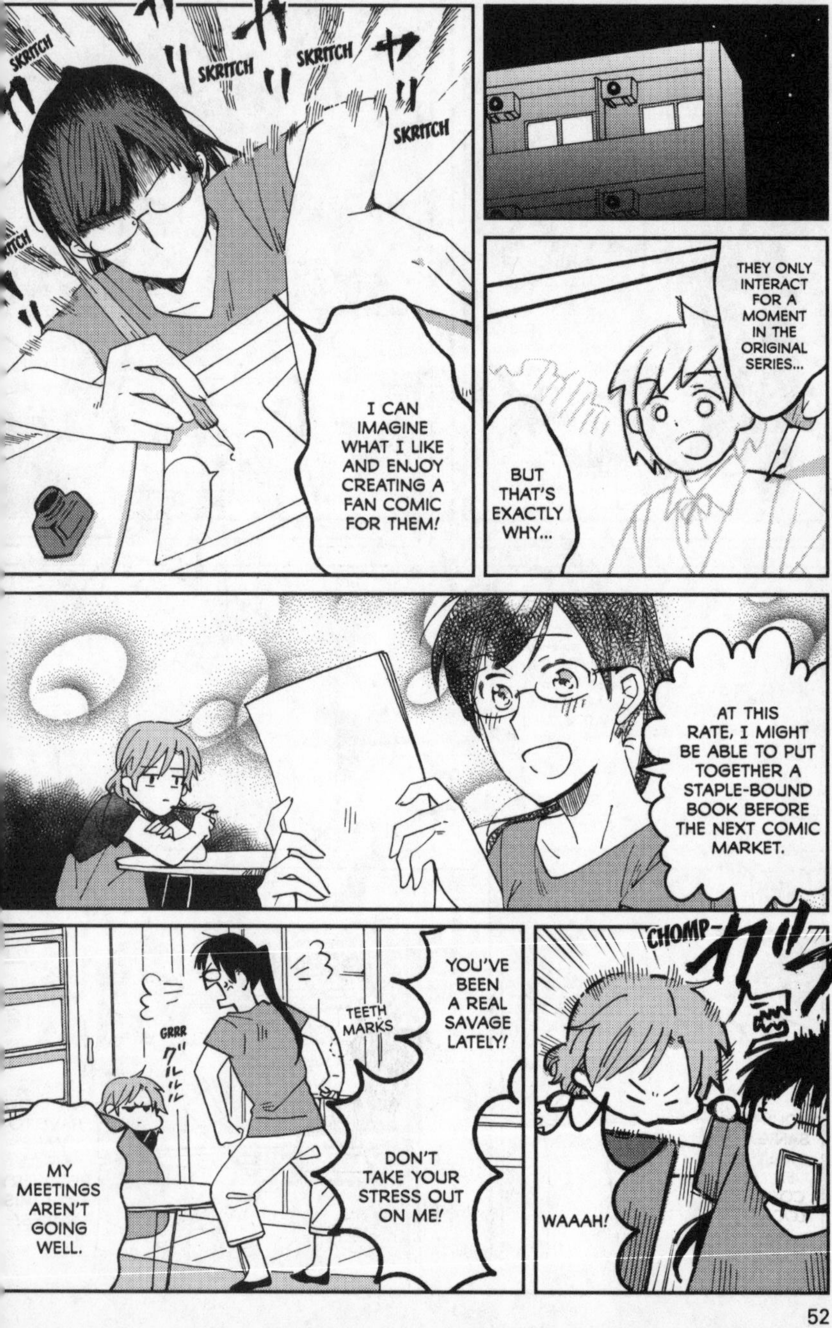
THEY ONLY INTERACT FOR A MOMENT IN THE ORIGINAL SERIES...
BUT THAT'S EXACTLY WHY...
SKRITCH
SKRITCH
SKRITCH
SKRITCH
I CAN IMAGINE WHAT I LIKE AND ENJOY CREATING A FAN COMIC FOR THEM!
AT THIS RATE, I MIGHT BE ABLE TO PUT TOGETHER A STAPLE-BOUND BOOK BEFORE THE NEXT COMIC MARKET.
CHOMP
WAAAH!
YOU'VE BEEN A REAL SAVAGE LATELY!
TEETH MARKS
DON'T TAKE YOUR STRESS OUT ON ME!
GRRR
MY MEETINGS AREN'T GOING WELL.

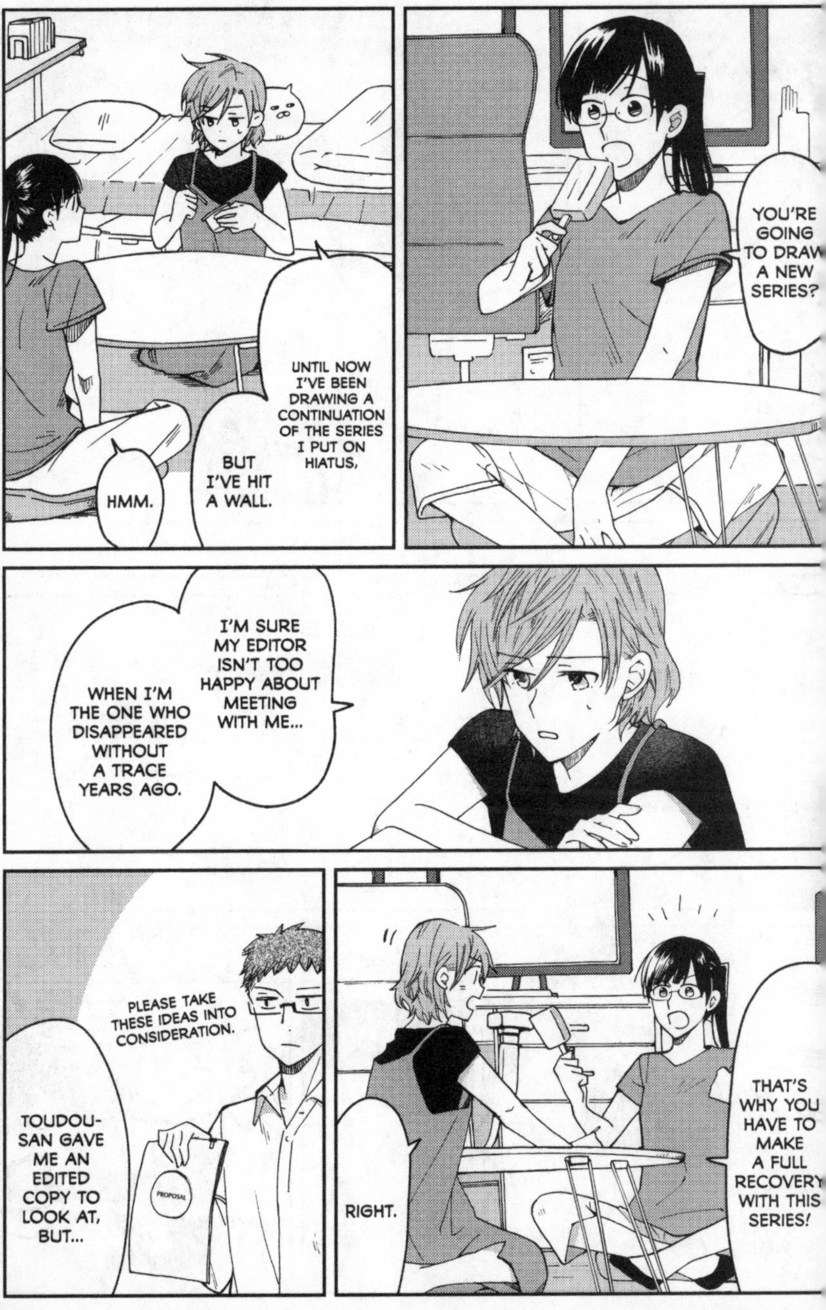
YOU'RE GOING TO DRAW A NEW SERIES?
UNTIL NOW I'VE BEEN DRAWING A CONTINUATION OF THE SERIES I PUT ON HIATUS,
BUT I'VE HIT A WALL.
HMM.
I'M SURE MY EDITOR ISN'T TOO HAPPY ABOUT MEETING WITH ME...
WHEN I'M THE ONE WHO DISAPPEARED WITHOUT A TRACE YEARS AGO.
THAT'S WHY YOU HAVE TO MAKE A FULL RECOVERY WITH THIS SERIES!
RIGHT.
PLEASE TAKE THESE IDEAS INTO CONSIDERATION.
PROPOSAL
TOUDOU-SAN GAVE ME AN EDITED COPY TO LOOK AT, BUT...

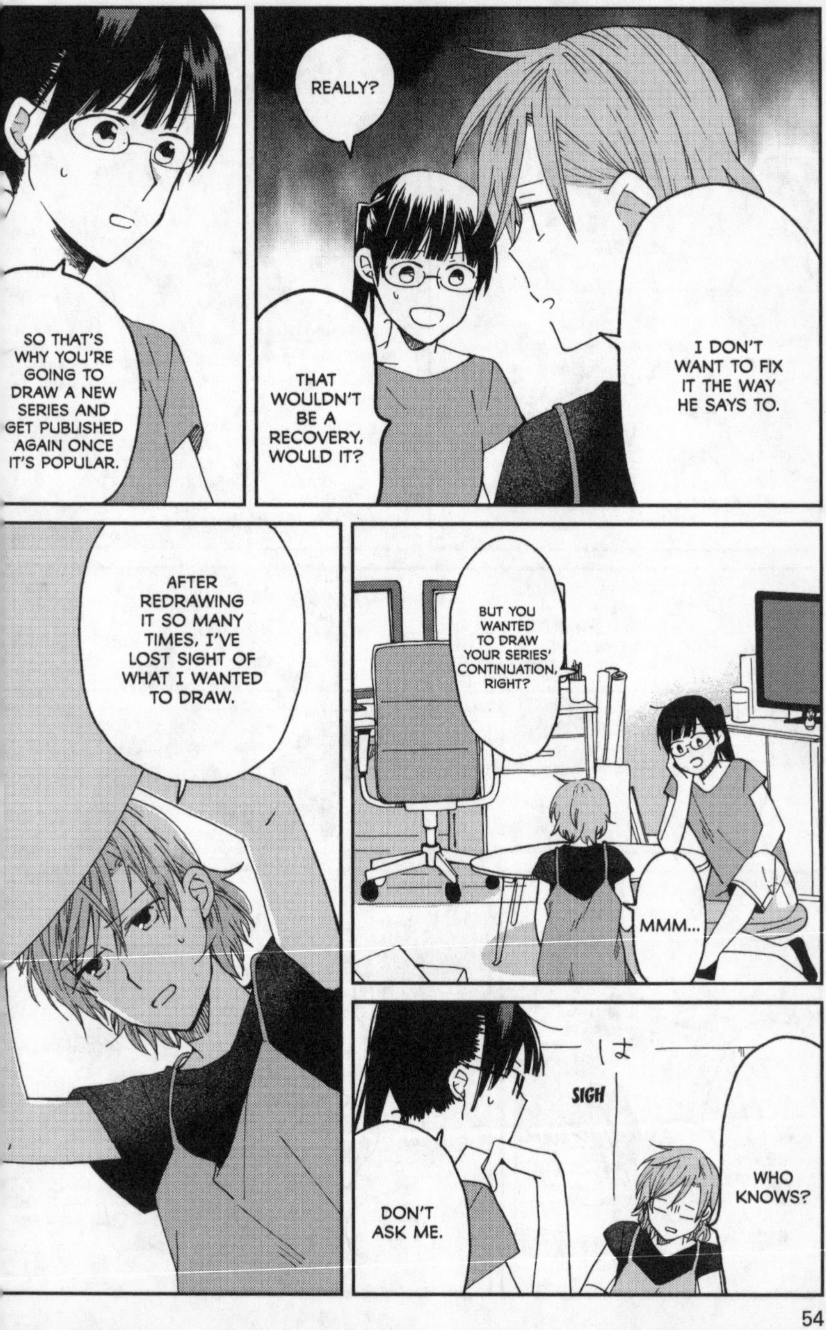
I DON'T WANT TO FIX IT THE WAY HE SAYS TO.
REALLY?
THAT WOULDN'T BE A RECOVERY, WOULD IT?
SO THAT'S WHY YOU'RE GOING TO DRAW A NEW SERIES AND GET PUBLISHED AGAIN ONCE IT'S POPULAR.
BUT YOU WANTED TO DRAW YOUR SERIES' CONTINUATION, RIGHT?
MMM...
WHO KNOWS?
は
SIGH
DON'T ASK ME.
AFTER REDRAWING IT SO MANY TIMES, I'VE LOST SIGHT OF WHAT I WANTED TO DRAW.

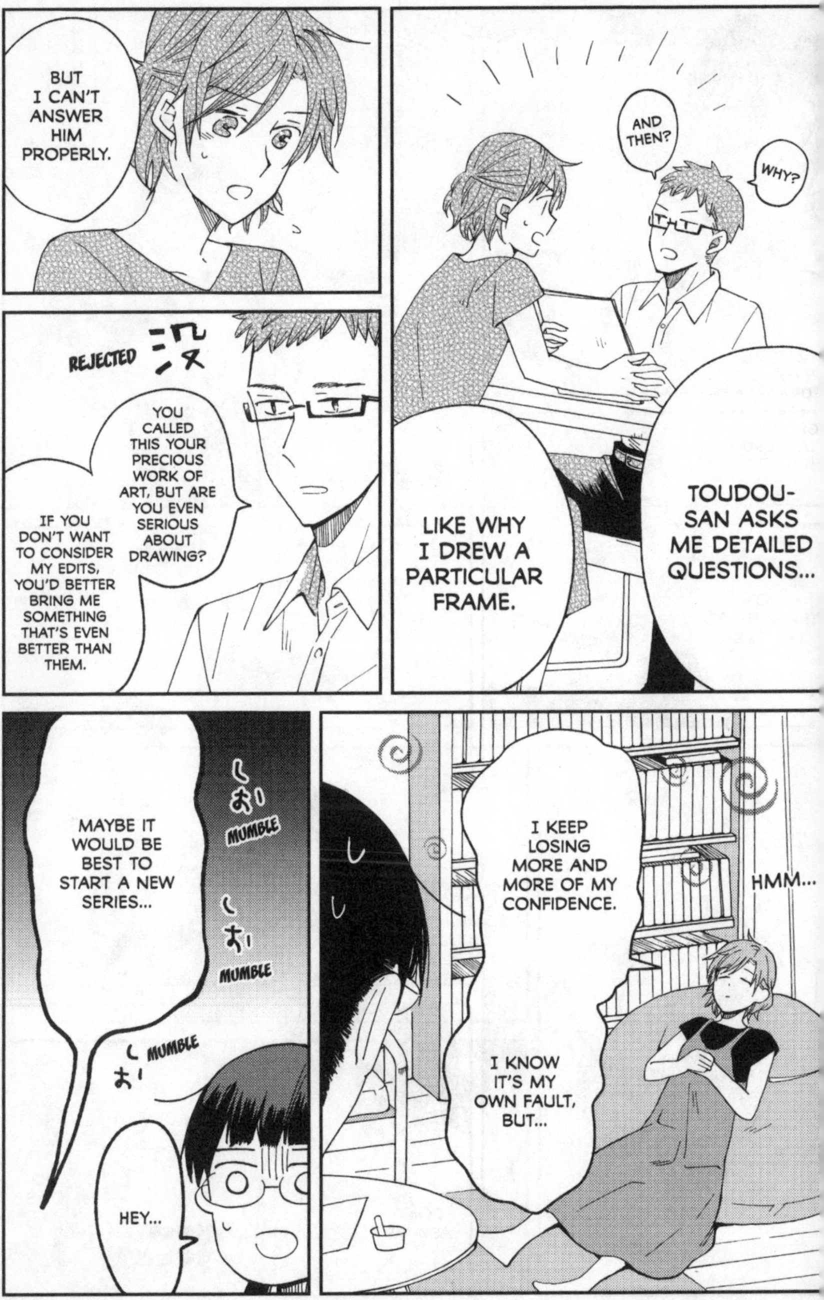
AND THEN?
WHY?
TOUDOU-SAN ASKS ME DETAILED QUESTIONS...
LIKE WHY I DREW A PARTICULAR FRAME.
BUT I CAN'T ANSWER HIM PROPERLY.
REJECTED
YOU CALLED THIS YOUR PRECIOUS WORK OF ART, BUT ARE YOU EVEN SERIOUS ABOUT DRAWING?
IF YOU DON'T WANT TO CONSIDER MY EDITS, YOU'D BETTER BRING ME SOMETHING THAT'S EVEN BETTER THAN THEM.
HMM...
I KEEP LOSING MORE AND MORE OF MY CONFIDENCE.
I KNOW IT'S MY OWN FAULT, BUT...
MUMBLE
MUMBLE
MAYBE IT WOULD BE BEST TO START A NEW SERIES...
MUMBLE
HEY...

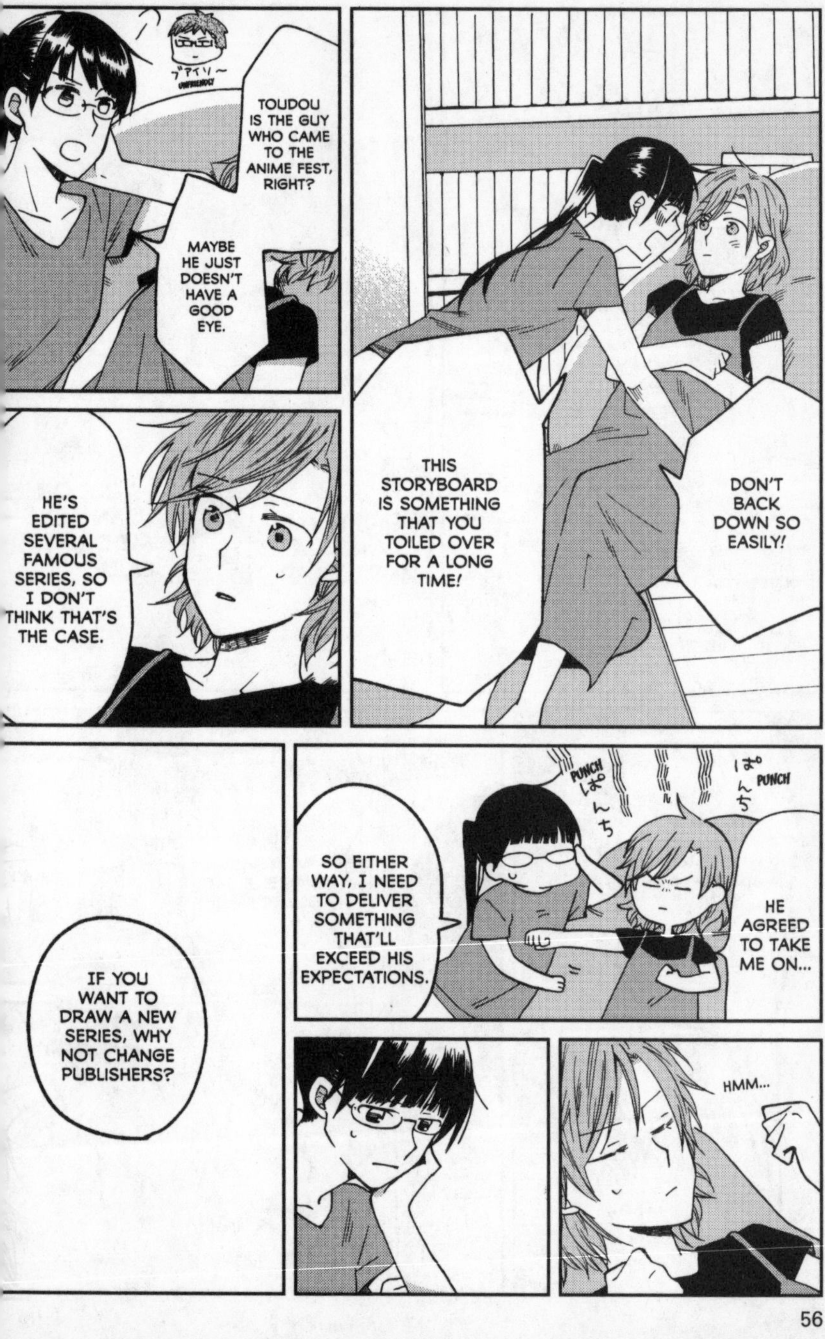
DON'T BACK DOWN SO EASILY!
THIS STORYBOARD IS SOMETHING THAT YOU TOILED OVER FOR A LONG TIME!
ブアイソ～
UNFRIENDLY
TOUDOU IS THE GUY WHO CAME TO THE ANIME FEST, RIGHT?
MAYBE HE JUST DOESN'T HAVE A GOOD EYE.
HE'S EDITED SEVERAL FAMOUS SERIES, SO I DON'T THINK THAT'S THE CASE.
ぱんち
PUNCH
ぱんち
PUNCH
HE AGREED TO TAKE ME ON...
SO EITHER WAY, I NEED TO DELIVER SOMETHING THAT'LL EXCEED HIS EXPECTATIONS.
HMM...
IF YOU WANT TO DRAW A NEW SERIES, WHY NOT CHANGE PUBLISHERS?

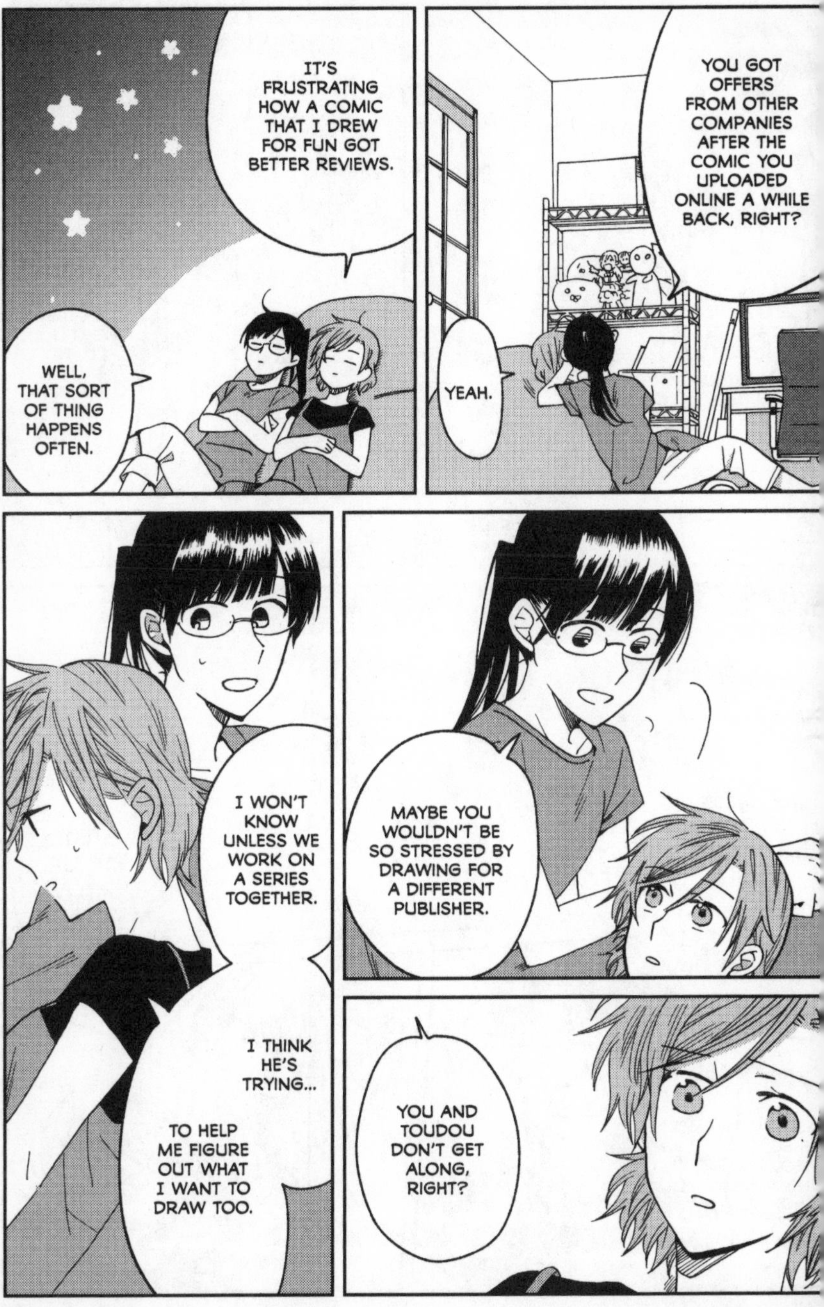
YOU GOT OFFERS FROM OTHER COMPANIES AFTER THE COMIC YOU UPLOADED ONLINE A WHILE BACK, RIGHT?
YEAH.
IT'S FRUSTRATING HOW A COMIC THAT I DREW FOR FUN GOT BETTER REVIEWS.
WELL, THAT SORT OF THING HAPPENS OFTEN.
MAYBE YOU WOULDN'T BE SO STRESSED BY DRAWING FOR A DIFFERENT PUBLISHER.
YOU AND TOUDOU DON'T GET ALONG, RIGHT?
I WON'T KNOW UNLESS WE WORK ON A SERIES TOGETHER.
I THINK HE'S TRYING...
TO HELP ME FIGURE OUT WHAT I WANT TO DRAW TOO.

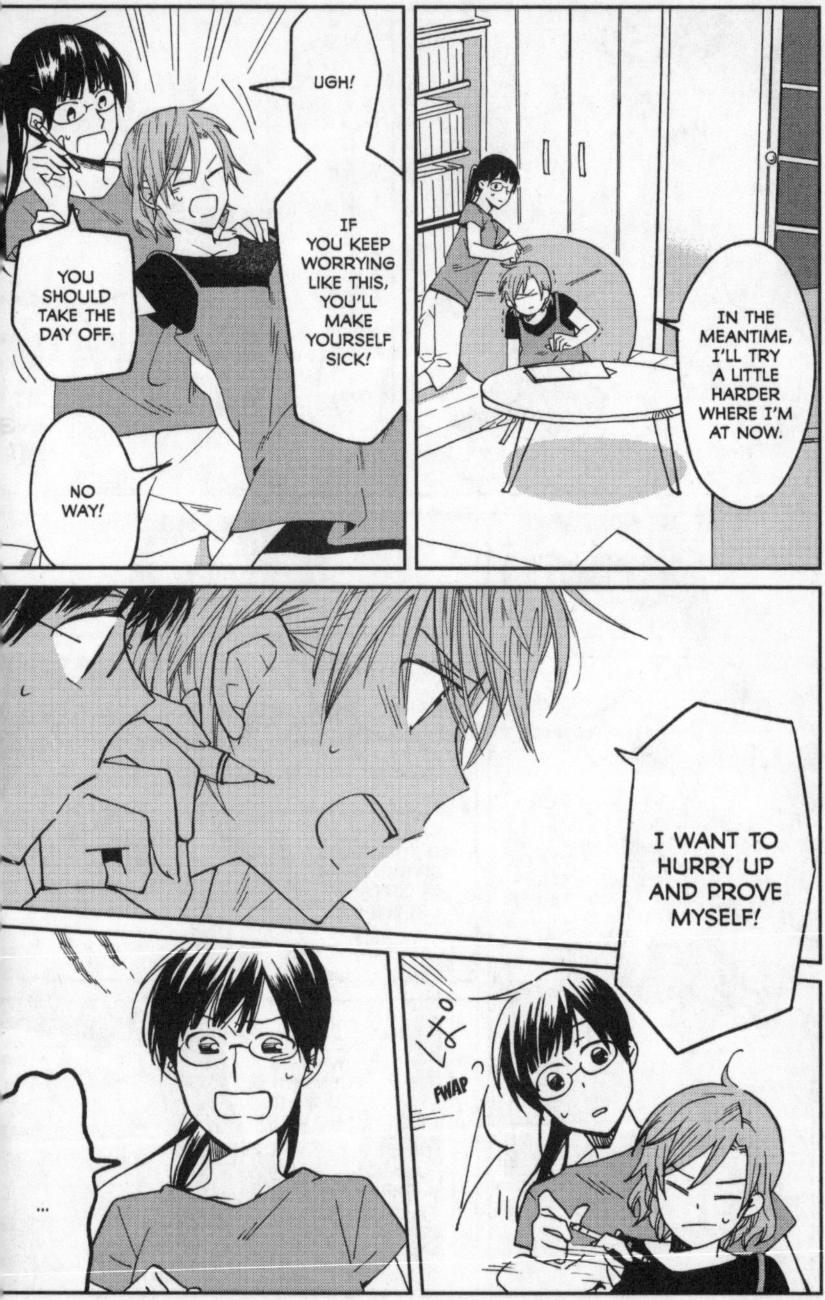
IN THE MEANTIME, I'LL TRY A LITTLE HARDER WHERE I'M AT NOW.
UGH!
IF YOU KEEP WORRYING LIKE THIS, YOU'LL MAKE YOURSELF SICK!
YOU SHOULD TAKE THE DAY OFF.
NO WAY!
I WANT TO HURRY UP AND PROVE MYSELF!
FWAP
...

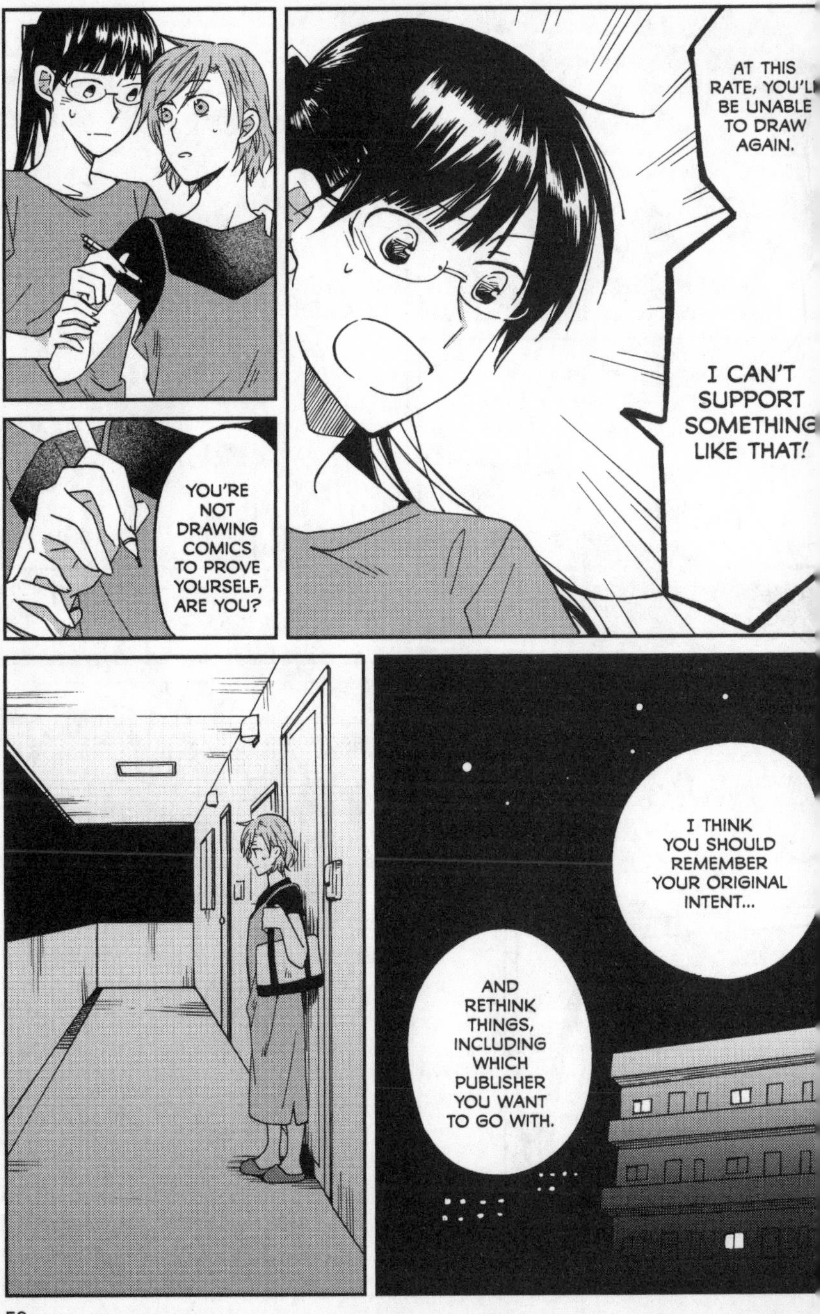
AT THIS RATE, YOU'LL BE UNABLE TO DRAW AGAIN.
I CAN'T SUPPORT SOMETHING LIKE THAT!
YOU'RE NOT DRAWING COMICS TO PROVE YOURSELF, ARE YOU?
I THINK YOU SHOULD REMEMBER YOUR ORIGINAL INTENT...
AND RETHINK THINGS, INCLUDING WHICH PUBLISHER YOU WANT TO GO WITH.

I'M EVEN MORE CONFUSED NOW.

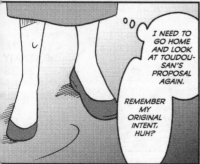

I NEED TO GO HOME AND LOOK AT TOUDOU-SAN'S PROPOSAL AGAIN.

REMEMBER MY ORIGINAL INTENT, HUH?

AH...

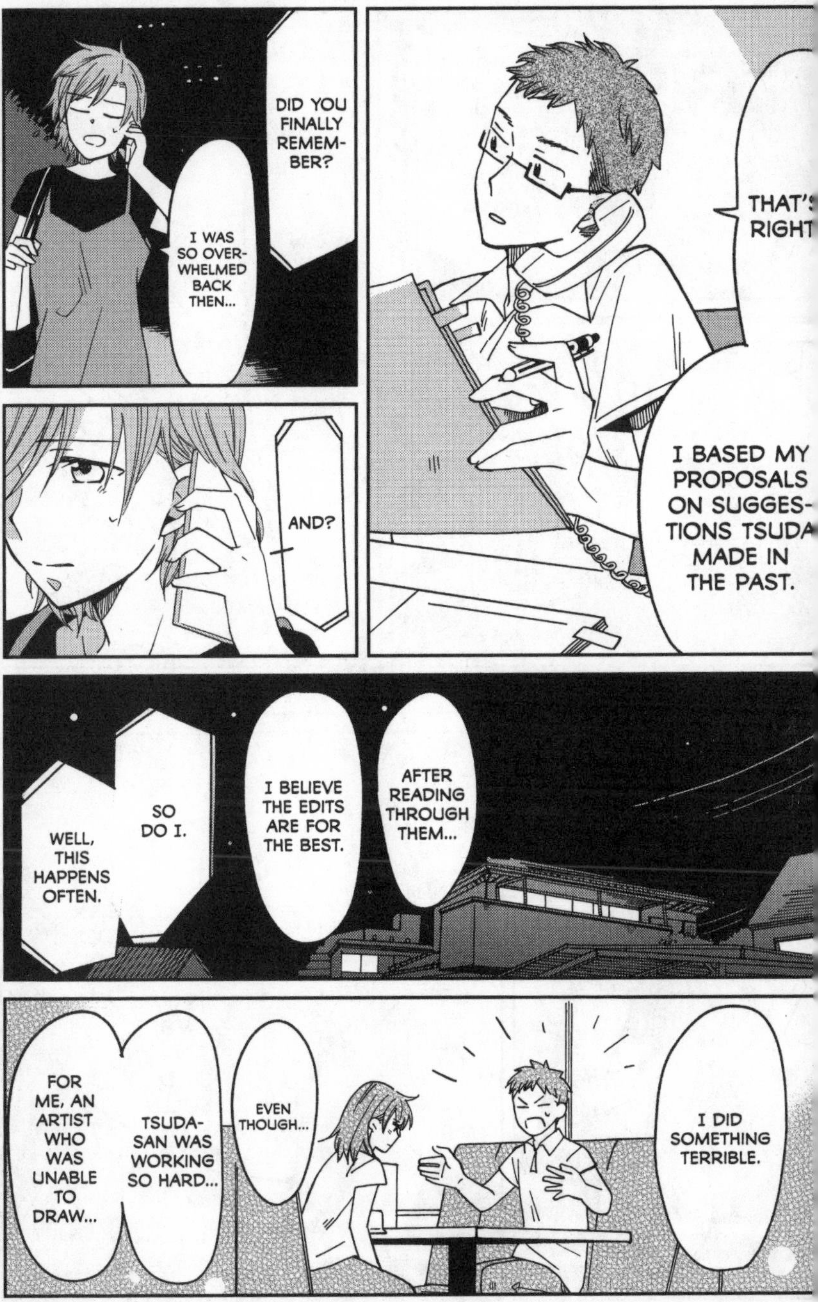
THAT'S RIGHT
I BASED MY PROPOSALS ON SUGGESTIONS TSUDA MADE IN THE PAST.
DID YOU FINALLY REMEMBER?
I WAS SO OVERWHELMED BACK THEN...
AND?
AFTER READING THROUGH THEM...
I BELIEVE THE EDITS ARE FOR THE BEST.
SO DO I.
WELL, THIS HAPPENS OFTEN.
I DID SOMETHING TERRIBLE.
EVEN THOUGH...
TSUDA-SAN WAS WORKING SO HARD...
FOR ME, AN ARTIST WHO WAS UNABLE TO DRAW...

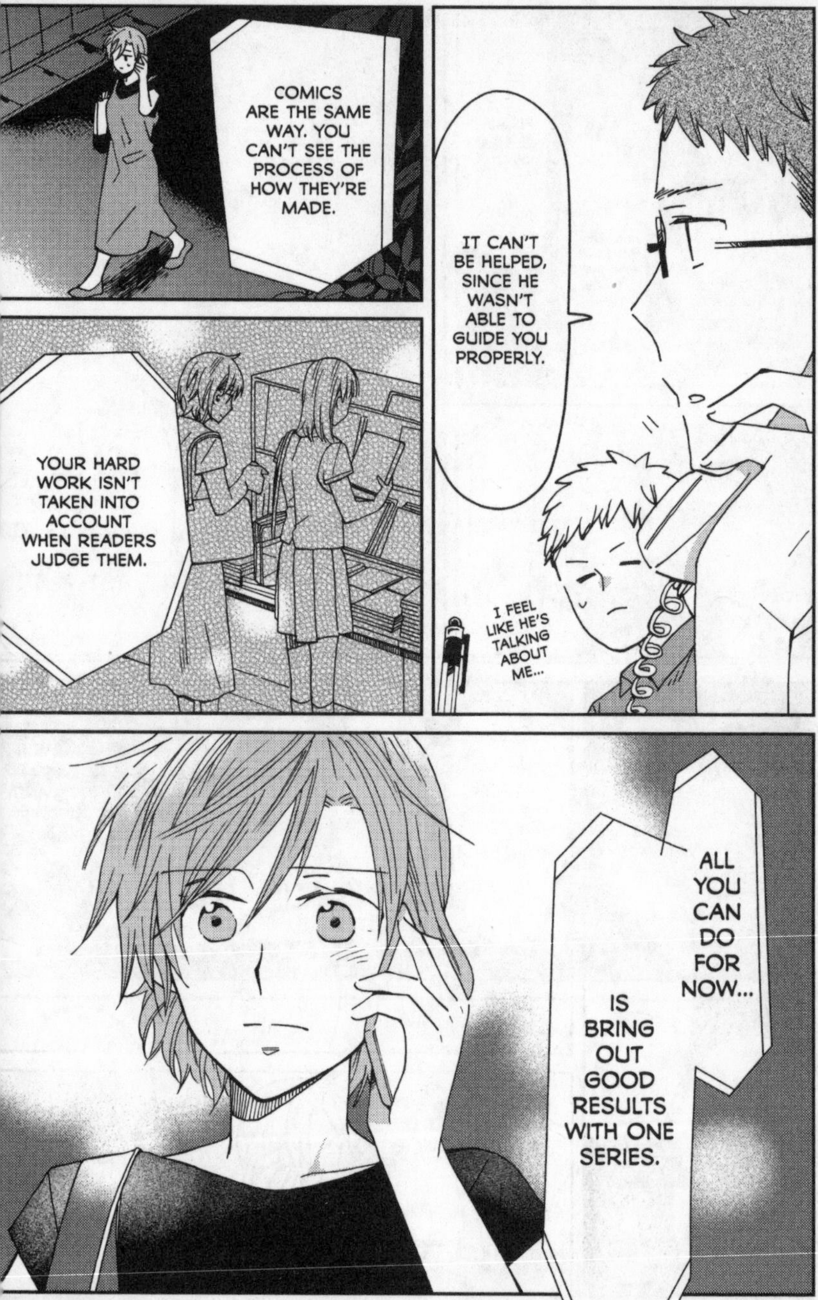
IT CAN'T BE HELPED, SINCE HE WASN'T ABLE TO GUIDE YOU PROPERLY.
I FEEL LIKE HE'S TALKING ABOUT ME...
COMICS ARE THE SAME WAY. YOU CAN'T SEE THE PROCESS OF HOW THEY'RE MADE.
YOUR HARD WORK ISN'T TAKEN INTO ACCOUNT WHEN READERS JUDGE THEM.
ALL YOU CAN DO FOR NOW...
IS BRING OUT GOOD RESULTS WITH ONE SERIES.

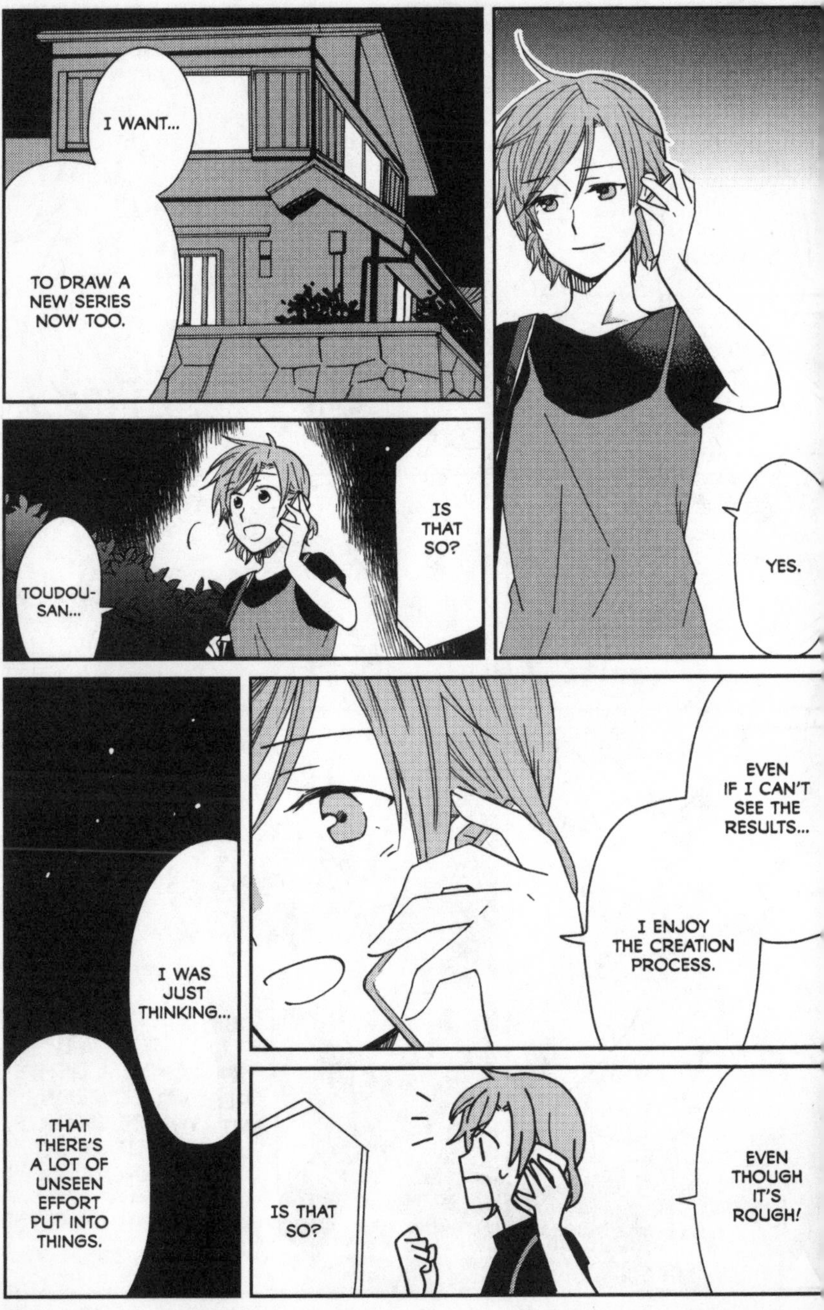
I WANT...
TO DRAW A NEW SERIES NOW TOO.
IS THAT SO?
TOUDOU-SAN...
YES.
EVEN IF I CAN'T SEE THE RESULTS...
I ENJOY THE CREATION PROCESS.
EVEN THOUGH IT'S ROUGH!
IS THAT SO?
I WAS JUST THINKING...
THAT THERE'S A LOT OF UNSEEN EFFORT PUT INTO THINGS.

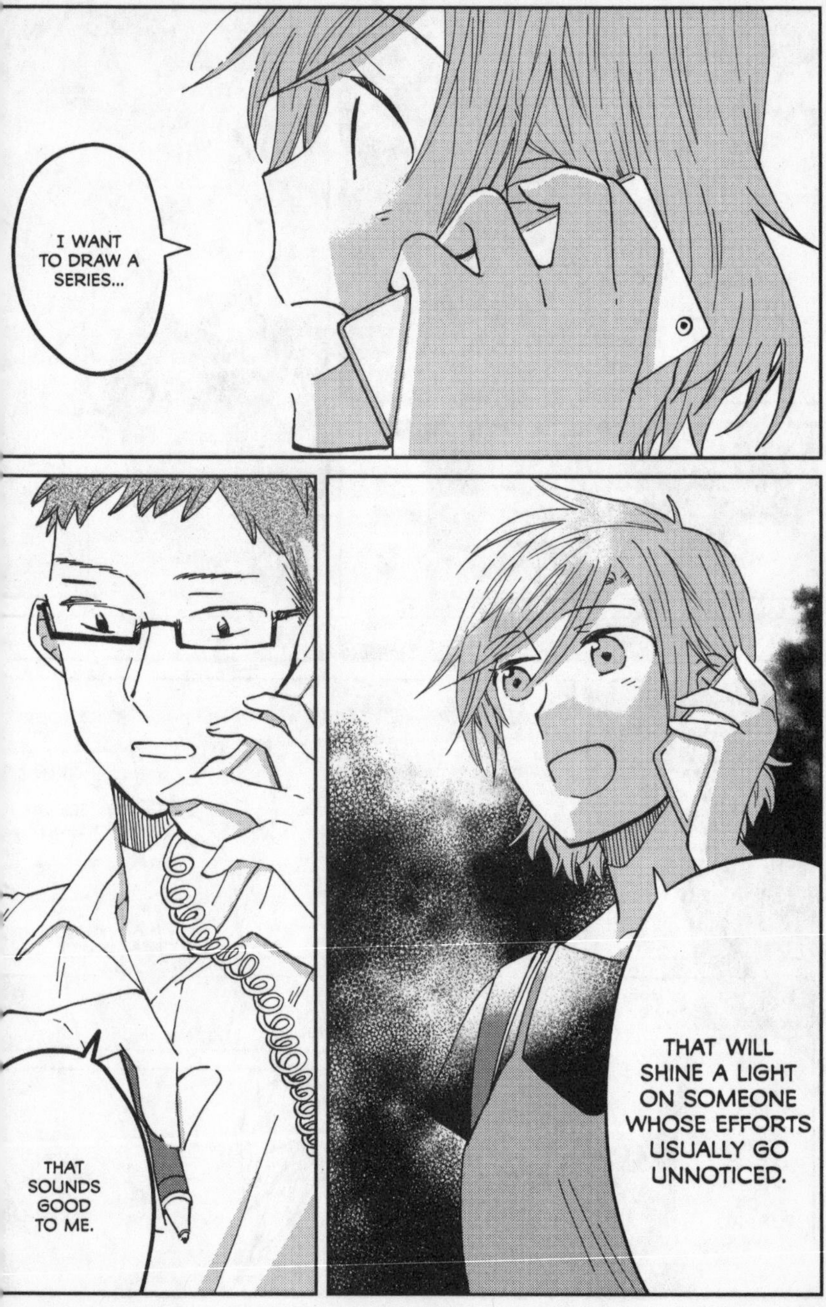
I WANT TO DRAW A SERIES...
THAT WILL SHINE A LIGHT ON SOMEONE WHOSE EFFORTS USUALLY GO UNNOTICED.
THAT SOUNDS GOOD TO ME.

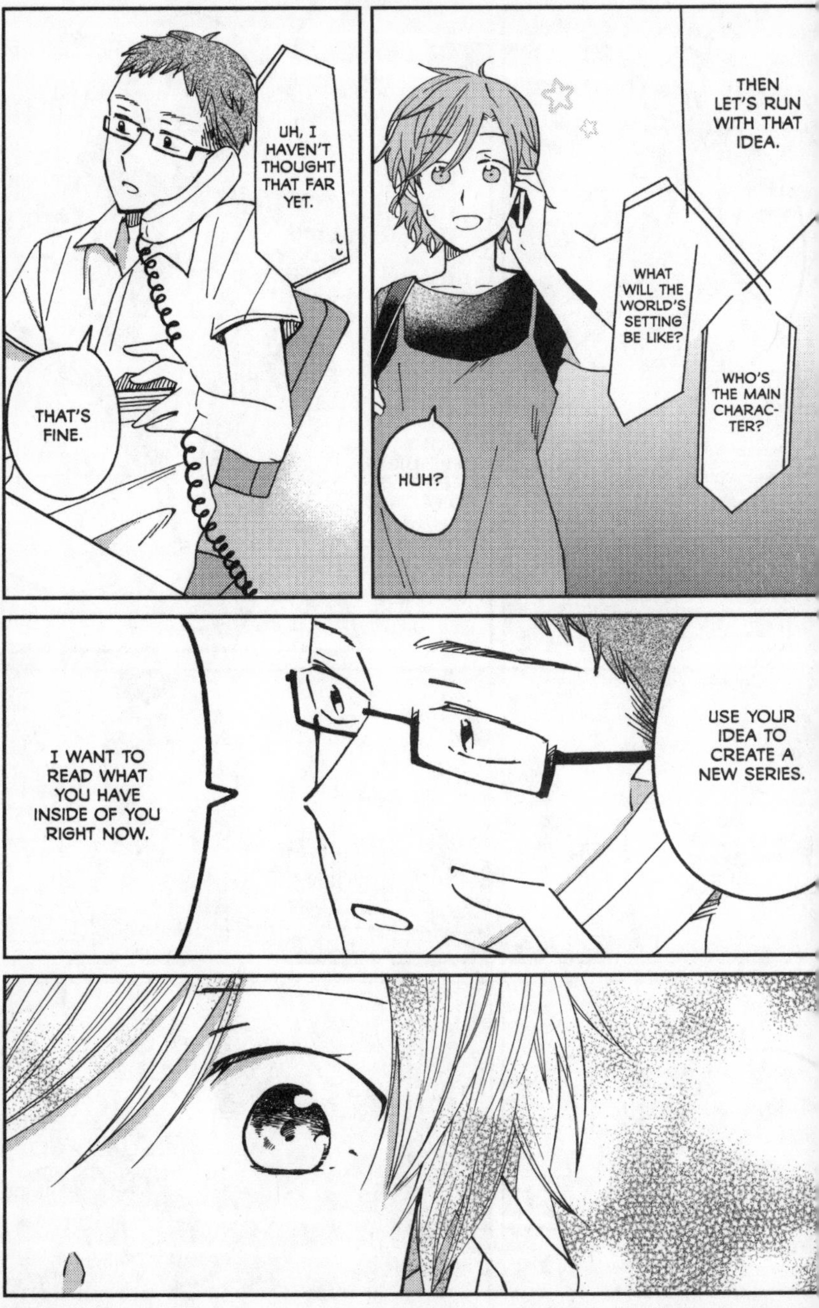
THEN LET'S RUN WITH THAT IDEA.
WHAT WILL THE WORLD'S SETTING BE LIKE?
WHO'S THE MAIN CHARACTER?
HUH?
UH, I HAVEN'T THOUGHT THAT FAR YET.
THAT'S FINE.
USE YOUR IDEA TO CREATE A NEW SERIES.
I WANT TO READ WHAT YOU HAVE INSIDE OF YOU RIGHT NOW.

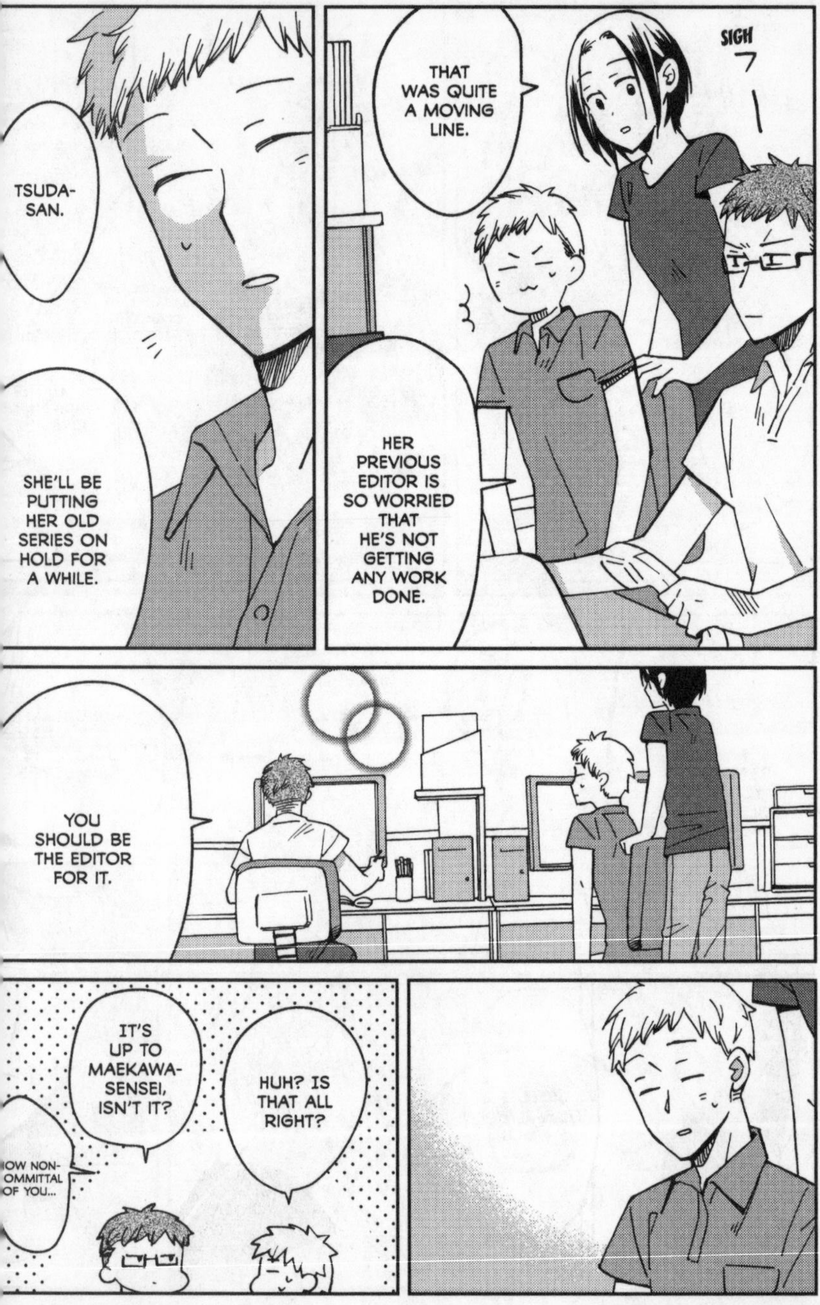
SIGH
THAT WAS QUITE A MOVING LINE.
HER PREVIOUS EDITOR IS SO WORRIED THAT HE'S NOT GETTING ANY WORK DONE.
TSUDA-SAN.
SHE'LL BE PUTTING HER OLD SERIES ON HOLD FOR A WHILE.
YOU SHOULD BE THE EDITOR FOR IT.
IT'S UP TO MAEKAWA-SENSEI, ISN'T IT?
HUH? IS THAT ALL RIGHT?
OW NON-OMMITTAL OF YOU...

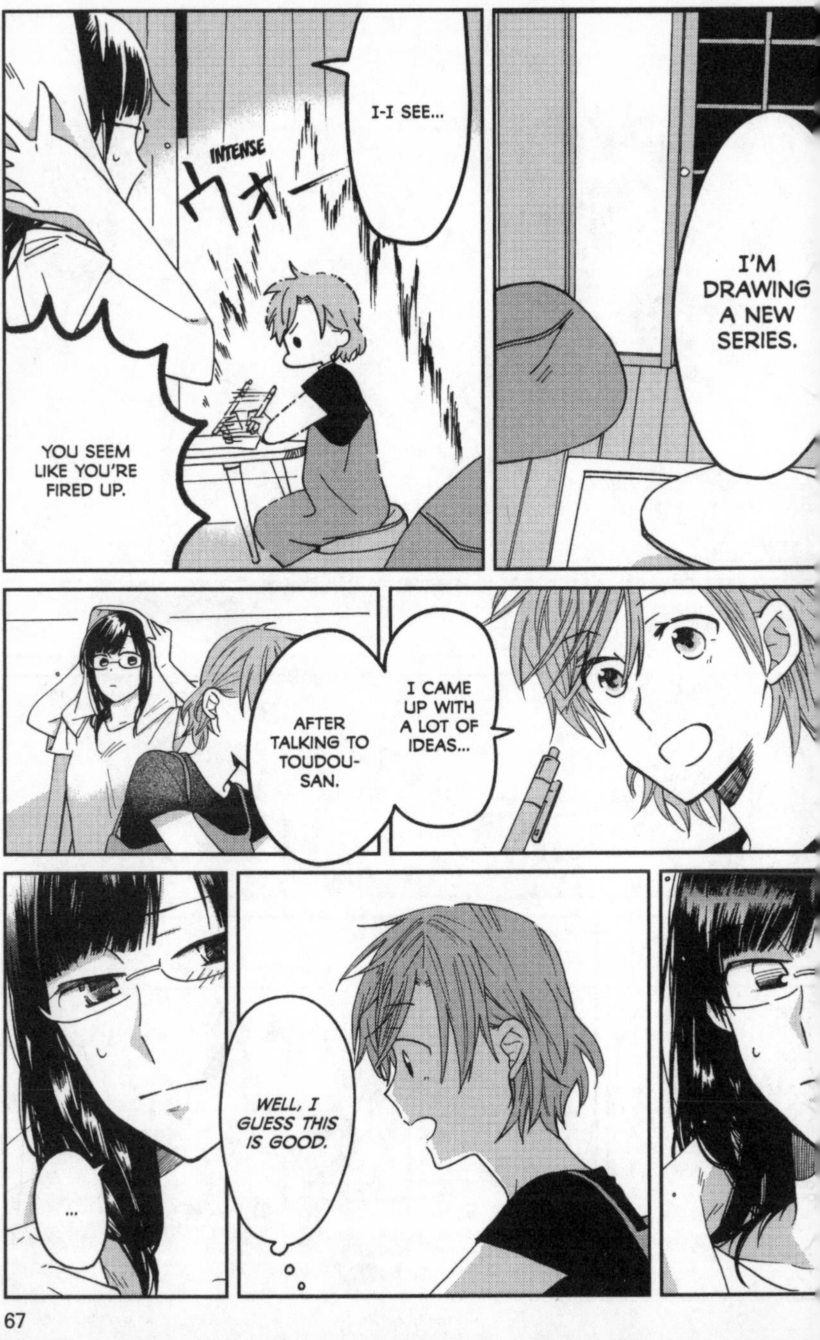
I'M DRAWING A NEW SERIES.
I-I SEE...
INTENSE
ウオー
YOU SEEM LIKE YOU'RE FIRED UP.
I CAME UP WITH A LOT OF IDEAS...
AFTER TALKING TO TOUDOU-SAN.
WELL, I GUESS THIS IS GOOD.
...

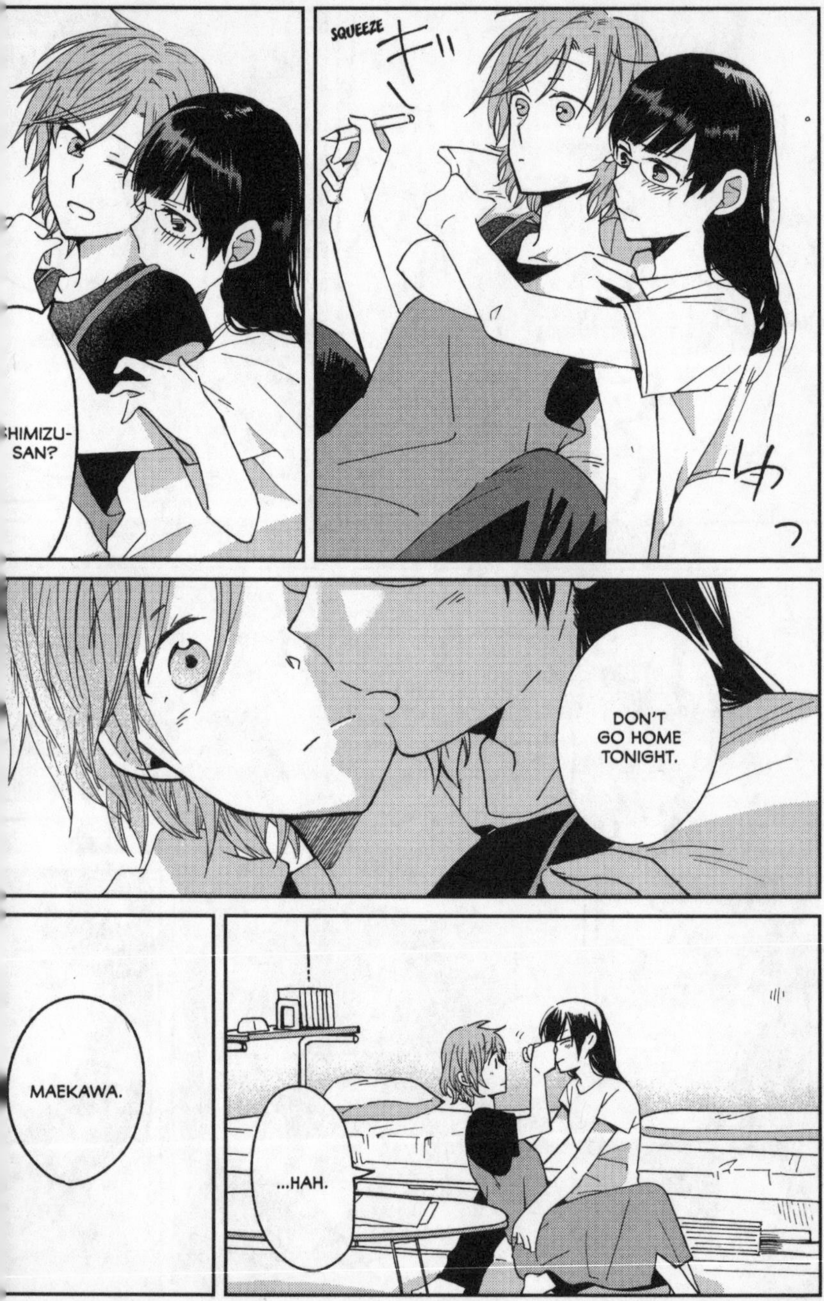
SQUEEZE
SHIMIZU-SAN?
DON'T GO HOME TONIGHT.
...HAH.
MAEKAWA.

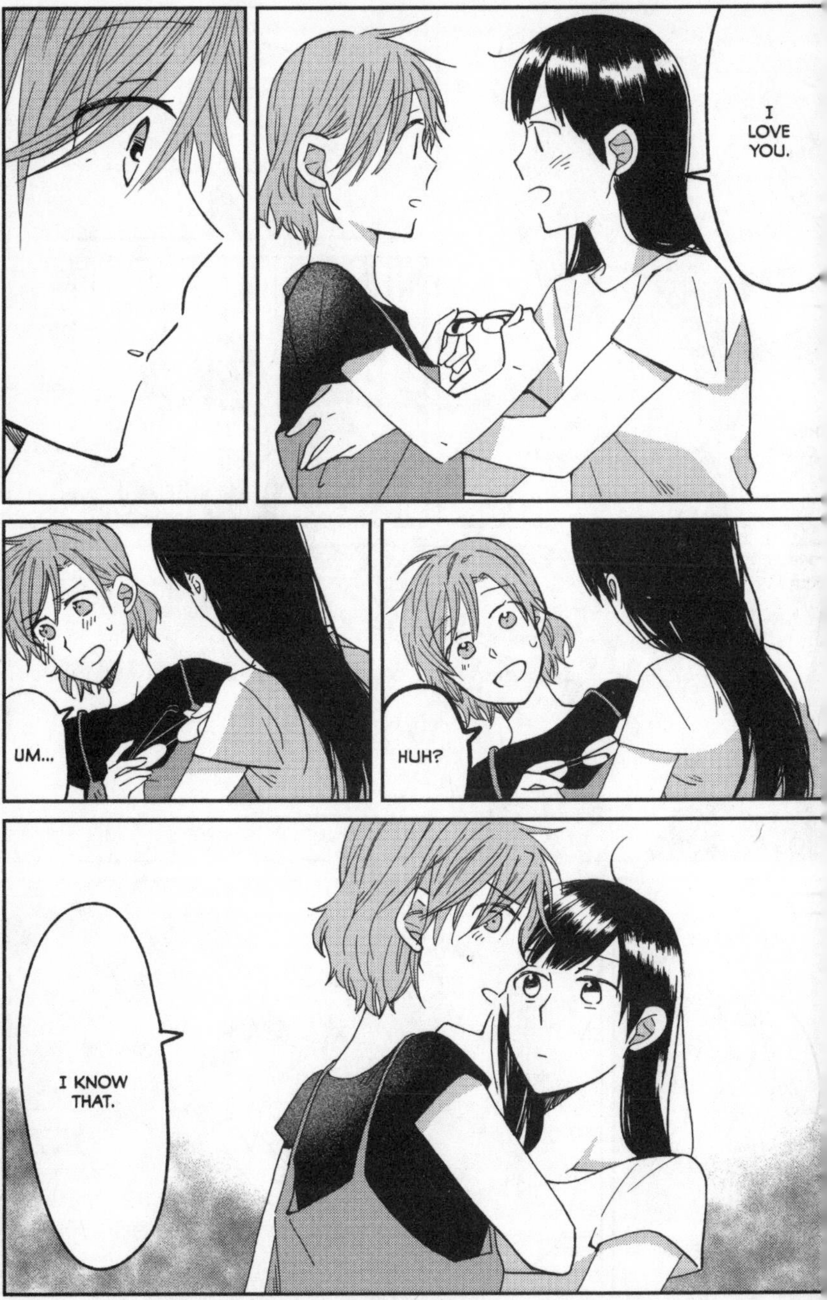
I LOVE YOU.
HUH?
UM...
I KNOW THAT.

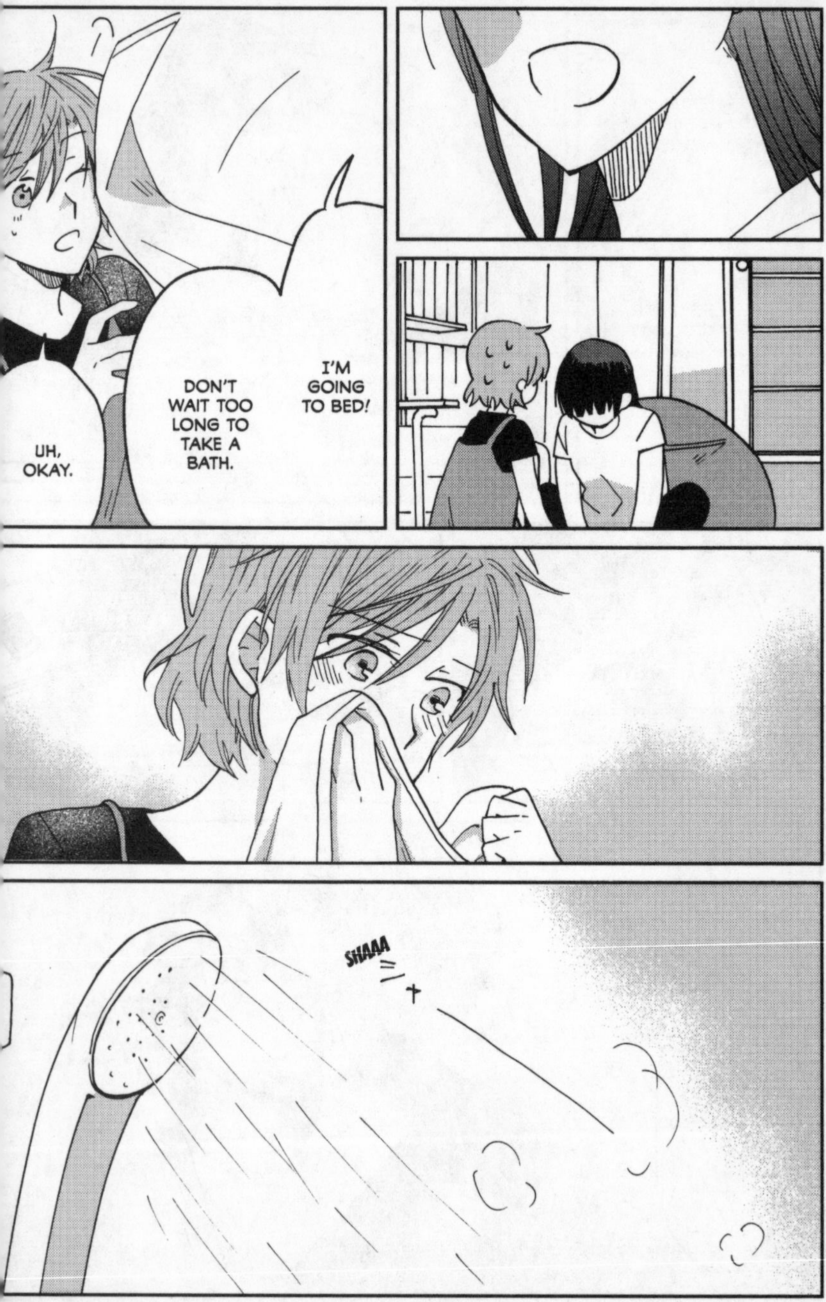
I'M GOING TO BED!
DON'T WAIT TOO LONG TO TAKE A BATH.
UH, OKAY.
SHAAA

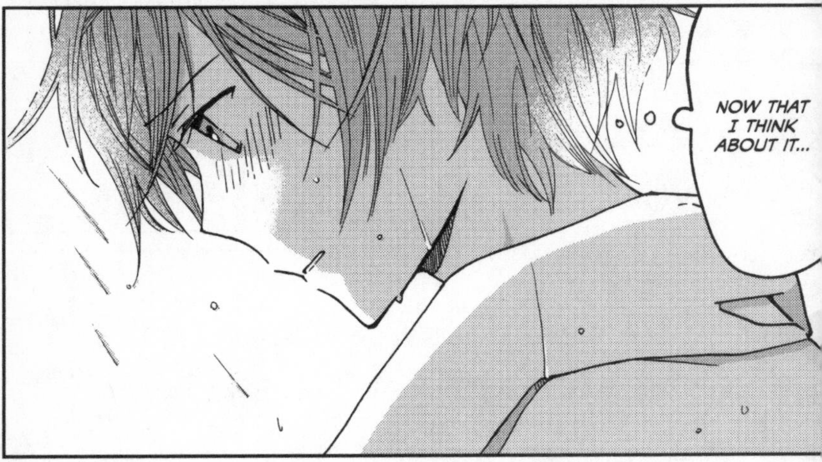
NOW THAT I THINK ABOUT IT...

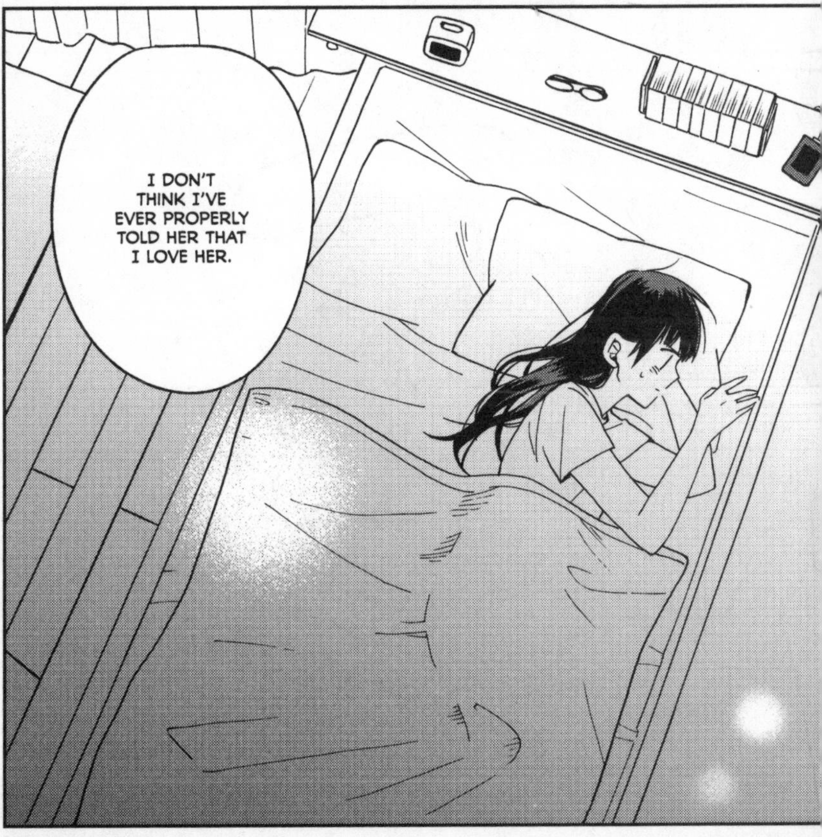
I DON'T THINK I'VE EVER PROPERLY TOLD HER THAT I LOVE HER.

Chapter 18

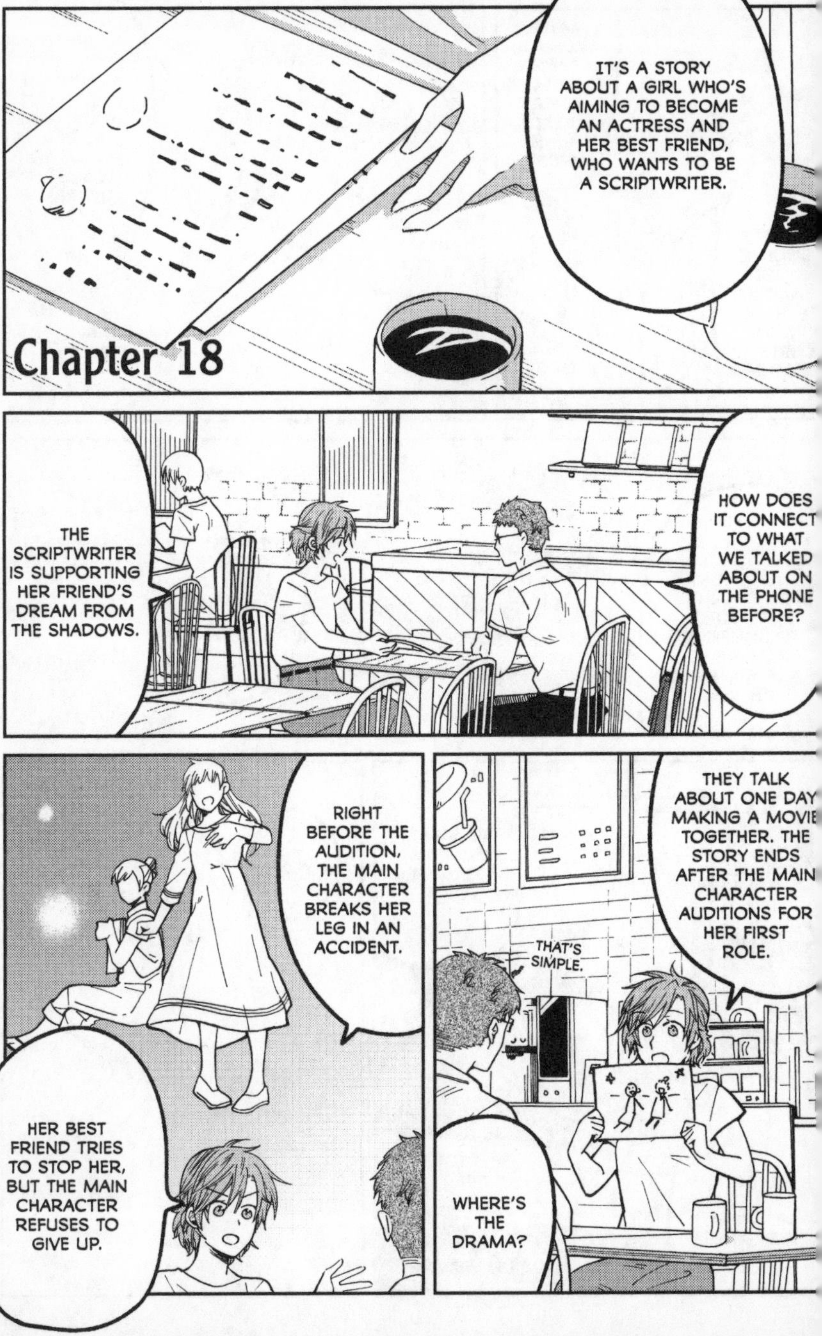
IT'S A STORY ABOUT A GIRL WHO'S AIMING TO BECOME AN ACTRESS AND HER BEST FRIEND, WHO WANTS TO BE A SCRIPTWRITER.
HOW DOES IT CONNECT TO WHAT WE TALKED ABOUT ON THE PHONE BEFORE?
THE SCRIPTWRITER IS SUPPORTING HER FRIEND'S DREAM FROM THE SHADOWS.
THEY TALK ABOUT ONE DAY MAKING A MOVIE TOGETHER. THE STORY ENDS AFTER THE MAIN CHARACTER AUDITIONS FOR HER FIRST ROLE.
THAT'S SIMPLE.
WHERE'S THE DRAMA?
RIGHT BEFORE THE AUDITION, THE MAIN CHARACTER BREAKS HER LEG IN AN ACCIDENT.
HER BEST FRIEND TRIES TO STOP HER, BUT THE MAIN CHARACTER REFUSES TO GIVE UP.

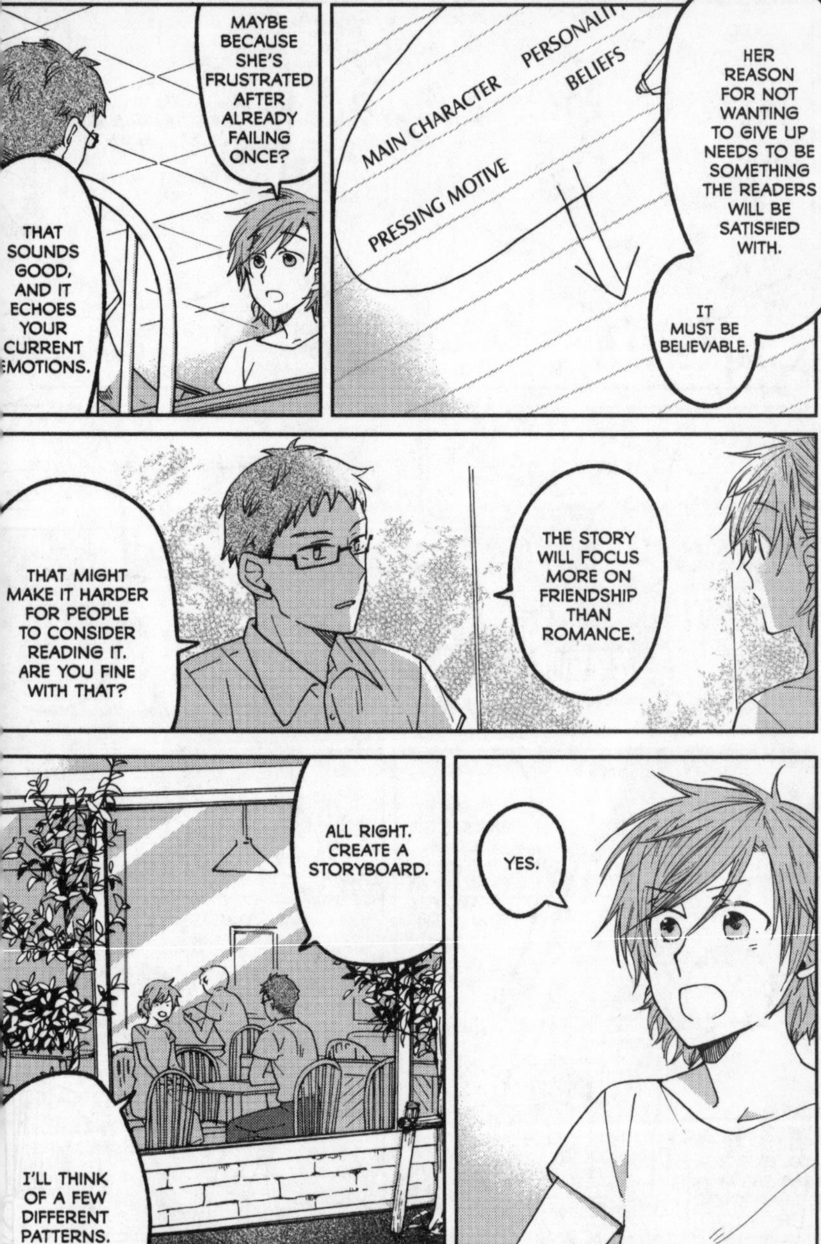
HER REASON FOR NOT WANTING TO GIVE UP NEEDS TO BE SOMETHING THE READERS WILL BE SATISFIED WITH.
IT MUST BE BELIEVABLE.
MAIN CHARACTER
PERSONALIT
BELIEFS
PRESSING MOTIVE
MAYBE BECAUSE SHE'S FRUSTRATED AFTER ALREADY FAILING ONCE?
THAT SOUNDS GOOD, AND IT ECHOES YOUR CURRENT EMOTIONS.
THE STORY WILL FOCUS MORE ON FRIENDSHIP THAN ROMANCE.
THAT MIGHT MAKE IT HARDER FOR PEOPLE TO CONSIDER READING IT. ARE YOU FINE WITH THAT?
YES.
ALL RIGHT. CREATE A STORYBOARD.
I'LL THINK OF A FEW DIFFERENT PATTERNS.

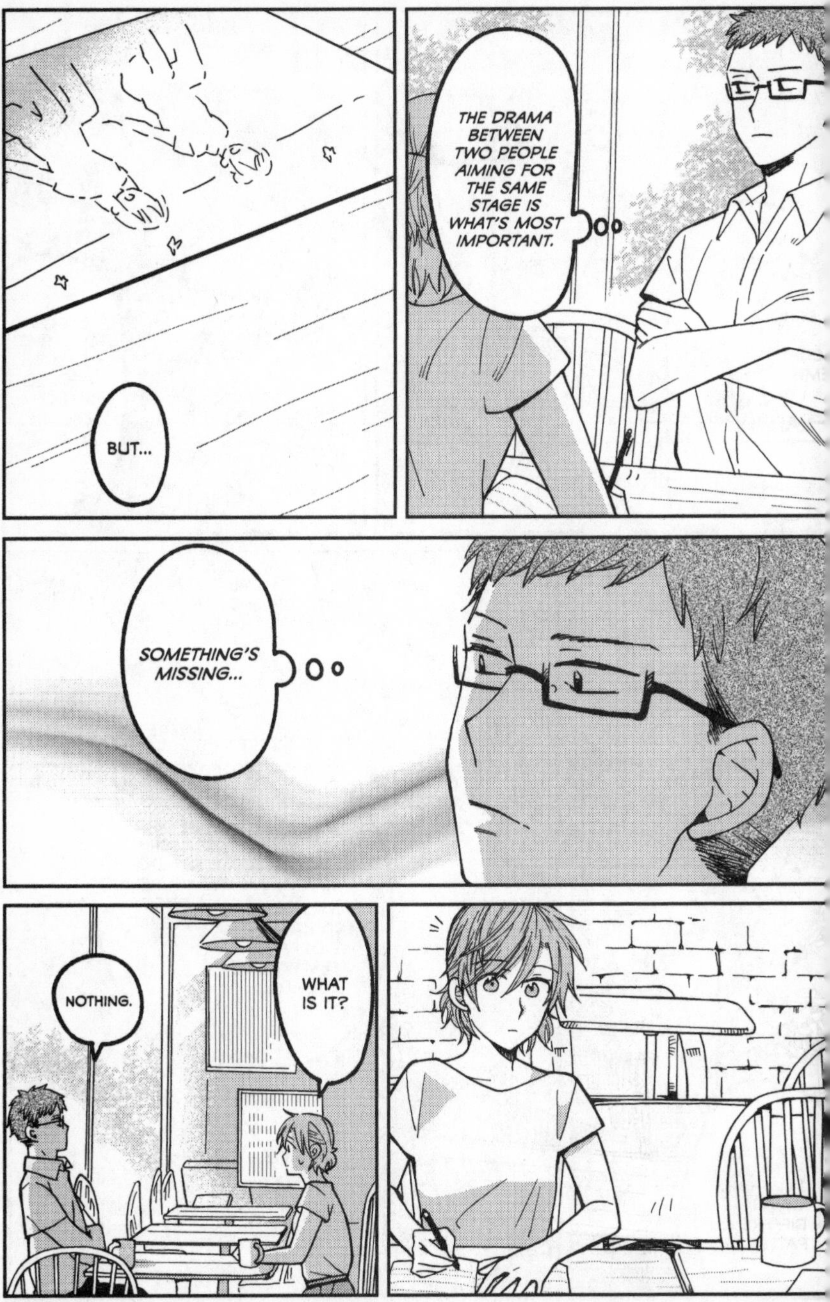
THE DRAMA BETWEEN TWO PEOPLE AIMING FOR THE SAME STAGE IS WHAT'S MOST IMPORTANT.
BUT...
SOMETHING'S MISSING...
WHAT IS IT?
NOTHING.

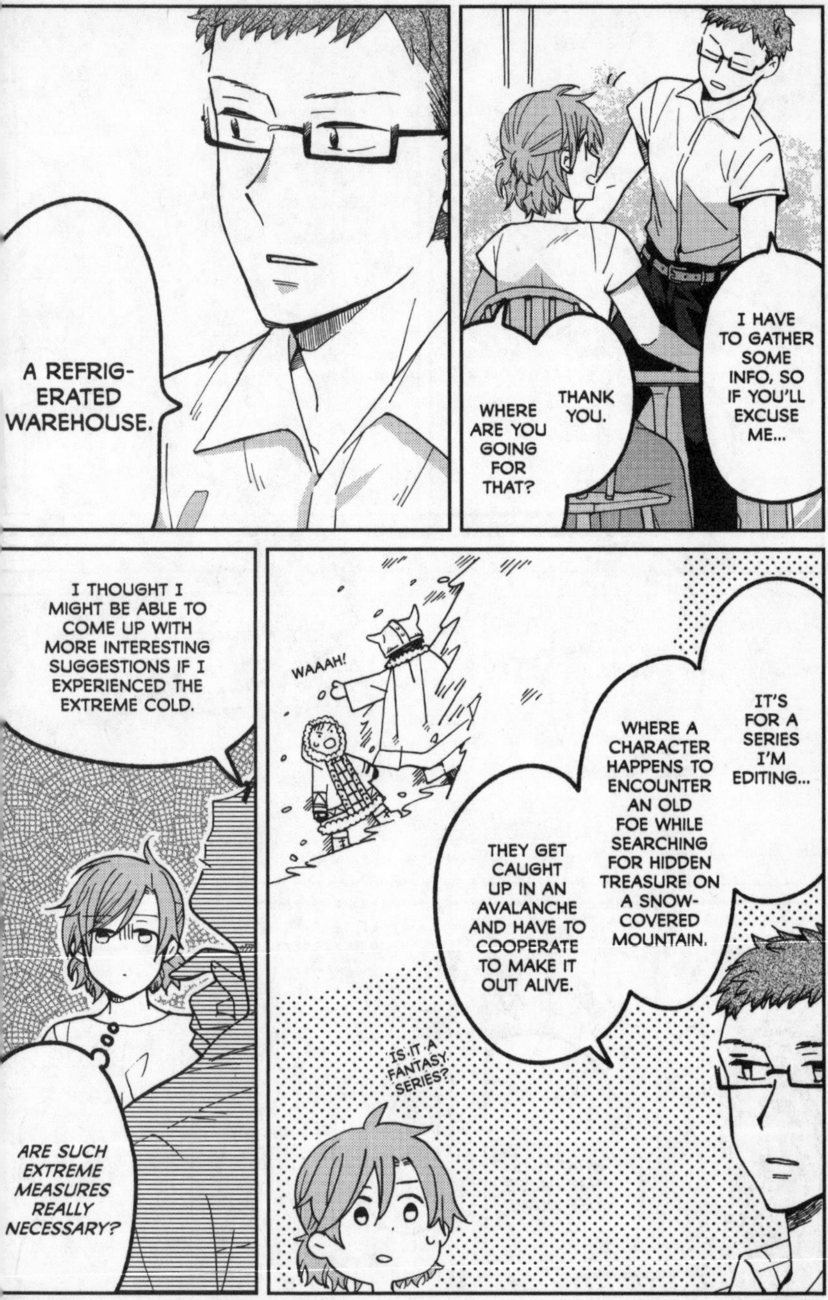
I HAVE TO GATHER SOME INFO, SO IF YOU'LL EXCUSE ME...
THANK YOU.
WHERE ARE YOU GOING FOR THAT?
A REFRIG-ERATED WAREHOUSE.
IT'S FOR A SERIES I'M EDITING...
WHERE A CHARACTER HAPPENS TO ENCOUNTER AN OLD FOE WHILE SEARCHING FOR HIDDEN TREASURE ON A SNOW-COVERED MOUNTAIN.
THEY GET CAUGHT UP IN AN AVALANCHE AND HAVE TO COOPERATE TO MAKE IT OUT ALIVE.
WAAAH!
IS IT A FANTASY SERIES?
I THOUGHT I MIGHT BE ABLE TO COME UP WITH MORE INTERESTING SUGGESTIONS IF I EXPERIENCED THE EXTREME COLD.
ARE SUCH EXTREME MEASURES REALLY NECESSARY?

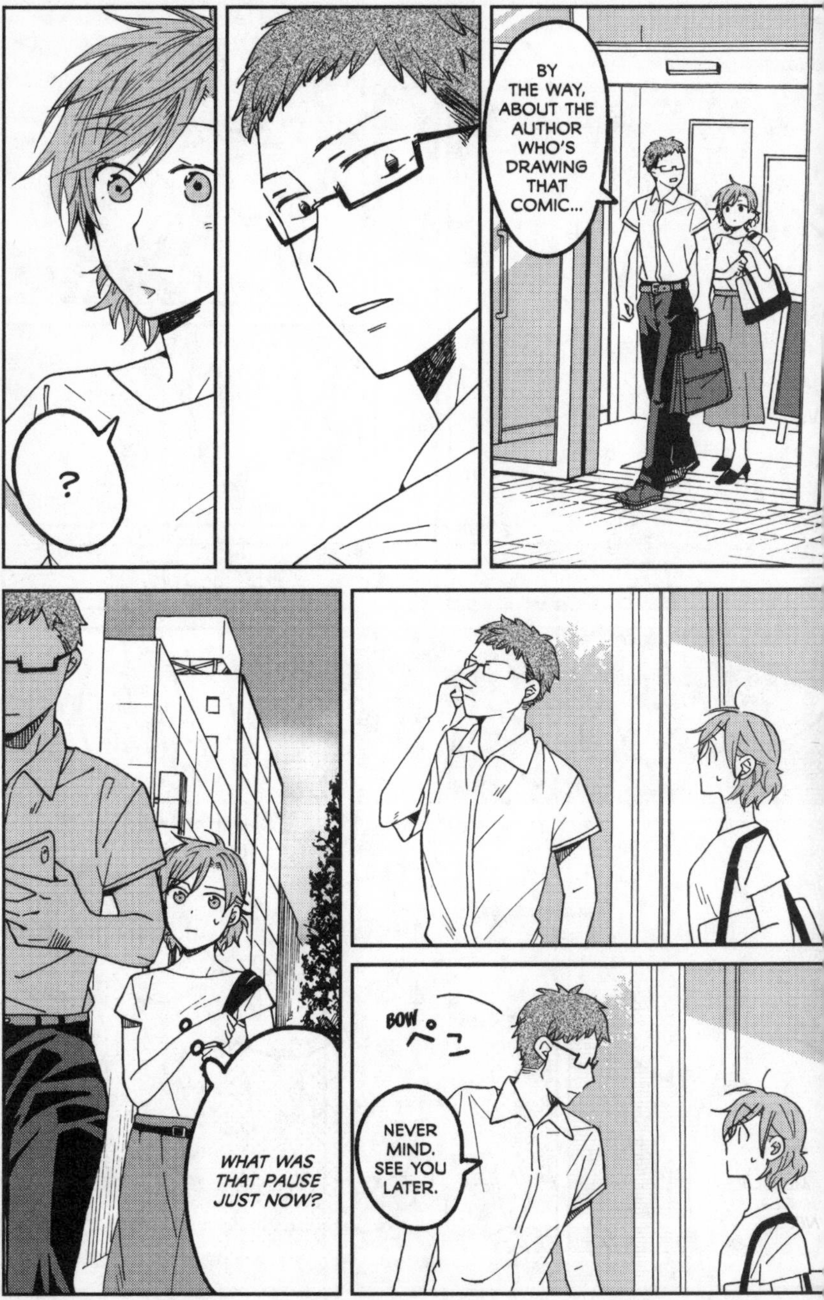
BY THE WAY, ABOUT THE AUTHOR WHO'S DRAWING THAT COMIC...
?
BOW
NEVER MIND. SEE YOU LATER.
WHAT WAS THAT PAUSE JUST NOW?

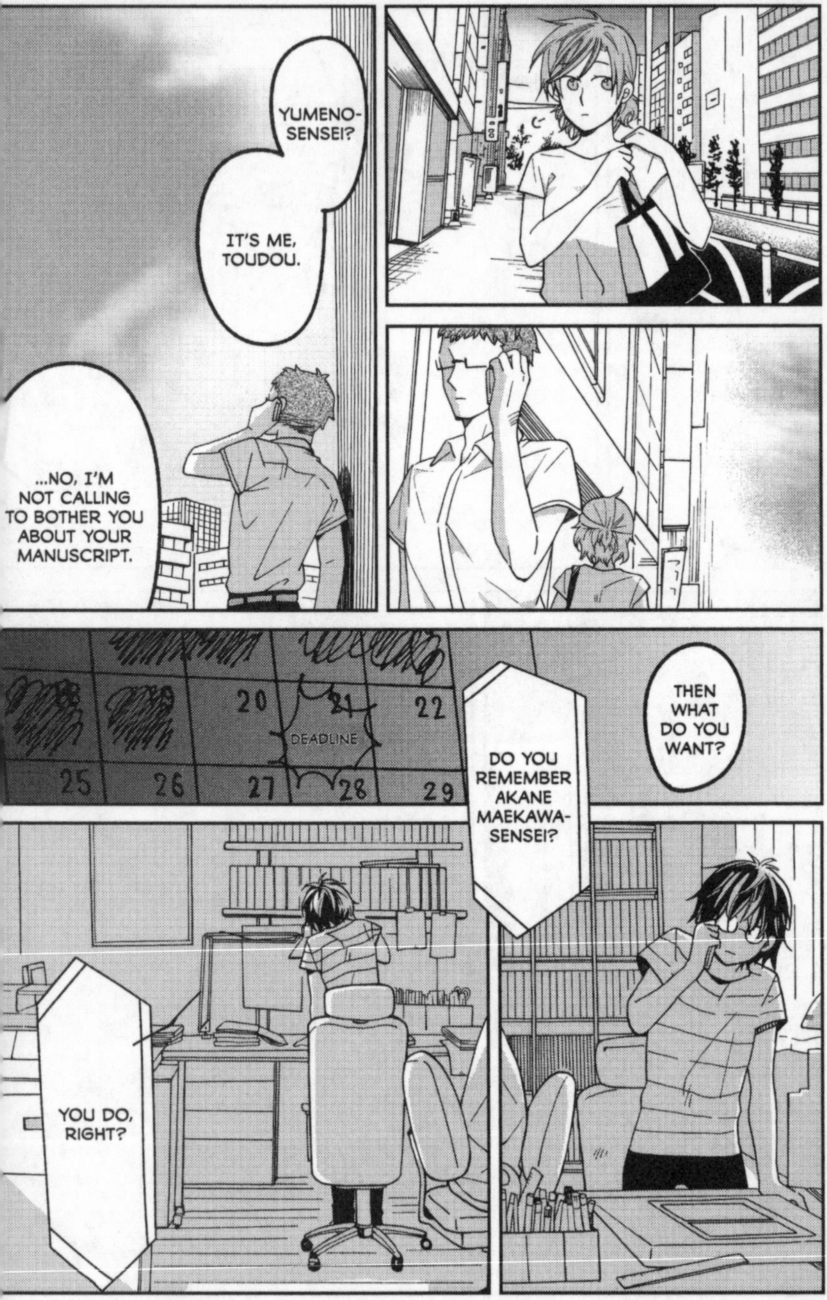
YUMENO-SENSEI?
IT'S ME, TOUDOU.
...NO, I'M NOT CALLING TO BOTHER YOU ABOUT YOUR MANUSCRIPT.
THEN WHAT DO YOU WANT?
20 21 22
DEADLINE
25 26 27 28 29
DO YOU REMEMBER AKANE MAEKAWA-SENSEI?
YOU DO, RIGHT?

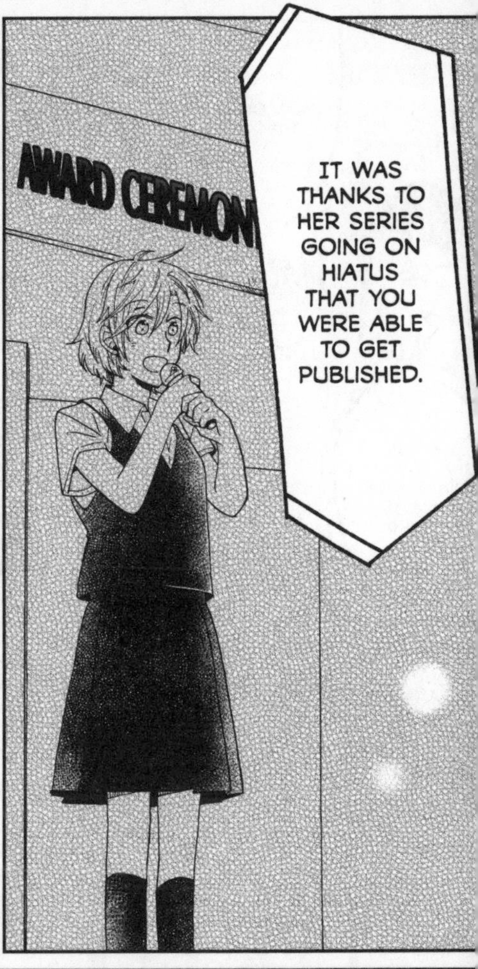
AWARD CEREMON
IT WAS THANKS TO HER SERIES GOING ON HIATUS THAT YOU WERE ABLE TO GET PUBLISHED.

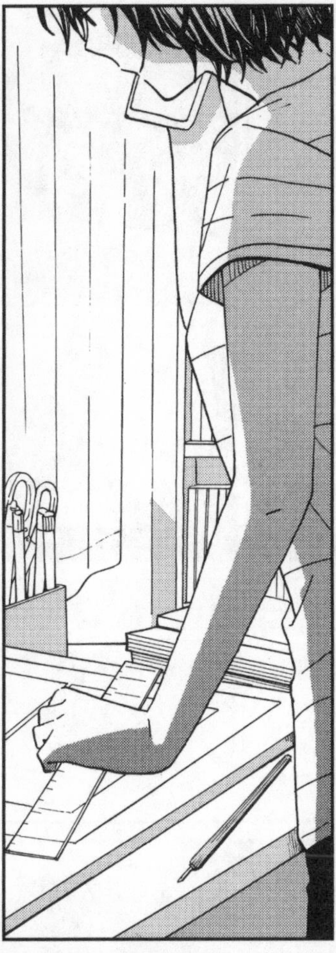

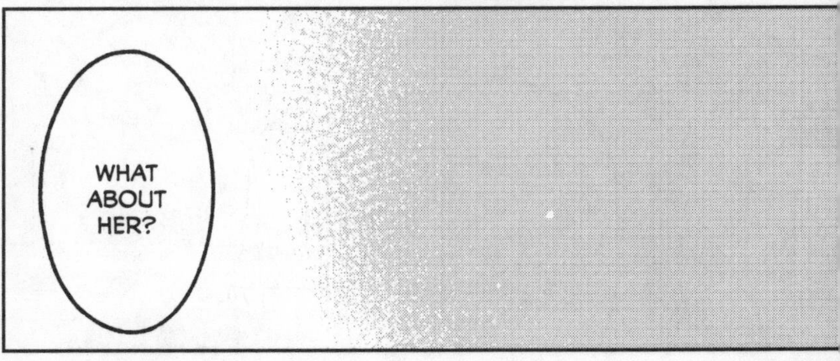
WHAT ABOUT HER?

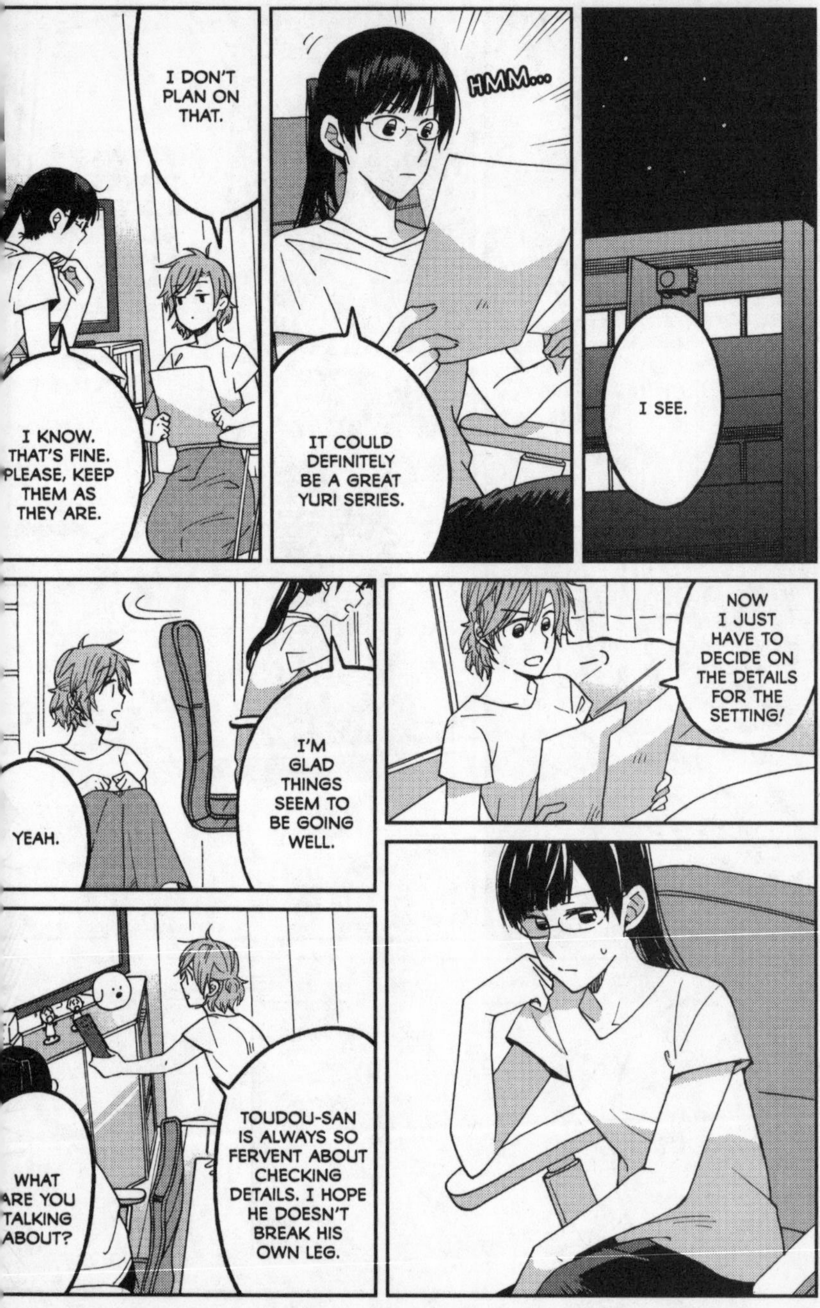
I SEE.
HMM...
IT COULD DEFINITELY BE A GREAT YURI SERIES.
I DON'T PLAN ON THAT.
I KNOW. THAT'S FINE. PLEASE, KEEP THEM AS THEY ARE.
NOW I JUST HAVE TO DECIDE ON THE DETAILS FOR THE SETTING!
I'M GLAD THINGS SEEM TO BE GOING WELL.
YEAH.
TOUDOU-SAN IS ALWAYS SO FERVENT ABOUT CHECKING DETAILS. I HOPE HE DOESN'T BREAK HIS OWN LEG.
WHAT ARE YOU TALKING ABOUT?

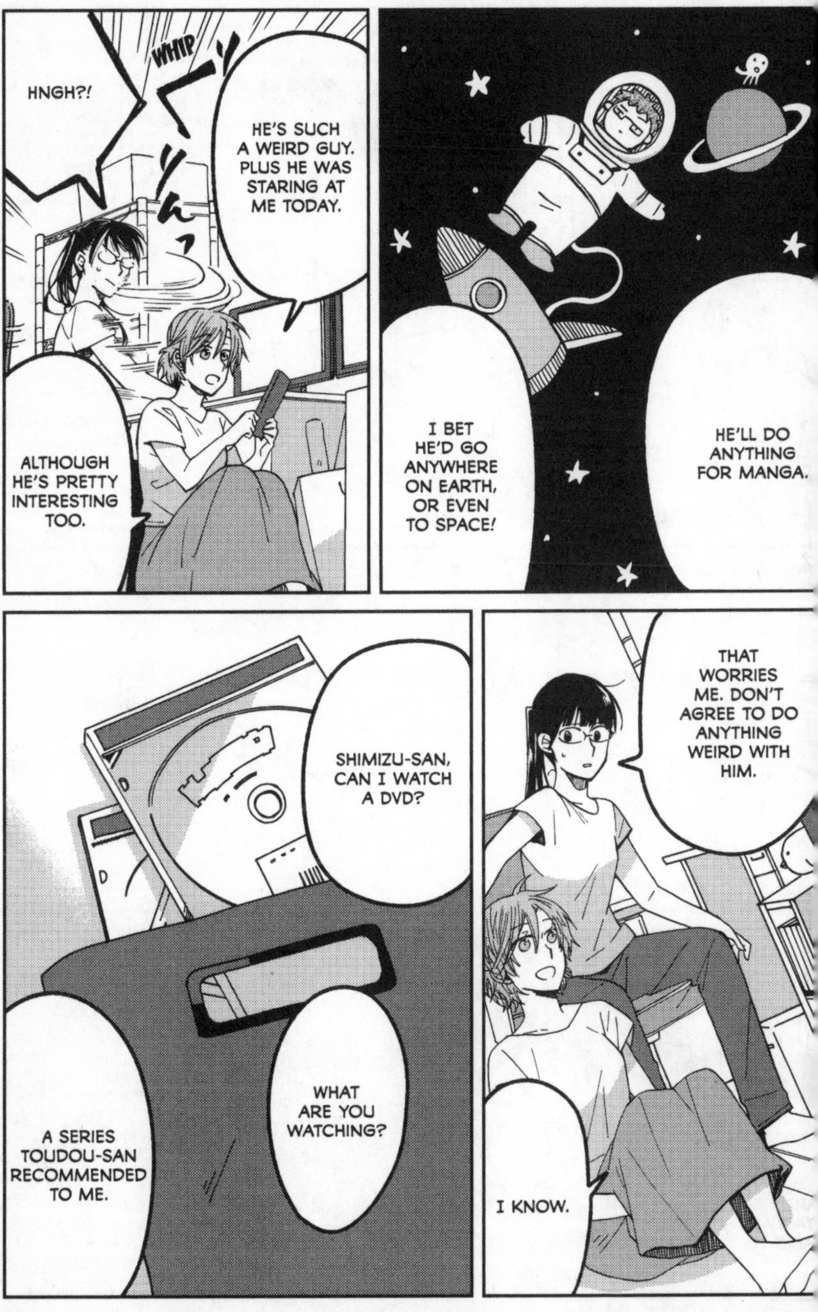
HE'LL DO ANYTHING FOR MANGA.
I BET HE'D GO ANYWHERE ON EARTH, OR EVEN TO SPACE!
HE'S SUCH A WEIRD GUY. PLUS HE WAS STARING AT ME TODAY.
WHIP
HNGH?!
ALTHOUGH HE'S PRETTY INTERESTING TOO.
THAT WORRIES ME. DON'T AGREE TO DO ANYTHING WEIRD WITH HIM.
I KNOW.
SHIMIZU-SAN, CAN I WATCH A DVD?
WHAT ARE YOU WATCHING?
A SERIES TOUDOU-SAN RECOMMENDED TO ME.

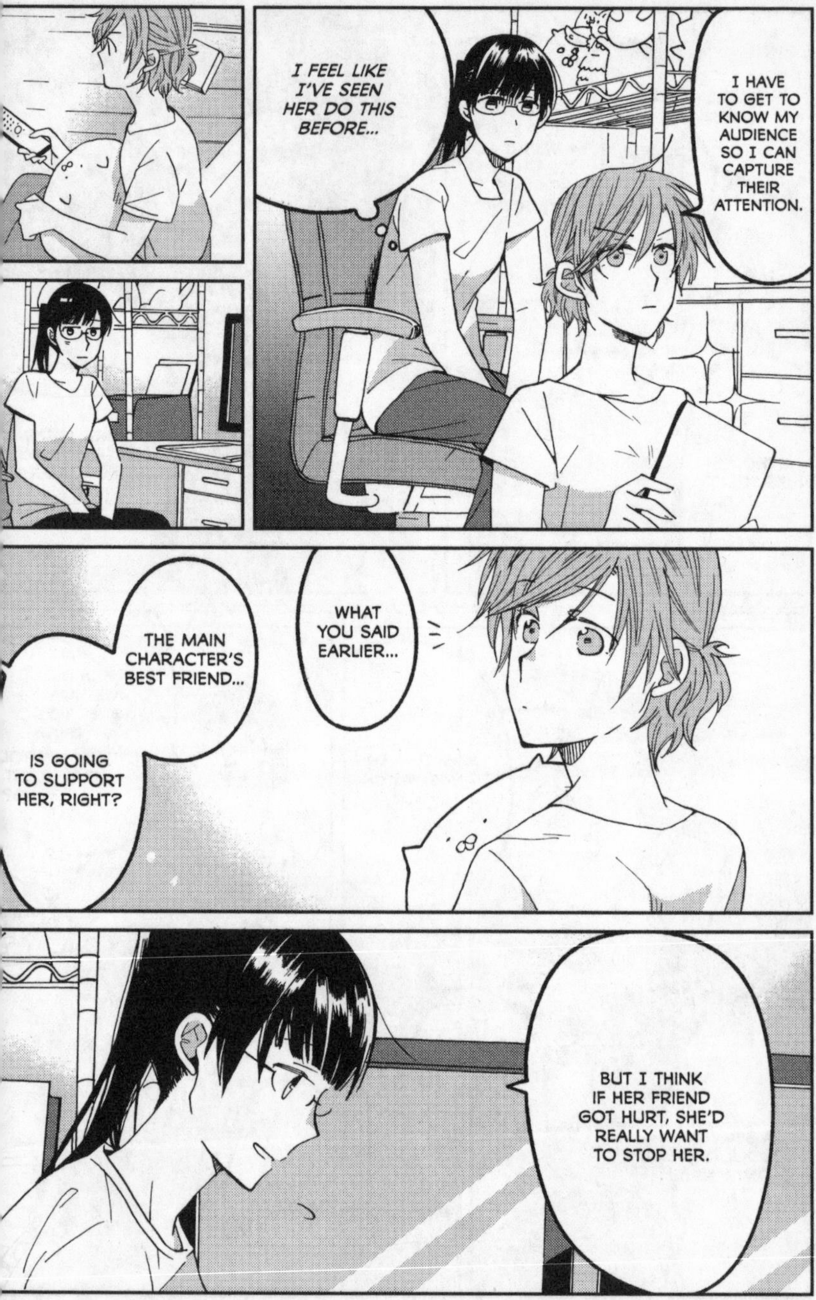
I HAVE TO GET TO KNOW MY AUDIENCE SO I CAN CAPTURE THEIR ATTENTION.
I FEEL LIKE I'VE SEEN HER DO THIS BEFORE...
WHAT YOU SAID EARLIER...
THE MAIN CHARACTER'S BEST FRIEND...
IS GOING TO SUPPORT HER, RIGHT?
BUT I THINK IF HER FRIEND GOT HURT, SHE'D REALLY WANT TO STOP HER.

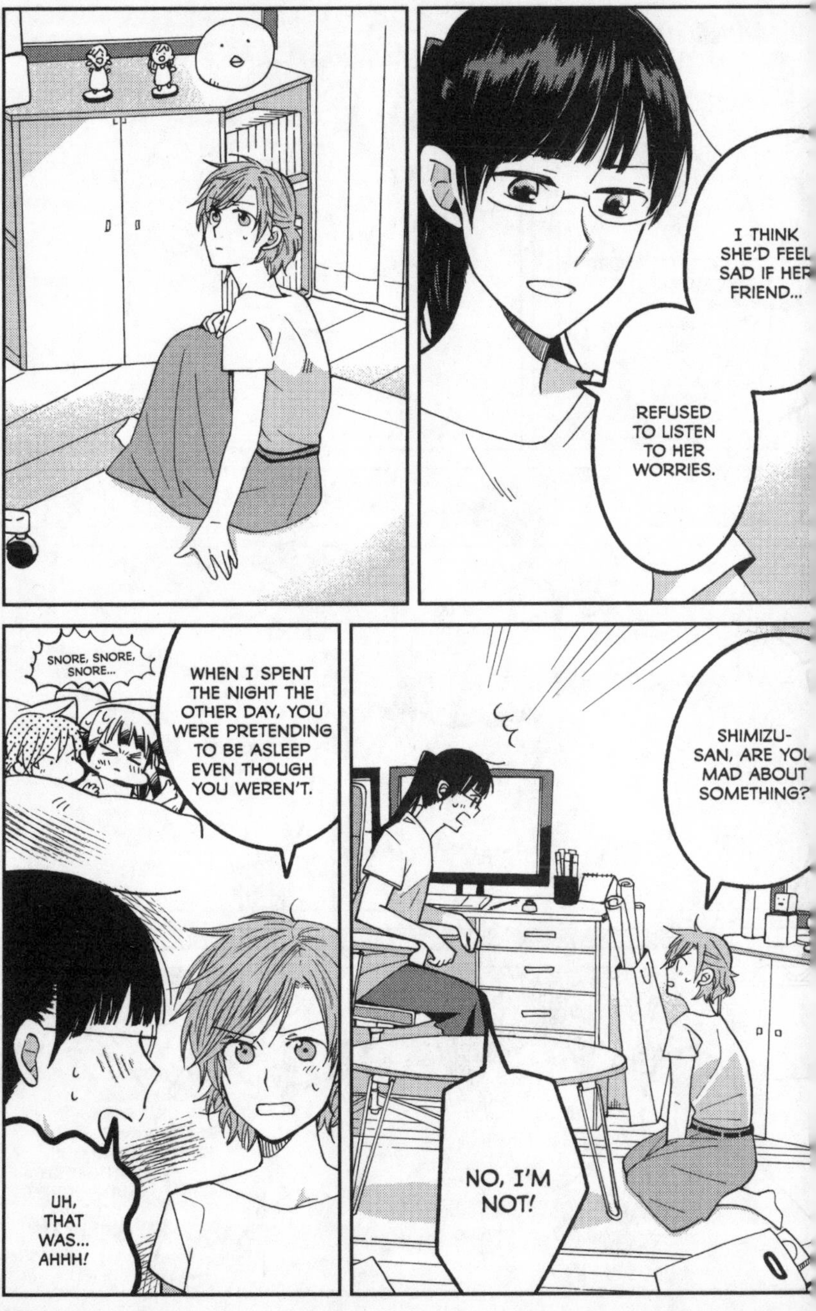
I THINK SHE'D FEEL SAD IF HER FRIEND...
REFUSED TO LISTEN TO HER WORRIES.
SHIMIZU-SAN, ARE YOU MAD ABOUT SOMETHING?
NO, I'M NOT!
SNORE, SNORE, SNORE...
WHEN I SPENT THE NIGHT THE OTHER DAY, YOU WERE PRETENDING TO BE ASLEEP EVEN THOUGH YOU WEREN'T.
UH, THAT WAS... AHHH!

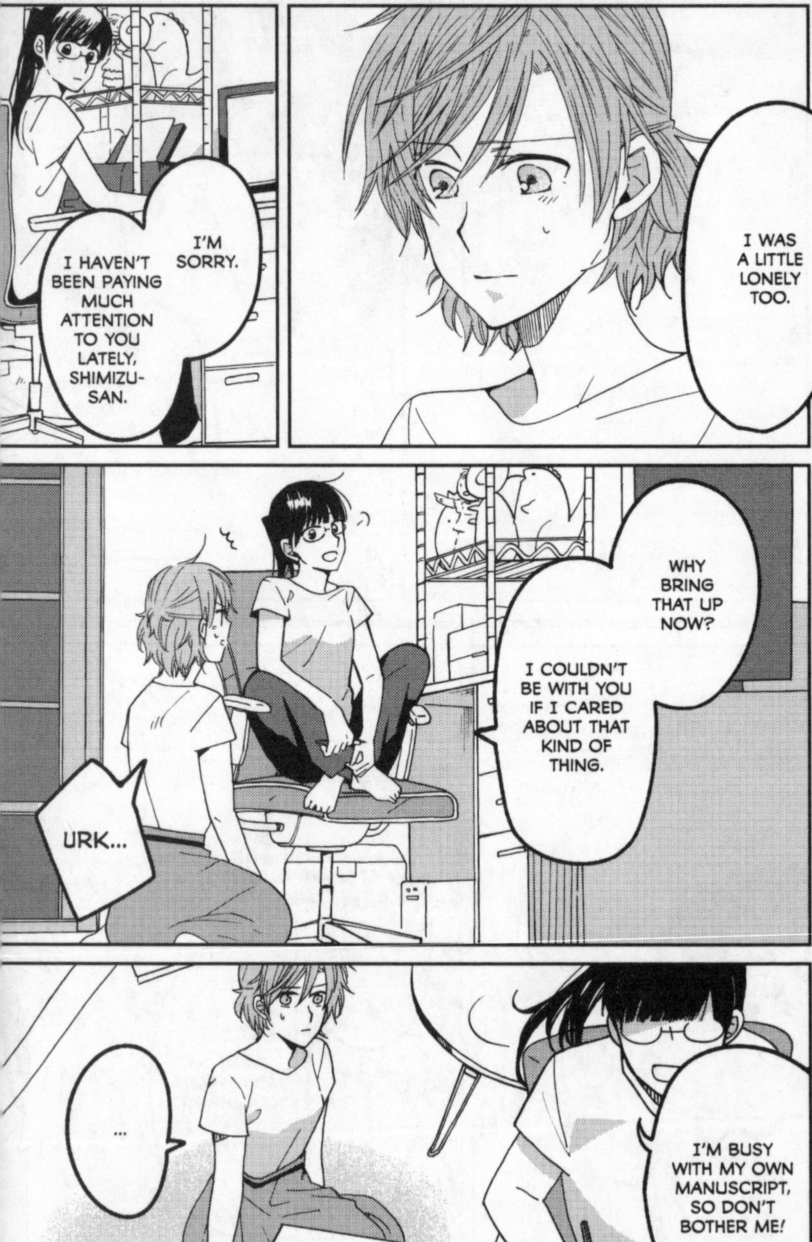
I WAS A LITTLE LONELY TOO.
I'M SORRY.
I HAVEN'T BEEN PAYING MUCH ATTENTION TO YOU LATELY, SHIMIZU-SAN.
WHY BRING THAT UP NOW?
I COULDN'T BE WITH YOU IF I CARED ABOUT THAT KIND OF THING.
URK...
I'M BUSY WITH MY OWN MANUSCRIPT, SO DON'T BOTHER ME!
...

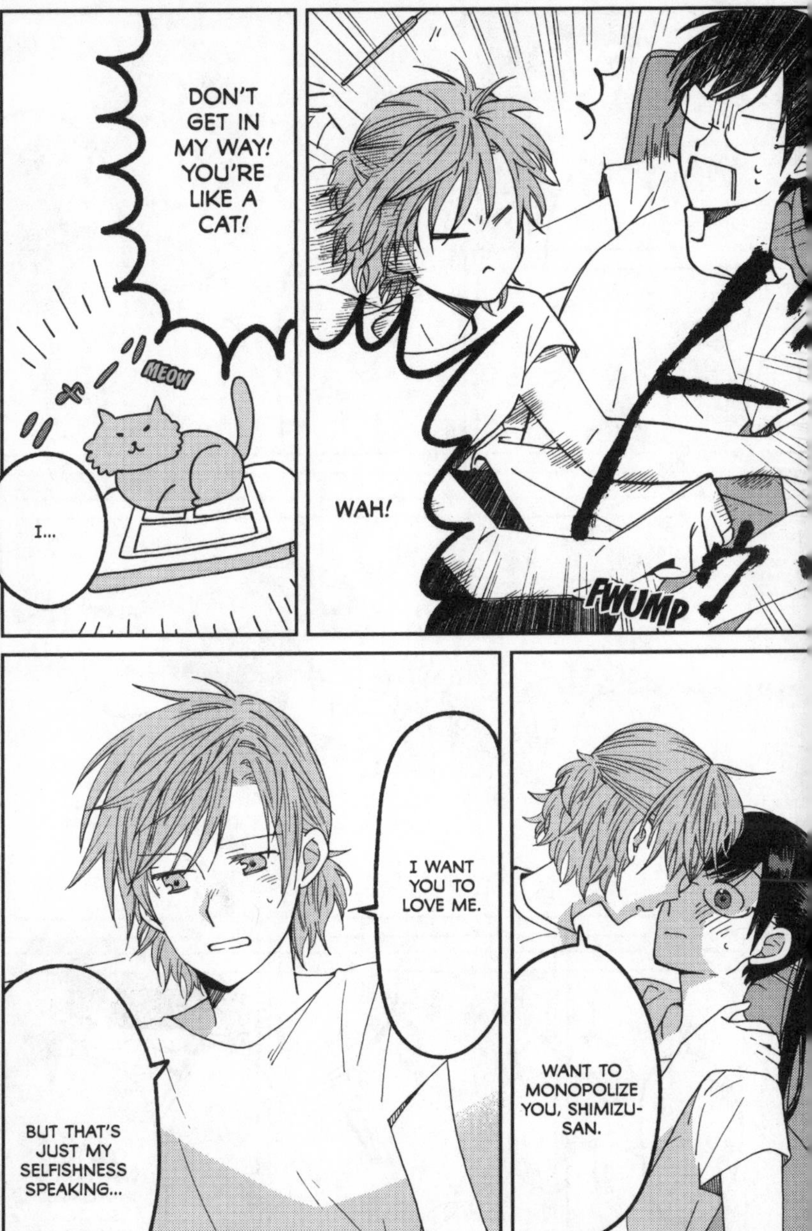
WAH!
FWUMP
DON'T GET IN MY WAY! YOU'RE LIKE A CAT!
MEOW
I...
WANT TO MONOPOLIZE YOU, SHIMIZU-SAN.
I WANT YOU TO LOVE ME.
BUT THAT'S JUST MY SELFISHNESS SPEAKING...

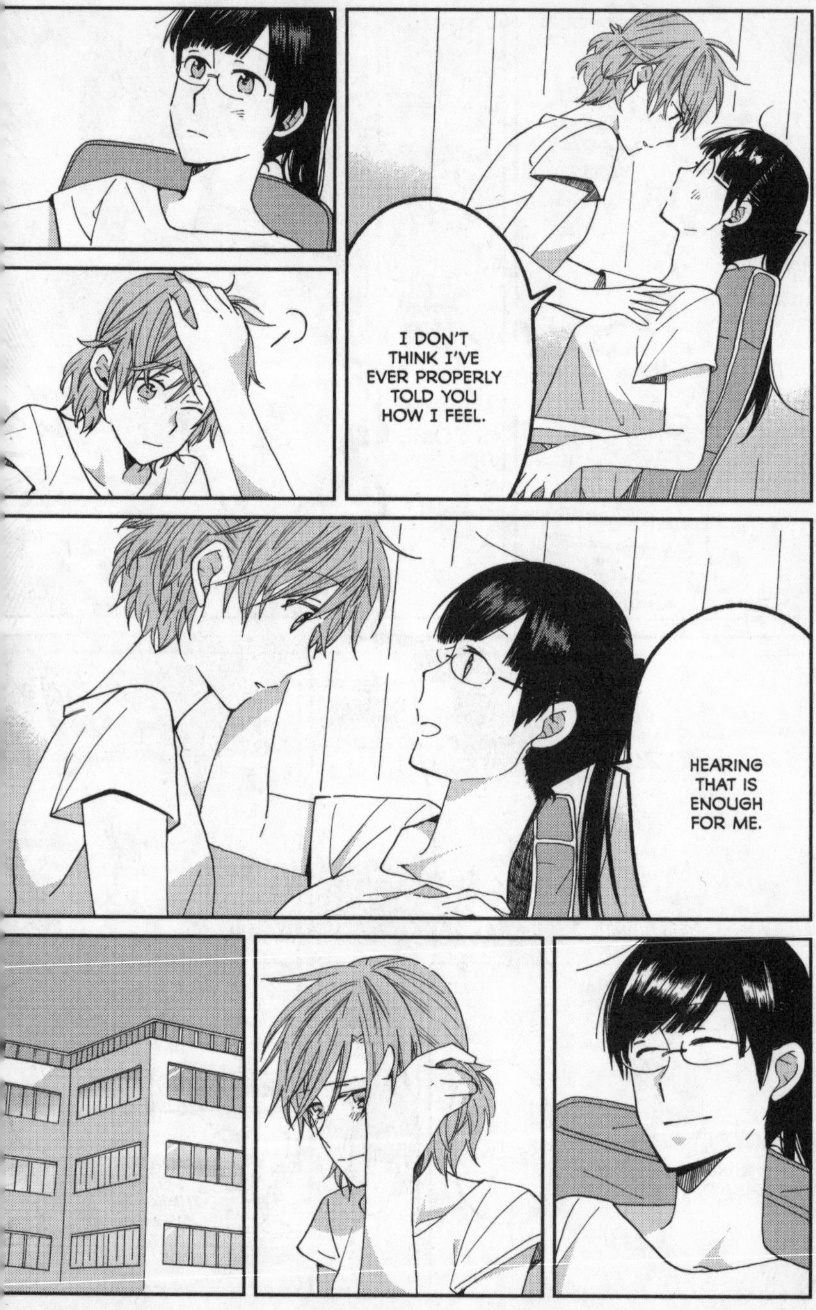
I DON'T THINK I'VE EVER PROPERLY TOLD YOU HOW I FEEL.
HEARING THAT IS ENOUGH FOR ME.

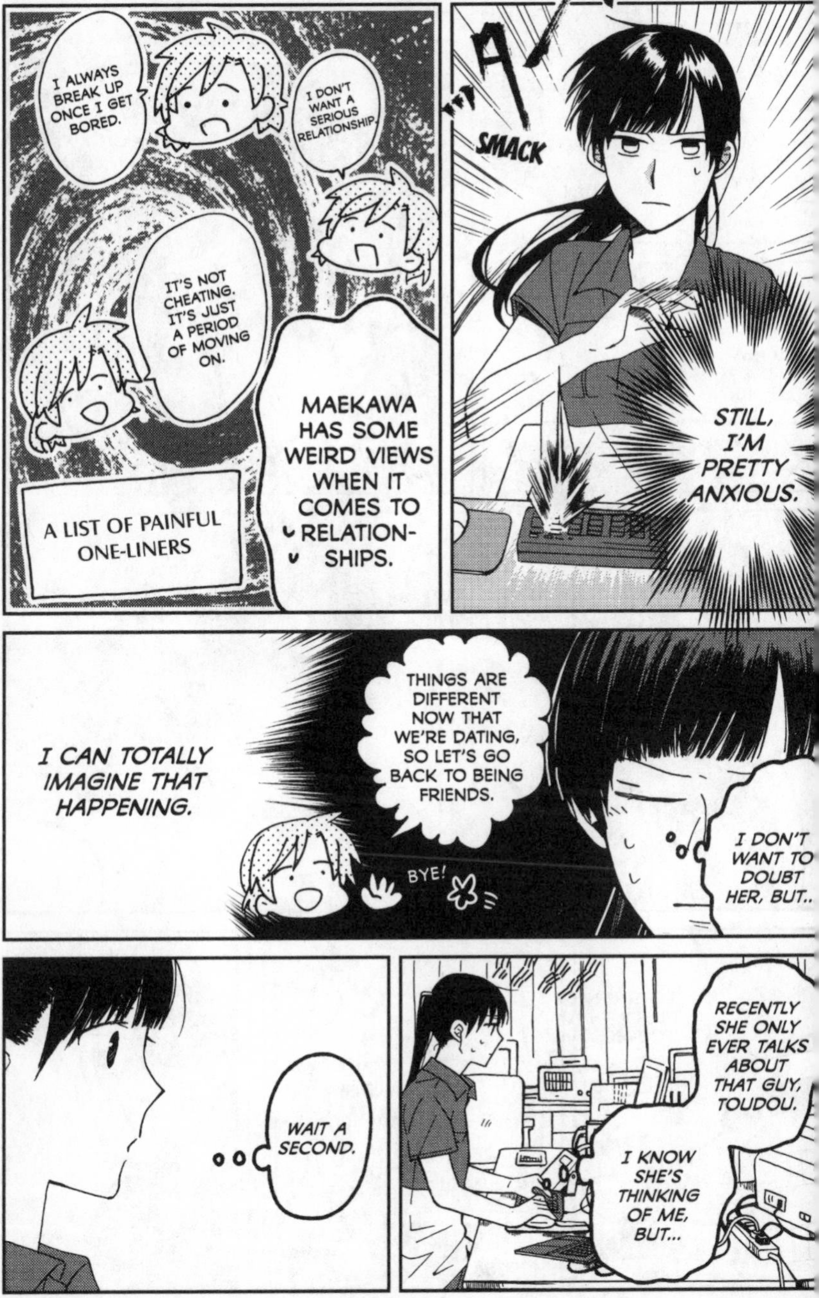
SMACK
STILL, I'M PRETTY ANXIOUS.
I DON'T WANT A SERIOUS RELATIONSHIP.
I ALWAYS BREAK UP ONCE I GET BORED.
IT'S NOT CHEATING. IT'S JUST A PERIOD OF MOVING ON.
MAEKAWA HAS SOME WEIRD VIEWS WHEN IT COMES TO RELATION-SHIPS.
A LIST OF PAINFUL ONE-LINERS
I DON'T WANT TO DOUBT HER, BUT..
THINGS ARE DIFFERENT NOW THAT WE'RE DATING, SO LET'S GO BACK TO BEING FRIENDS.
BYE!
I CAN TOTALLY IMAGINE THAT HAPPENING.
RECENTLY SHE ONLY EVER TALKS ABOUT THAT GUY, TOUDOU.
I KNOW SHE'S THINKING OF ME, BUT...
WAIT A SECOND.

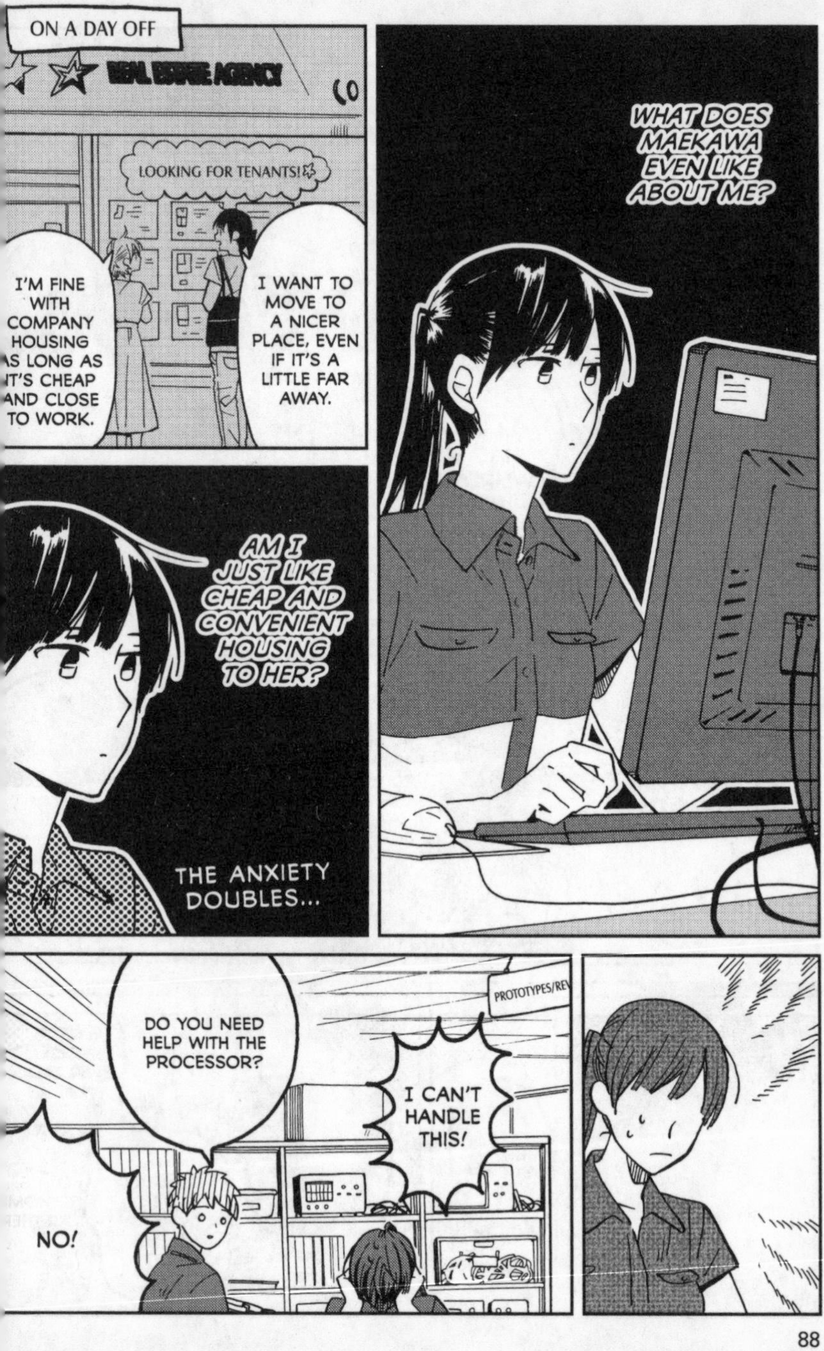
ON A DAY OFF
REAL ESTATE AGENCY
LOOKING FOR TENANTS!
I'M FINE WITH COMPANY HOUSING AS LONG AS IT'S CHEAP AND CLOSE TO WORK.
I WANT TO MOVE TO A NICER PLACE, EVEN IF IT'S A LITTLE FAR AWAY.
WHAT DOES MAEKAWA EVEN LIKE ABOUT ME?
AM I JUST LIKE CHEAP AND CONVENIENT HOUSING TO HER?
THE ANXIETY DOUBLES...
PROTOTYPES/REV
DO YOU NEED HELP WITH THE PROCESSOR?
I CAN'T HANDLE THIS!
NO!

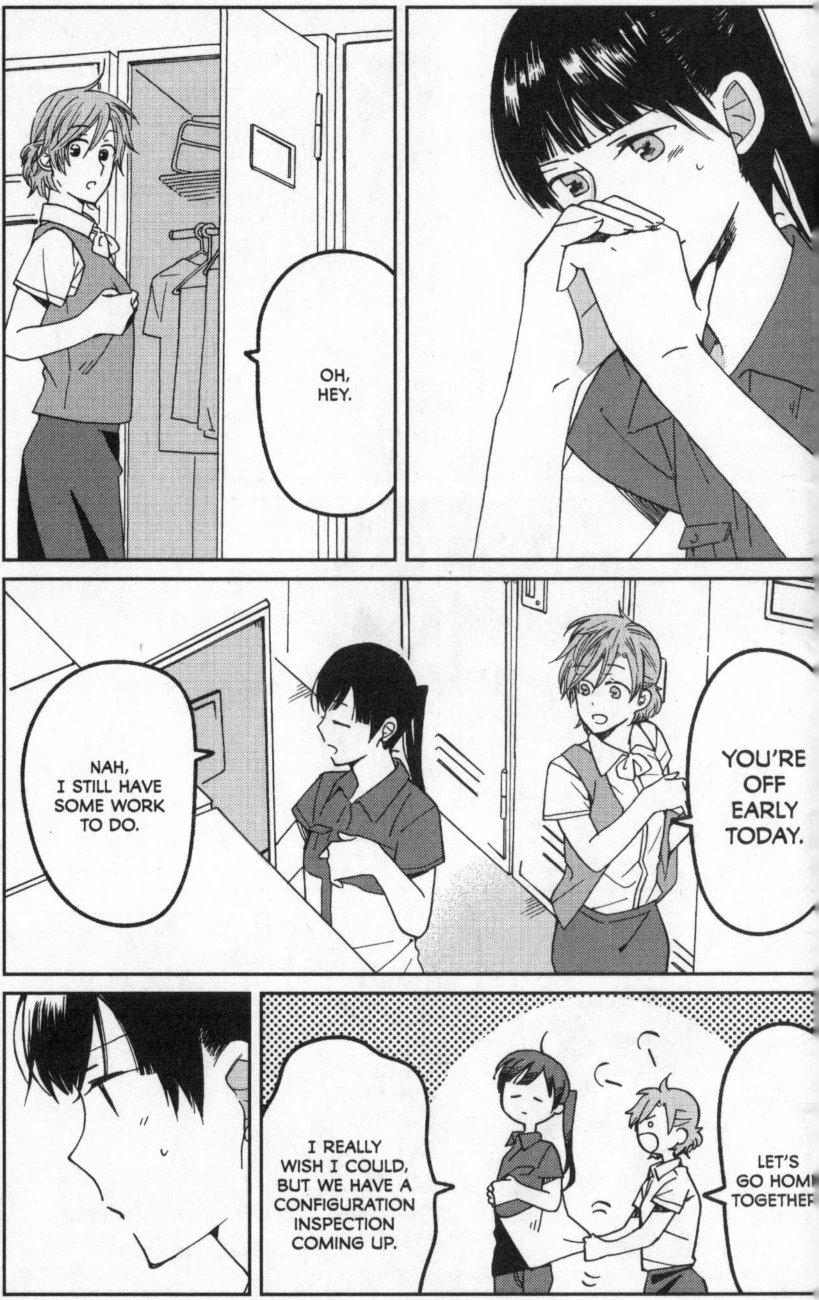
OH, HEY.
YOU'RE OFF EARLY TODAY.
NAH, I STILL HAVE SOME WORK TO DO.
LET'S GO HOM TOGETHE
I REALLY WISH I COULD, BUT WE HAVE A CONFIGURATION INSPECTION COMING UP.

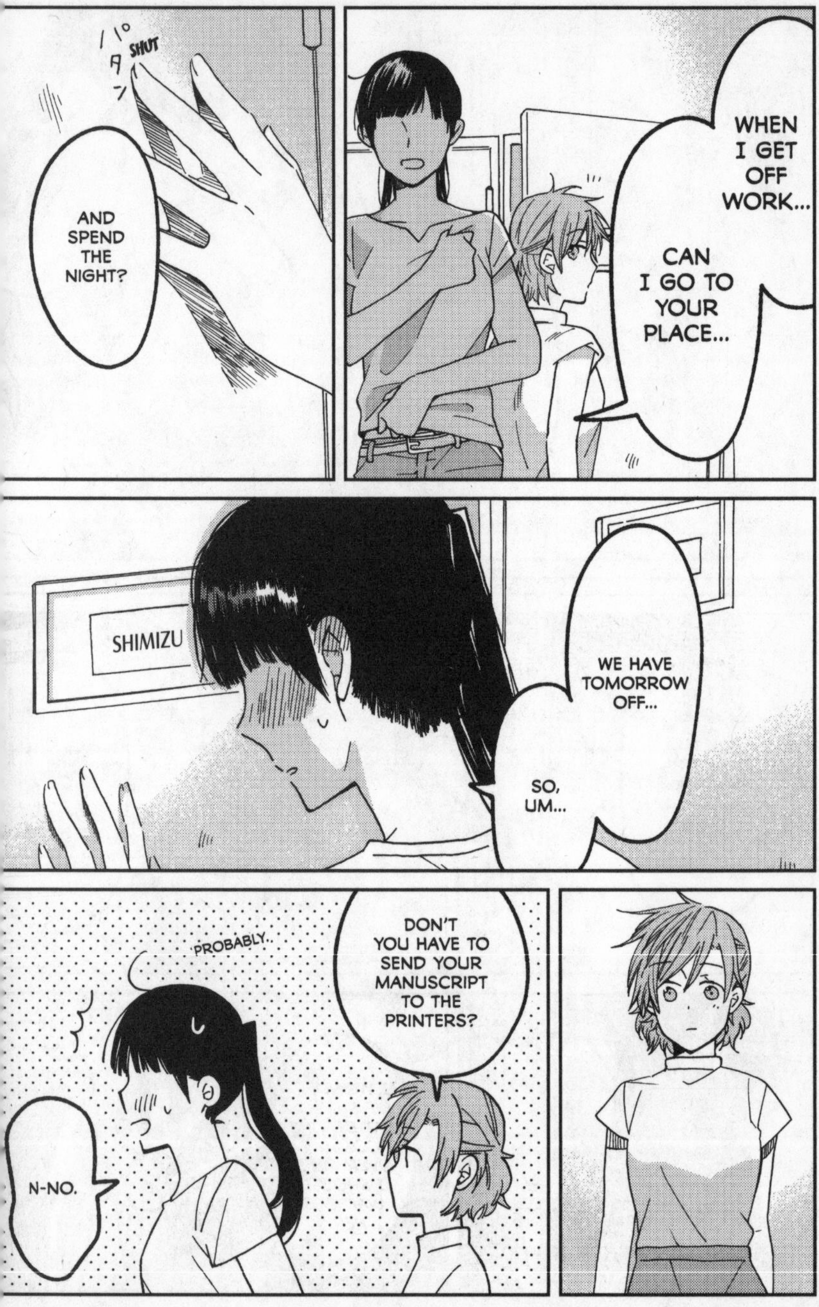
WHEN I GET OFF WORK...
CAN I GO TO YOUR PLACE...
パタン
SHUT
AND SPEND THE NIGHT?
WE HAVE TOMORROW OFF...
SO, UM...
SHIMIZU
DON'T YOU HAVE TO SEND YOUR MANUSCRIPT TO THE PRINTERS?
PROBABLY..
N-NO.

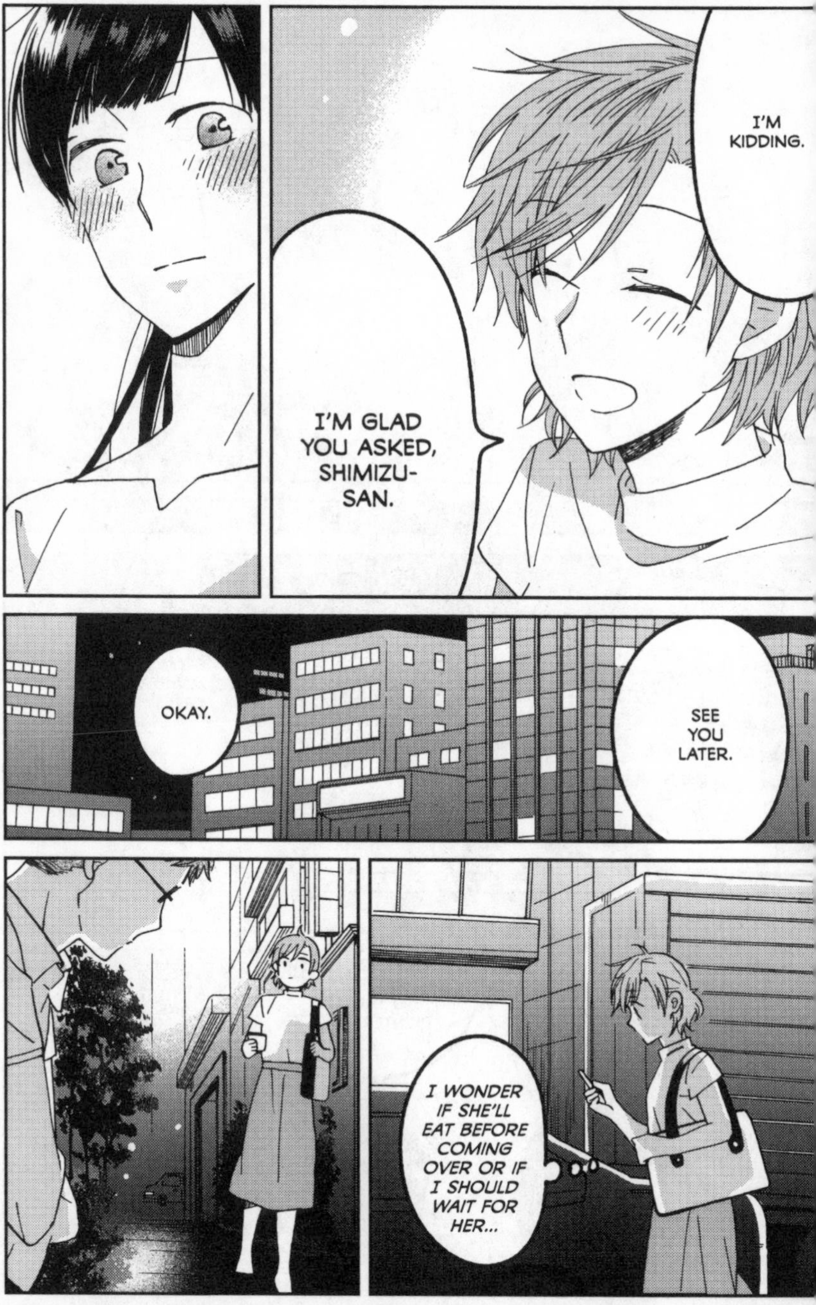
I'M KIDDING.
I'M GLAD YOU ASKED, SHIMIZU-SAN.
SEE YOU LATER.
OKAY.
I WONDER IF SHE'LL EAT BEFORE COMING OVER OR IF I SHOULD WAIT FOR HER...

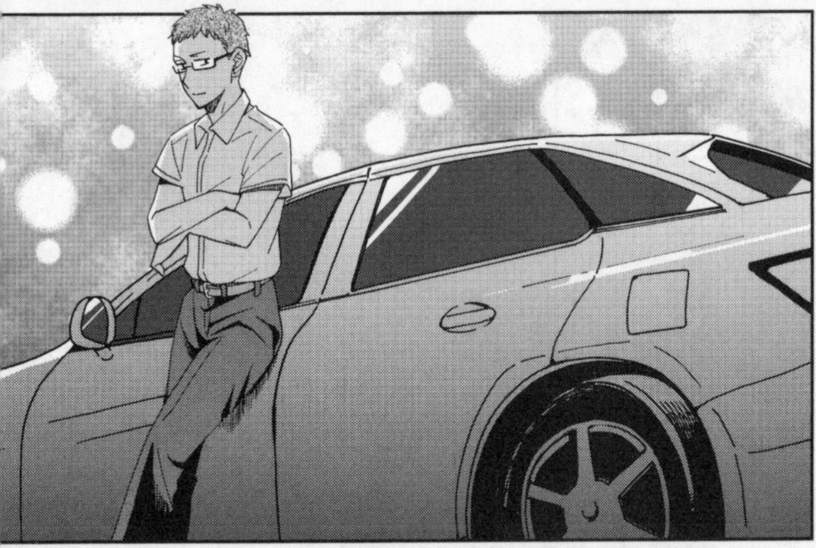

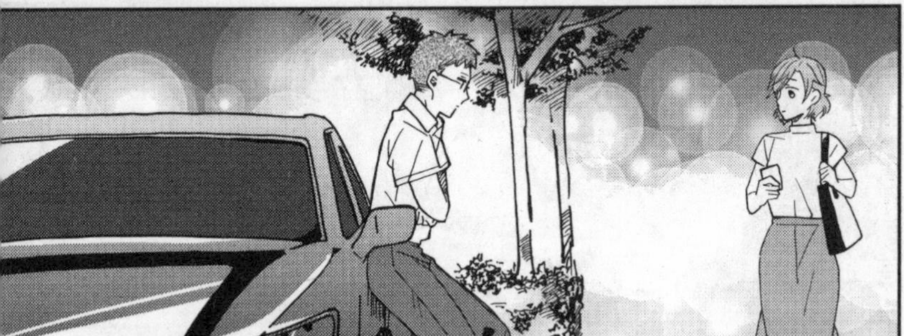

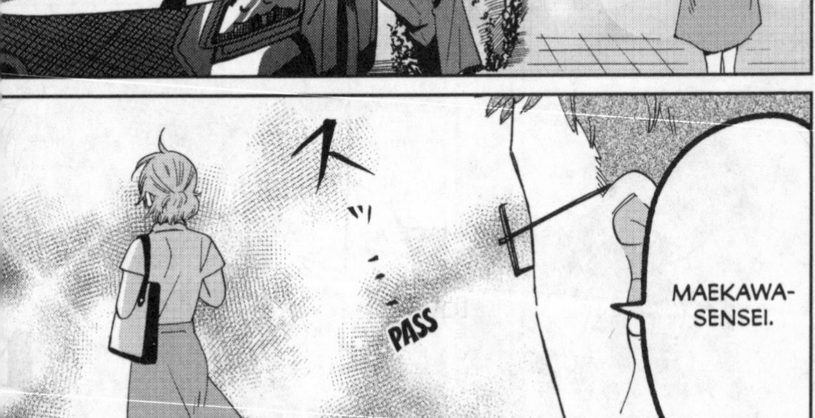
MAEKAWA-SENSEI.
PASS

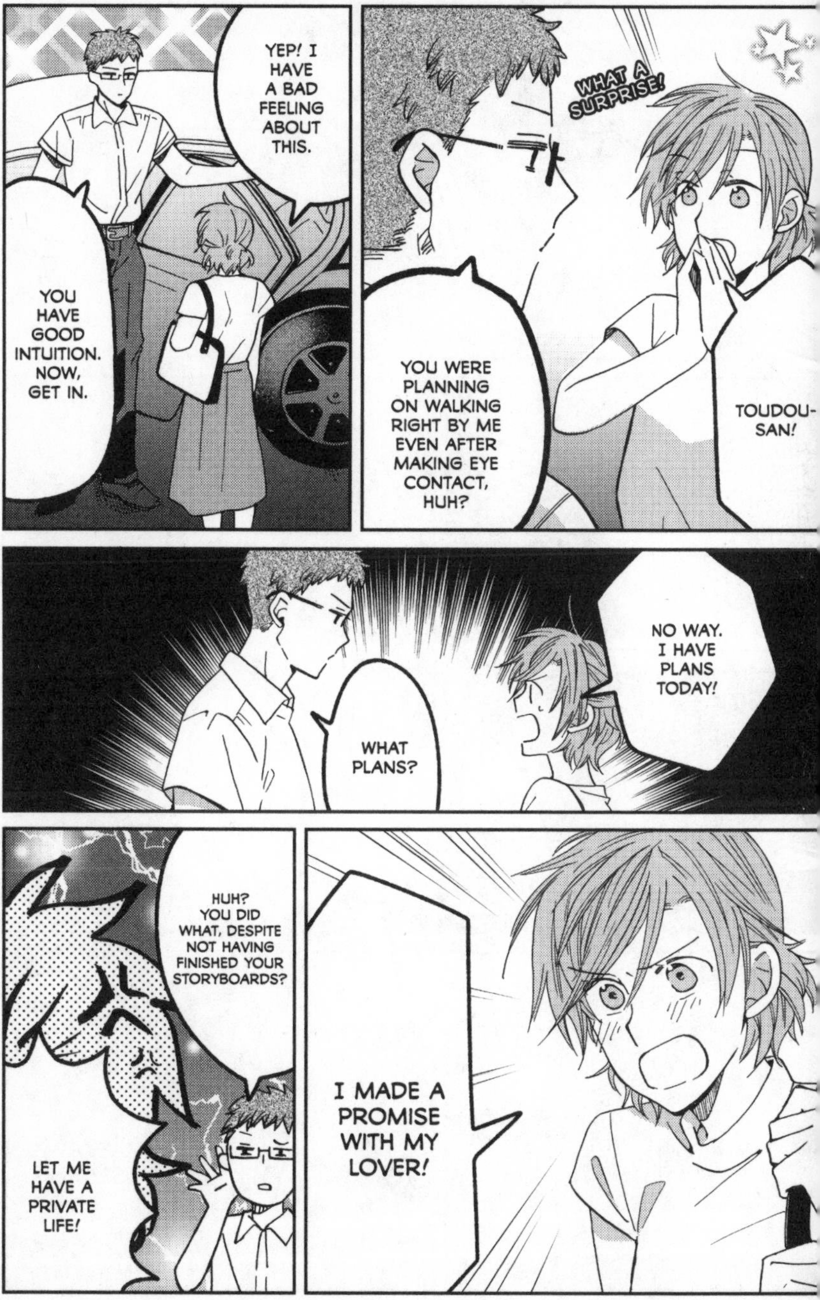
WHAT A SURPRISE!
TOUDOU-SAN!
YOU WERE PLANNING ON WALKING RIGHT BY ME EVEN AFTER MAKING EYE CONTACT, HUH?
YEP! I HAVE A BAD FEELING ABOUT THIS.
YOU HAVE GOOD INTUITION. NOW, GET IN.
NO WAY. I HAVE PLANS TODAY!
WHAT PLANS?
I MADE A PROMISE WITH MY LOVER!
HUH? YOU DID WHAT, DESPITE NOT HAVING FINISHED YOUR STORYBOARDS?
LET ME HAVE A PRIVATE LIFE!

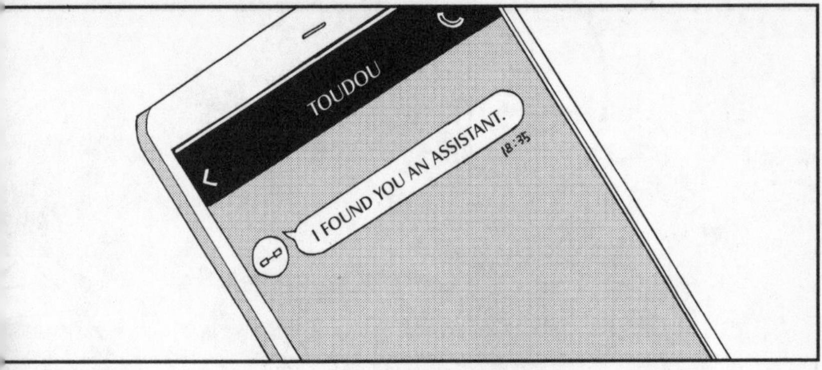
TOUDOU
I FOUND YOU AN ASSISTANT.
18:35

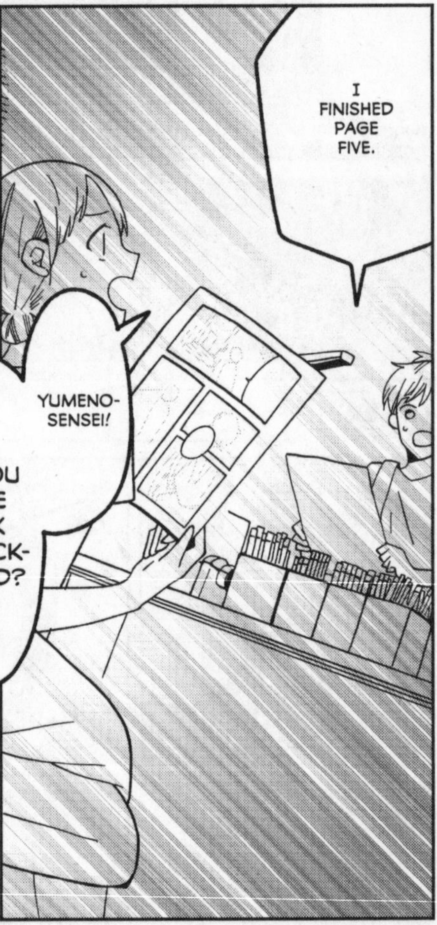
I FINISHED PAGE FIVE.
YUMENO-SENSEI! CAN YOU PLEASE CHECK THIS BACK-GROUND?

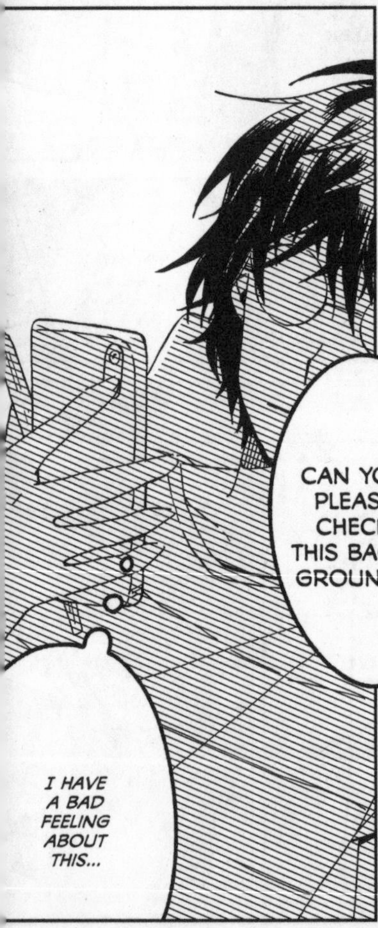
I HAVE A BAD FEELING ABOUT THIS...

Chapter 19

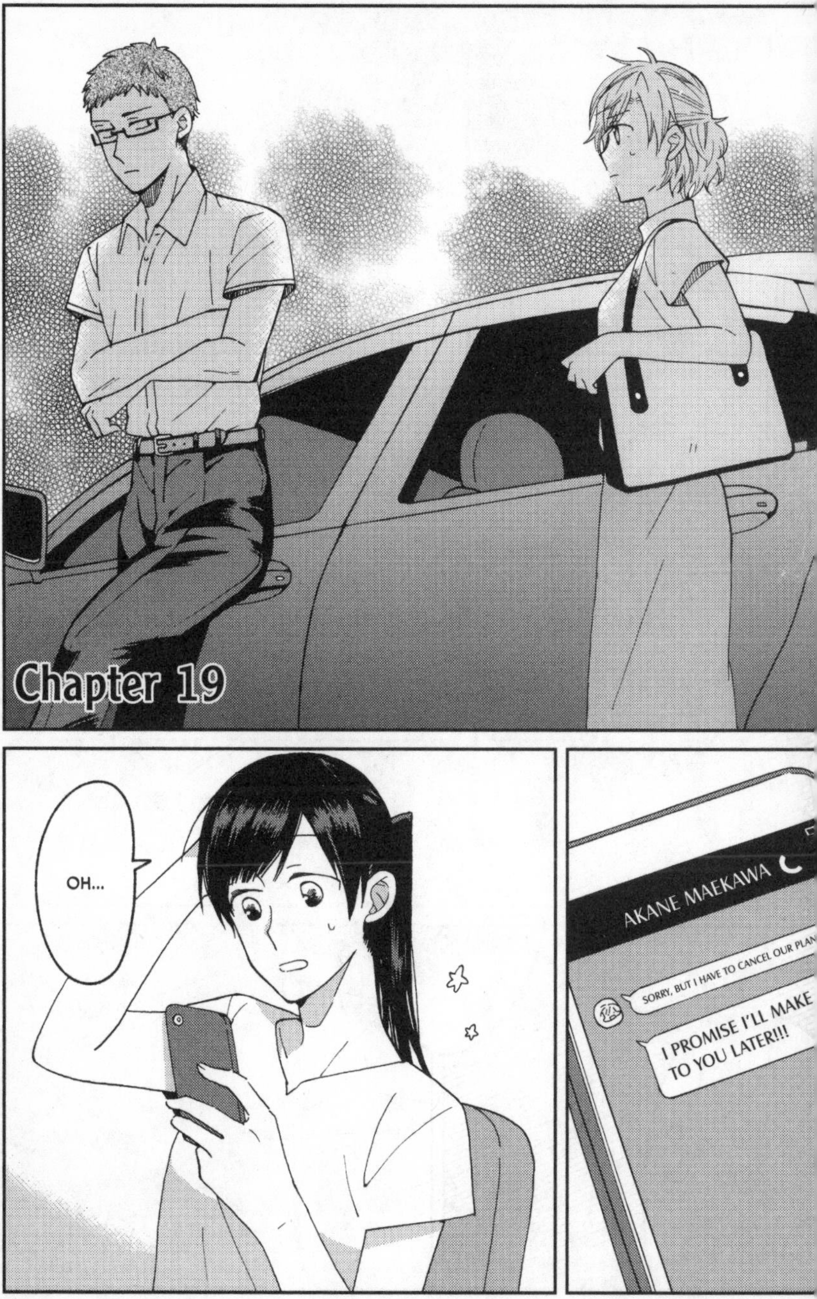
AKANE MAEKAWA
SORRY, BUT I HAVE TO CANCEL OUR PLAN
I PROMISE I'LL MAKE TO YOU LATER!!!
OH...

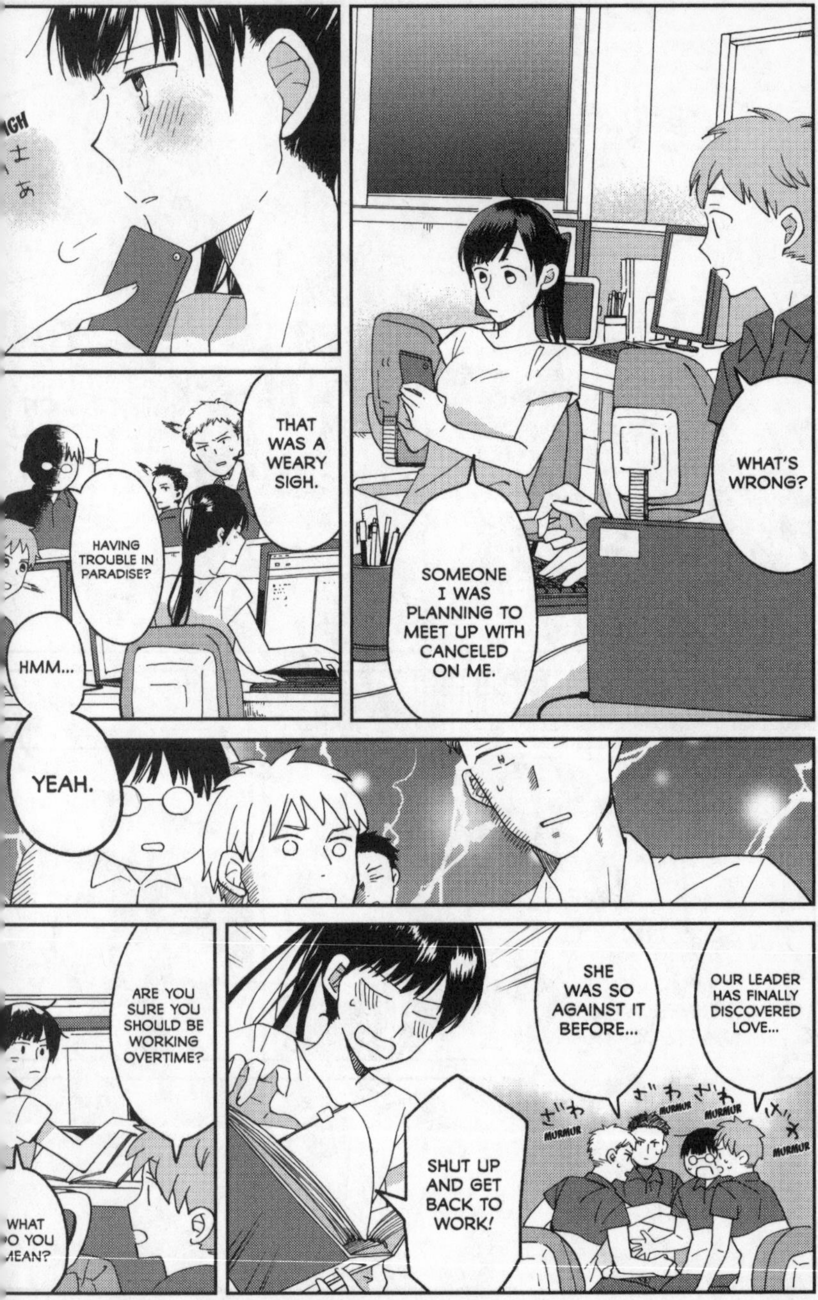
WHAT'S WRONG?
SOMEONE I WAS PLANNING TO MEET UP WITH CANCELED ON ME.
はあ
THAT WAS A WEARY SIGH.
HAVING TROUBLE IN PARADISE?
HMM...
YEAH.
OUR LEADER HAS FINALLY DISCOVERED LOVE...
SHE WAS SO AGAINST IT BEFORE...
ざわざわ MURMUR MURMUR
ざわ MURMUR
MURMUR
SHUT UP AND GET BACK TO WORK!
ARE YOU SURE YOU SHOULD BE WORKING OVERTIME?
WHAT O YOU MEAN?

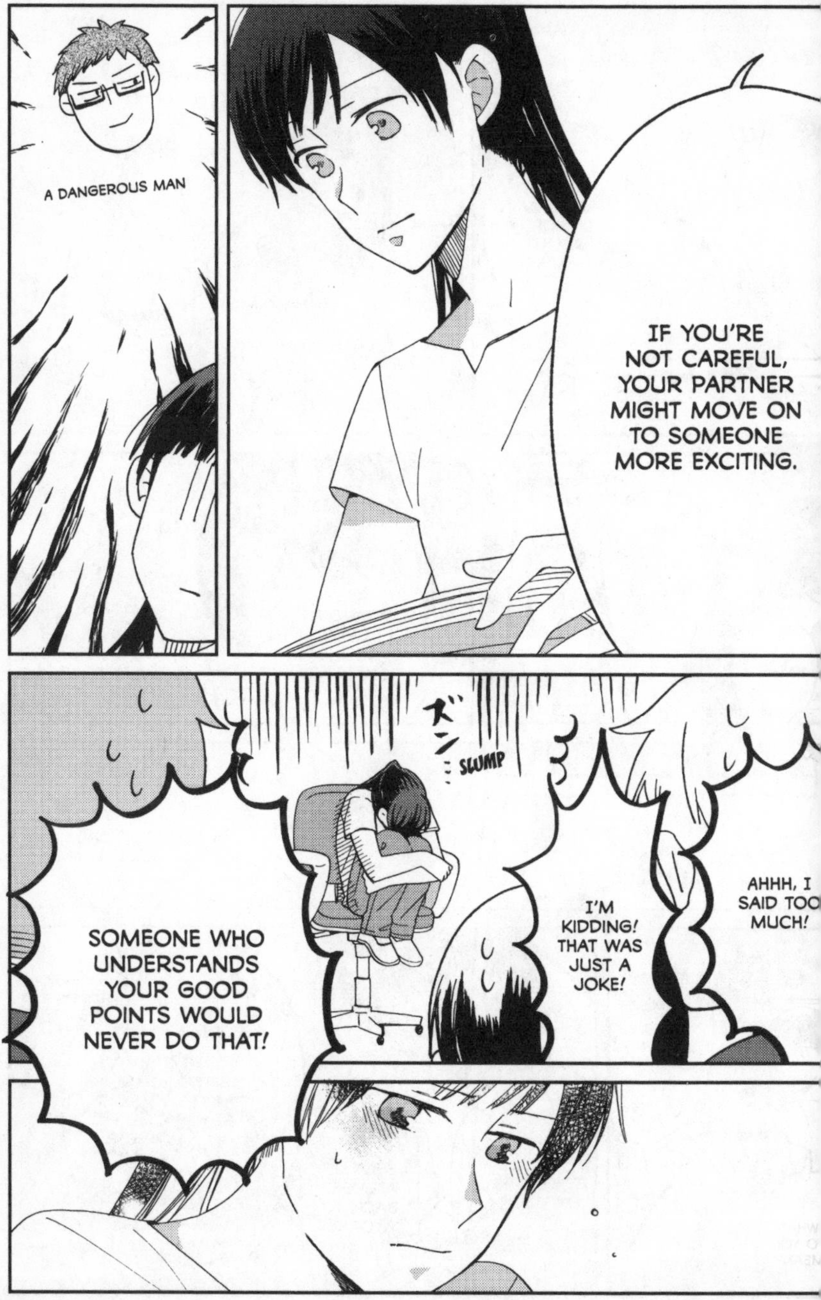
IF YOU'RE NOT CAREFUL, YOUR PARTNER MIGHT MOVE ON TO SOMEONE MORE EXCITING.
A DANGEROUS MAN
AHHH, I SAID TOO MUCH!
I'M KIDDING! THAT WAS JUST A JOKE!
ズン
SLUMP
SOMEONE WHO UNDERSTANDS YOUR GOOD POINTS WOULD NEVER DO THAT!

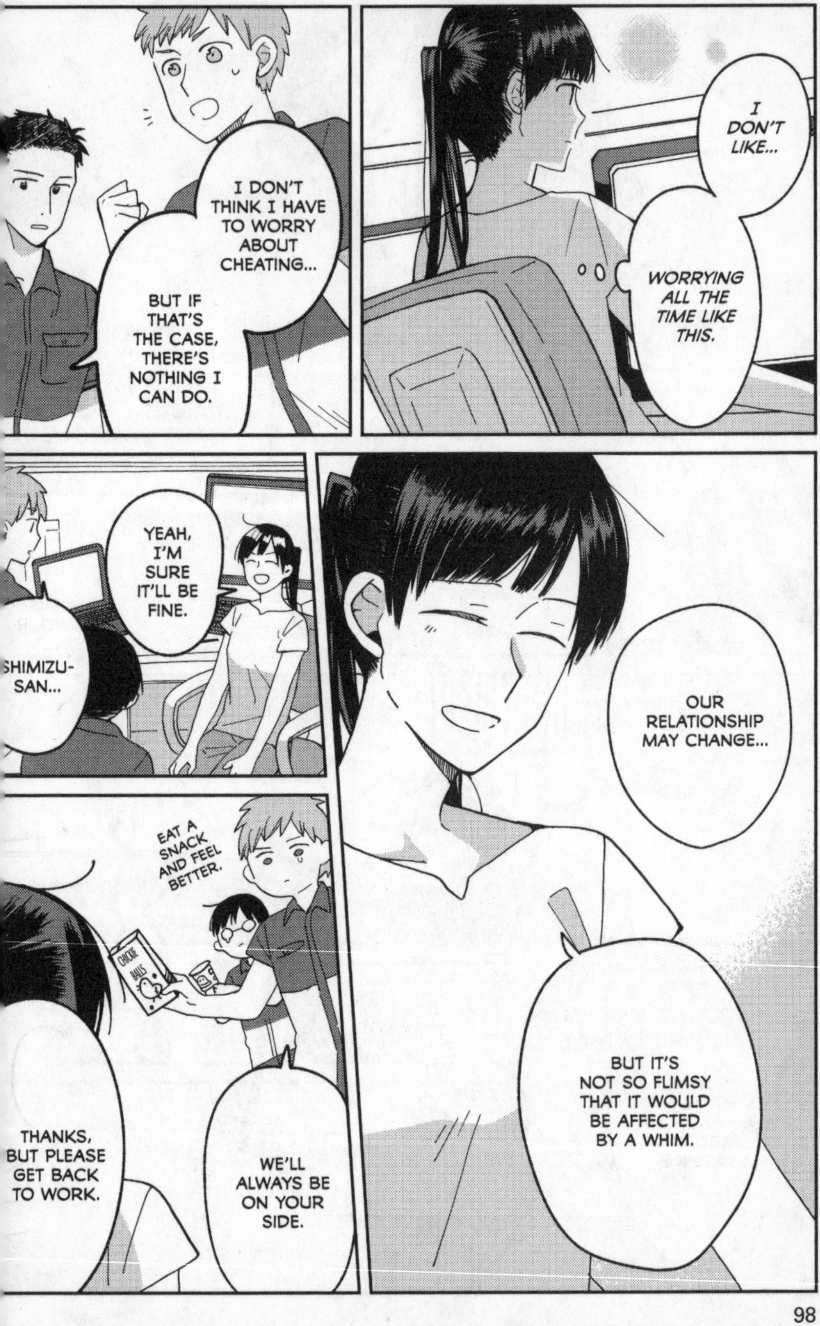
I DON'T LIKE...
WORRYING ALL THE TIME LIKE THIS.
I DON'T THINK I HAVE TO WORRY ABOUT CHEATING...
BUT IF THAT'S THE CASE, THERE'S NOTHING I CAN DO.
OUR RELATIONSHIP MAY CHANGE...
BUT IT'S NOT SO FLIMSY THAT IT WOULD BE AFFECTED BY A WHIM.
YEAH, I'M SURE IT'LL BE FINE.
SHIMIZU-SAN...
EAT A SNACK AND FEEL BETTER.
CHICKIE BALLS
WE'LL ALWAYS BE ON YOUR SIDE.
THANKS, BUT PLEASE GET BACK TO WORK.

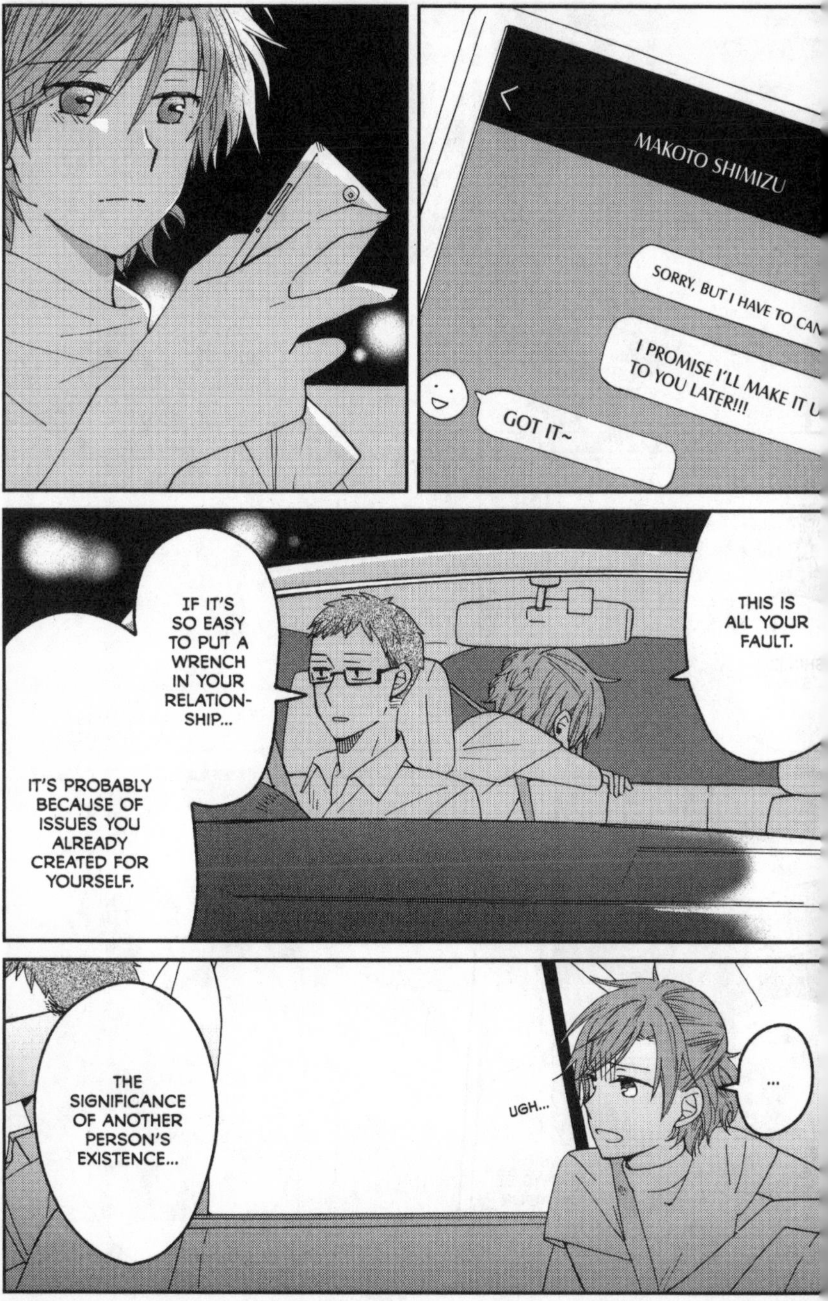
MAKOTO SHIMIZU
SORRY, BUT I HAVE TO CAN
I PROMISE I'LL MAKE IT U
TO YOU LATER!!!
GOT IT~
THIS IS ALL YOUR FAULT.
IF IT'S SO EASY TO PUT A WRENCH IN YOUR RELATIONSHIP...
IT'S PROBABLY BECAUSE OF ISSUES YOU ALREADY CREATED FOR YOURSELF.
...
UGH...
THE SIGNIFICANCE OF ANOTHER PERSON'S EXISTENCE...

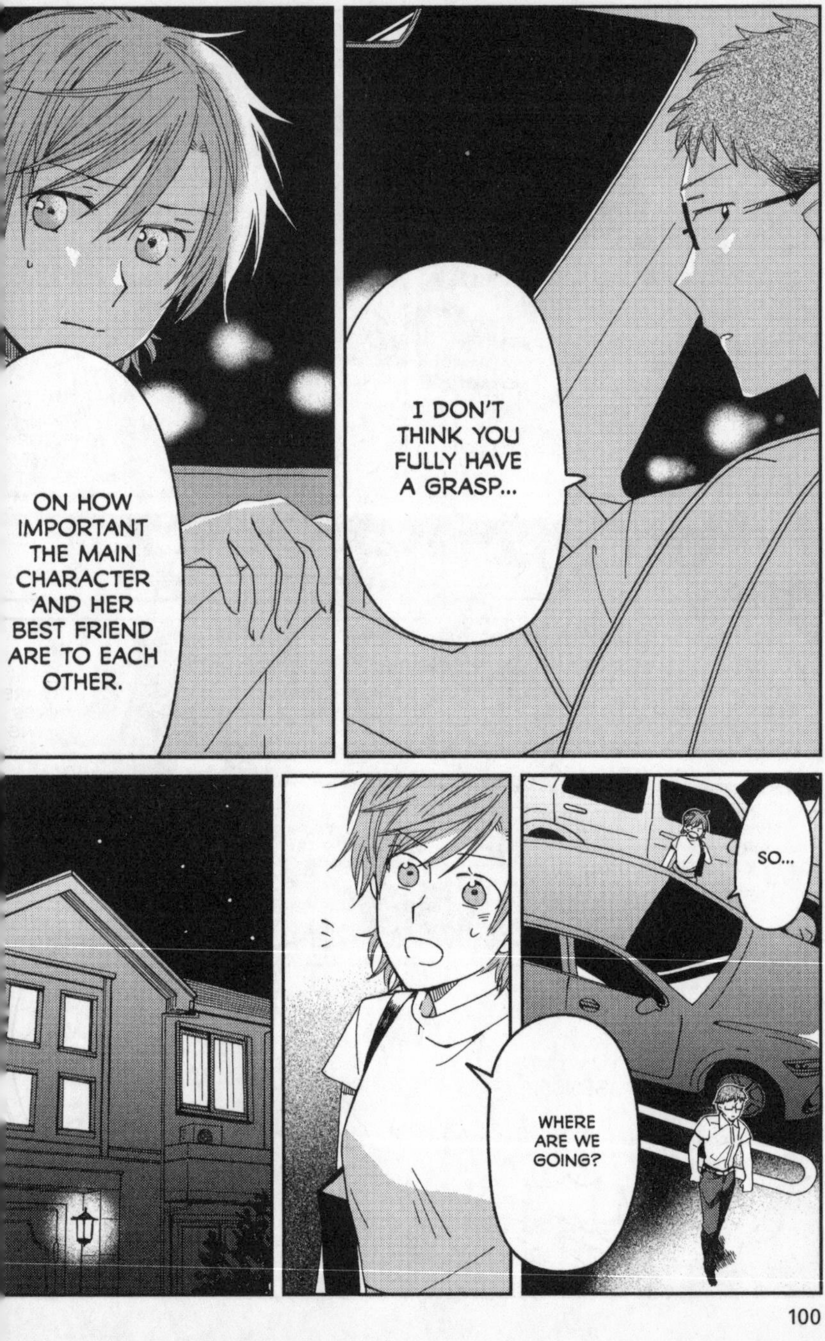
I DON'T THINK YOU FULLY HAVE A GRASP...
ON HOW IMPORTANT THE MAIN CHARACTER AND HER BEST FRIEND ARE TO EACH OTHER.
SO...
WHERE ARE WE GOING?

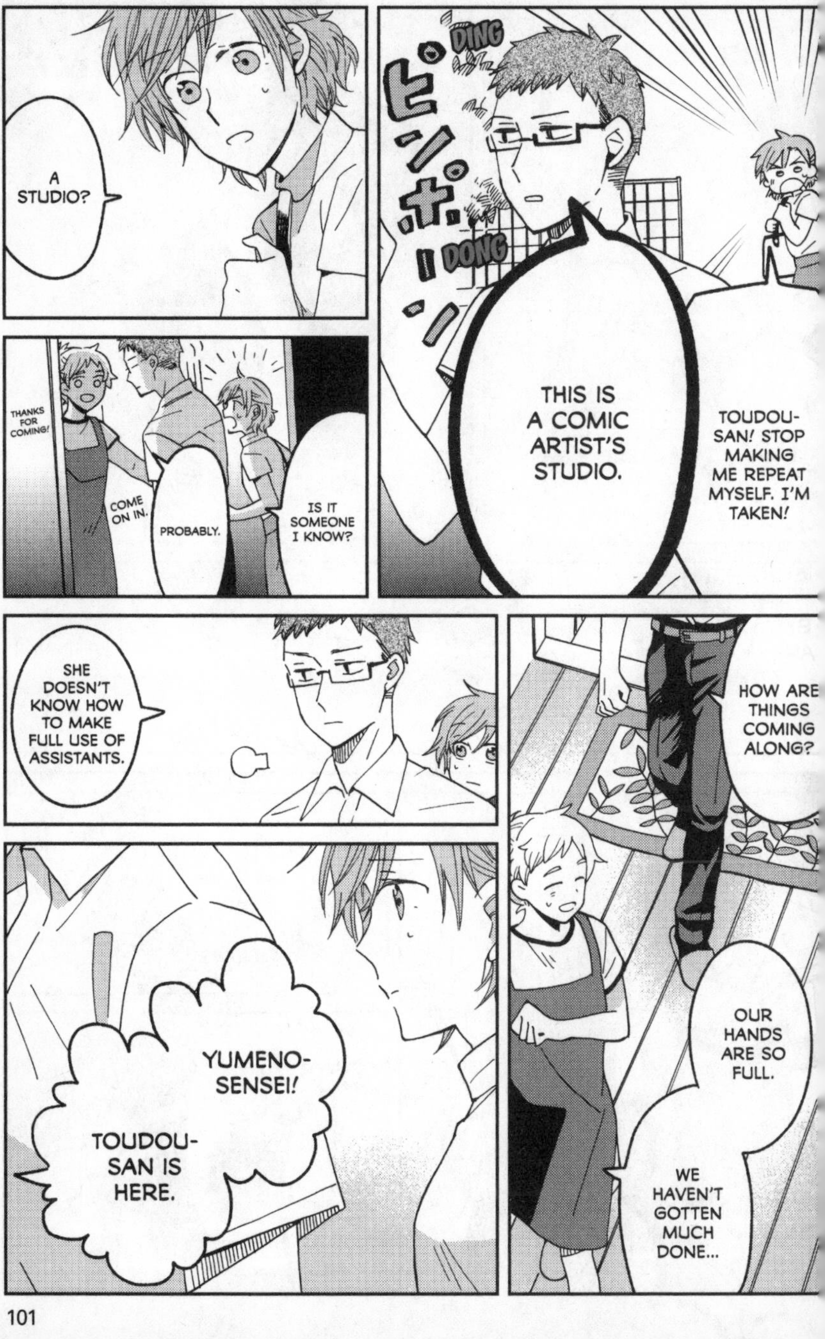
DING
DONG
TOUDOU-SAN! STOP MAKING ME REPEAT MYSELF. I'M TAKEN!
THIS IS A COMIC ARTIST'S STUDIO.
A STUDIO?
IS IT SOMEONE I KNOW?
PROBABLY.
COME ON IN.
THANKS FOR COMING!
HOW ARE THINGS COMING ALONG?
SHE DOESN'T KNOW HOW TO MAKE FULL USE OF ASSISTANTS.
OUR HANDS ARE SO FULL.
WE HAVEN'T GOTTEN MUCH DONE...
YUMENO-SENSEI!
TOUDOU-SAN IS HERE.

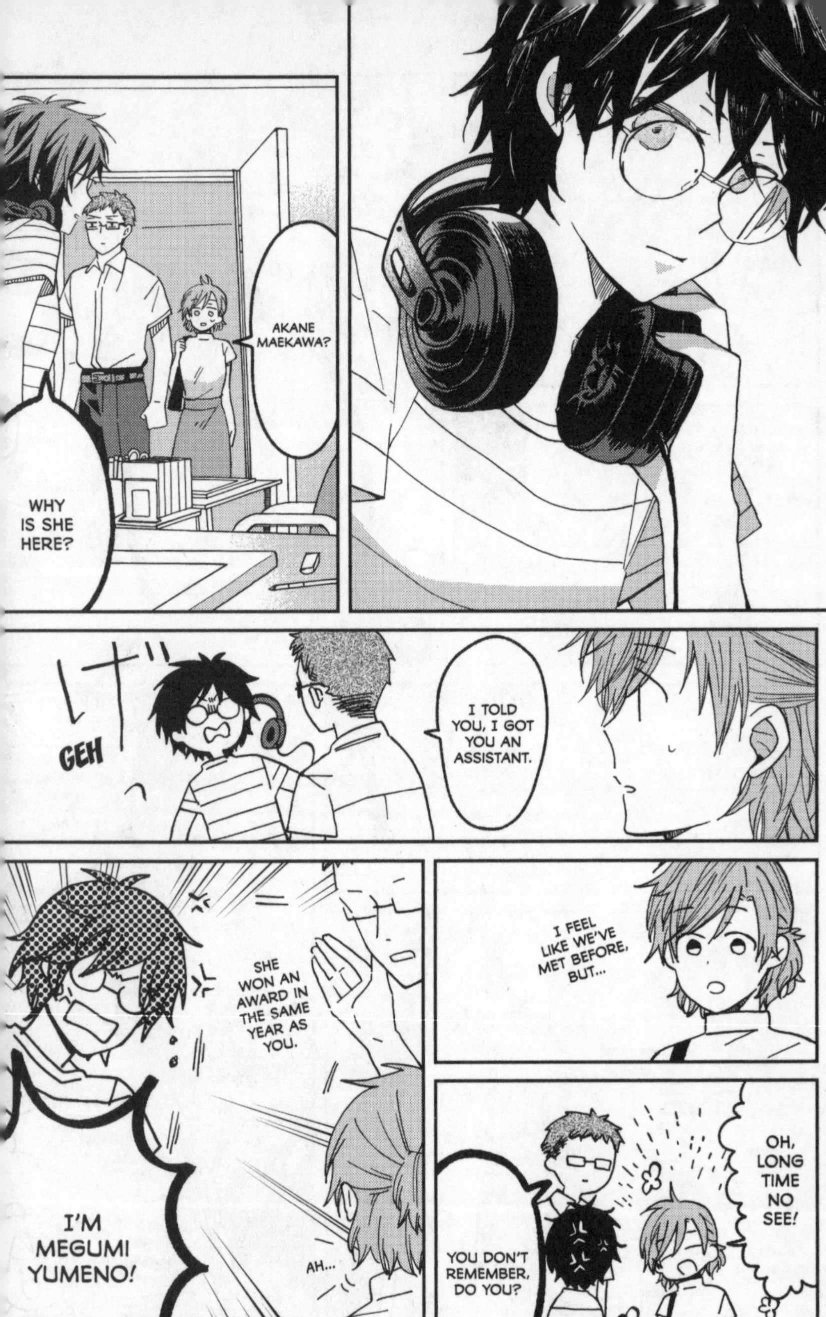
AKANE MAEKAWA?
WHY IS SHE HERE?
I TOLD YOU, I GOT YOU AN ASSISTANT.
GEH
I FEEL LIKE WE'VE MET BEFORE, BUT...
OH, LONG TIME NO SEE!
YOU DON'T REMEMBER, DO YOU?
SHE WON AN AWARD IN THE SAME YEAR AS YOU.
AH...
I'M MEGUMI YUMENO!

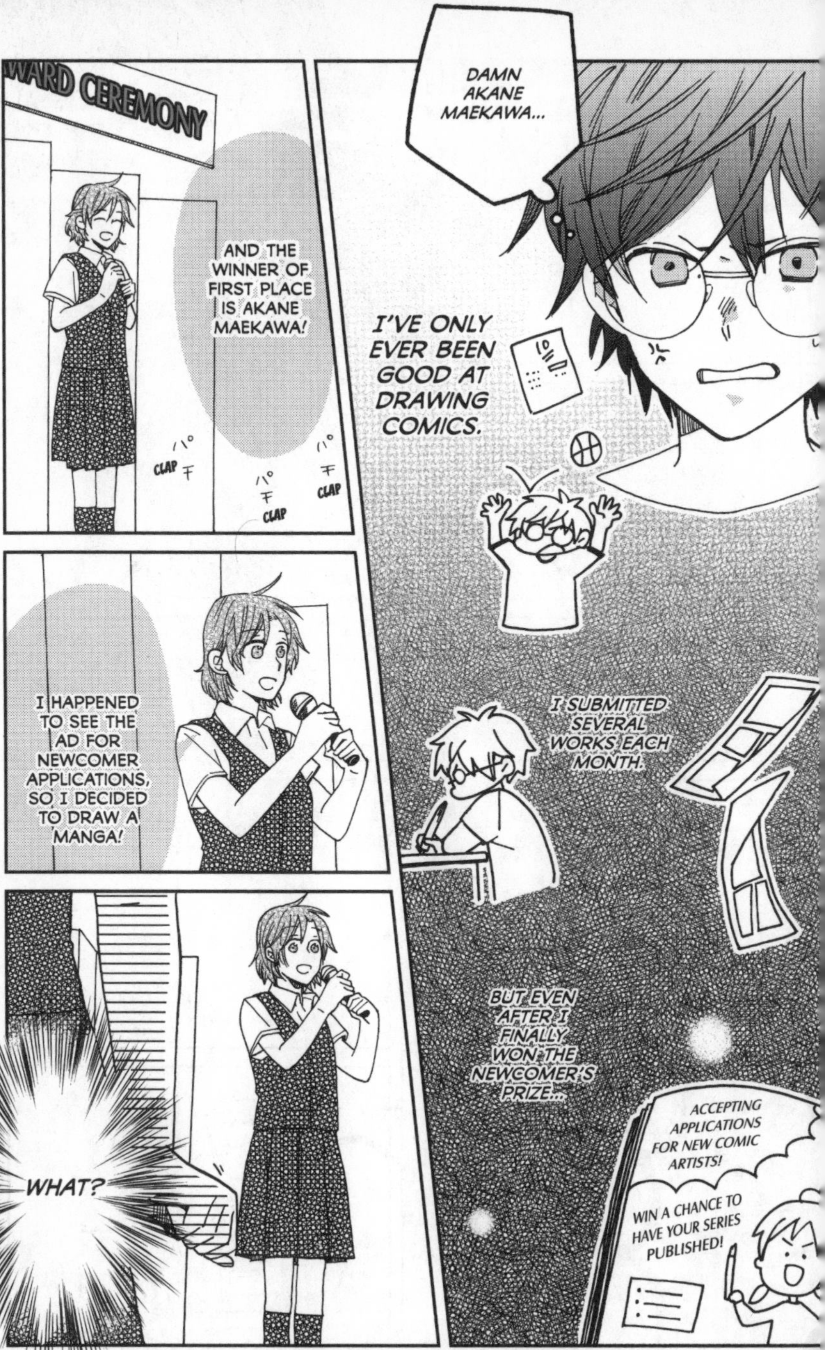
DAMN AKANE MAEKAWA...
I'VE ONLY EVER BEEN GOOD AT DRAWING COMICS.
I SUBMITTED SEVERAL WORKS EACH MONTH.
BUT EVEN AFTER I FINALLY WON THE NEWCOMER'S PRIZE...
ACCEPTING APPLICATIONS FOR NEW COMIC ARTISTS!
WIN A CHANCE TO HAVE YOUR SERIES PUBLISHED!
WARD CEREMONY
AND THE WINNER OF FIRST PLACE IS AKANE MAEKAWA!
パチ
CLAP
パチ
CLAP
パチ
CLAP
I HAPPENED TO SEE THE AD FOR NEWCOMER APPLICATIONS, SO I DECIDED TO DRAW A MANGA!
WHAT?

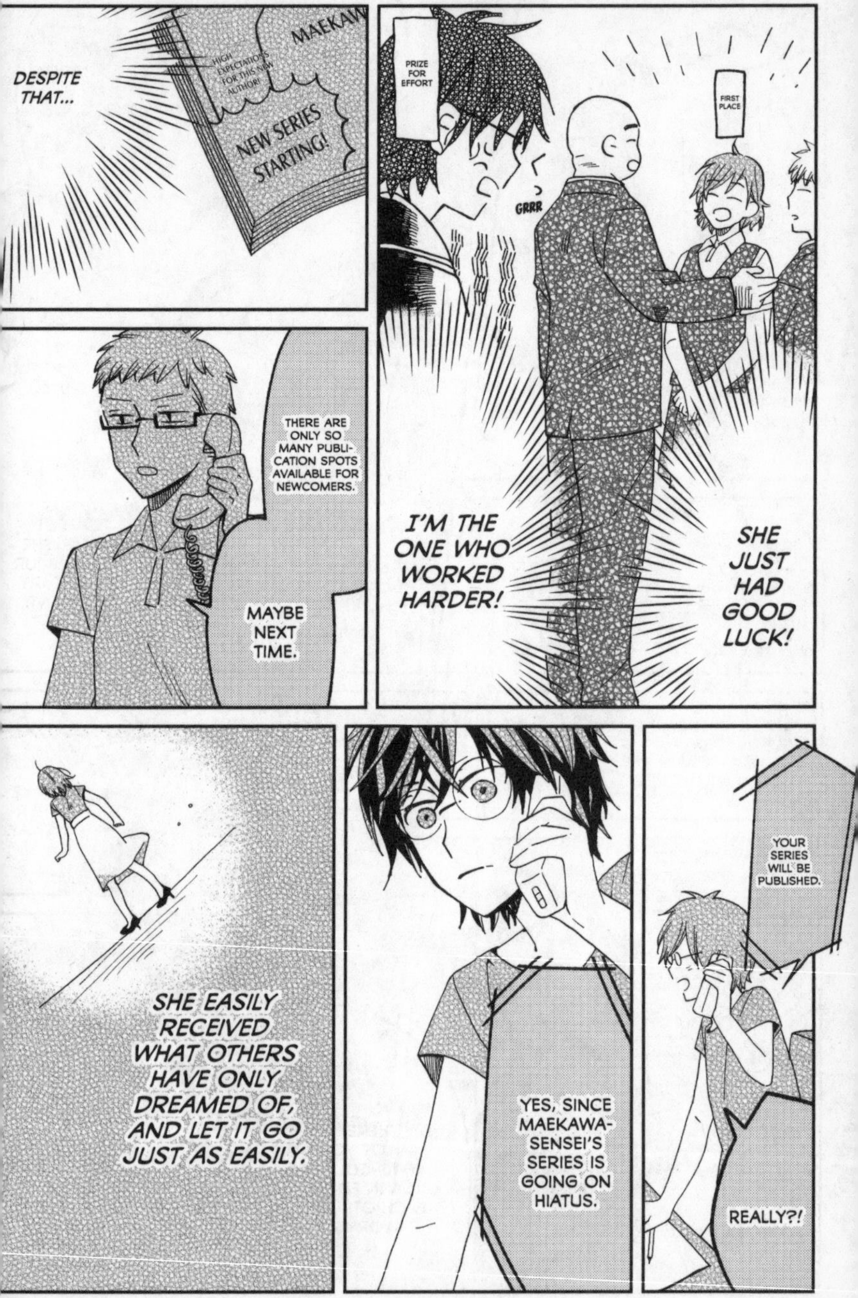
FIRST PLACE
PRIZE FOR EFFORT
GRRR
SHE JUST HAD GOOD LUCK!
I'M THE ONE WHO WORKED HARDER!
MAEKAWA
HIGH EXPECTATIONS FOR THIS NEW AUTHOR!
NEW SERIES STARTING!
DESPITE THAT...
THERE ARE ONLY SO MANY PUBLI-CATION SPOTS AVAILABLE FOR NEWCOMERS.
MAYBE NEXT TIME.
YOUR SERIES WILL BE PUBLISHED.
REALLY?!
YES, SINCE MAEKAWA-SENSEI'S SERIES IS GOING ON HIATUS.
SHE EASILY RECEIVED WHAT OTHERS HAVE ONLY DREAMED OF, AND LET IT GO JUST AS EASILY.

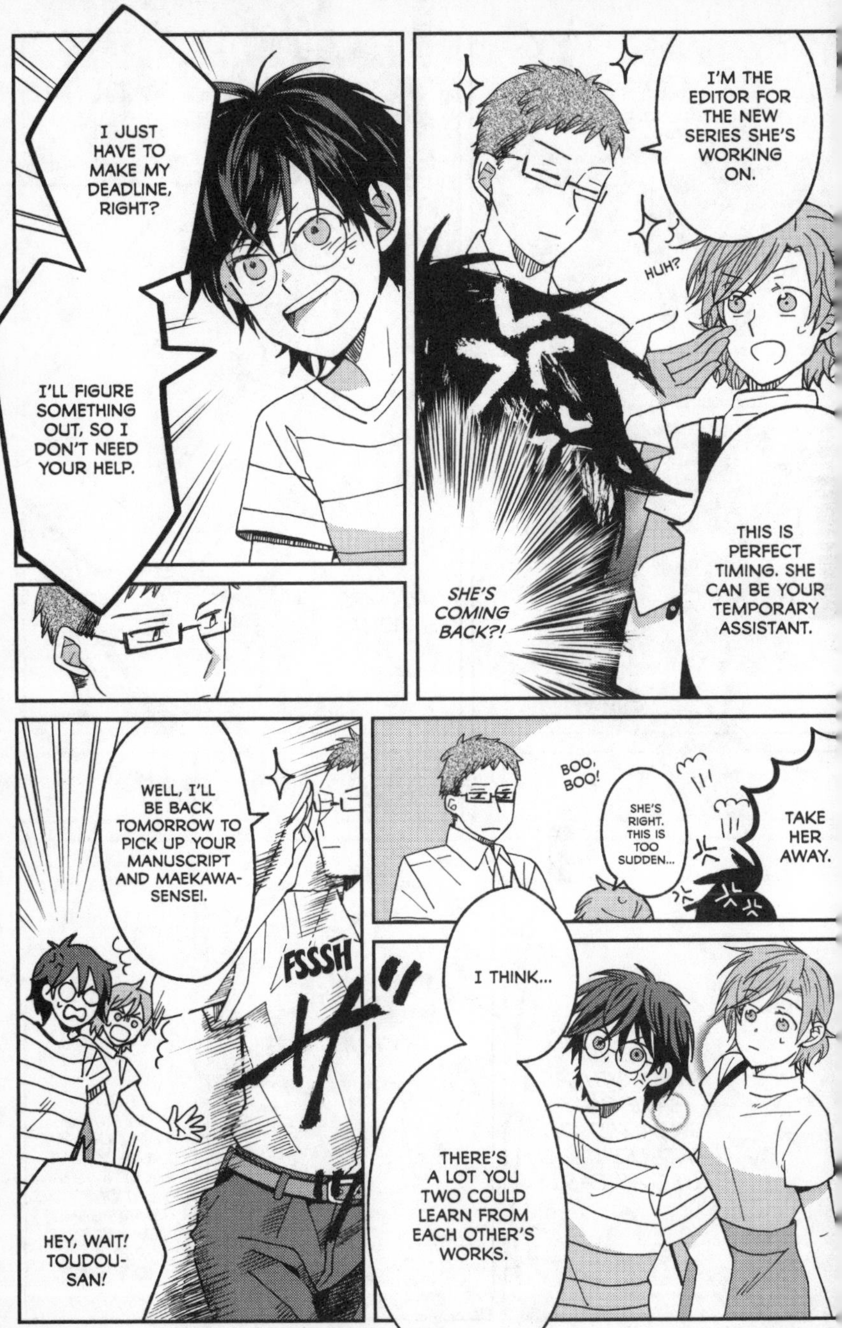
I'M THE EDITOR FOR THE NEW SERIES SHE'S WORKING ON.
HUH?
THIS IS PERFECT TIMING. SHE CAN BE YOUR TEMPORARY ASSISTANT.
SHE'S COMING BACK?!
I JUST HAVE TO MAKE MY DEADLINE, RIGHT?
I'LL FIGURE SOMETHING OUT, SO I DON'T NEED YOUR HELP.
TAKE HER AWAY.
SHE'S RIGHT. THIS IS TOO SUDDEN...
BOO, BOO!
I THINK...
THERE'S A LOT YOU TWO COULD LEARN FROM EACH OTHER'S WORKS.
WELL, I'LL BE BACK TOMORROW TO PICK UP YOUR MANUSCRIPT AND MAEKAWA-SENSEI.
FSSSH
HEY, WAIT! TOUDOU-SAN!

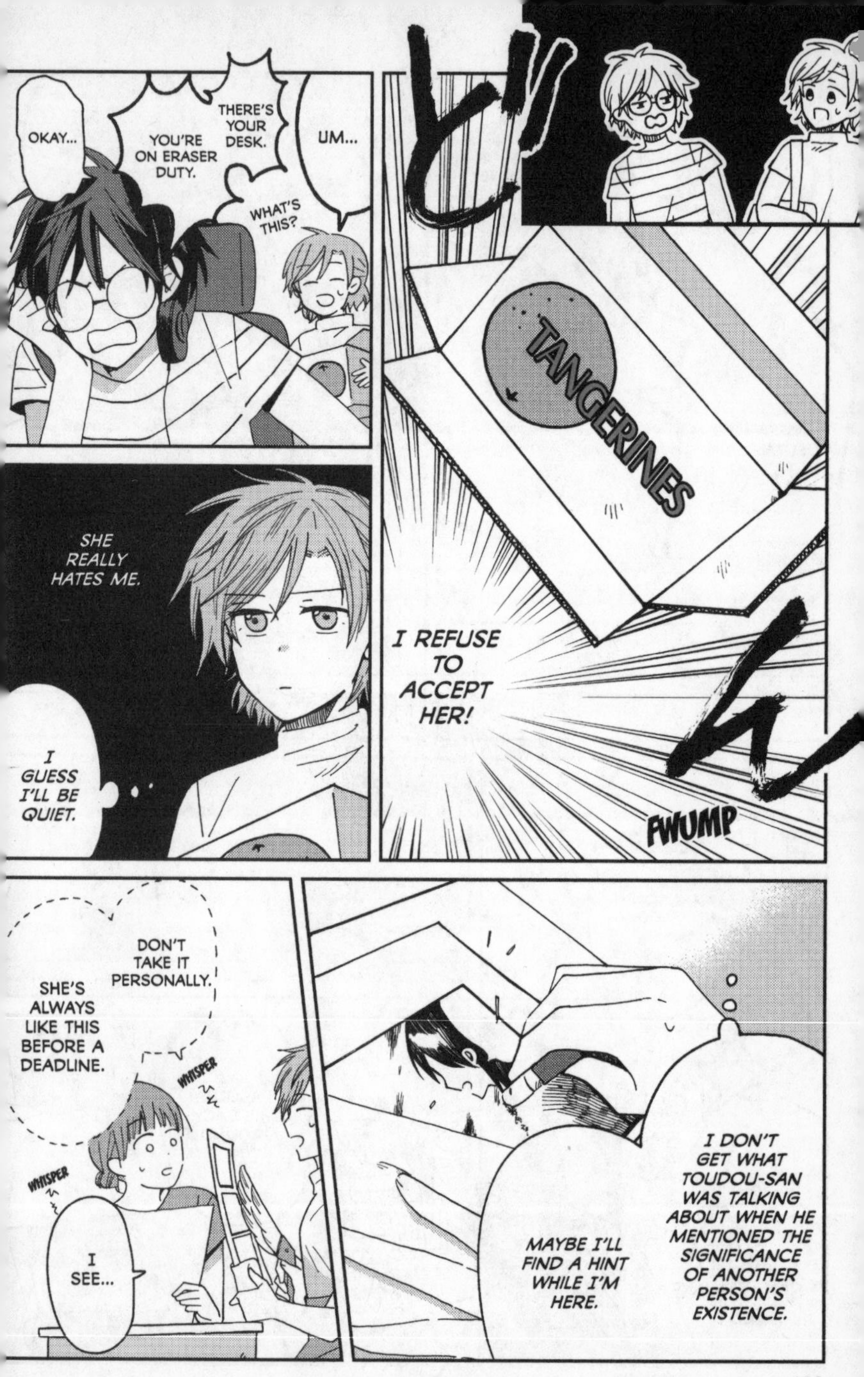
UM...
WHAT'S THIS?
THERE'S YOUR DESK.
YOU'RE ON ERASER DUTY.
OKAY...
TANGERINES
I REFUSE TO ACCEPT HER!
FWUMP
SHE REALLY HATES ME.
I GUESS I'LL BE QUIET.
I DON'T GET WHAT TOUDOU-SAN WAS TALKING ABOUT WHEN HE MENTIONED THE SIGNIFICANCE OF ANOTHER PERSON'S EXISTENCE.
MAYBE I'LL FIND A HINT WHILE I'M HERE.
DON'T TAKE IT PERSONALLY.
SHE'S ALWAYS LIKE THIS BEFORE A DEADLINE.
WHISPER
WHISPER
I SEE...

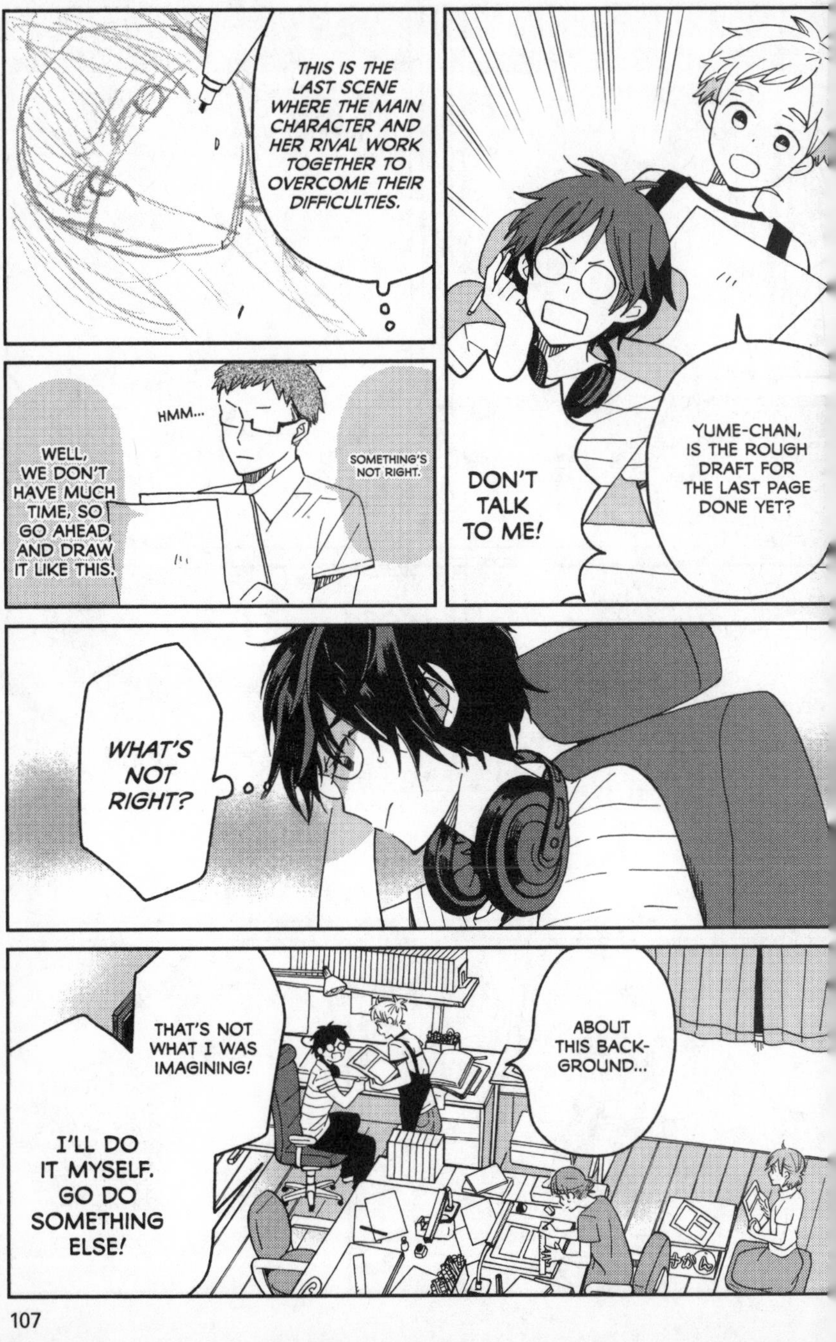
YUME-CHAN, IS THE ROUGH DRAFT FOR THE LAST PAGE DONE YET?
DON'T TALK TO ME!
THIS IS THE LAST SCENE WHERE THE MAIN CHARACTER AND HER RIVAL WORK TOGETHER TO OVERCOME THEIR DIFFICULTIES.
SOMETHING'S NOT RIGHT.
HMM...
WELL, WE DON'T HAVE MUCH TIME, SO GO AHEAD AND DRAW IT LIKE THIS.
WHAT'S NOT RIGHT?
ABOUT THIS BACK-GROUND...
THAT'S NOT WHAT I WAS IMAGINING!
I'LL DO IT MYSELF. GO DO SOMETHING ELSE!

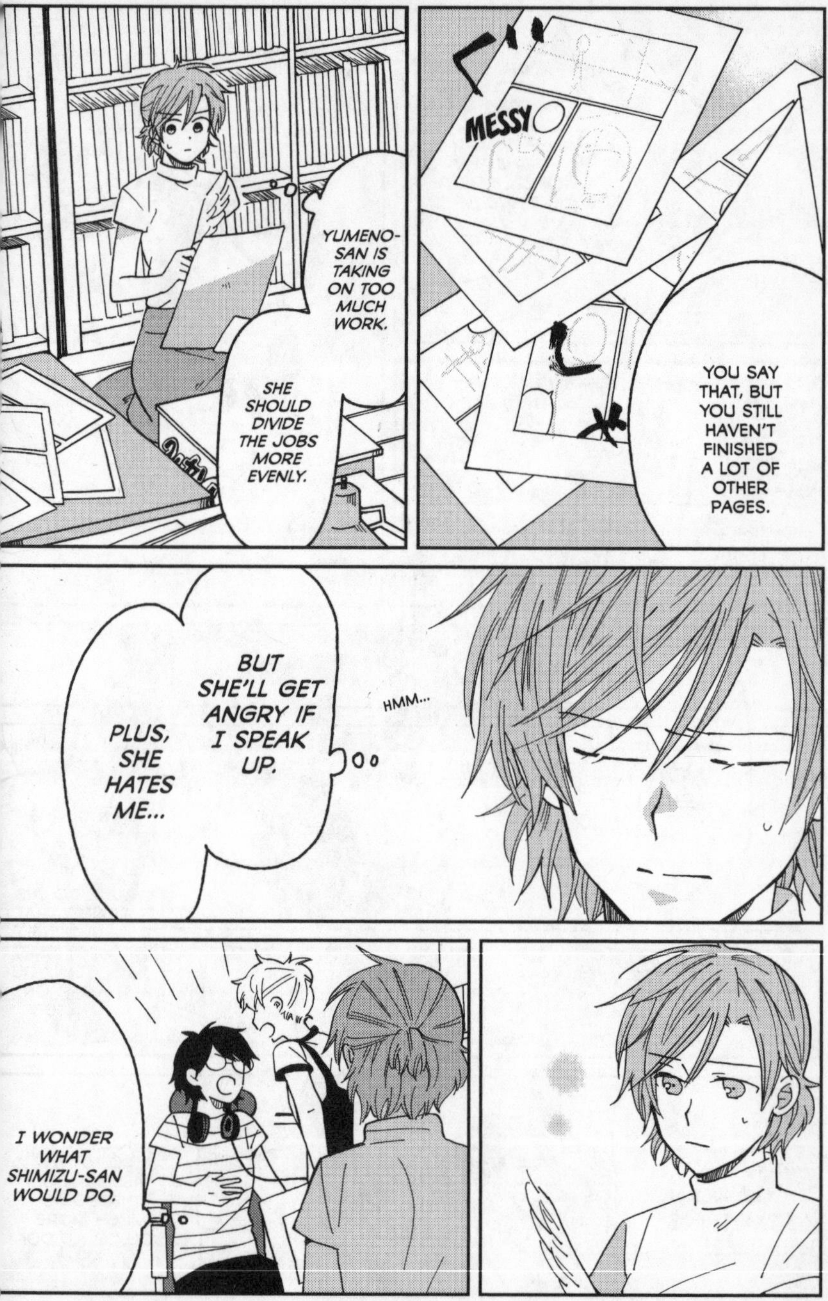
YUMENO-SAN IS TAKING ON TOO MUCH WORK.
SHE SHOULD DIVIDE THE JOBS MORE EVENLY.
MESSY
YOU SAY THAT, BUT YOU STILL HAVEN'T FINISHED A LOT OF OTHER PAGES.
BUT SHE'LL GET ANGRY IF I SPEAK UP.
PLUS, SHE HATES ME...
HMM...
I WONDER WHAT SHIMIZU-SAN WOULD DO.

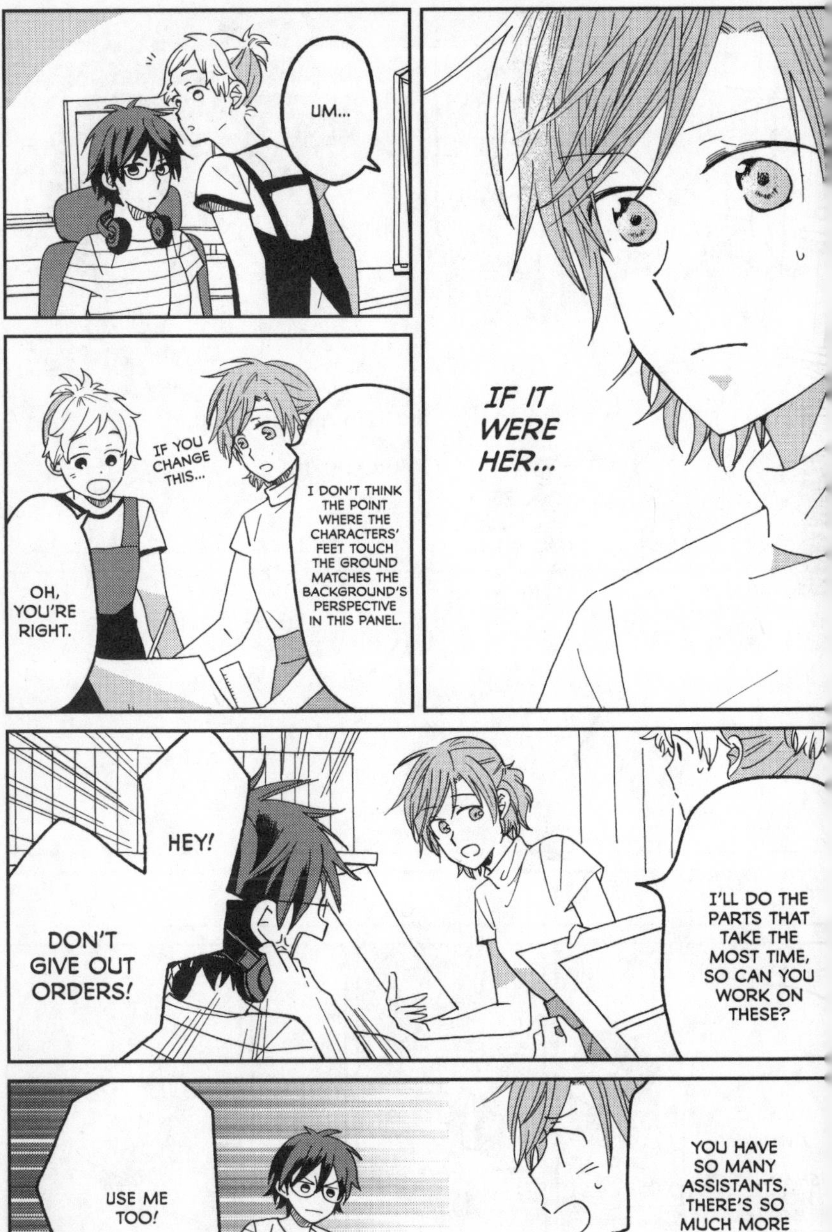
IF IT WERE HER...
UM...
I DON'T THINK THE POINT WHERE THE CHARACTERS' FEET TOUCH THE GROUND MATCHES THE BACKGROUND'S PERSPECTIVE IN THIS PANEL.
IF YOU CHANGE THIS...
OH, YOU'RE RIGHT.
I'LL DO THE PARTS THAT TAKE THE MOST TIME, SO CAN YOU WORK ON THESE?
HEY!
DON'T GIVE OUT ORDERS!
YOU HAVE SO MANY ASSISTANTS. THERE'S SO MUCH MORE YOU COULD DO!
USE ME TOO!

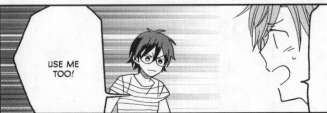

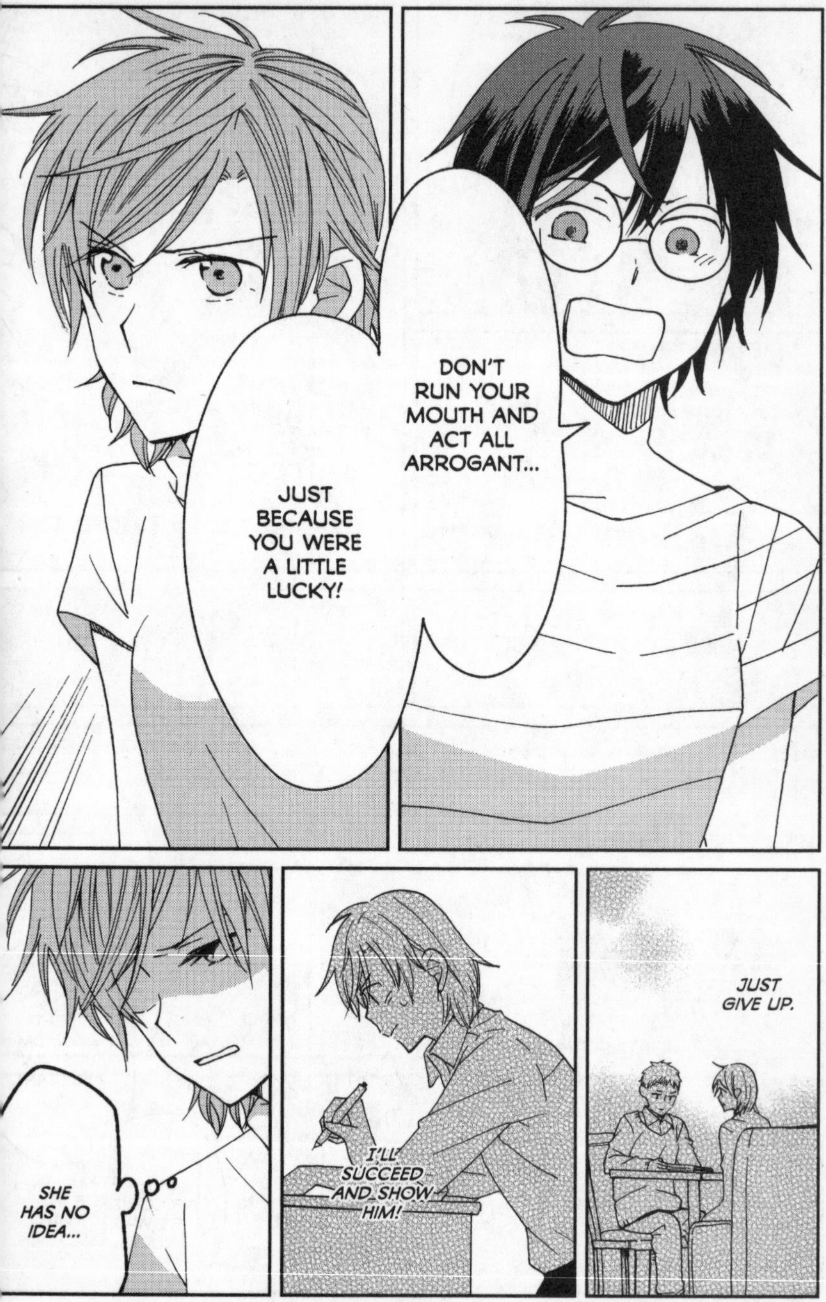
DON'T RUN YOUR MOUTH AND ACT ALL ARROGANT...
JUST BECAUSE YOU WERE A LITTLE LUCKY!
JUST GIVE UP.
I'LL SUCCEED AND SHOW HIM!
SHE HAS NO IDEA...

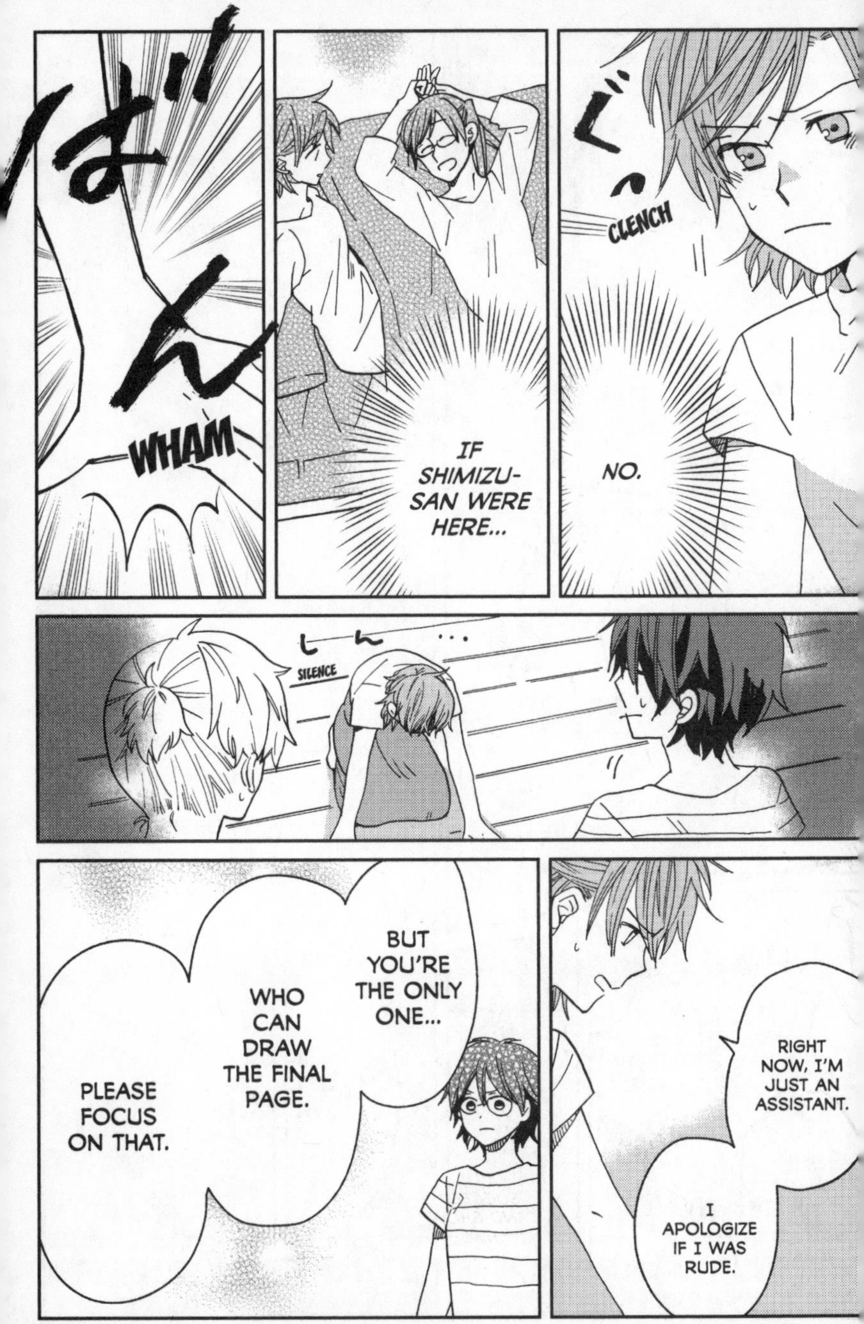
ぐっ
CLENCH
NO.
IF SHIMIZU-SAN WERE HERE...
ばんっ
WHAM
しん…
SILENCE
RIGHT NOW, I'M JUST AN ASSISTANT.
I APOLOGIZE IF I WAS RUDE.
BUT YOU'RE THE ONLY ONE...
WHO CAN DRAW THE FINAL PAGE.
PLEASE FOCUS ON THAT.

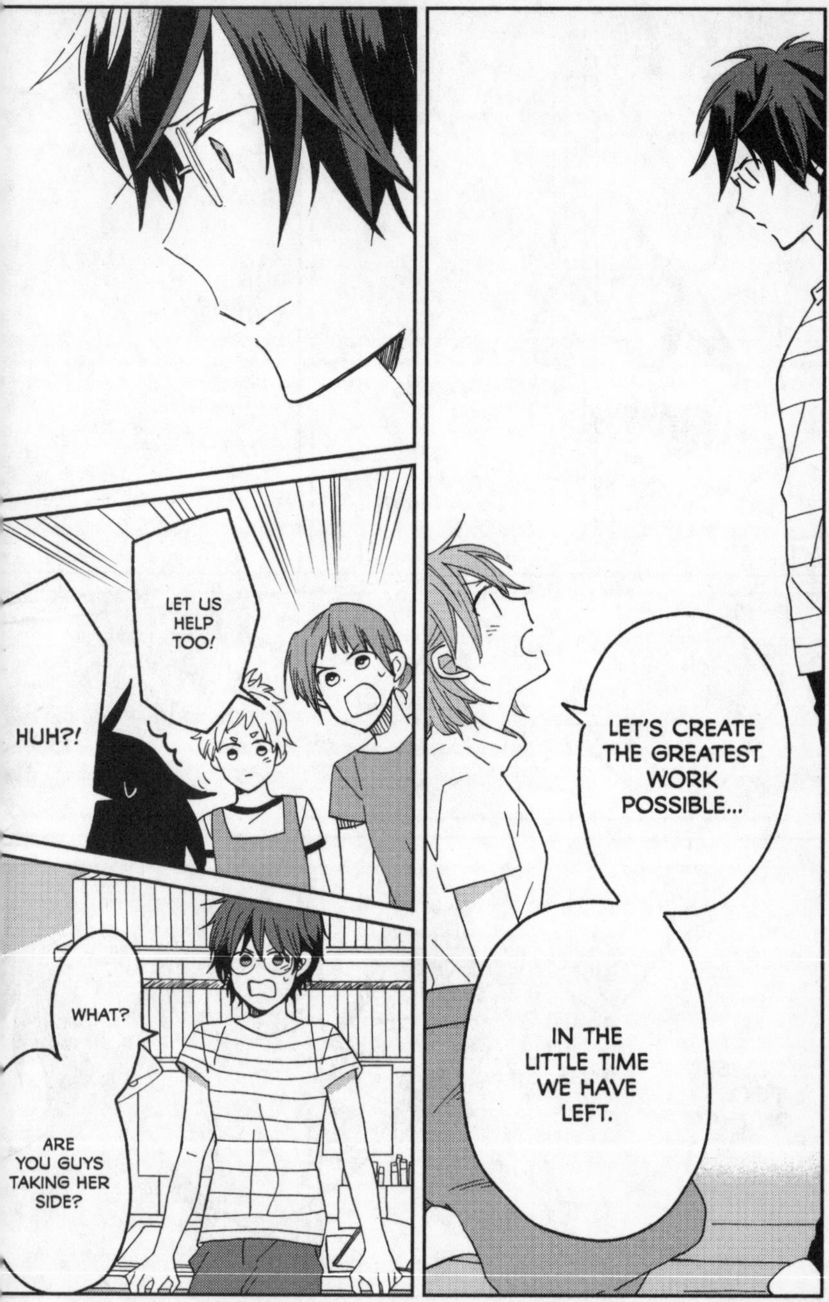
LET'S CREATE THE GREATEST WORK POSSIBLE...
IN THE LITTLE TIME WE HAVE LEFT.
LET US HELP TOO!
HUH?!
WHAT?
ARE YOU GUYS TAKING HER SIDE?

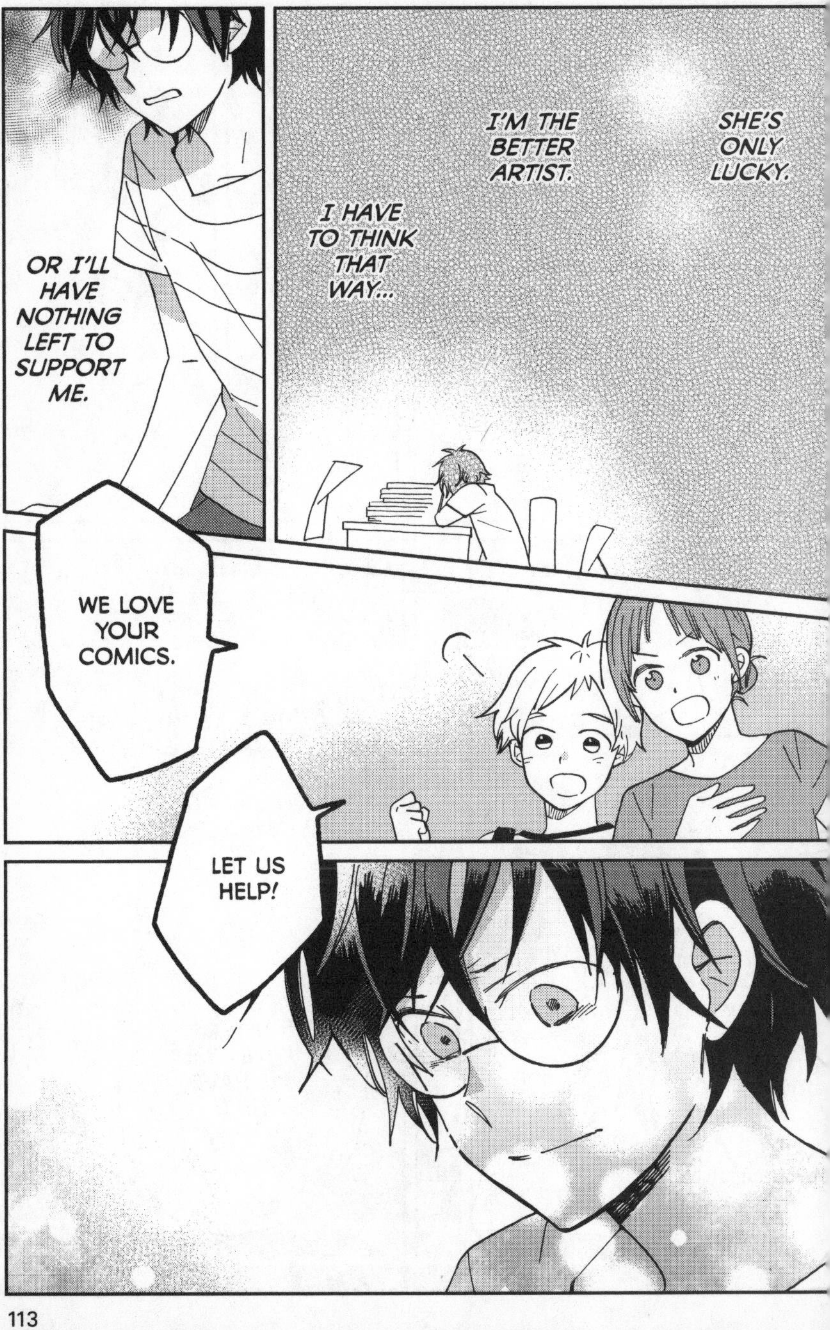
SHE'S ONLY LUCKY.
I'M THE BETTER ARTIST.
I HAVE TO THINK THAT WAY...
OR I'LL HAVE NOTHING LEFT TO SUPPORT ME.
WE LOVE YOUR COMICS.
LET US HELP!

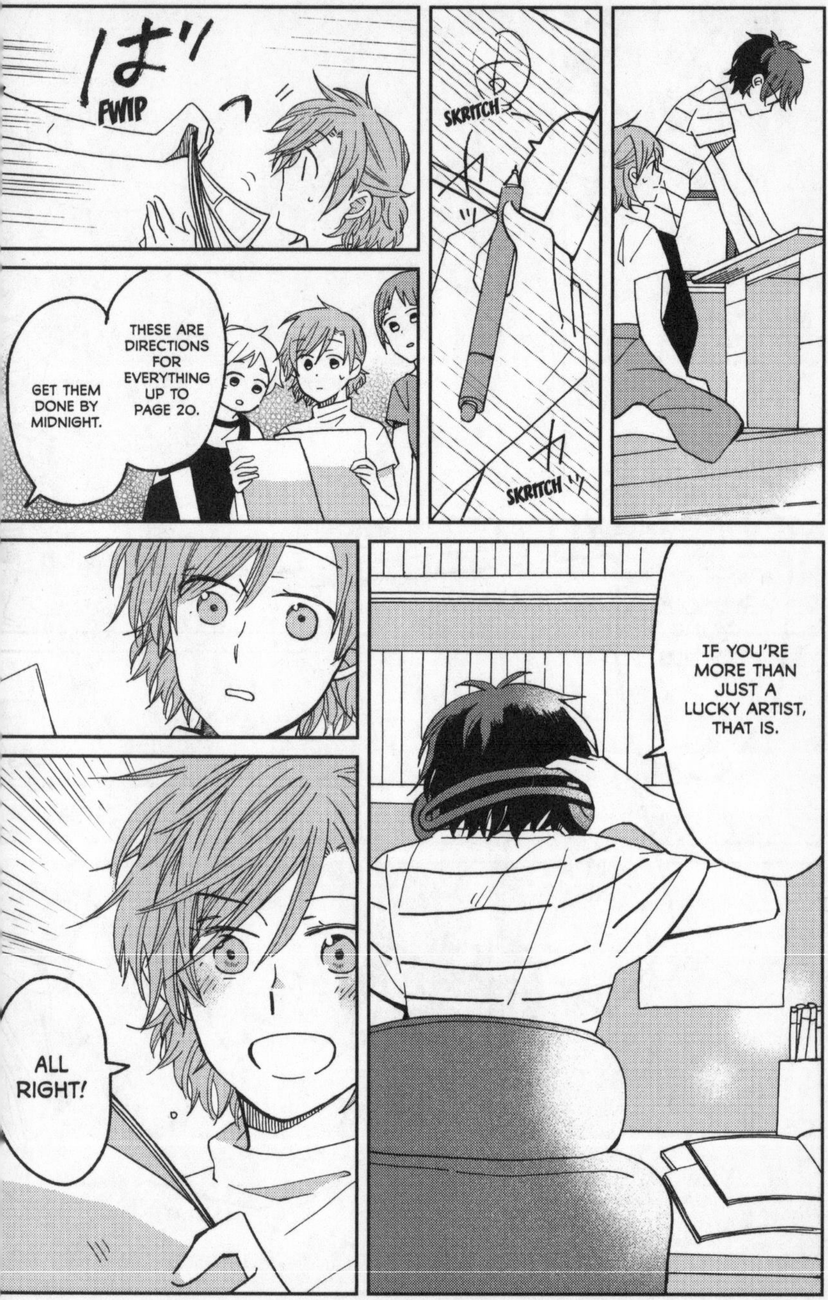

SKRITCH
SKRITCH
はり
FWIP
THESE ARE DIRECTIONS FOR EVERYTHING UP TO PAGE 20.
GET THEM DONE BY MIDNIGHT.
IF YOU'RE MORE THAN JUST A LUCKY ARTIST, THAT IS.
ALL RIGHT!

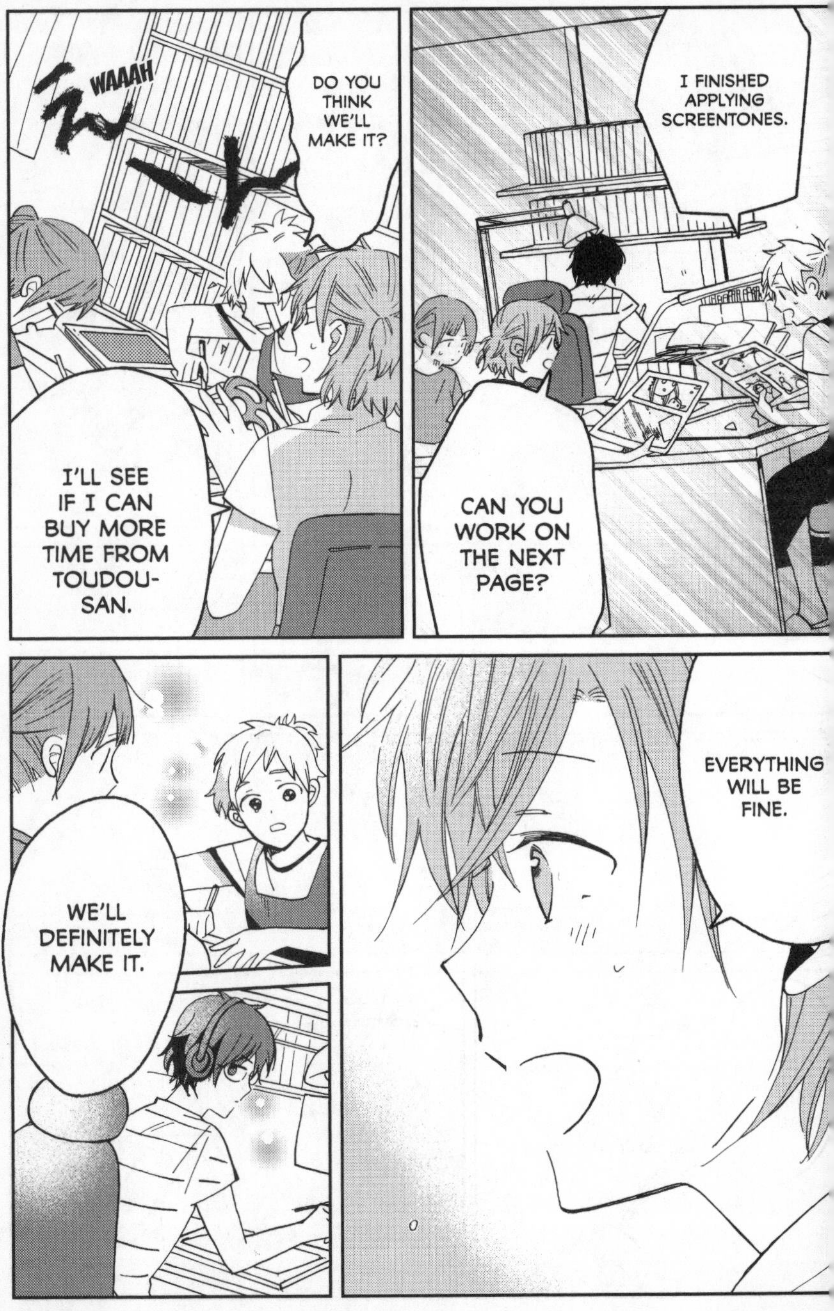
I FINISHED APPLYING SCREENTONES.
CAN YOU WORK ON THE NEXT PAGE?
WAAAH
DO YOU THINK WE'LL MAKE IT?
I'LL SEE IF I CAN BUY MORE TIME FROM TOUDOU-SAN.
EVERYTHING WILL BE FINE.
WE'LL DEFINITELY MAKE IT.

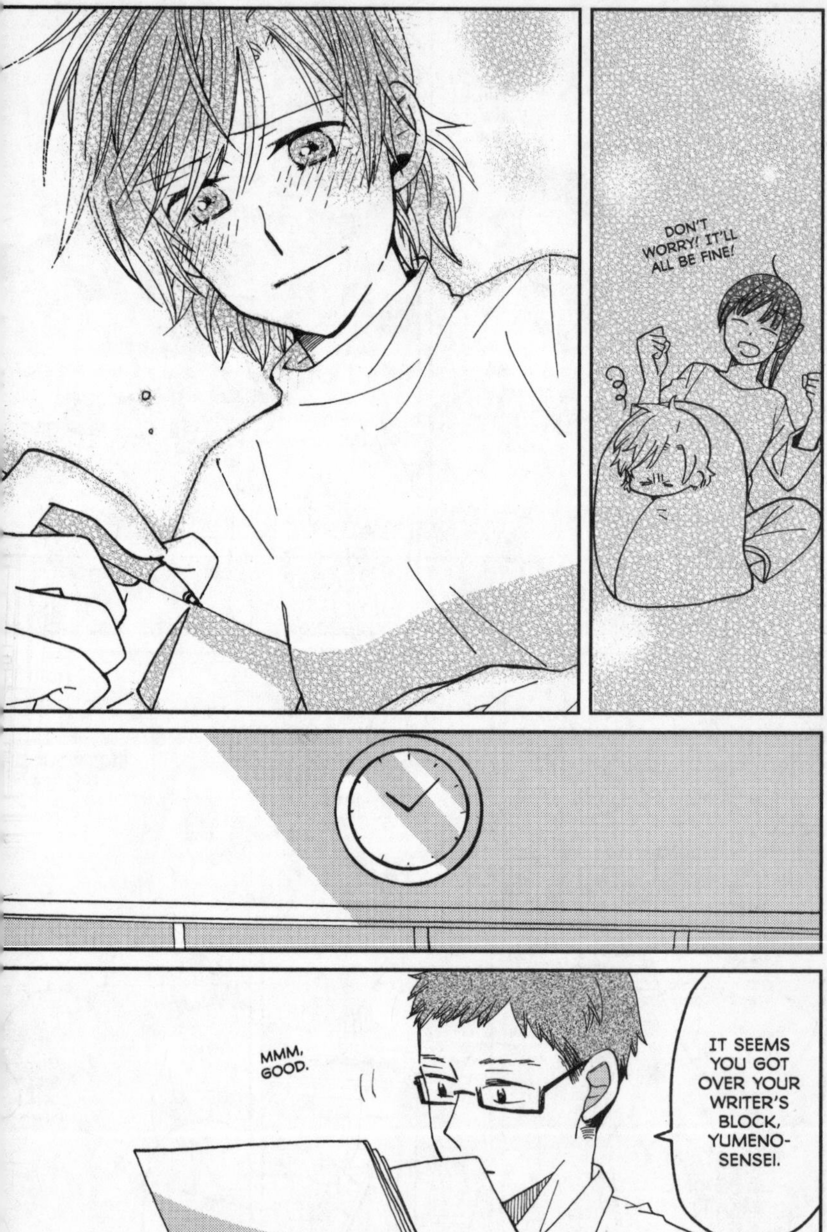
DON'T WORRY! IT'LL ALL BE FINE!
IT SEEMS YOU GOT OVER YOUR WRITER'S BLOCK, YUMENO-SENSEI.
MMM, GOOD.

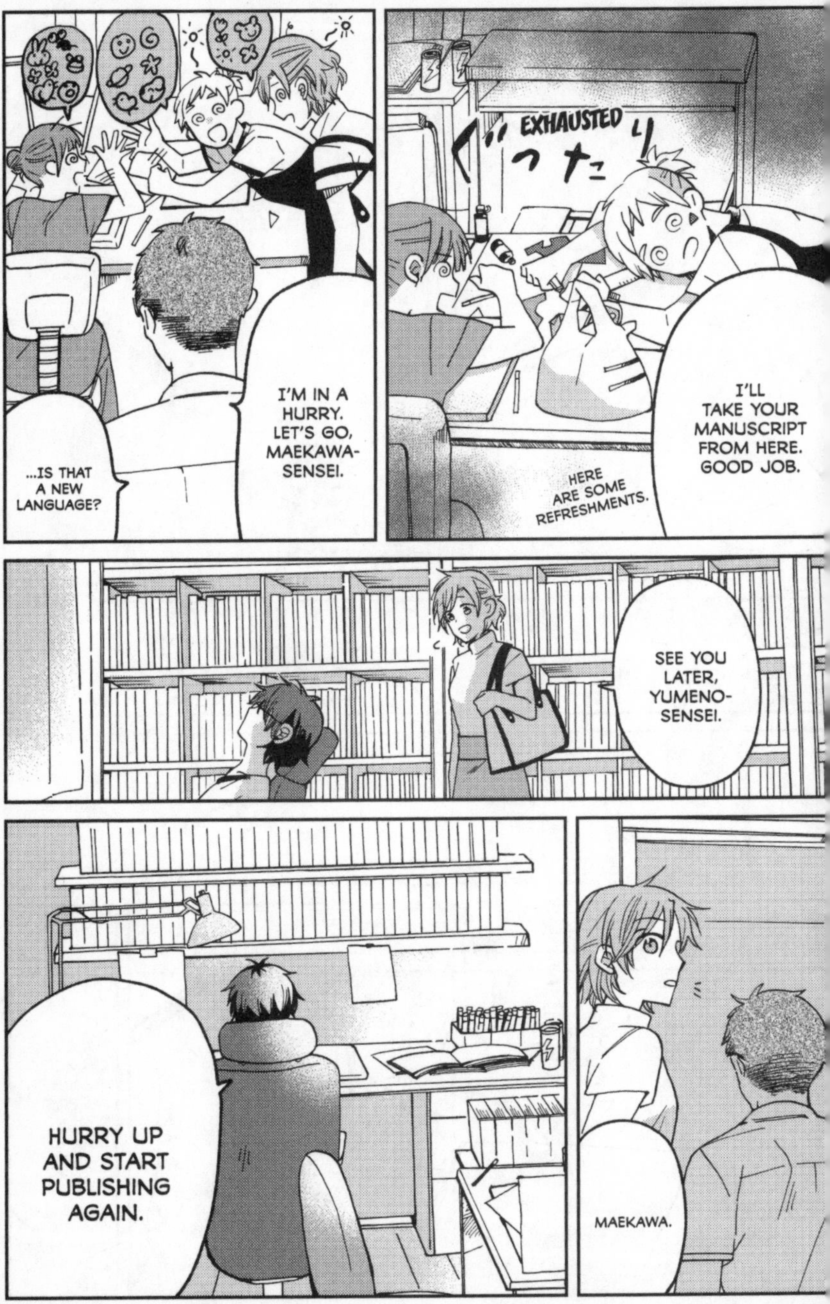
EXHAUSTED
I'LL TAKE YOUR MANUSCRIPT FROM HERE. GOOD JOB.
HERE ARE SOME REFRESHMENTS.
I'M IN A HURRY. LET'S GO, MAEKAWA-SENSEI.
...IS THAT A NEW LANGUAGE?
SEE YOU LATER, YUMENO-SENSEI.
MAEKAWA.
HURRY UP AND START PUBLISHING AGAIN.

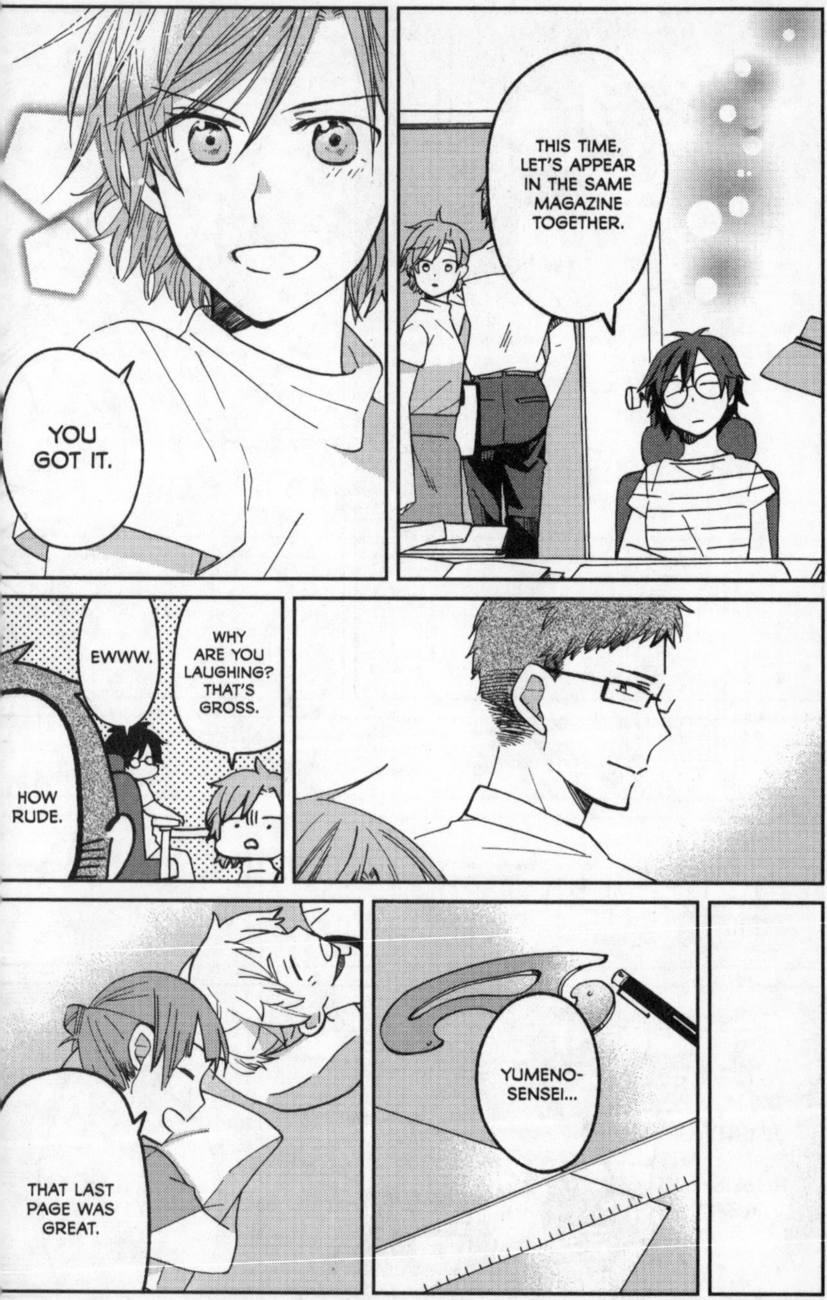
THIS TIME, LET'S APPEAR IN THE SAME MAGAZINE TOGETHER.
YOU GOT IT.
WHY ARE YOU LAUGHING? THAT'S GROSS.
EWWW.
HOW RUDE.
YUMENO-SENSEI...
THAT LAST PAGE WAS GREAT.

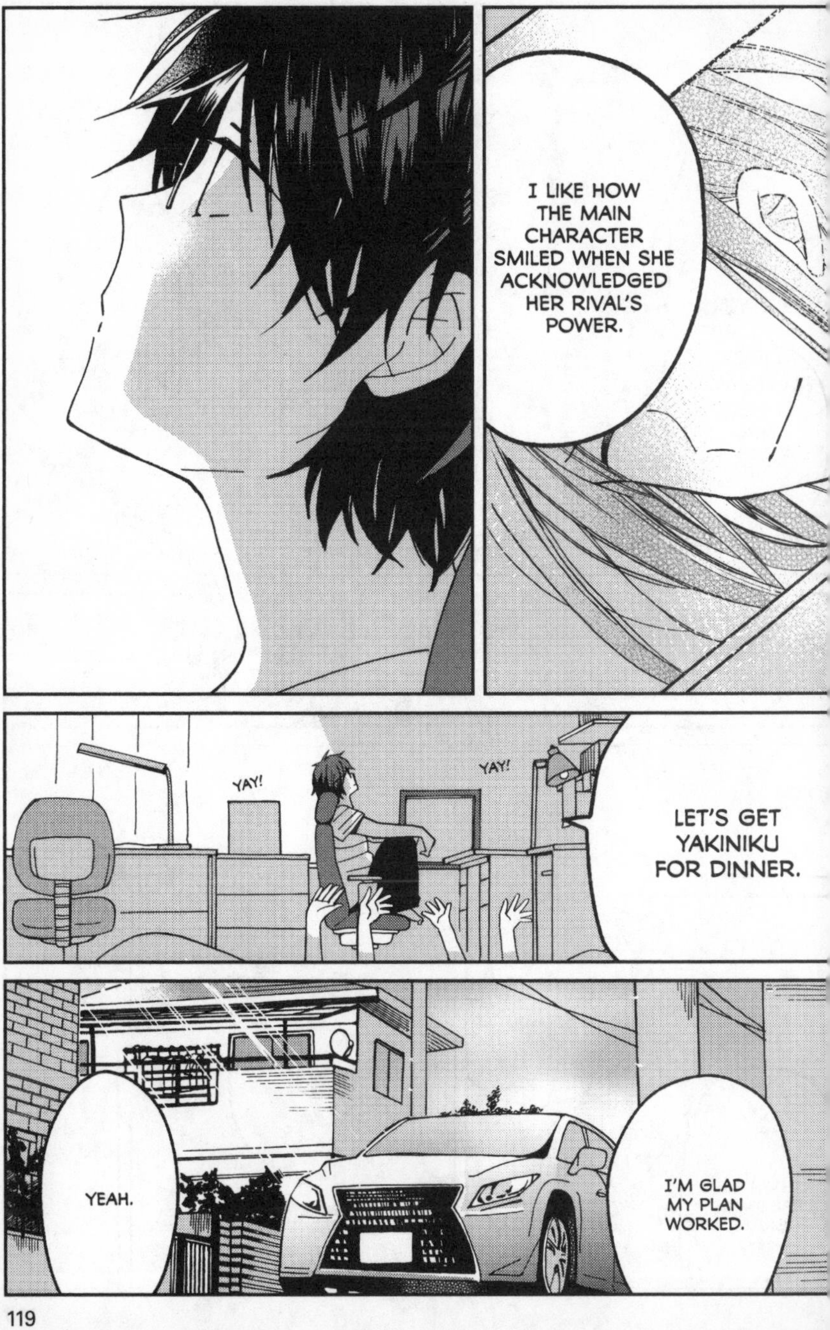
I LIKE HOW THE MAIN CHARACTER SMILED WHEN SHE ACKNOWLEDGED HER RIVAL'S POWER.
LET'S GET YAKINIKU FOR DINNER.
YAY!
YAY!
I'M GLAD MY PLAN WORKED.
YEAH.

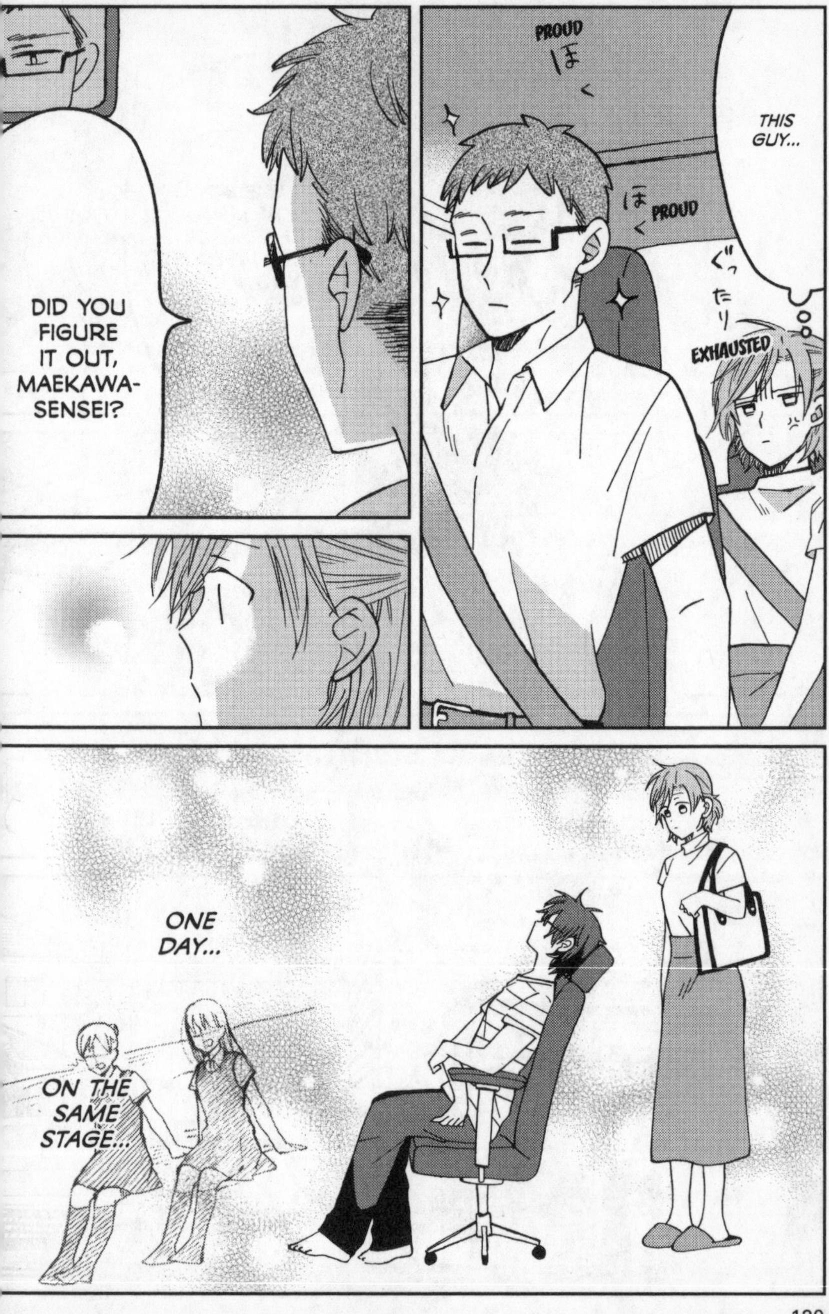
PROUD
ほく
ほく
PROUD
THIS GUY...
ぐったり
EXHAUSTED
DID YOU FIGURE IT OUT, MAEKAWA-SENSEI?
ONE DAY...
ON THE SAME STAGE...

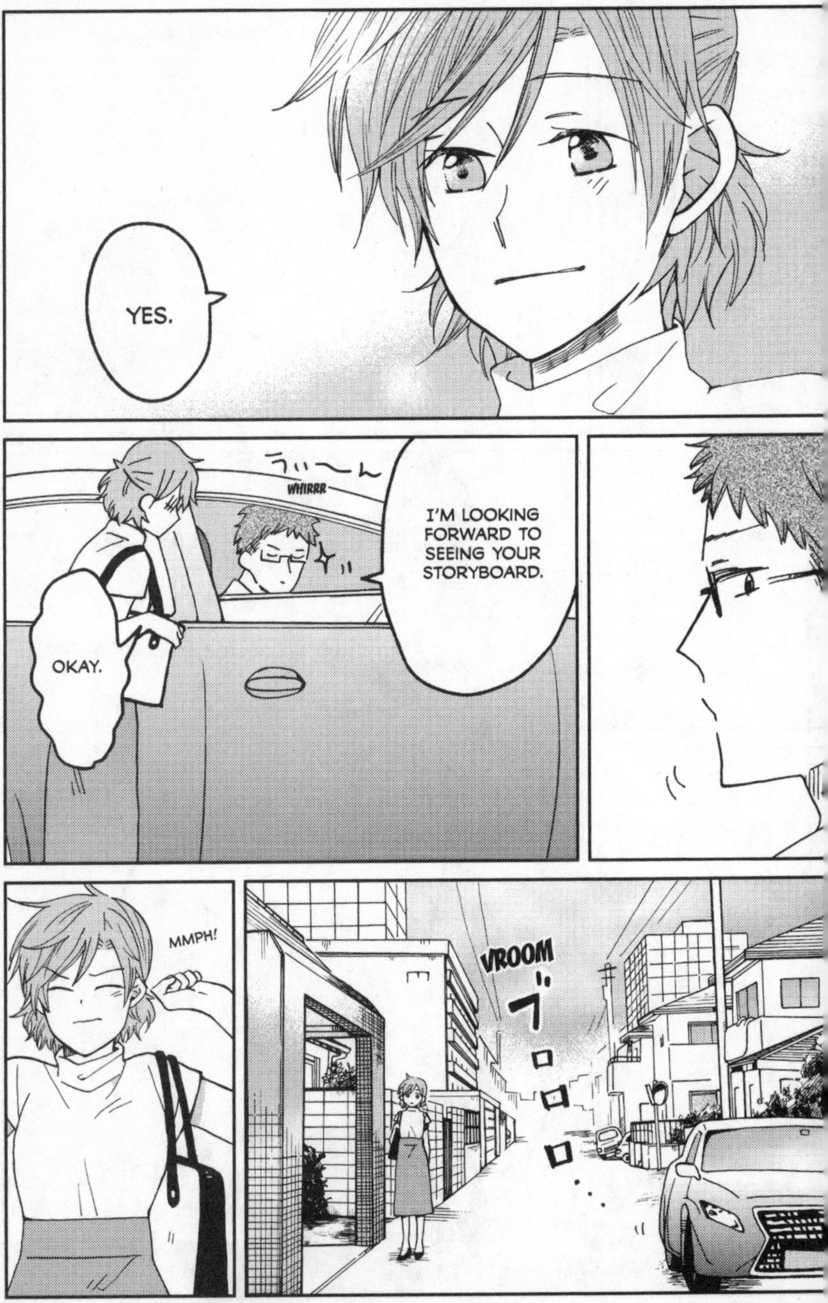
YES.
うぃ〜ん
WHIRRR
I'M LOOKING FORWARD TO SEEING YOUR STORYBOARD.
OKAY.
VROOM
ブロロロ
MMPH!

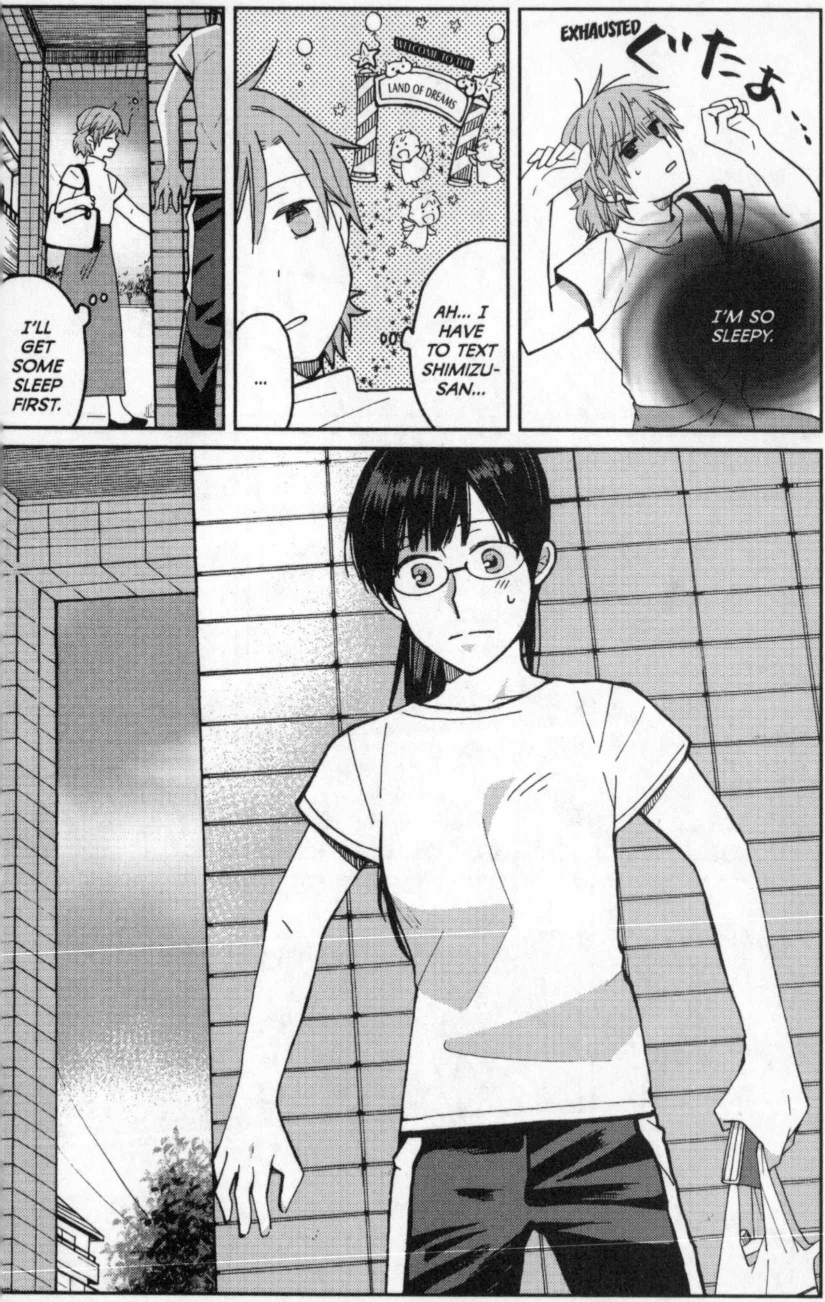
EXHAUSTED
ぐたぁ…
I'M SO SLEEPY.
WELCOME TO THE
LAND OF DREAMS
AH... I HAVE TO TEXT SHIMIZU-SAN...
...
I'LL GET SOME SLEEP FIRST.

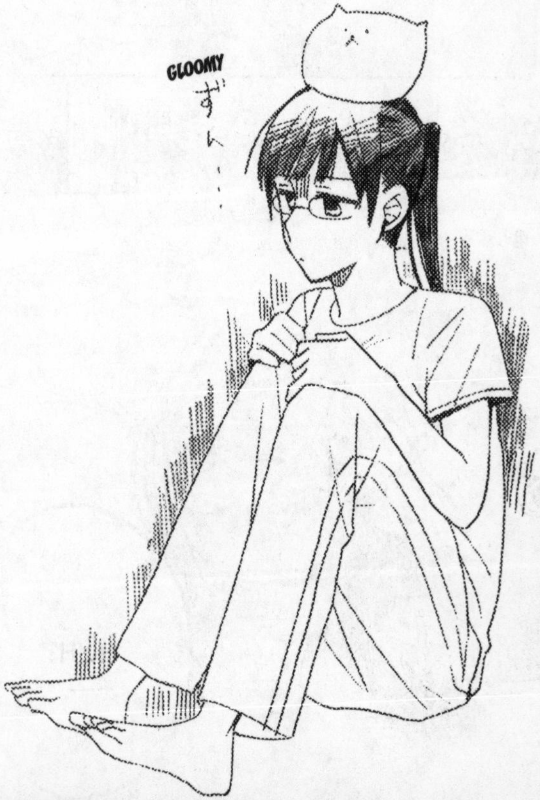
GLOOMY
ずん…

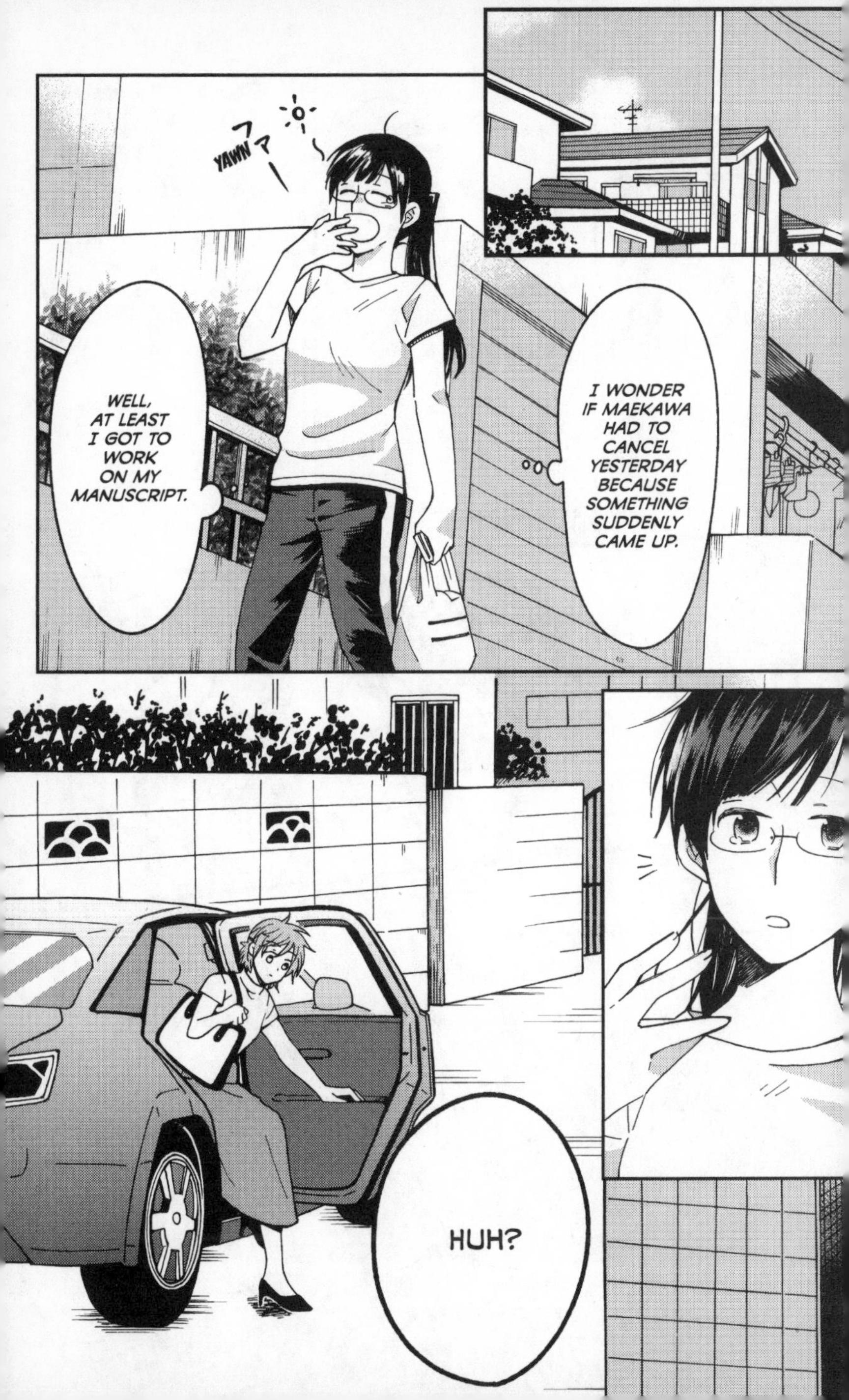
YAWN
I WONDER IF MAEKAWA HAD TO CANCEL YESTERDAY BECAUSE SOMETHING SUDDENLY CAME UP.
WELL, AT LEAST I GOT TO WORK ON MY MANUSCRIPT.
HUH?

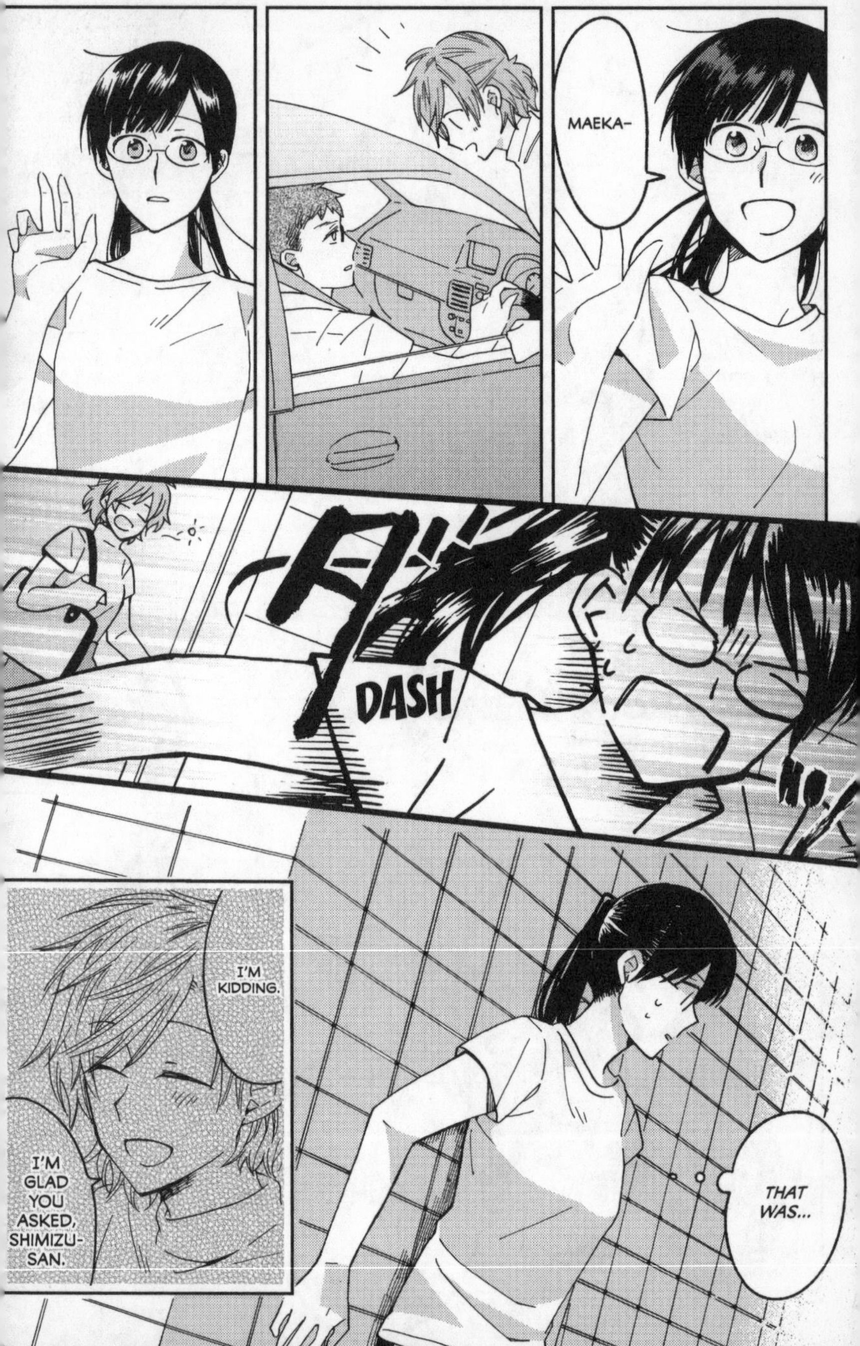
MAEKA-
DASH
THAT WAS...
I'M KIDDING.
I'M GLAD YOU ASKED, SHIMIZU-SAN.

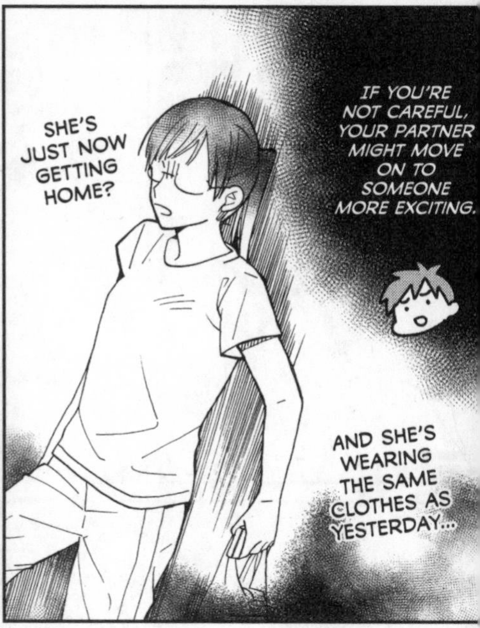
IF YOU'RE NOT CAREFUL, YOUR PARTNER MIGHT MOVE ON TO SOMEONE MORE EXCITING.
SHE'S JUST NOW GETTING HOME?
AND SHE'S WEARING THE SAME CLOTHES AS YESTERDAY...
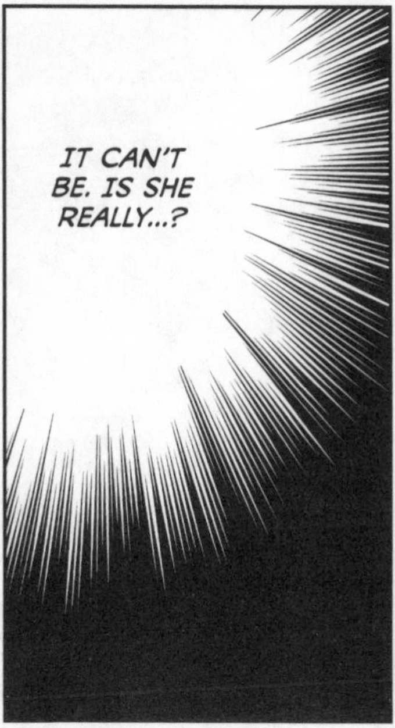
IT CAN'T BE. IS SHE REALLY...?

Chapter 20

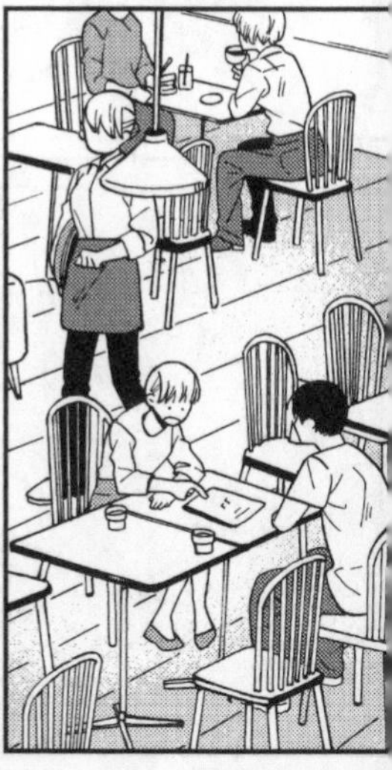
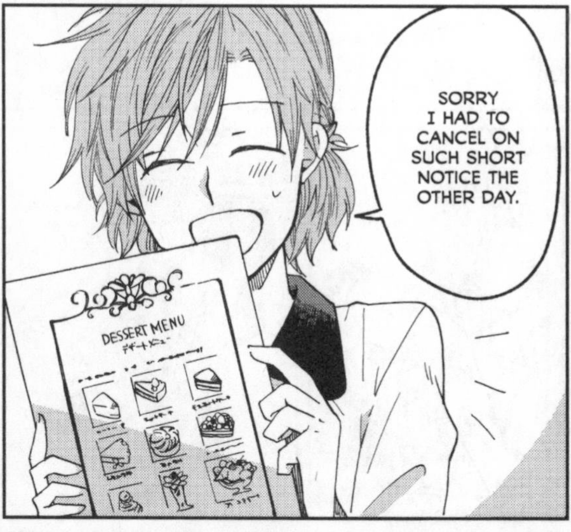
SORRY I HAD TO CANCEL ON SUCH SHORT NOTICE THE OTHER DAY.
DESSERT MENU

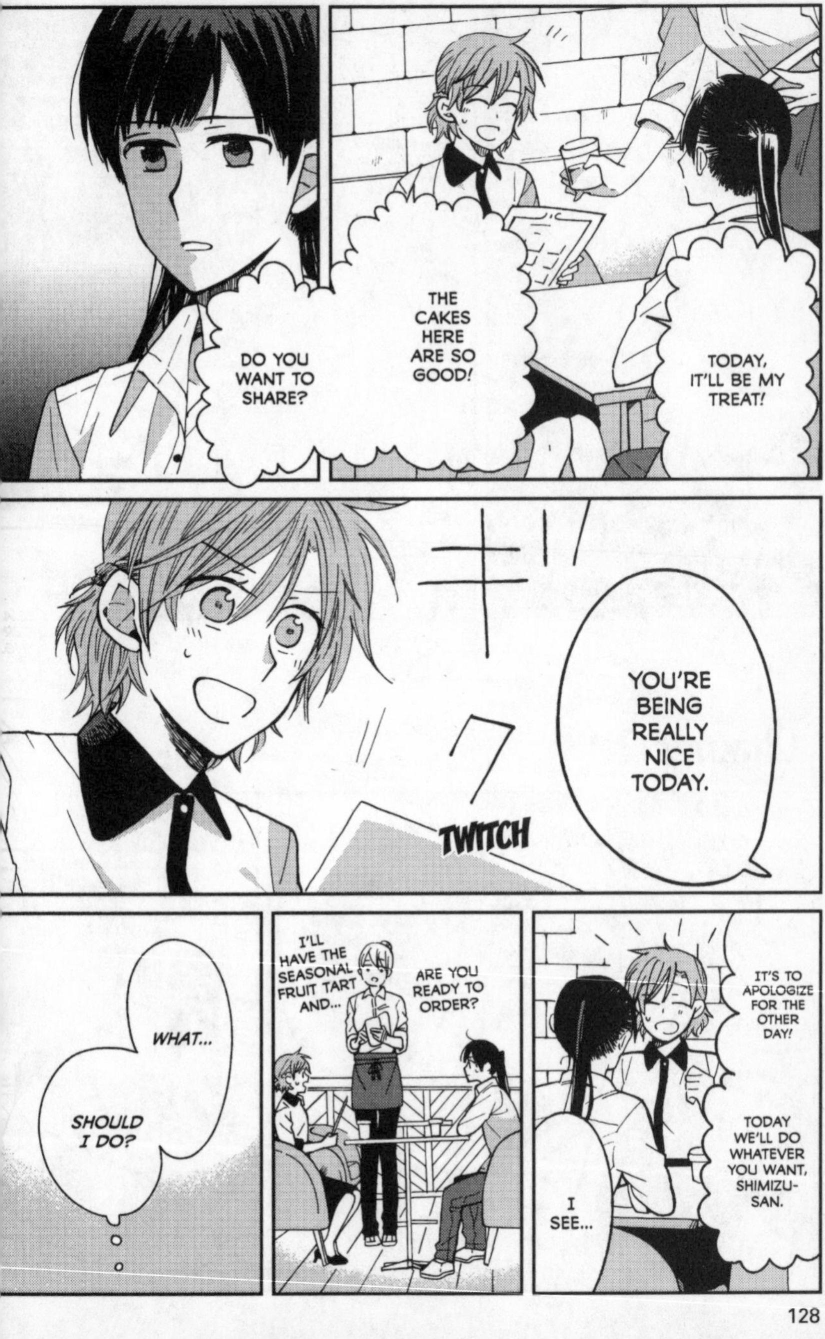
TODAY, IT'LL BE MY TREAT!
THE CAKES HERE ARE SO GOOD!
DO YOU WANT TO SHARE?
YOU'RE BEING REALLY NICE TODAY.
TWITCH
IT'S TO APOLOGIZE FOR THE OTHER DAY!
TODAY WE'LL DO WHATEVER YOU WANT, SHIMIZU-SAN.
I SEE...
ARE YOU READY TO ORDER?
I'LL HAVE THE SEASONAL FRUIT TART AND...
WHAT...
SHOULD I DO?

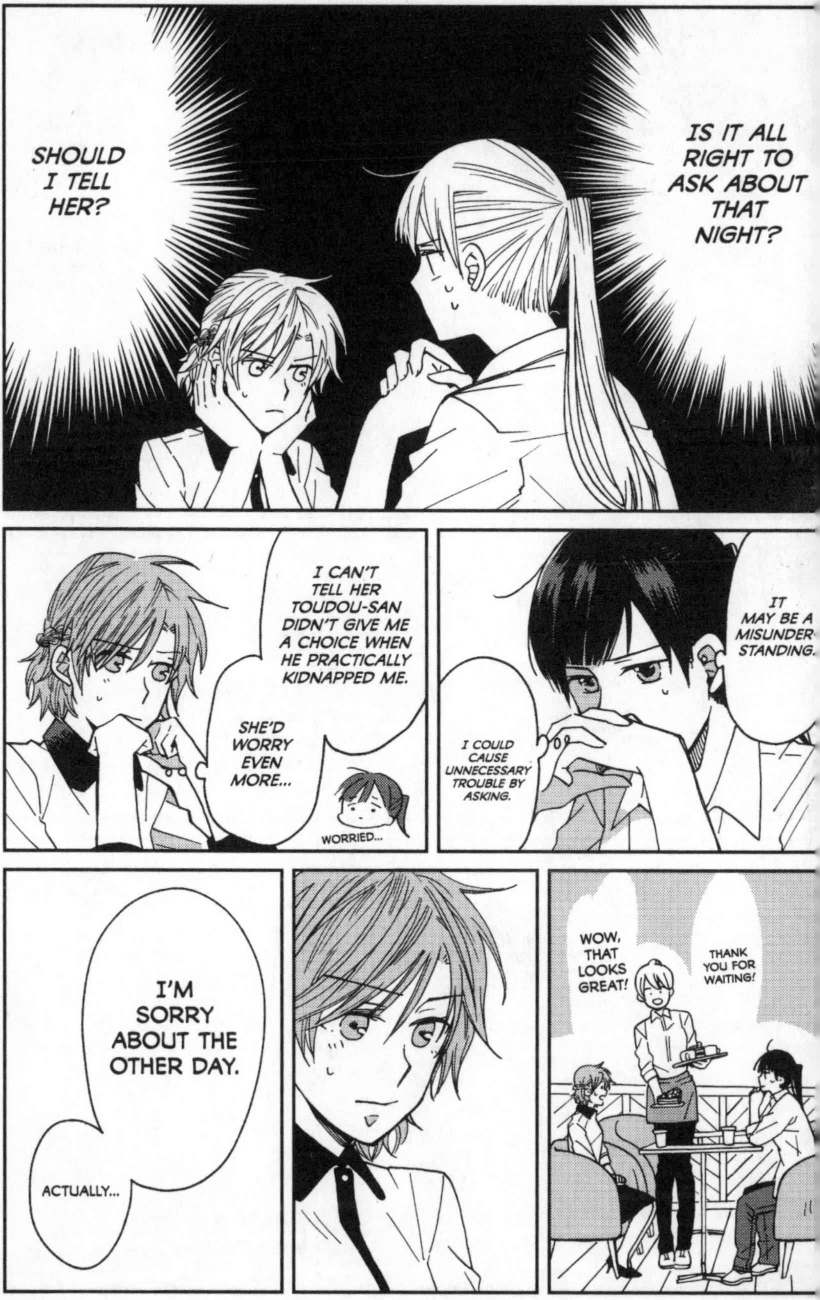
IS IT ALL RIGHT TO ASK ABOUT THAT NIGHT?
SHOULD I TELL HER?
IT MAY BE A MISUNDERSTANDING.
I COULD CAUSE UNNECESSARY TROUBLE BY ASKING.
I CAN'T TELL HER TOUDOU-SAN DIDN'T GIVE ME A CHOICE WHEN HE PRACTICALLY KIDNAPPED ME.
SHE'D WORRY EVEN MORE...
WORRIED...
THANK YOU FOR WAITING!
WOW, THAT LOOKS GREAT!
I'M SORRY ABOUT THE OTHER DAY.
ACTUALLY...

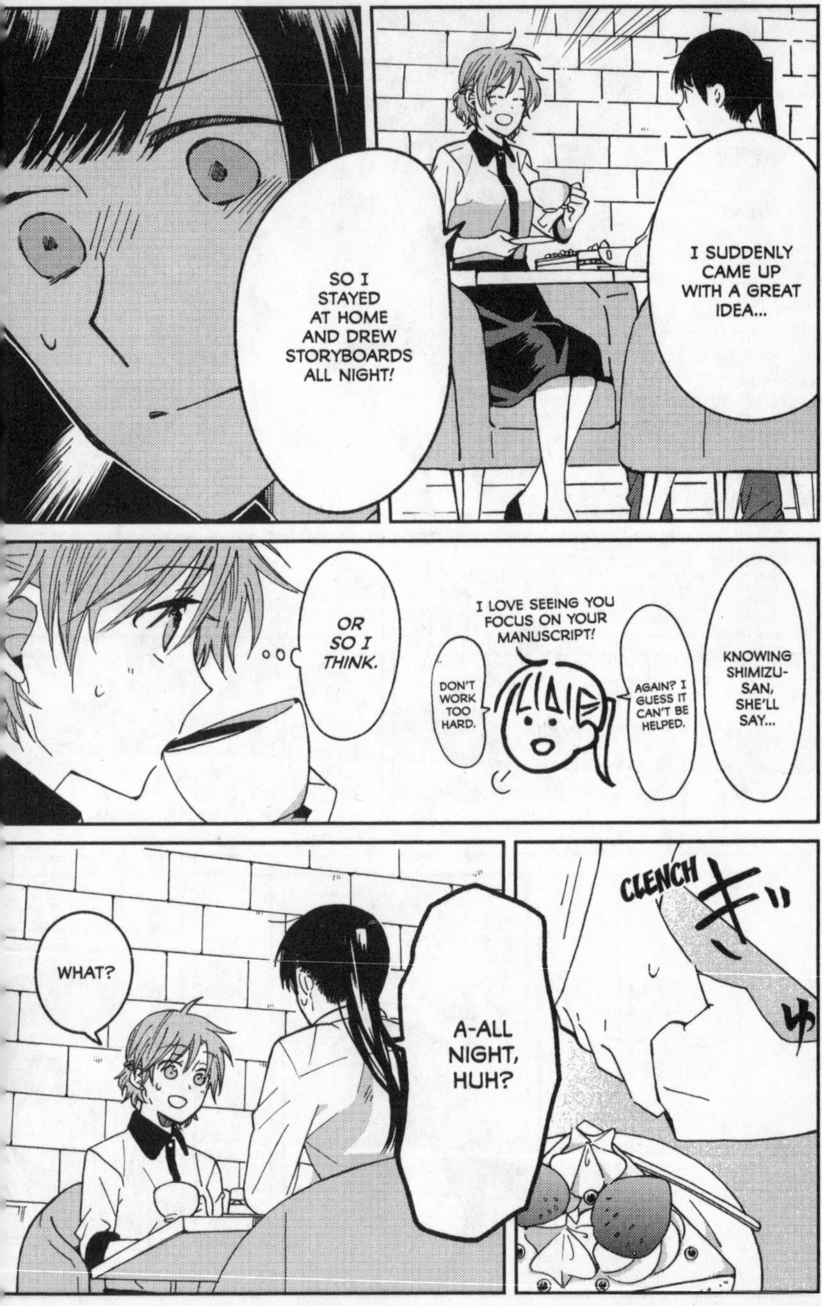
I SUDDENLY CAME UP WITH A GREAT IDEA...
SO I STAYED AT HOME AND DREW STORYBOARDS ALL NIGHT!
KNOWING SHIMIZU-SAN, SHE'LL SAY...
AGAIN? I GUESS IT CAN'T BE HELPED.
I LOVE SEEING YOU FOCUS ON YOUR MANUSCRIPT!
DON'T WORK TOO HARD.
OR SO I THINK.
CLENCH
A-ALL NIGHT, HUH?
WHAT?

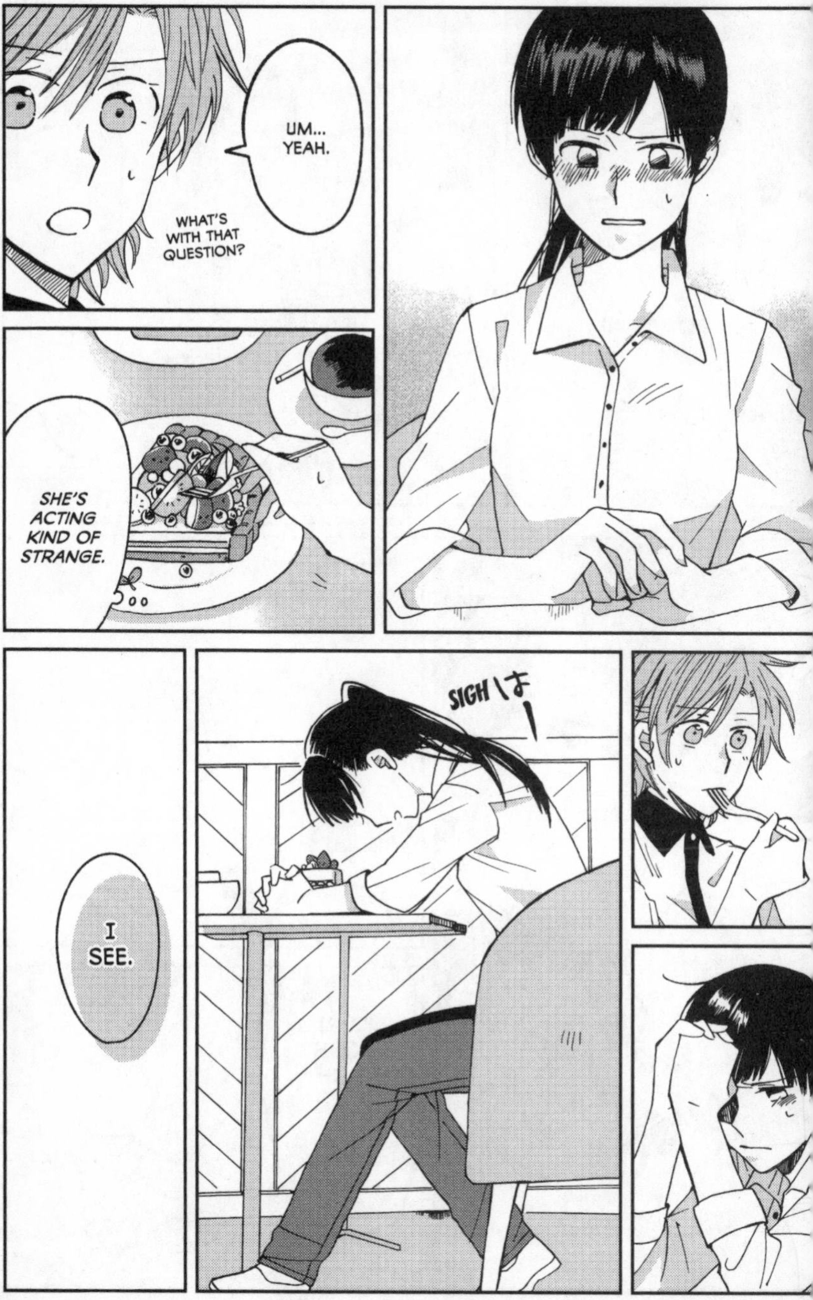
UM... YEAH.
WHAT'S WITH THAT QUESTION?
SHE'S ACTING KIND OF STRANGE.
SIGH はー
I SEE.

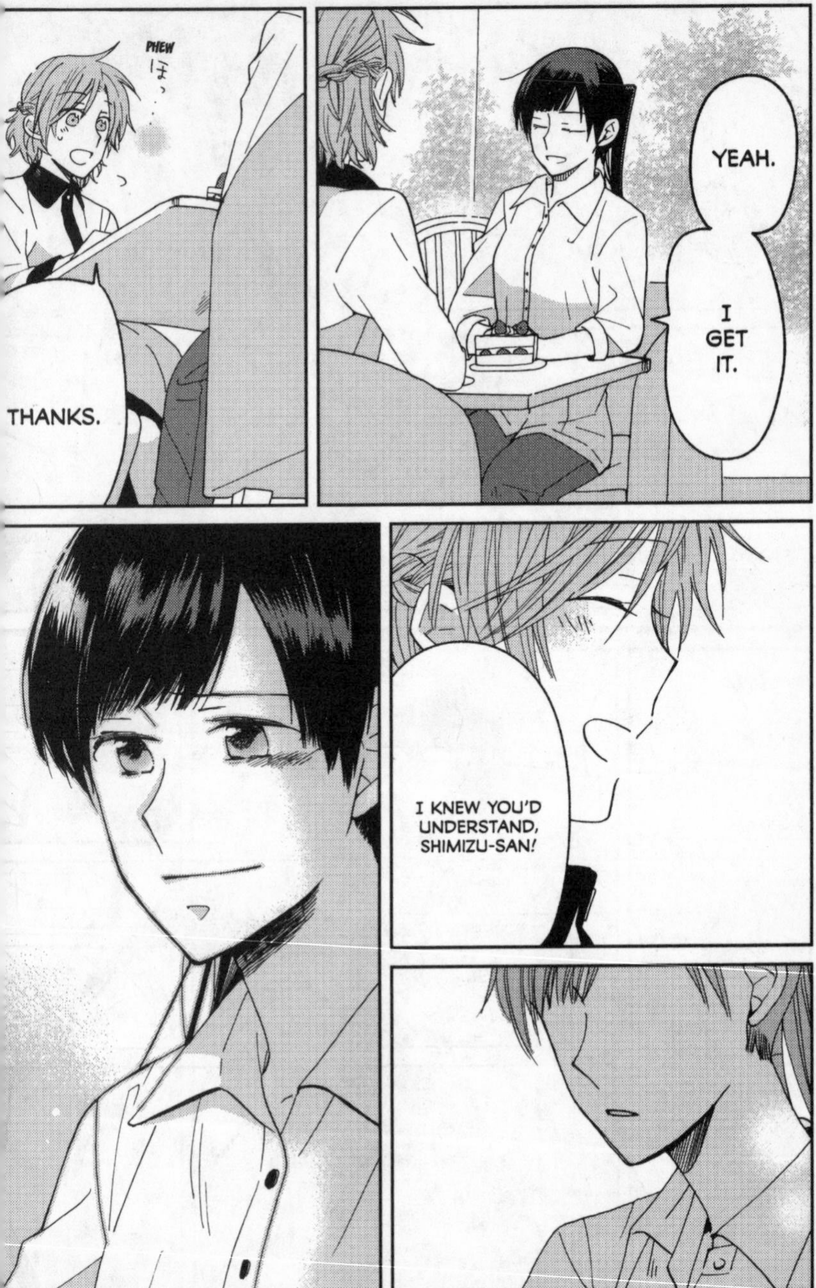
YEAH.
I GET IT.
PHEW
ほっ
THANKS.
I KNEW YOU'D UNDERSTAND, SHIMIZU-SAN!

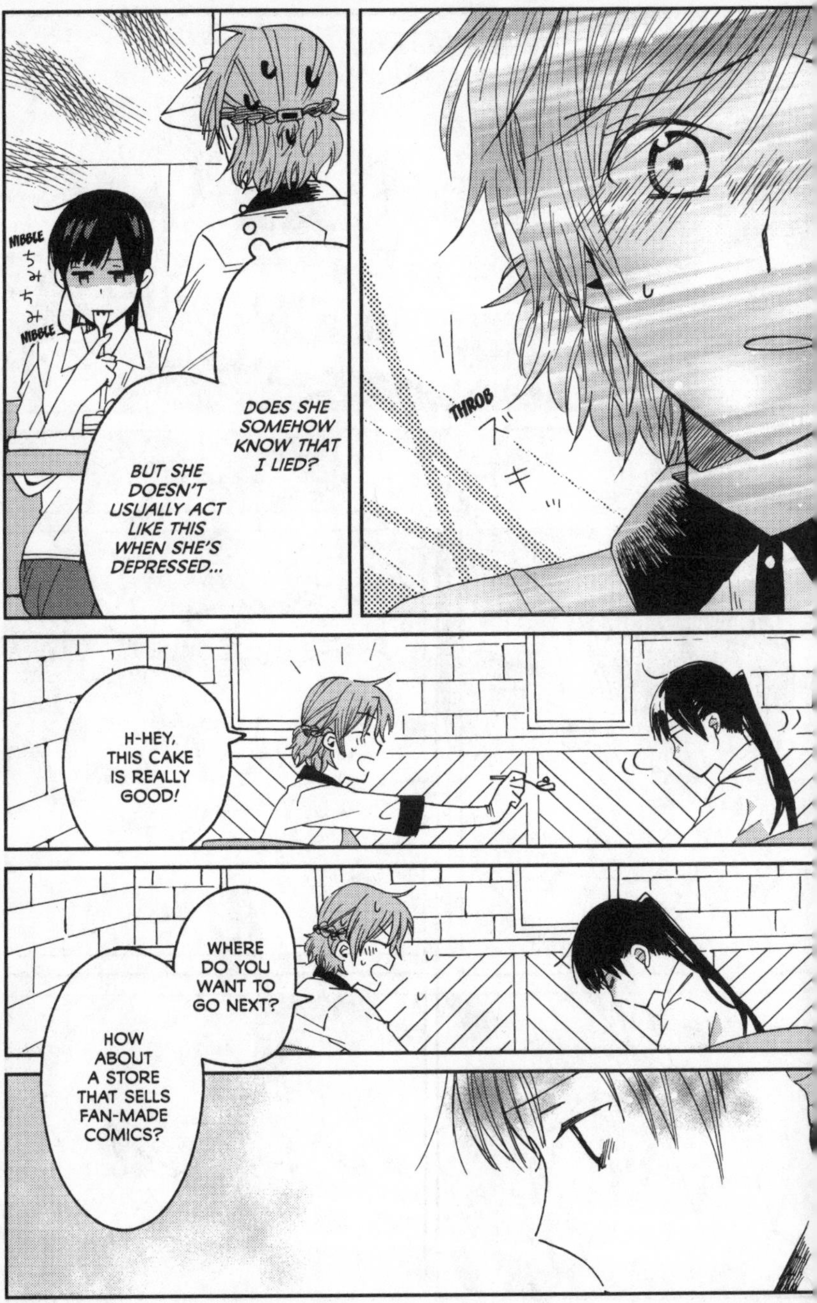
THROB
ズキッ
DOES SHE SOMEHOW KNOW THAT I LIED?
BUT SHE DOESN'T USUALLY ACT LIKE THIS WHEN SHE'S DEPRESSED...
NIBBLE
ちみちみ
NIBBLE
H-HEY, THIS CAKE IS REALLY GOOD!
WHERE DO YOU WANT TO GO NEXT?
HOW ABOUT A STORE THAT SELLS FAN-MADE COMICS?

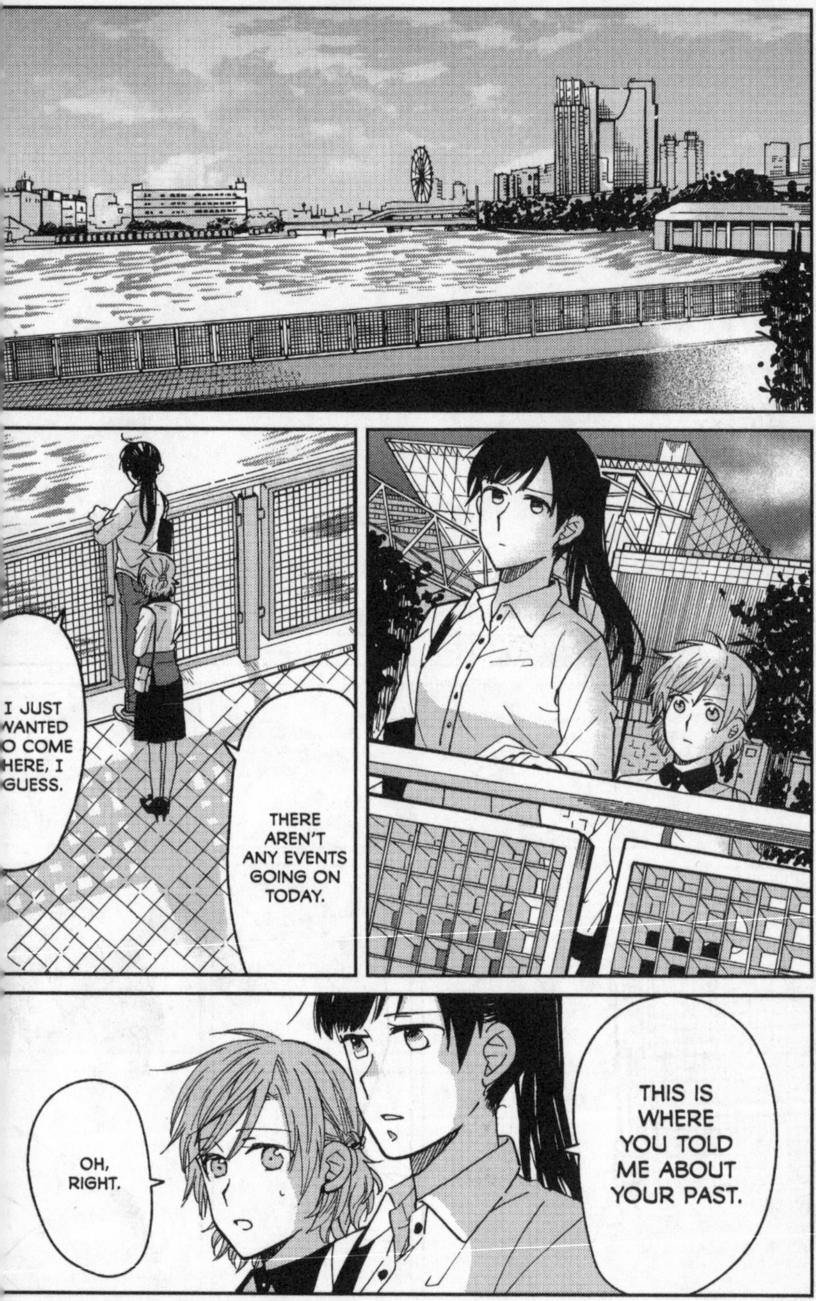
THERE AREN'T ANY EVENTS GOING ON TODAY.
I JUST WANTED O COME HERE, I GUESS.
THIS IS WHERE YOU TOLD ME ABOUT YOUR PAST.
OH, RIGHT.

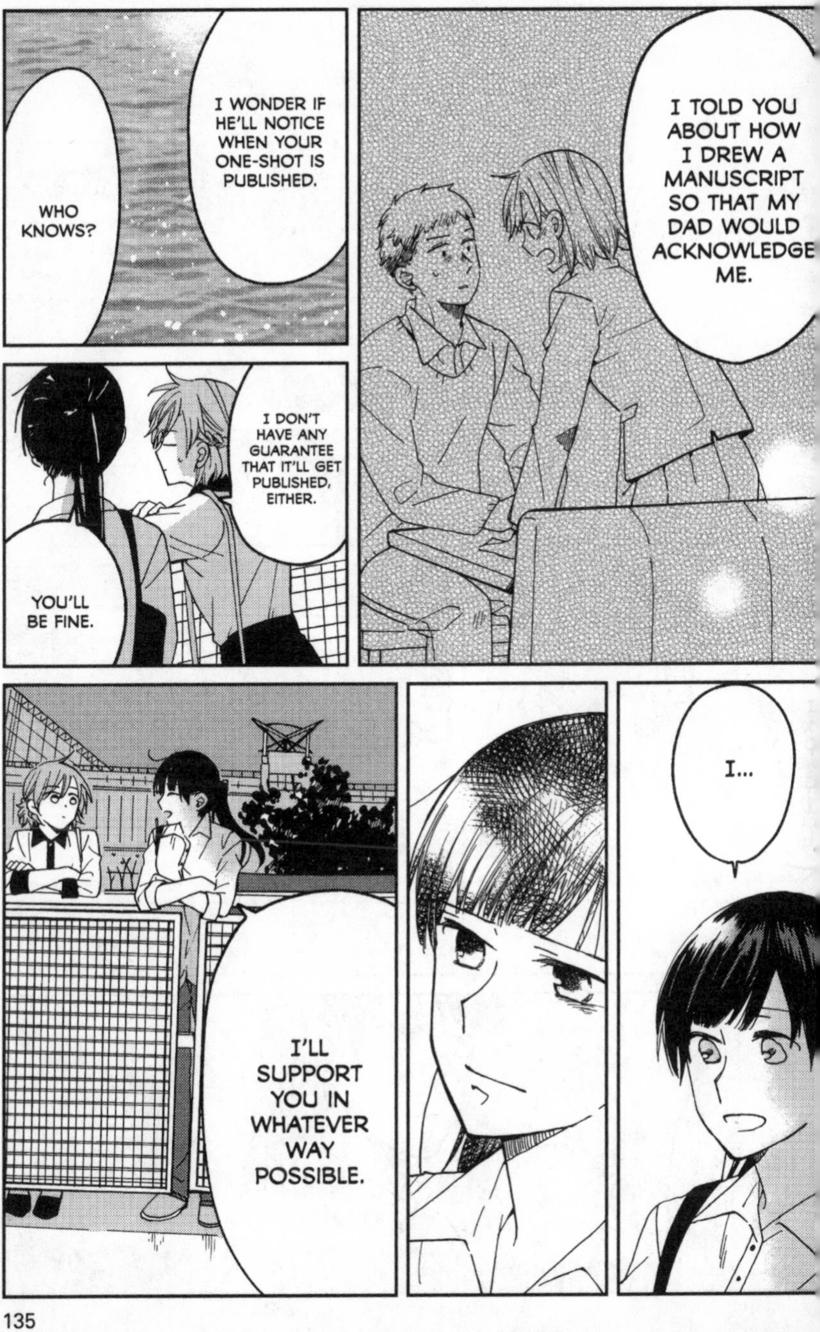
I TOLD YOU ABOUT HOW I DREW A MANUSCRIPT SO THAT MY DAD WOULD ACKNOWLEDGE ME.
I WONDER IF HE'LL NOTICE WHEN YOUR ONE-SHOT IS PUBLISHED.
WHO KNOWS?
I DON'T HAVE ANY GUARANTEE THAT IT'LL GET PUBLISHED, EITHER.
YOU'LL BE FINE.
I...
I'LL SUPPORT YOU IN WHATEVER WAY POSSIBLE.

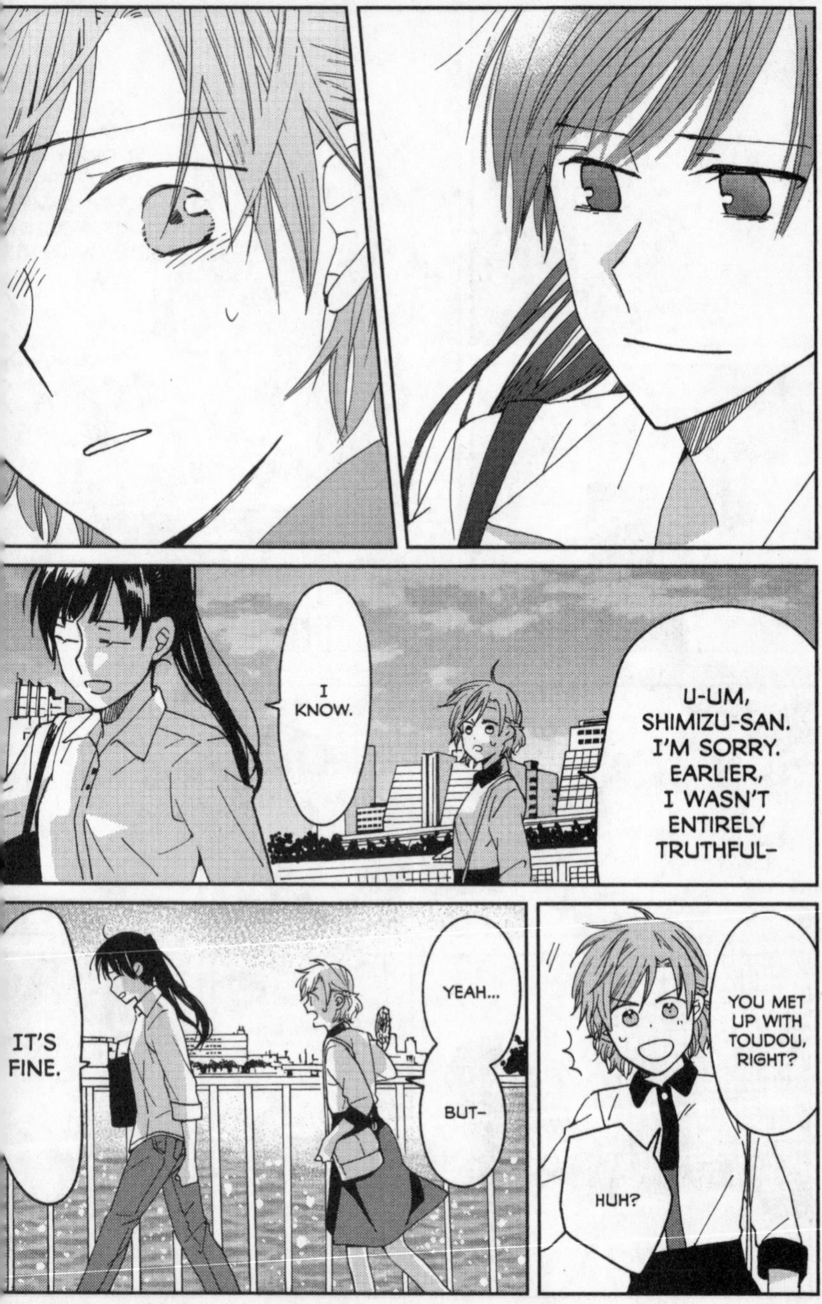
U-UM, SHIMIZU-SAN. I'M SORRY. EARLIER, I WASN'T ENTIRELY TRUTHFUL-
I KNOW.
YOU MET UP WITH TOUDOU, RIGHT?
HUH?
YEAH...
BUT-
IT'S FINE.

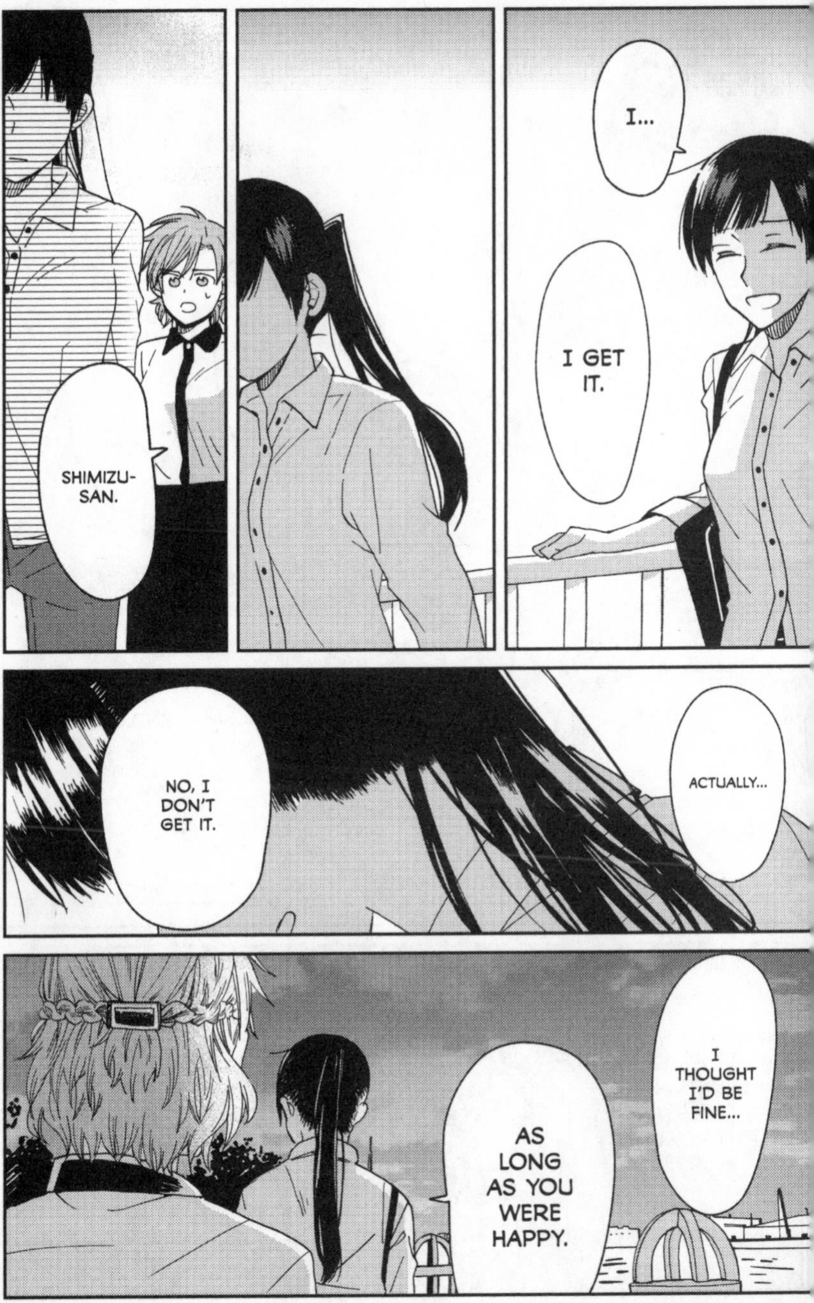
I...
I GET IT.
SHIMIZU-SAN.
ACTUALLY...
NO, I DON'T GET IT.
I THOUGHT I'D BE FINE...
AS LONG AS YOU WERE HAPPY.

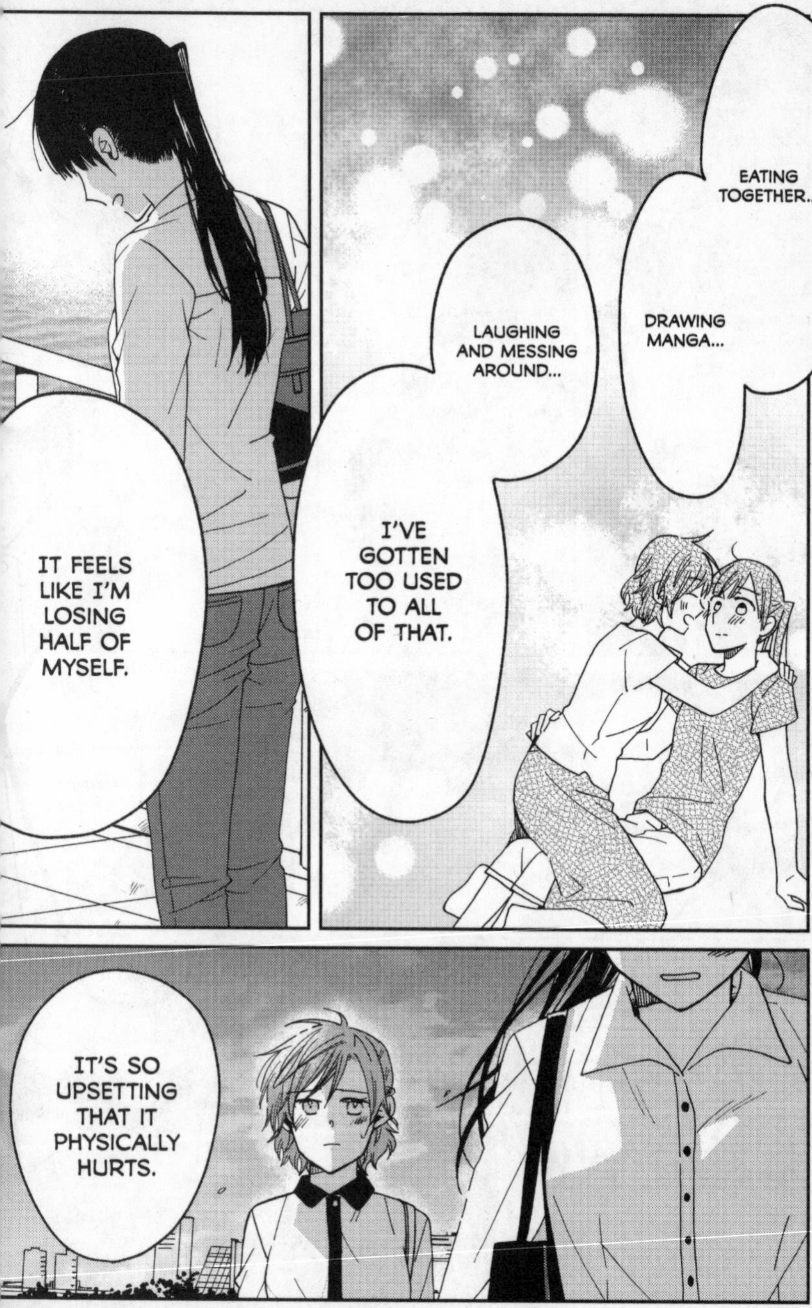
EATING TOGETHER...
DRAWING MANGA...
LAUGHING AND MESSING AROUND...
I'VE GOTTEN TOO USED TO ALL OF THAT.
IT FEELS LIKE I'M LOSING HALF OF MYSELF.
IT'S SO UPSETTING THAT IT PHYSICALLY HURTS.

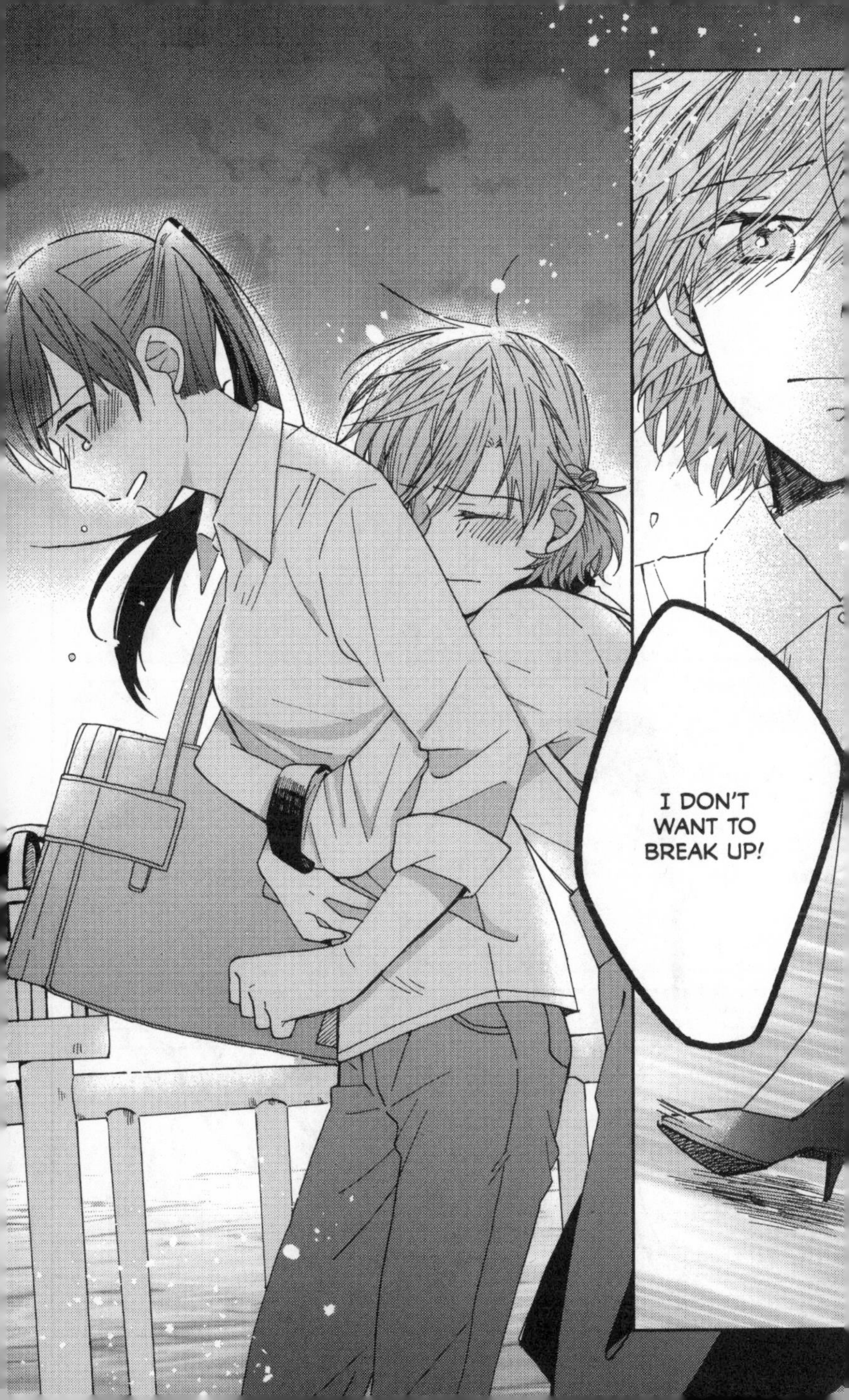
I DON'T WANT TO BREAK UP!

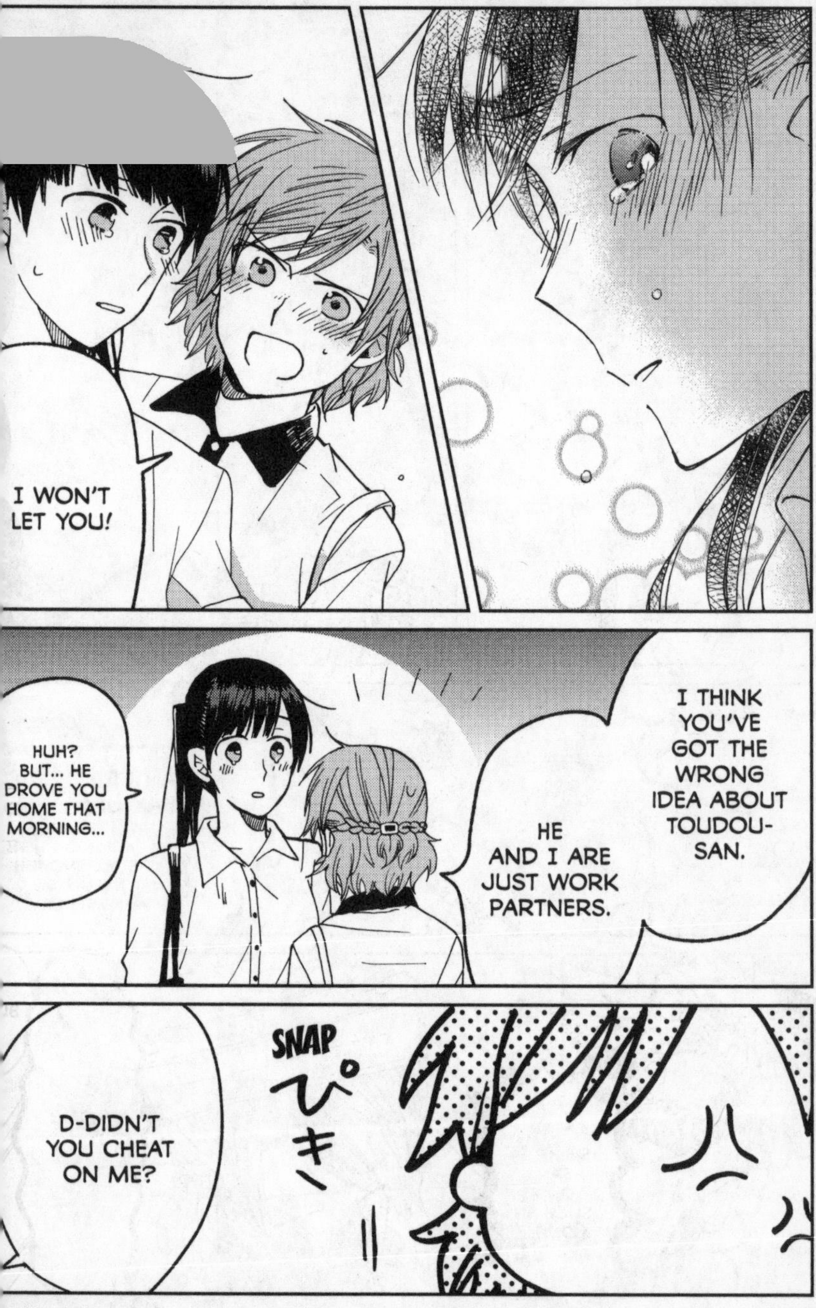
I WON'T LET YOU!
I THINK YOU'VE GOT THE WRONG IDEA ABOUT TOUDOU-SAN.
HE AND I ARE JUST WORK PARTNERS.
HUH? BUT... HE DROVE YOU HOME THAT MORNING...
SNAP
ぴき
D-DIDN'T YOU CHEAT ON ME?

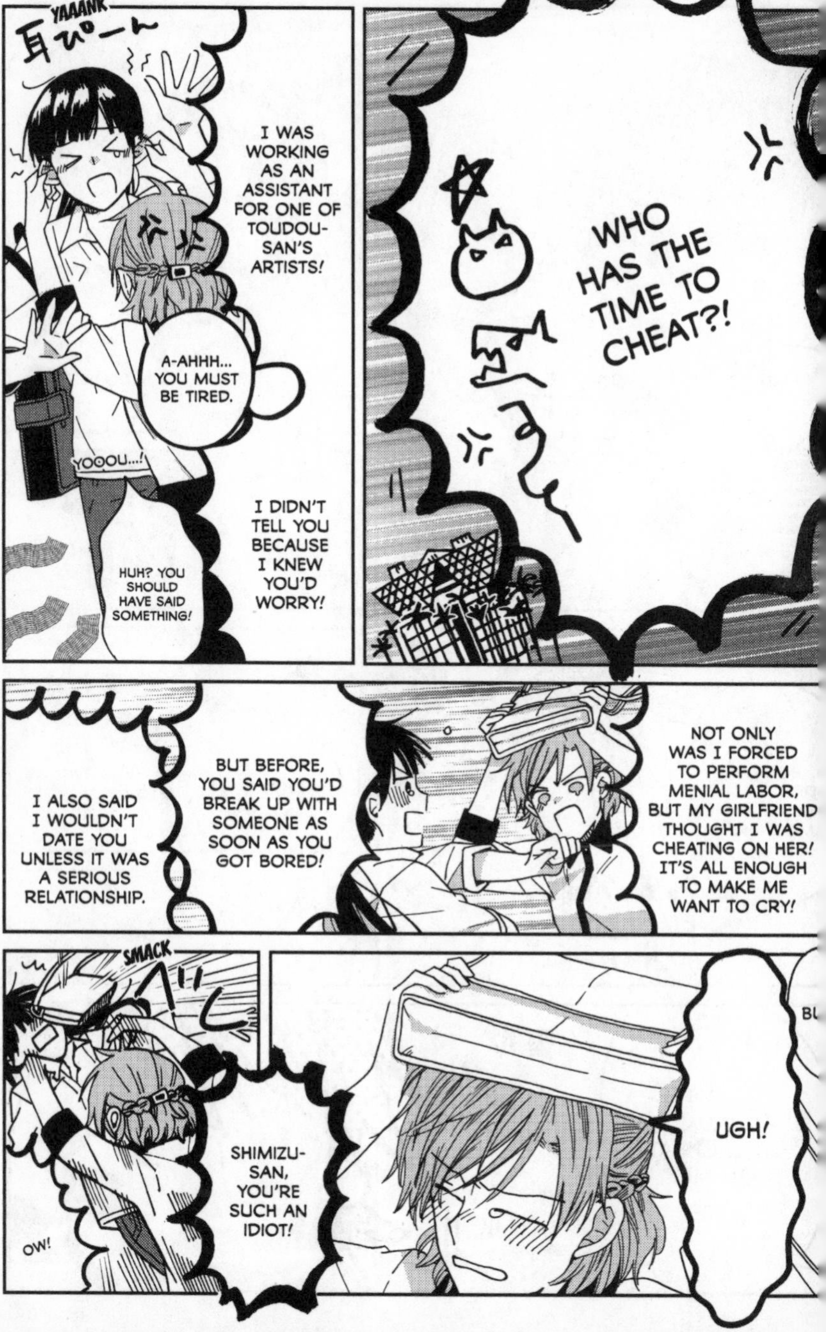
WHO HAS THE TIME TO CHEAT?!
YAAANK
耳ぴーん
I WAS WORKING AS AN ASSISTANT FOR ONE OF TOUDOU-SAN'S ARTISTS!
A-AHHH... YOU MUST BE TIRED.
YOOOU...!
I DIDN'T TELL YOU BECAUSE I KNEW YOU'D WORRY!
HUH? YOU SHOULD HAVE SAID SOMETHING!
NOT ONLY WAS I FORCED TO PERFORM MENIAL LABOR, BUT MY GIRLFRIEND THOUGHT I WAS CHEATING ON HER! IT'S ALL ENOUGH TO MAKE ME WANT TO CRY!
BUT BEFORE, YOU SAID YOU'D BREAK UP WITH SOMEONE AS SOON AS YOU GOT BORED!
I ALSO SAID I WOULDN'T DATE YOU UNLESS IT WAS A SERIOUS RELATIONSHIP.
UGH!
SMACK
SHIMIZU-SAN, YOU'RE SUCH AN IDIOT!
OW!

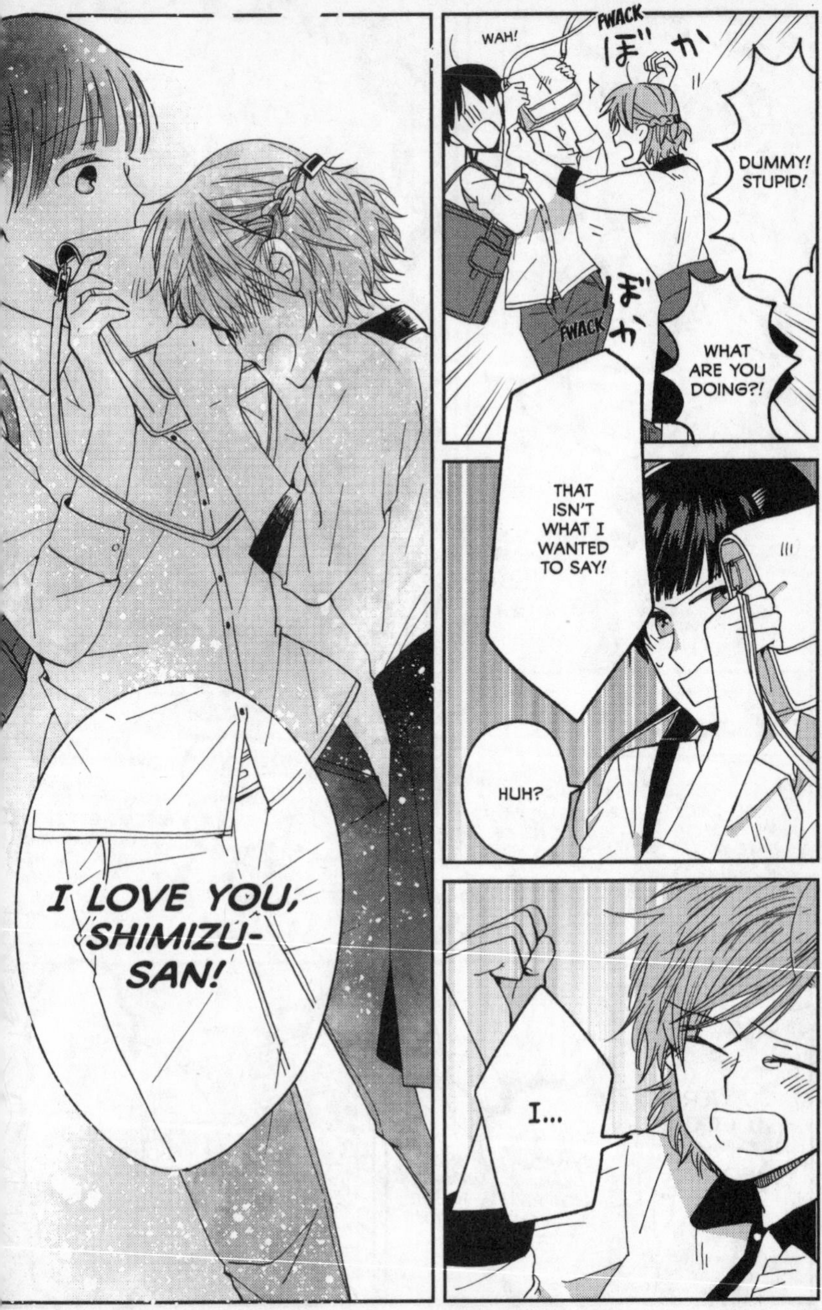
FWACK
ぼか
DUMMY! STUPID!
WAH!
FWACK
ぼか
WHAT ARE YOU DOING?!
THAT ISN'T WHAT I WANTED TO SAY!
HUH?
I...
I LOVE YOU, SHIMIZU-SAN!

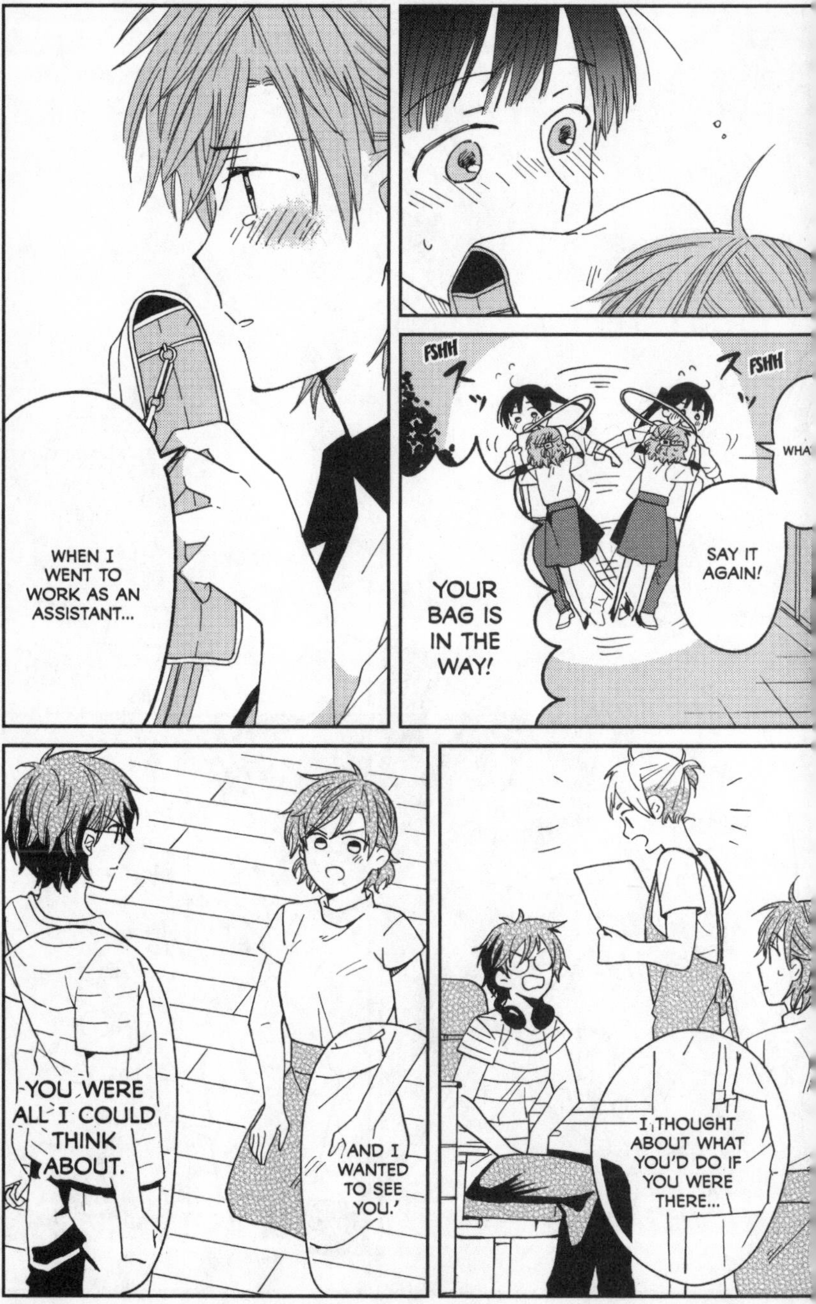
FSHH
ス ッ
FSHH
ス ッ
WHA
SAY IT AGAIN!
YOUR BAG IS IN THE WAY!
WHEN I WENT TO WORK AS AN ASSISTANT...
I THOUGHT ABOUT WHAT YOU'D DO IF YOU WERE THERE...
YOU WERE ALL I COULD THINK ABOUT.
AND I WANTED TO SEE YOU.'

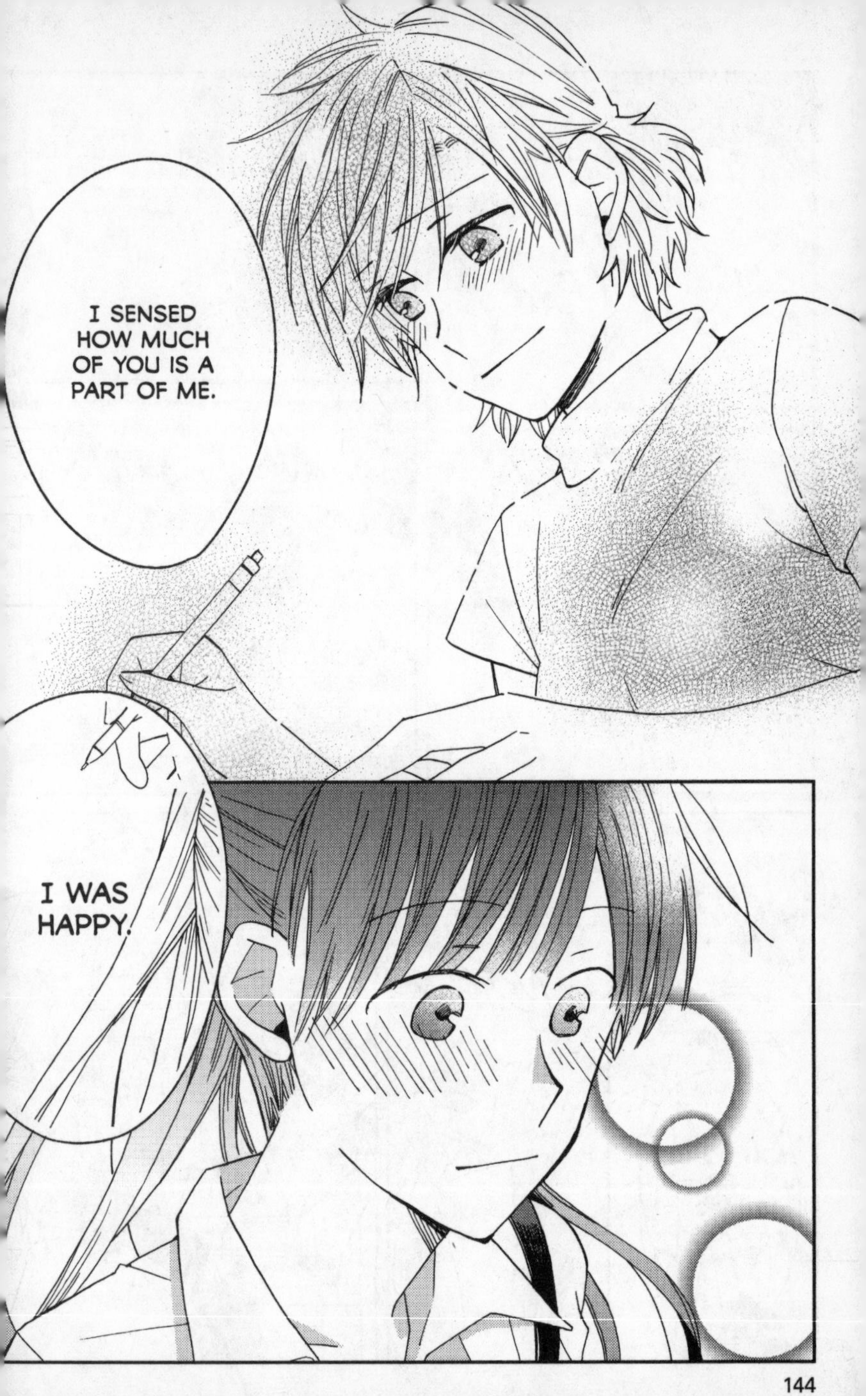
I SENSED HOW MUCH OF YOU IS A PART OF ME.
I WAS HAPPY.

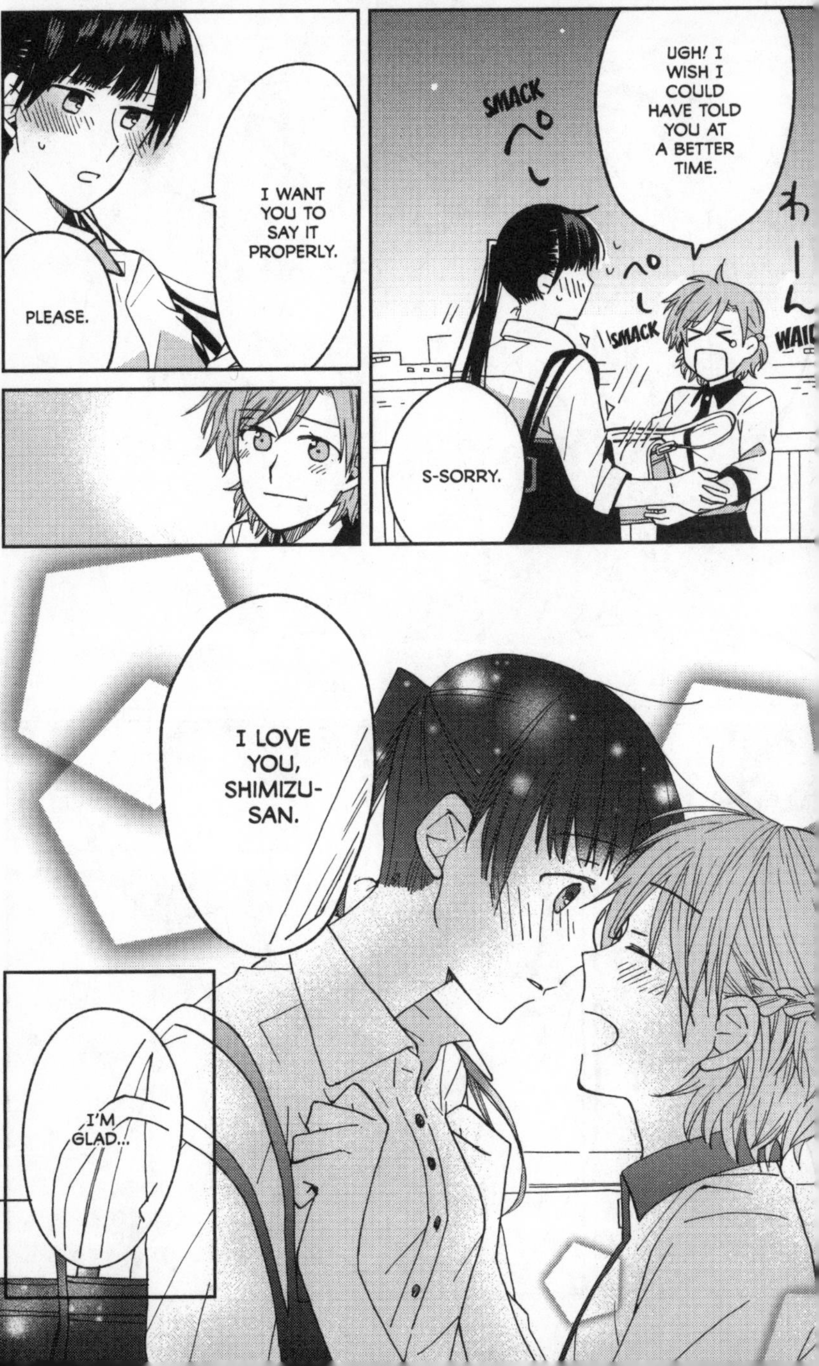
わーん
UGH! I WISH I COULD HAVE TOLD YOU AT A BETTER TIME.
SMACK
ぺし
ぺし
SMACK
S-SORRY.
I WANT YOU TO SAY IT PROPERLY.
PLEASE.
I LOVE YOU, SHIMIZU-SAN.
I'M GLAD...

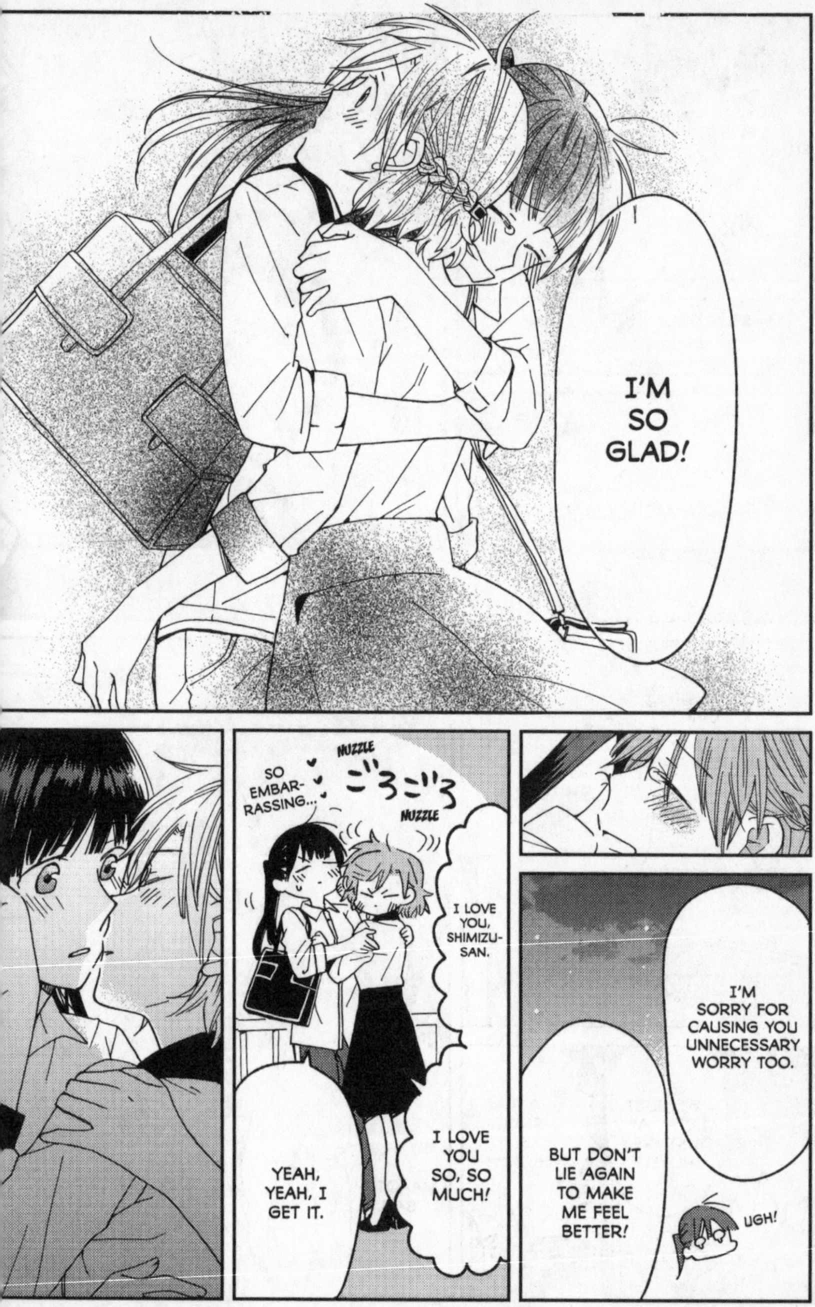
I'M SO GLAD!
I'M SORRY FOR CAUSING YOU UNNECESSARY WORRY TOO.
BUT DON'T LIE AGAIN TO MAKE ME FEEL BETTER!
UGH!
NUZZLE
ごろごろ
NUZZLE
SO EMBAR-RASSING...
I LOVE YOU, SHIMIZU-SAN.
I LOVE YOU SO, SO MUCH!
YEAH, YEAH, I GET IT.

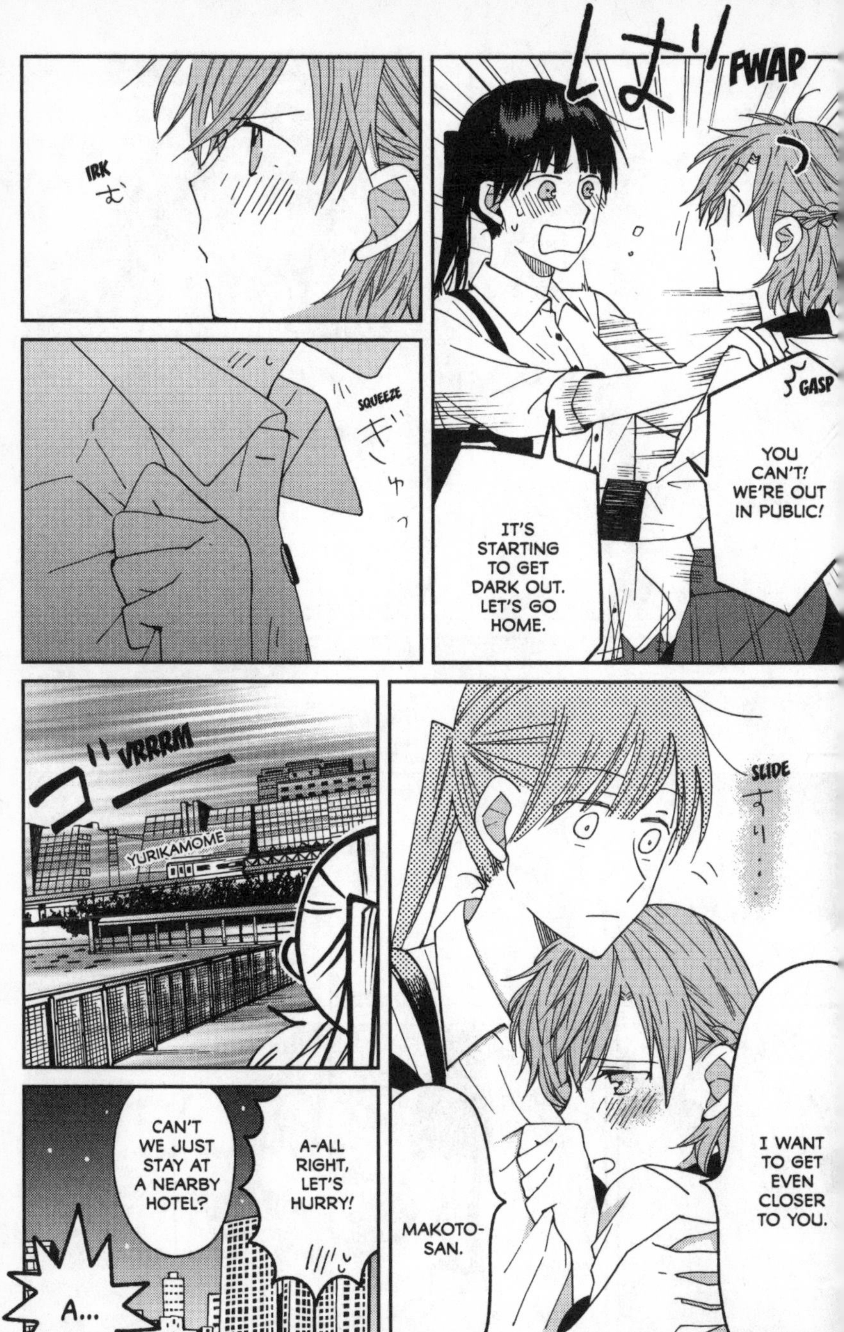
FWAP
GASP
YOU CAN'T! WE'RE OUT IN PUBLIC!
IT'S STARTING TO GET DARK OUT. LET'S GO HOME.
IRK
SQUEEZE
SLIDE
I WANT TO GET EVEN CLOSER TO YOU.
MAKOTO-SAN.
VRRRM
YURIKAMOME
CAN'T WE JUST STAY AT A NEARBY HOTEL?
A...
A-ALL RIGHT, LET'S HURRY!

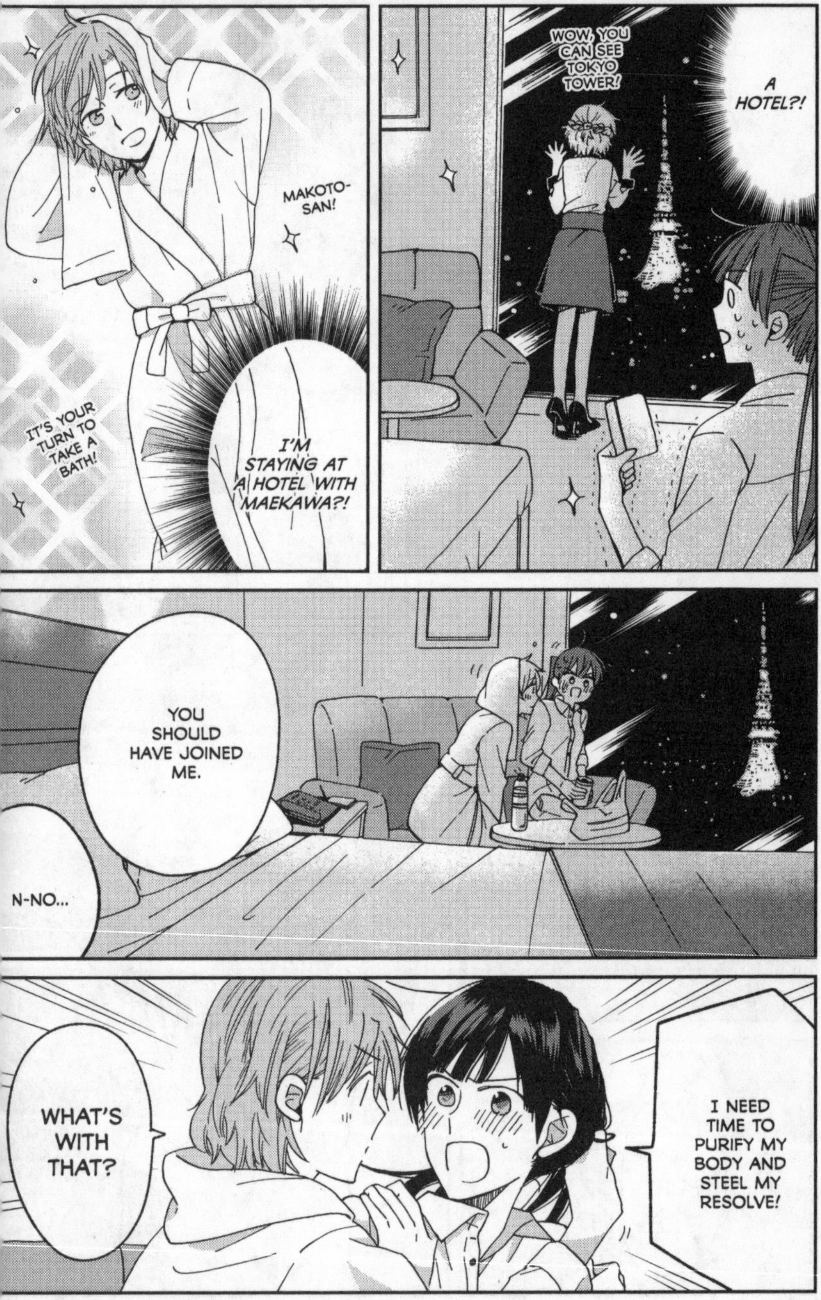
WOW, YOU CAN SEE TOKYO TOWER!
A HOTEL?!
MAKOTO-SAN!
IT'S YOUR TURN TO TAKE A BATH!
I'M STAYING AT A HOTEL WITH MAEKAWA?!
YOU SHOULD HAVE JOINED ME.
N-NO...
I NEED TIME TO PURIFY MY BODY AND STEEL MY RESOLVE!
WHAT'S WITH THAT?

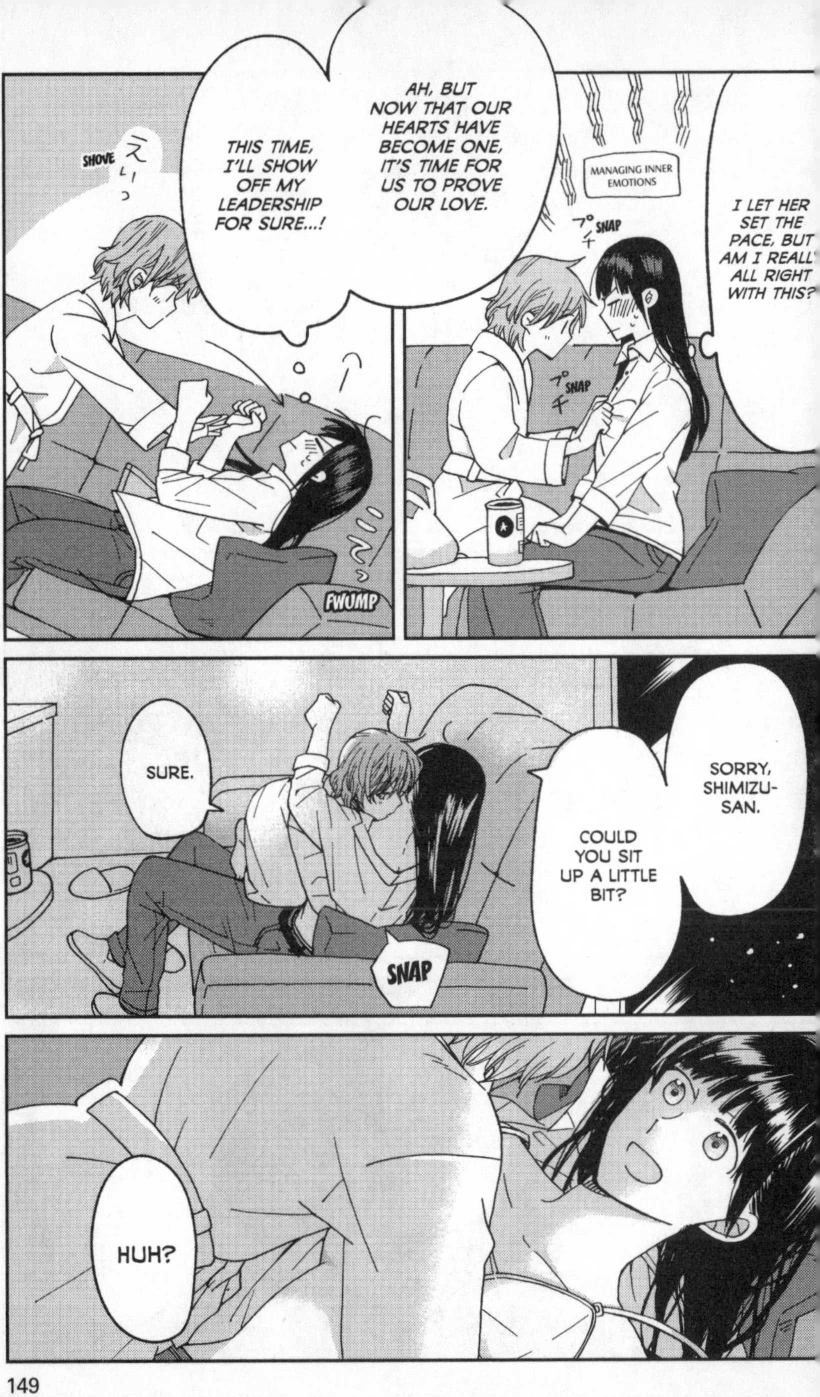
MANAGING INNER EMOTIONS
I LET HER SET THE PACE, BUT AM I REALL ALL RIGHT WITH THIS?
SNAP
SNAP
AH, BUT NOW THAT OUR HEARTS HAVE BECOME ONE, IT'S TIME FOR US TO PROVE OUR LOVE.
THIS TIME, I'LL SHOW OFF MY LEADERSHIP FOR SURE...!
SHOVE
FWUMP
SORRY, SHIMIZU-SAN.
COULD YOU SIT UP A LITTLE BIT?
SURE.
SNAP
HUH?

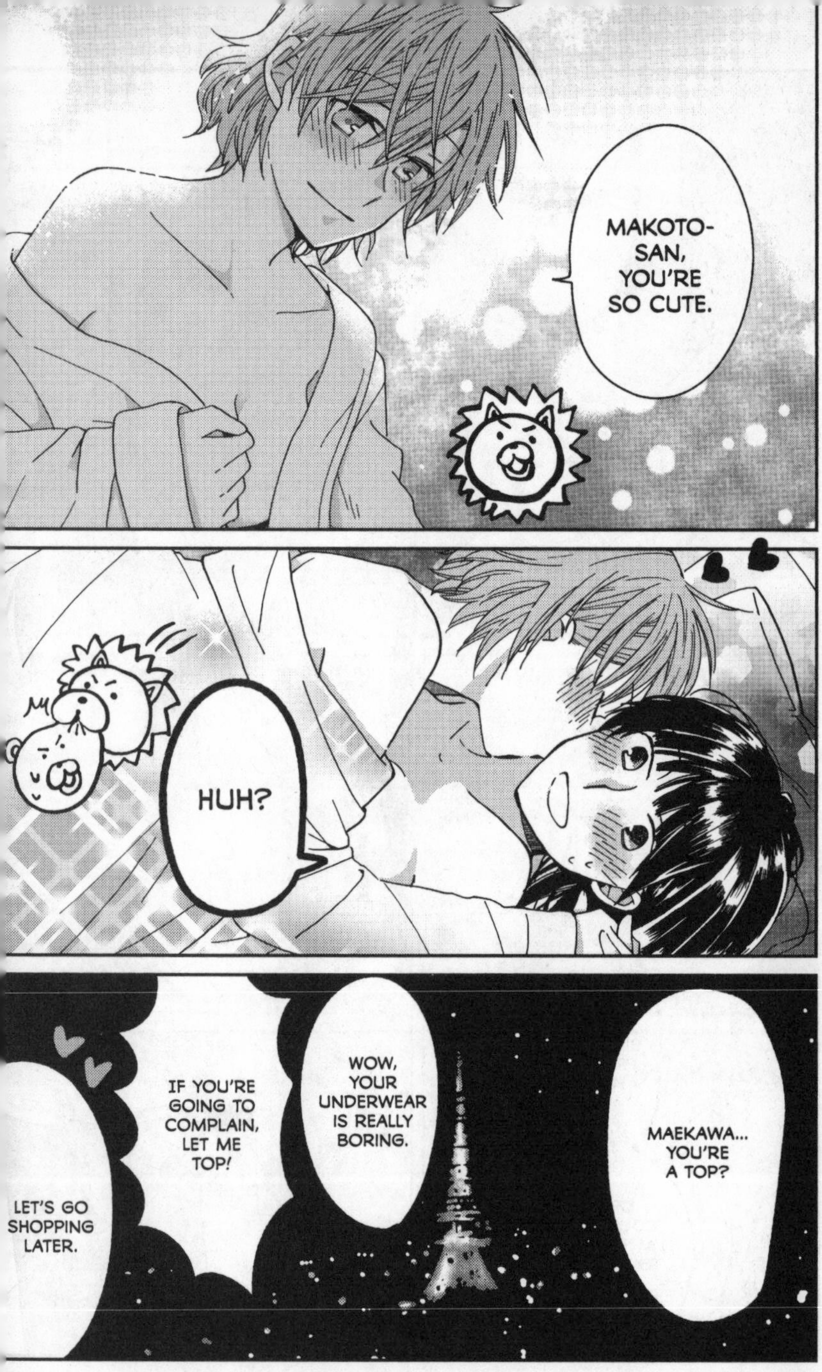
MAKOTO-SAN, YOU'RE SO CUTE.
HUH?
MAEKAWA... YOU'RE A TOP?
WOW, YOUR UNDERWEAR IS REALLY BORING.
IF YOU'RE GOING TO COMPLAIN, LET ME TOP!
LET'S GO SHOPPING LATER.

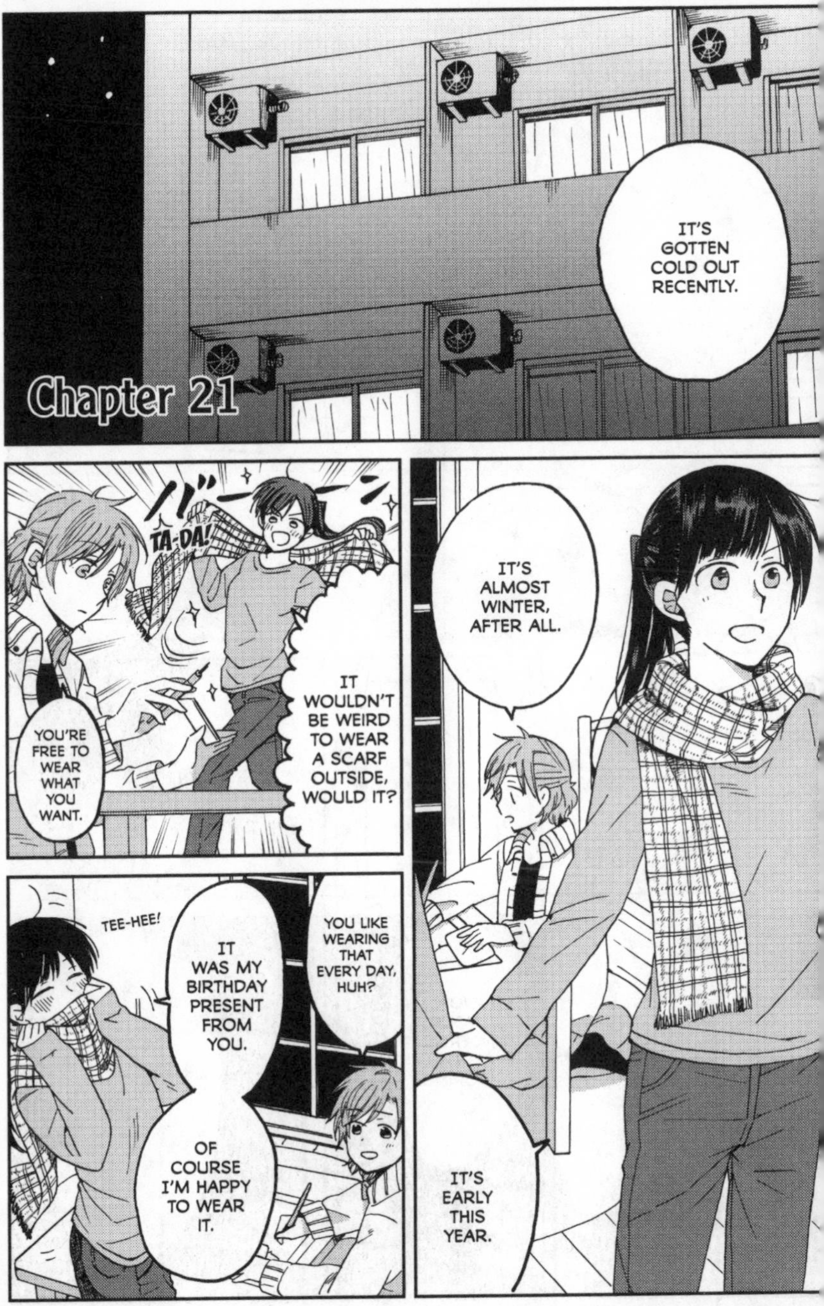
IT'S GOTTEN COLD OUT RECENTLY.
Chapter 21
IT'S ALMOST WINTER, AFTER ALL.
IT'S EARLY THIS YEAR.
IT WOULDN'T BE WEIRD TO WEAR A SCARF OUTSIDE, WOULD IT?
TA-DA!
YOU'RE FREE TO WEAR WHAT YOU WANT.
YOU LIKE WEARING THAT EVERY DAY, HUH?
IT WAS MY BIRTHDAY PRESENT FROM YOU.
TEE-HEE!
OF COURSE I'M HAPPY TO WEAR IT.

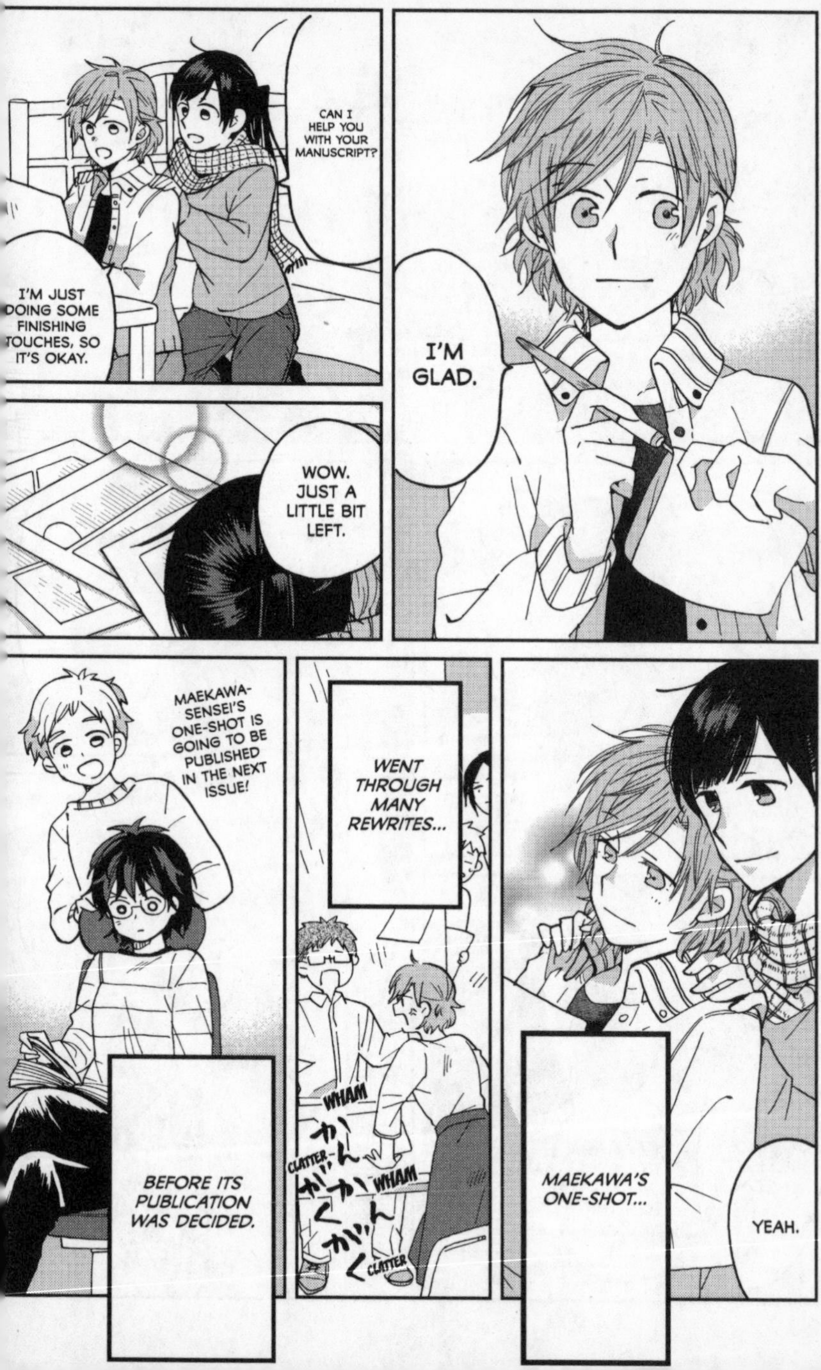
I'M GLAD.
CAN I HELP YOU WITH YOUR MANUSCRIPT?
I'M JUST DOING SOME FINISHING TOUCHES, SO IT'S OKAY.
WOW. JUST A LITTLE BIT LEFT.
MAEKAWA'S ONE-SHOT...
YEAH.
WENT THROUGH MANY REWRITES...
WHAM
CLATTER
WHAM
CLATTER
MAEKAWA-SENSEI'S ONE-SHOT IS GOING TO BE PUBLISHED IN THE NEXT ISSUE!
BEFORE ITS PUBLICATION WAS DECIDED.

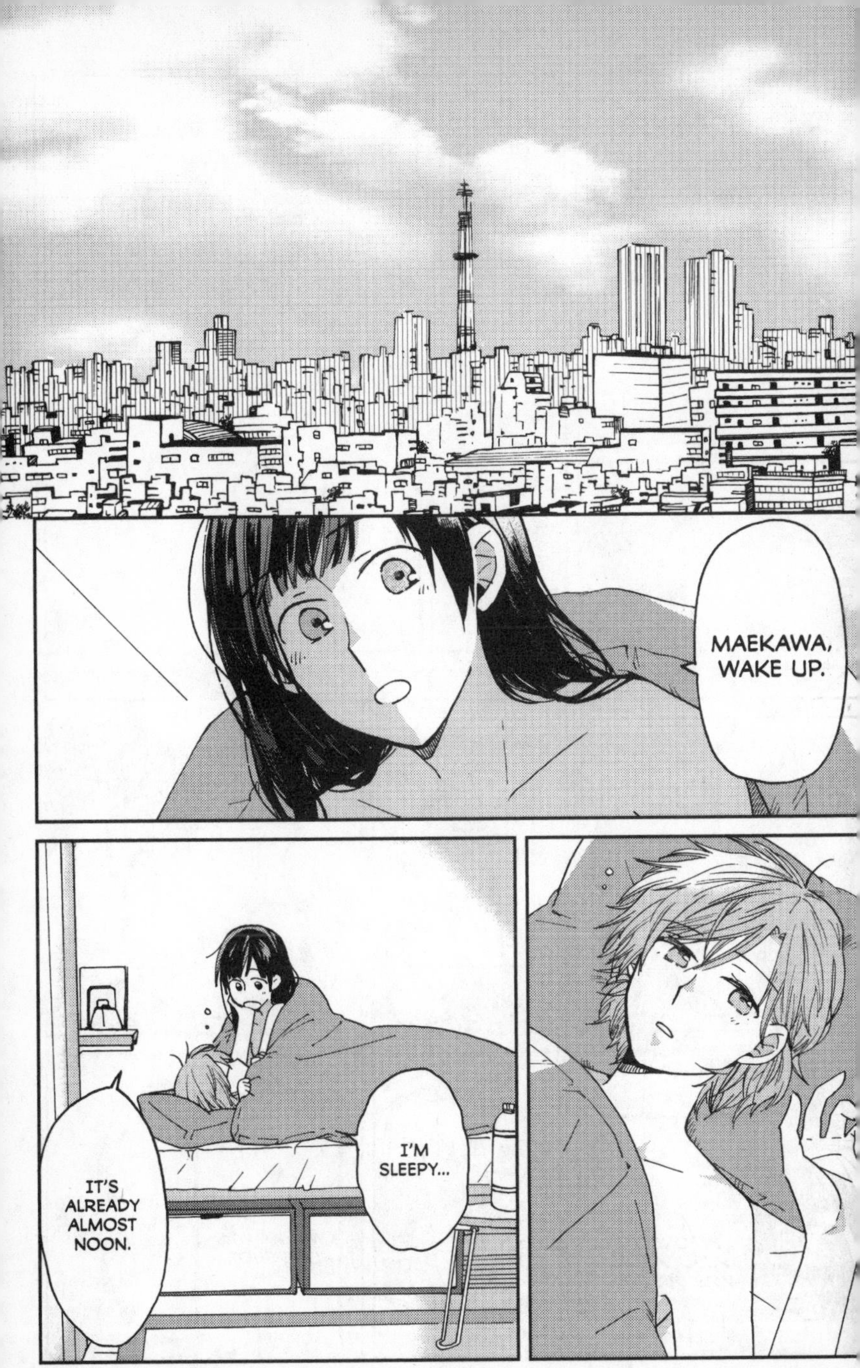
MAEKAWA, WAKE UP.
I'M SLEEPY...
IT'S ALREADY ALMOST NOON.

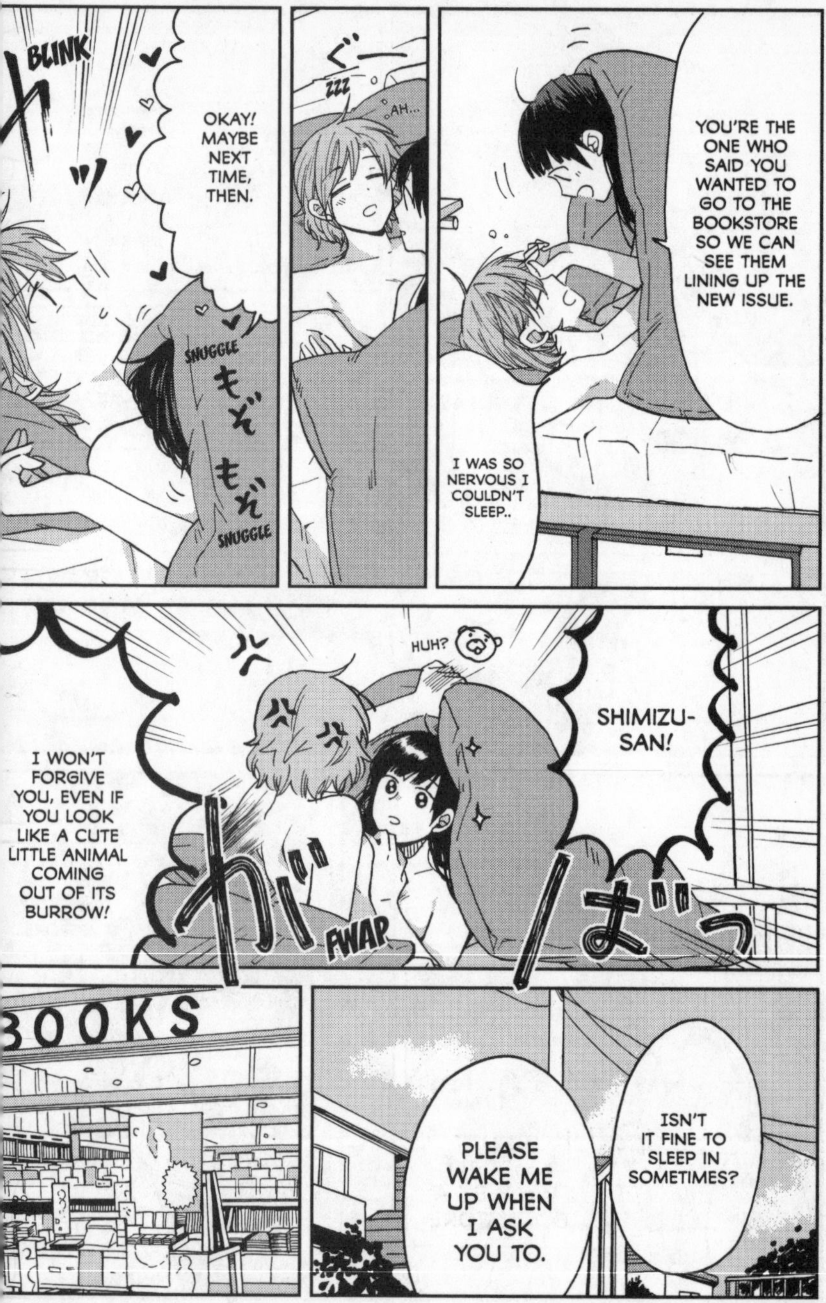
YOU'RE THE ONE WHO SAID YOU WANTED TO GO TO THE BOOKSTORE SO WE CAN SEE THEM LINING UP THE NEW ISSUE.
I WAS SO NERVOUS I COULDN'T SLEEP..
ぐー
ZZZ
AH...
BLINK
OKAY! MAYBE NEXT TIME, THEN.
SNUGGLE
もぞもぞ
SNUGGLE
SHIMIZU-SAN!
HUH?
I WON'T FORGIVE YOU, EVEN IF YOU LOOK LIKE A CUTE LITTLE ANIMAL COMING OUT OF ITS BURROW!
がばっ
FWAP
ISN'T IT FINE TO SLEEP IN SOMETIMES?
PLEASE WAKE ME UP WHEN I ASK YOU TO.
BOOKS

IT'S GOING ON SALE IN BOOKSTORES AROUND THE COUNTRY, RIGHT?

DON'T TEASE ME.

THAT'S PRETTY AMAZING, MAEKAWA-SENSEI.

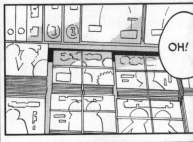

OH!

HERE IT IS!

IT HURT JUST TO WALK BY A BOOKSTORE.

BUT NOW...

BEFORE...

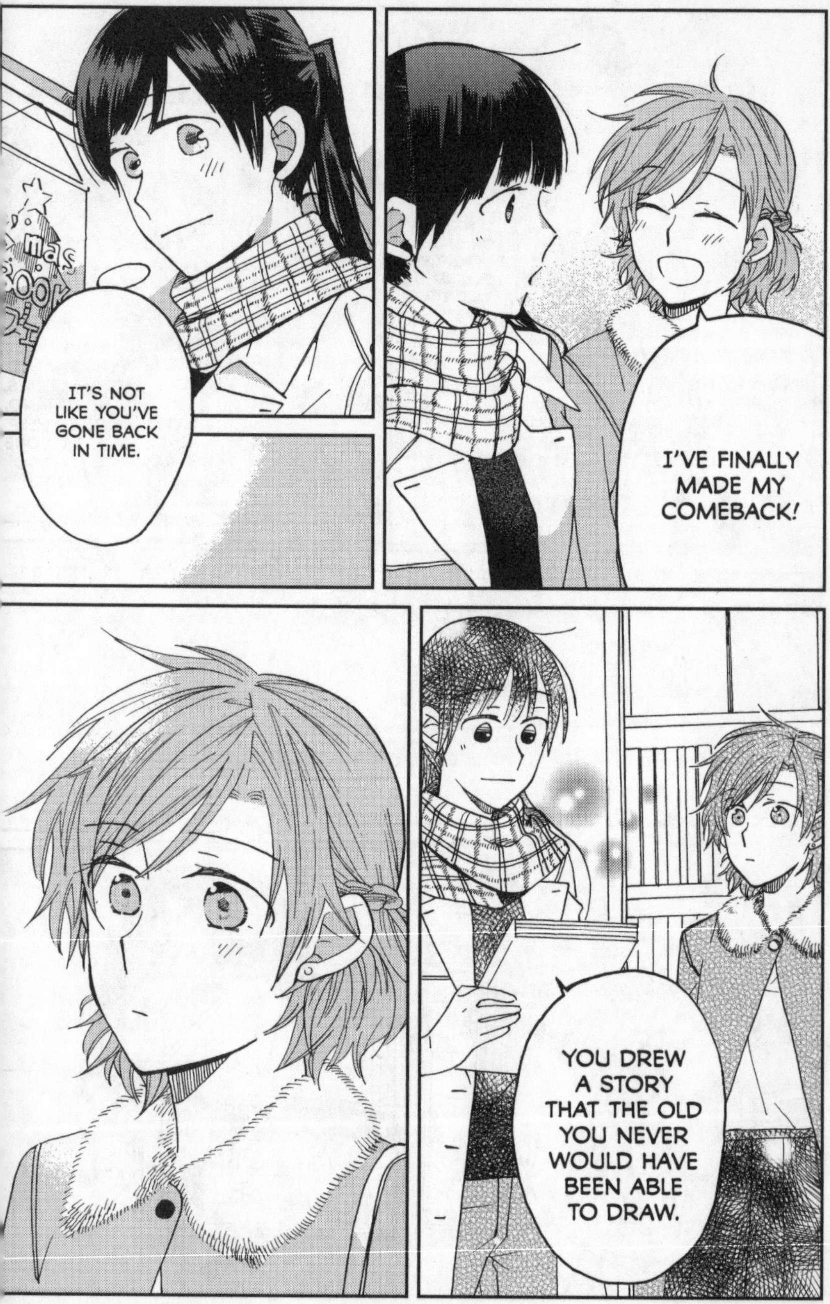
I'VE FINALLY MADE MY COMEBACK!
IT'S NOT LIKE YOU'VE GONE BACK IN TIME.
YOU DREW A STORY THAT THE OLD YOU NEVER WOULD HAVE BEEN ABLE TO DRAW.

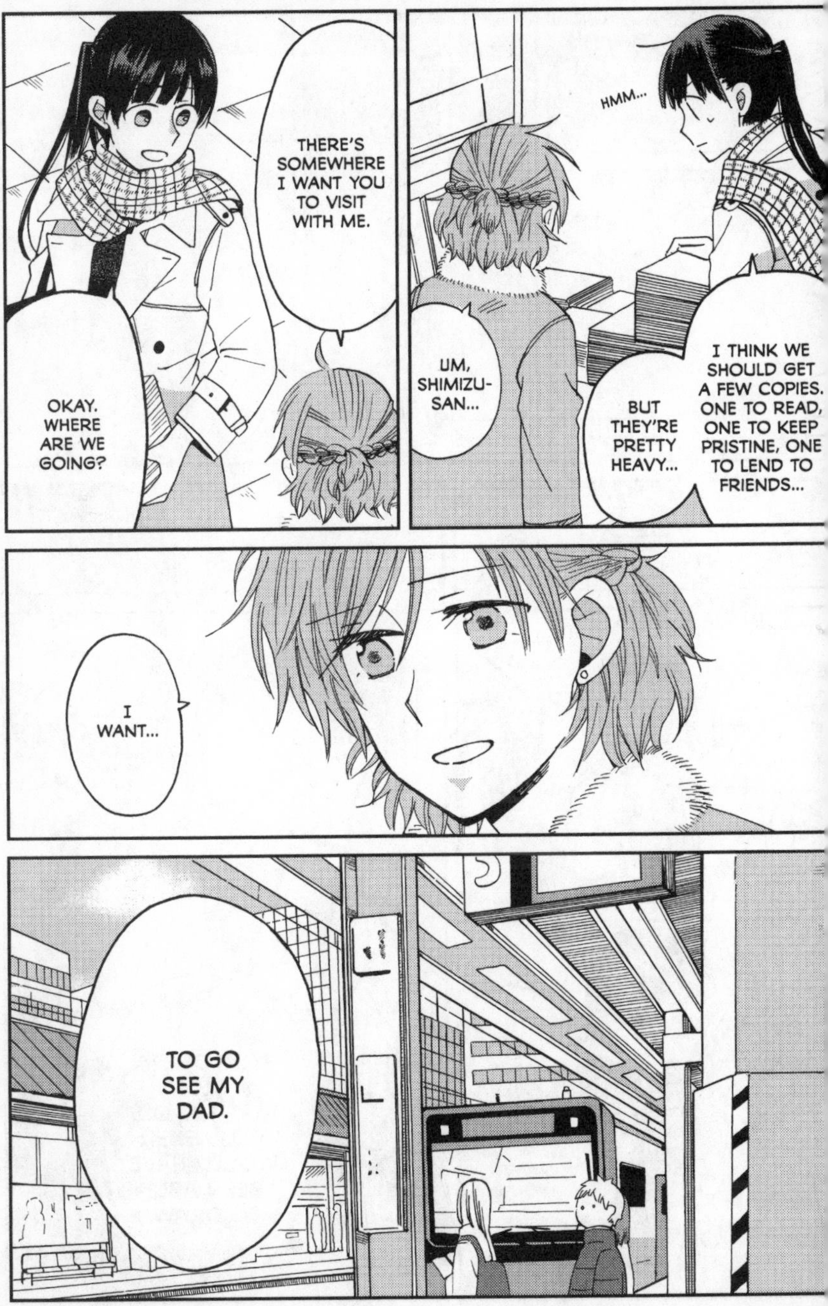
HMM...
I THINK WE SHOULD GET A FEW COPIES. ONE TO READ, ONE TO KEEP PRISTINE, ONE TO LEND TO FRIENDS...
BUT THEY'RE PRETTY HEAVY...
UM, SHIMIZU-SAN...
THERE'S SOMEWHERE I WANT YOU TO VISIT WITH ME.
OKAY. WHERE ARE WE GOING?
I WANT...
TO GO SEE MY DAD.

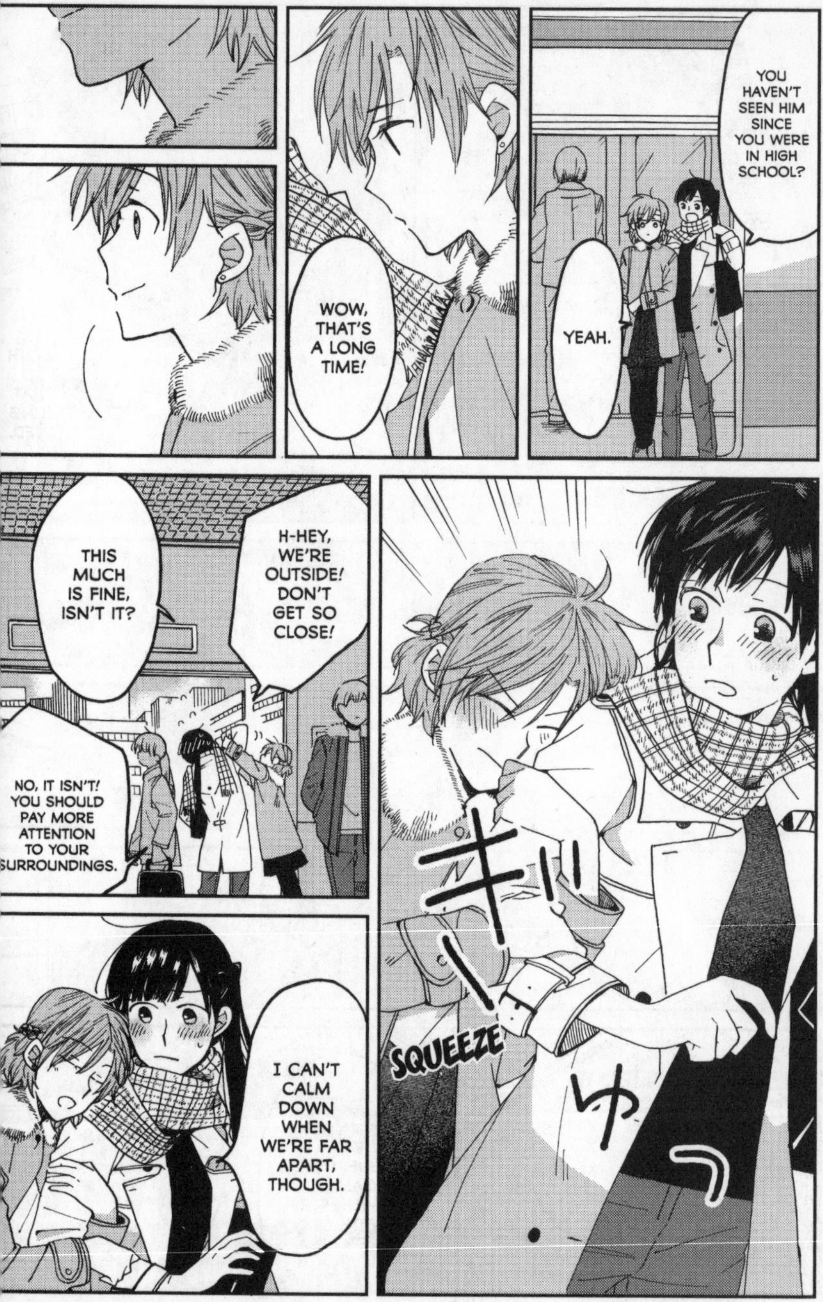
YOU HAVEN'T SEEN HIM SINCE YOU WERE IN HIGH SCHOOL?
YEAH.
WOW, THAT'S A LONG TIME!
SQUEEZE
H-HEY, WE'RE OUTSIDE! DON'T GET SO CLOSE!
THIS MUCH IS FINE, ISN'T IT?
NO, IT ISN'T! YOU SHOULD PAY MORE ATTENTION TO YOUR SURROUNDINGS.
I CAN'T CALM DOWN WHEN WE'RE FAR APART, THOUGH.

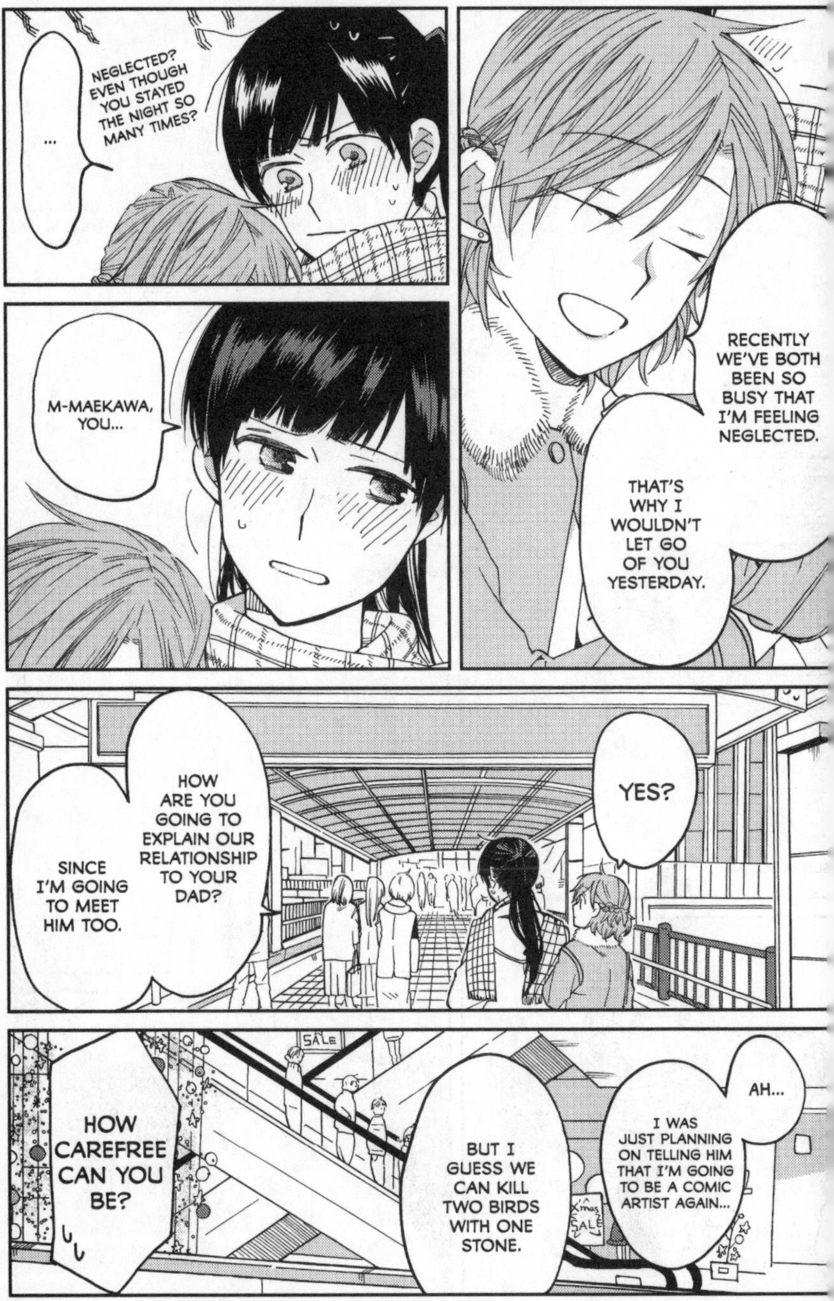
RECENTLY WE'VE BOTH BEEN SO BUSY THAT I'M FEELING NEGLECTED.
THAT'S WHY I WOULDN'T LET GO OF YOU YESTERDAY.
NEGLECTED? EVEN THOUGH YOU STAYED THE NIGHT SO MANY TIMES?
...
M-MAEKAWA, YOU...
YES?
HOW ARE YOU GOING TO EXPLAIN OUR RELATIONSHIP TO YOUR DAD?
SINCE I'M GOING TO MEET HIM TOO.
SALE
AH...
I WAS JUST PLANNING ON TELLING HIM THAT I'M GOING TO BE A COMIC ARTIST AGAIN...
X'mas SALE
BUT I GUESS WE CAN KILL TWO BIRDS WITH ONE STONE.
HOW CAREFREE CAN YOU BE?

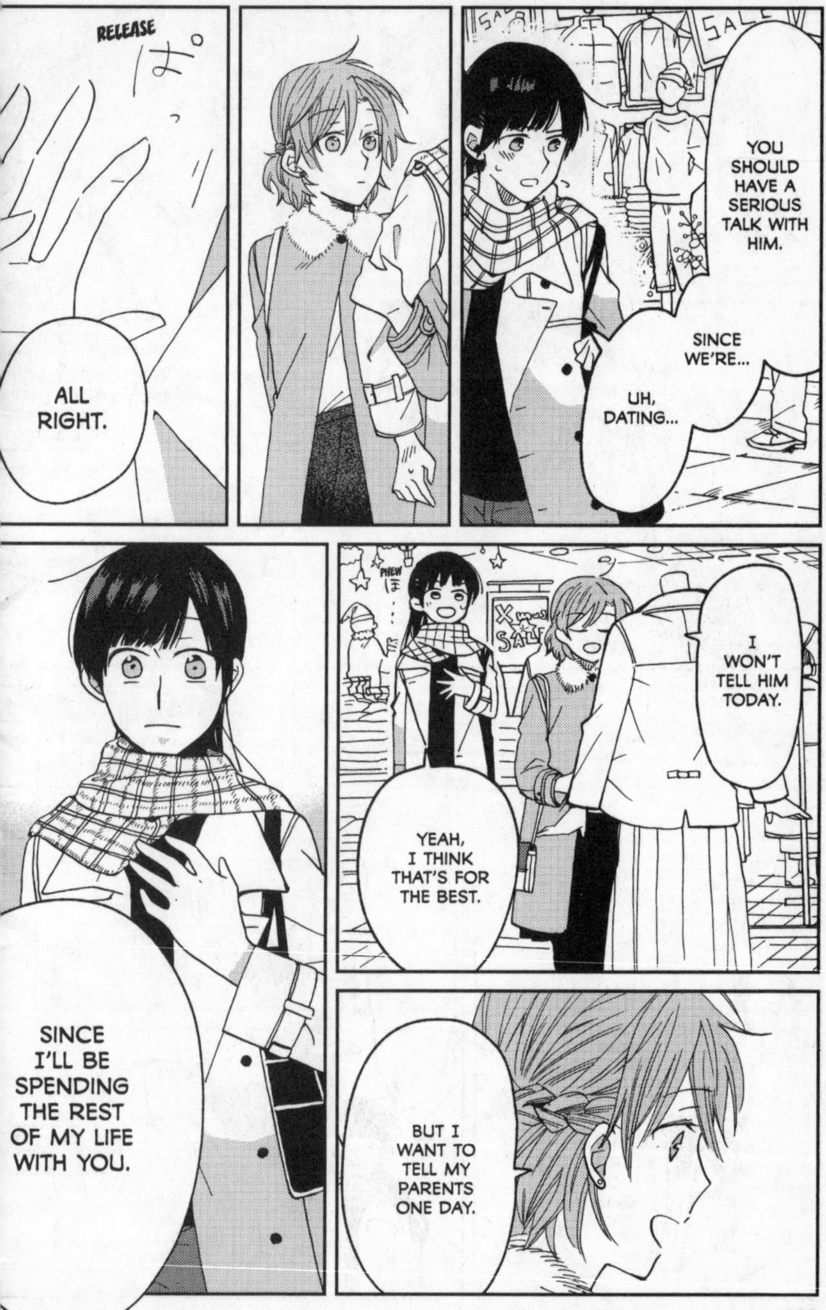
YOU SHOULD HAVE A SERIOUS TALK WITH HIM.
SINCE WE'RE...
UH, DATING...
RELEASE
ぱっ
ALL RIGHT.
PHEW
ほ
I WON'T TELL HIM TODAY.
YEAH, I THINK THAT'S FOR THE BEST.
BUT I WANT TO TELL MY PARENTS ONE DAY.
SINCE I'LL BE SPENDING THE REST OF MY LIFE WITH YOU.

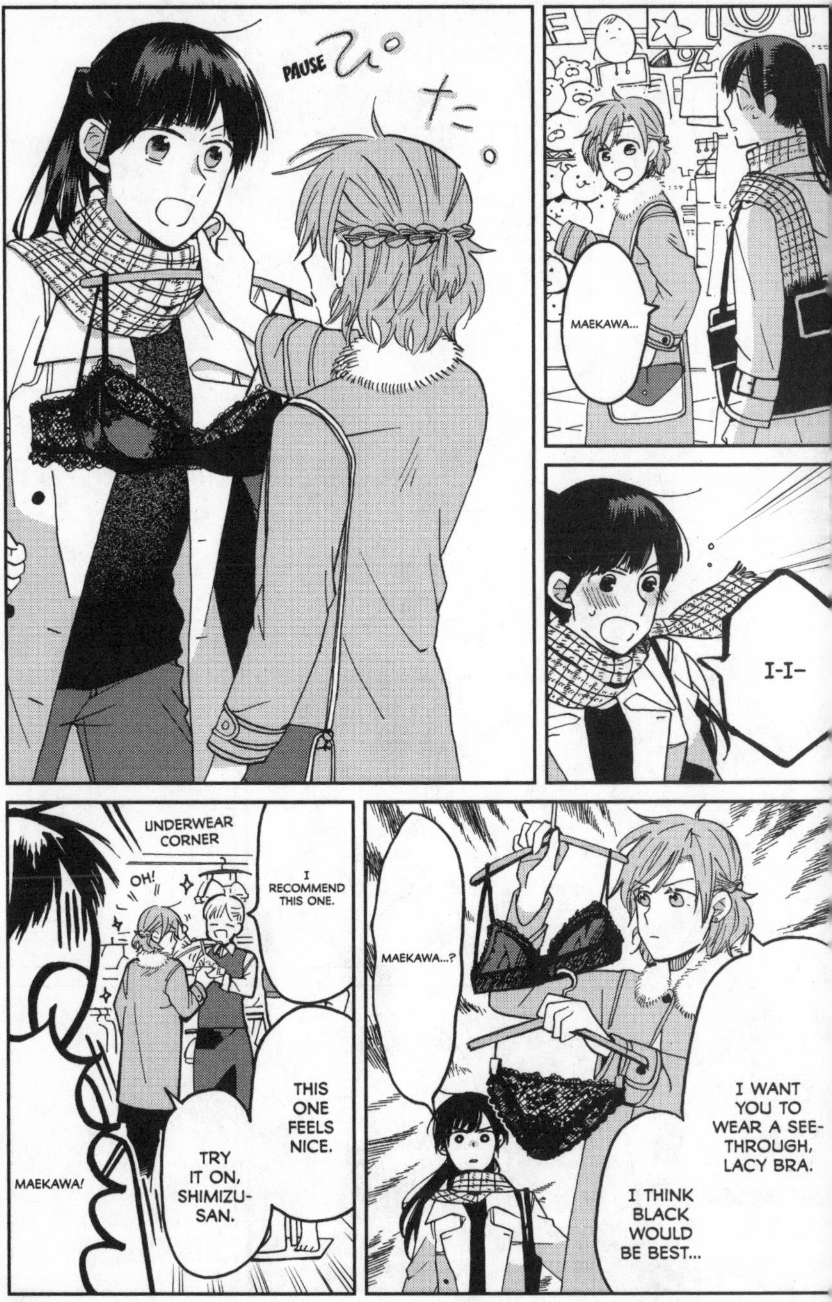
MAEKAWA...
I-I-
PAUSE
MAEKAWA...?
I WANT YOU TO WEAR A SEE-THROUGH, LACY BRA.
I THINK BLACK WOULD BE BEST...
UNDERWEAR CORNER
I RECOMMEND THIS ONE.
OH!
THIS ONE FEELS NICE.
TRY IT ON, SHIMIZU-SAN.
MAEKAWA!

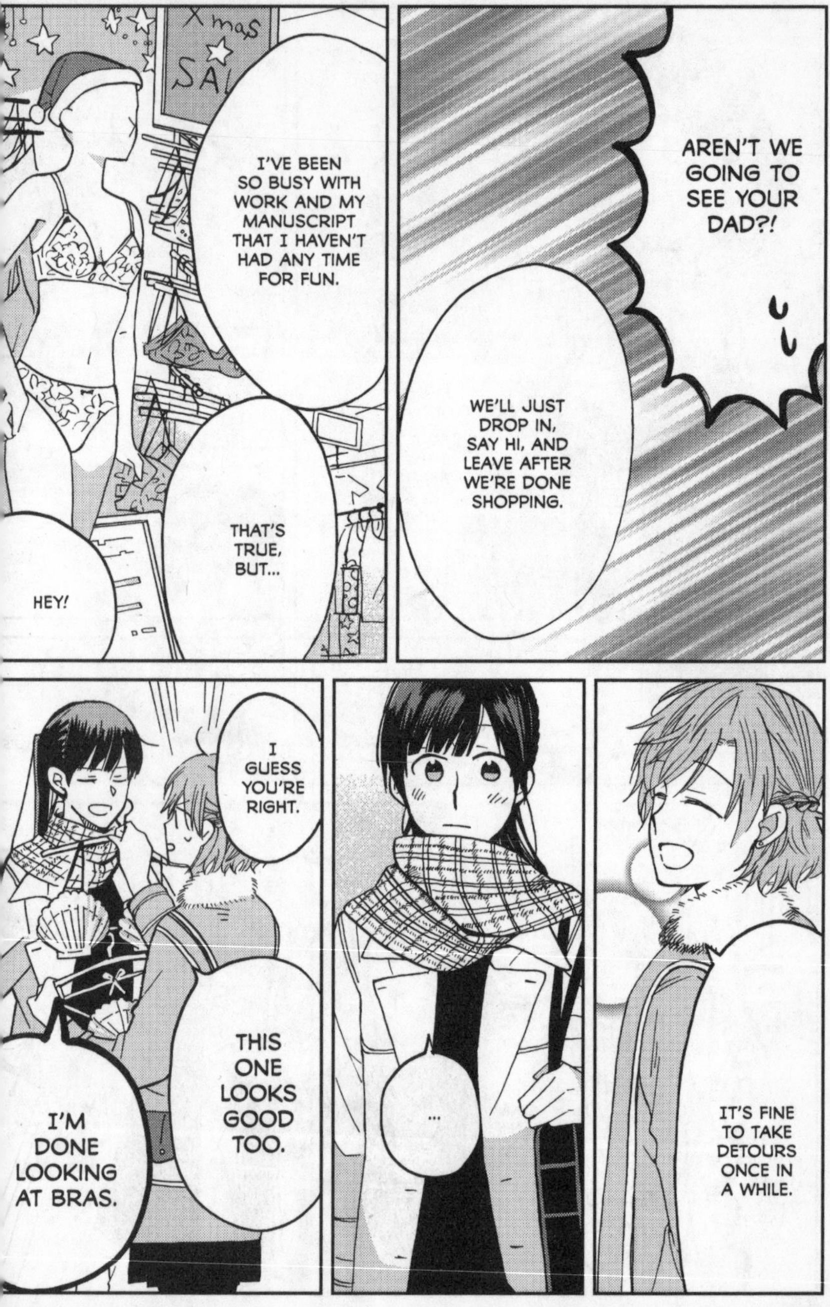
AREN'T WE GOING TO SEE YOUR DAD?!
WE'LL JUST DROP IN, SAY HI, AND LEAVE AFTER WE'RE DONE SHOPPING.
I'VE BEEN SO BUSY WITH WORK AND MY MANUSCRIPT THAT I HAVEN'T HAD ANY TIME FOR FUN.
THAT'S TRUE, BUT...
HEY!
IT'S FINE TO TAKE DETOURS ONCE IN A WHILE.
...
I GUESS YOU'RE RIGHT.
THIS ONE LOOKS GOOD TOO.
I'M DONE LOOKING AT BRAS.

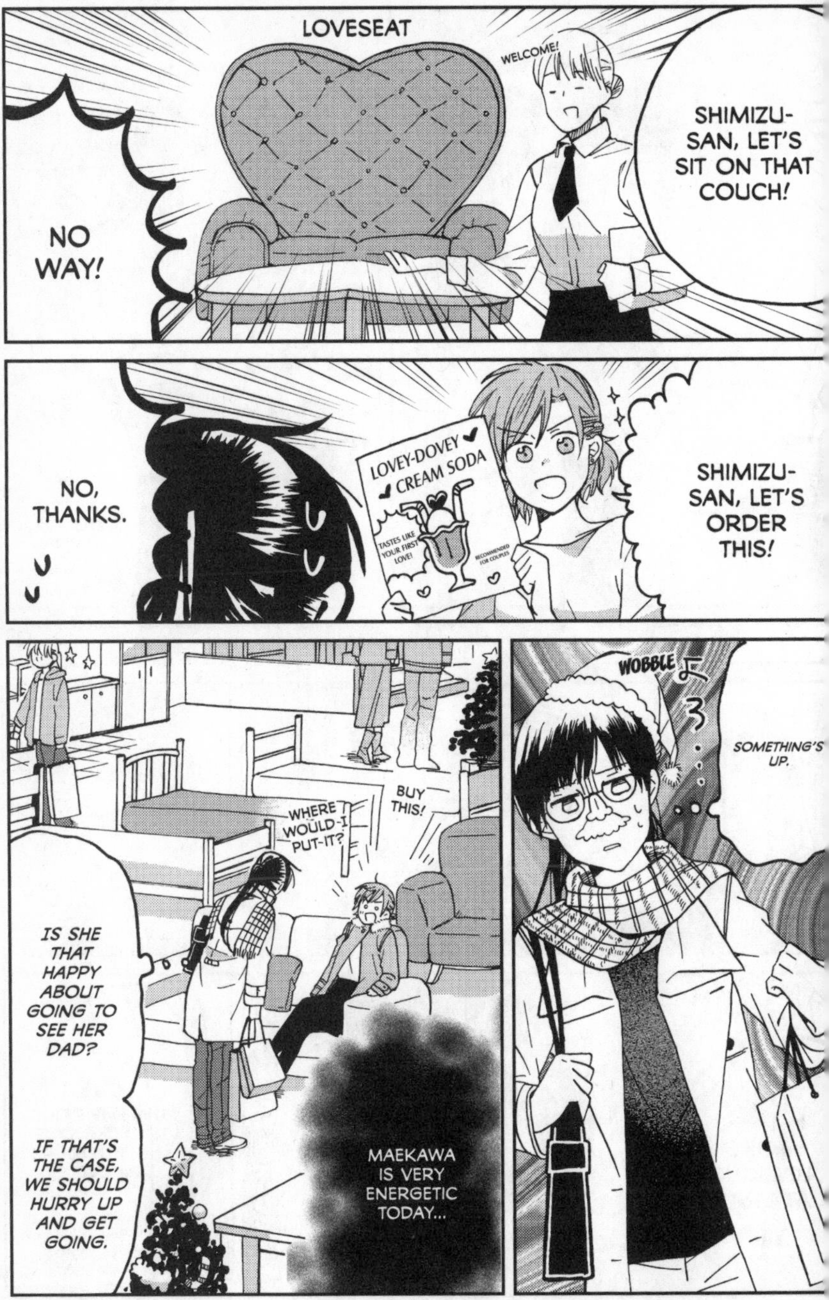
SHIMIZU-SAN, LET'S SIT ON THAT COUCH!
WELCOME!
LOVESEAT
NO WAY!
SHIMIZU-SAN, LET'S ORDER THIS!
LOVEY-DOVEY CREAM SODA
TASTES LIKE YOUR FIRST LOVE!
RECOMMENDED FOR COUPLES
NO, THANKS.
WOBBLE
SOMETHING'S UP.
BUY THIS!
WHERE WOULD I PUT IT?
MAEKAWA IS VERY ENERGETIC TODAY...
IS SHE THAT HAPPY ABOUT GOING TO SEE HER DAD?
IF THAT'S THE CASE, WE SHOULD HURRY UP AND GET GOING.

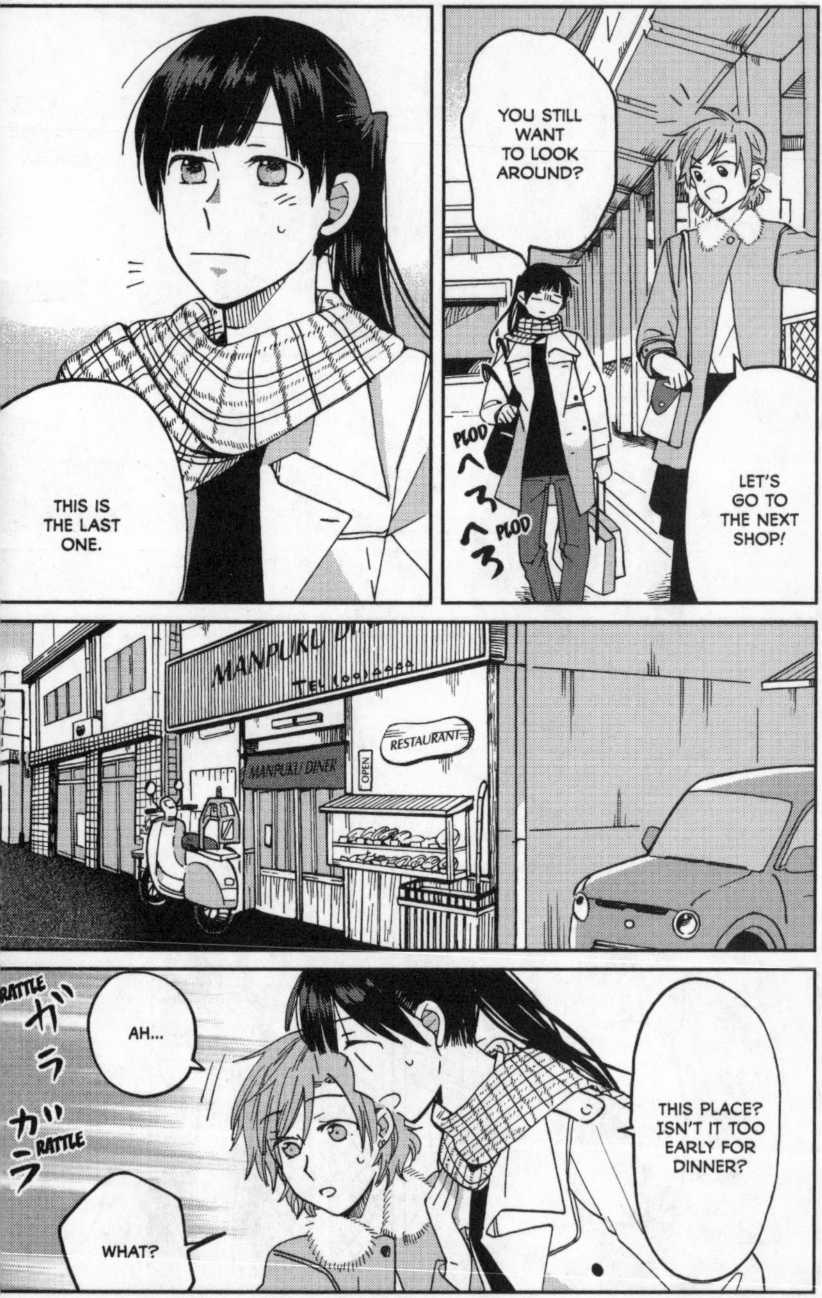
YOU STILL WANT TO LOOK AROUND?
LET'S GO TO THE NEXT SHOP!
PLOD
へろへろ
PLOD
THIS IS THE LAST ONE.
MANPUKU DINER
RESTAURANT
MANPUKU DINER
OPEN
THIS PLACE? ISN'T IT TOO EARLY FOR DINNER?
AH...
RATTLE
ガラガラ
RATTLE
WHAT?

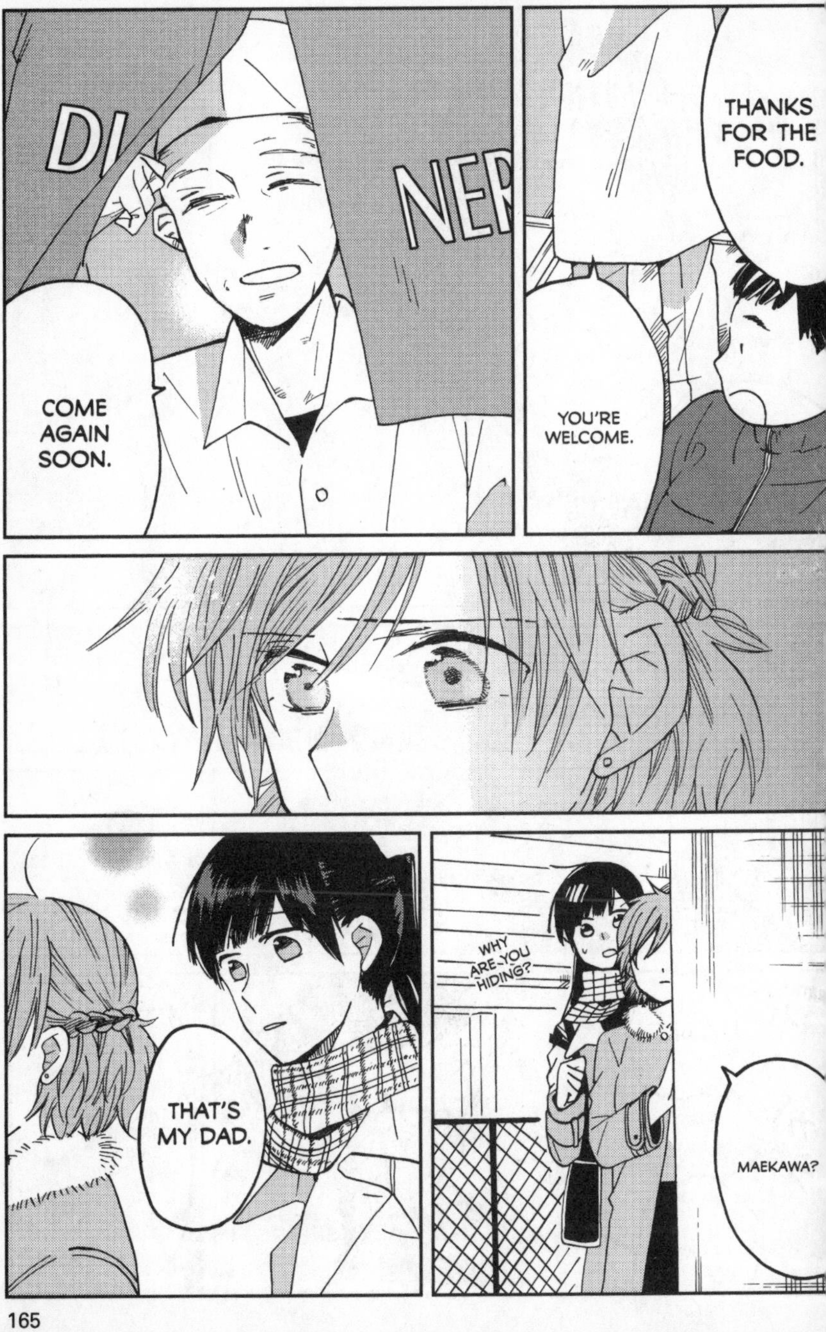
THANKS FOR THE FOOD.
YOU'RE WELCOME.
DI
NER
COME AGAIN SOON.
WHY ARE YOU HIDING?
MAEKAWA?
THAT'S MY DAD.

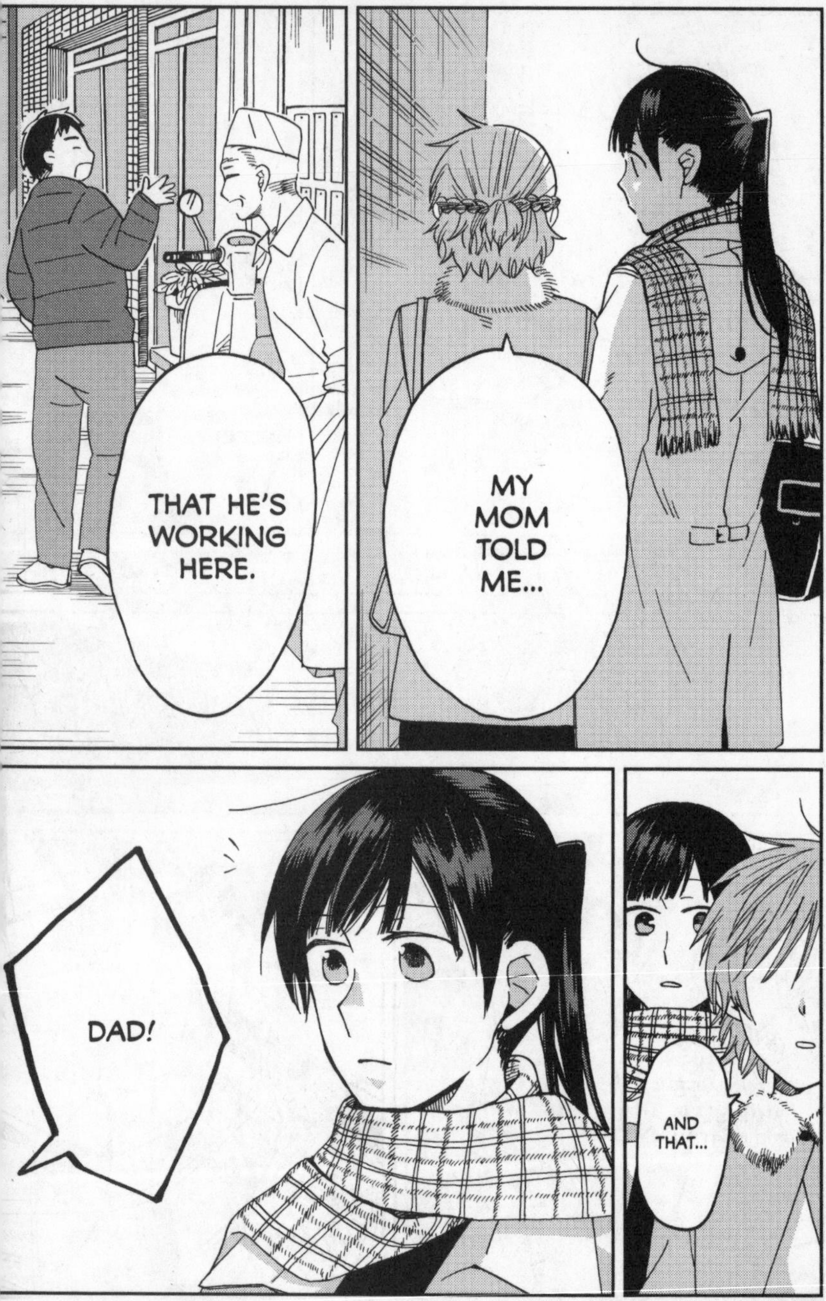
MY MOM TOLD ME...
THAT HE'S WORKING HERE.
AND THAT...
DAD!

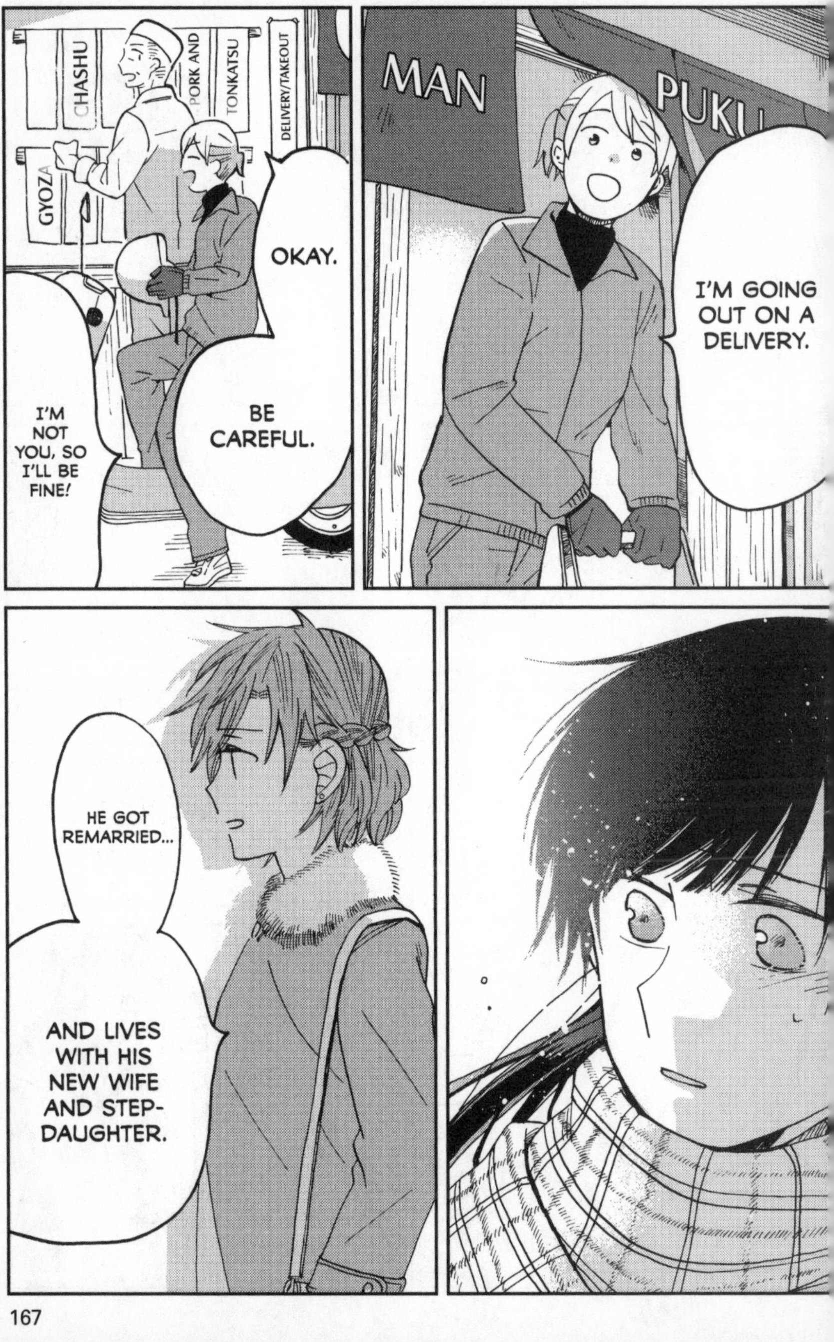
MAN
PUKU
I'M GOING OUT ON A DELIVERY.
DELIVERY/TAKEOUT
PORK AND
TONKATSU
CHASHU
GYOZA
OKAY.
BE CAREFUL.
I'M NOT YOU, SO I'LL BE FINE!
HE GOT REMARRIED...
AND LIVES WITH HIS NEW WIFE AND STEP-DAUGHTER.

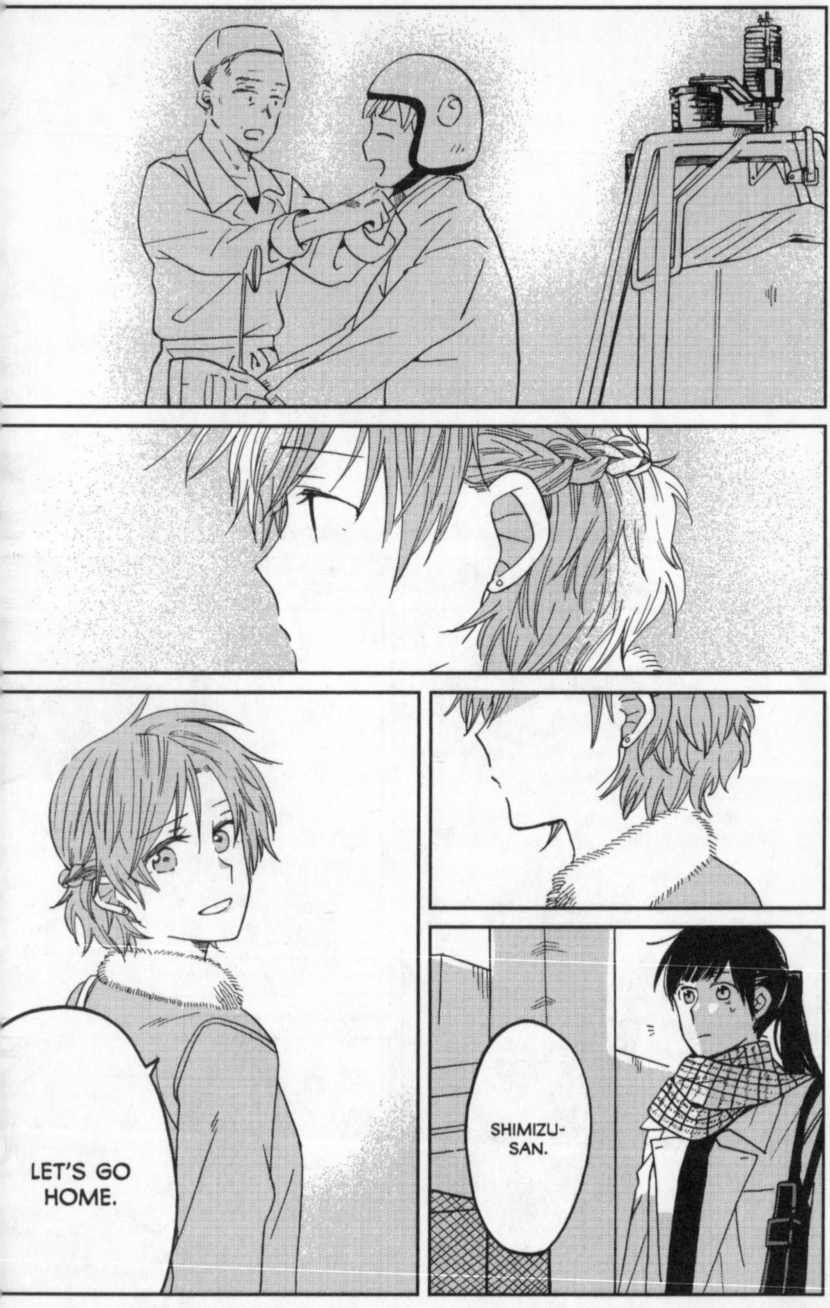
SHIMIZU-SAN.
LET'S GO HOME.

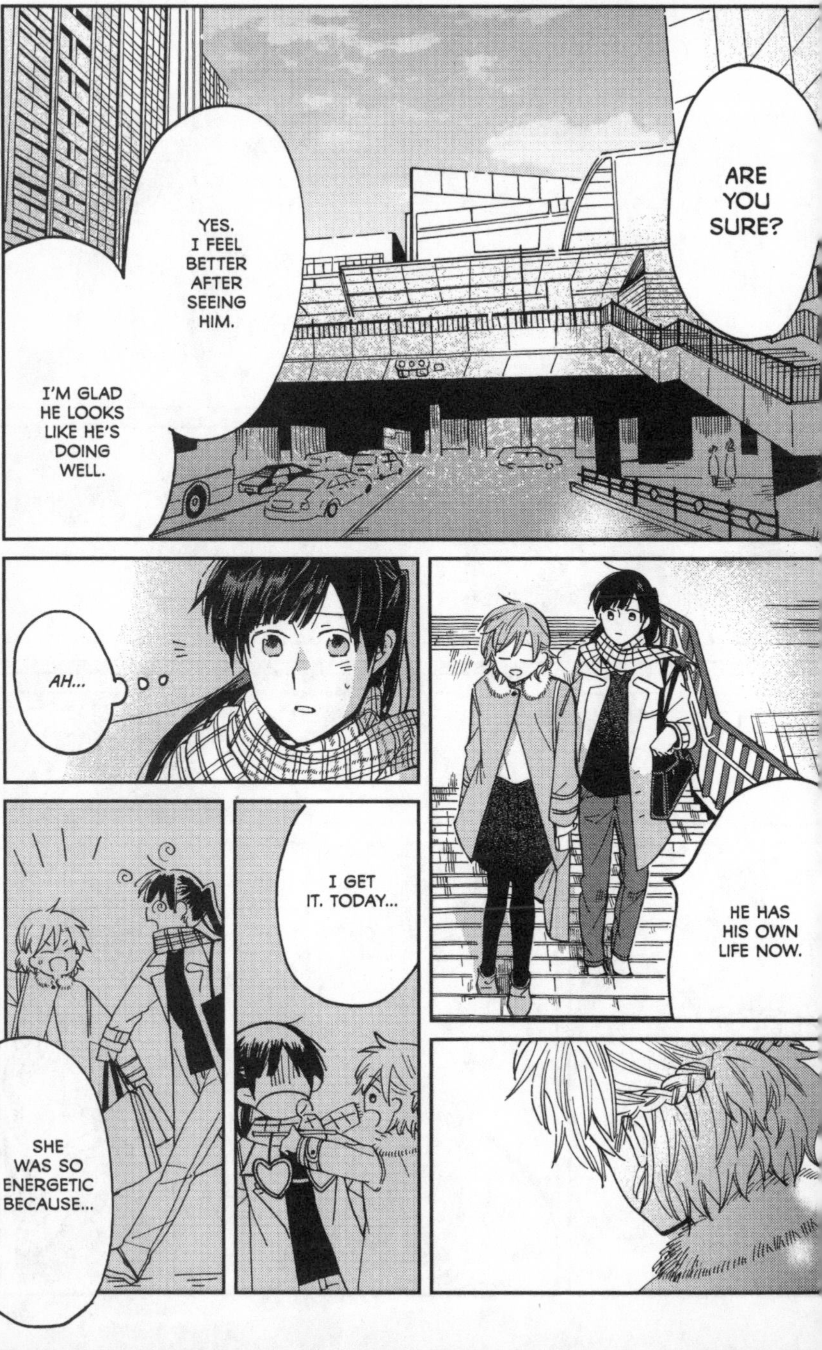
ARE YOU SURE?
YES. I FEEL BETTER AFTER SEEING HIM.
I'M GLAD HE LOOKS LIKE HE'S DOING WELL.
HE HAS HIS OWN LIFE NOW.
AH...
I GET IT. TODAY...
SHE WAS SO ENERGETIC BECAUSE...

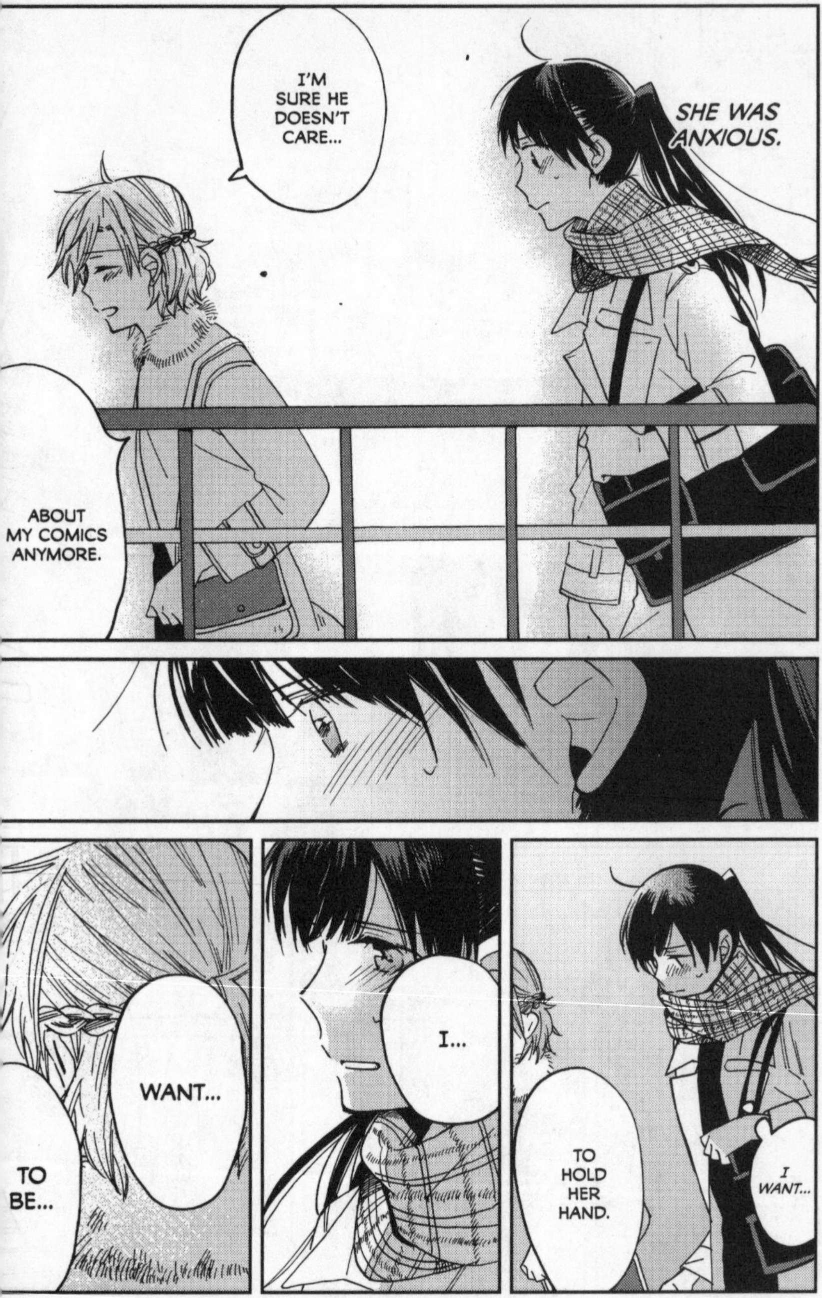
SHE WAS ANXIOUS.
I'M SURE HE DOESN'T CARE...
ABOUT MY COMICS ANYMORE.
I WANT...
TO HOLD HER HAND.
I...
WANT...
TO BE...

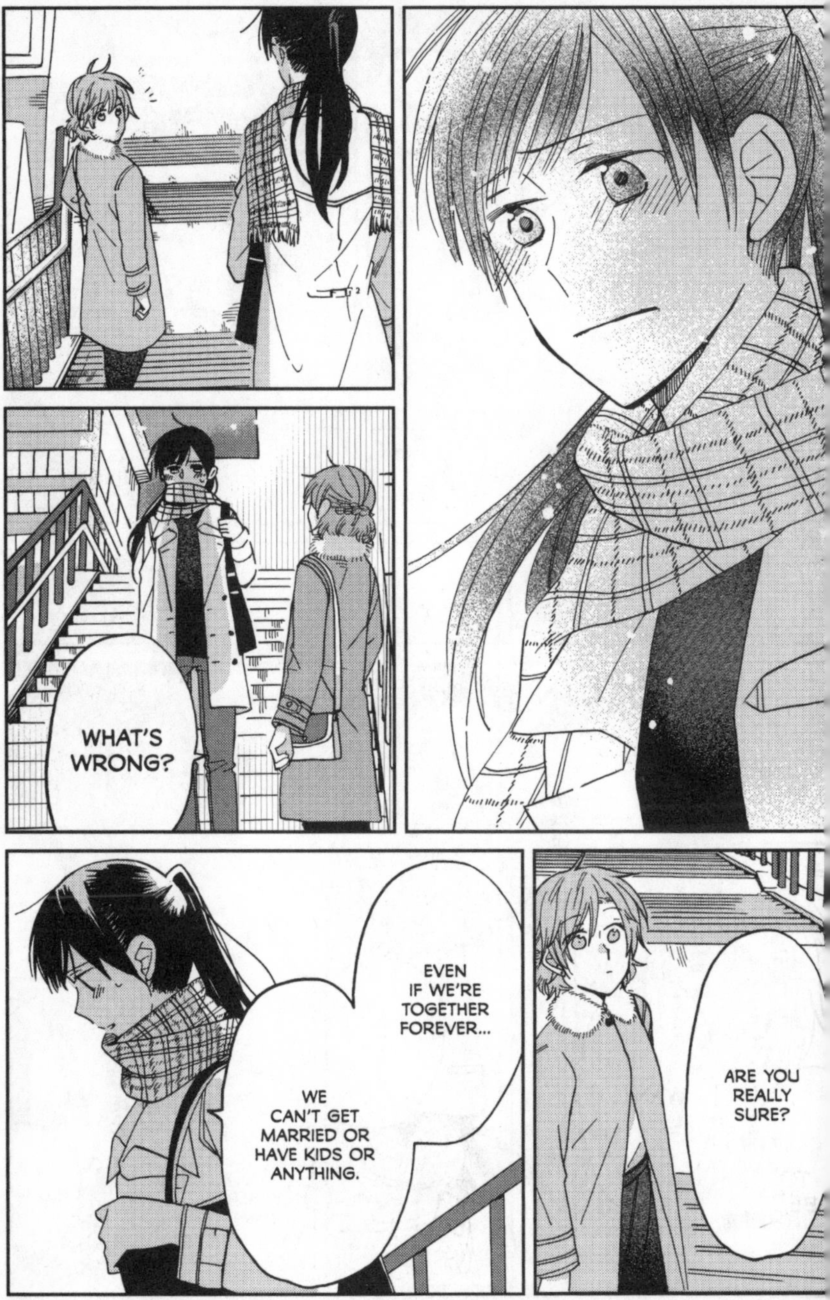
WHAT'S WRONG?
ARE YOU REALLY SURE?
EVEN IF WE'RE TOGETHER FOREVER...
WE CAN'T GET MARRIED OR HAVE KIDS OR ANYTHING.

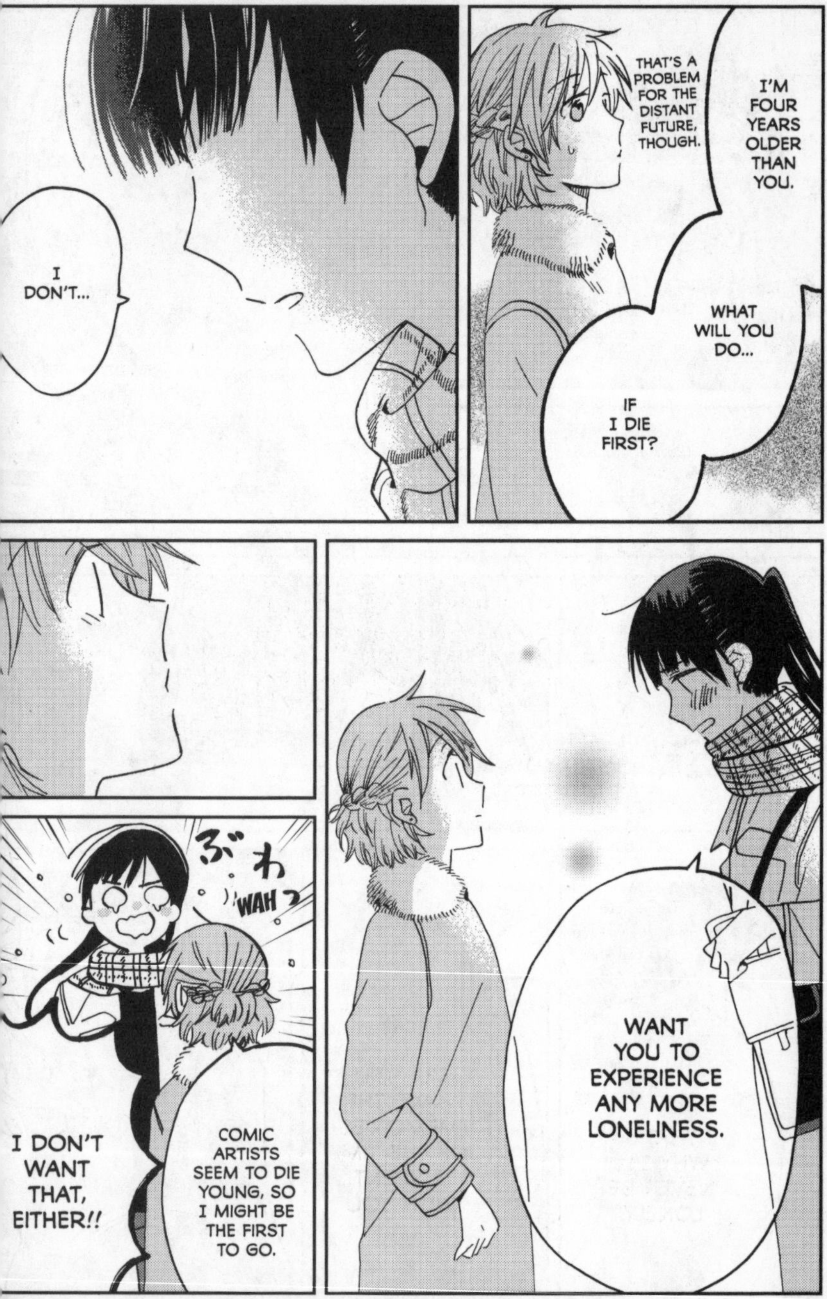
I'M FOUR YEARS OLDER THAN YOU.
THAT'S A PROBLEM FOR THE DISTANT FUTURE, THOUGH.
WHAT WILL YOU DO...
IF I DIE FIRST?
I DON'T...
WANT YOU TO EXPERIENCE ANY MORE LONELINESS.
COMIC ARTISTS SEEM TO DIE YOUNG, SO I MIGHT BE THE FIRST TO GO.
ぶわ
WAH
I DON'T WANT THAT, EITHER!!

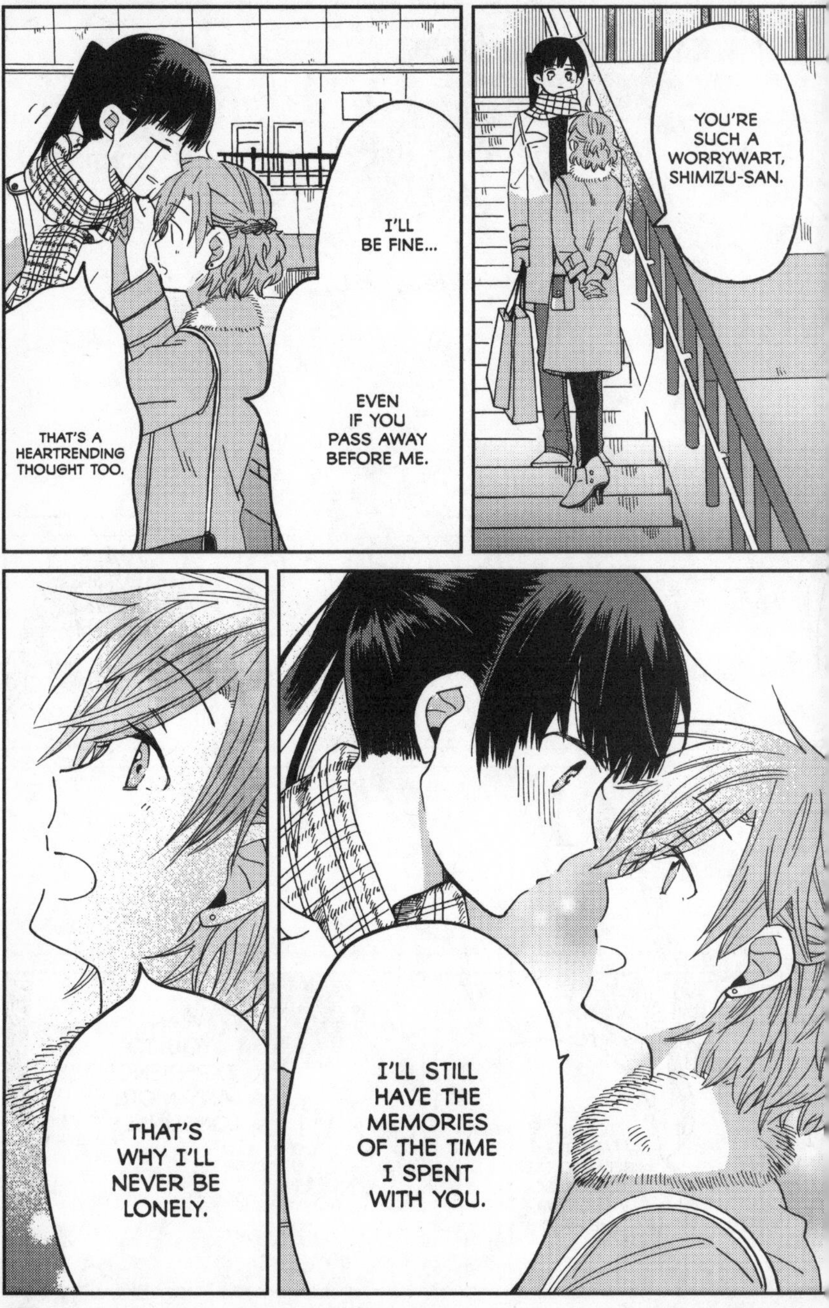
YOU'RE SUCH A WORRYWART, SHIMIZU-SAN.
I'LL BE FINE...
EVEN IF YOU PASS AWAY BEFORE ME.
THAT'S A HEARTRENDING THOUGHT TOO.
I'LL STILL HAVE THE MEMORIES OF THE TIME I SPENT WITH YOU.
THAT'S WHY I'LL NEVER BE LONELY.

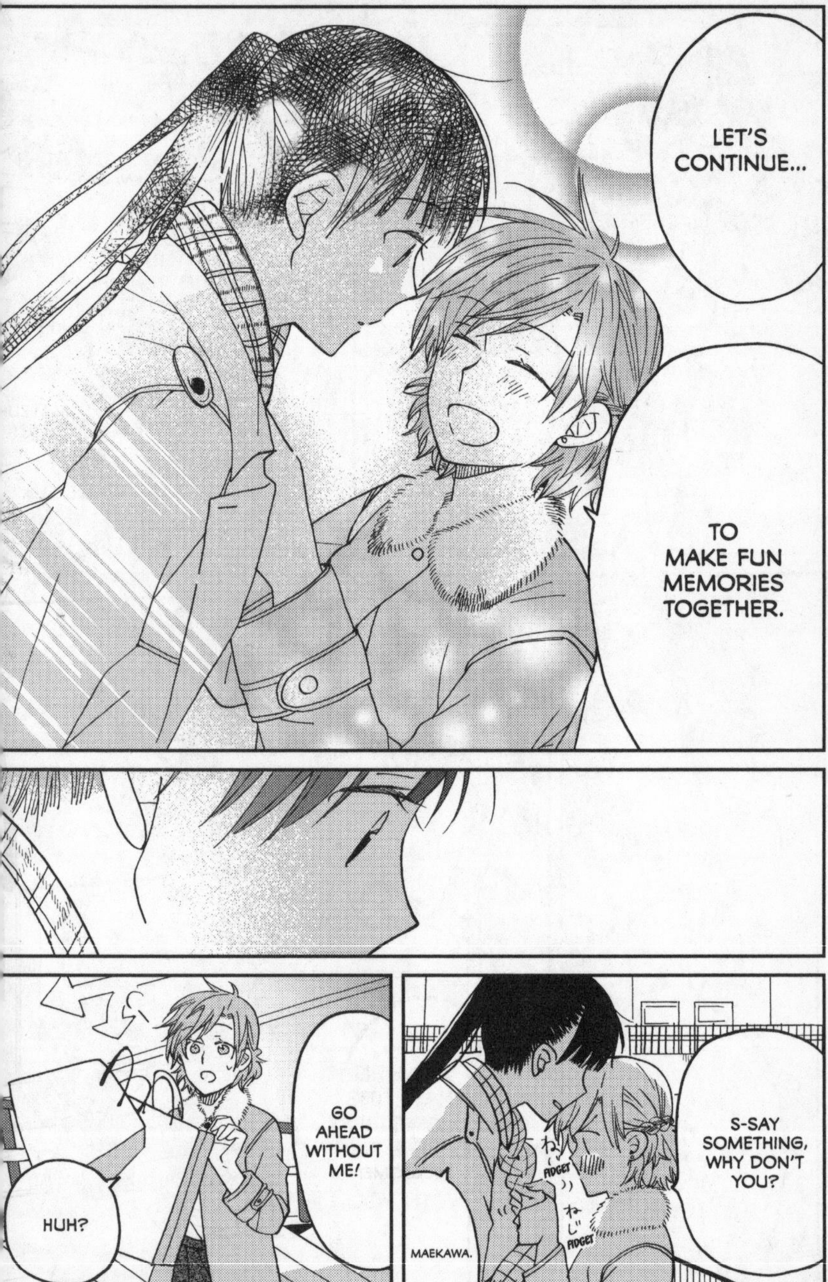
LET'S CONTINUE...
TO MAKE FUN MEMORIES TOGETHER.
S-SAY SOMETHING, WHY DON'T YOU?
FIDGET
FIDGET
MAEKAWA.
GO AHEAD WITHOUT ME!
HUH?

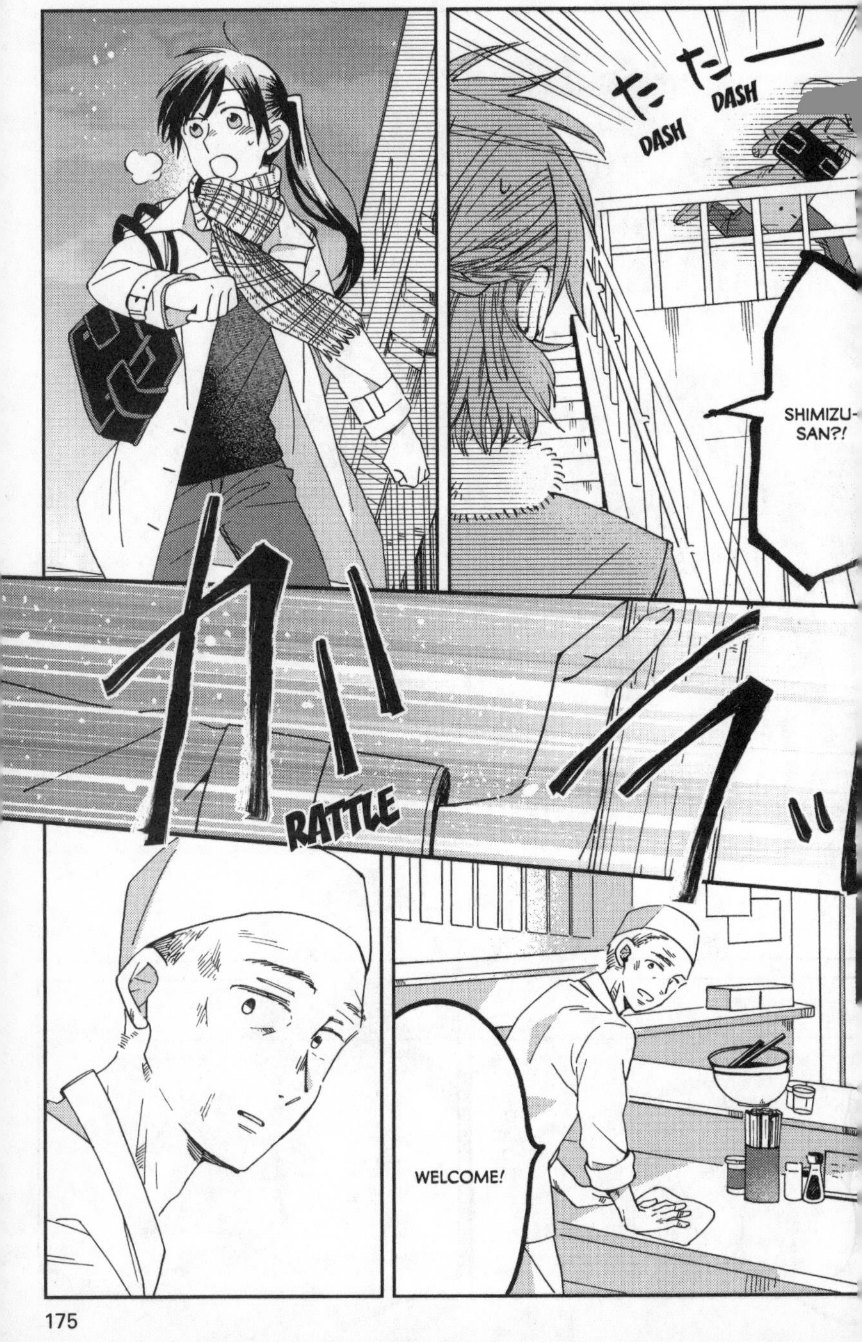

た たー
DASH
DASH
SHIMIZU-SAN?!
RATTLE
WELCOME!

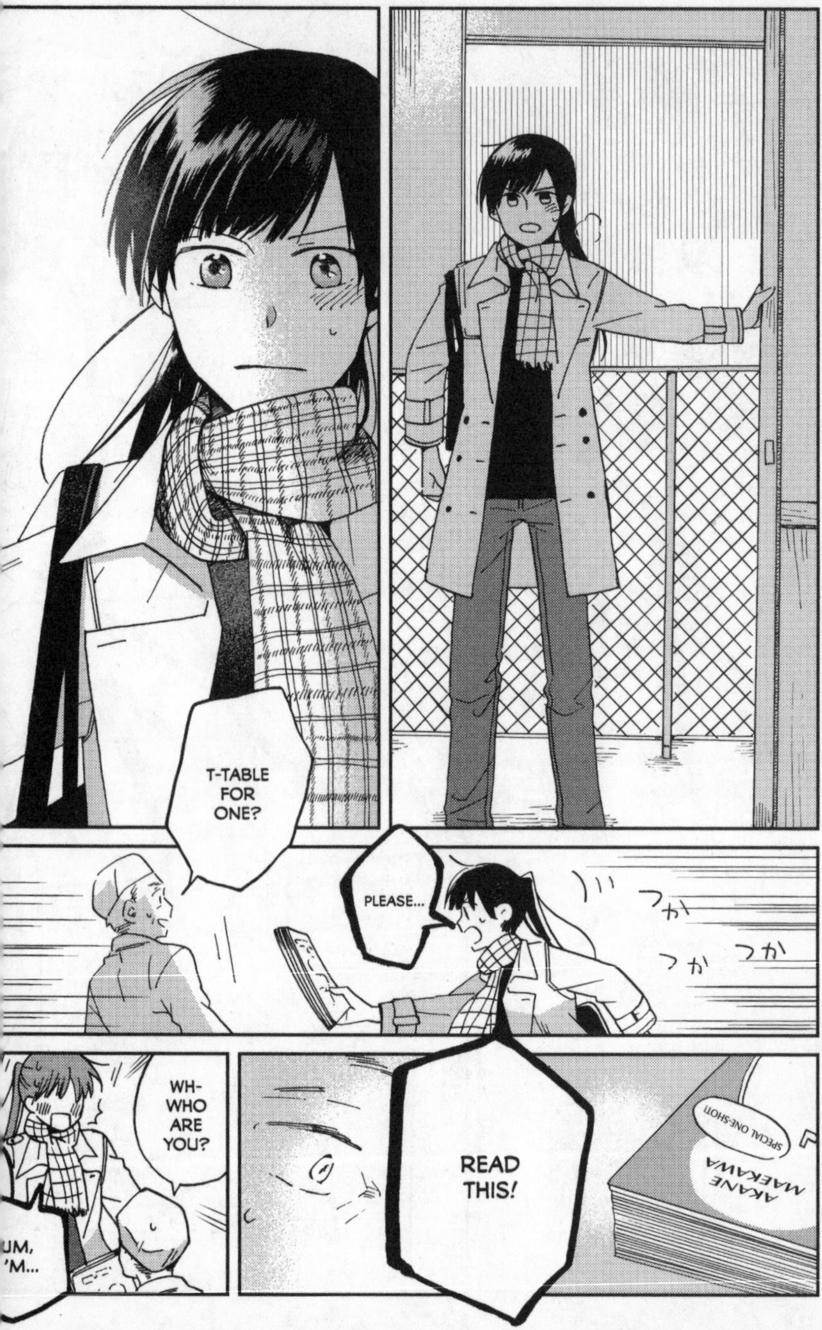
T-TABLE FOR ONE?
PLEASE...
つか
つか
つか
READ THIS!
AKANE MAEKAWA
SPECIAL ONE-SHOT!
WH- WHO ARE YOU?
UM, 'M...

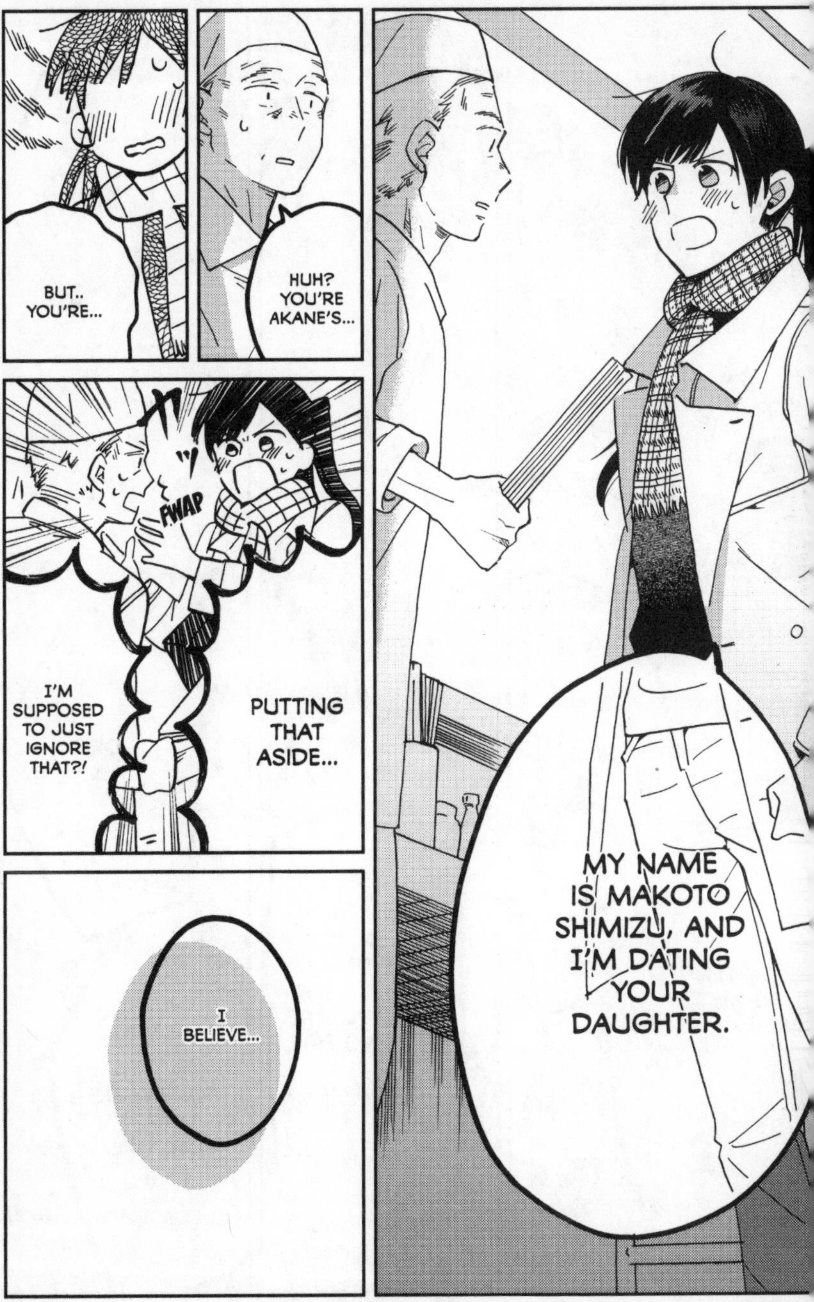
MY NAME IS MAKOTO SHIMIZU, AND I'M DATING YOUR DAUGHTER.
HUH? YOU'RE AKANE'S...
BUT.. YOU'RE...
FWAP
PUTTING THAT ASIDE...
I'M SUPPOSED TO JUST IGNORE THAT?!
I BELIEVE...

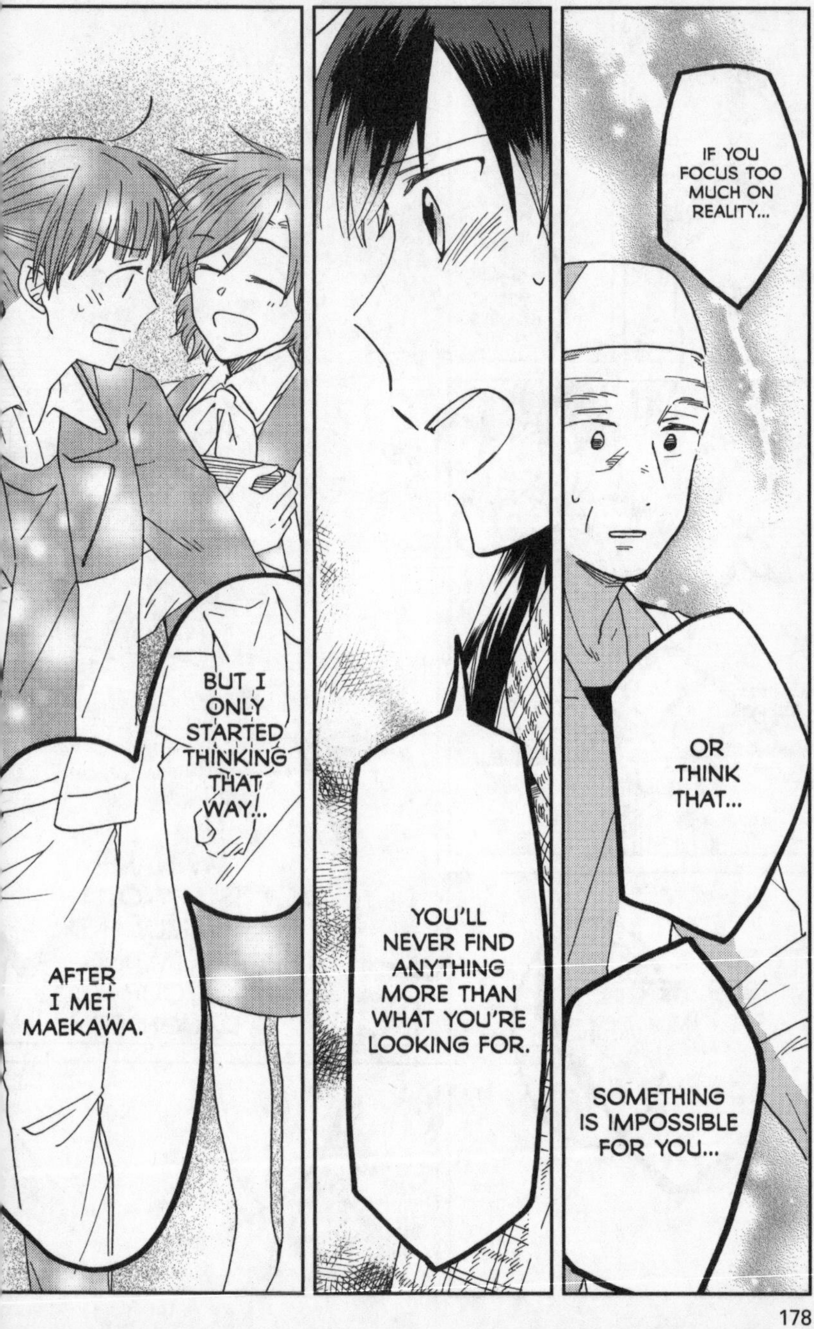
IF YOU FOCUS TOO MUCH ON REALITY...
OR THINK THAT...
SOMETHING IS IMPOSSIBLE FOR YOU...
YOU'LL NEVER FIND ANYTHING MORE THAN WHAT YOU'RE LOOKING FOR.
BUT I ONLY STARTED THINKING THAT WAY...
AFTER I MET MAEKAWA.

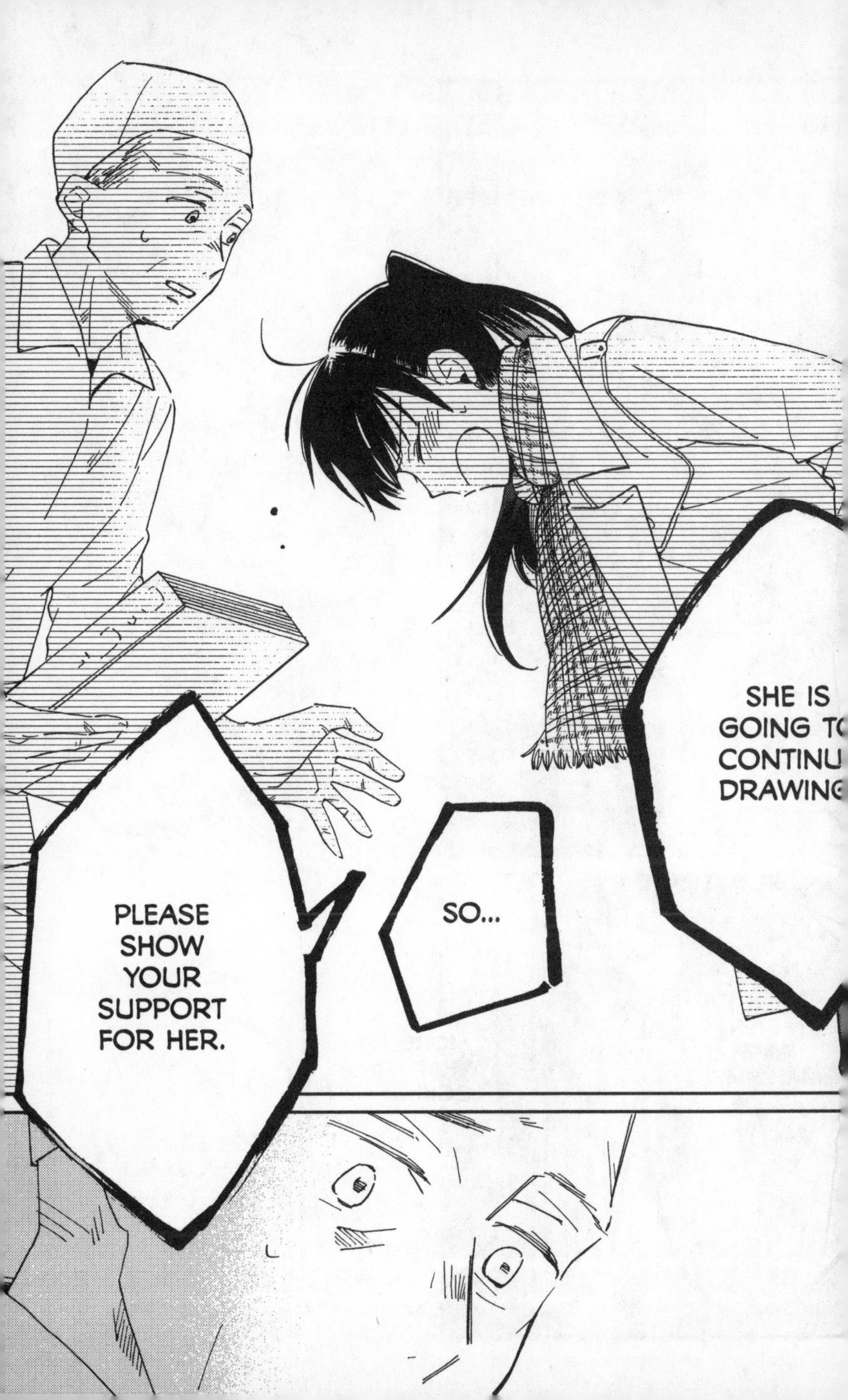
SHE IS GOING TO CONTINU DRAWING
SO...
PLEASE SHOW YOUR SUPPORT FOR HER.

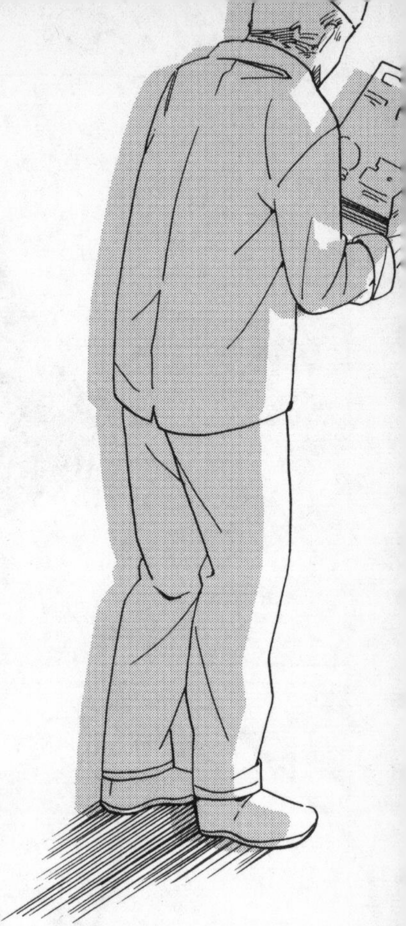

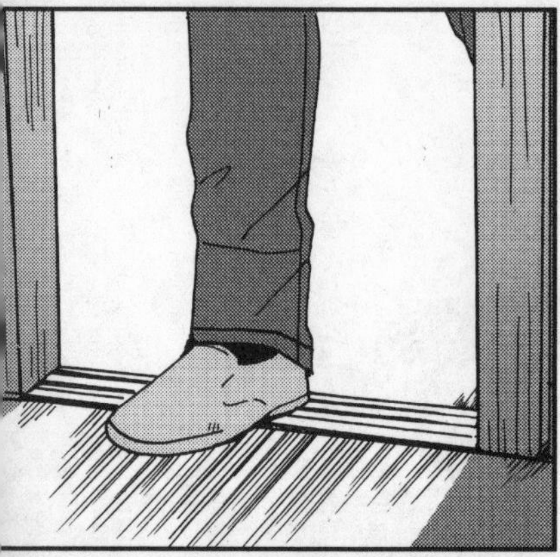

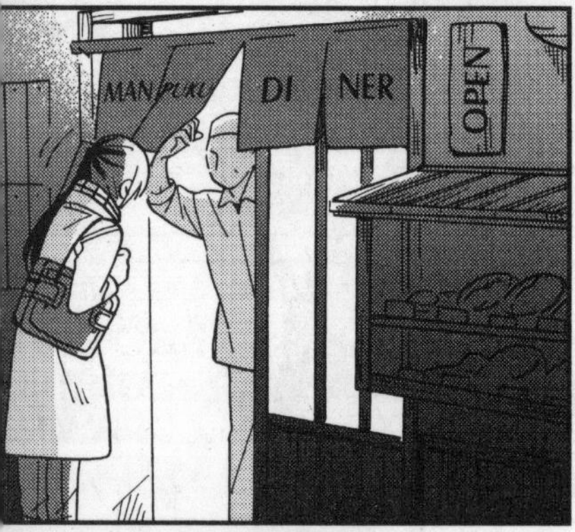
MANPUKU DINER
OPEN

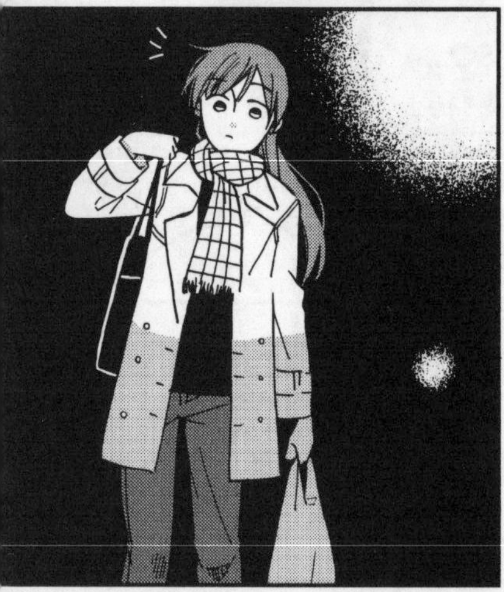

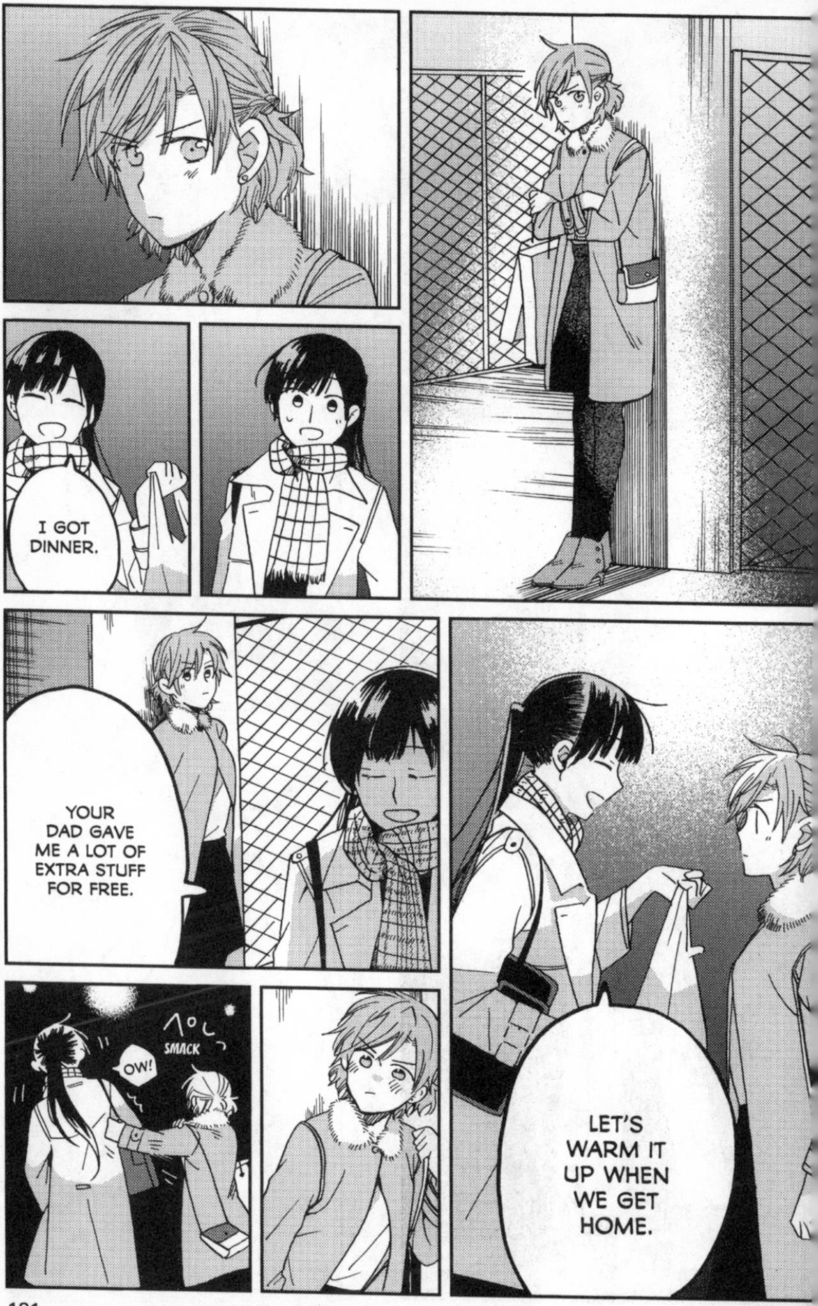

I GOT DINNER.
YOUR DAD GAVE ME A LOT OF EXTRA STUFF FOR FREE.
LET'S WARM IT UP WHEN WE GET HOME.
SMACK
OW!

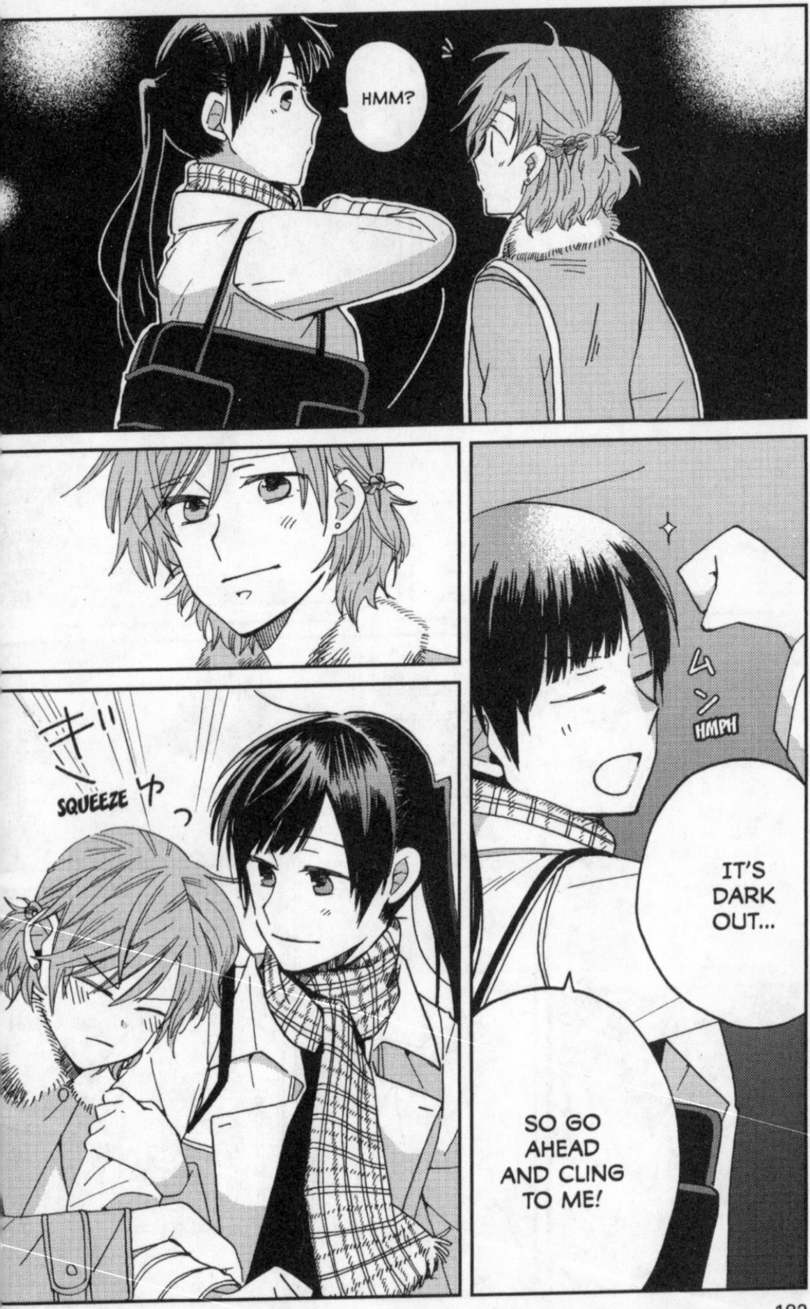
HMM?
HMPH
IT'S DARK OUT...
SO GO AHEAD AND CLING TO ME!
SQUEEZE

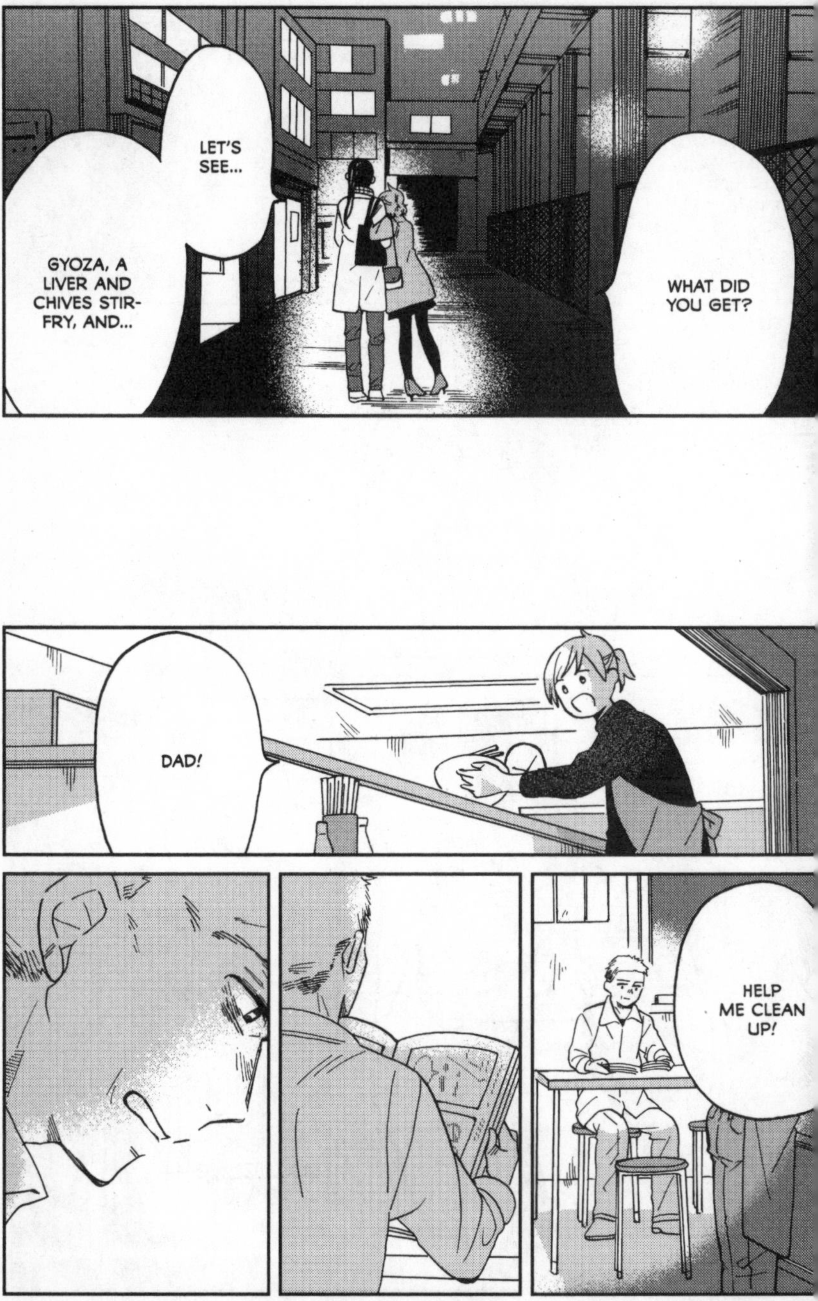
WHAT DID YOU GET?
LET'S SEE...
GYOZA, A LIVER AND CHIVES STIR-FRY, AND...
DAD!
HELP ME CLEAN UP!

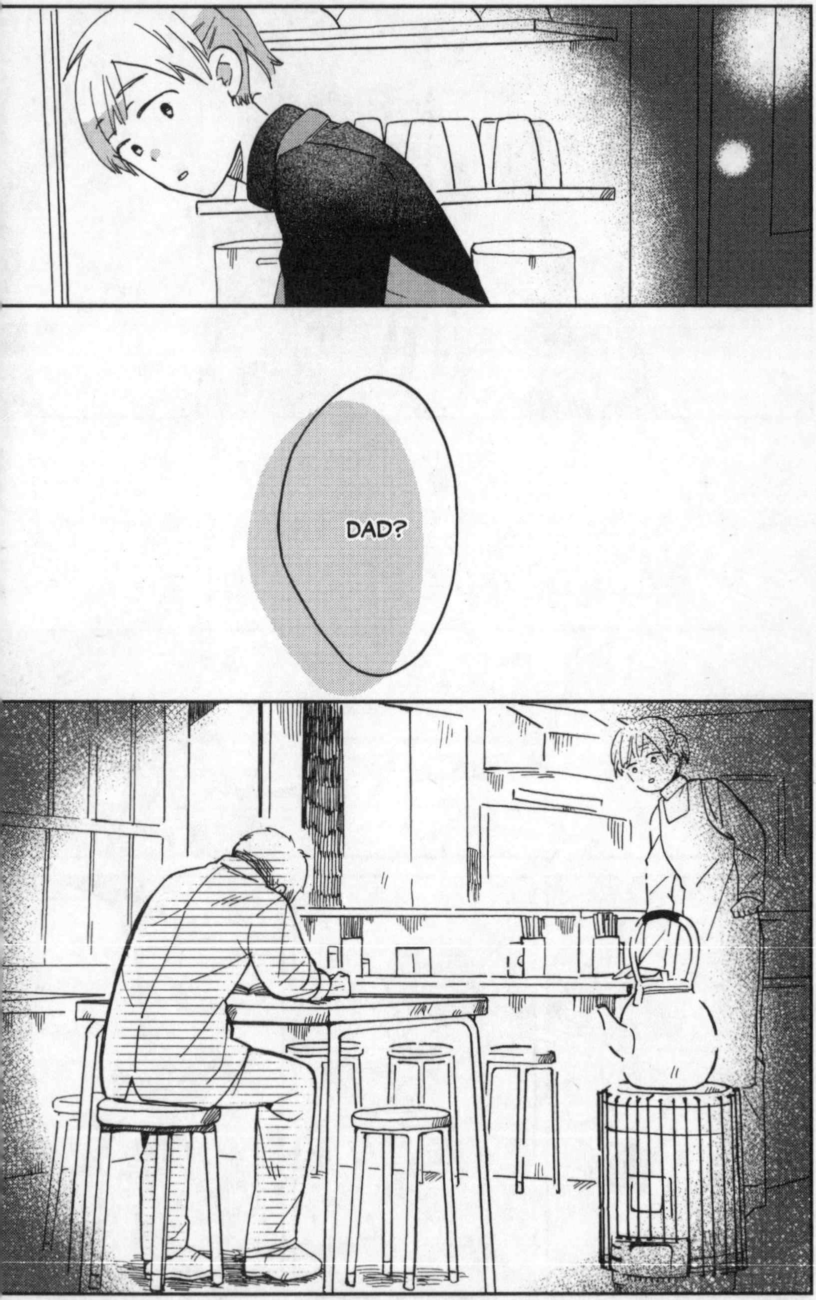
DAD?

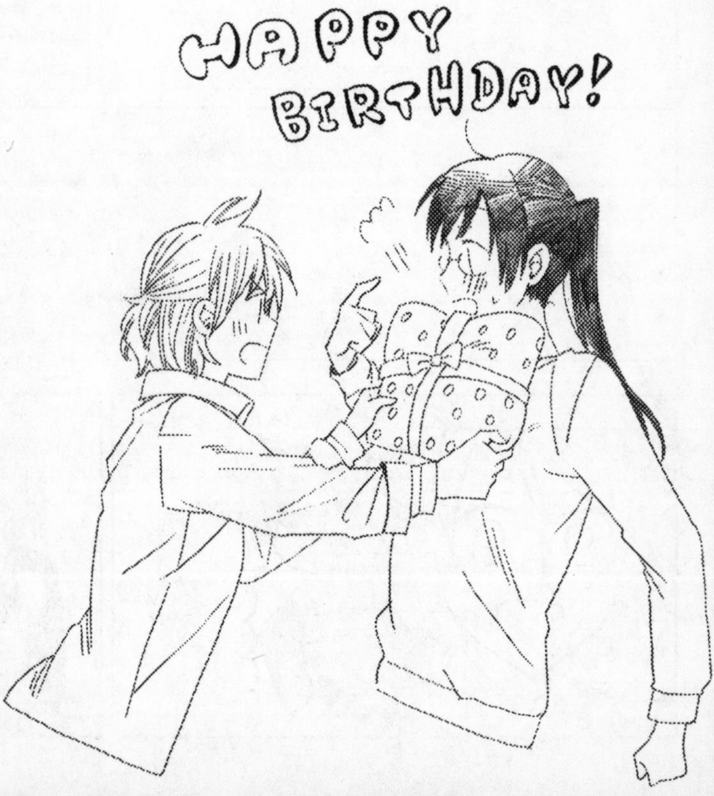
HAPPY BIRTHDAY!

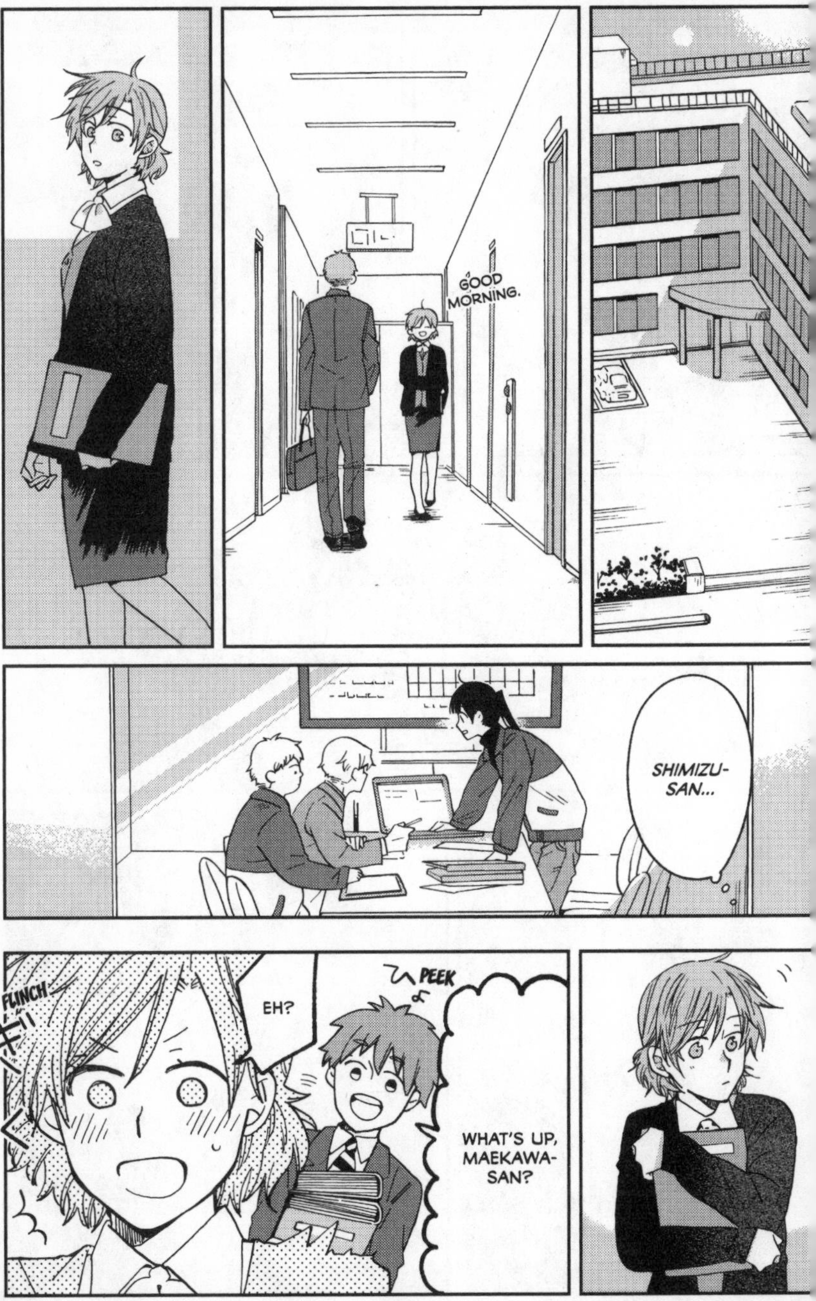
GOOD MORNING.
SHIMIZU-SAN...
PEEK
WHAT'S UP, MAEKAWA-SAN?
EH?
FLINCH

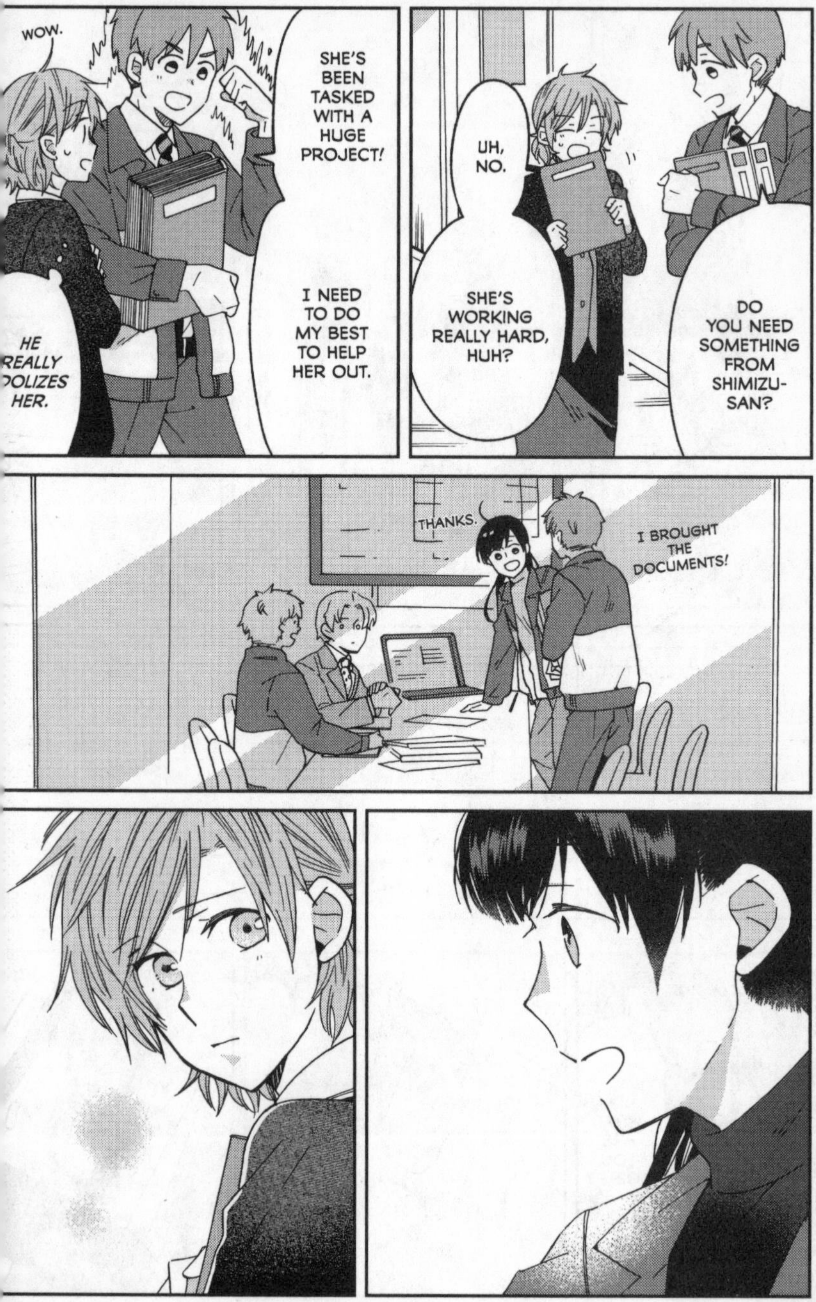
DO YOU NEED SOMETHING FROM SHIMIZU-SAN?
UH, NO.
SHE'S WORKING REALLY HARD, HUH?
SHE'S BEEN TASKED WITH A HUGE PROJECT!
I NEED TO DO MY BEST TO HELP HER OUT.
WOW.
HE REALLY DOLIZES HER.
I BROUGHT THE DOCUMENTS!
THANKS.

Chapter 22

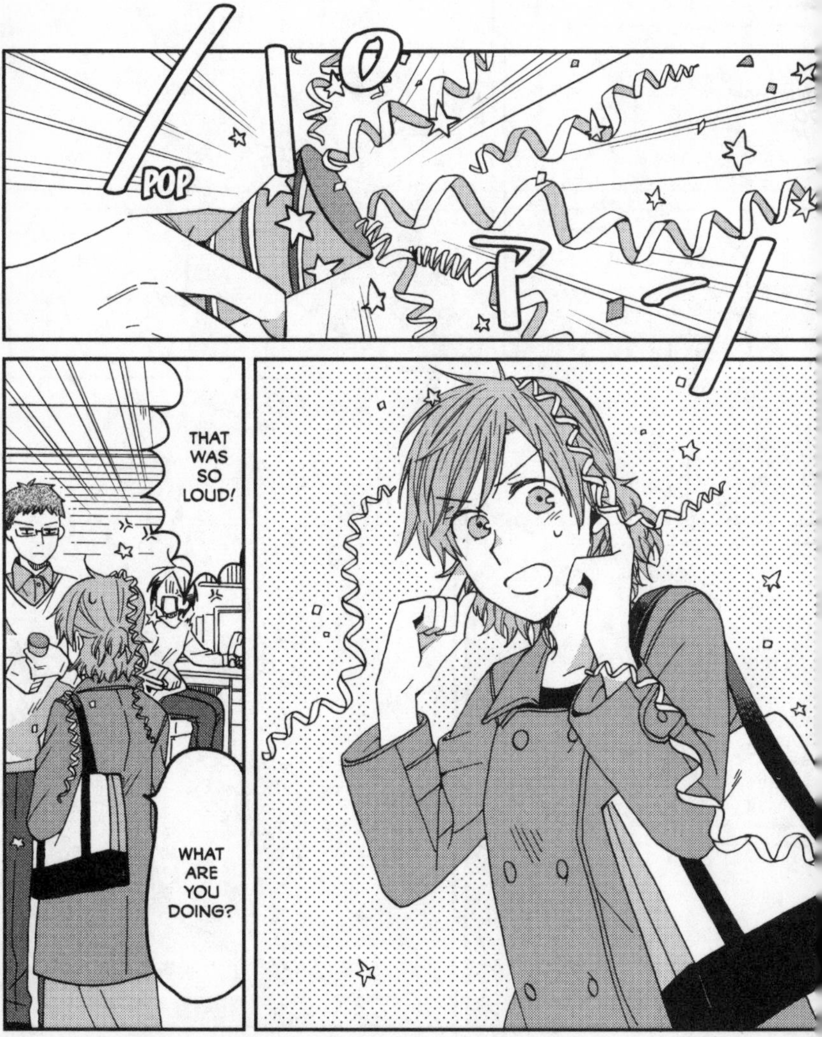
POP
THAT WAS SO LOUD!
WHAT ARE YOU DOING?

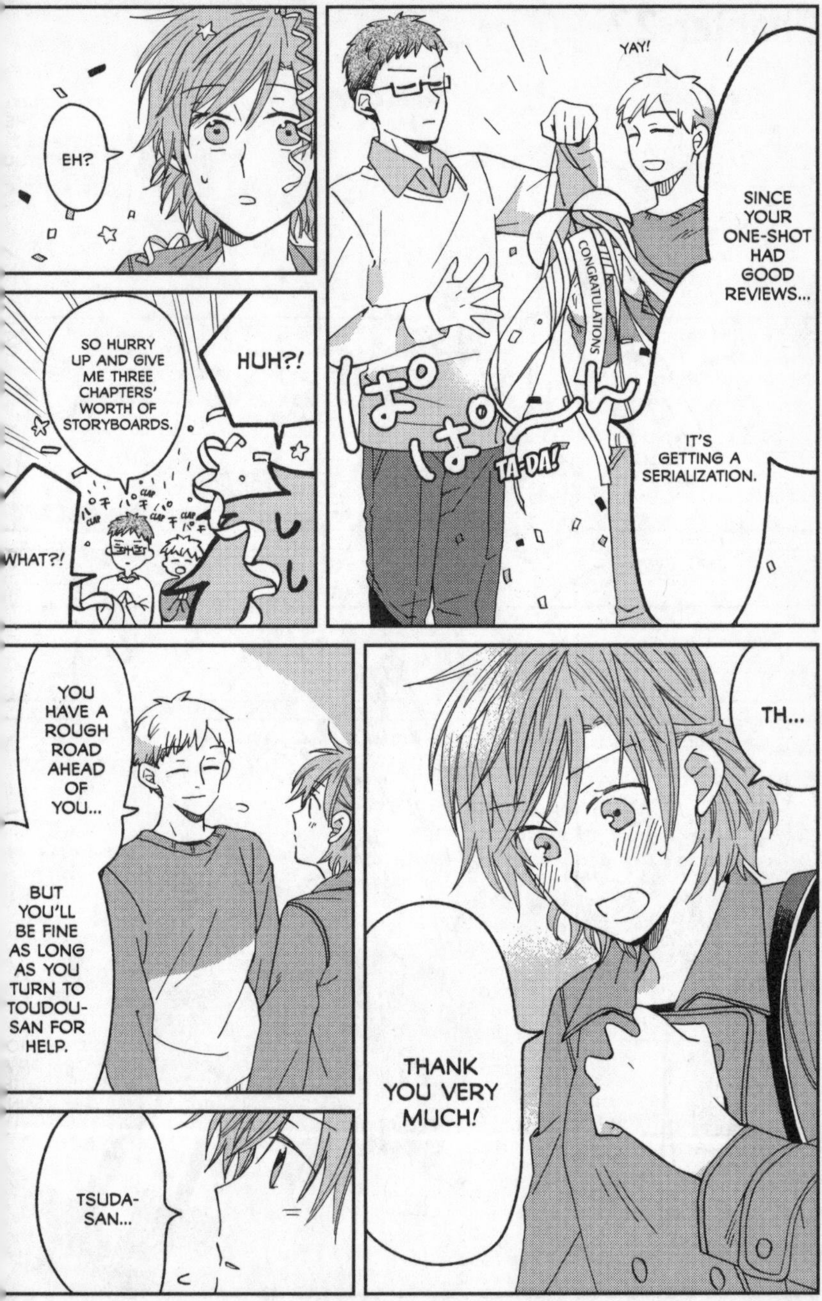

SINCE YOUR ONE-SHOT HAD GOOD REVIEWS...
YAY!
IT'S GETTING A SERIALIZATION.
ぱぱーん
TA-DA!
CONGRATULATIONS
EH?
HUH?!
SO HURRY UP AND GIVE ME THREE CHAPTERS' WORTH OF STORYBOARDS.
パチパチ
CLAP
WHAT?!
TH...
THANK YOU VERY MUCH!
YOU HAVE A ROUGH ROAD AHEAD OF YOU...
BUT YOU'LL BE FINE AS LONG AS YOU TURN TO TOUDOU-SAN FOR HELP.
TSUDA-SAN...

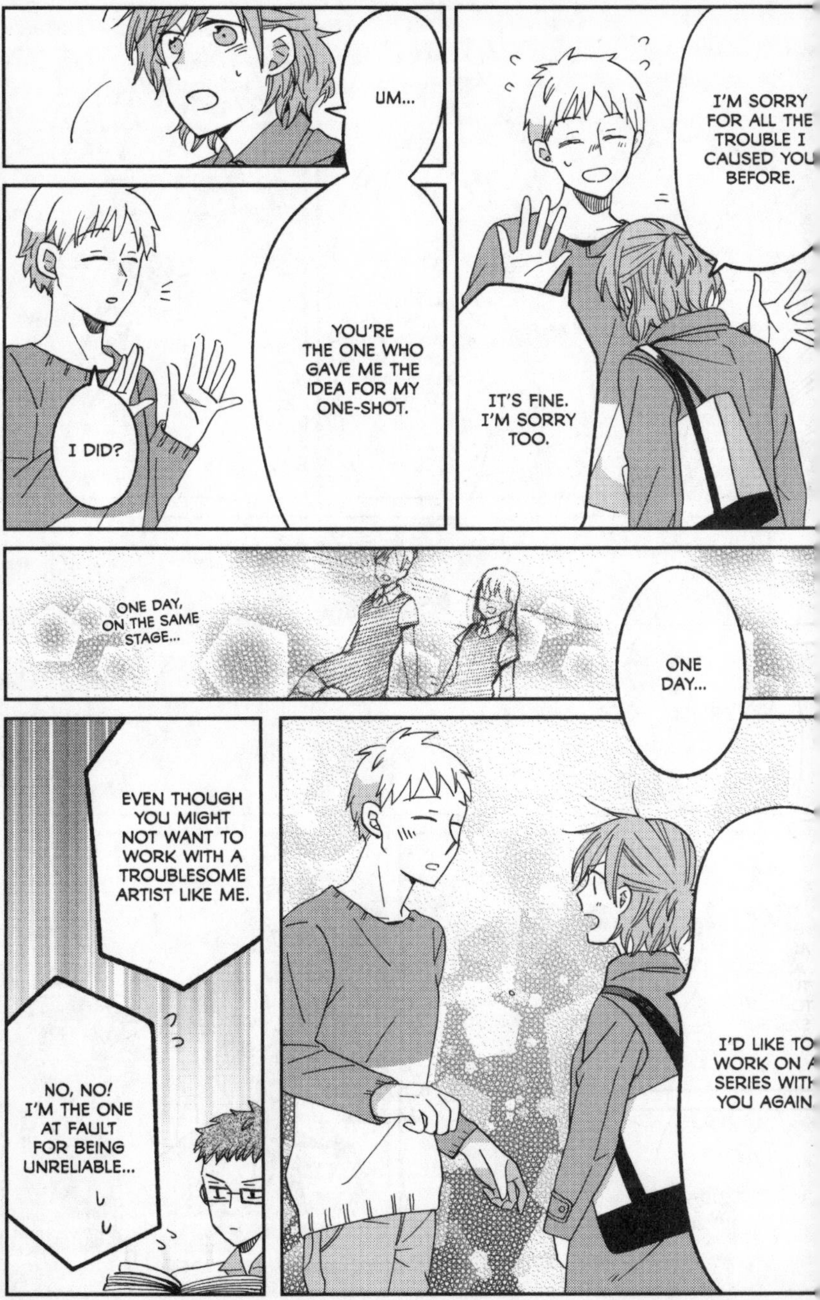
I'M SORRY FOR ALL THE TROUBLE I CAUSED YOU BEFORE.
IT'S FINE. I'M SORRY TOO.
UM...
YOU'RE THE ONE WHO GAVE ME THE IDEA FOR MY ONE-SHOT.
I DID?
ONE DAY...
ONE DAY, ON THE SAME STAGE...
I'D LIKE TO WORK ON A SERIES WITH YOU AGAIN
EVEN THOUGH YOU MIGHT NOT WANT TO WORK WITH A TROUBLESOME ARTIST LIKE ME.
NO, NO! I'M THE ONE AT FAULT FOR BEING UNRELIABLE...

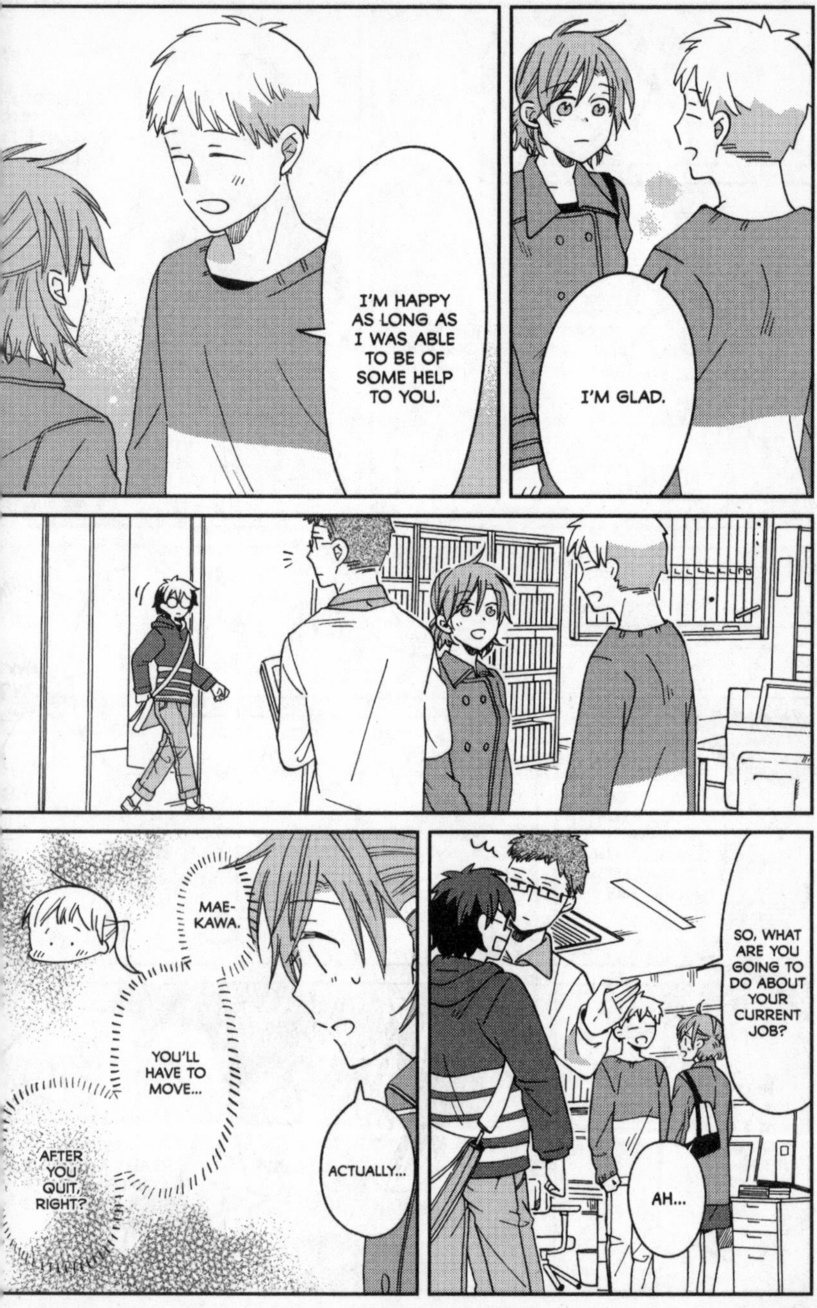
I'M GLAD.
I'M HAPPY AS LONG AS I WAS ABLE TO BE OF SOME HELP TO YOU.
SO, WHAT ARE YOU GOING TO DO ABOUT YOUR CURRENT JOB?
AH...
ACTUALLY...
MAE-KAWA.
YOU'LL HAVE TO MOVE...
AFTER YOU QUIT, RIGHT?

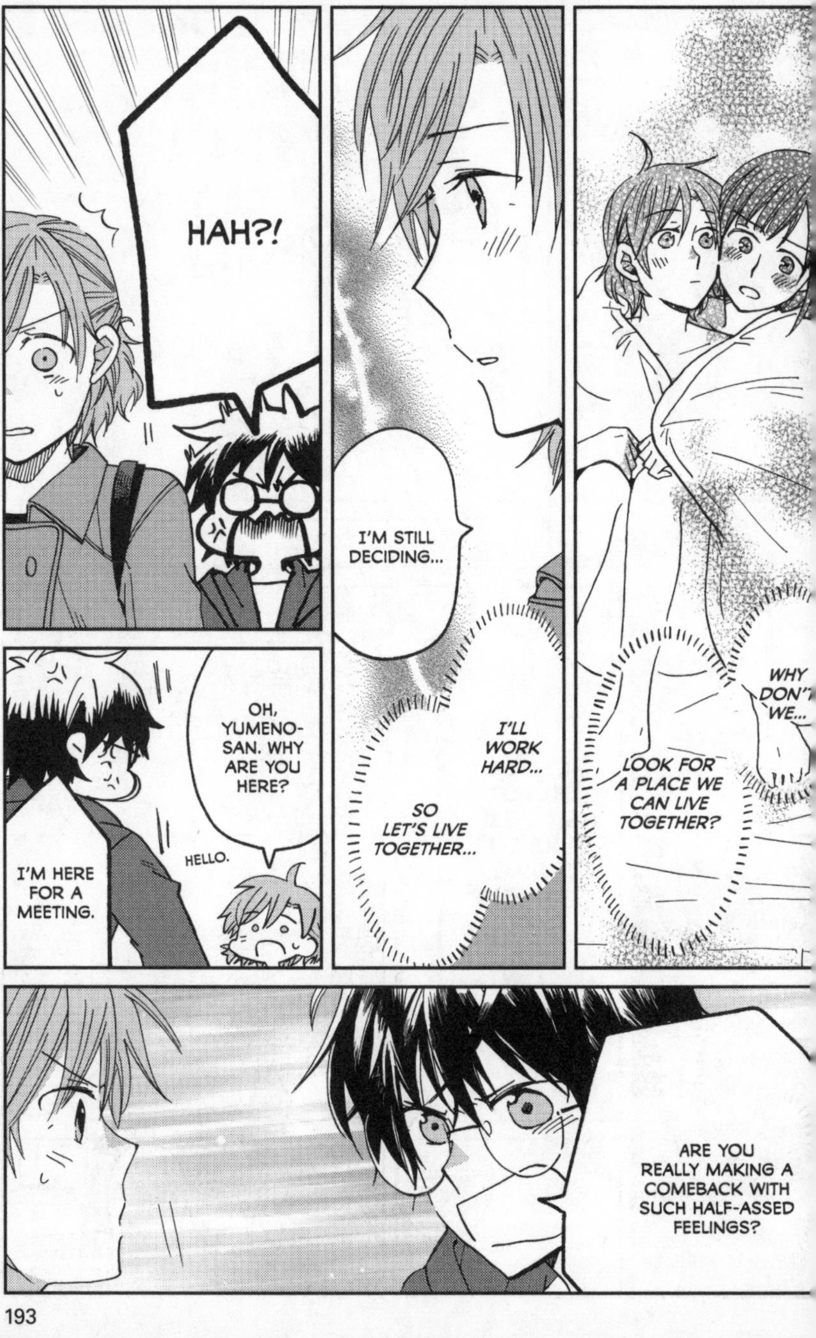
WHY DON'T WE...
LOOK FOR A PLACE WE CAN LIVE TOGETHER?
I'M STILL DECIDING...
I'LL WORK HARD...
SO LET'S LIVE TOGETHER...
HAH?!
OH, YUMENO-SAN. WHY ARE YOU HERE?
HELLO.
I'M HERE FOR A MEETING.
ARE YOU REALLY MAKING A COMEBACK WITH SUCH HALF-ASSED FEELINGS?

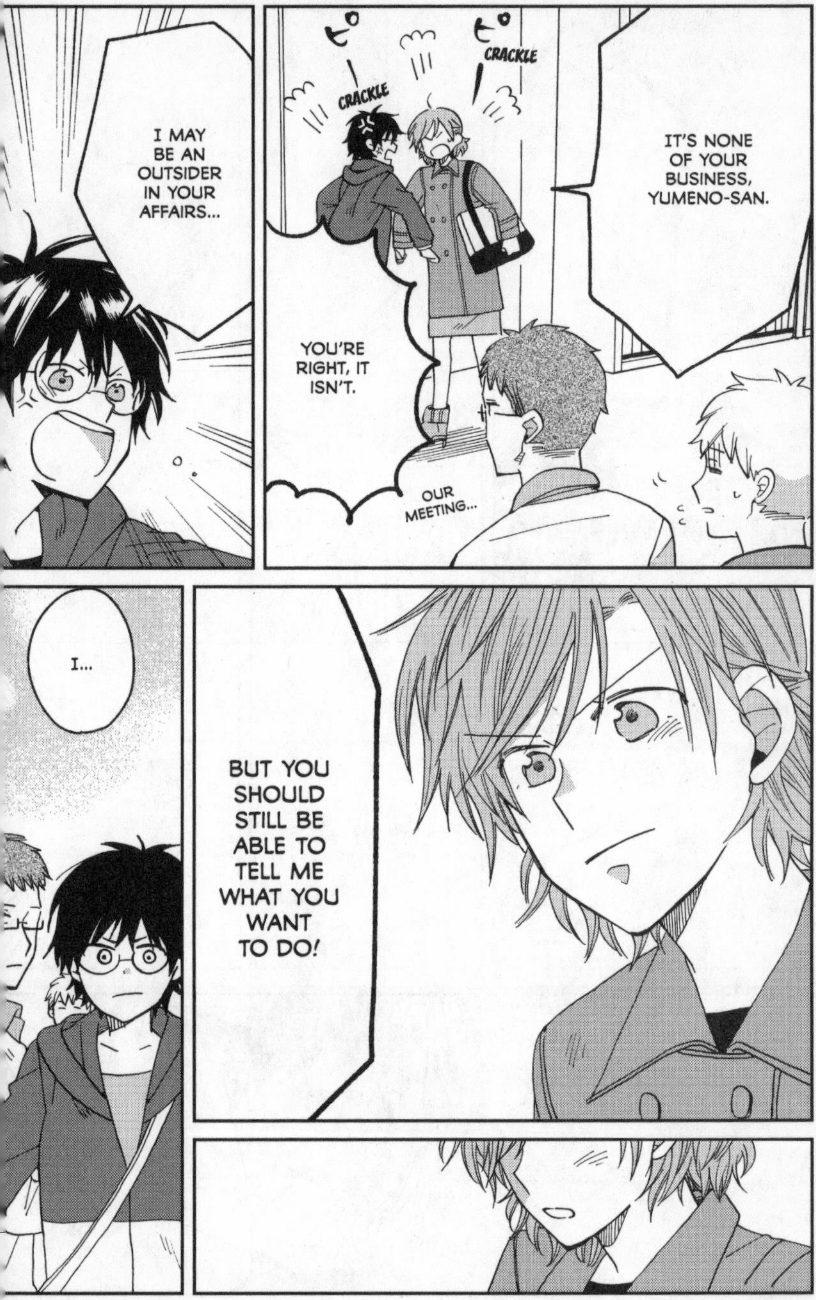
CRACKLE
CRACKLE
IT'S NONE OF YOUR BUSINESS, YUMENO-SAN.
YOU'RE RIGHT, IT ISN'T.
OUR MEETING...
I MAY BE AN OUTSIDER IN YOUR AFFAIRS...
BUT YOU SHOULD STILL BE ABLE TO TELL ME WHAT YOU WANT TO DO!
I...

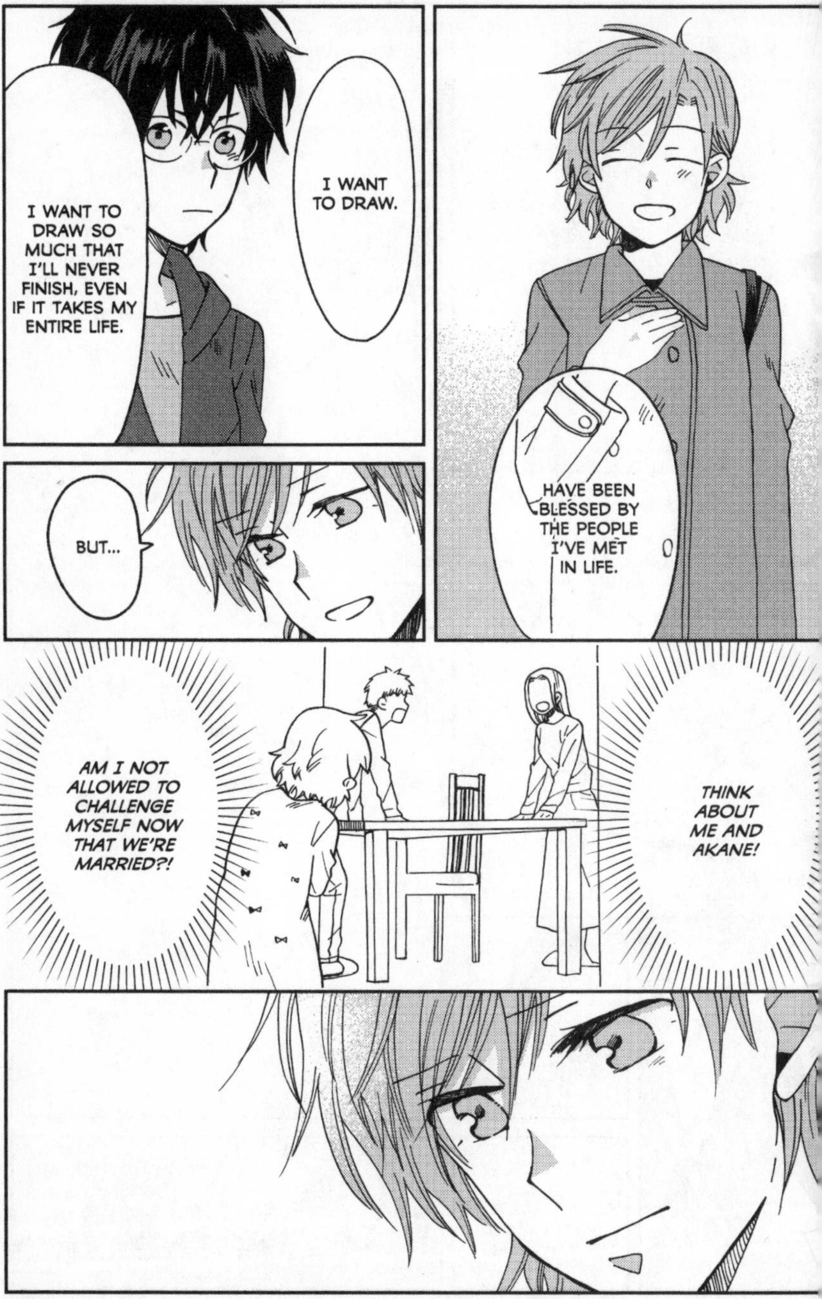
HAVE BEEN BLESSED BY THE PEOPLE I'VE MET IN LIFE.
I WANT TO DRAW.
I WANT TO DRAW SO MUCH THAT I'LL NEVER FINISH, EVEN IF IT TAKES MY ENTIRE LIFE.
BUT...
THINK ABOUT ME AND AKANE!
AM I NOT ALLOWED TO CHALLENGE MYSELF NOW THAT WE'RE MARRIED?!

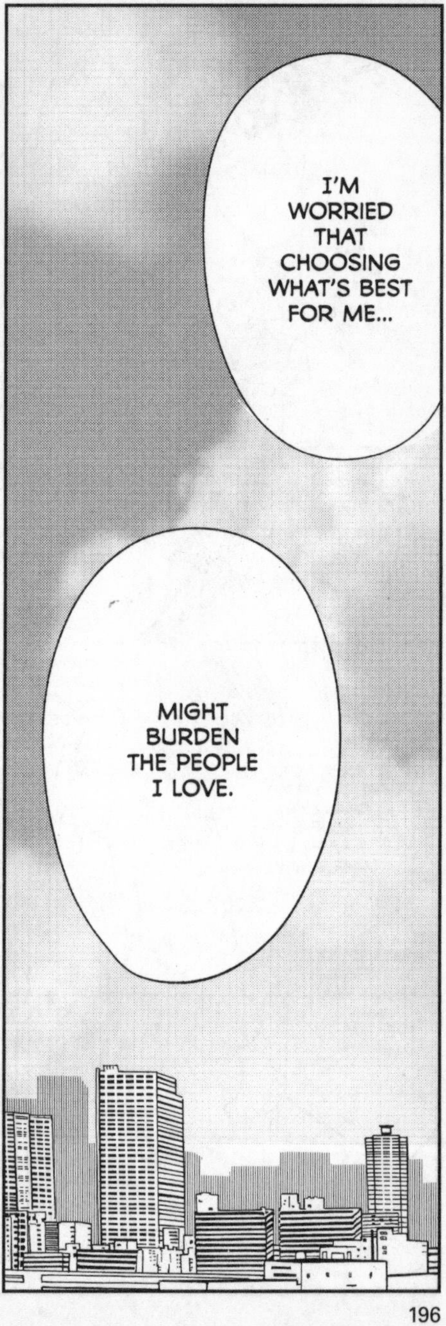
I'M WORRIED THAT CHOOSING WHAT'S BEST FOR ME...
MIGHT BURDEN THE PEOPLE I LOVE.
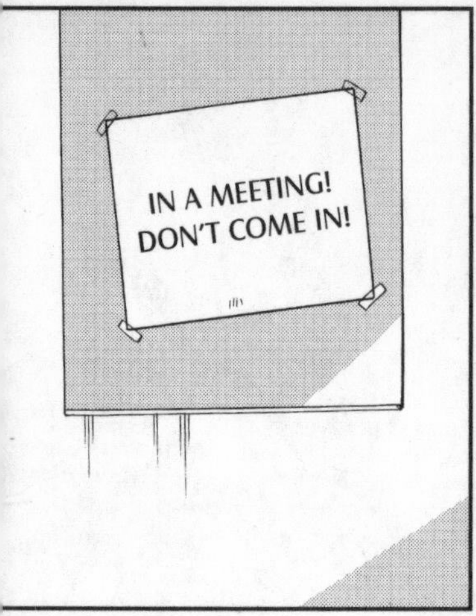
IN A MEETING! DON'T COME IN!
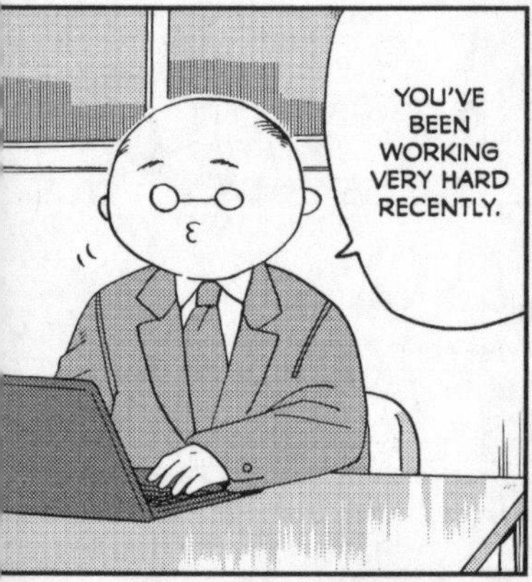
YOU'VE BEEN WORKING VERY HARD RECENTLY.
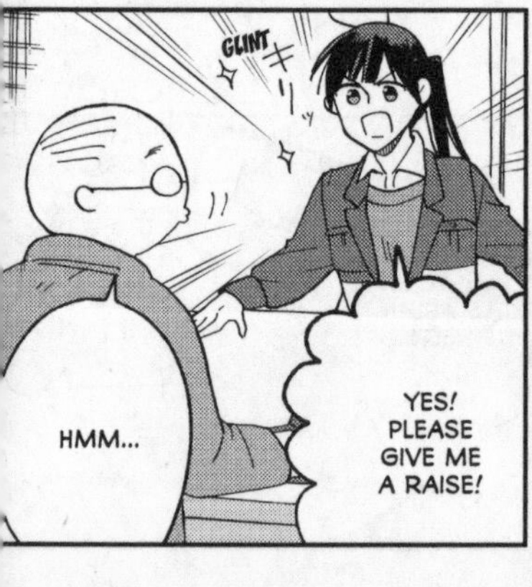
GLINT
YES! PLEASE GIVE ME A RAISE!
HMM...

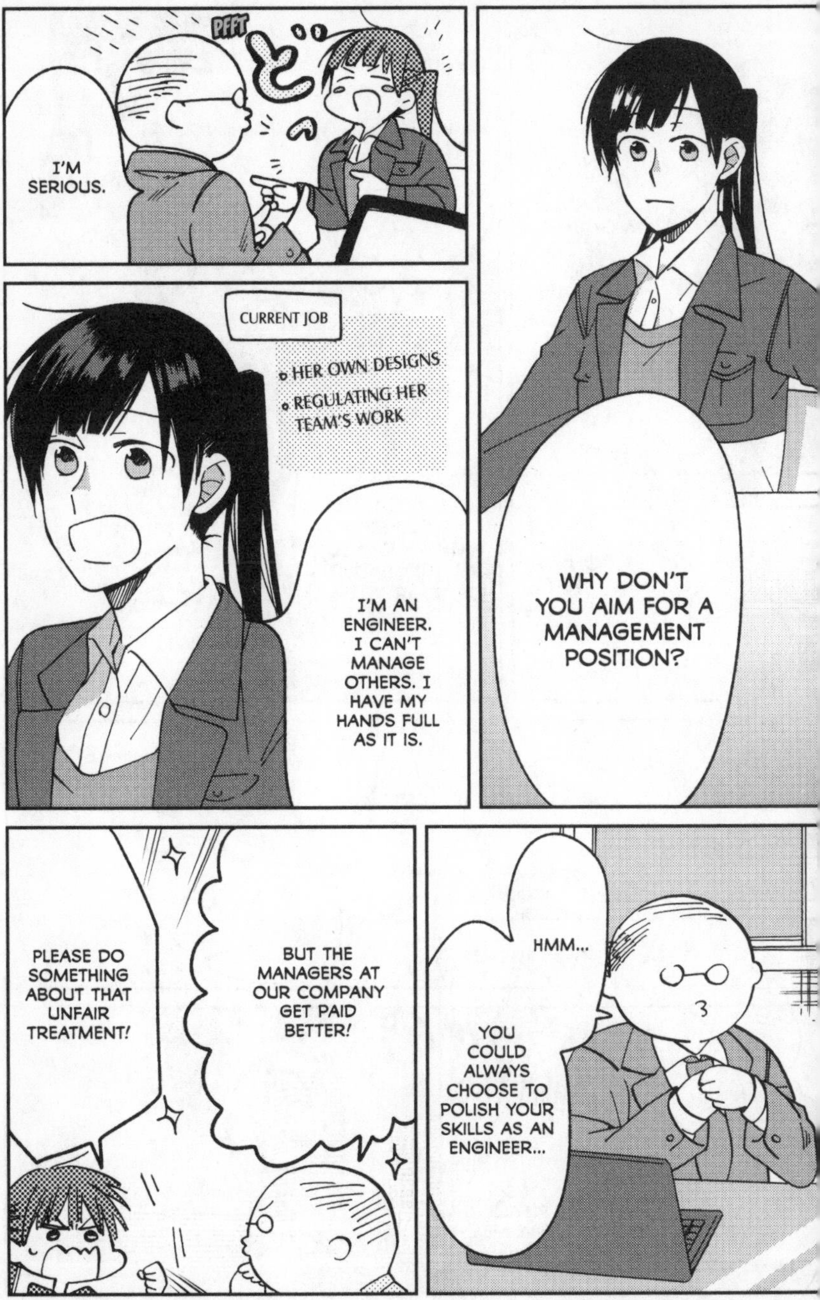
WHY DON'T YOU AIM FOR A MANAGEMENT POSITION?
PFFT
I'M SERIOUS.
CURRENT JOB
HER OWN DESIGNS
REGULATING HER TEAM'S WORK
I'M AN ENGINEER. I CAN'T MANAGE OTHERS. I HAVE MY HANDS FULL AS IT IS.
HMM...
YOU COULD ALWAYS CHOOSE TO POLISH YOUR SKILLS AS AN ENGINEER...
BUT THE MANAGERS AT OUR COMPANY GET PAID BETTER!
PLEASE DO SOMETHING ABOUT THAT UNFAIR TREATMENT!

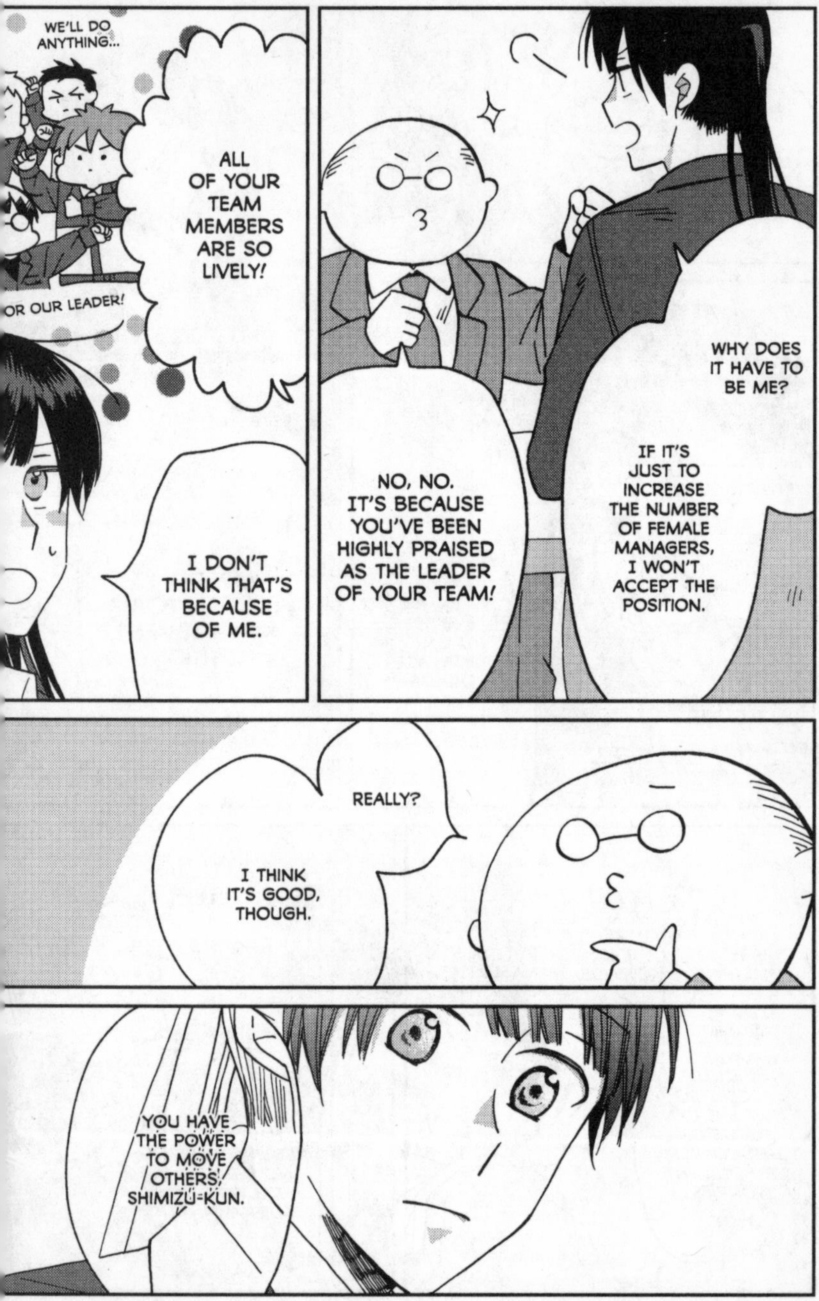
WHY DOES IT HAVE TO BE ME?
IF IT'S JUST TO INCREASE THE NUMBER OF FEMALE MANAGERS, I WON'T ACCEPT THE POSITION.
NO, NO. IT'S BECAUSE YOU'VE BEEN HIGHLY PRAISED AS THE LEADER OF YOUR TEAM!
ALL OF YOUR TEAM MEMBERS ARE SO LIVELY!
WE'LL DO ANYTHING...
OR OUR LEADER!
I DON'T THINK THAT'S BECAUSE OF ME.
REALLY?
I THINK IT'S GOOD, THOUGH.
YOU HAVE THE POWER TO MOVE OTHERS, SHIMIZU-KUN.

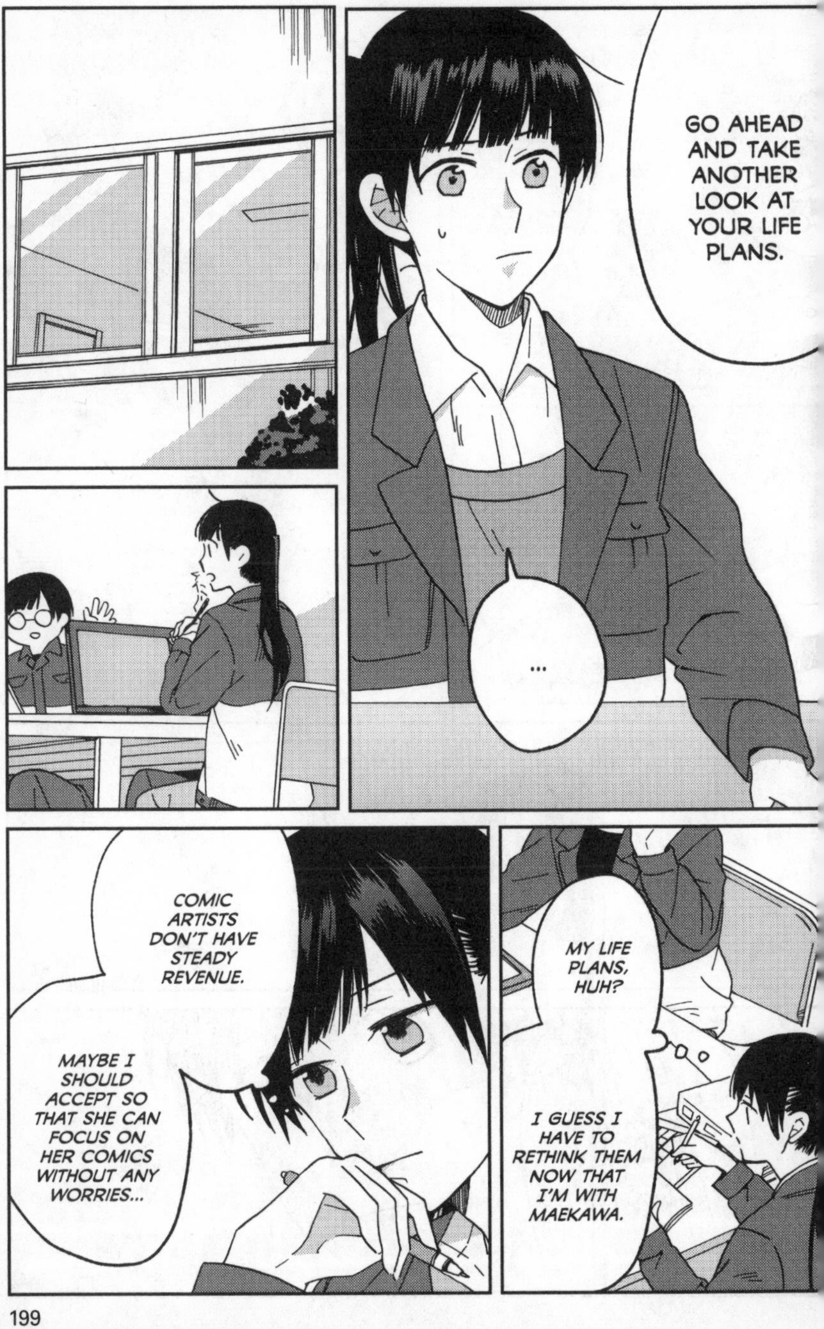
GO AHEAD AND TAKE ANOTHER LOOK AT YOUR LIFE PLANS.
...
MY LIFE PLANS, HUH?
I GUESS I HAVE TO RETHINK THEM NOW THAT I'M WITH MAEKAWA.
COMIC ARTISTS DON'T HAVE STEADY REVENUE.
MAYBE I SHOULD ACCEPT SO THAT SHE CAN FOCUS ON HER COMICS WITHOUT ANY WORRIES...

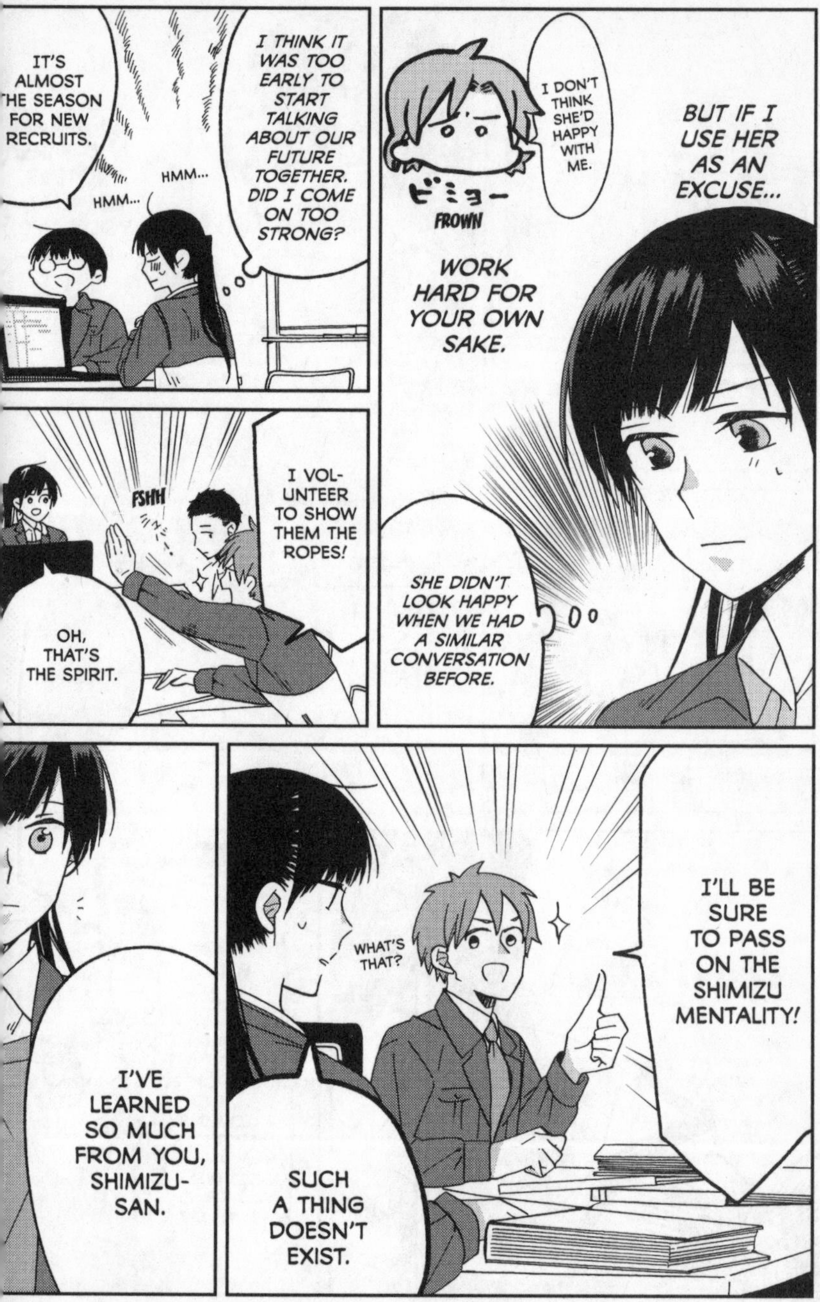
BUT IF I USE HER AS AN EXCUSE...
I DON'T THINK SHE'D HAPPY WITH ME.
ビミョー
FROWN
WORK HARD FOR YOUR OWN SAKE.
SHE DIDN'T LOOK HAPPY WHEN WE HAD A SIMILAR CONVERSATION BEFORE.
IT'S ALMOST THE SEASON FOR NEW RECRUITS.
I THINK IT WAS TOO EARLY TO START TALKING ABOUT OUR FUTURE TOGETHER. DID I COME ON TOO STRONG?
HMM...
HMM...
I VOL-UNTEER TO SHOW THEM THE ROPES!
FSHH
OH, THAT'S THE SPIRIT.
I'LL BE SURE TO PASS ON THE SHIMIZU MENTALITY!
WHAT'S THAT?
SUCH A THING DOESN'T EXIST.
I'VE LEARNED SO MUCH FROM YOU, SHIMIZU-SAN.

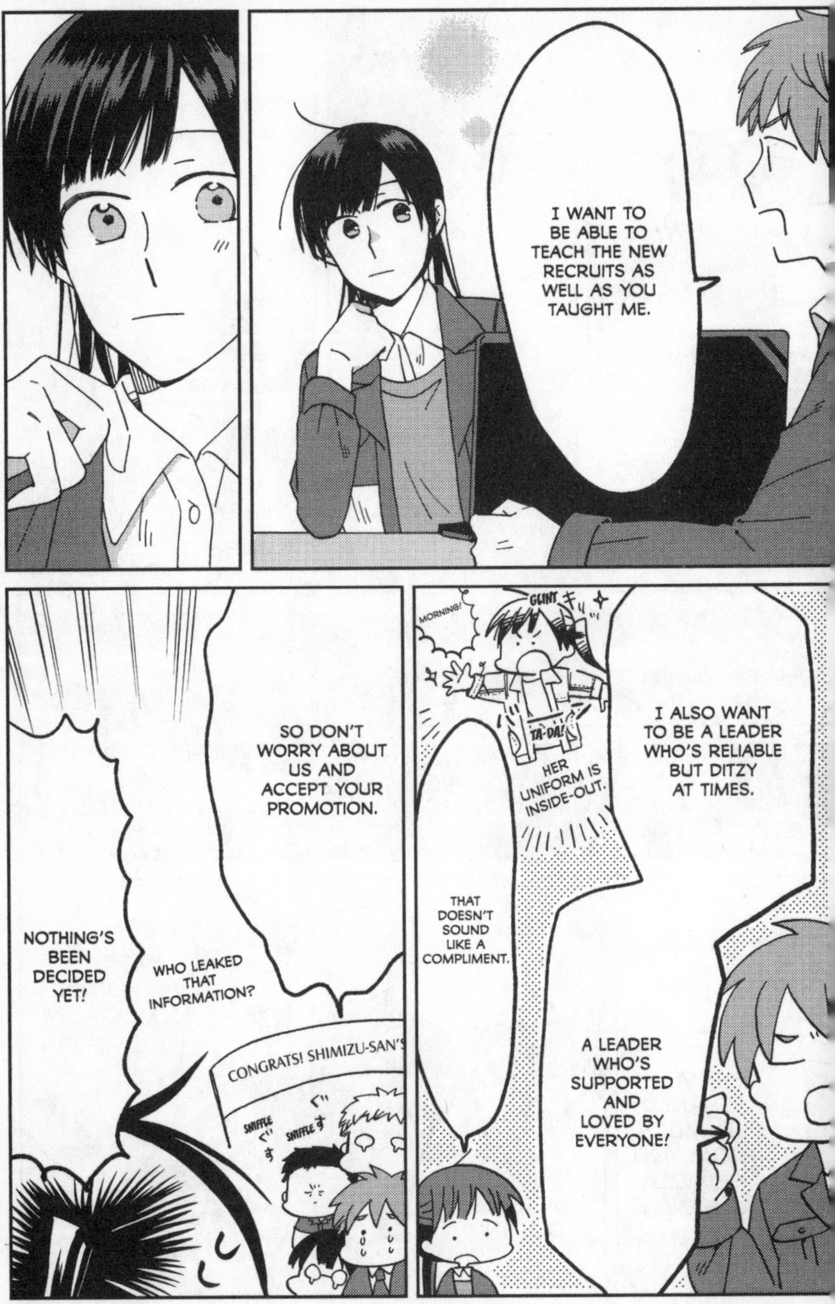
I WANT TO BE ABLE TO TEACH THE NEW RECRUITS AS WELL AS YOU TAUGHT ME.
I ALSO WANT TO BE A LEADER WHO'S RELIABLE BUT DITZY AT TIMES.
MORNING!
GLINT
TA-DA!
HER UNIFORM IS INSIDE-OUT.
A LEADER WHO'S SUPPORTED AND LOVED BY EVERYONE!
THAT DOESN'T SOUND LIKE A COMPLIMENT.
SO DON'T WORRY ABOUT US AND ACCEPT YOUR PROMOTION.
CONGRATS! SHIMIZU-SAN'S
SNIFFLE
SNIFFLE
WHO LEAKED THAT INFORMATION?
NOTHING'S BEEN DECIDED YET!

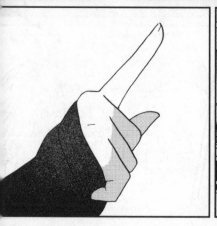

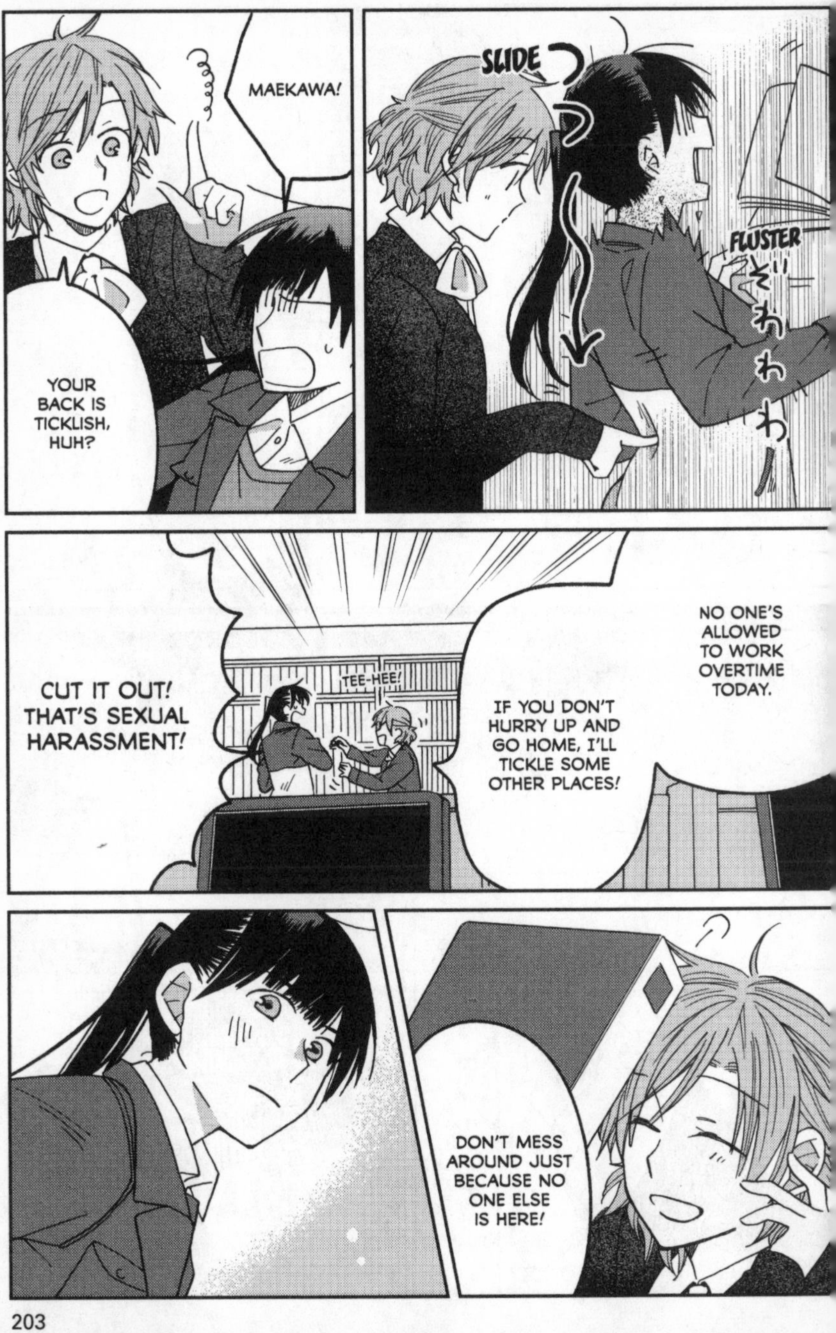
SLIDE
FLUSTER
そわわわ
MAEKAWA!
YOUR BACK IS TICKLISH, HUH?
NO ONE'S ALLOWED TO WORK OVERTIME TODAY.
IF YOU DON'T HURRY UP AND GO HOME, I'LL TICKLE SOME OTHER PLACES!
TEE-HEE!
CUT IT OUT! THAT'S SEXUAL HARASSMENT!
DON'T MESS AROUND JUST BECAUSE NO ONE ELSE IS HERE!

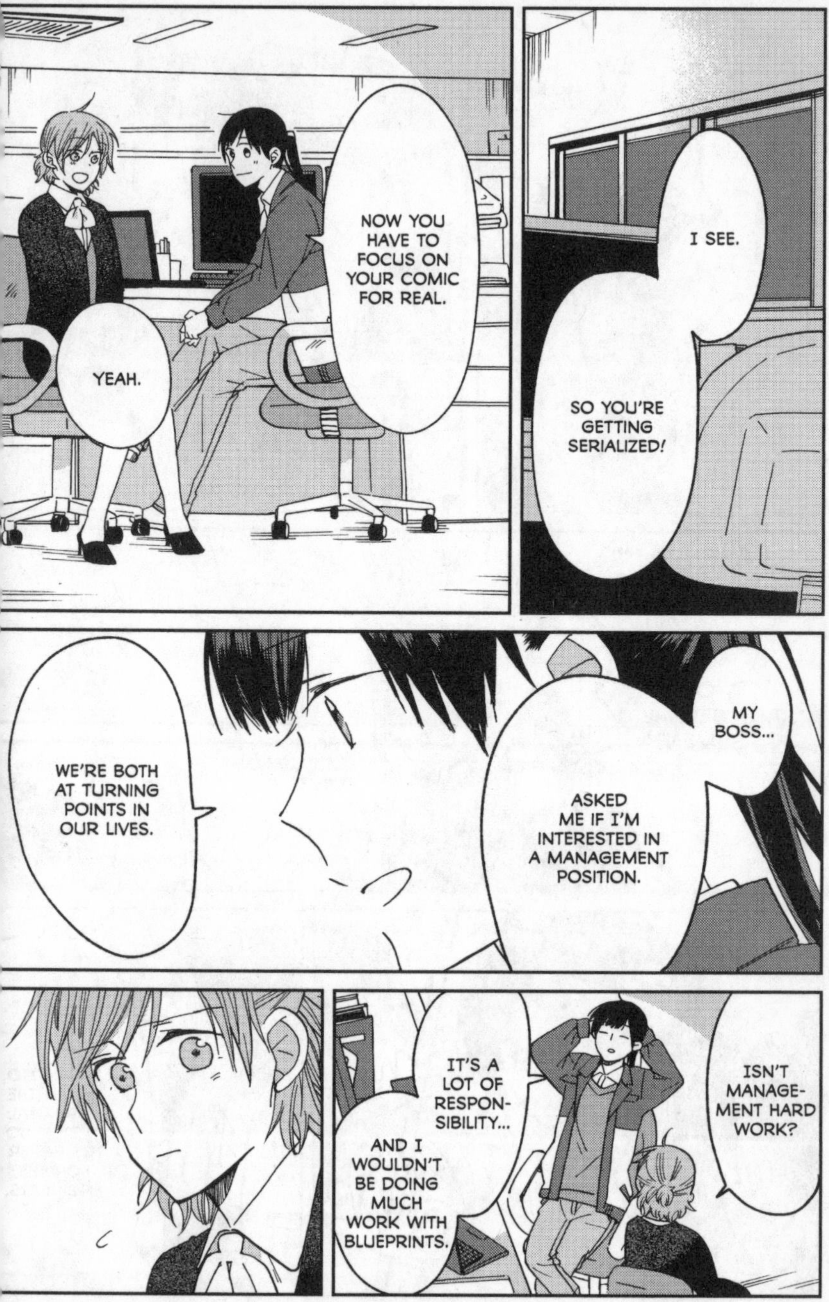
I SEE.
SO YOU'RE GETTING SERIALIZED!
NOW YOU HAVE TO FOCUS ON YOUR COMIC FOR REAL.
YEAH.
MY BOSS...
ASKED ME IF I'M INTERESTED IN A MANAGEMENT POSITION.
WE'RE BOTH AT TURNING POINTS IN OUR LIVES.
ISN'T MANAGEMENT HARD WORK?
IT'S A LOT OF RESPONSIBILITY...
AND I WOULDN'T BE DOING MUCH WORK WITH BLUEPRINTS.

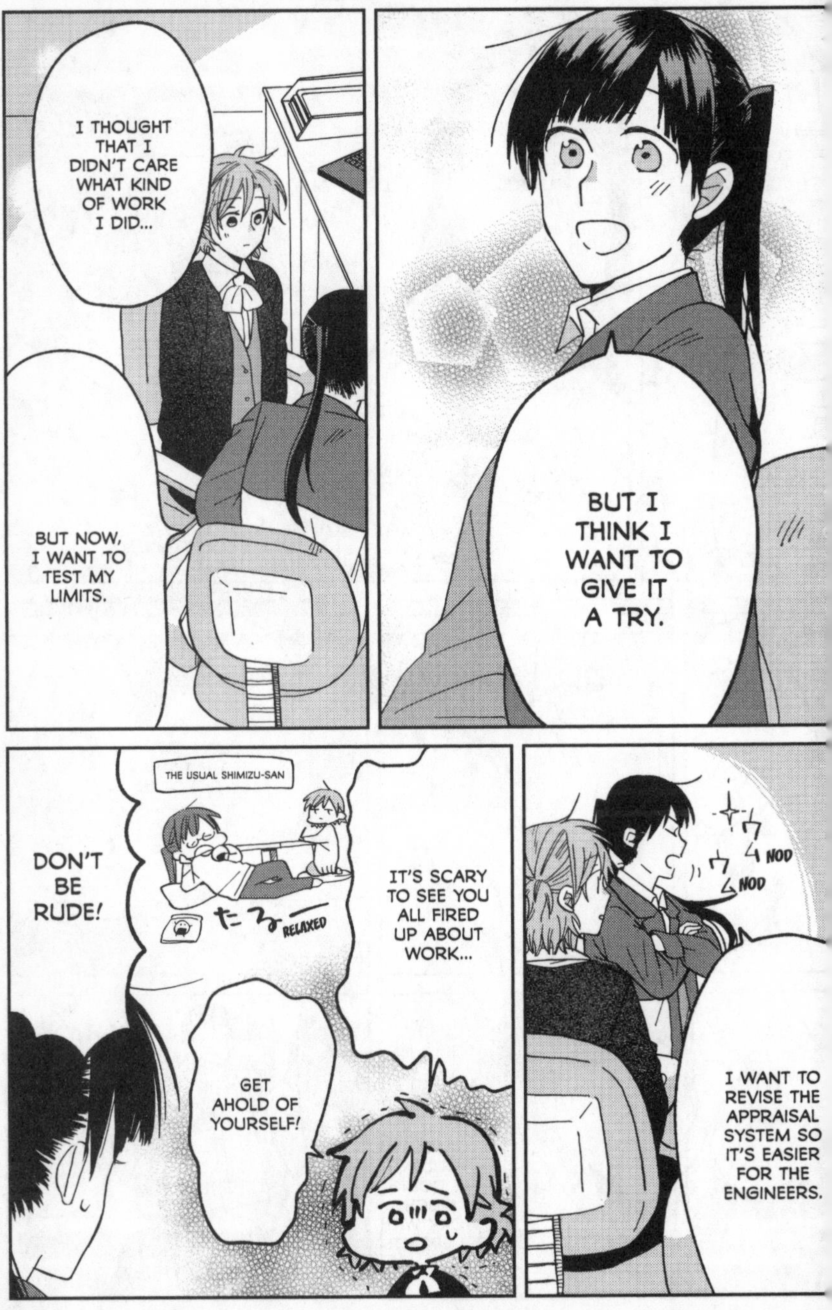
BUT I THINK I WANT TO GIVE IT A TRY.
I THOUGHT THAT I DIDN'T CARE WHAT KIND OF WORK I DID...
BUT NOW, I WANT TO TEST MY LIMITS.
I WANT TO REVISE THE APPRAISAL SYSTEM SO IT'S EASIER FOR THE ENGINEERS.
ウム NOD
ウム NOD
IT'S SCARY TO SEE YOU ALL FIRED UP ABOUT WORK...
THE USUAL SHIMIZU-SAN
たる～ RELAXED
DON'T BE RUDE!
GET AHOLD OF YOURSELF!

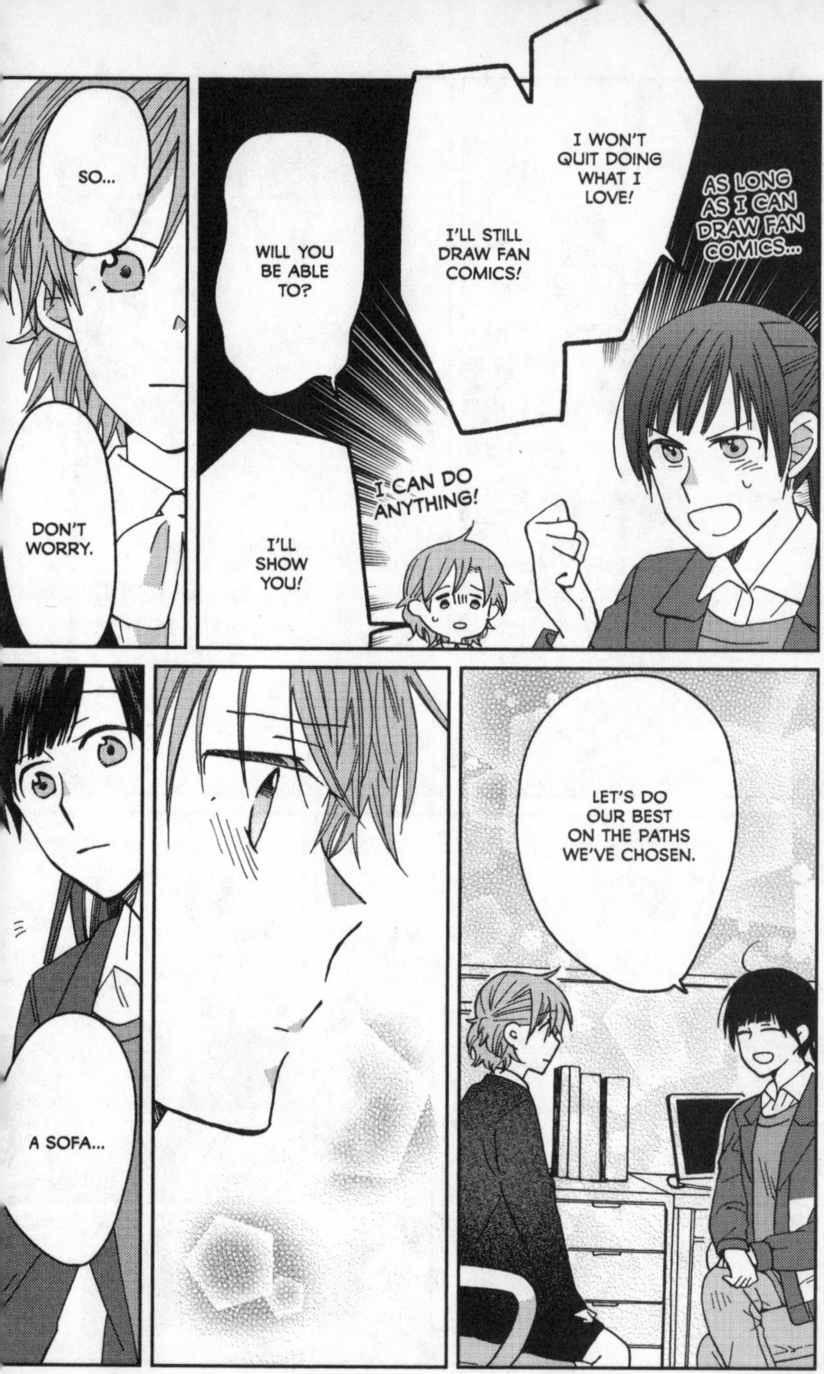
AS LONG AS I CAN DRAW FAN COMICS...
I WON'T QUIT DOING WHAT I LOVE!
I'LL STILL DRAW FAN COMICS!
WILL YOU BE ABLE TO?
I CAN DO ANYTHING!
I'LL SHOW YOU!
SO...
DON'T WORRY.
LET'S DO OUR BEST ON THE PATHS WE'VE CHOSEN.
A SOFA...

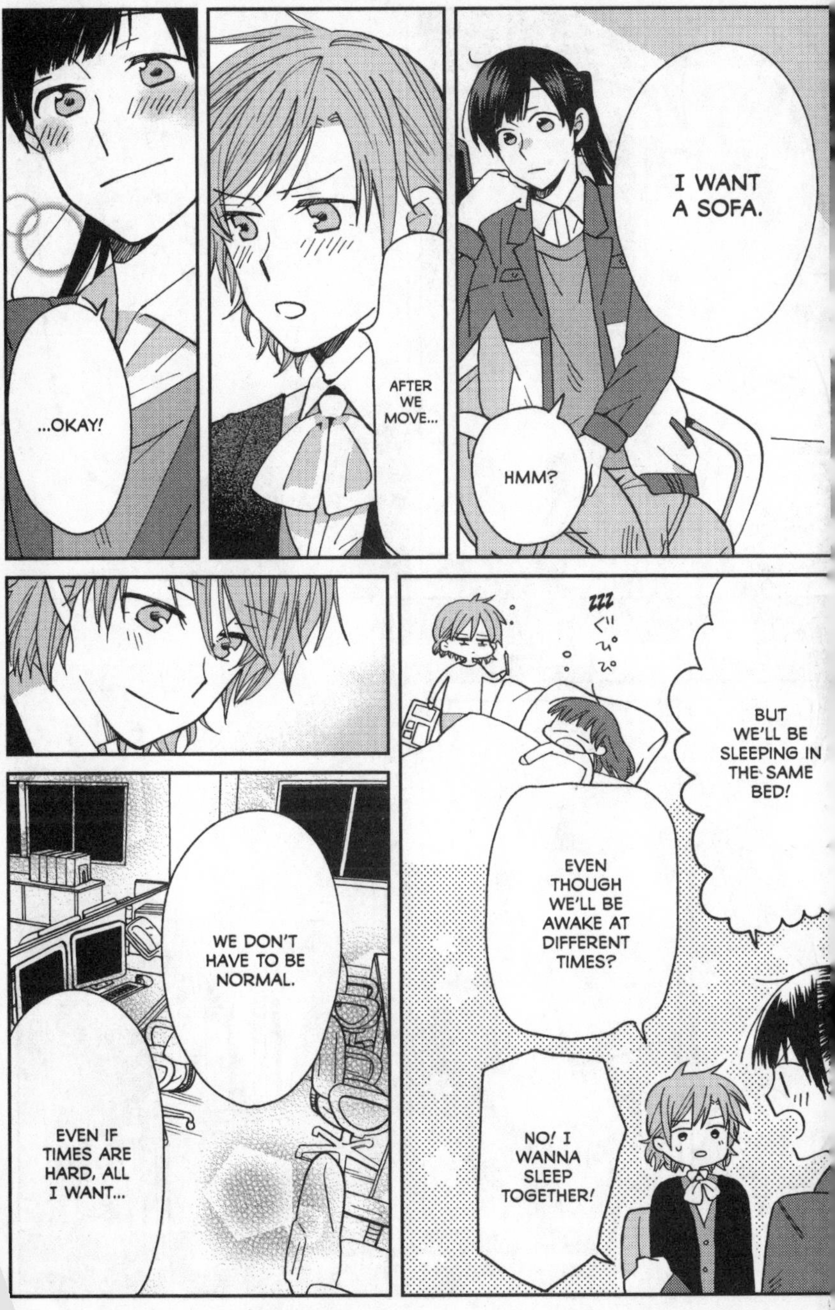
I WANT A SOFA.
HMM?
AFTER WE MOVE...
...OKAY!
ZZZ
BUT WE'LL BE SLEEPING IN THE SAME BED!
EVEN THOUGH WE'LL BE AWAKE AT DIFFERENT TIMES?
NO! I WANNA SLEEP TOGETHER!
WE DON'T HAVE TO BE NORMAL.
EVEN IF TIMES ARE HARD, ALL I WANT...

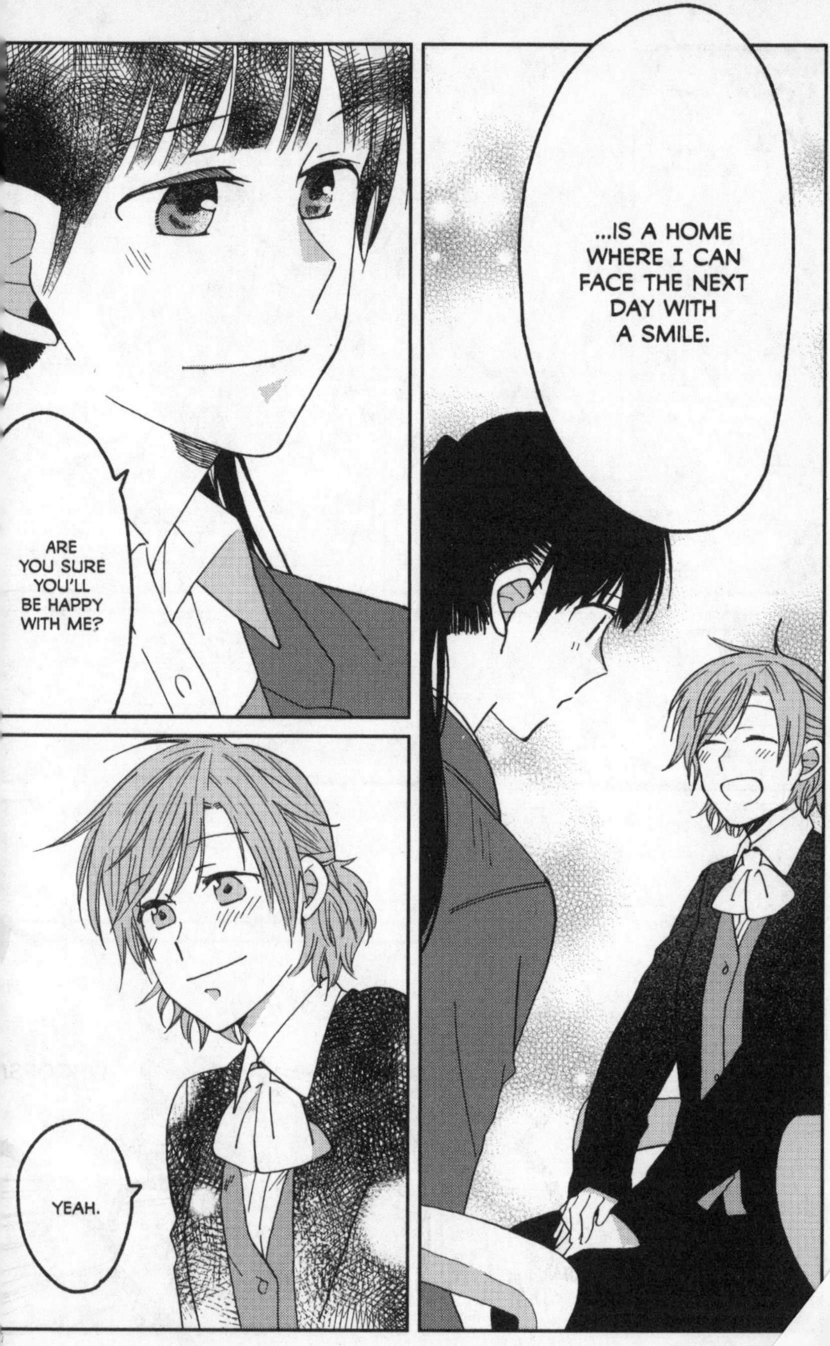
...IS A HOME WHERE I CAN FACE THE NEXT DAY WITH A SMILE.
ARE YOU SURE YOU'LL BE HAPPY WITH ME?
YEAH.

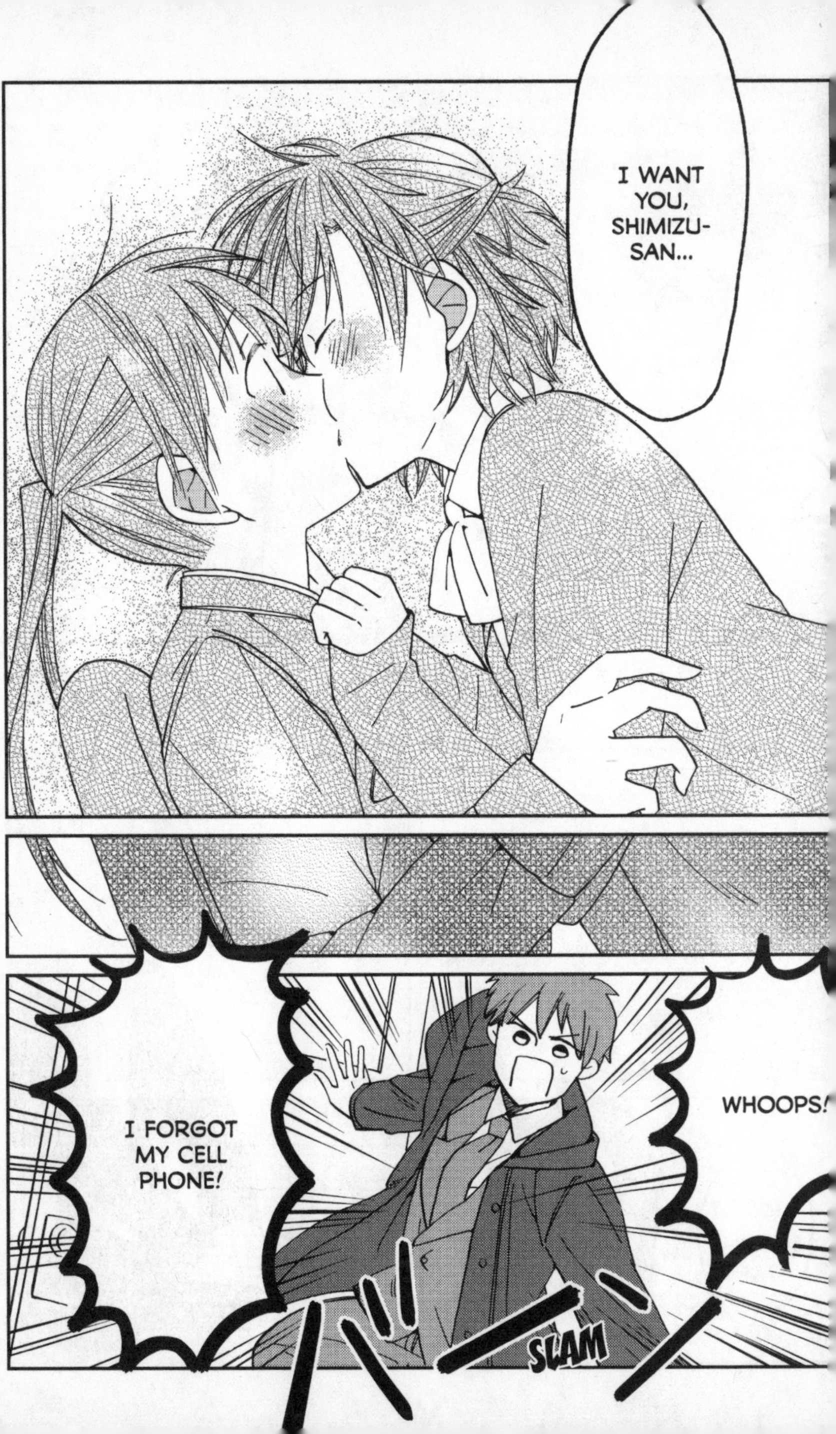
I WANT YOU, SHIMIZU-SAN...
WHOOPS!
I FORGOT MY CELL PHONE!
SLAM

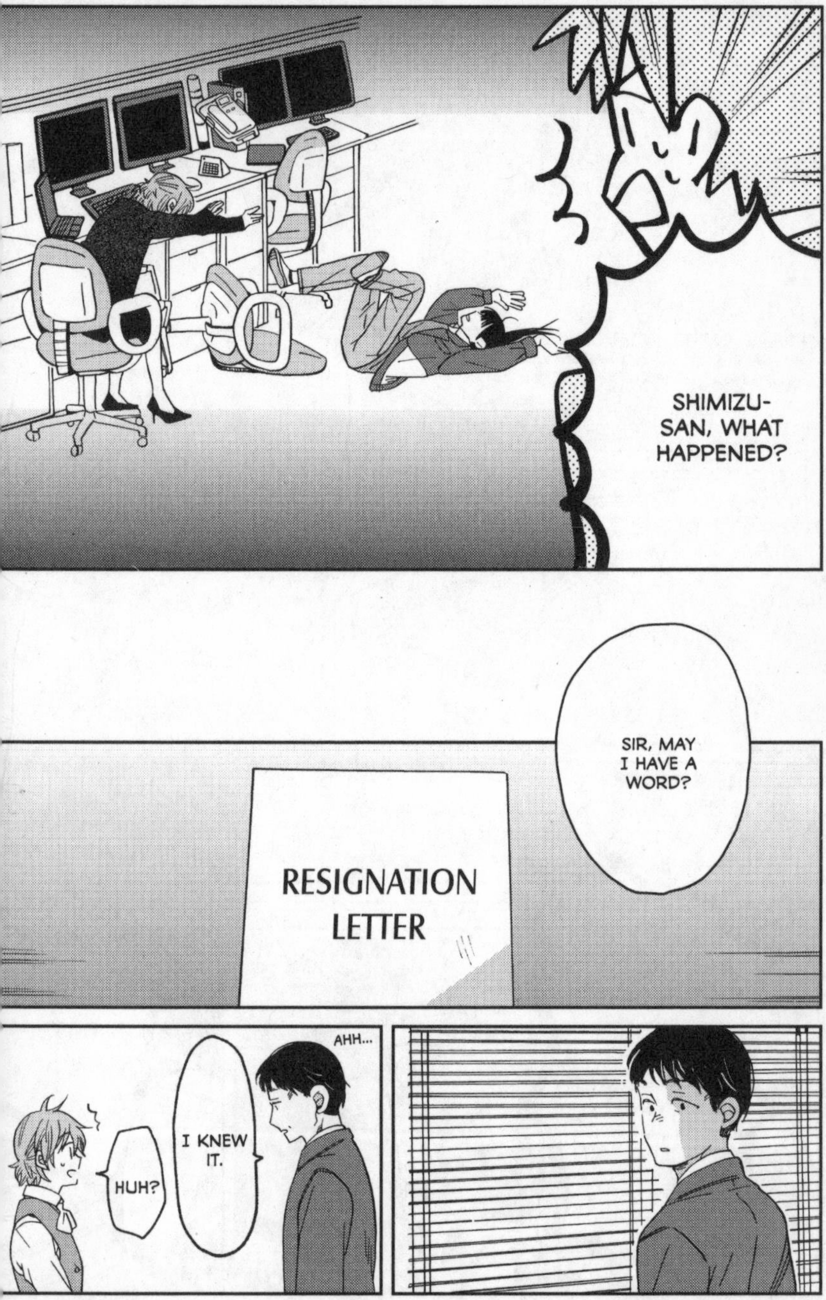
SHIMIZU-SAN, WHAT HAPPENED?
SIR, MAY I HAVE A WORD?
RESIGNATION LETTER
AHH...
I KNEW IT.
HUH?

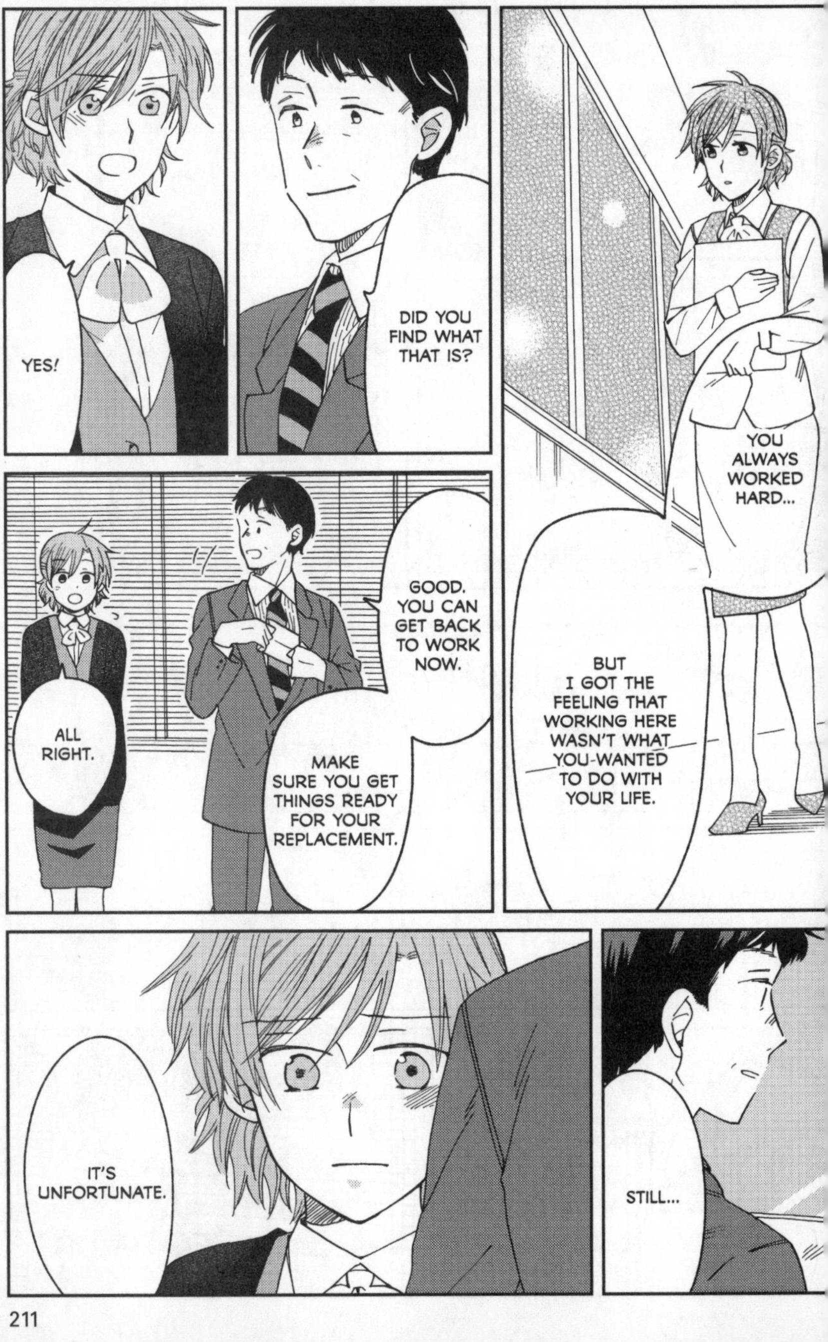
YOU ALWAYS WORKED HARD...
BUT I GOT THE FEELING THAT WORKING HERE WASN'T WHAT YOU WANTED TO DO WITH YOUR LIFE.
DID YOU FIND WHAT THAT IS?
YES!
GOOD. YOU CAN GET BACK TO WORK NOW.
MAKE SURE YOU GET THINGS READY FOR YOUR REPLACEMENT.
ALL RIGHT.
STILL...
IT'S UNFORTUNATE.

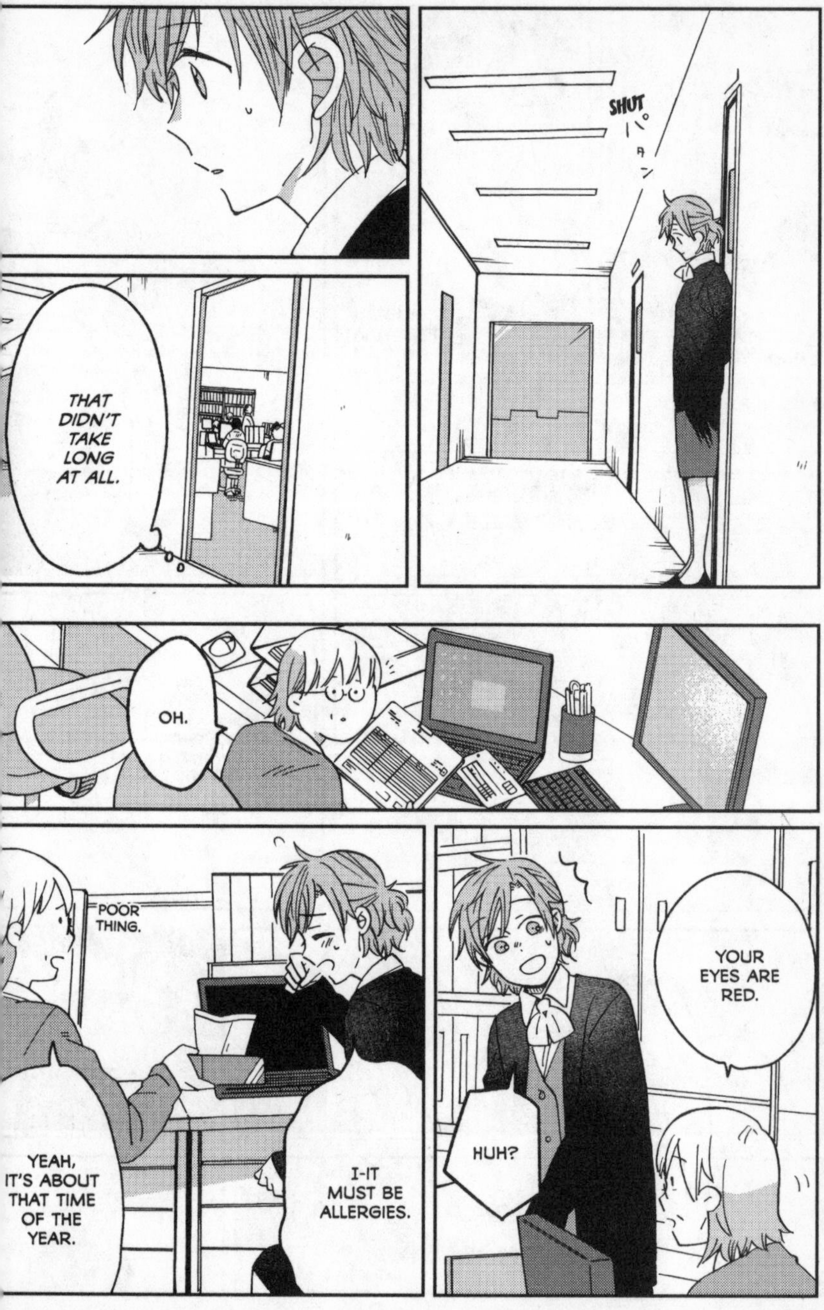
SHUT
パタン
THAT DIDN'T TAKE LONG AT ALL.
OH.
YOUR EYES ARE RED.
HUH?
I-IT MUST BE ALLERGIES.
YEAH, IT'S ABOUT THAT TIME OF THE YEAR.
POOR THING.

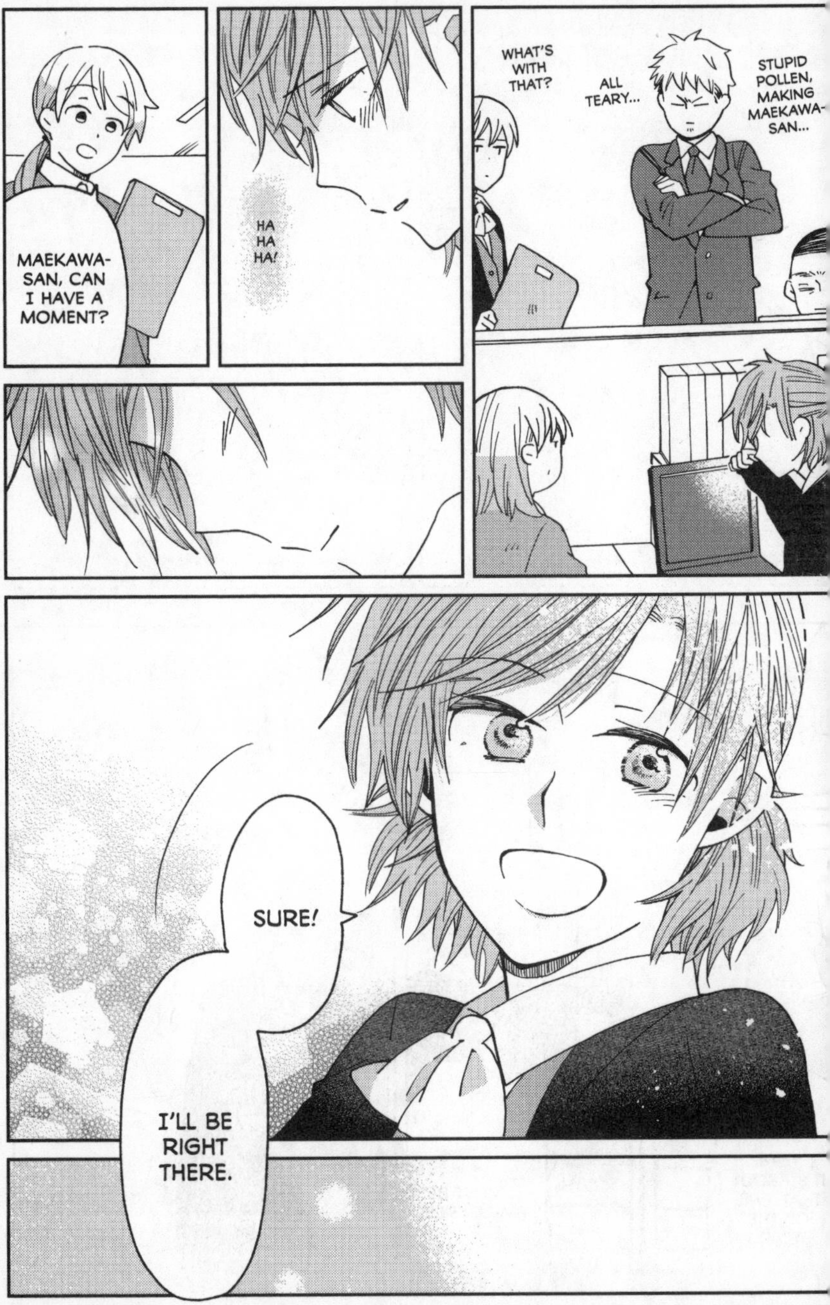
STUPID POLLEN, MAKING MAEKAWA-SAN...
ALL TEARY...
WHAT'S WITH THAT?
HA HA HA!
MAEKAWA-SAN, CAN I HAVE A MOMENT?
SURE!
I'LL BE RIGHT THERE.

THE PACKING
NEVER ENDS...

manga

fan comics

fan comics

manga

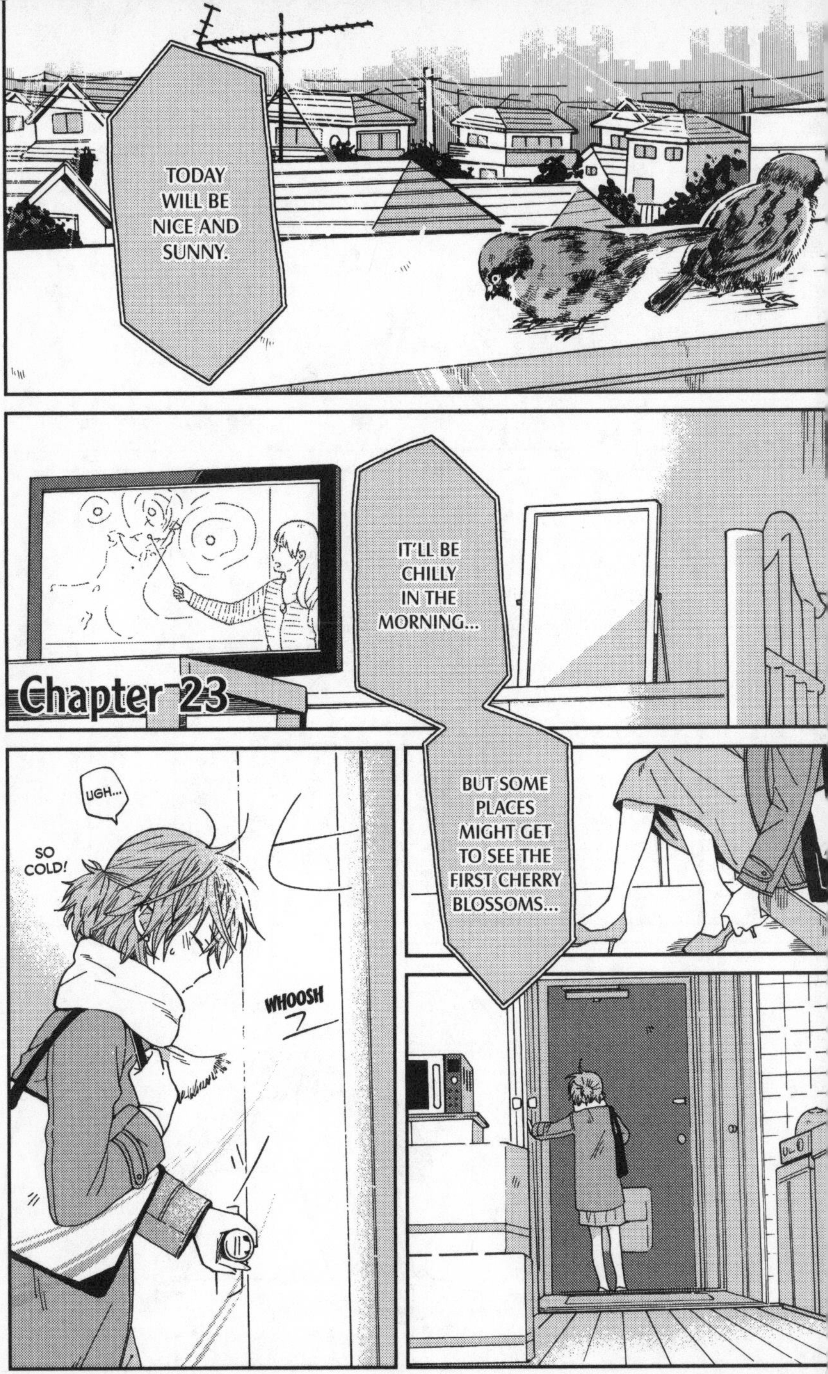
TODAY WILL BE NICE AND SUNNY.
IT'LL BE CHILLY IN THE MORNING...
Chapter 23
BUT SOME PLACES MIGHT GET TO SEE THE FIRST CHERRY BLOSSOMS...
UGH...
SO COLD!
WHOOSH

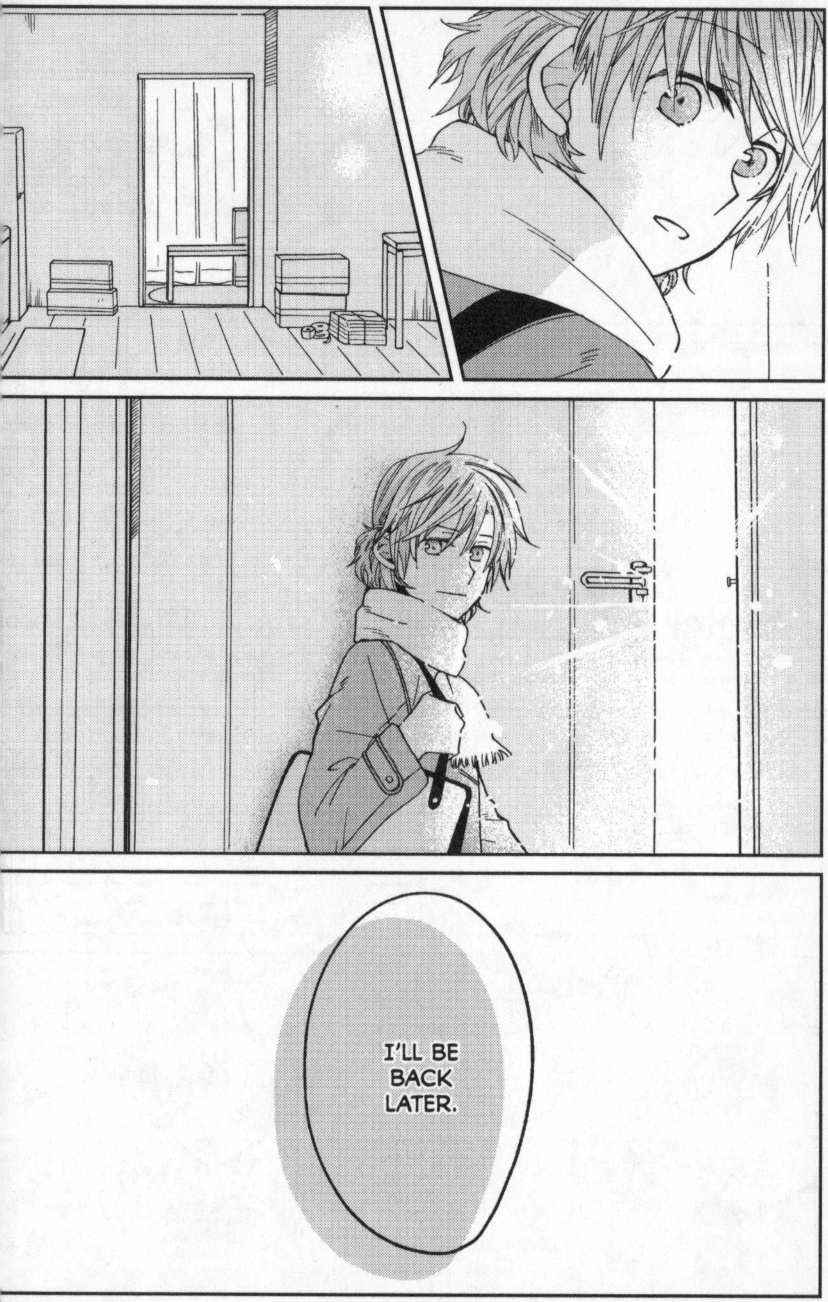
I'LL BE BACK LATER.

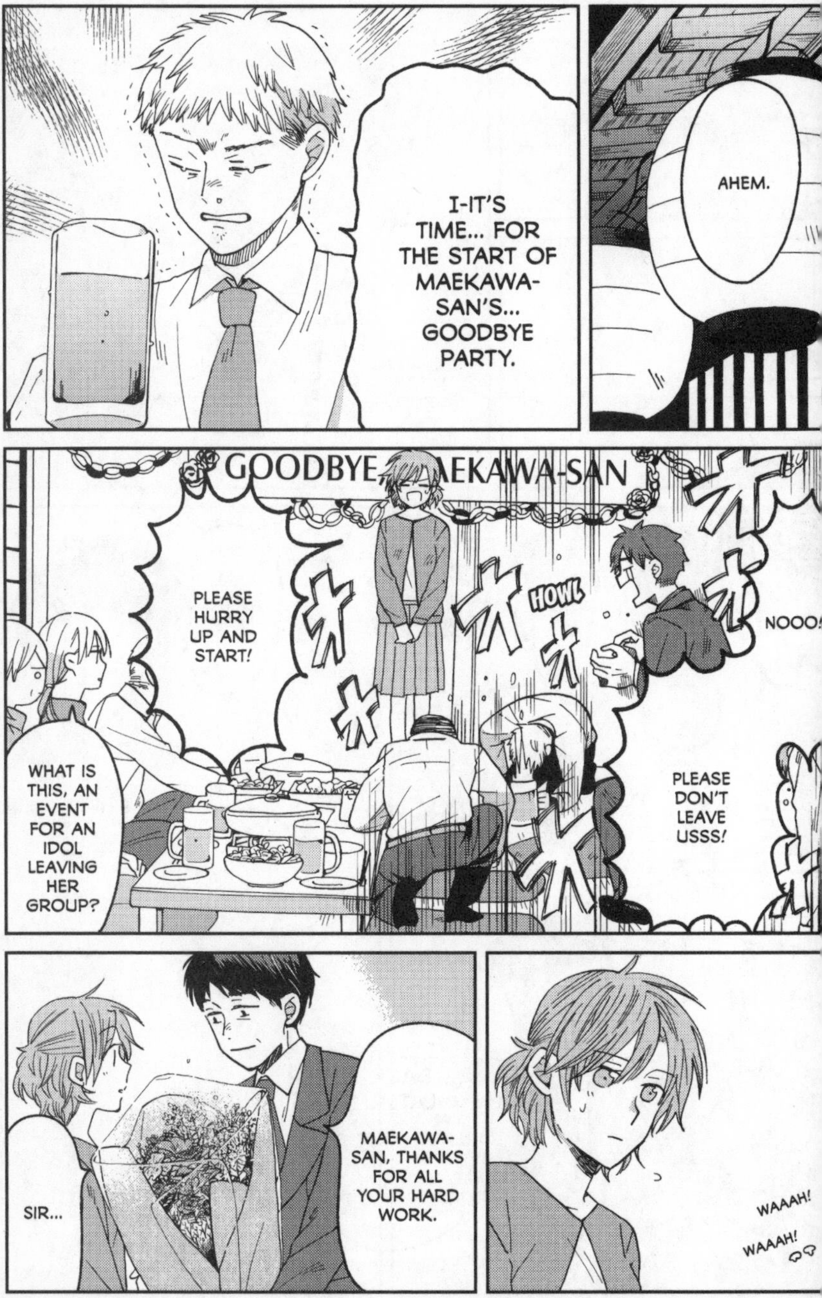
AHEM.
I-IT'S TIME... FOR THE START OF MAEKAWA-SAN'S... GOODBYE PARTY.
NOOO!
PLEASE DON'T LEAVE USSS!
HOWL
GOODBYE, AEKAWA-SAN
PLEASE HURRY UP AND START!
WHAT IS THIS, AN EVENT FOR AN IDOL LEAVING HER GROUP?
WAAAH!
WAAAH!
MAEKAWA-SAN, THANKS FOR ALL YOUR HARD WORK.
SIR...

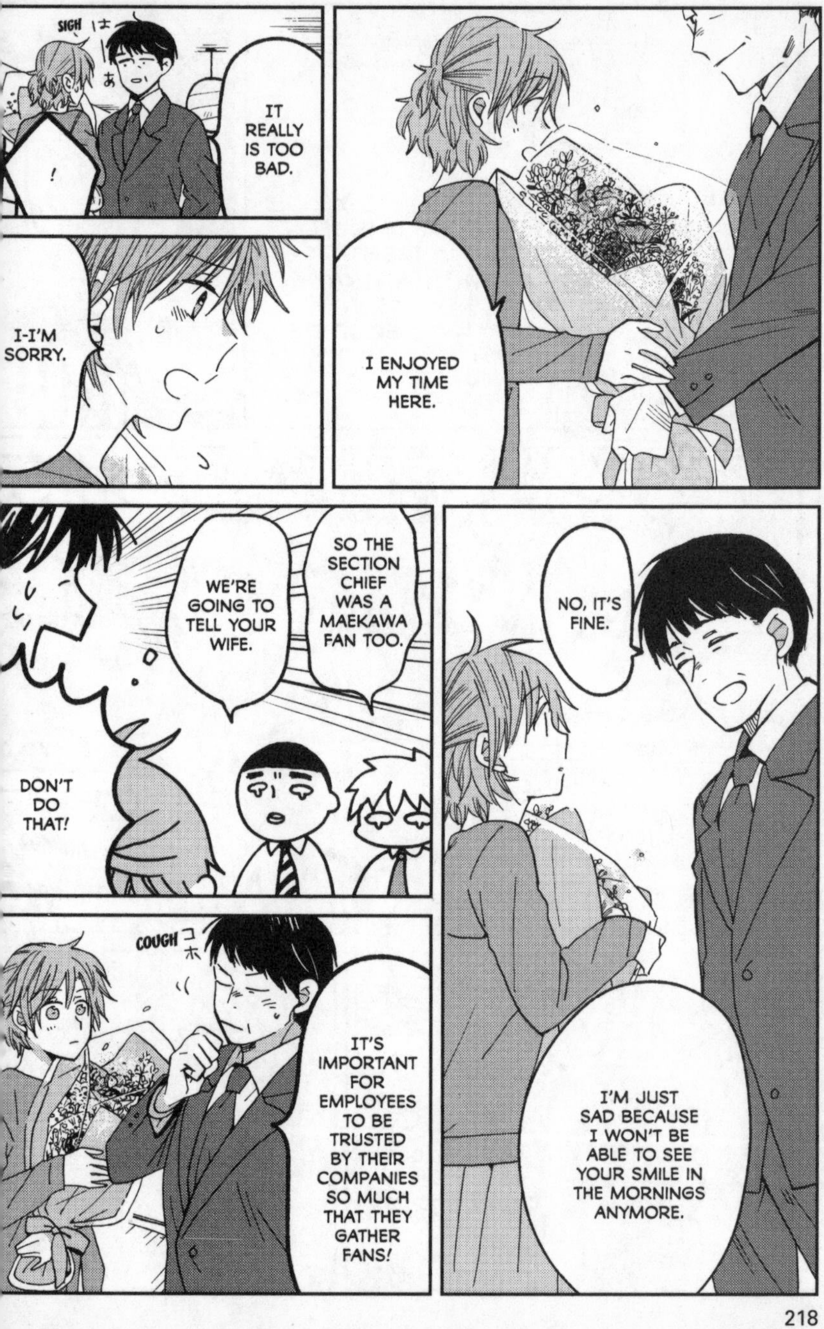
I ENJOYED MY TIME HERE.
SIGH は
あ
IT REALLY IS TOO BAD.
!
I-I'M SORRY.
NO, IT'S FINE.
I'M JUST SAD BECAUSE I WON'T BE ABLE TO SEE YOUR SMILE IN THE MORNINGS ANYMORE.
SO THE SECTION CHIEF WAS A MAEKAWA FAN TOO.
WE'RE GOING TO TELL YOUR WIFE.
DON'T DO THAT!
COUGH コホ
IT'S IMPORTANT FOR EMPLOYEES TO BE TRUSTED BY THEIR COMPANIES SO MUCH THAT THEY GATHER FANS!

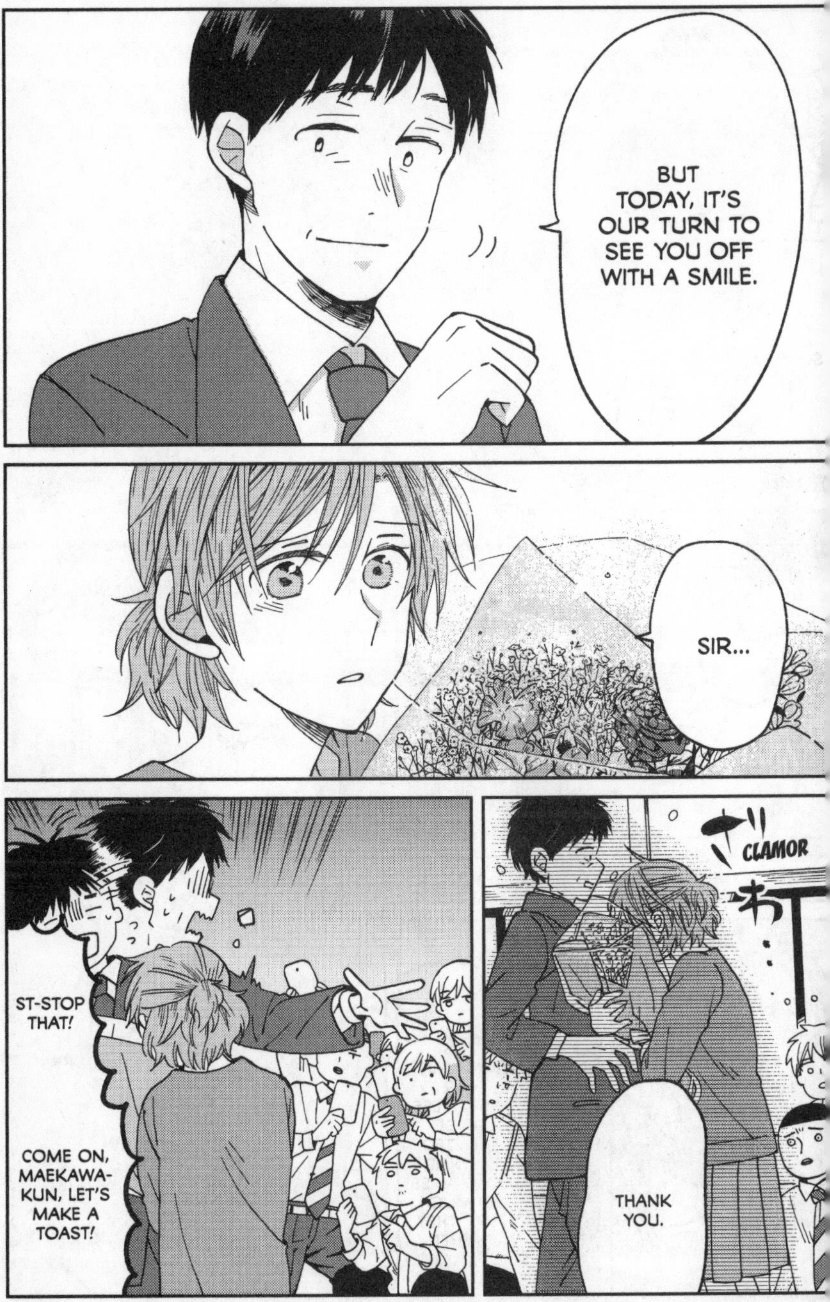
BUT TODAY, IT'S OUR TURN TO SEE YOU OFF WITH A SMILE.
SIR...
CLAMOR
THANK YOU.
ST-STOP THAT!
COME ON, MAEKAWA-KUN, LET'S MAKE A TOAST!

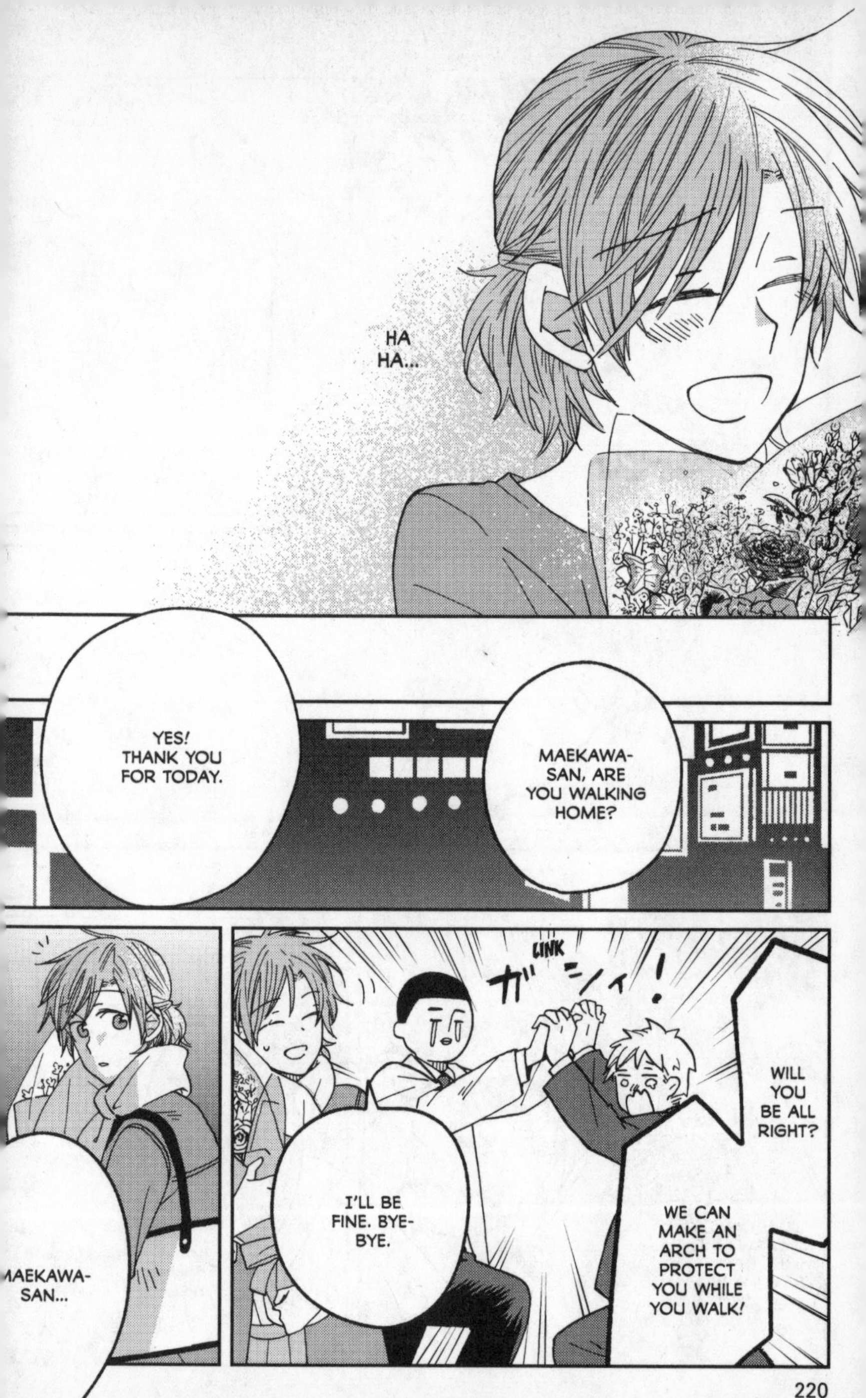
HA HA...
MAEKAWA-SAN, ARE YOU WALKING HOME?
YES! THANK YOU FOR TODAY.
LINK
ガシィ!
WILL YOU BE ALL RIGHT?
WE CAN MAKE AN ARCH TO PROTECT YOU WHILE YOU WALK!
I'LL BE FINE. BYE-BYE.
MAEKAWA-SAN...

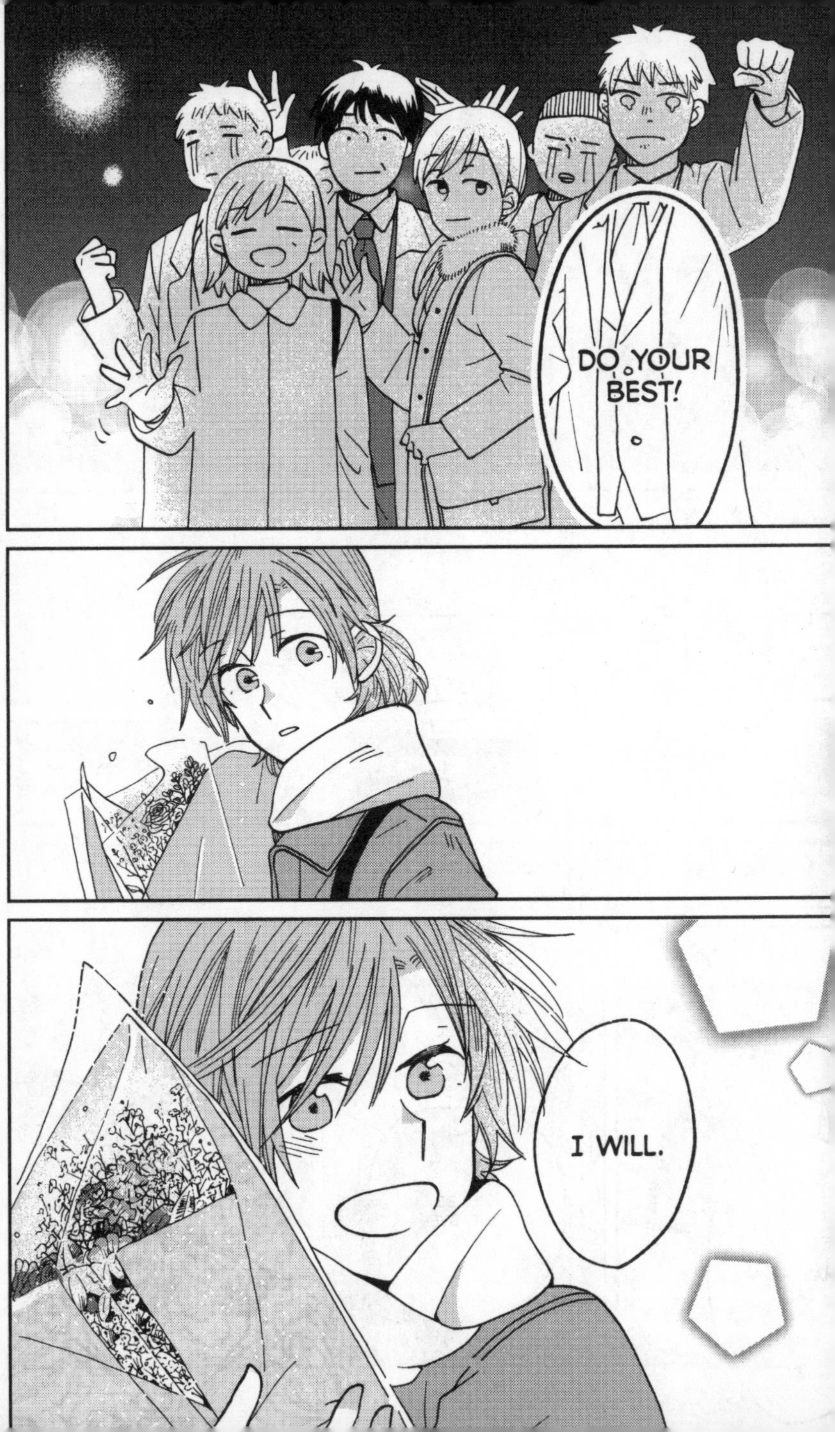
DO YOUR BEST!
I WILL.

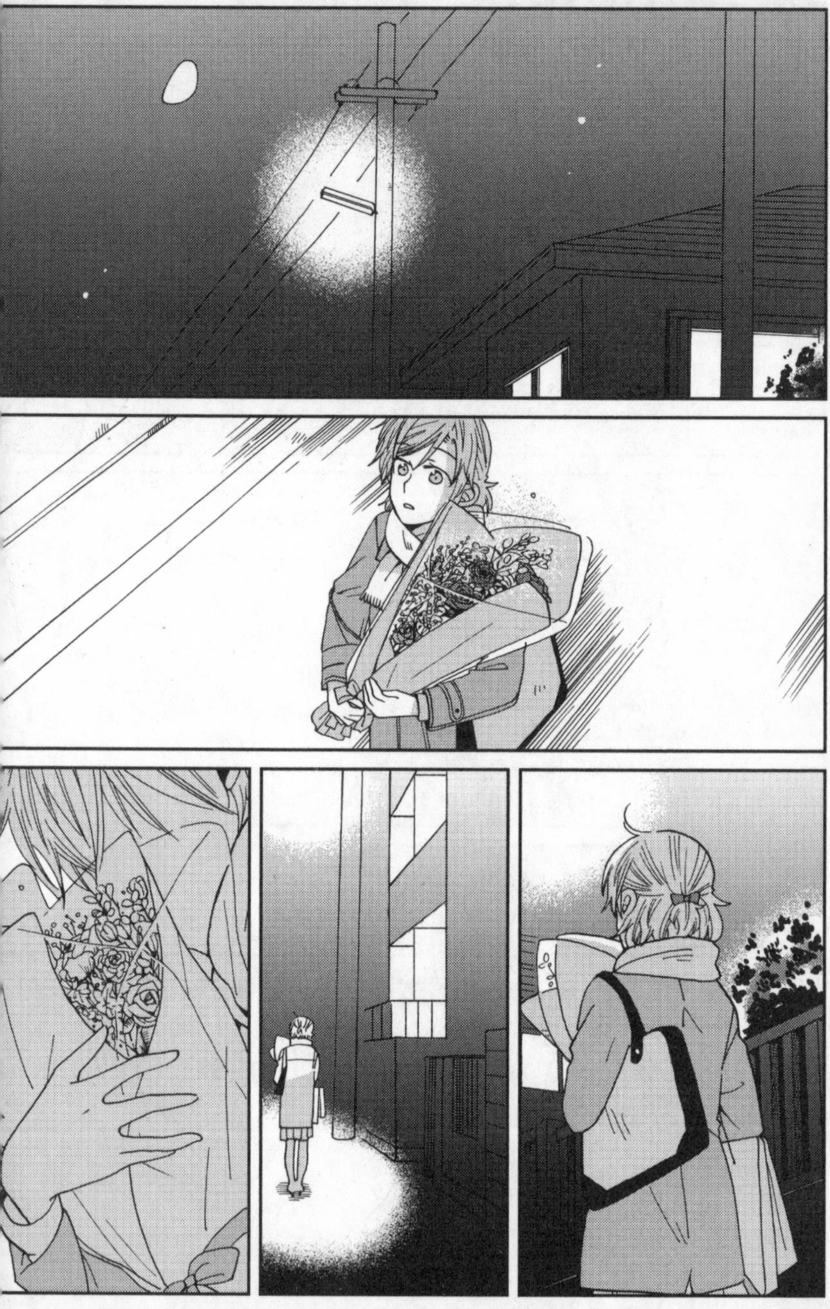

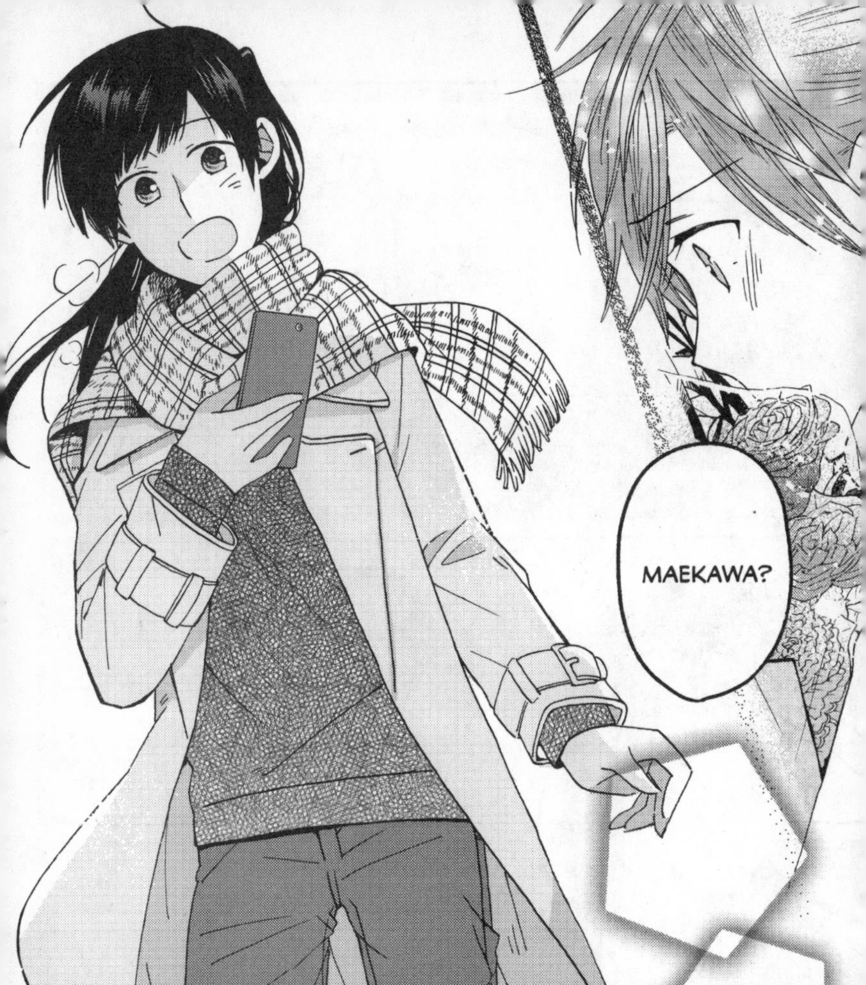
MAEKAWA?
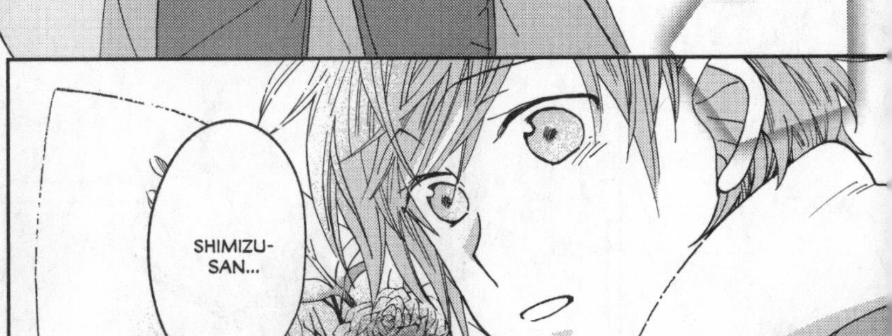
SHIMIZU-SAN...

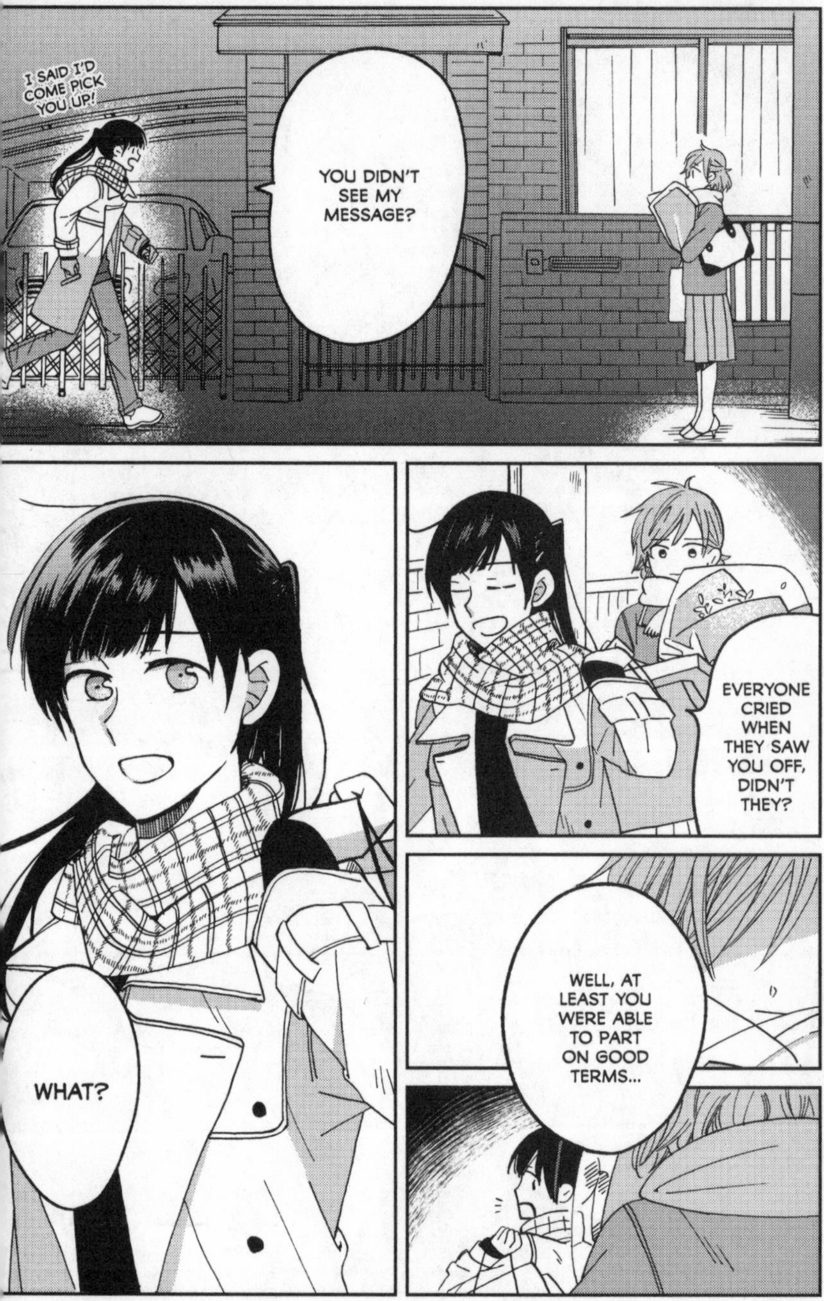
YOU DIDN'T SEE MY MESSAGE?
I SAID I'D COME PICK YOU UP!
EVERYONE CRIED WHEN THEY SAW YOU OFF, DIDN'T THEY?
WELL, AT LEAST YOU WERE ABLE TO PART ON GOOD TERMS...
WHAT?

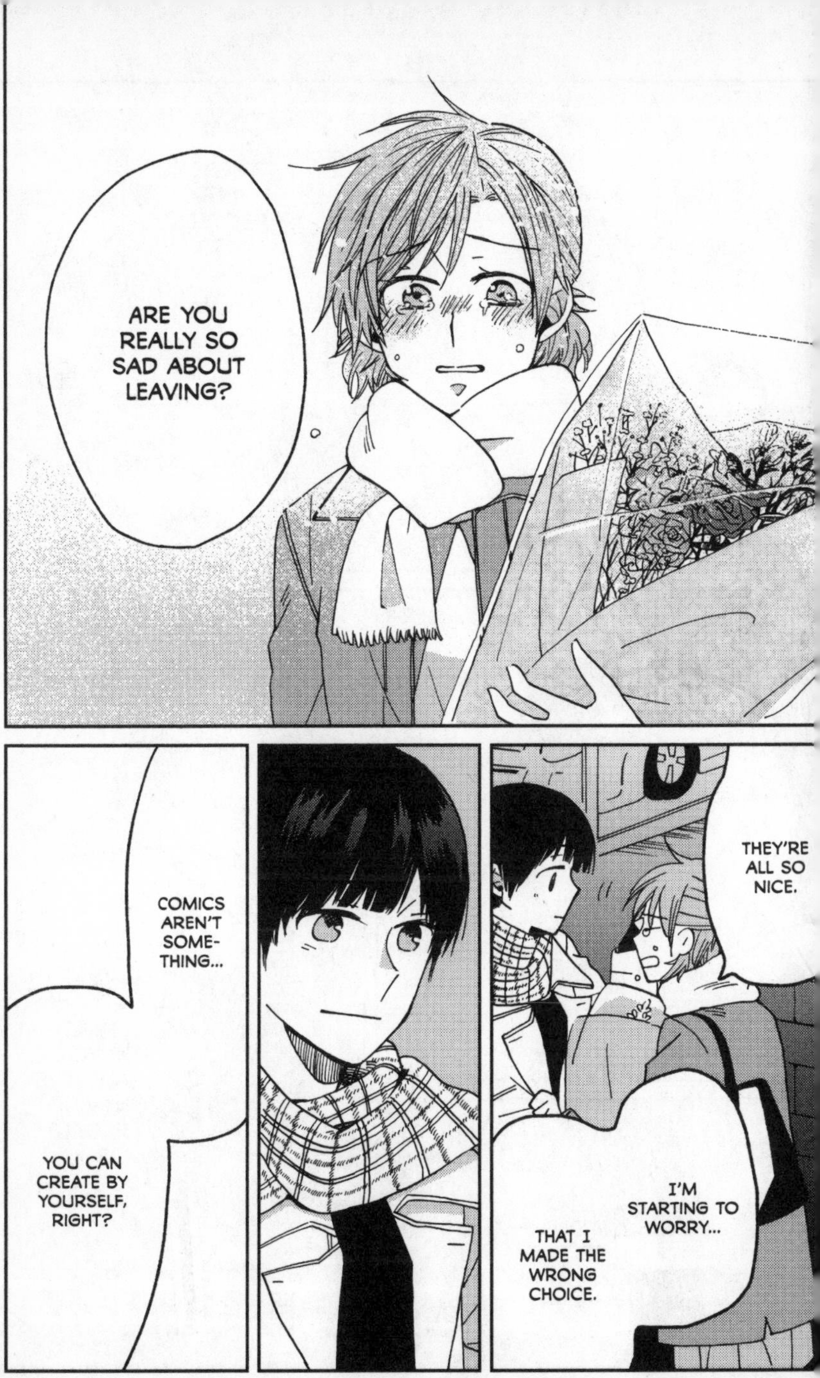
ARE YOU REALLY SO SAD ABOUT LEAVING?
THEY'RE ALL SO NICE.
I'M STARTING TO WORRY...
THAT I MADE THE WRONG CHOICE.
COMICS AREN'T SOME-THING...
YOU CAN CREATE BY YOURSELF, RIGHT?

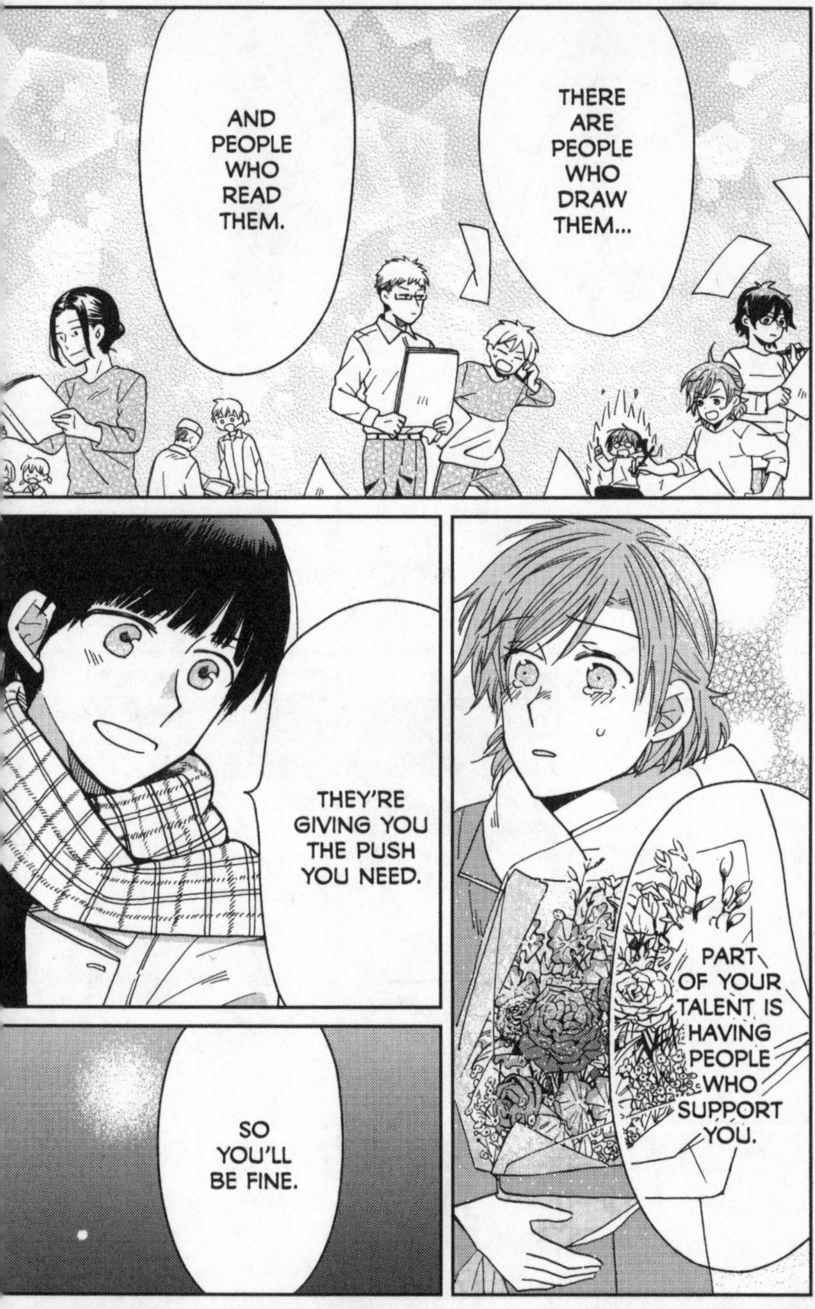
THERE ARE PEOPLE WHO DRAW THEM...
AND PEOPLE WHO READ THEM.
PART OF YOUR TALENT IS HAVING PEOPLE WHO SUPPORT YOU.
THEY'RE GIVING YOU THE PUSH YOU NEED.
SO YOU'LL BE FINE.

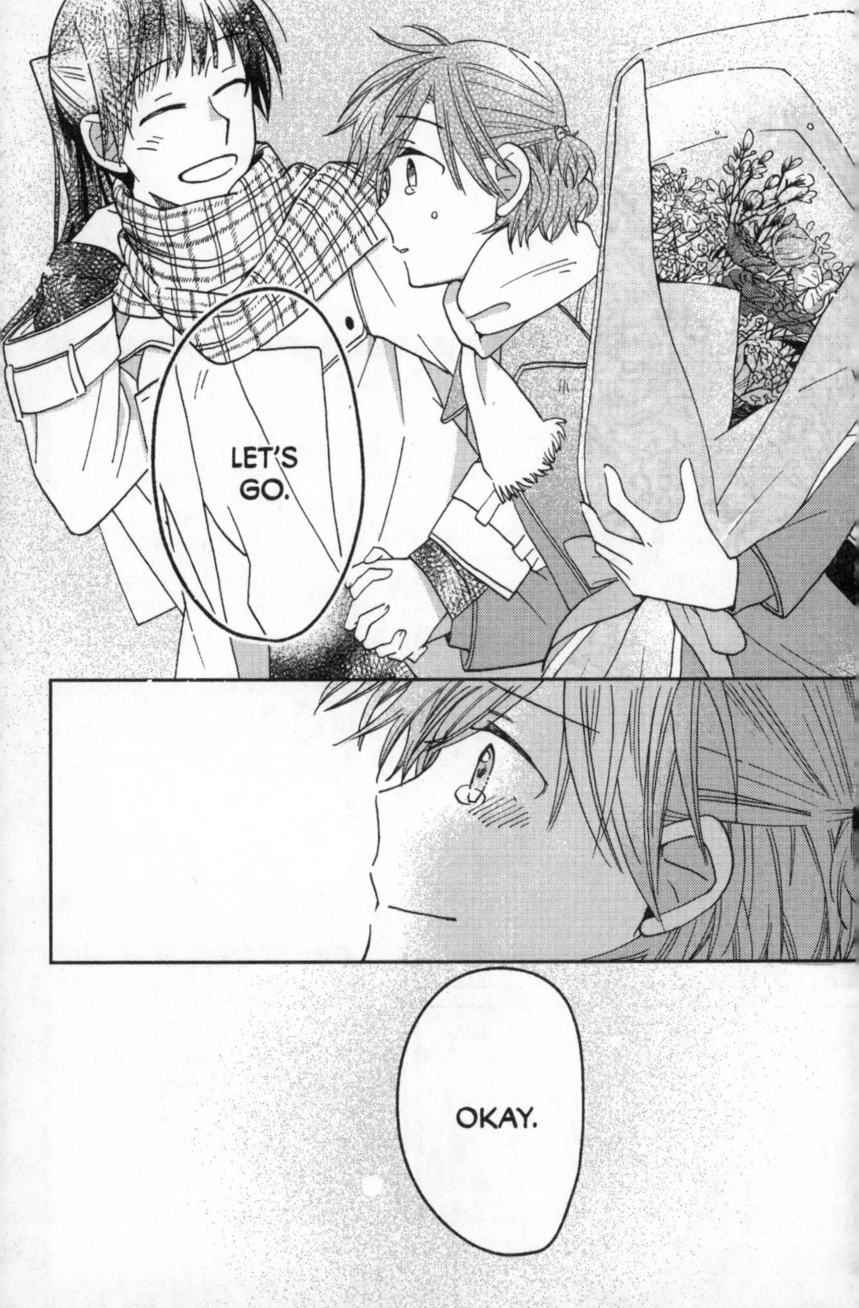
LET'S GO.
OKAY.

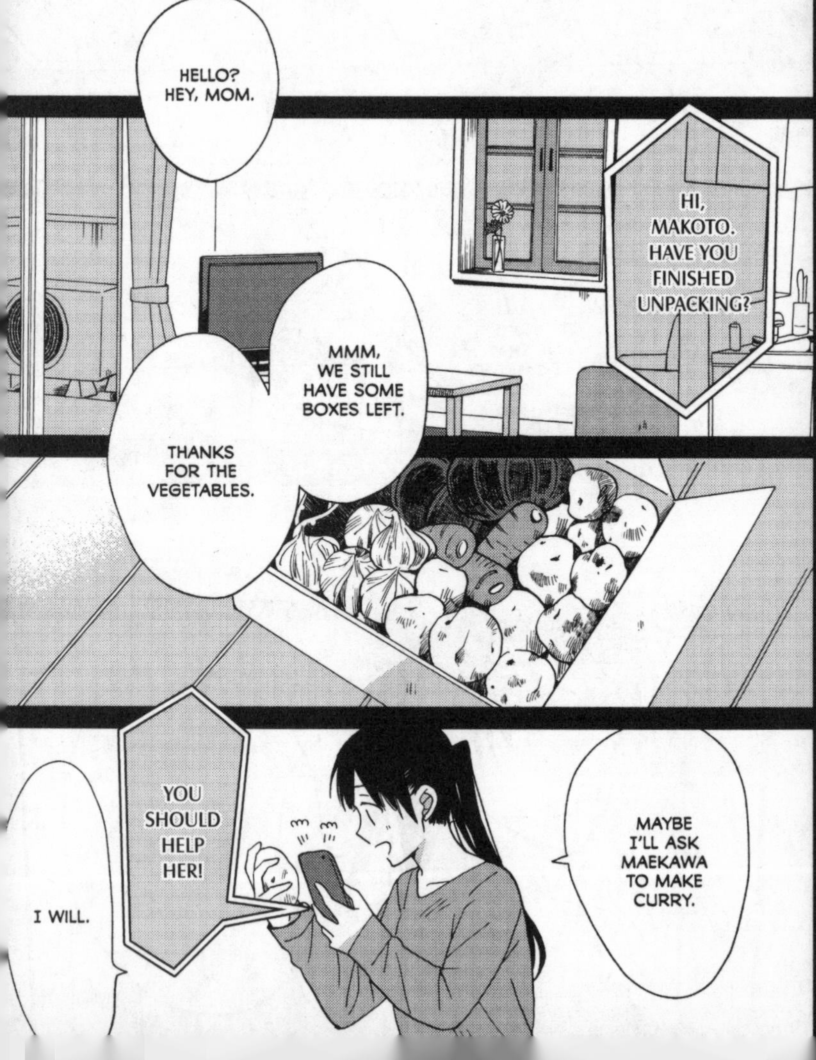
HELLO? HEY, MOM.
HI, MAKOTO. HAVE YOU FINISHED UNPACKING?
MMM, WE STILL HAVE SOME BOXES LEFT.
THANKS FOR THE VEGETABLES.
MAYBE I'LL ASK MAEKAWA TO MAKE CURRY.
YOU SHOULD HELP HER!
I WILL.

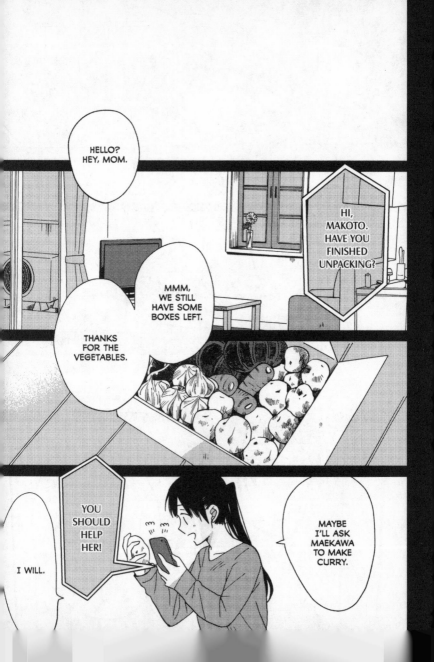

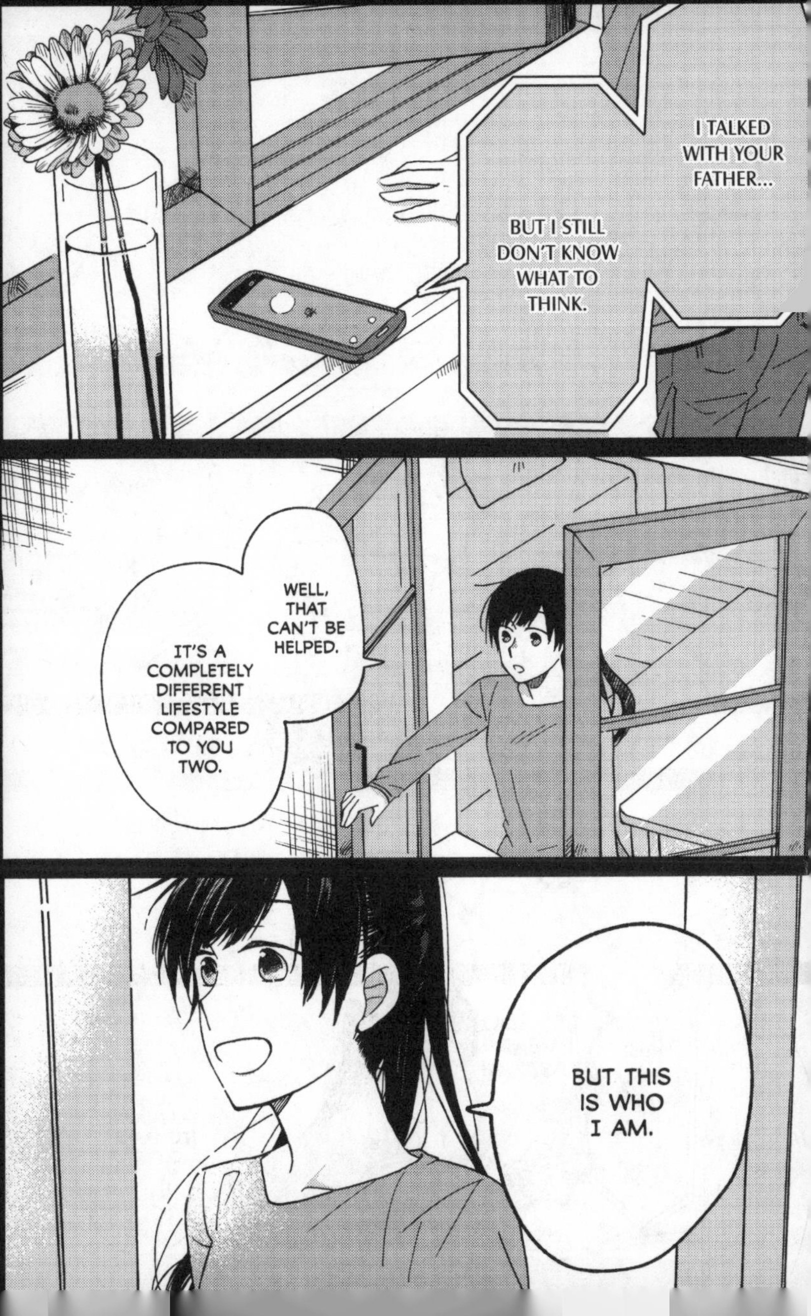
I TALKED WITH YOUR FATHER...
BUT I STILL DON'T KNOW WHAT TO THINK.
WELL, THAT CAN'T BE HELPED.
IT'S A COMPLETELY DIFFERENT LIFESTYLE COMPARED TO YOU TWO.
BUT THIS IS WHO I AM.

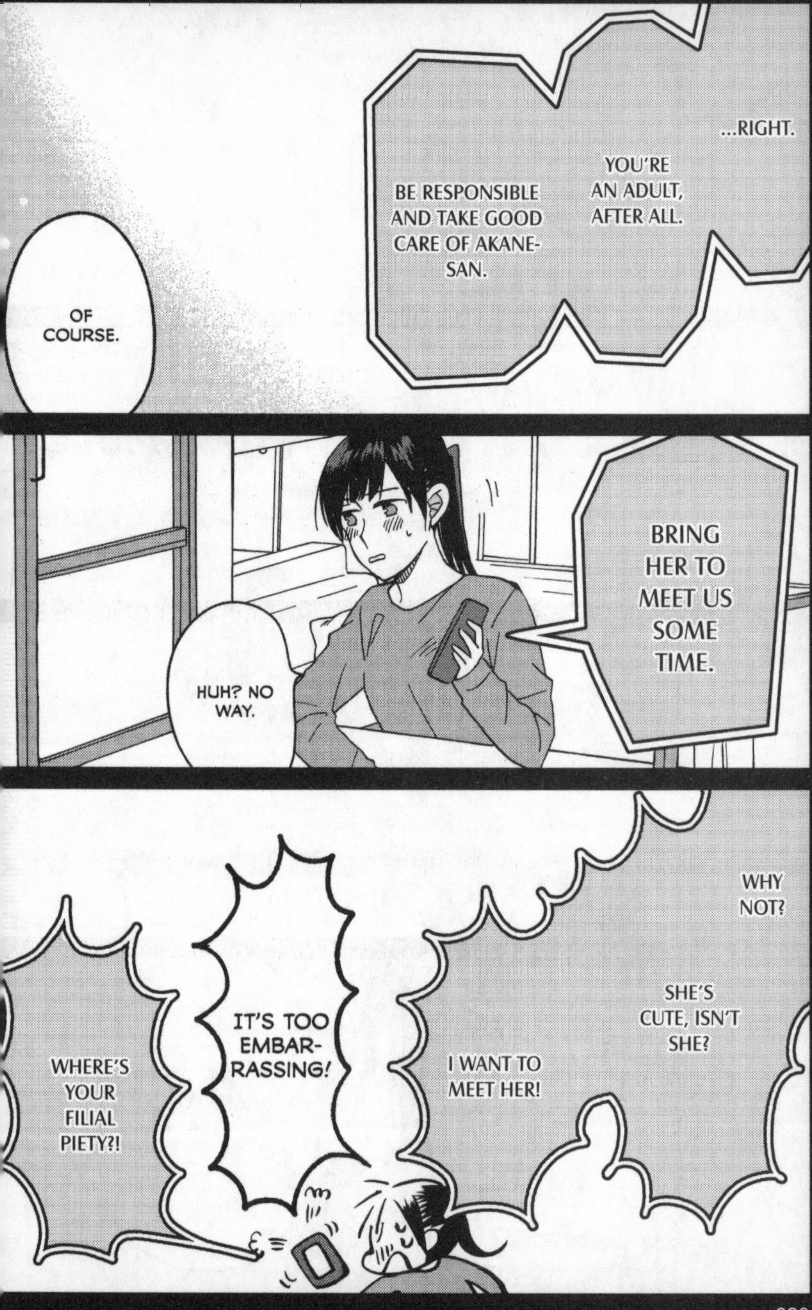
...RIGHT.
YOU'RE AN ADULT, AFTER ALL.
BE RESPONSIBLE AND TAKE GOOD CARE OF AKANE-SAN.
OF COURSE.
BRING HER TO MEET US SOME TIME.
HUH? NO WAY.
WHY NOT?
SHE'S CUTE, ISN'T SHE?
I WANT TO MEET HER!
IT'S TOO EMBARRASSING!
WHERE'S YOUR FILIAL PIETY?!

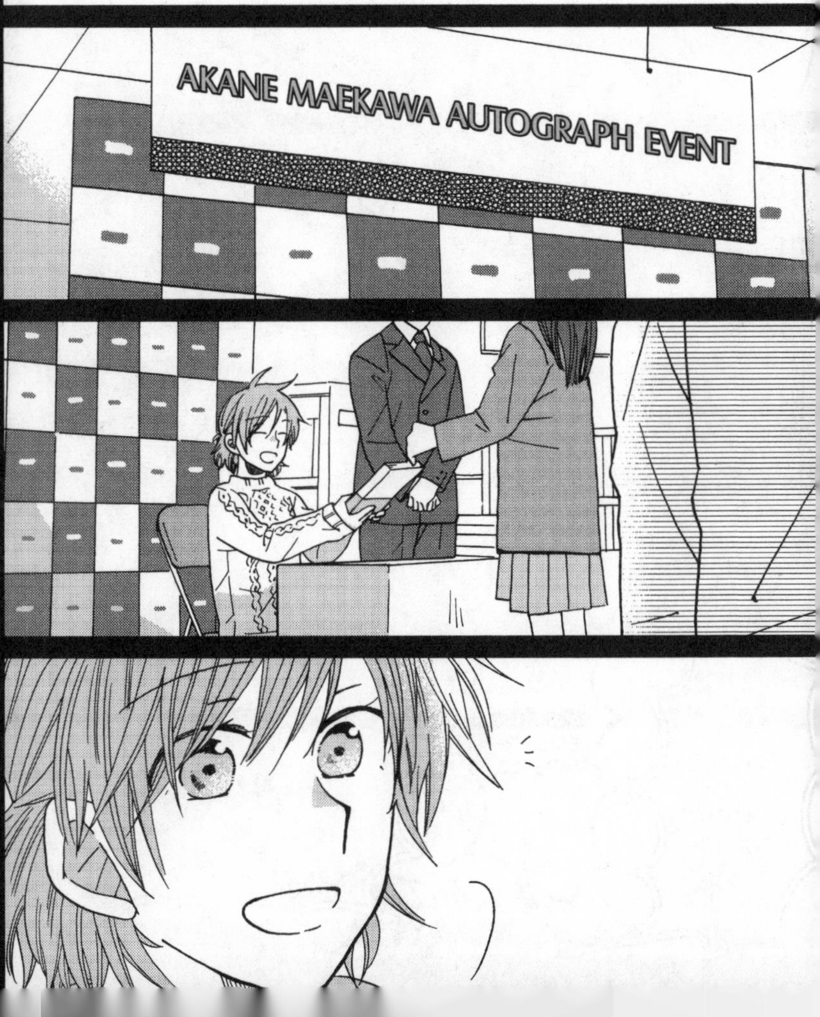
AKANE MAEKAWA AUTOGRAPH EVENT

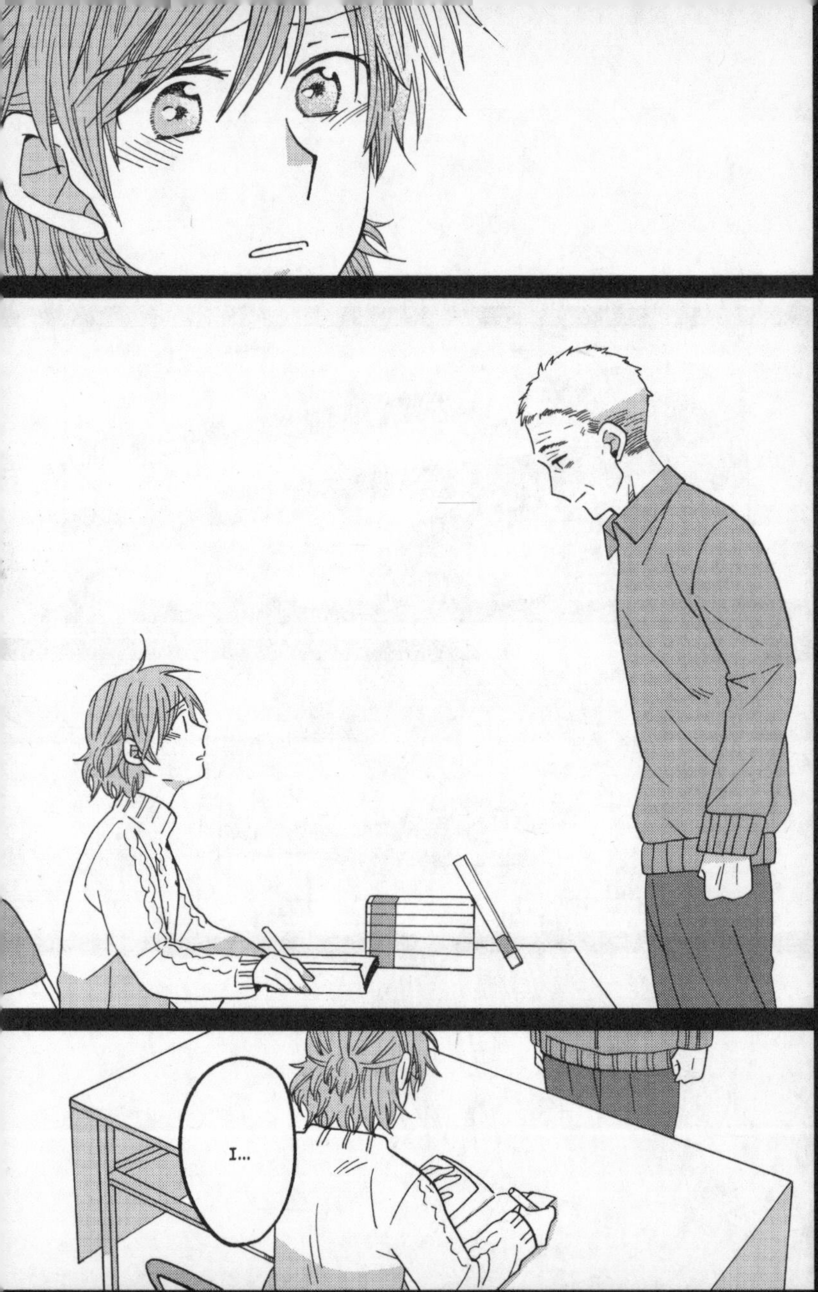
I...

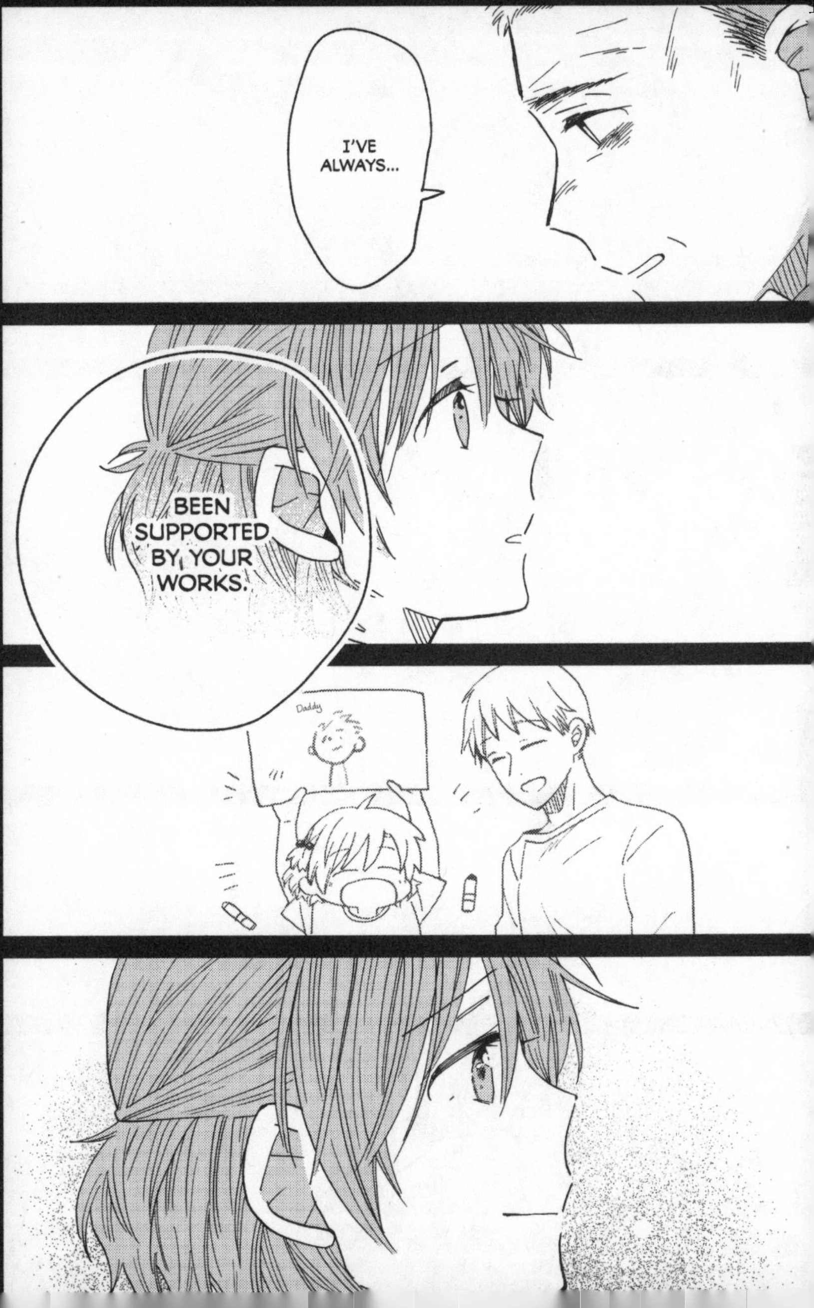
I'VE ALWAYS...
BEEN SUPPORTED BY YOUR WORKS.
Daddy

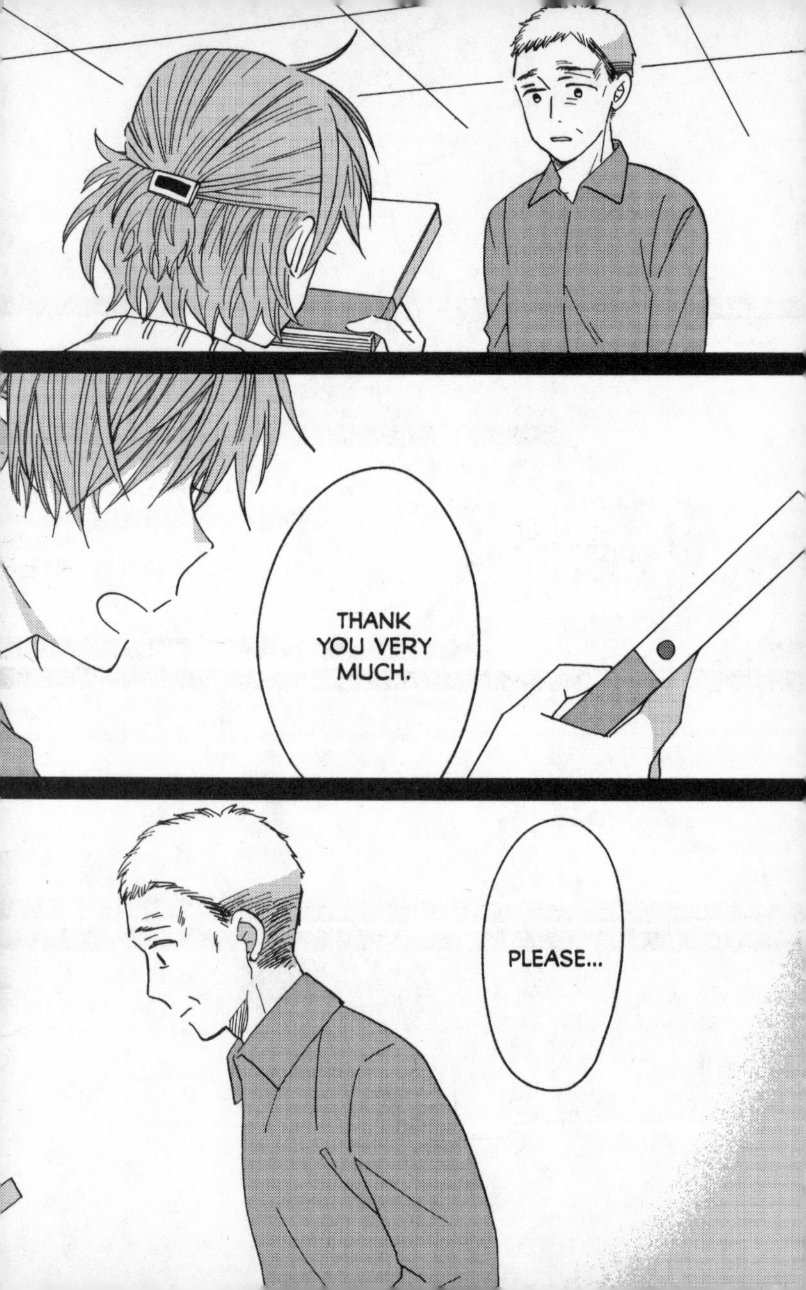
THANK YOU VERY MUCH.
PLEASE...

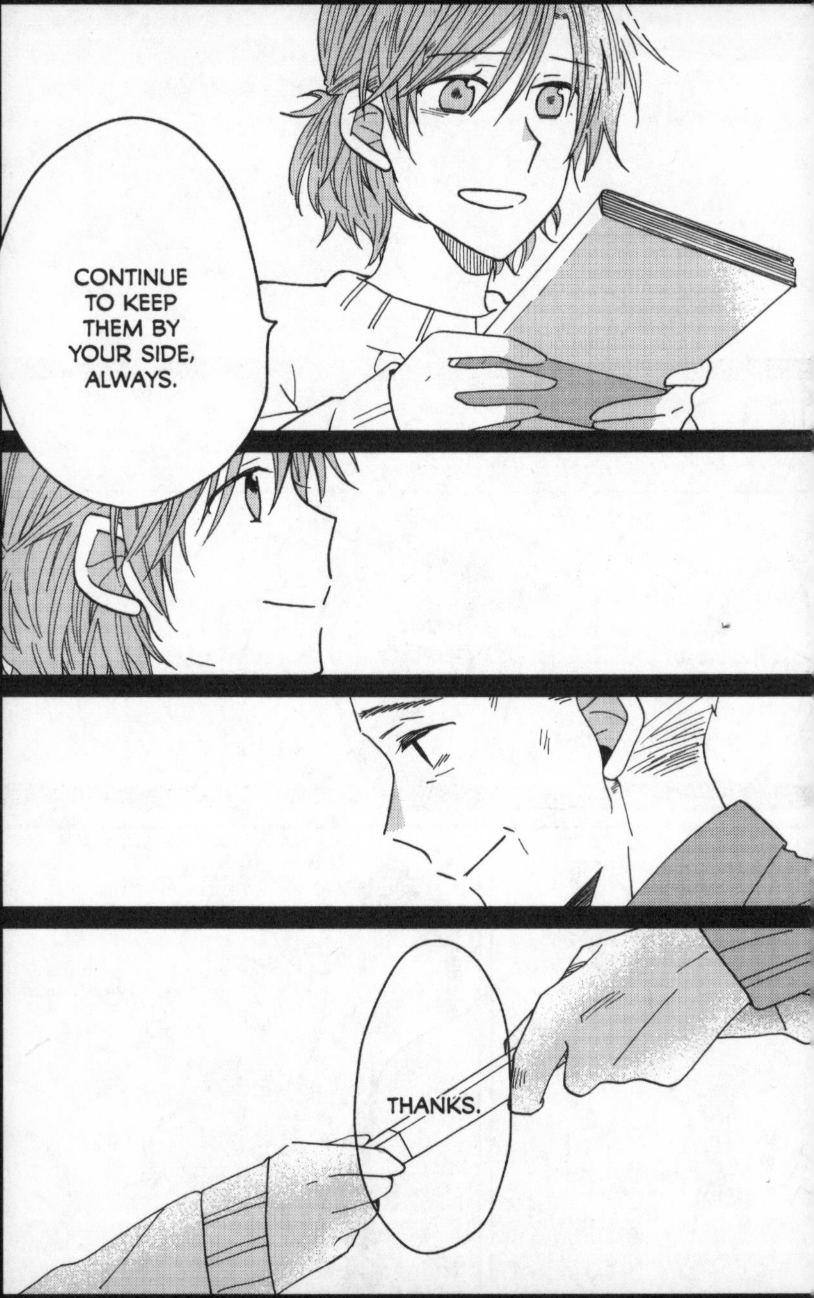
CONTINUE TO KEEP THEM BY YOUR SIDE, ALWAYS.
THANKS.

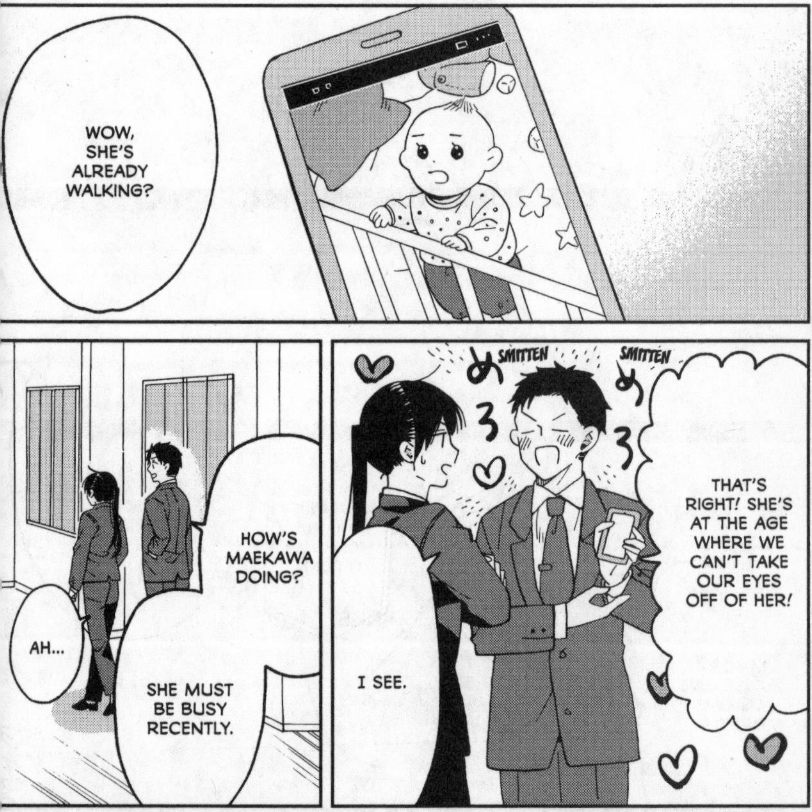
WOW, SHE'S ALREADY WALKING?
SMITTEN
SMITTEN
THAT'S RIGHT! SHE'S AT THE AGE WHERE WE CAN'T TAKE OUR EYES OFF OF HER!
I SEE.
HOW'S MAEKAWA DOING?
AH...
SHE MUST BE BUSY RECENTLY.

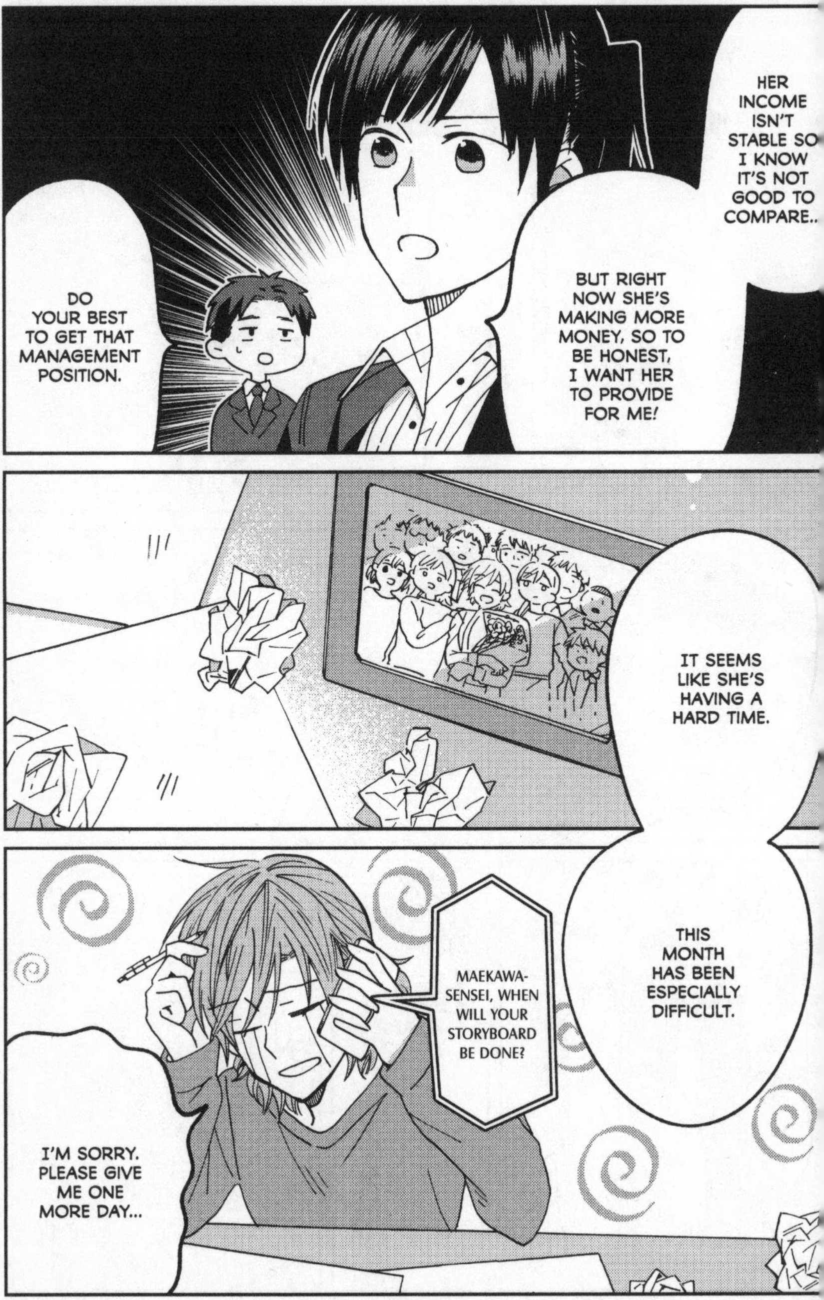
HER INCOME ISN'T STABLE SO I KNOW IT'S NOT GOOD TO COMPARE..
BUT RIGHT NOW SHE'S MAKING MORE MONEY, SO TO BE HONEST, I WANT HER TO PROVIDE FOR ME!
DO YOUR BEST TO GET THAT MANAGEMENT POSITION.
IT SEEMS LIKE SHE'S HAVING A HARD TIME.
THIS MONTH HAS BEEN ESPECIALLY DIFFICULT.
MAEKAWA-SENSEI, WHEN WILL YOUR STORYBOARD BE DONE?
I'M SORRY. PLEASE GIVE ME ONE MORE DAY...

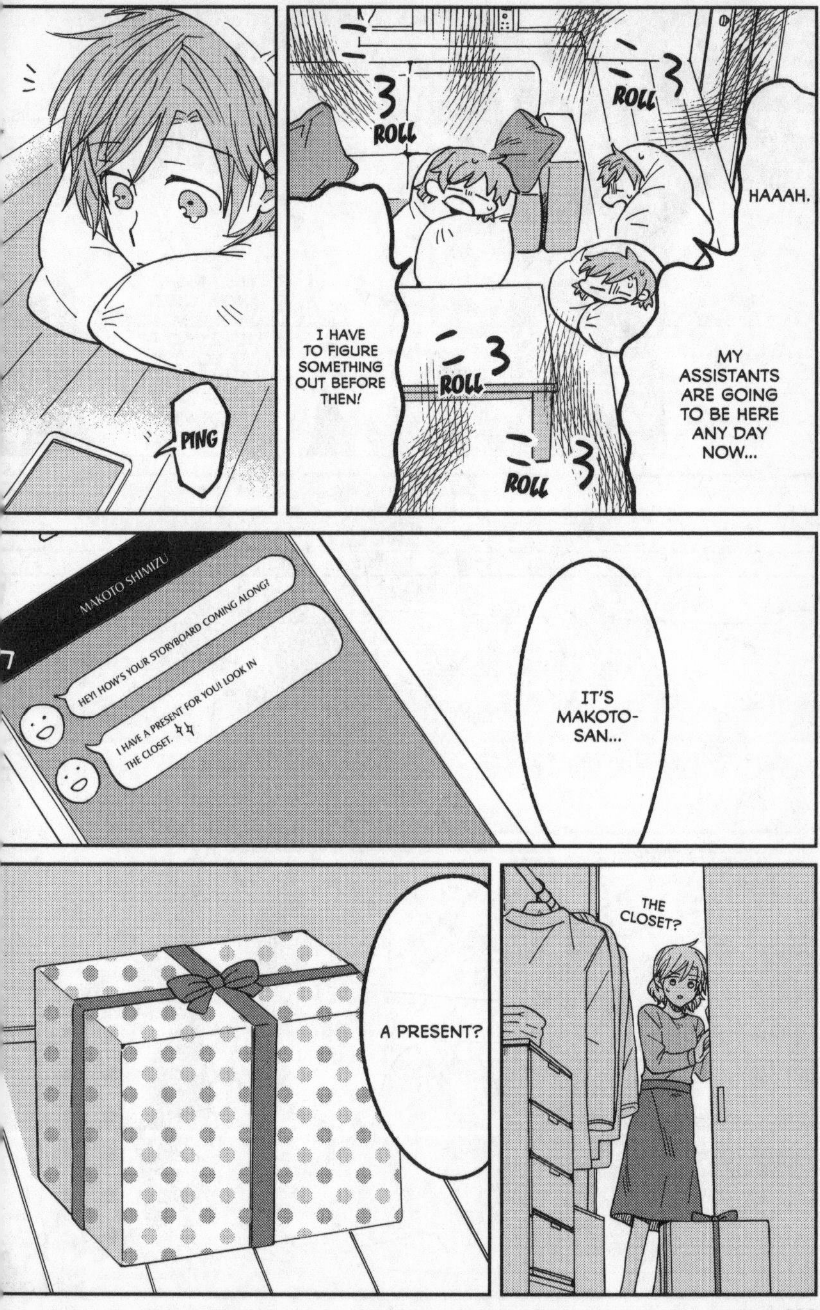
HAAAH.
ROLL
ROLL
MY ASSISTANTS ARE GOING TO BE HERE ANY DAY NOW...
I HAVE TO FIGURE SOMETHING OUT BEFORE THEN!
ROLL
ROLL
PING
IT'S MAKOTO-SAN...
MAKOTO SHIMIZU
HEY! HOW'S YOUR STORYBOARD COMING ALONG?
I HAVE A PRESENT FOR YOU! LOOK IN THE CLOSET.
THE CLOSET?
A PRESENT?

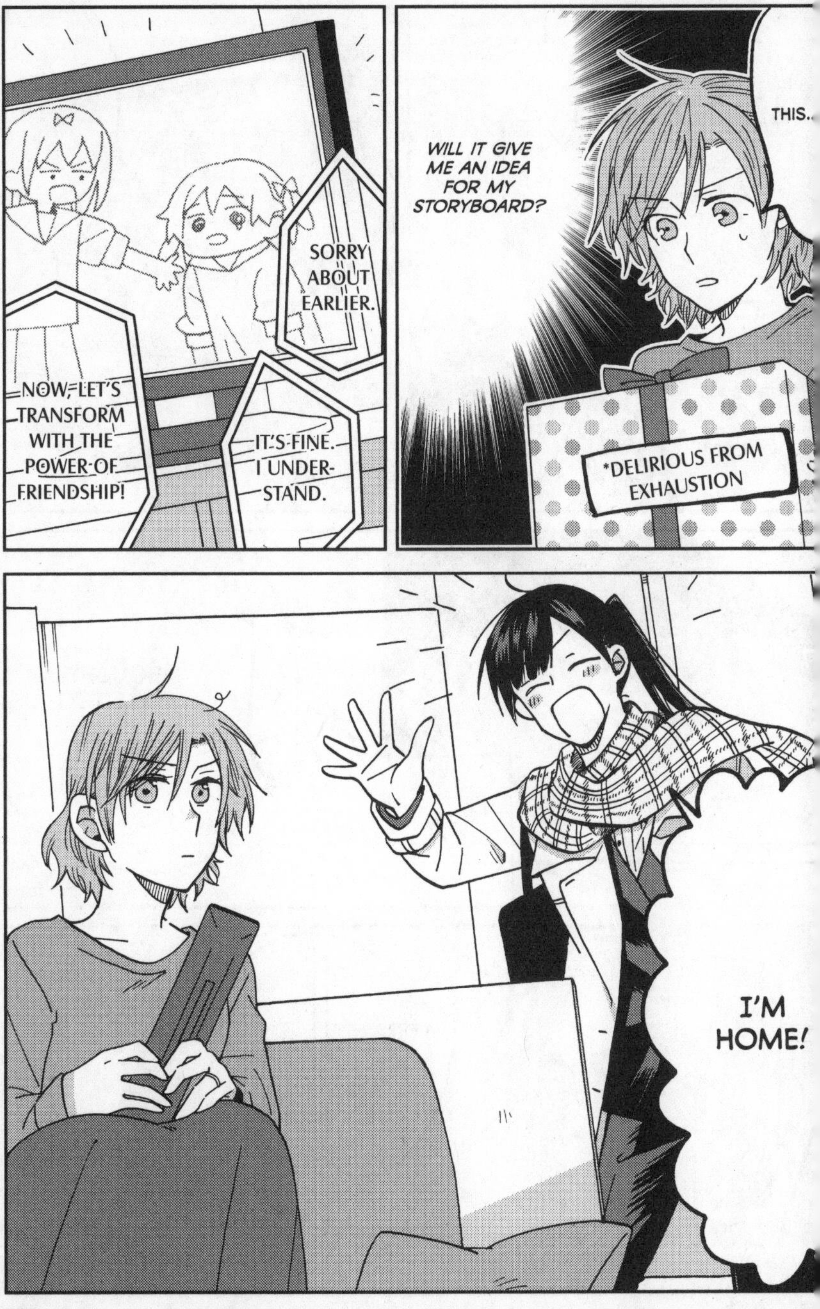
THIS...
WILL IT GIVE ME AN IDEA FOR MY STORYBOARD?
*DELIRIOUS FROM EXHAUSTION
SORRY ABOUT EARLIER.
IT'S FINE. I UNDERSTAND.
NOW, LET'S TRANSFORM WITH THE POWER OF FRIENDSHIP!
I'M HOME!

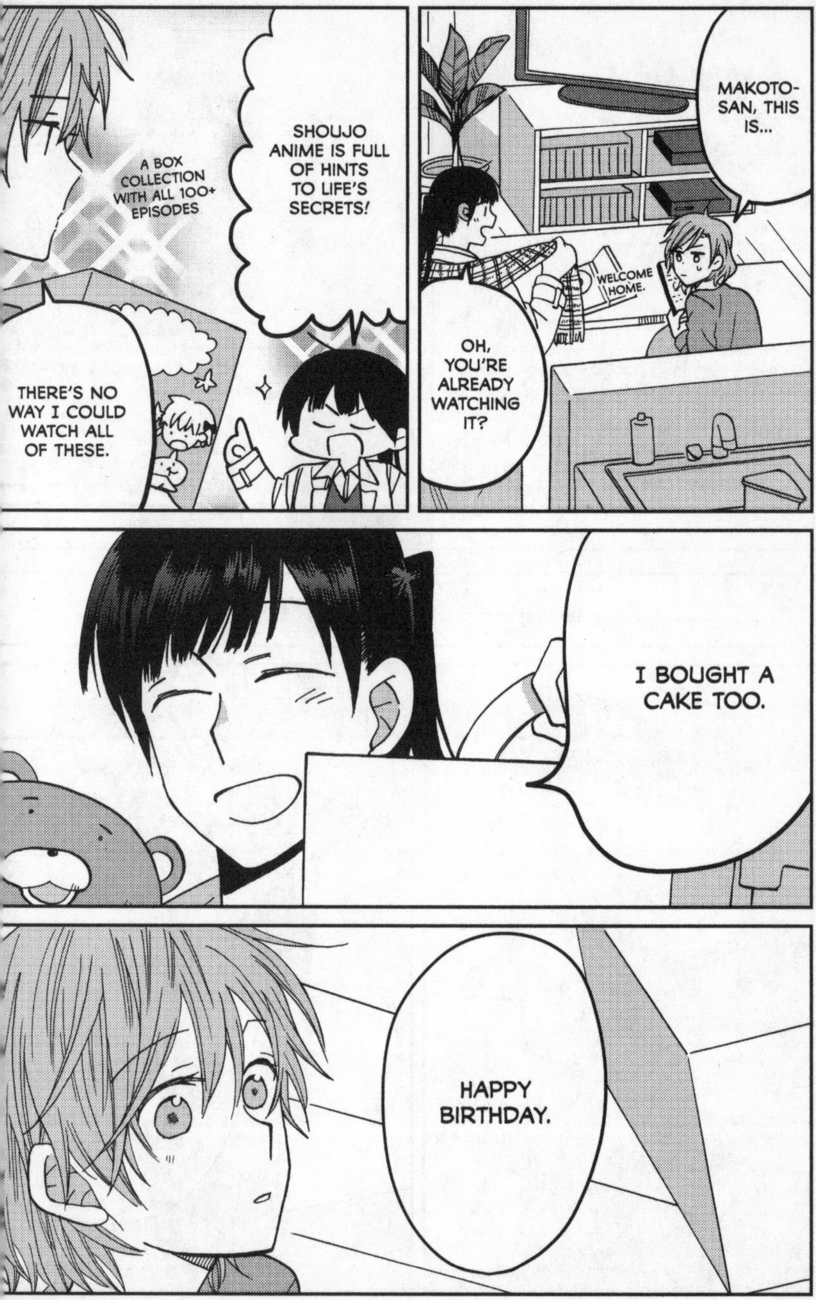
MAKOTO-SAN, THIS IS...
WELCOME HOME.
OH, YOU'RE ALREADY WATCHING IT?
SHOUJO ANIME IS FULL OF HINTS TO LIFE'S SECRETS!
A BOX COLLECTION WITH ALL 100+ EPISODES
THERE'S NO WAY I COULD WATCH ALL OF THESE.
I BOUGHT A CAKE TOO.
HAPPY BIRTHDAY.

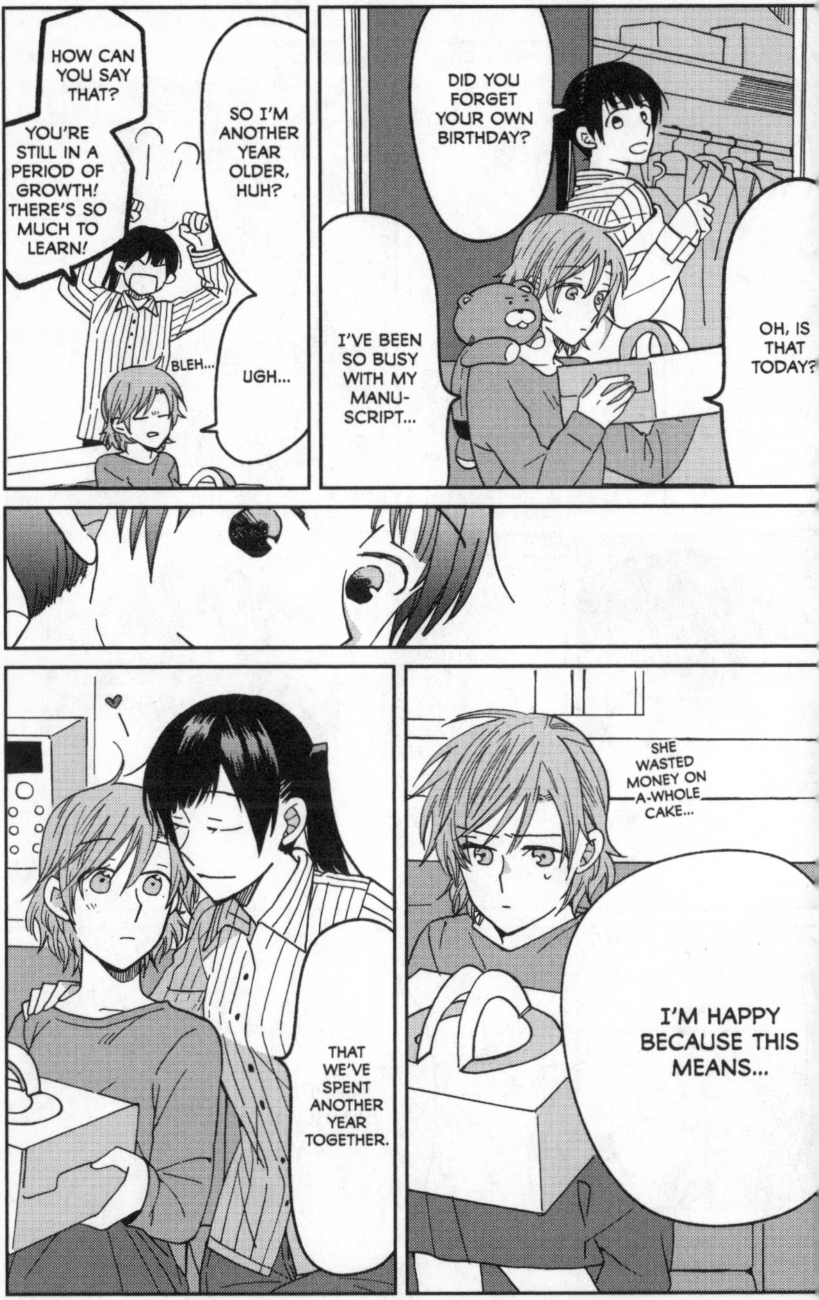
DID YOU FORGET YOUR OWN BIRTHDAY?
OH, IS THAT TODAY?
I'VE BEEN SO BUSY WITH MY MANU-SCRIPT...
SO I'M ANOTHER YEAR OLDER, HUH?
HOW CAN YOU SAY THAT?
YOU'RE STILL IN A PERIOD OF GROWTH! THERE'S SO MUCH TO LEARN!
UGH...
BLEH...
SHE WASTED MONEY ON A WHOLE CAKE...
I'M HAPPY BECAUSE THIS MEANS...
THAT WE'VE SPENT ANOTHER YEAR TOGETHER.

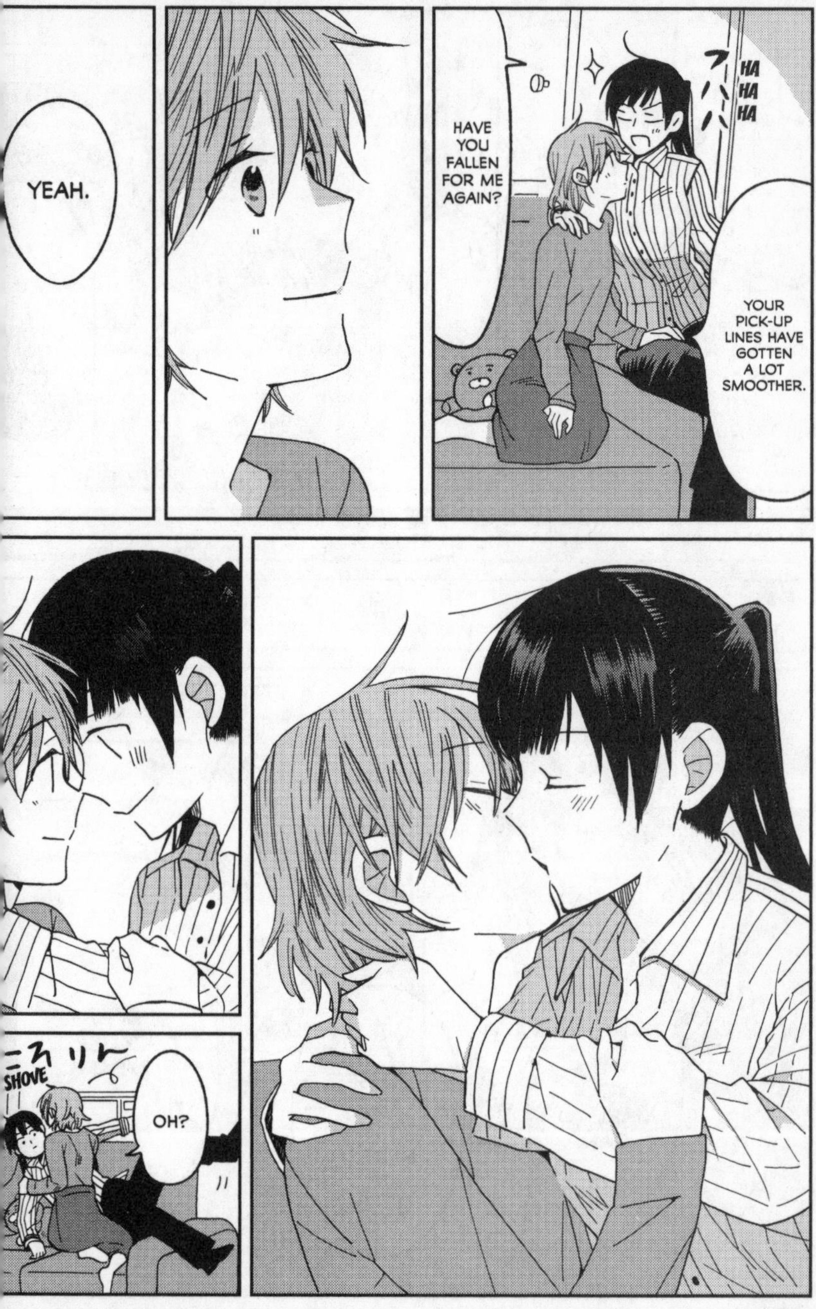
HA HA HA
YOUR PICK-UP LINES HAVE GOTTEN A LOT SMOOTHER.
HAVE YOU FALLEN FOR ME AGAIN?
YEAH.
SHOVE
OH?

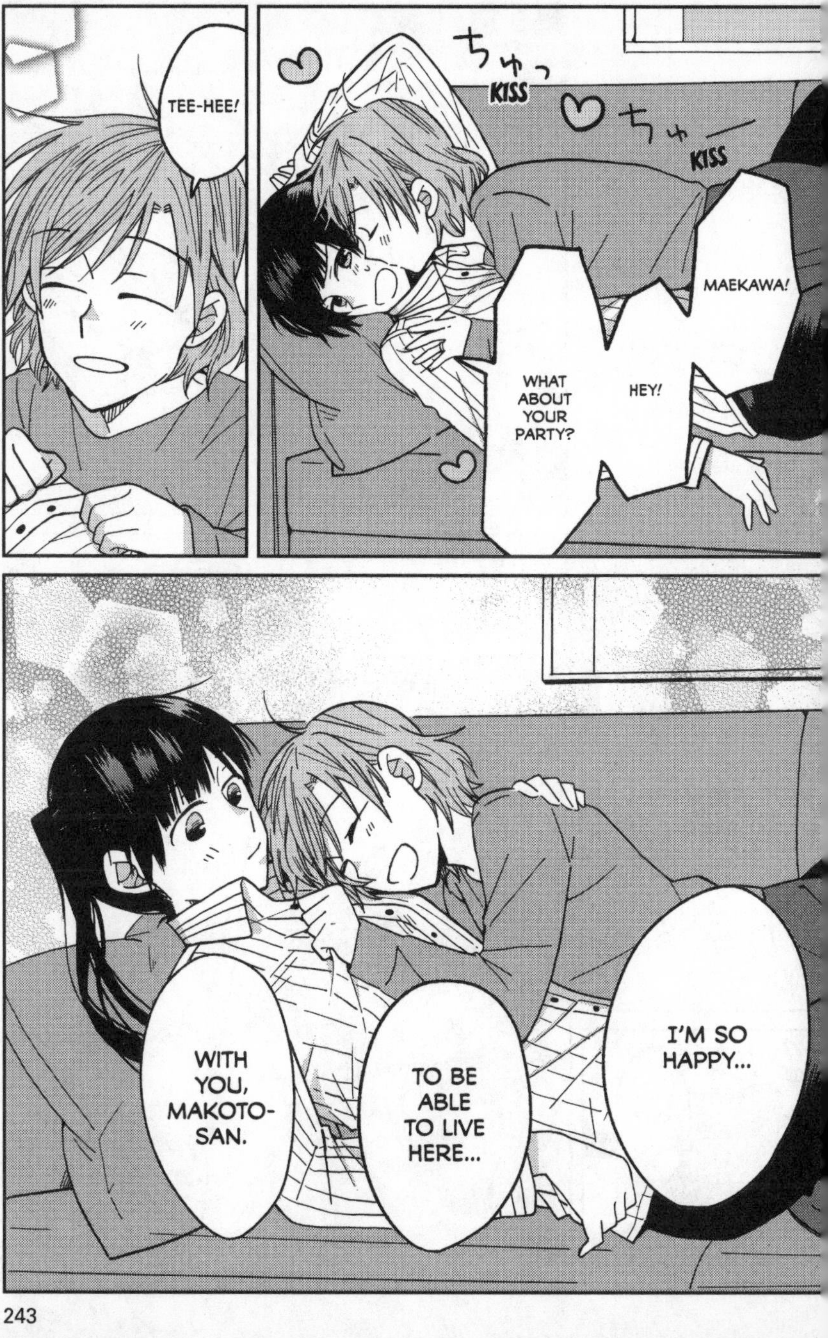
ちゅっ
KISS
ちゅー
KISS
MAEKAWA!
HEY!
WHAT ABOUT YOUR PARTY?
TEE-HEE!
I'M SO HAPPY...
TO BE ABLE TO LIVE HERE...
WITH YOU, MAKOTO-SAN.

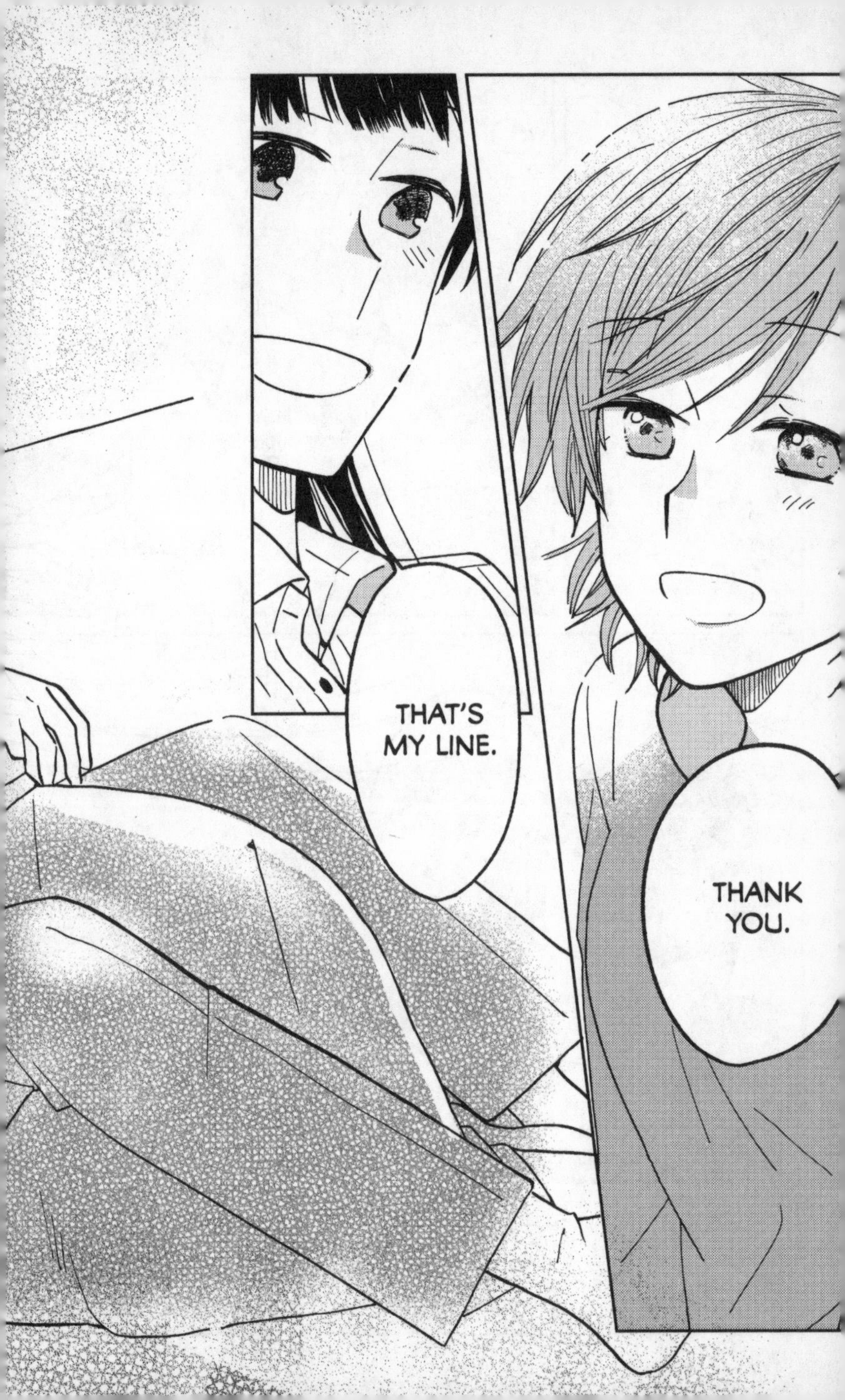
THANK YOU.
THAT'S MY LINE.

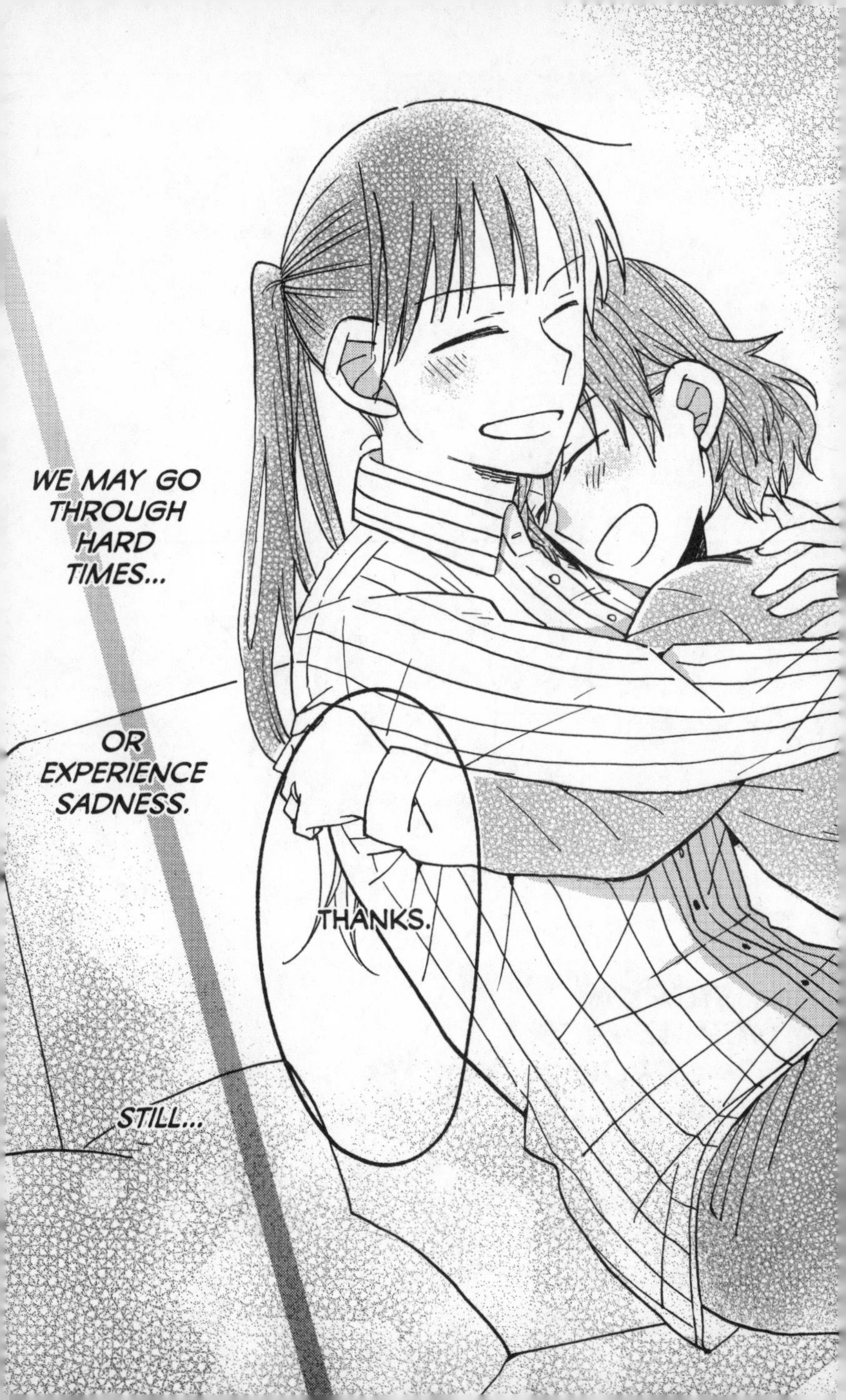
WE MAY GO THROUGH HARD TIMES...
OR EXPERIENCE SADNESS.
THANKS.
STILL...

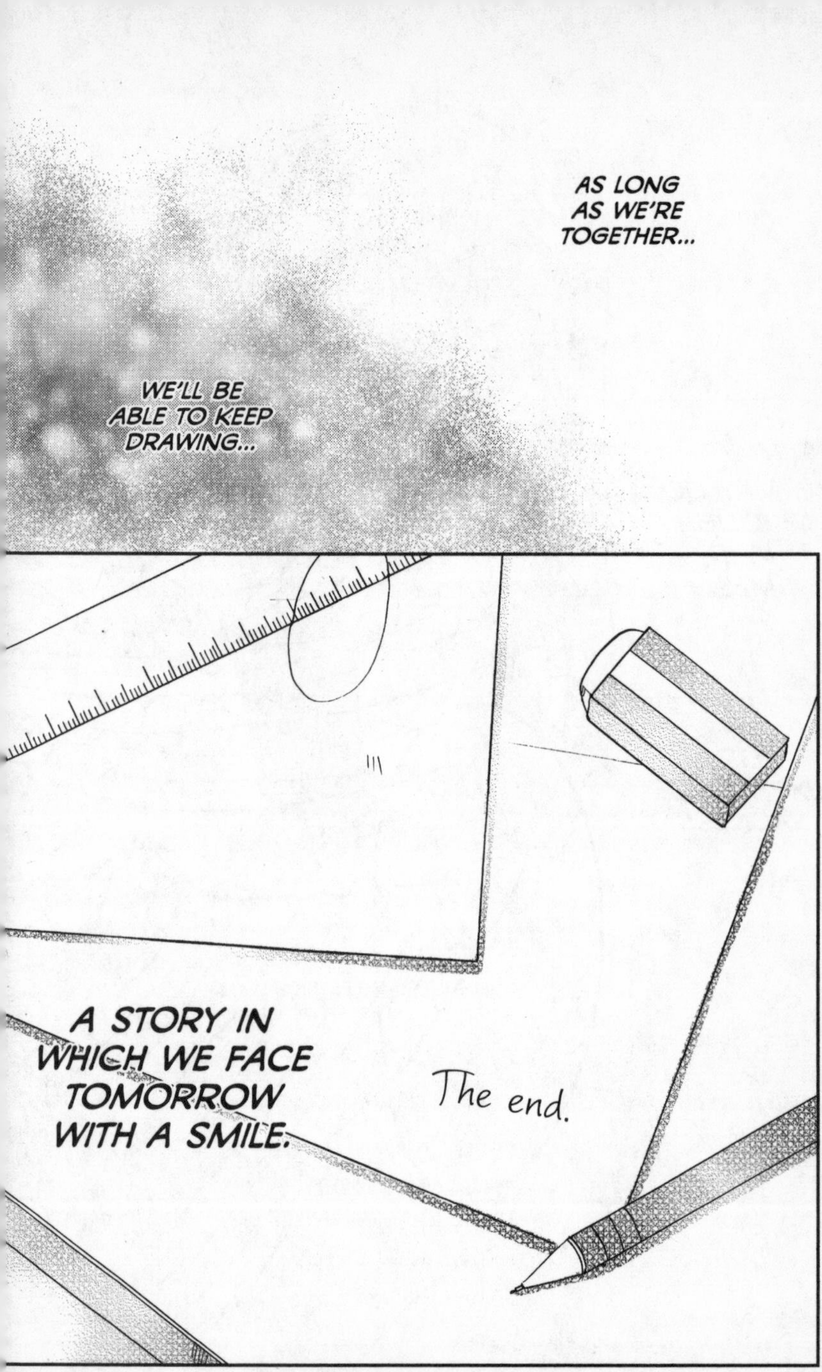
AS LONG AS WE'RE TOGETHER...
WE'LL BE ABLE TO KEEP DRAWING...
A STORY IN WHICH WE FACE TOMORROW WITH A SMILE.
The end.

Still Sick - The End

**THANK YOU FOR
SUPPORTING THIS SERIES!**

I would like to thank
everyone who read this series,
supported me on Twitter and Pixiv,
those who left comments with their
opinions, as well as my editor,
Kokuba-sama, and everyone else
who was involved in
its publication.

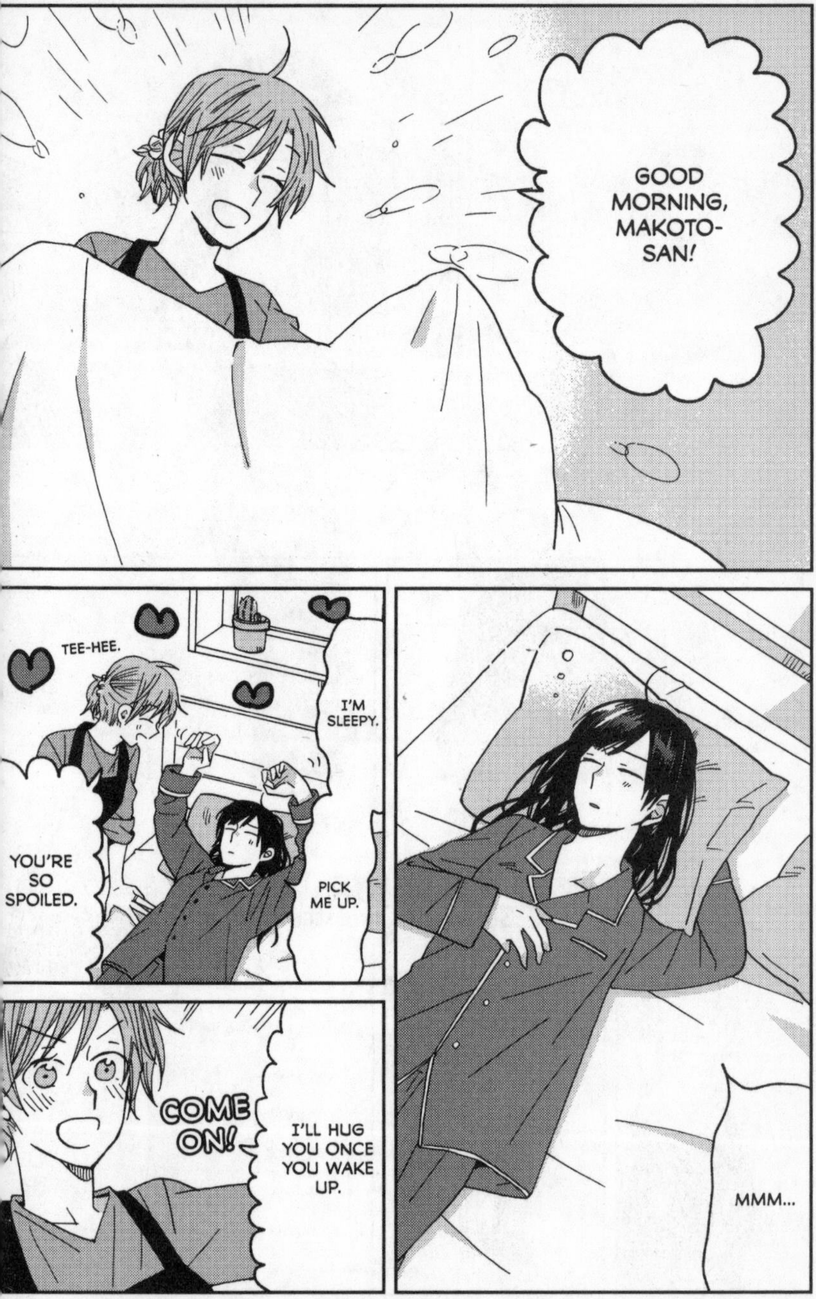
GOOD MORNING, MAKOTO-SAN!
MMM...
I'M SLEEPY.
PICK ME UP.
TEE-HEE.
YOU'RE SO SPOILED.
COME ON!
I'LL HUG YOU ONCE YOU WAKE UP.

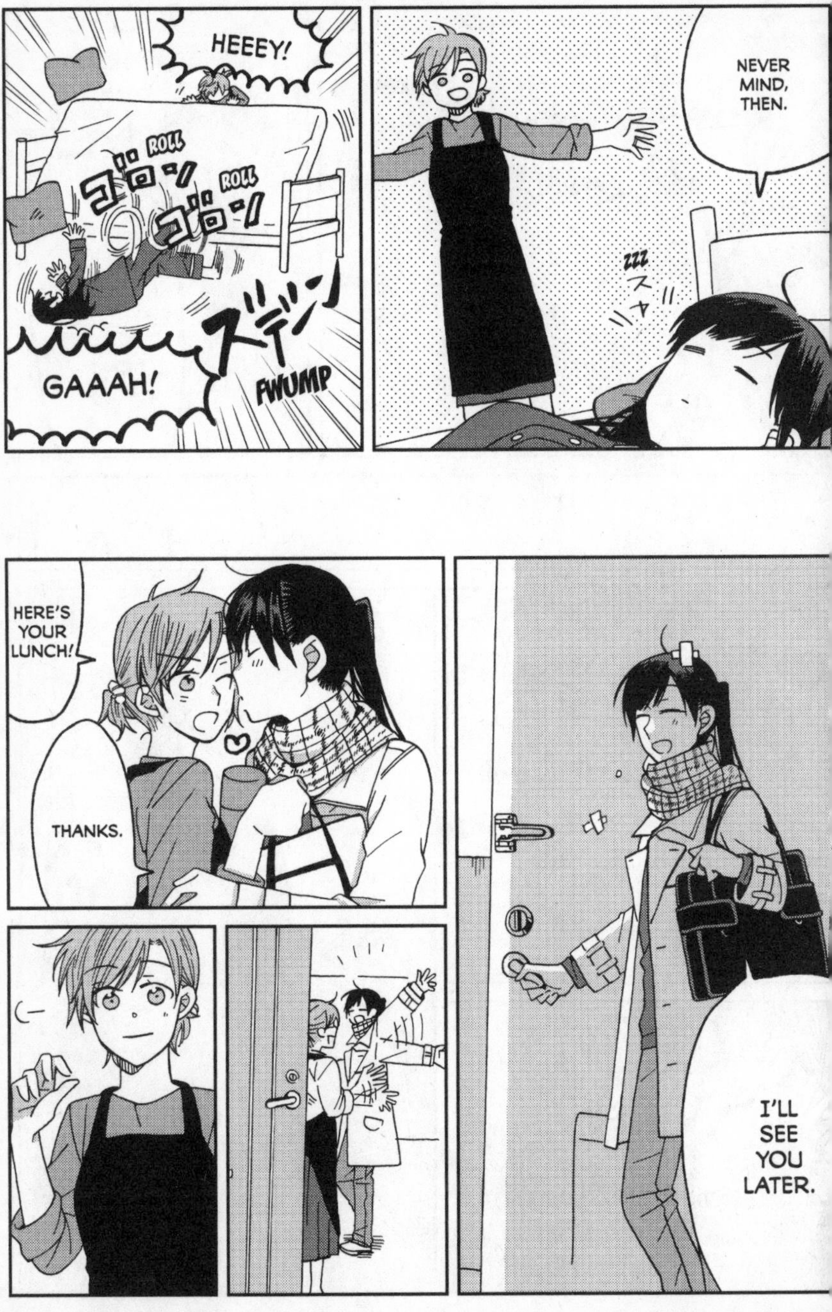
NEVER MIND, THEN.
ZZZ
スヤ
HEEEY!
ROLL
ROLL
ズデン
GAAAH!
FWUMP
I'LL SEE YOU LATER.
HERE'S YOUR LUNCH!
THANKS.

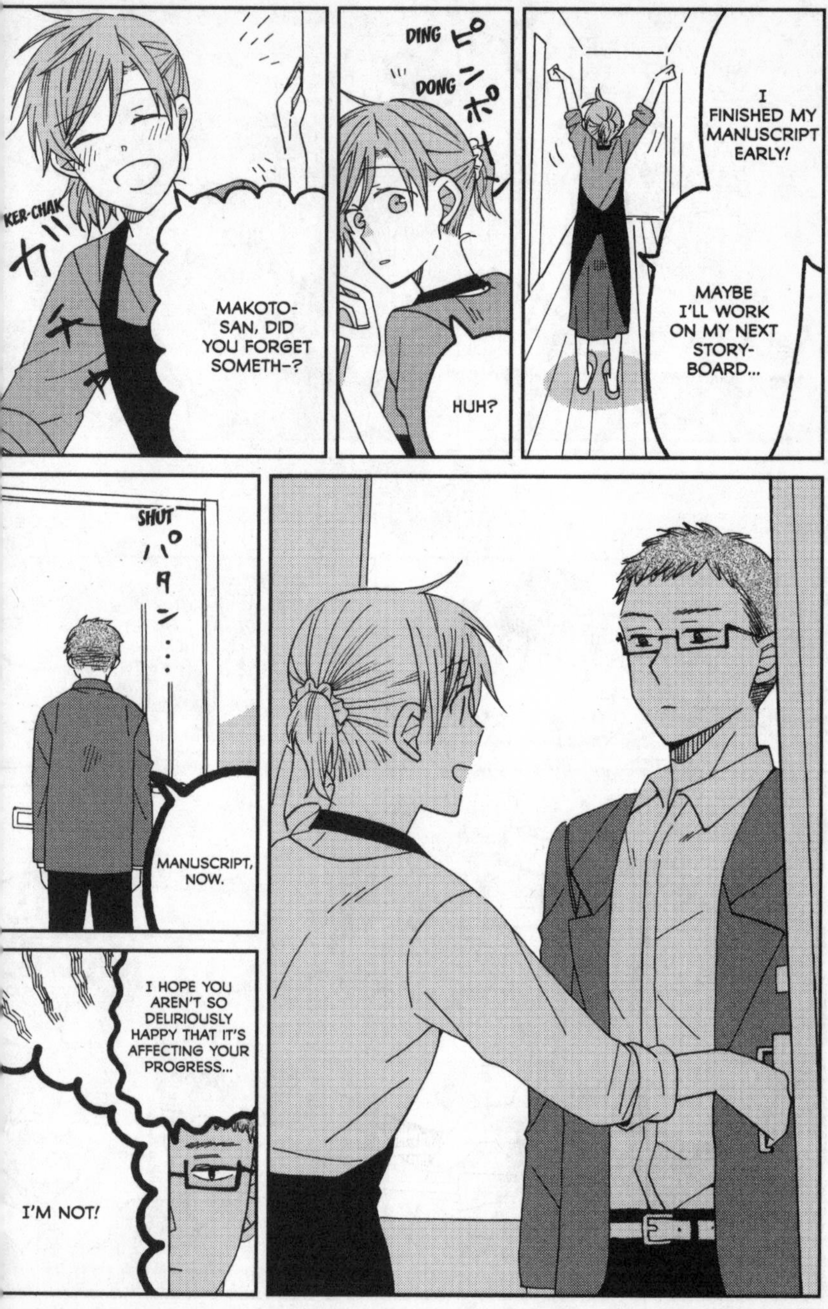
I FINISHED MY MANUSCRIPT EARLY!
MAYBE I'LL WORK ON MY NEXT STORY-BOARD...
DING
DONG
ピンポ
HUH?
KER-CHAK
カチャ
MAKOTO-SAN, DID YOU FORGET SOMETH-?
SHUT
パタン・・・
MANUSCRIPT, NOW.
I HOPE YOU AREN'T SO DELIRIOUSLY HAPPY THAT IT'S AFFECTING YOUR PROGRESS...
I'M NOT!

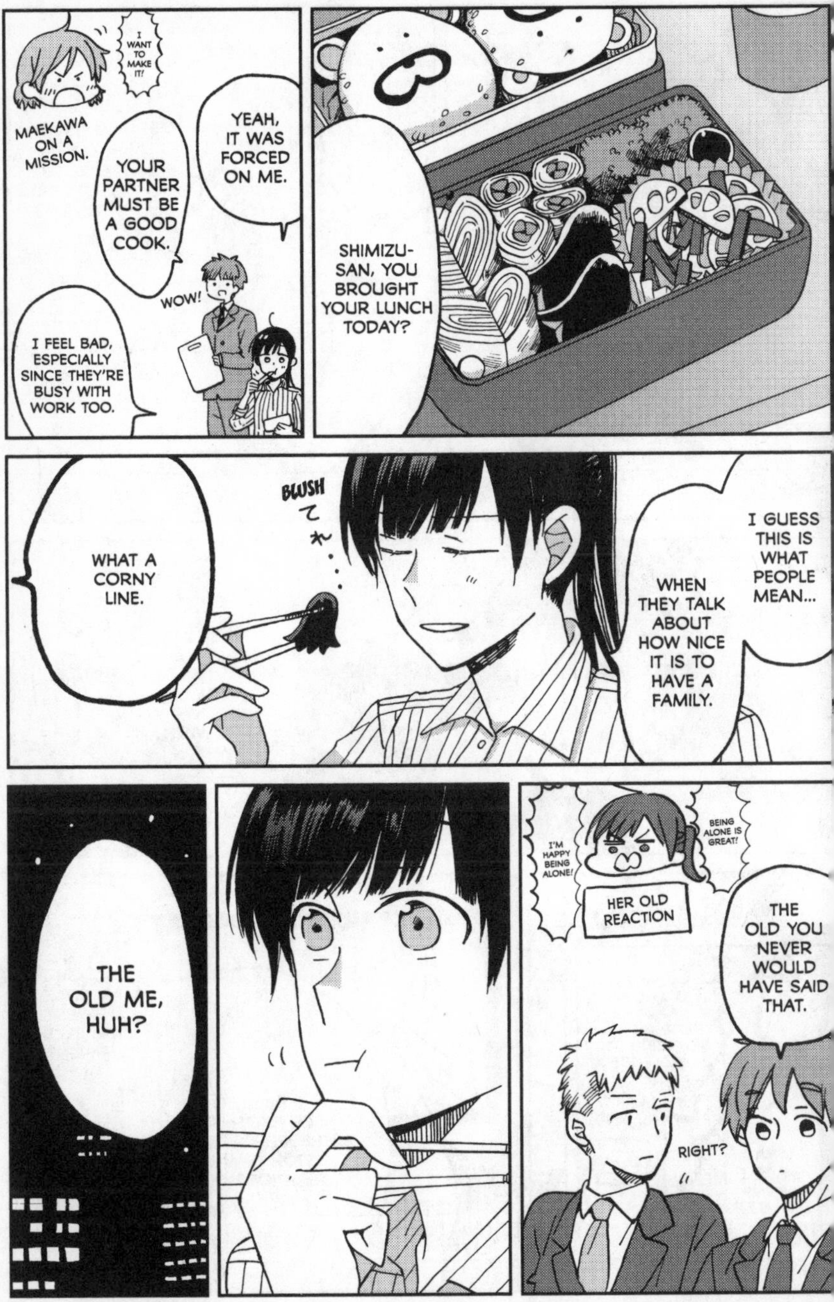
SHIMIZU-SAN, YOU BROUGHT YOUR LUNCH TODAY?
YEAH, IT WAS FORCED ON ME.
YOUR PARTNER MUST BE A GOOD COOK.
I WANT TO MAKE IT!
MAEKAWA ON A MISSION.
WOW!
I FEEL BAD, ESPECIALLY SINCE THEY'RE BUSY WITH WORK TOO.
I GUESS THIS IS WHAT PEOPLE MEAN...
WHEN THEY TALK ABOUT HOW NICE IT IS TO HAVE A FAMILY.
BLUSH
てれ・・・
WHAT A CORNY LINE.
THE OLD YOU NEVER WOULD HAVE SAID THAT.
RIGHT?
BEING ALONE IS GREAT!
I'M HAPPY BEING ALONE!
HER OLD REACTION
THE OLD ME, HUH?

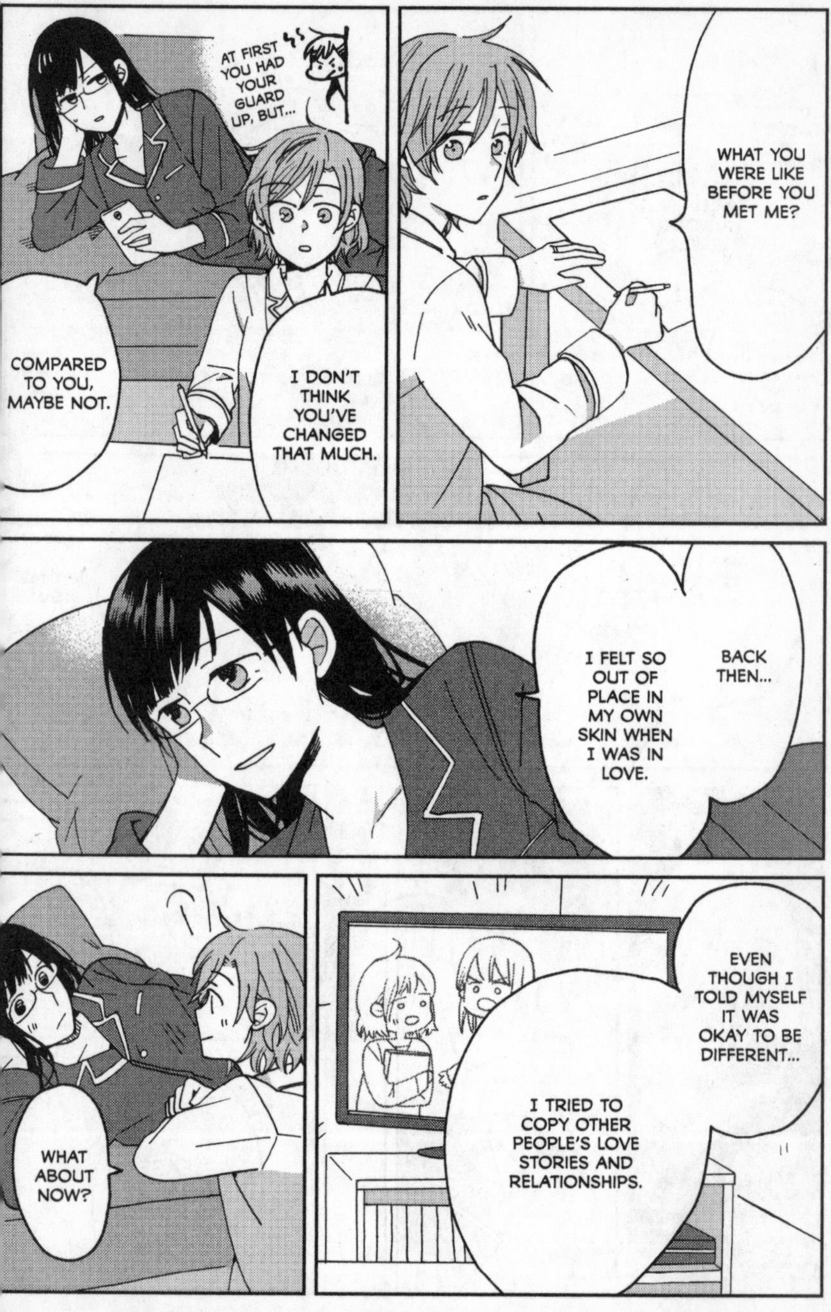
WHAT YOU WERE LIKE BEFORE YOU MET ME?
AT FIRST YOU HAD YOUR GUARD UP, BUT...
I DON'T THINK YOU'VE CHANGED THAT MUCH.
COMPARED TO YOU, MAYBE NOT.
BACK THEN...
I FELT SO OUT OF PLACE IN MY OWN SKIN WHEN I WAS IN LOVE.
EVEN THOUGH I TOLD MYSELF IT WAS OKAY TO BE DIFFERENT...
I TRIED TO COPY OTHER PEOPLE'S LOVE STORIES AND RELATIONSHIPS.
WHAT ABOUT NOW?

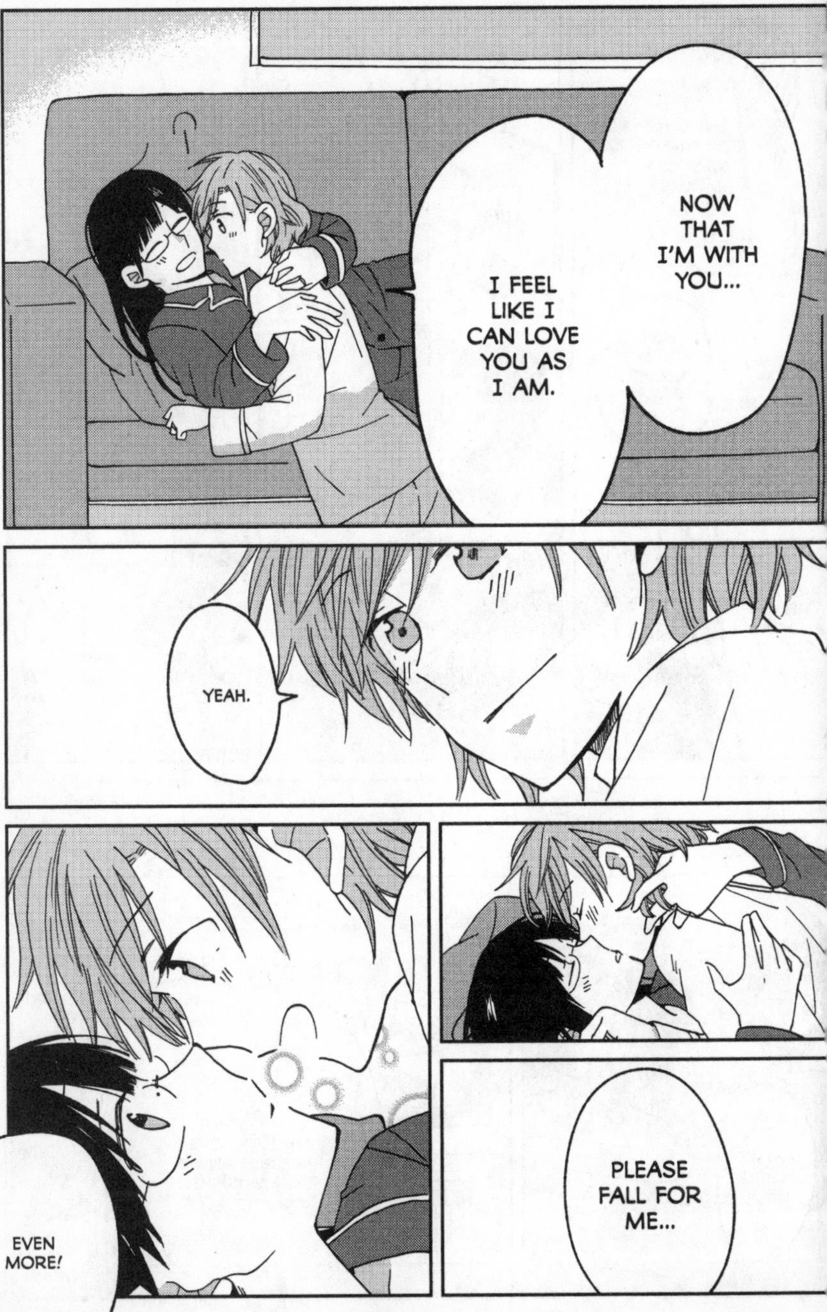
NOW THAT I'M WITH YOU...
I FEEL LIKE I CAN LOVE YOU AS I AM.
YEAH.
PLEASE FALL FOR ME...
EVEN MORE!

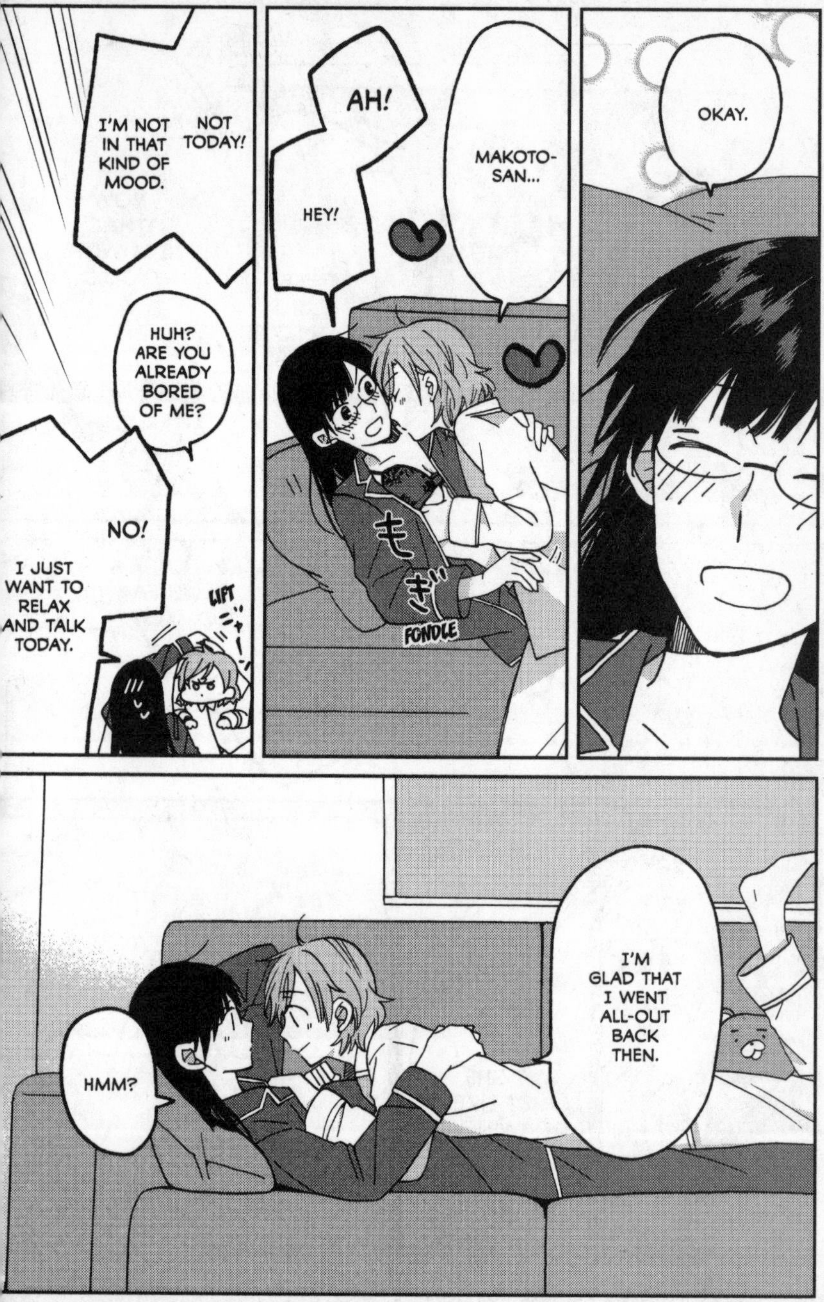
OKAY.
MAKOTO-SAN...
AH!
HEY!
もぎ
FONDLE
NOT TODAY!
I'M NOT IN THAT KIND OF MOOD.
HUH? ARE YOU ALREADY BORED OF ME?
NO!
I JUST WANT TO RELAX AND TALK TODAY.
LIFT
ニャ
I'M GLAD THAT I WENT ALL-OUT BACK THEN.
HMM?

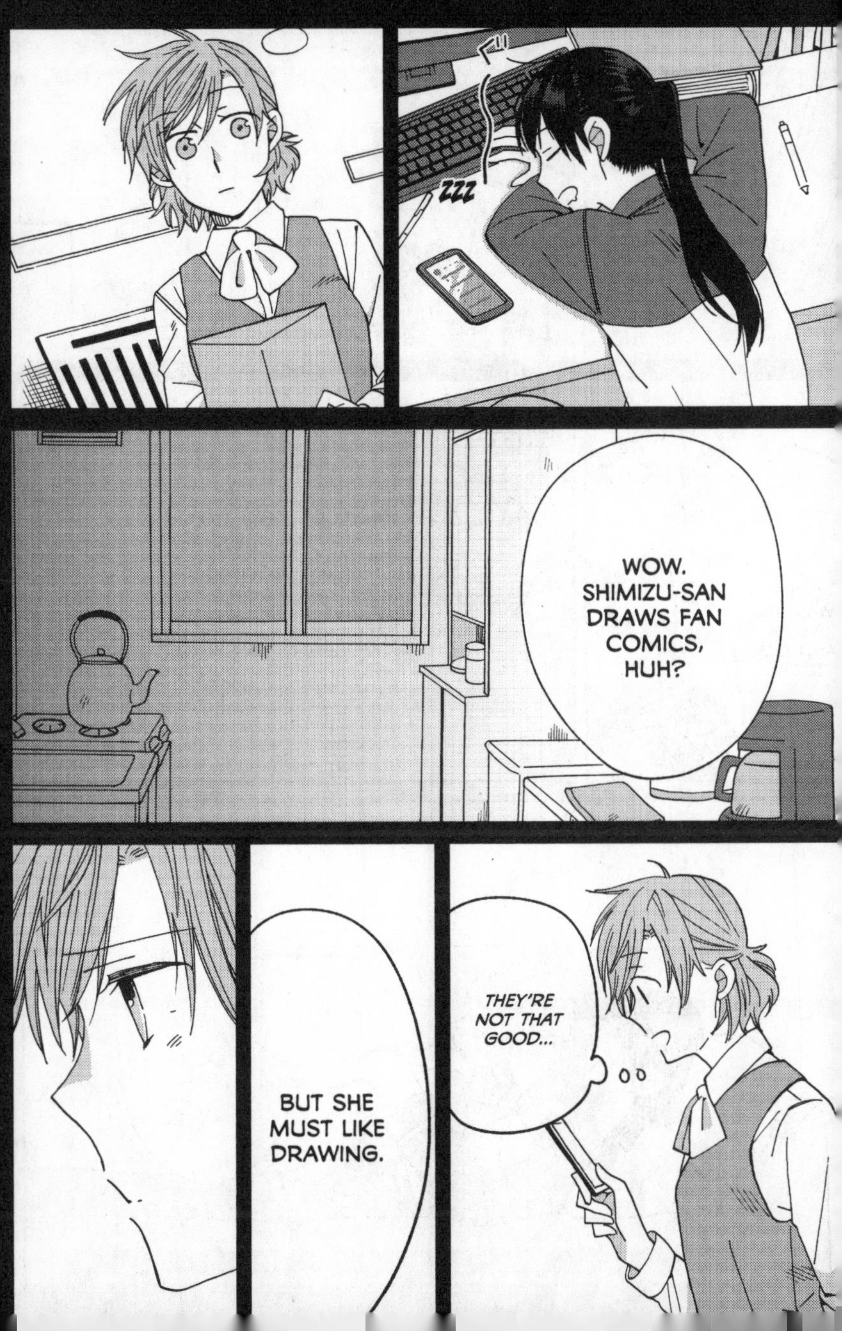
ZZZ
WOW. SHIMIZU-SAN DRAWS FAN COMICS, HUH?
THEY'RE NOT THAT GOOD...
BUT SHE MUST LIKE DRAWING.

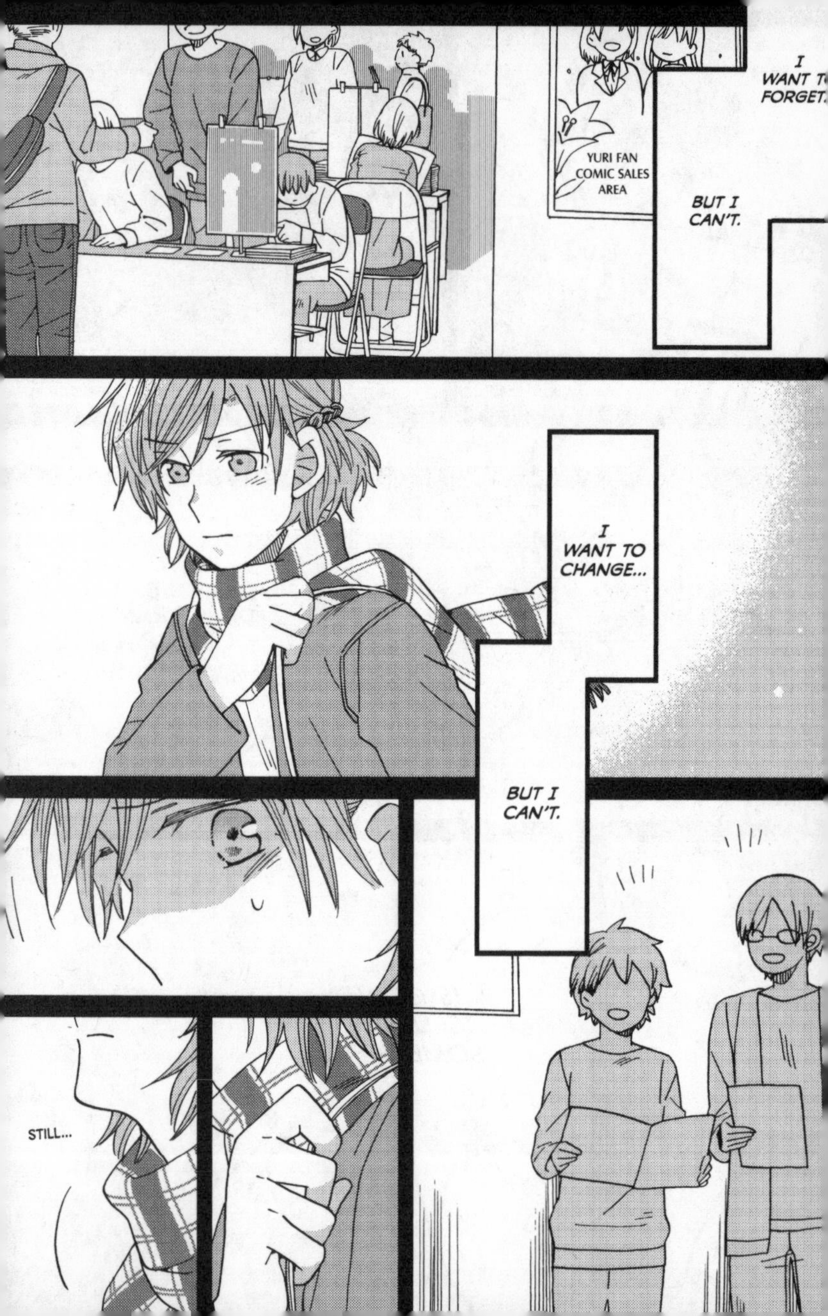
I WANT T FORGET.
BUT I CAN'T.
YURI FAN COMIC SALES AREA
I WANT TO CHANGE...
BUT I CAN'T.
STILL...

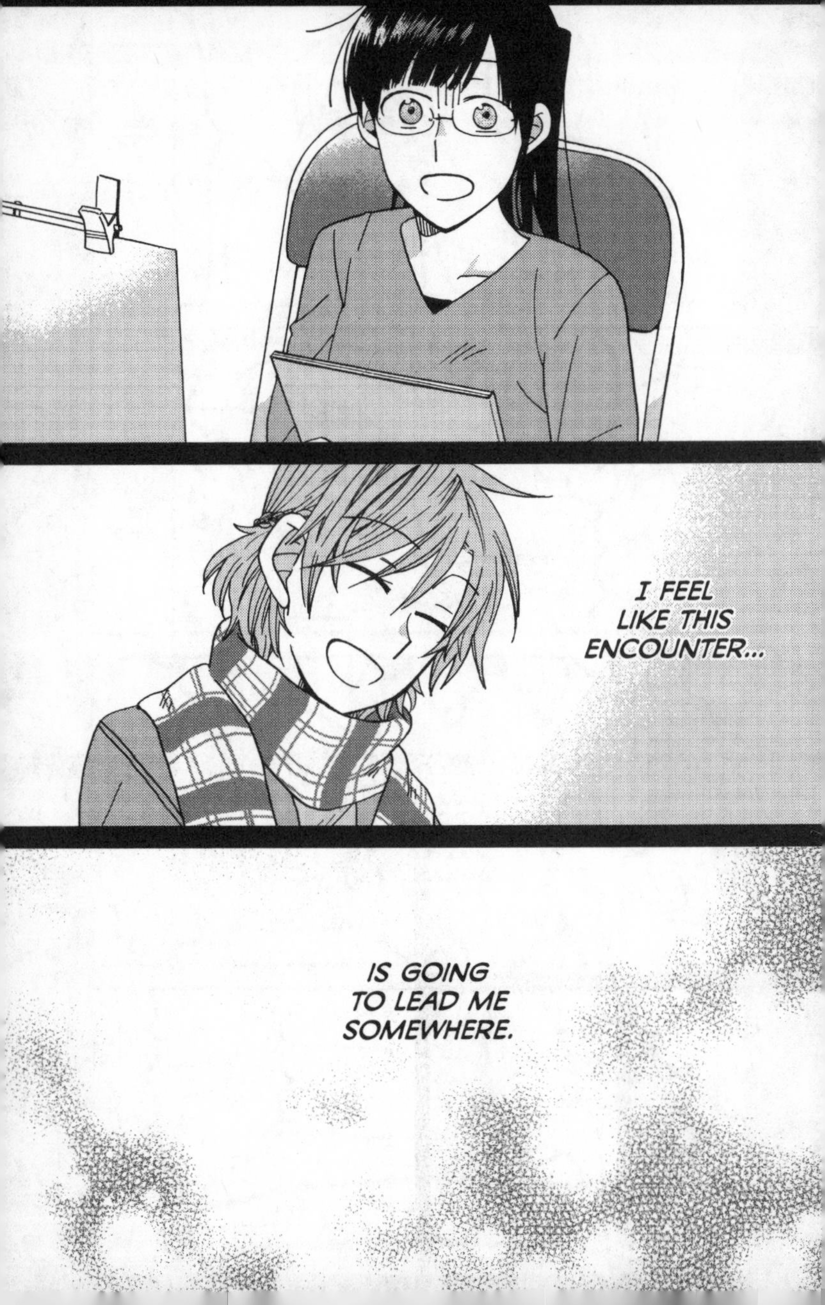
I FEEL LIKE THIS ENCOUNTER...
IS GOING TO LEAD ME SOMEWHERE.

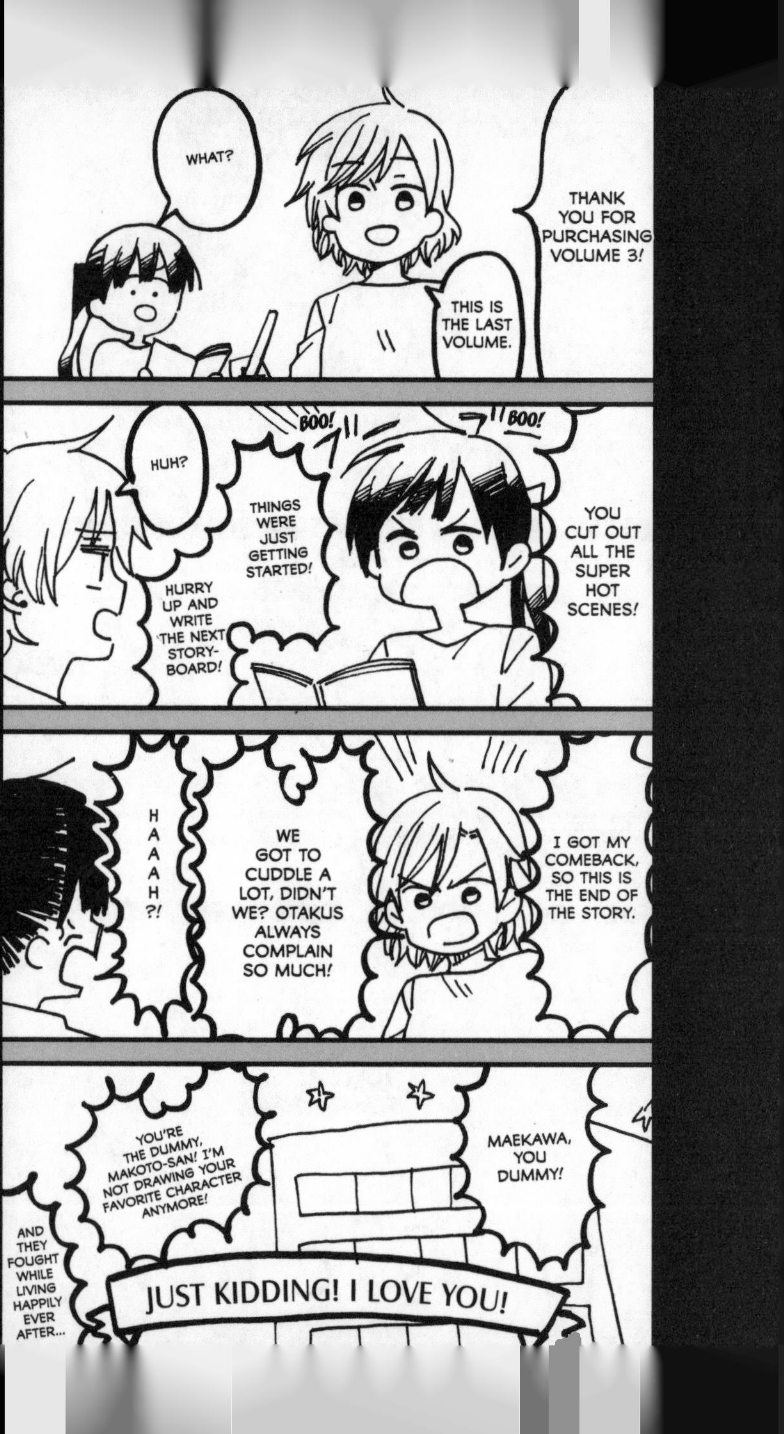
THANK YOU FOR PURCHASING VOLUME 3!
THIS IS THE LAST VOLUME.
WHAT?
BOO!
BOO!
YOU CUT OUT ALL THE SUPER HOT SCENES!
THINGS WERE JUST GETTING STARTED!
HURRY UP AND WRITE THE NEXT STORY-BOARD!
HUH?
I GOT MY COMEBACK, SO THIS IS THE END OF THE STORY.
WE GOT TO CUDDLE A LOT, DIDN'T WE? OTAKUS ALWAYS COMPLAIN SO MUCH!
HAAAAH?!
MAEKAWA, YOU DUMMY!
YOU'RE THE DUMMY, MAKOTO-SAN! I'M NOT DRAWING YOUR FAVORITE CHARACTER ANYMORE!
AND THEY FOUGHT WHILE LIVING HAPPILY EVER AFTER...
JUST KIDDING! I LOVE YOU!

Still Sick

The End

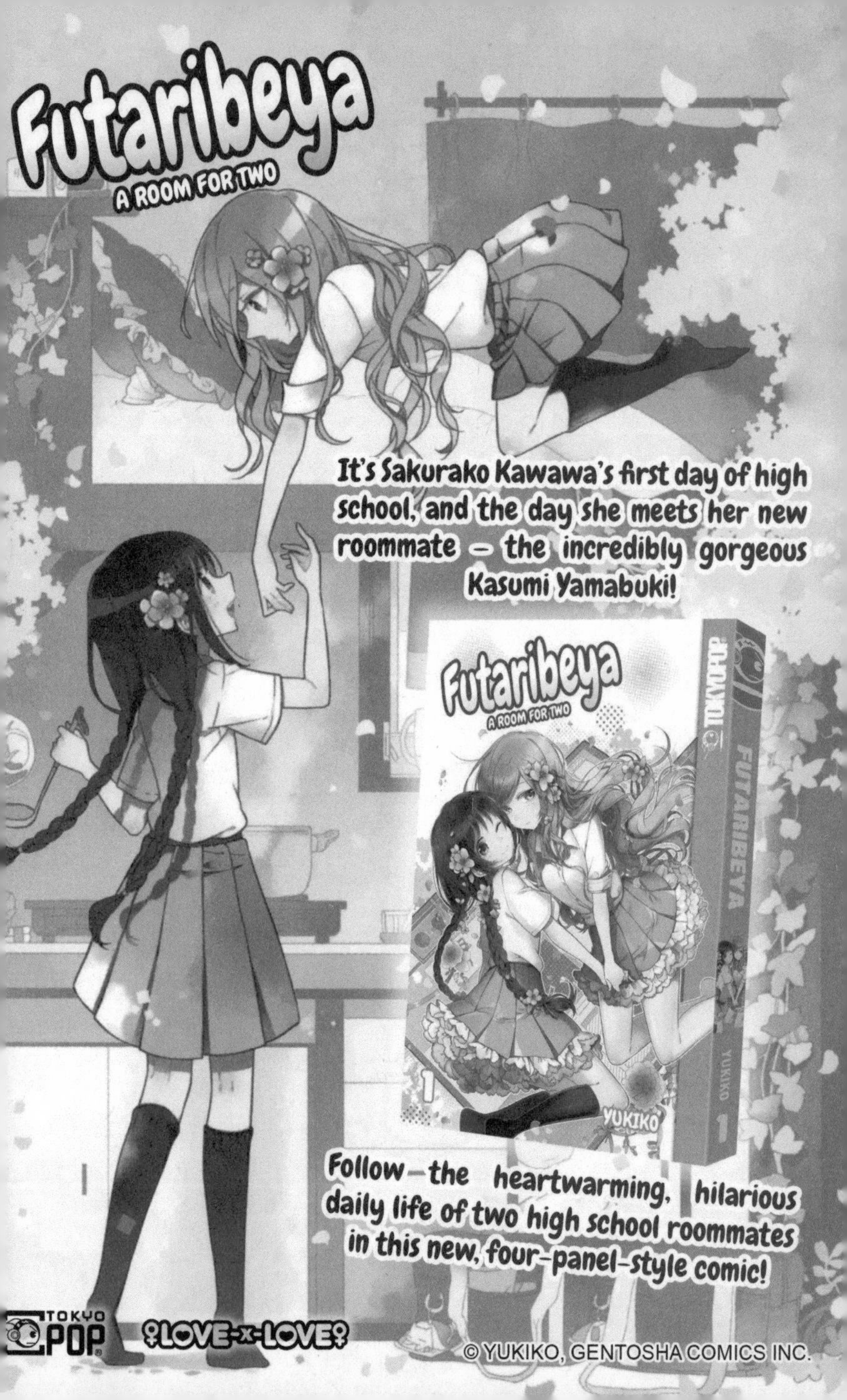
Futaribeya
A ROOM FOR TWO
It's Sakurako Kawawa's first day of high school, and the day she meets her new roommate – the incredibly gorgeous Kasumi Yamabuki!
Futaribeya
A ROOM FOR TWO
TOKYOPOP
FUTARIBEYA
YUKIKO
1
YUKIKO
1
Follow the heartwarming, hilarious daily life of two high school roommates in this new, four-panel-style comic!
TOKYO POP
LOVE x LOVE
© YUKIKO, GENTOSHA COMICS INC.

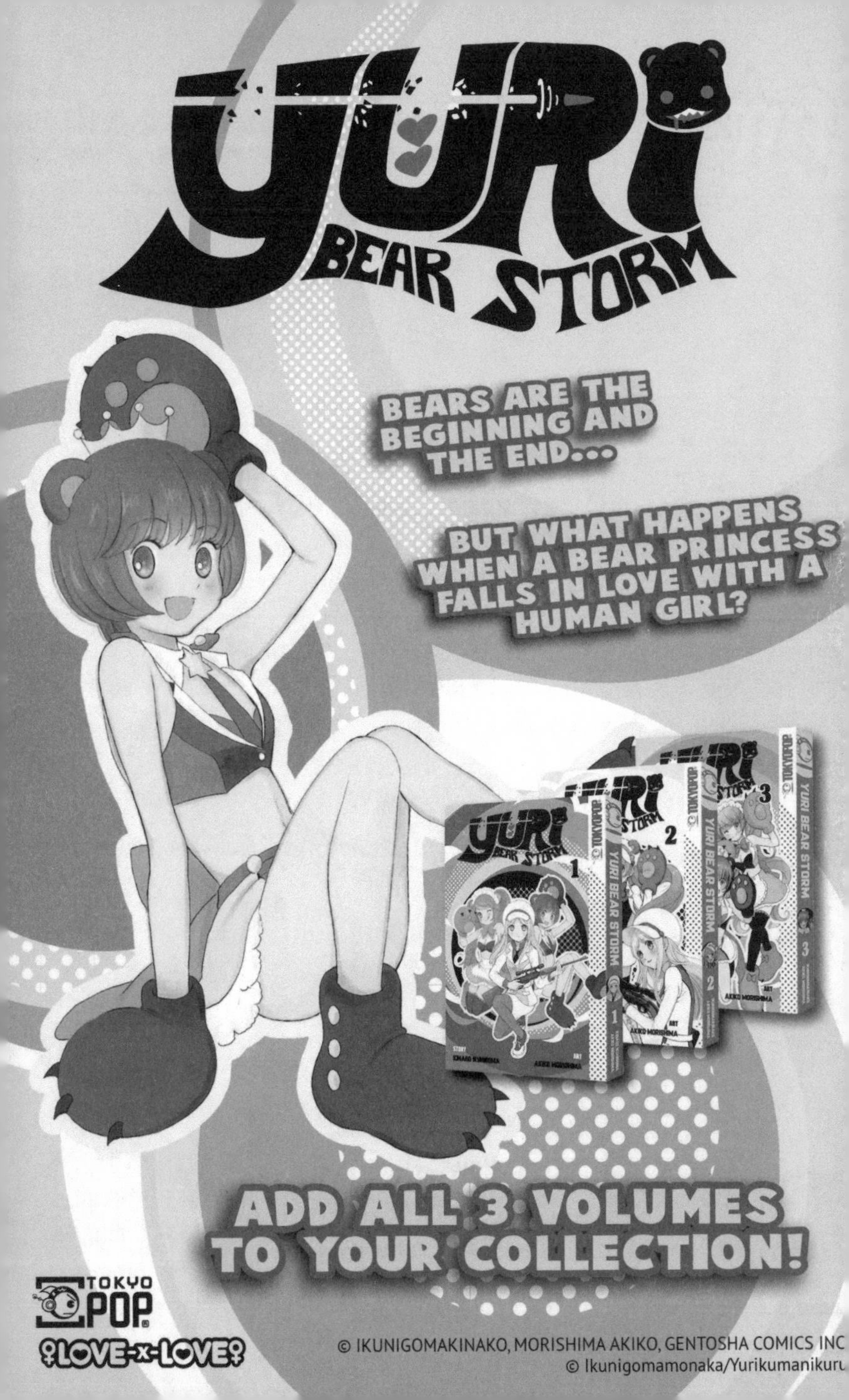
YURI BEAR STORM
BEARS ARE THE BEGINNING AND THE END...
BUT WHAT HAPPENS WHEN A BEAR PRINCESS FALLS IN LOVE WITH A HUMAN GIRL?
ADD ALL 3 VOLUMES TO YOUR COLLECTION!
TOKYO POP
LOVE x LOVE
© IKUNIGOMAKINAKO, MORISHIMA AKIKO, GENTOSHA COMICS INC
© Ikunigomamonaka/Yurikumanikuru

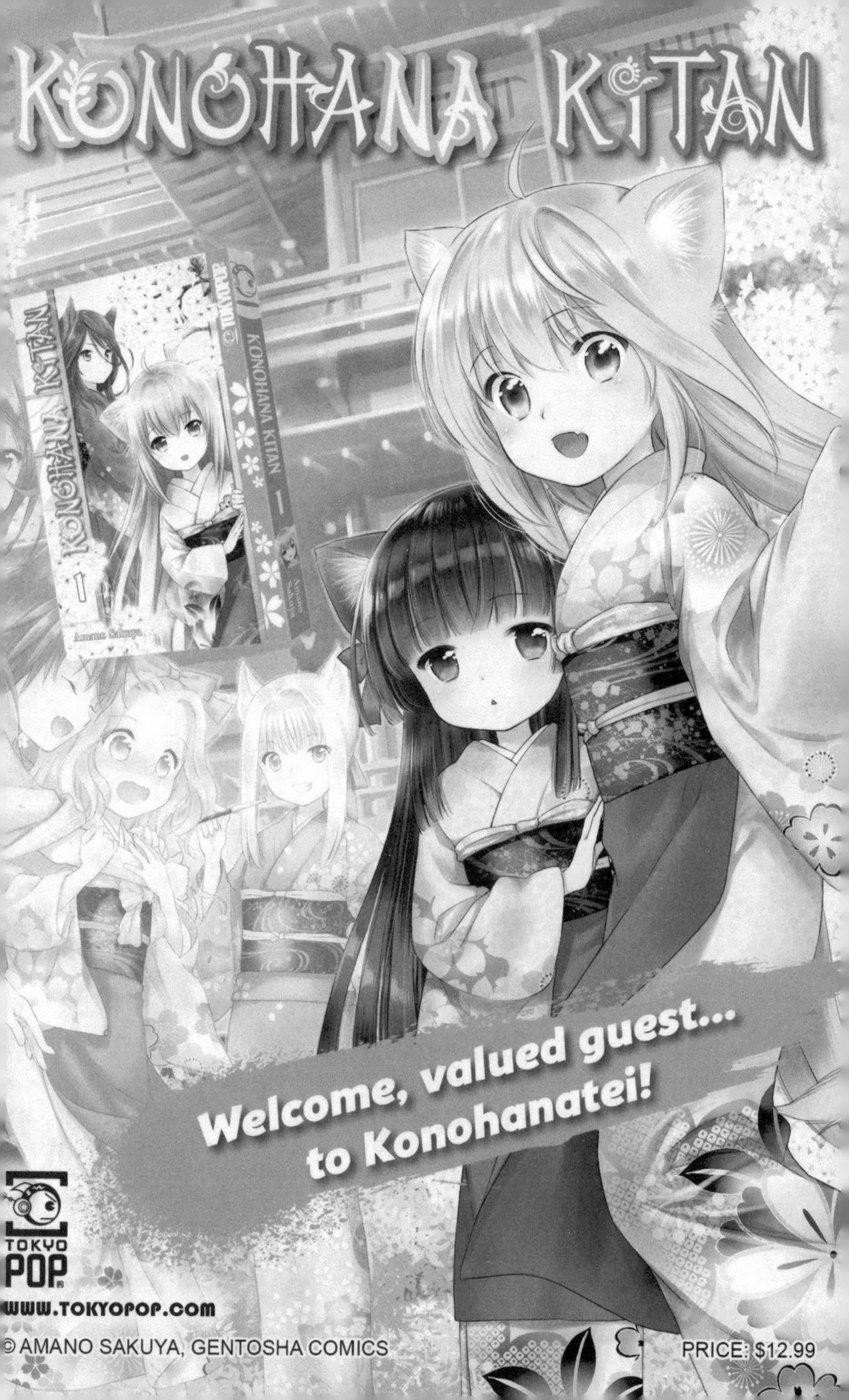
KONOHANA KITAN
KONOHANA KITAN 1
Amano Sakuya
TOKYOPOP
Welcome, valued guest...
to Konohanatei!
TOKYO POP
www.tokyopop.com
© AMANO SAKUYA, GENTOSHA COMICS
PRICE: $12.99

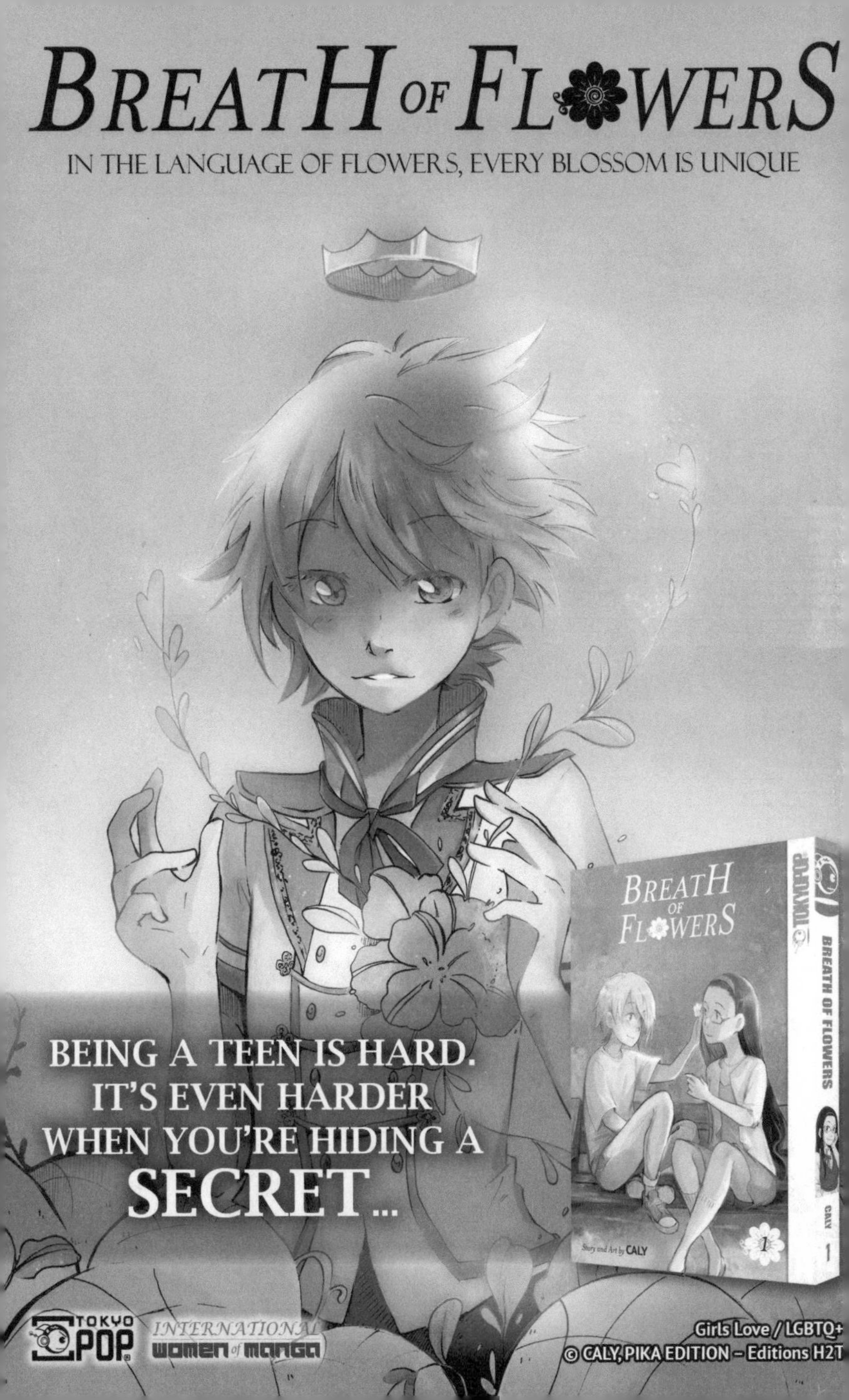
BREATH OF FLOWERS
IN THE LANGUAGE OF FLOWERS, EVERY BLOSSOM IS UNIQUE
BEING A TEEN IS HARD.
IT'S EVEN HARDER
WHEN YOU'RE HIDING A
SECRET...
BREATH OF FLOWERS
Story and Art by CALY
1
TOKYOPOP
BREATH OF FLOWERS
CALY
1
TOKYOPOP
INTERNATIONAL
WOMEN of MANGA
Girls Love / LGBTQ+
© CALY, PIKA EDITION – Editions H2T

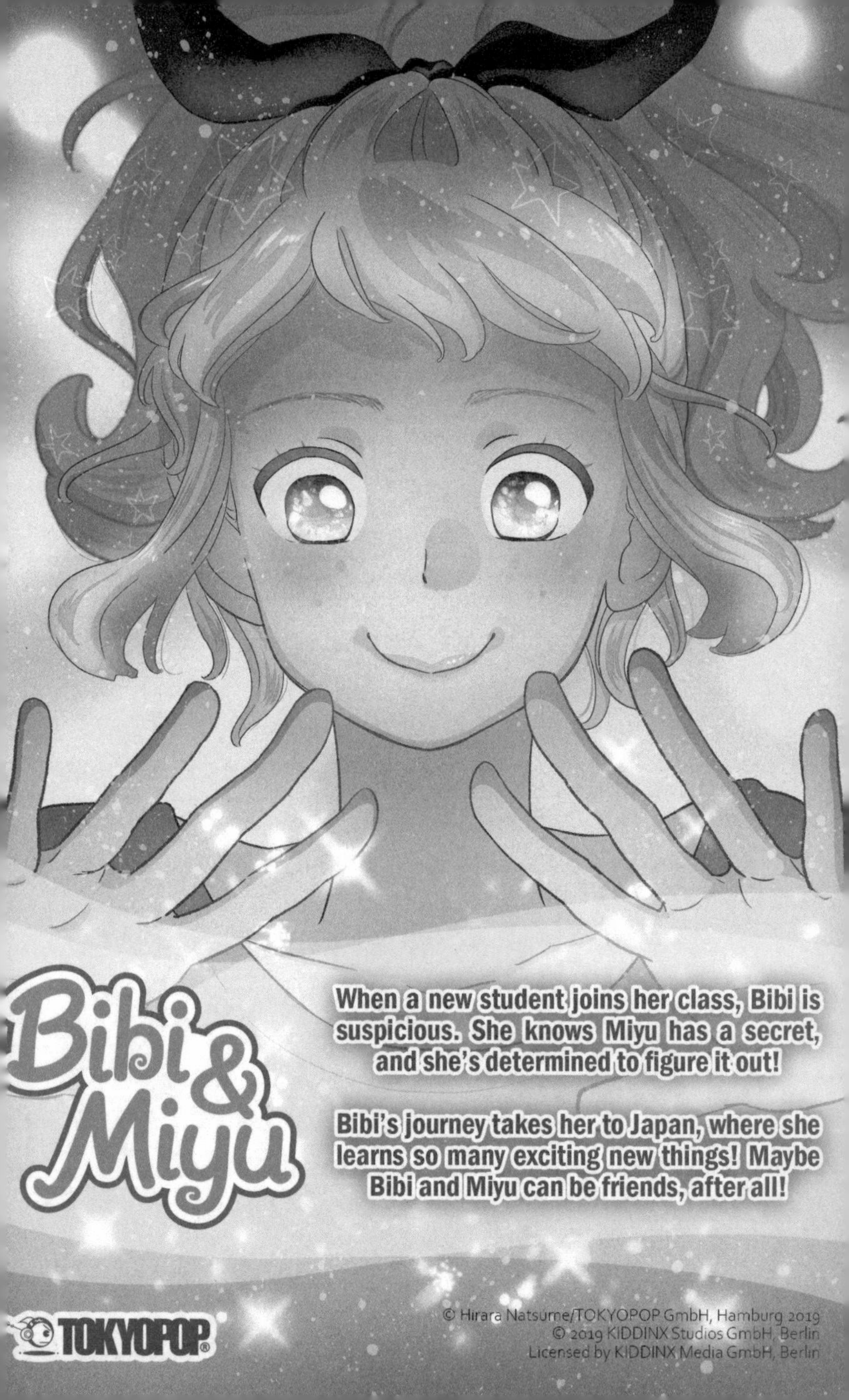
Bibi & Miyu
When a new student joins her class, Bibi is suspicious. She knows Miyu has a secret, and she's determined to figure it out!
Bibi's journey takes her to Japan, where she learns so many exciting new things! Maybe Bibi and Miyu can be friends, after all!
TOKYOPOP
© Hirara Natsume/TOKYOPOP GmbH, Hamburg 2019
© 2019 KIDDINX Studios GmbH, Berlin
Licensed by KIDDINX Media GmbH, Berlin

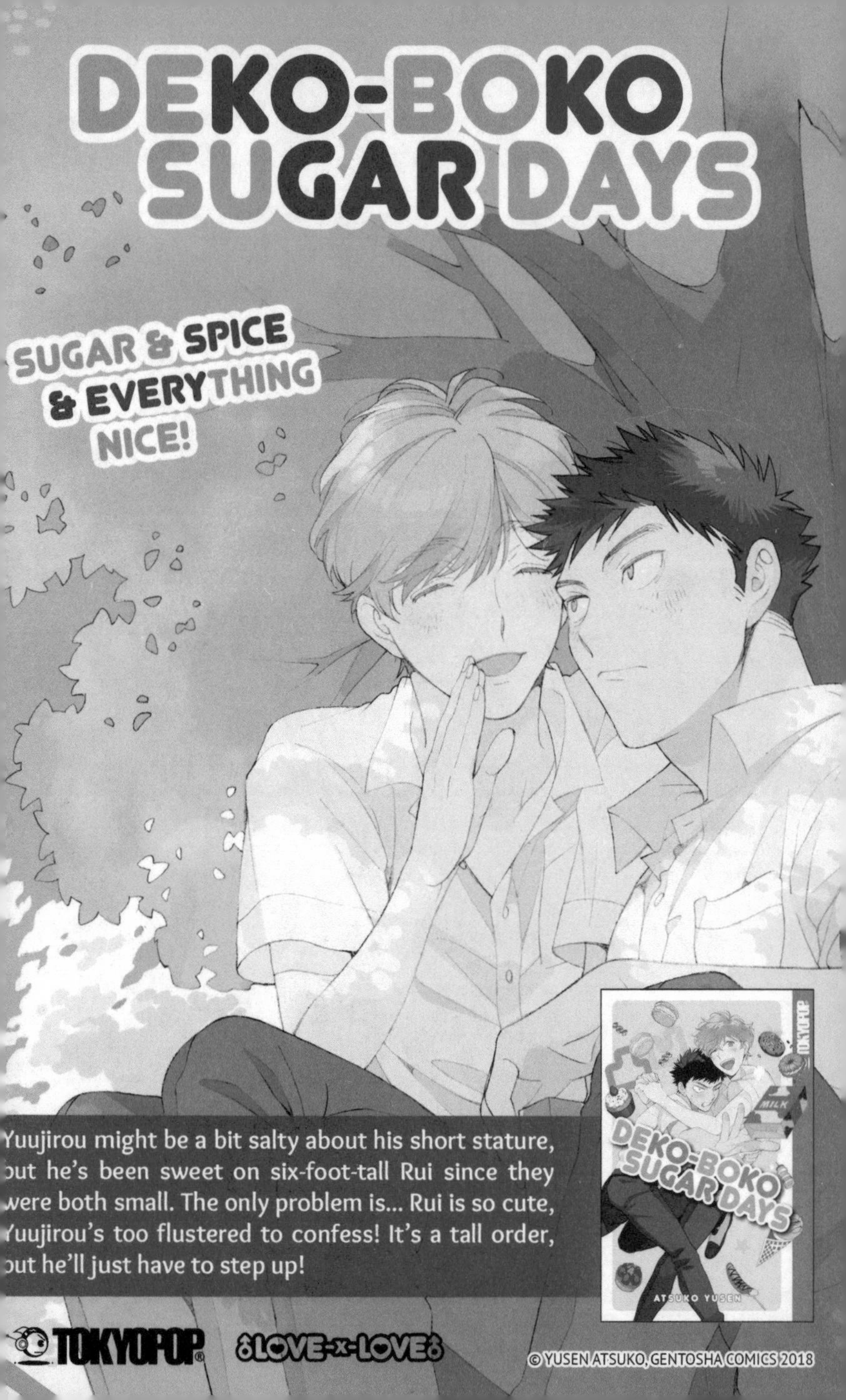
DEKO-BOKO SUGAR DAYS
SUGAR & SPICE & EVERYTHING NICE!
Yuujirou might be a bit salty about his short stature, but he's been sweet on six-foot-tall Rui since they were both small. The only problem is... Rui is so cute, Yuujirou's too flustered to confess! It's a tall order, but he'll just have to step up!
MILK
DEKO-BOKO SUGAR DAYS
ATSUKO YUSEN
TOKYOPOP
TOKYOPOP®
LOVE-x-LOVE
© YUSEN ATSUKO, GENTOSHA COMICS 2018

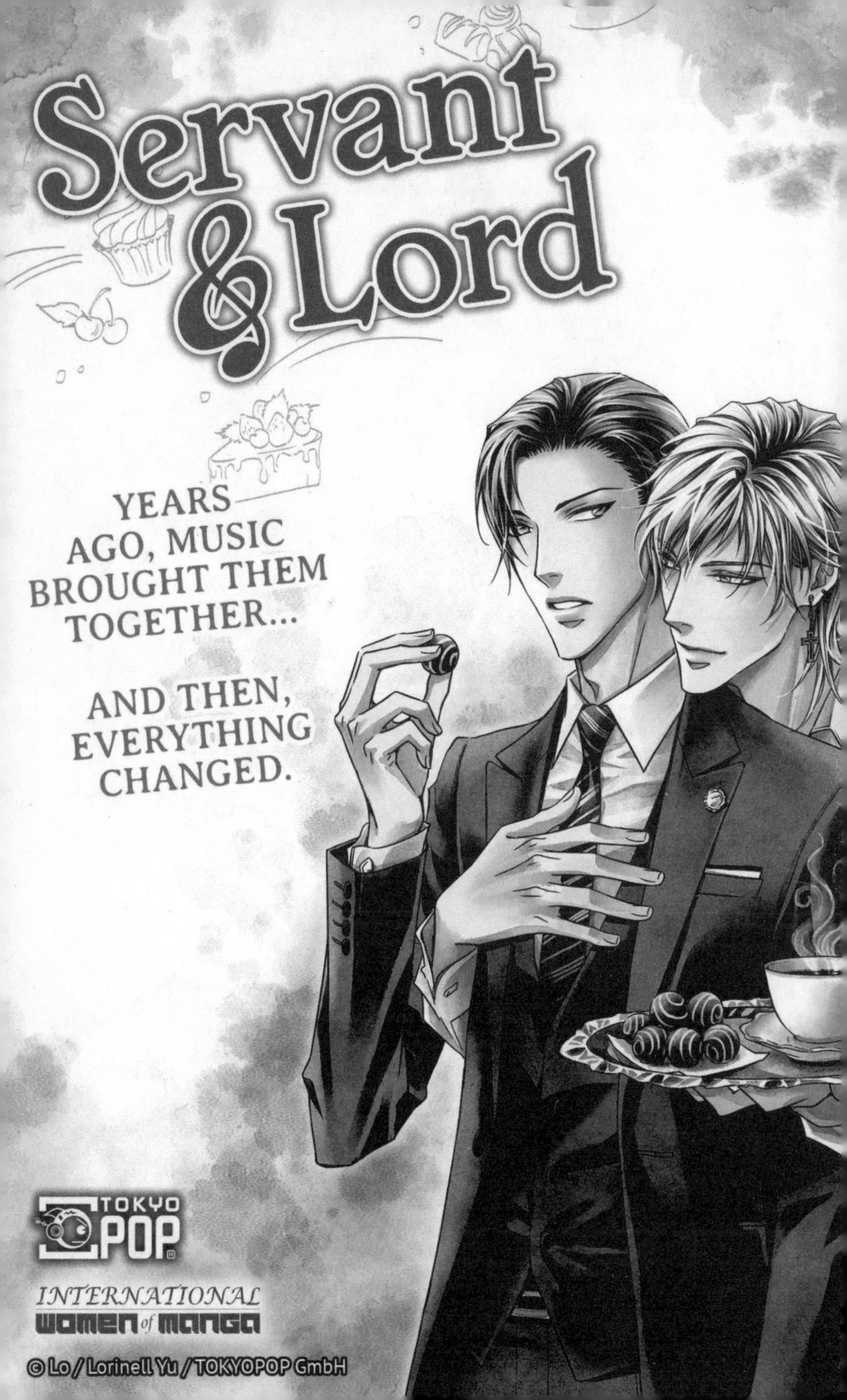
Servant & Lord
YEARS AGO, MUSIC BROUGHT THEM TOGETHER...
AND THEN, EVERYTHING CHANGED.
TOKYO POP
INTERNATIONAL WOMEN of MANGA
© Lo / Lorinell Yu / TOKYOPOP GmbH

DON'T CALL ME DIRTY

Shouji is gay. Hama is homeless. Two men trying to make their way in a society that labels each of them as 'dirty' find a connection with one another — and a special relationship blossoms.

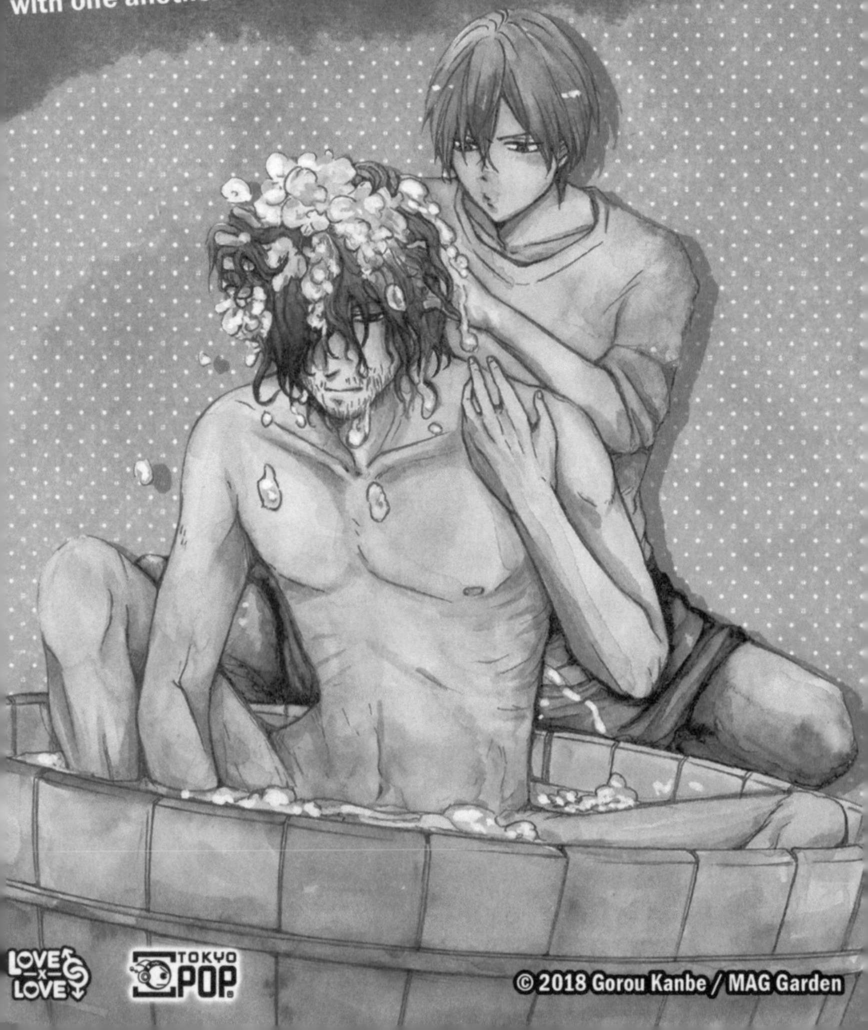

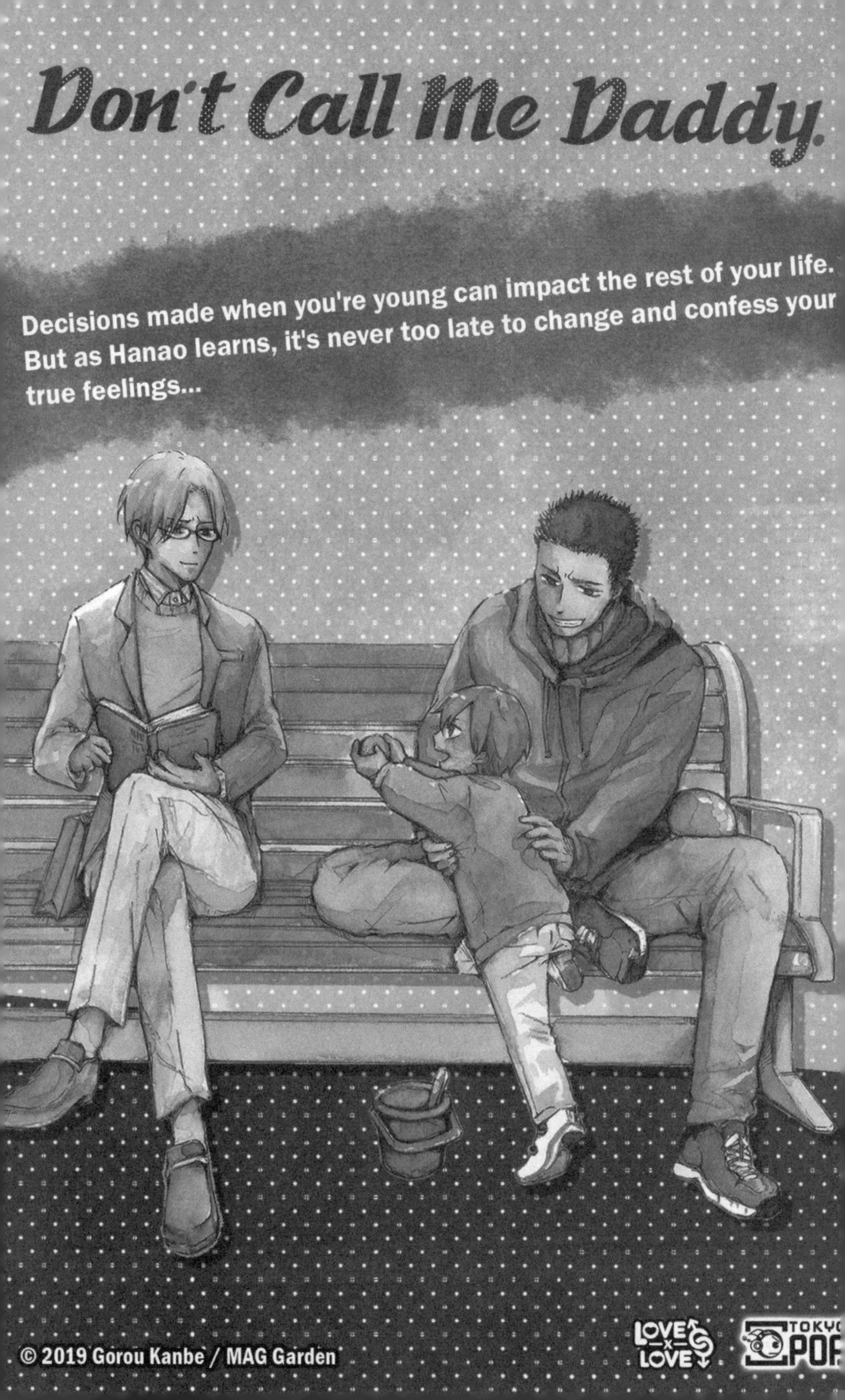
Don't Call Me Daddy.
Decisions made when you're young can impact the rest of your life. But as Hanao learns, it's never too late to change and confess your true feelings...
© 2019 Gorou Kanbe / MAG Garden
LOVE x LOVE
TOKYOPOP

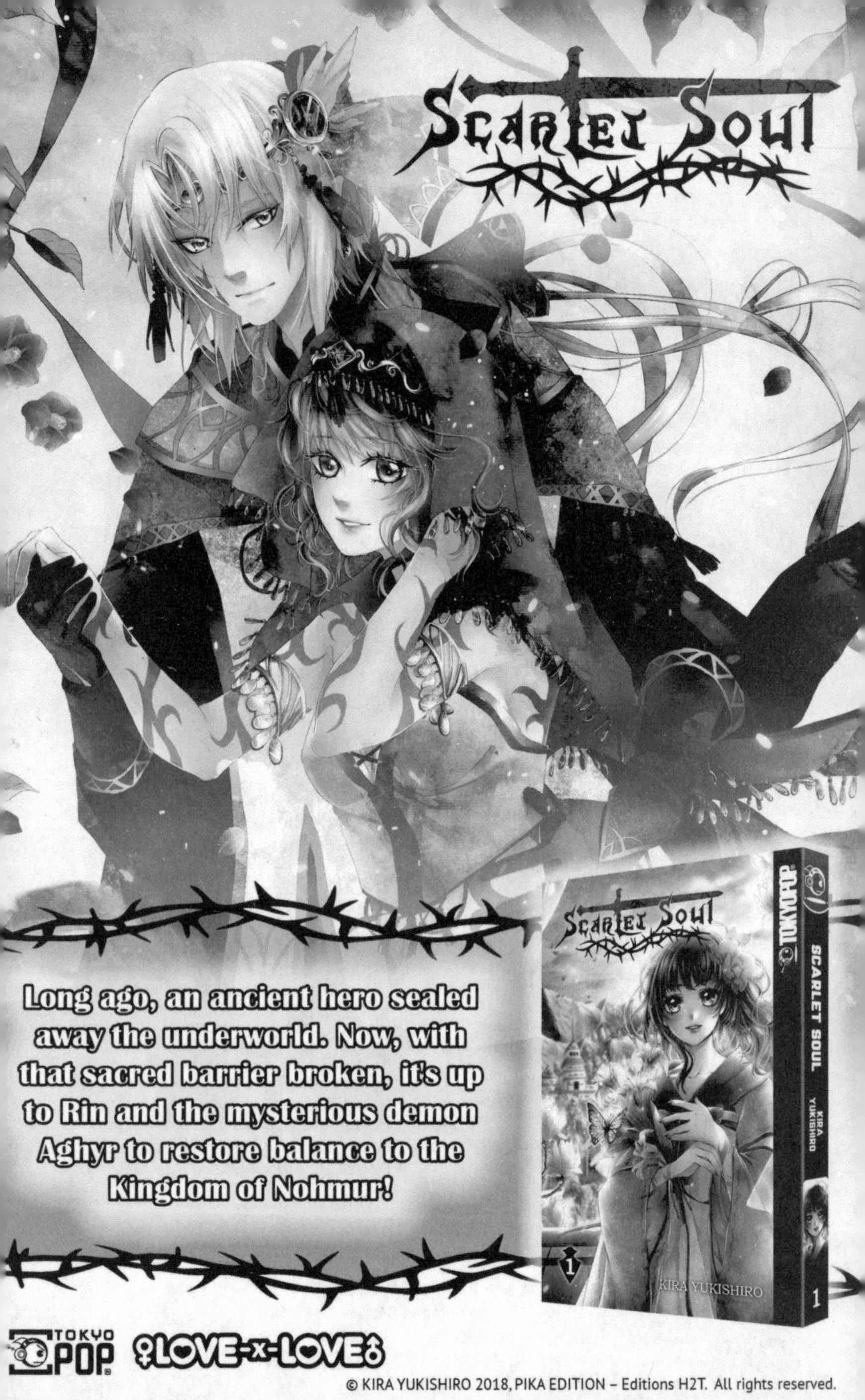
SCARLET SOUL
Long ago, an ancient hero sealed away the underworld. Now, with that sacred barrier broken, it's up to Rin and the mysterious demon Aghyr to restore balance to the Kingdom of Nohmur!
SCARLET SOUL
TOKYOPOP
SCARLET SOUL
KIRA YUKISHIRO
1
KIRA YUKISHIRO
1
TOKYO POP
LOVE x LOVE

Still Sick Volume 3
Akashi

Editor - Lena Atanassova
Marketing Associate - Kae Winters
Translator - Katie Kimura
Copy Editor - Massiel Gutierrez
QC - Daichi Nemoto
Cover Designer - Sol DeLeo & Soodam Lee
Retouching and Lettering - Vibrraant Publishing Studio
Editor-in-Chief & Publisher - Stu Levy

A  Manga

TOKYOPOP and 🐱 are trademarks or registered trademarks of TOKYOPOP Inc.

TOKYOPOP
5200 W Century Blvd
Suite 705
Los Angeles, CA 90045 USA

E-mail: info@TOKYOPOP.com
Come visit us online at www.TOKYOPOP.com

f www.facebook.com/TOKYOPOP
🐦 www.twitter.com/TOKYOPOP
📌 www.pinterest.com/TOKYOPOP
📷 www.instagram.com/TOKYOPOP

ISBN: 978-1-4278-6750-6
First TOKYOPOP Printing: January 2021
10 9 8 7 6 5 4 3 2 1
Printed in CANADA

STOP

THIS IS THE BACK OF THE BOOK!

How do you read manga-style? It's simple! Let's practice -- just start in the top right panel and follow the numbers below!

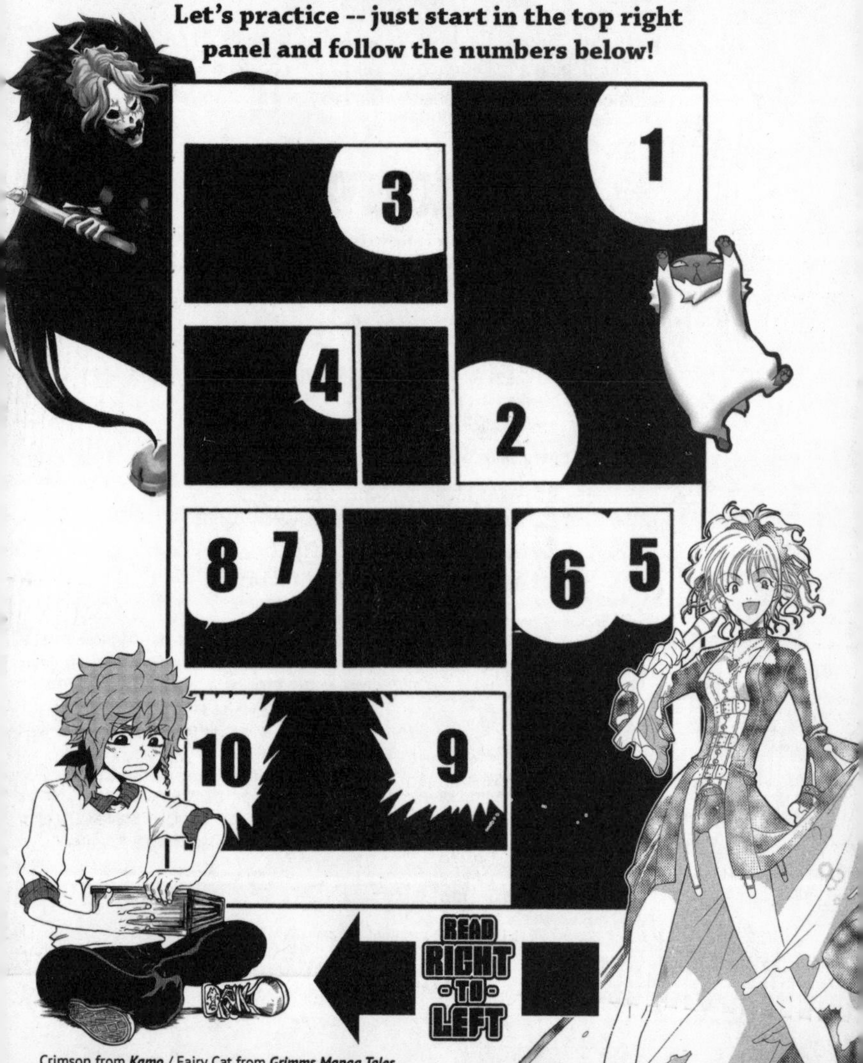

1
2
3
4
5
6
7
8
9
10
READ
RIGHT
-TO-
LEFT

Crimson from ***Kamo*** / Fairy Cat from ***Grimms Manga Tales***
Morrey from ***Goldfisch*** / Princess Ai from ***Princess Ai***